Early History of the Israelite People

Early History of the Israelite People

from the Written & Archaeological Sources

Thomas L. Thompson

BRILL

LEIDEN · BOSTON · KOLN

This journal is printed on acid-free paper.

Design: TopicA (Antoinette Hanekuyk), Leiden

Library of Congress Cataloging-in-Publication Data

The Library of Congress Cataloging-in-Publication Data
are also available.

ISBN 90 04 11943 4

To

Shirley and Sarah

CONTENTS

ACKNOWLEDGEMENTS

This book has many debts. Its initial research is largely due to a 1988 National Endowment of the Humanities Fellowship which enabled me to spend nine months of uninterrupted study. During the course of this fellowship, Luther Northwestern Seminary kindly provided housing, for which I am grateful. Gratitude is also due to the Midwest Faculty Seminar for their generous appointment of Occasional Fellowships in 1988 and 1989, enabling me to spend three weeks of research at the University of Chicago's Oriental Institute. I wish to thank Lawrence University for defraying part of my research costs during the 1988–1989 academic year in the form of a grant. Much of the later research for this book was funded by travel and research grants from Marquette University, the American Philosophical Society, the Deutsche Akademische Austauschdienst, and the National Endowment for the Humanities. I wish also to thank the staffs of the Luther Northwestern Seminary library in St. Paul, of the Oriental Institute Archives in Chicago, and of the libraries at the universities of Tübingen and Heidelberg for their unstinting help. I am grateful to Vicki Koessl of Lawrence University and Patrick Russell, Pam Young, Ardie Evenson and Ed Maniscalco of Marquette University for typing the manuscript. Julian Hills and Ed Maniscalco gave me much help in preparing the finished text and fonts for printing, generously giving both their time and patience. I wish also to thank Manfred Weippert and Dr. F.Th. Dijkema for their editorial assistance and for accepting this work in the Brill series: *Studies in the History of the Ancient Near East.*

Nobody works in a vacuum, and a book like this accumulates some very heavy intellectual debts to the insights of others which can only rarely be specifically acknowledged in footnotes. In this way, I am seriously indebted to the late Gösta Ahlström, to Niels Peter Lemche, Diana Edelman, Julian Hills, Becky Kasper, Axel Knauf, Andrea Molinari, Shirley Janke, Philip Davies, Thomas Bolin, Ed Maniscalco, and Max Miller. They are all to be thanked for their painstaking comments and criticisms, their advice and their detailed suggestions and improvements of various drafts of my manuscript. I am thoroughly indebted to their instruction and to the breadth of their scholarship. The students of my graduate classes at Marquette will notice that this work has been substantially improved by our discussions and debates. The mistakes I hid from them are, of course, my own responsibility.

There are also personal debts which I wish to acknowledge, debts which cannot be repaid: to the Catholic Biblical Association and the fathers of the École Biblique who first made it possible for me to return to the academy. I also wish to acknowledge how much this book owes to the generosity of Gösta Ahlström, who allowed me to use the manuscript of his great history of Palestine before it was published and gave me so much advice and support in the last two years of his life. I also thank Philip Davies, Axel Knauf, Max Miller and Jack Sasson, whose friendship and generous letter writing has supported me when I was most isolated. My spouse and closest friend, Shirley Janke, has not only been the good wife of Proverbs, but has been my best critic and adviser. From her more careful scholarship I have stolen many good ideas and insights (as well as data and bibliography) in the writing of this book. Through this help and her personal support I have been able to return to research in my field after a long absence. I wish to dedicate this work to her and to Sarah, born May 8, 1989, the daughter of Amy and Marty Stone, friends whose cooperation with my wife's felicitous kidnapping of me in 1987 did so much to make my life more interesting.

Thomas L. Thompson
Milwaukee
April 15, 1992

ABBREVIATIONS

AASOR	*Annualof the American Schools of Oriental Research*
ÄAT	*Ägypten und Altes Testament*
ADAJ	*Annual of the Department of Antiquities of Jordan*
ADPV	*Abhandlungen des deutschen Palästinavereins*
AfO	*Archiv für Orientforschung*
AJA	*American Journal of Archaeology*
AJBA	*Australian Journal of Biblical Archaeology*
ANET	*Ancient Near Eastern Texts Related to the Old Testament*
AOAT	*Alter Orient und altes Testament*
ASORDS	*American Schools of Oriental Research Dissertation Series*
AThANT	*Abhandlungen zur Theologie des alten und neuen Testaments*
AUSS	*Andrews University Seminar Studies*
BA	*Biblical Archaeologist*
BAR	*Biblical Archaeology Review*
BASOR	*Bulletin of the American Schools of Oriental Research*
BAT	*Biblical Archaeology Today*
Bb	*Biblica*
BBB	*Bonner biblische Beiträge*
BN	*Biblische Notizen*
BRL	*Biblisches Reallexikon*
BTAVO	*Beihefte zum Tübinger Atlas des vorderen Orients*
BWANT	*Beiträge zur Wissenschaft vom alten und neuen Testament*
BZAW	*Beihefte zur Zeitschrift für die alttestamentliche Wissenschaft*
CAH	*Cambridge Ancient History*
CBQMS	*Catholic Biblical Quarterly Monograph Series*
CRB	*Cahiers de la Revue Biblique*
DBAT	*Dielheimer Blätter zum alten Testament*
DBS	*Dictionnaire de la Bible Supplément*
DTT	*Dansk teologisk Tidsskrift*
EAEHL	*Encyclopedia of Archaeological Excavations in the Holy Land*

EI	Eretz Israel
FRLANT	Forschungen zur Religion und Literatur des alten und neuen Testaments
HSM	Harvard Semitic Monographs
HSS	Harvard Semitic Series
IEJ	Israel Exploration Journal
IJNA	International Journal of Nautical Archaeology
JANESCU	Journal of the Ancient Near Eastern Society of Columbia University
JAOS	Journal of the American Oriental Society
JBL	Journal of Biblical Literature
JEOL	Journal, Ex Oriente Lux
JESHO	Journal of Economic and Social History of the Orient
JNES	Journal of Near Eastern Studies
JSOT	Journal for the Study of the Old Testament
JSOTS	Journal for the Study of the Old Testament Supplements
JSS	Journal of Semitic Studies
OA	Oriens Antiquus
PEQ	Palestine Exploration Quarterly
RB	Revue Biblique
SBL	Society of Biblical Literature
SBLDS	Society of Biblical Literature Dissertation Series
SBLMS	Society of Biblical Literature Monograph Series
SBT	Studies in Biblical Theology
SHAJ	Studies in the History and Antiquities of Jordan
SJOT	Scandinavian Journal of the Old Testament
SSAWL	Sitzungsberichte der Sächsigen Akademie der Wissenschaft zu Leipzig
StTh	Studia Theologica
SWBAS	Social World of Biblical Antiquity Series
TAVO	Tübinger Atlas des vorderen Orients
ThZ	Theologische Zeitschrift
TRE	Theologische Realenzyklopädie
VT	Vetus Testamentum
VTS	Vetus Testamentum Supplements
WMANT	Wissenschaftliche Monographien zum alten und neuen Testament
ZA	Zeitschrift für Assyriologie
ZAW	Zeitschrift für die alttestamentliche Wissenschaft

ZDMG   *Zeitschrift der deutschen morgenländischen Gesellschaft*
ZDPV   *Zeitschrift des deutschen Palästina-Vereins*

CHAPTER ONE

HISTORICAL-CRITICAL RESEARCH AND EXTRABIBLICAL SOURCES[1]

1. *The Documentary Hypothesis*

About a century ago, J. Wellhausen[2] synthesized the results of more than two generations of Old Testament historical-critical scholarship on the sources of the pentateuch into the "documentary hypothesis." This synthesis concluded that the pentateuch and indeed the first six books of the bible had been formed from a composite of four originally independent documents (commonly referred to by scholars as J, E, D and P: the Yahwist, the Elohist, the Deuteronomist and the Priestly sources), dating successively from the early monarchic period to postexilic times.[3]

---

[1] Summaries of scholarship presumed by this study that I have consciously avoided repeating: M. Weippert, *Die Landnahme der israelitischen Stämme in der neueren wissenschaftlichen Diskussion* (Göttingen, 1967); J.M. Miller, "The Israelite Occupation of Canaan," in *Israelite and Judaean History*, ed. by J.M. Miller and J.H. Hayes (Philadelphia, 1977), pp.213-284. G.W. Ramsey, *The Quest for the Historical Israel: Reconstructing Israel's Early History* (Atlanta, 1981); N.P. Lemche, *Early Israel: Anthropological and Historical Studies on Israelite Society in Premonarchical Times* (Leiden, 1985); and Th.L. Thompson, *The Origin Tradition of Ancient Israel I, JSOTS* 55 (Sheffield, 1987) pp.11-40.

[2] J. Wellhausen, *Geschichte Israels* (Berlin, 1878; 2nd. ed. =*Prolegomena zur Geschichte Israels*, 1883); *idem, Israelitische und jüdische Geschichte* (Berlin, 1894); *idem, Skizzen und Vorarbeiten*, vols. 1-6 (Berlin, 1884-1899); *idem, Die Composition des Hexateuchs und der historischen Bücher des alten Testaments* 3d. ed. (Berlin, 1899); *idem, Grundrisse zum alten Testament*, ed. by R. Smend (Munich, 1965); see also D.A. Knight, *Julius Wellhausen and His Prolegomena to the History of Israel, Semeia* 25 (Chico, 1983). Wellhausen's work on the pentateuch was closely associated with that of K. Graf (*Die geschichtlichen Bücher des alten Testaments: Zwei Historisch-kritische Untersuchungen*, Leipzig, 1866) and A. Kuenen (*Historisch-kritische Einleitung in die Bücher des alten Testaments hinsichtlich ihrer Entstehung und Sammlung I. Die Entstehung des Hexateuch*, Leipzig, 1887).

[3] For a summary of recent discussions of the documentary hypothesis, S. de Vries, "A Review of Recent Research in the Tradition History of the Pentateuch," *SBL Seminar Papers* 26 (1987), pp.459-502; N. Whybray, *The Making of the Pentateuch, JSOTS* 53 (Sheffield, 1987).

The thrust of Wellhausen's critical analysis of the pentateuch was essentially historical: to establish through an understanding of the history of the pentateuch's composition and development as a composite text evidence for an evolutionary history of the religion of ancient Israel. In this, he sought to outline a stepped chronological development, away from primitive forms of religious beliefs through henotheism to the mature understanding of prophetic monotheism and ending in what he understood as the narrow sectarianism of a priestly, cult-oriented legalism. Essential to this historical and evolutionary goal of Wellhausen and others was the isolation of discrete independent sources and their chronological and ideological association with major epochal transitions in Israel's history: J with the United Monarchy, *Judah* and the Davidic dynasty; E with the Divided Monarchy and the State of *Israel*; D with the reforms of Josiah, the late preexilic period and the prophetic movement; and P with the exilic and postexilic periods and the priestly circles from *Jerusalem*.

However, while the orientation of Wellhausen's work was decidedly in the direction of a positive historical reconstruction of a history of Israel's religion, the implications of the documentary hypothesis largely eliminated any acceptance of the historicity of the referents of the pentateuchal narrative, which includes not only the creation and origin narratives of Genesis 1–11 but also the patriarchal stories and the Mosaic traditions. This aspect of his historical-critical research rendered a polemical component to the acceptance and rejection of Wellhausen's documentary hypothesis that has rarely been absent in the subsequent discussions of his work.

Essential to the history of scholarship expressed in Wellhausen's synthesis was that these four discrete sources of the pentateuch were to be understood as literary documents created at the time of their written composition, and hence as compositions reflecting the understanding and knowledge of their authors and their world. This assumption contained the disturbing corollary that nothing historically dependable about earlier periods in Israel's history could be gained from them. The usefulness of the pentateuch for reconstructing the early history of Israel prior to the time of composition was thereby decidedly curtailed. After two decades of intense and often personal attacks on his work, the "Graf-Wellhausen approach" to the so-called historical books of the Old Testament had become the dominant critical interpretation by the end of the century.

Wellhausen's contributions to the history of critical scholarship were immense. But none was as great or as lasting as this on the pentateuch. It is hardly an exaggeration to state that most of the next century of research on the pentateuch and the prehistory of Israel developed either from Wellhausen's synthesis or was consciously in reaction against it. In the century of scholarship following Wellhausen, and largely as a result of the documentary hypothesis's dominance, many pivotal assumptions and tendencies now common in the field have achieved the status of axioms, moving historical-critical scholarship along a path away from theology and giving it an orientation that is increasingly historical and secular. While these tendencies and assumptions are products of the enlightenment and of the nineteenth-century success of historicism in Western thought, it was this work of Wellhausen, his colleagues and successors that provided the fulcrum of change in biblical studies.

The broad acceptance of Wellhausen's and Graf's historical-critical reconstruction of the composition of the pentateuch quickly influenced the understanding of the rest of the Old Testament corpus, particularly in the perception of sources, in compositional theory and in the chronological analysis of the literary development of the Bible. Most productive were the discussions about the extension of the pentateuch's sources (or the assertion of comparable sources) in the collection of the narrative traditions of the "Former Prophets" of Joshua–2 Kings. Derivative methods were used in the analysis of the relationship of Joshua–2 Kings to the composition of Chronicles and the association of Chronicles with the books of both Ezra and Nehemiah. Ultimately, the methods that were developed in the study of the pentateuchal sources gave a significant historical bent to the interpretation of the prophetic corpus, especially in regards to Isaiah, and rendered chronological depth to the collection of the psalms.

This comprehensive revision of biblical interpretation, following upon the acceptance of the Graf-Wellhausen-Kuenen paradigm, was not entirely dependent on the conclusions drawn from (or the ideological implications of) their work. Nevertheless, the acceptance of the efficient and practical methods and techniques of analysis, of which—even today—Wellhausen's works illustrate his mastery, influenced the entire field. The concentration on details and anomalies, linguistic variations and the theological and ideological plurality of the received text enabled distinctions between the implied and received literary contexts of the sources. It fostered a concentration on the composition of a text and its implied point of departure, and firmly established lasting and important distinctions between the contexts and referents of these texts. Such methods encouraged a discriminating avoidance of harmonies and an increasing understanding of the composition of these complex traditions in terms of process. The acceptance of these and like techniques of scholarship were, in the debates that followed, of far more importance than any of the controverted issues, such as the implicit rejection of the pentateuch's historicity, around which so many of the debates centered. In the course of this still current debate, many of Wellhausen's specific conclusions and ideological positions foundered and were with justice rejected. The methods and principles of his analysis, however, representing as they did some of the best of nineteenth-century historical analysis, laid the foundation of the scholarship of even his most trenchant critics.

The success of this nineteenth-century alternative to the Mosaic authorship of the pentateuch gave increasing strength and acceptance to the recognition of human authorship as a point of departure for all biblical scholarship, and concurrent support for the growing separation of critical academic scholarship from religiously and theologically motivated biblical interpretation. Nevertheless, in the century that followed Wellhausen, many efforts were made to bridge this ever widening gap, and the context of biblical scholarship within university and seminary departments of theology ensured a steady stream of theologians committed to such a bridge. Yet, the dichotomy has remained. The new role of historically critical, biblical research, centered within a post-Enlightenment understanding of exegesis as a critical intellectual discipline with its own independent role in the academy, makes it exceedingly difficult to maintain biblical studies as a subdiscipline of theology. As long as theology has dogmatically insisted on maintaining the historical facticity or historicity of ancient biblical historiographies, the challenge that historical research has posed for theology has been inexorable.

Cumulative historical-critical research over the past century has, at its best and methodologically most rigorous, increasingly undermined any theological enterprise that laid its foundation on the interpretation of the past as normative. This union of the abiding interest in the past with efforts to reconstuct a critical understanding of that past has been one of the most lasting results of the critical approaches espoused by Wellhausen, and is perhaps the most far-reaching benefit of any of

Wellhausen's many contributions to biblical research. If it is still possible for a theological approach to biblical research to take a legitimately critical place within the academy, it must face with integrity the historical-critical questions that both historians and theologians have inherited from Wellhausen.

2. Synthesis of Biblical Tradition and History of the Ancient Near East

It was a younger colleague and close friend of Wellhausen's at Halle, E. Meyer, who, building on both Wellhausen's documentary analysis and his own broad anthropological interests in Arab culture, added a complexity to Wellhausen's discussion by creating a synthesis with the then known history and geography of the ancient world.[4] This developed into the first successful departure from Wellhausen's more hypothetical literary criticism. Especially in his *Die Israeliten and ihre Nachbarstämme*, Meyer argued that it is impossible to maintain, with Wellhausen and other documentary critics, that the pentateuchal sources of J, E and P had been independently coherent documents, since these sources were so obviously lacking in any unifying self-coherent structures.

Meyer saw the traditions from which the documentary sources had derived as having originated in oral traditions and collections of narrative that consisted largely of folktale, legend and saga. The narratives of Genesis, in particular, he saw as having little to do with history,[5] belonging rather to the world of fiction. On grounds of literary form and perhaps a historian's strong distaste for easy parallels, Meyer strongly rejected the radical mythological interpretations of H. Winkler[6] and the entire *Babel-Bibel* school then so popular, which saw so much of Old Testament narrative as the refraction of cuneiform literature.[7]

---

[4] E. Meyer, *Geschichte des Altertums* I-V (Stuttgart, 1884-1902); *idem, Forschungen zur alten Geschichte* (Halle, 1892); *idem, Die Israeliten und ihre Nachbarstämme* (Halle, 1906); but also, *idem, Die Entstehung des Judenthums* (Halle, 1896); *idem, Julius Wellhausen und meine Schrift Die Entstehung des Judenthums: Eine Erwiderung* (Halle, 1897).

[5] E. Meyer, *op.cit.*, 1906, pp.130f.

[6] H. Winkler, *Altorientalische Forschungen* I-III (Leipzig, 1893-1906); *See also idem, Religionsgeschichtlicher und Geschichtlicher Orient* (Leipzig, 1906).

[7] E. Meyer, *op.cit.* 1906, pp.146-148. The closure of this peculiar chapter of biblical exegesis came with the *reductio ad absurdum* of A. Jepsen's two-volume work, *Das Gilgamesch-Epos* (Berlin, 1924-1926).

In this, Meyer's work was very closely aligned with the writings of H. Gunkel (who taught with him at Halle as a lecturer from 1889 to 1894), who explored the relationship of Old Testament narrative with what was known of world literature and folklore and developed his well-known understanding of oral traditions that he early argued lay at the foundations of biblical narrative.[8] Following Meyer, Gunkel's wide ranging historical interests and, in particular, his attempt to understand the history of Israel more in terms of world history and comparative studies than solely in terms of literary criticism, found mature expression in his editorial work and articles in the first[9] and second[10] editions of the immeasurably influential encyclopedia, *Religion in Geschichte und Gegenwart*.

Although Gunkel was by far the more renowned scholar in his day, it was primarily through the work of orientalists, especially H. Gressmann, a student of Wellhausen's, that the growing influence of this group—widely known as the "Religionsgeschichtliche Schule"—was very quickly extended into ancient Near Eastern studies generally. This radically altered the almost exclusively biblical orientation to the history of Israel of the literary critical followers of Wellhausen. Gressmann's important publication of *Altorientalische Texte zum alten Testament* and of *Altorientalische Bilder zum alten Testament*,[11] as well as his close collaboration with Gunkel's narrative and folklore studies, had an influence in Europe comparable to that of J.B. Pritchard's more recent *ANET* in America after World War II, and extended the comparative approach to the history of Israel to include the entire Near East.

---

[8] H. Gunkel, *Genesis, Handkommentar zum alten Testament* (Göttingen, 1901), passim. This early position of Gunkel, subsequently abandoned, was most emphatically argued by F. Delitzsch (*Genesiskommentor*) and subsequently underlay G. Dalman's search for an anthropological and sociological context for biblical narrative, expressed in his magnum opus, *Arbeit und Sitte in Palästina* (originally published in Gütersloh, 1928-1942 and reprinted in seven volumes in Hildesheim, 1964-1987). Dalman's pioneering work in this field (reflected also in the more liberally oriented work of the Scandinavian J. Pedersen, *Early Israel*, vols. I-IV, Copenhagen, 1926-40) was supported by his influence in the Deutscher Evangelische Institut fur Altertumswissenschaft des heiligen Landes (Palästina-Institut) and his founding and editing of the *Palästinajahrbuch* from 1905, which helped develop wider interests in biblical studies in both geography and anthropology.

[9] 1909 ff.

[10] 1927 ff.

[11] H. Gressmann, *Altorientalische Texte zum alten Testament* and *Altorientalische Bilder zum alten Testament*, 2nd. ed. (Berlin, 1926f.).

This group of scholars was deeply involved in the flood of newly discovered and newly translated texts of the ancient Near East. It is to a great extent the influence of these new materials, coupled with a freedom from the theological narrowness of the predominantly biblical orientation of both liberal and conservative protestant scholarship that led to a new understanding of the early history of Israel. Some of the adherents of this "history of religions school" made major contributions to comparative literature and folklore studies as well. Others hoped through archaeological and comparative cultural studies to develop an understanding of the sociological context or "world" of the Bible[12] as a starting point of biblical studies.

Without directly challenging the major theses of the documentary hypothesis,[13] these scholars decisively undercut its impact on the issue

---

[12] In more recent times, the historical-critical influence of this school has continued not only in the work of Alt and Alt's students, such as M. Noth, K. Elliger, S. Hermann, A. Kuschke, and H. Donner, but also in that of Gressman's student K. Galling, of French scholars such as R. de Vaux and J. Tournay, Scandinavians such as S. Mowinckel, E. Nielsen, J. Pedersen, and more recently G. Ahlström, T. Mettinger and N.P. Lemche, and a number of such younger German scholars as V. Fritz, S. Mittmann, H. and M. Weippert, P. Welten, M. Wüst, S. Timm and E.A. Knauf and their students.

[13] The pivotal studies of M. Noth (*Überlieferungsgeschichte des Pentateuch, Stuttgart,* 1948; *idem, Überlieferungsgeschichtliche Studien I,* Halle, 1943) and G. von Rad (*Theologie des Alten Testaments,* Munich, 1957, *idem, The Problem of the Pentateuch and Other Essays,* Edinburgh, 1966; *Das erste Buch Mose: Genesis übersetzt und erklärt,* Göttingen, 1949-1953) brought about a decisive shift in the understanding of the sources involved in the formation of the narrative traditions of Genesis-2 Kings away from a perception of them as creative literary works, and gave attention rather to an extended process of tradition formation, concentrating efforts on identifying the originating creative core of the complex tradition as well as the historical contexts which gave rise to both individual tradition complexes and their transposition through long histories of redaction. Pivotal in the history of scholarship were both von Rad's "kleines Credo" as an originating core of the pentateuchal tradition and Noth's thesis of a *Grundlage* of tradition prior to the multiple variants of the received traditions. K. Galling's (*Die Erwählungstraditionen Israels, BZAW* 48, Berlin, 1928) separation of the formation of the Mosaic tradition from that of the patriarchs also had a lasting influence in German scholarship's efforts to understand the pentateuch as a complex of independent traditions which had had distinct and separable histories long preceding their written forms. The use of the documentary hypothesis as an explanation for the composition of the written traditions of the received texts has only been challenged decisively in recent years by von Rad's student R. Rendtorff (*Das über-lieferungsgeschichtliche Problem des Pentateuch, BZAW* 147, Berlin, 1977) and the recent study of Rendtorff's student E. Blum (*Die Komposition der Vätergeschichte,* Neukirchen, 1984); further N. Whybray (*The Making of the Pentateuch, JSOTS* 53, Sheffield 1987) and Th.L. Thompson (*op.cit.,* 1987). However, a comprehensive alternative to the documentary

of the history and origins of Israel by arguing persuasively that the written documents (from which the narrative traditions of the Bible had been formed) had an oral folk history long antedating their literary composition. While accepting that the Yahwistic and Elohistic sources reflected the period of the monarchy, they argued that this late context was decisively applicable only to the final editorial additions and harmonizations involved in the process of unifying a previously oral tradition. The Yahwist and Elohist were not understood as authors, let alone as historians of Israel's past, but much more restrictively as collectors and editors of a variety of legends and folk traditions of disparate date and origin.[14] The patriarchal narratives of Genesis, for example, were first understood by Gunkel—fully concurring in Wellhausen's adamant dating of them to the time of the monarchy—as originally ahistorical family tales that had only secondarily and gradually become historicized and understood by the Israelites as part of the history of their past.

I would place the initial turning point of the conservative reaction to the "history of religions school"—ironically enough—in O. Eissfeldt's championing of source criticism in his successful debate with Gunkel over the role of the documentary hypothesis in form criticism as well as of its function in the reconstruction of Israel's earliest history.[15] Gunkel's capitulation to Eissfeldt's critique[16] led to the far-reaching and still widely accepted assumption in Old Testament studies that form and source criticism were in practice complementary procedures. Rather than alternative and conflicting approaches, form and source criticism became a joint effort in critical exegesis. Now, with Eissfeldt, the history of the pentateuchal tradition no longer led back to an ever more fragmented and inaccessible folklore, populated by myths and other tall tales. The

---

hypothesis with the persuasive power of Wellhausen's *Prolegomena* has not yet been written.

[14] E. Meyer 1906, p.vii; H. Gunkel, esp. *op.cit.* 1901, p.19; H. Gressmann, esp. "Sage und Geschichte in den Patriarchenerzählungen," *ZAW* 30 (1910), pp.1-34; *idem*, "Ursprung und Entwicklung der Joseph-Sage," in *Eucharisterion*, Festschrift H. Gunkel (Leipzig, 1923) pp.1-55; and K. Galling, *op.cit.*

[15] O. Eissfeldt, "Stammessage und Novelle in den Geschichten von Jakob und von seinen Söhnen," *Eucharisterion* (1923) pp.56-77; *idem*, "Achronische, anachronische, und synchronische Elemente in der Genesis," *JEOL* 17 (1963), pp.148-164; *idem*, "Stammessage und Menscheitserzählung in der Genesis," *SSAWL* 110, 4 (1965), pp.5-21.

[16] H. Gunkel, *opera citata*, 1917, 1919, 1922; further, Th.L. Thompson, "The Conflict Themes in the Jacob Narratives," *Semeia* 15 (1979), pp.5-11.

pentateuchal legends were now judged to have been in their earliest forms tales about historical individuals: folk histories, which, because of their mode of transmission as relatively unfixed oral traditions, continuously attracted secondary inflations of what was asserted as an original historical account, eventually achieving a resemblance to fictive tales. That is, one had in the Old Testament not historicized fiction, but fictionalized history. Eissfeldt established the immensely influential doctrine that originating events lay behind the early biblical traditions wherever more than a single variant or account of a tradition was extant in the received text. An original historical event, which was thought to have given rise to such a complex tradition, could be recovered, so Eissfeldt argued, by discounting and removing the later, secondary accretions, until ultimately one discovered the historical nucleus that was hidden in all significant early traditions. It was only a short step to the assumption—long confirmed by scholarly practice and authority in both Germany and the United States—that the discovery of the primary or original core of a tradition was a discovery of the historical event itself. Its converse implication was also important: that the designation of an element of the tradition as secondary marked it, *ipso facto,* as unhistorical.[17]

Eissfeldt thus maintained the value of the early patriarchal traditions as history. The historical nuclei of the traditions were now sought in the process of a long *Traditionsgeschichte* that Old Testament scholarship widely asserted must lay behind our received text. In this search, secondary expansions were sharply distinguished by scholars from what was (frequently mistakenly) thought to be more original, primary, cores of tradition that were inevitably given great historical weight, since such primary traditions were understood to originate in events which they purportedly portrayed. It was often thought that to isolate the original form of a tradition was to write the prehistory both of the biblical text and of Israel as well. In this process, the thrust of Wellhausen's and Meyer's efforts to construct a critical history of early Israel was decisively parried, as historical-critical scholarship accepted an essential doctrine of fundamentalism, namely, that in the Bible one discovered history.[18]

---

[17] Only recently has it become widely recognized that neither assumption is probable; see J.M. Miller and J.H. Hayes, *A History of Ancient Israel and Judah* (Philadelphia, 1986), esp. pp. 74-79; and Th.L. Thompson, *op.cit.,* 1987, pp.11ff.

[18] B.O. Long, "On Finding the Hidden Premises," *JSOT* 39 (1987), pp.10-14.

At the time, there seemed no question whatever but that these earliest traditions were in fact direct reflections of the historical origins of Israel.

Eissfeldt argued further that the earlier the pentateuchal source or document in which a tradition was found, the more likely that tradition was to be close to the originating events. Thus the earlier J and E documents were given paramount importance as the primary historical sources for Israel's early history. Eissfeldt attributed many of the patriarchal sagas of Genesis to a specific literary type of narrative that he called a *Stammessage*. In this he understood the patriarchal stories to have their origin, not in historically irrelevant family tales that had, as Gunkel earlier suggested, only later become historicized. He understood them rather to have their nuclei and points of origin in the events of historical tribes and nations that had been fictively personified as individuals in the stories through fictionalized eponymic ancestors.[19] What in the extant text often gives the appearance of heroic tales reflects rather the historical activities of groups. Not Jacob's sons but the tribes of an historical Israel lay behind the originating events of Genesis.

By means of this union of source and form criticism, Old Testament historical-critical scholarship was able to redirect in the analysis of tradition history what originally had seemed to many to have been a destructive, negative trend in the higher criticism of Wellhausen, Meyer and others, towards a consensus in search of an historically positive synthesis. The correlative assumptions, that the traditional narratives of the pentateuch were fictionalized history and that the originating events of this tradition reflected the history of peoples of the ancient Near East, were quickly assimilated in a new generation of scholars as unquestioned—and to a great extent unquestionable—presuppositions of nearly all historical scholarship about the Bible and early Israel. With Eissfeldt and his generation, the pendulum of common opinion swung decisively in a conservative direction.

3. *The Rise of Biblical Archaeology*

The gains for Israelite history of this conservative swing in scholarship were immense. During the late 1920s, and increasingly through the

---

[19] O. Eissfeldt, *op.cit.*, 1923; see further *opera citata*, 1963, 1965. On eponomy generally, Th.L. Thompson, *op.cit.*, 1974, chapter 12a.

1930s, supported by the proven illustrative power of geographical research and anthropological studies strongly supported by such religiously conservative scholars as Dalman,[20] the influx of a very large number of remarkable epigraphic and archaeological discoveries from the ancient Near East permanently transformed the historical component of biblical studies. Systematic archaeological explorations and major excavations throughout *Palestine* and its neighboring regions brought a flood of new information to both biblical exegesis and to the history of Israel, affecting particularly biblical scholarship's understanding of the early history of Israel. As is also the case today, the problem of the synthesis of a mass of new data (and the relative inadequacy of methods in the field for integrating new types of historical information) was pivotal to the interpretation of details. This unfortunately depended largely on the research and imagination of only a handful of scholars. While Eissfeldt's major contributions to Old Testament scholarship lay in literary criticism, the work and methods of two of his contemporaries strongly influenced the future development of historical studies on both sides of the Atlantic for nearly a half-century: W.F. Albright in the United States and A. Alt in Germany.

Although Albright was more conservative and Alt more liberal than Eissfeldt, both shared his essential union of source and form criticism. They also shared his conservative presuppositions that the biblical tradition was generally historical in origin and that the historical events which lay behind any tradition could theoretically be discovered in the earliest forms of that tradition. Albright and Alt shared a common goal of constructing a history of early Israel on the basis of a critical appraisal and synthesis of biblical, archaeological and ancient Near Eastern studies. To uncover the historical events of Israel's past was the task which both men hoped to find resolved through the new extrabiblical sources now becoming available. Unlike Eissfeldt, neither of these scholars was much interested in the problems of source criticism. Alt was openly pious towards Wellhausen's work but, in practice, a successor more of E. Meyer or of the early Gunkel. For him, the oral prehistory of the text was of immense importance for historical reconstruction. The documents of the pentateuch were perhaps necessary assumptions, but were of limited use. Albright, on the other hand, after an initial flirtation with the panbabylonianism of the *Babel-Bibel* school and with form

---

[20] See above, note 8.

criticism,[21] was openly hostile to Wellhausen and his successors,
particularly to their source-critically and form-critically based rejection
of the historicity of what were for Albright many of Israel's earliest
traditions. Although Albright never attempted a sustained criticism of
the documentary hypothesis, he, like Alt, held a strong brief for a
preliterary oral transmission, and openly espoused the tradition history
promoted by many Scandinavian scholars.[22] In the wide range of studies
that Albright undertook, covering nearly the entire field of ancient Near
Eastern studies, he created an accumulating list of new historical hypotheses based on a direct correlation of biblical tradition with
extrabiblical data. On the strength of these theses, he was able to
conclude that the early history and prehistory of Israel—from a
patriarchal period to the time of the monarchy—had been in outline
confirmed by the historical archaeological information from *Palestine,
Egypt, Mesopotamia, Palestine* and *Syria* of the second-millennium B.C.[23]
Albright's goal was to fit the early history of Israel into the framework
of the history of the ancient Near East.[24] The biblical narrative, already
assumed to be motivated by a comprehensive historiography originating
from approximately the same time as, or immediately after, the historical
events which it portrayed, provided for Albright both an interpretive
structure and a framework for hundreds of complex and fragmentary
discoveries throughout the many distinct fields of oriental studies which
had been newly created during his very productive career.

The unfortunate but understandable shallowness of Albright's
historical perspective, the essential circuity of his comparisons, the lack
of a clear method of analysis and of explicit principles of verification and
the attraction to reconstructions in which every new element in his
hypothesis changed the constellation of the whole as new perspectives
were gained in related fields, ultimately destroyed his every attempt at

---

[21] W.F. Albright, "Historical and Mythical Elements in the Joseph Story," *JBL* 37 (1918),
pp.111-143. H. Winckler, *opera citata*.

[22] W.F. Albright, "Albrecht Alt," *JBL* 75 (1956), pp.169-173.

[23] For summary accounts, See esp. W.F. Albright, *From the Stone Age to Christianity*
(Garden City, 1940, [3]1957); *idem, Archaeology and the Religion of Israel* (Baltimore, 1953);
idem, The Biblical Period from Abraham to Ezra (New York, 1963); *idem, Yahweh and the
Gods of Canaan* (London, 1968).

[24] W.F. Albright, *op.cit.* 1940.

synthesis[25] and resulted in many of the later contributions of his life incoherently contradicting much of his earlier work.[26] Albright was neither an historian nor an exegete, but rather an antiquarian, an archaeologist of great originality and a philologist of breadth. The field of Semitic studies generally was poorly developed and allowed a range of speculation that is of course impossible today. His great influence on research in the fields of the archaeology and history of *Palestine* has, however, been immense and extraordinarily creative. The wide range of his interests, his productivity, and the quickness of his mind dominated for both good and ill nearly two generations of American scholarship.

Albright's work had a major impact on the development of three critical theses in the history of Israel's origins: a) the establishment and delineation of an historical patriarchal period within the context of ancient Near Eastern history. While Albright's latest synthesis, in which he attempted to portray Abraham as a donkey caravaneer of the Middle Bronze I period, did not gain widespread support,[27] and while his earlier arguments for Abraham's historicity on the basis of the "Amorite" hypothesis and the nomadic character of Middle Bronze I were strongly disputed and overturned in the mid-seventies,[28] many of the details of our history of the second-millennium B.C., especially as they relate to chronology, archaeological stratigraphy and ceramic typology are still today rooted in Albright's often pioneering work. To some extent this has been due to an ideologically saturated indifference to any history of *Palestine* that does not directly involve the history of Israel in biblical exegesis; b) an argument against an evolutionary view of the origins of Israelite religion, coupled with the assertion of the origins of Israelite monotheism in the Mosaic tradition.[29] The negative

---

[25] Th.L. Thompson, *The Historicity of the Patriarchal Narratives, BZAW* 133 (Berlin, 1974), pp.52-57. See also, more recently, *idem*, "W.F. Albright as Historian," *Proceedings of the Midwest Regional Meeting of SBL* (1992 forthcoming).

[26] Esp. W.F. Albright, "Abram the Hebrew, A New Archaeological Interpretation," *BASOR* 163 (1961), pp.36-54; but also substantial portions of *idem, op.cit.*, 1968.

[27] M. Weippert, "Abraham der Hebräer? Bemerkungen zu W.F. Albright's Deutung der Väter Israels," *Bb* 52 (1971), pp.407-432.

[28] Th.L. Thompson, *Historicity* (1974), pp.17-186; *idem, The Settlement of Sinai and the Negev in the Bronze Age, BTAVO* 8 (Wiesbaden, 1975); *idem, The Settlement of Palestine in the Bronze Age, BTAVO* 34 (Wiesbaden, 1979); J. Van Seters, *Abraham in History and Tradition* (New Haven, 1975).

[29] *Op.cit.*, 1940, p.45; 1942, p.68.

focus of Albright's arguments was primarily directed against the spector of Wellhausen's understanding of Israelite religion, beginning from an original polytheism reflected in the patriarchal narratives, through the henotheism of Joshua and Judges to the monotheism of the prophets. Albright correctly saw this as severely undermining both the historicity of the Mosaic tradition[30] and the perspective of most of biblical historiography.[31] It is perhaps this issue of *Religionsgeschichte* more than any other that separated Albright (who had been a student of the ultraconservative P. Haupt) from Alt (strongly influenced by Gunkel). On most issues, Albright's views were very close to those of Alt, especially to Alt's understanding of the "God of the Fathers" as a distinctively proto-Israelite, pre-monotheistic religious conception. Albright also accepted Alt's distinction in ancient Israelite law between pre-Canaanite apodictic and originally Canaanite casuistic forms of laws, and argued further that this distinction definitively established an historical basis for an original Mosaic lawgiving. Albright also accepted Alt's concept of amphictyony as an essential, unifying political structure of early Israel—attributing Israel's amphictyony, however, to a preconquest period, and dating it prior to Israel's entry into the land. Finally, Albright echoed Alt's understanding of charismatic leadership as the primary ideological and sociopolitical foundation for the period of the Judges.[32]

On the question of the historicity of the Mosaic tradition, however, Alt was generally more skeptical than Albright, as his understanding of a gradual and peaceful settlement of originally unrelated tribal groups (which had become Israel only after their establishment in *Palestine* under an amphictyony) was thoroughly irreconcilable with either an historical patriarchal period or an understanding of Moses as the actual founder of Israelite religion. While Albright recognized the essential improbability of establishing extrabiblical evidence for the Israel of Moses in *Egypt* or *Sinai* of the Late Bronze period, he used source and form criticism[33] to argue that the documentary sources of the bible's pentateuchal tradition originated from a single eleventh-century epic narrative. Since J, E and P gave independent affirmation of the essential

---

[30] *Op.cit.*, 1968, pp.153ff.

[31] *Ibid.*, p.183.

[32] On Alt, see below, Chapter 2.

[33] A. Alt, *op.cit.*, 1940, pp.189–193.

structure of the Mosaic tradition, he argued that the historicity of this epic narrative could be accepted as likely. Once historicity could be assumed, then the various Egyptian motifs of the Joseph and Moses stories could function as supportive evidence. In Albright's argument for the authenticity and historicity of the Mosaic tradition, he began to use a principle of argumentation that in subsequent years became increasingly common throughout both American and German biblical scholarship; namely, that if the biblical "witness" was "unanimous," the events recounted could be regarded as likely or probable.[34] Albright reconciled his Mosaic period with an independent and prior patriarchal period in *Palestine* by pointing to such stories as Genesis 34[35] (which involved only some of the Israelite tribes) as evidence for a preconquest presence of these tribes in Palestine. This tradition Albright associated with extrabiblical "evidence" by understanding the *'apiru* of the Late Bronze *Amarna* tablets as reflecting a continuous Hebrew presence in *Palestine* even during the period of sojourn. Albright's argument closed with the observation that only some of the Hebrew tribes had been directly associated with Moses in *Egypt* and *Sinai*.[36]

While few scholars today would care to support Wellhausen's view of the evolutionary development of Israelite religion that had dominated scholarly understanding of Israelite religion prior to the publication of

---

[34] W.F. Albright, *op.cit.*, 1940, p.196. Critical in the assumption of unanimity is of course that Albright's 'independent' witnesses are the so-called J, E and P of the documentary hypothesis, a theory which had largely been established on the "principle" that the large number of doublet traditions in the pentateuch reflected multiple independent sources. The circuity of this logic escapes many still today. Whether this theory of Albright's was initially independent of Noth's *Grundlage* theory is uncertain. The two hypotheses served different functions: while Noth's *Grundlage* functioned as a base from which disparate oral traditions developed, Albright's oral epic served a harmonizing function for extant biblical traditions. Speiser's "Tradition" in his Anchor Bible commentary (*Genesis*, Garden City, 1965, esp. his "Introduction") adopts much of Albright's theory, but largely through the lens of Noth's *Grundlage*. F.M. Cross's hypothesis of an epical "Divine Warrior" tradition (*Canaanite Myth and Hebrew Epic*, Cambridge, 1973) is a more sophisticated version of Albright's theories, allowing for an early dating of several early Hebrew poems, harmonistically read along a continuum of epic poetry rooted in Ugaritic literature. Such interpretations stand or fall neither on their heuristic value nor on the quality of the analogies with Ugarit but on their wholly arbitrary historical assumptions.

[35] *Op.cit.*, 1940, pp.179-183.

[36] A position already put forward by Eissfeldt and by Meyer before him.

Alt's "Der Gott der Väter" in 1929,[37] an understanding of development and change in Israelite religion and of the creative role played by Old Testament prophecy in the origins of monotheism, while not as yet dominant interpretations, are nevertheless strong tendencies.[38] A fully developed Mosaic period in Israelite history has hardly survived in today's scholarship,[39] and many of the positions that Albright had accepted from Alt are no longer widely held. Nevertheless, several of Albright's seminal views have been further explored and strongly supported by his students. Certainly the concept of the radical distinctiveness of Israelite faith and tradition from its ancient Near Eastern matrix is unfortunately widely assumed in detail. G.E. Wright,[40] F.M. Cross[41] and W.W. Hallo[42] have argued adamantly and expansively for the uniqueness of Israelite culture and tradition both in contrast to and in conflict with its "Canaanite" neighbors. It is most clearly in the "revolt model" of Israel's origins that many of these ideas are put forward by G.E. Mendenhall and N.K. Gottwald. Fundamental to their "revolt" theory is the acceptance of a "Moses group" separate from the rest of Israel as the originators of "Yahwistic" faith.[43] The historicity of the Exodus[44] and the existence of an Israelite amphictyony as the

---

[37] A. Alt, *Kleine Schriften I*, pp.1–78 (Munich, 1953).

[38] J.A. Emerton, "New Light on the Israelite Religion: the Implications of the Inscriptions from Kuntillet Ajrud," *ZAW* 94 (1982), pp.2–20; G. Ahlström, *An Archaeological Picture of Iron Age Religions in Ancient Palestine*, Studia Orientalia 55/3 (Helsinki, 1984); *idem, Who Were the Israelites?* (Winona Lake, 1986).

[39] For a brief survey see Th.L. Thompson, "The Joseph and Moses Narratives," in *Israelite and Judaean History*, ed. by J.H. Hayes and J.M. Miller (Philadelphia, 1977) pp.149–179, 210–212. Also J.B. Geyer, "The Joseph and Moses Narrative: Folk-Tale and History," *JSOT* 15 (1980), pp.51–56 and Th.L. Thompson, "History and Tradition: A Response to J.B. Geyer," *JSOT* 15 (1980), pp.57–61.

[40] G.E. Wright, The Old Testament Against its Environment (London, 1955); *idem, God Who Acts* (London, 1962).

[41] F.M. Cross, *op.cit.*, esp. pp.79–90; see however more recently *idem*, "Biblical Archaeology: The Biblical Aspect," *Biblical Archaeology Today*, ed. by A. Biran (Jerusalem, 1985) pp.9–15.

[42] W.W. Hallo, "Biblical History in its Near Eastern Setting: the Contextual Approach," in *Scripture in Context*, ed. by W.W. Hallo (Winona Lake, 1980) pp.1–26.

[43] Above all, N.K. Gottwald, *The Tribes of Yahweh: A Sociology of the Religion of Liberated Israel*, 1250–1050 B.C. (New York, 1979) pp.33–40.

[44] Now supported by Mendenhall's theory of the Hittite origin of biblical concepts of covenant; G.E. Mendenhall, "Covenant Forms in Israelite Tradition," *BA* 17 (1954),

foundation of Israelite unity also remain as essential elements of this theory.[45] c) The third major thesis of Albright is the well known assertion that the biblical tradition of a united Israel conquering *Palestine* has been confirmed by our knowledge of the destruction of Late Bronze Canaanite cities by Israelite seminomads, resulting in the onset of Iron I, understood as an Israelite occupation.

There are at least five distinct complexes of issues in this hypothesis, which have often been viewed, even by Albright, as a single and univocal theory—with unfortunate consequences. The affirmation of one part of the hypothesis does not make the other aspects more probable nor does it confirm the hypothesis as a whole. Each aspect has a life of its own. The distinctiveness of the essential elements of this hypothesis has lent much to its ability to persuade and to survive over the years in spite of often trenchant and detailed criticism of various points of Albright's theories, which had been thoroughly reviewed in 1967 by M. Weippert and again with devastating implications by J.M. Miller in 1977.[46]

1) *Historiography.* When Albright argued that biblical historiography is confirmed by archaeology he had in mind a specific understanding of the biblical tradition. He believed that the biblical tradition is primarily an historiographical account of the past, very much in the terms of Eissfeldt.[47] He took for granted that the Bible's representations of the ancestors of Israel were not only as historical individuals, but were also literary representations of peoples, such as the Late Bronze 'apiru or the Middle Bronze "Amorites." Moreover, Albright presupposed that the affirmation of significant details of the tradition by extrabiblical sources established the historicity of the tradition as a whole, while an absence of affirmation and the contradiction of some elements of the tradition by such sources required a scholarly reinterpretation of the tradition which he understood to represent history through what was after all story, with its structural, fictionalizing bias. Good examples of this willingness to correct biblical tradition in the "light of history" are his interpretation of the traditional biblical account of the conquest of *Ai* and his dating of the conquest of *Canaan* to the Late Bronze–Iron Age transition, which he shared with many. Since the excavations of *at-Tall*

---

pp.50-76; Th.L. Thompson, *op.cit.*, 1977, pp.160-166.

[45] Above all Gottwald, *op.cit.*, 1979, pp.345-388.

[46] See above, note 1.

[47] *Op.cit.*, 1963, 1965.

(commonly identified with *Ai*) suggested that the site had been unoccupied between the Early Bronze period and Iron II, Albright suggested that the story about *Ai* in the Book of Joshua should be understood as referring historically to the conquest of nearby *Beitin*, and that this relatively minor adjustment of geographical perspective would permit the historical affirmation of the event. Similarly, since Albright believed that archaeological data relating to the destructions of Late Bronze cities in *Palestine* were best understood as a result of the Israelite conquest, he consequently corrected what had been understood as the traditional biblical chronology—which generally he otherwise was careful to maintain—and dated the conquest to the Late Bronze-Iron I transition rather than to an earlier date that might better follow the biblical chronologies.[48]

Not only did Albright view the biblical narratives as an adjustable history, his affirmation of historicity was specifically oriented to a select group of traditions, particularly those of Joshua 1–9. Other traditions, such as Judges 1[49] and Exodus 24:3–8,[50] which present a different picture of Israel's settlement in *Palestine,* were of little interest to Albright and were not included in his picture of what the biblical view of the conquest was. This of course was, in Albright's terms, fully legitimate, given his interpretation (following Eissfeldt) that the original histories in the Bible had only survived in fragmentary and partially fictionalized forms, of necessity limiting the scholar to an affirmation of only a "minimal" or "essential" historicity.

2) *Form Criticism.* Albright's confirmation of an essential historicity for the "biblical" framework of events rested independently on the poetically formulated "credal" summaries of Israel's past. While probably originating in the form-critical evaluation of credal formulas by Von Rad,[51] this seemingly complicated thesis rests on the entirely unjustified

---

[48] That this contradicted Albright's repeated assertions, that the historicity of the patriarchal narratives gained in plausibility because the prevalence of analogous evidence corresponded chronologically with a biblical dating of the patriarchs which presupposed a traditional dating of the conquest, is one of the more striking of the many anomalies of Albright's historical reconstructions, given the strong interests in chronological correlations that dominate so much of his published writings.

[49] M. Weippert, *op.cit.*, 1967, J.M. Miller, *op.cit.*, 1977.

[50] Th.L. Thompson, 1987, p.187.

[51] *Op.cit.*, 1966, pp.1–78, Th.L. Thompson, *op.cit.*, 1977, pp.162–166.

assumption—commonly held in Old Testament circles[52]—that generally speaking poems are early and prose is late. This is certainly rooted in the common sense observation that poetry is easier to remember; so that (and here logic weakens perceptibly) remembered history is more likely to be found in a form that is easier to remember. The jump in logic that then asserts a date "close to the events" on the grounds of assumed "early" forms for such poems as the songs of Miriam and Deborah is regrettable.[53] The far too common unconfirmed assertion in biblical studies derived from an oversimplistic concept: *Formgeschichte* (regnant throughout this entire period of biblical scholarship), which decrees that texts can be dated on the basis of their forms, supports a methodology that is wholly inappropriate to critical scholarship. The primary difficulty with this method is analogous to the problems of its daughter discipline *Redaktionsgeschichte*. That is, we do not have—by the furthest stretch of imagination—an adequate number of traditions and varieties of forms to say anything specific about their transposition and history.[54] Poetry—and especially highly dramatic epic poetry—gives no peculiarly formal warrant for assuming roots in historical events, let alone historicity (so also *The Odyssey, The Aeneid*). Nor does the particular form of songs that find themselves within prose narratives support the judgement that the song has a greater antiquity. Such an assumption with reference to such songs as the frequently cited Exodus 15:21 and Judges 5, which are refractions of a specific context within an appropriate prose narration, is particularly mind-boggling and needs to be understood as a product of a systematic, ideologically motivated scholarly agenda. Who would think of making any such claims for the barmaid's speech or for Ea's song to the reed hut of the Gilgamesh story, or indeed the biblical song of Genesis 3:14-19? It is form-critically characteristic of both biblical and ancient Near Eastern prose narratives to break into song, but it does nothing for us in terms of chronology. To assert that Ugaritic analogies to the song of Deborah help us date the biblical song early not only flies in the face of even closer parallels in the psalms but also ignores the proven durability of motifs, plot lines and literary narrative traditions across millennia in the ancient Near

---

[52] F.M. Cross, *op.cit.*, 1973, pp.112-144, esp, p.121.

[53] W.F. Albright 1956, *op.cit.*, p.172.

[54] See my comments on *Redaktionsgeschichte* in *op.cit.*, 1987, which are fully applicable here.

East. Neither the earliest examples of motifs or forms allows any precision of dating within the lifetime of that motif or form. Only if we can establish that a specific motif or form has ceased to exist in intellectual history can we render a "plus" factor of precision in our chronology, and we do not have that kind of information for any pre-hellenistic literature. Failing that capability in our sources, both *Formgeschichte* and *Redaktionsgeschichte* are exercises in futility.

Except for purposes of chronology, Albright made little use of any analysis of form or literary structure for the purpose of interpretation and historicization, though he readily accepted many of Eissfeldt's and Alt's conclusions and encouraged some of his students in this analysis.[55] These uncritical form-critical assumptions, however, often marred his otherwise open and critical perspective of historical questions[56] and have made constructive dialogue on many of his positions extremely difficult for critics of the "conquest model."[57] Indeed, Albright was admittedly least clear in his analysis of the Old Testament text itself, and any but the most vague references to what in fact he understood the biblical traditions to have been were rarely given.[58] This unfortunately

---

[55] Especially F.M. Cross, "Yahweh and the God of the Patriarchs," *HThR* 55 (1962), pp.225-259; *idem, op.cit.*, 1973, and G.E. Mendenhall, "Law and Covenant in Israel and the Ancient Near East," *BA* 17 (1954), pp.26-46; *idem*, "Covenant Forms in Israelite Tradition," *BA* 17 (1954), pp.50-76; *idem*, "The Hebrew Conquest of Palestine," *BA* 25 (1962), pp.66-87; *idem, The Tenth Generation* (Baltimore, 1973).

[56] In this freedom and openness towards extrabiblical presentation and a near total rejection of contemporary critical biblical research, Albright was followed by many of his students and close collaborators, such as G.E. Wright, *Biblical Archaeology* (Philadelphia, 1957), D.N. Freedman, "The Real Story of the Ebla Tablets: Ebla and the Cities of the Plain," *BA* 41 (1978), pp.143-164, and N. Glueck, *The Other Side of the Jordan* (New Haven, 1940); *idem, The River Jordan* (New York, 1946); and esp. *idem*, "The Age of Abraham in the Negev," *BA* 18 (1955), pp.10-22.

[57] Such as, e.g. G. Von Rad, "History and the Patriarchs," *Expository Times* 72 (1960/61), pp.213-216; and M. Noth, "Der Beitrag der Archäologie zur Geschichte Israels," *VTS* 7 (1960), pp.262-282; *idem, Die Ursprünge des alten Israel in Lichte neuer Quellen, AFLNW* 94 (1961).

[58] This lack of explicit reference and clarity is still a regrettable failing of some members of Albright's school, as for example in D.N. Freedman, *op.cit.*; H. Goedicke (see H. Shanks, "The Exodus and the Crossing of the Red Sea according to Hans Goedicke," *BAR* 7,5 (1981), pp.42-50), Y. Yadin, "Hazor" in *Archaeology and Old Testament Study*, ed. by D.W. Thomas (Edinburgh, 1967), 245-263; *idem, Hazor: The Head of All Those Kingdoms*, 1970 Schweich Lectures (Oxford, 1972); *idem, Hazor: The Rediscovery of a Great Citadel of the Bible* (London, 1975) and W. Dever, "The Patriarchal Traditions," in *Israelite and Judaean*

gave much of Albright's work an appearance of superficiality, and allowed it to be read with a greater dogmatic rigidity and flavor of neo-fundamentalism than it deserved.

3) *Nomadic Origins.* The third issue of Albright's historical reconstruction of Israel's origins rests in the identification of Joshua's conquest as a military campaign carried out by a unified invasion of Israelite nomads. This thesis rested on the assumption that both the destruction of the Late Bronze culture of the city-states and the establishment of the Iron Age cultural succession was caused by the belligerent incursion of nomads. In this, issues of the historicity of specific narratives like that about *Jericho* were functionally supportive rather than central to the argument as a whole. By this, I mean that Albright's hypothesis of conquest did not stand or fall on the question of historicity for any of the specific Joshua stories. That the historical debates of the 1950s and 1960s focussed on such immature perceptions was far more the result of the efforts of scholars such as J. Bright and G.E. Wright.[59]

The core of Albright's arguments centered in his understanding of the history of *Palestine.* In the current understanding of the Albright school, this assumption of Albright's has become very difficult to maintain and has been implicitly but forcefully rejected by Albright's student G. Mendenhall, as well as by C.H.J. de Geus, N. Gottwald, J.T. Luke, V. Matthews[60] and others in their critique of the nomadic background of the Israelite settlement that had been proposed by A. Alt, M. Noth and M. Weippert.[61]

History, ed. by J.H. Hayes and J.M. Miller (Philadelphia, 1977), esp. pp.104-120. Exceptions to this are many, most notably the often careful and detailed work of F.M. Cross (esp. *op.cit.*) 1973 and A. Malamat (e.g. "Die Frühgeschichte Israels: eine methodologische Studie," *ThZ* 39 (1983), pp.1-16).

[59] J. Bright, *op.cit.*, G.E. Wright, *Biblical Archaeology* (Westminster, 1956).

[60] C.H.J. de Geus, "The Amorites in the Archaeology of Palestine," *Ugarit-Forschung* 3 (1971), pp.41-60; *idem, The Tribes of Israel, Studia Semitica Neerlandica* 18 (Assen, 1976); N.K. Gottwald, "Domain Assumptions and Societal Models in the Study of Pre-Monarchic Israel," *VTS* 28 (1975), pp.89-100; idem, *op.cit.*, 1979; J.T. Luke, *Pastoralism and Politics in the Mari Period* (University of Michigan dissertation, 1965); V.H. Matthews, *Pastoral Nomadism in the Mari Kingdom (ca. 1830-1760 B.C.), ASORDS* 3 (Cambridge, 1978).

[61] N.P. Lemche, *Early Israel: Anthropological and Historical Studies on the Israelite Society Before the Monarchy, VTS* 37 (Leiden, 1985) pp.35-47.

I share the opinion that the concept of a nomadic movement at the beginning of Iron I (on a scale comparable to the equally questionable "Amorite migration" of Middle Bronze I) is no longer an adequate explanation for Israel's origin and needs to be thoroughly reexamined. Aside from the possible issue of naiveté and sociolinguistic outdatedness (which is of importance to Mendenhall and Gottwald),[62] the difficulties of asserting conquest and displacement, but above all a unity (as Albright in contrast to Alt did) among such invading tribes prior to the conquest, are formidable. Although the biblical historiography of a *Sinai* covenant and a prior Egyptian enslavement could theoretically supply that unity, the concept of the Israelites as nomadic in their economic and social structure hardly allows for their identification in the biblical tradition as refugees and fugitives lost in the wilderness. These difficulties of coherence have encouraged many scholars who would wish to support some element of conquest or settlement from outside of *Palestine* to reject the historicity of an Egyptian exodus and a source of tribal unity in the patriarchs, to describe a fragmented prehistory for Israel,[63] or to accept the *Shechem* legend of Joshua 24 (in spite of its deuteronomistic character) as alternative early historical bases for Israelite unity.[64] The issue of the role of nomads in Israel's origins, in spite of strong reservations by most scholars, remains nevertheless formidable. The assumption of a nomadic invasion and conquest, however, is today rare.[65]

4) *Canaanite-Israelite Dichotomy*. A fourth issue raised by Albright, already referred to above, was that the destroyers of the Late Bronze city-states were the settlers of the Iron age villages excavated in subsequent strata. This was for Albright almost always an issue of relative chronology, namely, that the destruction of the Late Bronze "Canaanite" levels was followed by Iron Age "Israelite" strata. Given the method of pottery chronology by key forms slotted to chronologically perceived categories or "blocks of time," the stratigraphic sequence lent

---

[62] See above all, N.P. Lemche, *idem*, pp.84-94.

[63] With greatest elaboration by R. de Vaux, *The Early History of Israel* (Philadelphia, 1978) pp.153-290.

[64] N. Gottwald, *op.cit.*, 1979, pp.566f. and esp. p.216!

[65] Perhaps A. Malamat, *op.cit.*, 1978, 1983; J. Bright, *A History of Israel* (Philadelphia, [3]1981). On the issue of nomads, see below, chapters 6 & 7, and Th.L. Thompson, "Palestinian Pastoralism and Israel's Origins," *SJOT* 6 (1992), pp.1-13.

itself to the interpretation that the occupants of the Late Bronze city had been displaced by the subsequent and distinct settlers of the next discrete level. Unfortunately, careful observation of stratigraphy methodologically recognizes change and difference but is often blind to continuity. Stratigraphically, continuity is by definition a non-recognition of change. The difficulties in determining the ethnic identification of both the destroyers and the occupants of given strata is now widely recognized. With that awareness, scholars no longer find archaeological evidence for an Israelite conquest of Canaanite cities apparent. The early failure of major excavations to identify the destruction of Canaanite towns by Israelites on the sites of *Ai* and *Jericho* certainly weakened the force of Albright's argument.[66] The uncertainty of distinguishing archaeological criteria for ethnic groups of Israelites and Canaanites, therefore, renders the issue of the transition from Late Bronze to the Iron Age dysfunctional as evidence for an Israelite conquest.

Albright's questions regarding the transition from Late Bronze to Iron Age archaeological strata in *Palestine* are closely related to the assumption (held in common with Alt) that the question of Israel's origin is to be solved in the elucidation of an historical transition from a Canaanite to an Israelite *Palestine*. Since the early Iron Age strata have indeed been difficult[67] (some would say impossible)[68] to identify as peculiarly Israelite, the question inevitably has arisen whether this historical assumption is justified, lacking as we do clear evidence that Israelites and Canaanites are in fact ethnically distinct peoples.[69] Albright's view—largely shaped by his consistent opposition to Alt's

---

[66] M. Weippert, *op.cit.*, 1967, pp.24ff., 50ff. (ET), J.M. Miller, *op.cit.*, 1977, pp.270-276. For a different opinion, see A. Malamat, *op.cit.*, 1978.

[67] Esp. J.A. Callaway, "New Evidence on the Conquest of Ai," *JBL* 87 (1968), pp.312-320; *idem*, "The Significance of the Iron Age Village at Ai (et-Tell)," *Proceedings of the Fifth World Congress of Jewish Studies* (Jerusalem, 1969) pp.56-61; *idem*, "Village Subsistence at Ai and Raddana in Iron Age I," *The Answers Lie Below: Essays in Honor of Lawrence Edmund Toombs*, ed. by H.O. Thompson (Lanham, 1984) pp.51-66; *idem*, "A New Perspective on the Hill Country Settlement of Canaan in Iron Age I," *Palestine in the Bronze and Iron Ages: Papers in Honour of Olga Tufnell*, ed. by J.N. Tubb (London, 1985) pp.31-49; J.M. Miller, *op.cit.*, 1977; *idem*, "Approaches to the Bible through History and Archaeology: Biblical History as a Discipline," *BA* 45 (1982), pp.211-216.

[68] N.P. Lemche, *op.cit.*, 1985; G. Ahlström, *op.cit.*, 1986.

[69] C.H.J. De Geus, *op.cit.*, 1976. See further below the related discussion of Alt's theory regarding the geographical distinctiveness of the Israelite occupation, and most recently N.P. Lemche, *The Canaanites and Their Land* (Sheffield, 1991).

Territorialgeschichte and his identification of the Israelite settlement with the conquest of the already occupied Canaanite territories—establishes a diametric opposition between the concepts "Canaanite" and "Israelite." This is indeed central to Albright's theological understanding of ancient Israel, and is strongly linked to the polarity of monotheism (=Israelite) vs. polytheism (=Canaanite) that one finds throughout his work. The inability of Palestinian archaeology, however, clearly to distinguish Canaan from Israel, suggests that this polarity is rather biblically based, and remains unverified by extrabiblical evidence, a requirement for the assumption of historicity that Albright himself has frequently stressed.[70]

5) *Chronology*. Finally, finding a biblical event's "place in the past," within the history of the ancient world, was ever Albright's starting point. The biblical and archaeological periods established by Albright became mutually definable and cyclically dependent. The central goal of Albright's vision of "biblical archaeology," so clearly elucidated in his *From the Stone Age to Christianity*, and followed throughout his career, has been to find a context within the history of the ancient Near East in which the history of Israel might develop. It is in respect to this central goal that the final but central issue regarding Albright's reconstruction of Israel's origins is his chronology: the, for him, pivotal perspective that Israel came to exist[71] as a "dominant presence in *Palestine*" from about 1200 B.C., and that the conquest occurred at the end of the thirteenth- and the beginning of the twelfth-century B.C. Few scholars have challenged this chronology.[72] Indeed Alt wholly concurred in this assumption in spite of the fact that it was perhaps Albright's most radical departure from Old Testament tradition and which in fact offers a much earlier date. Most scholars today, whether conservative or liberal, accept this date unquestionly as their starting point. Indeed, increasingly the question of Israel's origin has become—at least from the extrabiblical and archaeological perspective—largely an issue of describing, examining and debating what we know of the region of *Palestine* from approximate-

---

[70] This does not of itself show that this polarity is false; however, the fabric of his extrabiblical confirmation of Joshua's historiography is thereby radically weakened, whether in favor of Judges 1 or some entirely distinct interpretation.

[71] As A. Malamat, *op.cit.*, 1983, expressed so well.

[72] Cf., however, J.J. Bimson, *Redating the Exodus and Conquest, JSOTS* 5 (Sheffield, 1981).

ly 1300 to 1000 B.C.[73] The relatively long period in recent scholarship
in which there has been a consensus on such a pivotal issue as
chronology has greatly—albeit only implicitly—strengthened all of the
mainline interpretations of Israel's origins. However else these
interpretations have contradicted each other about what occurred, they
have been consistently and resolutely in agreement on the issue of when
it happened. Involved in this issue is not only the fragile issue of the
historicity of a period of the Judges, which twenty years ago none
doubted, but the much more central issue of what is understood by
"Israel."

Very recently, and closely linked to the challenges to biblical
historicity, departures by A. Soggin and J.M. Miller from this consensus
reflect a shift away from the equation of history and biblical
historiography, drawing a line between history and prehistory rather at
the monarchy.[74] In his dissertation, J.J. Bimson also breaks ranks with
the consensus from the conservative side,[75] making it adamantly clear
both how far Albright and his followers disagree with common tenets of
biblical historiography and chronology and how much the interpretation
and the chronology of the archaeology of *Syria-Palestine* has been
harmonized on the basis of the scholarly consensus.[76] The assumption
that the history of Israel's origin can be understood as a history of the
chronological transition between Late Bronze Canaanite city-states and
Iron I Israelite highland settlement stands as a hypothesis to be tested
anew and not as an historical starting point from which we may proceed
with confidence.

In two brief articles, and again in his very thorough synthesis of the
sources for early Israelite history, R. de Vaux summed up the Albright-
Alt consensus, and few would have seriously disagreed with him then.[77]

---

[73] J.A. Callaway, esp. *op.cit.*, 1985; N.K. Gottwald, *op.cit.*, 1979; I. Finkelstein, *The Archaeology of the Israelite Settlement* (Jerusalem, 1988); D.C. Hopkins, *The Highlands of Canaan, SWBAS* 3 (Sheffield, 1985); R.B. Coote and K.W. Whitelam, *The Emergence of Early Israel in Historical Perspective, SWBAS* 5 (Sheffield, 1987).

[74] J.A. Soggin, *A History of Israel* (London, 1984); J.M. Miller and J.H. Hayes, *A History of Israel and Judah* (Philadelphia, 1986).

[75] J.J. Bimson, *op.cit.*

[76] With the weakening of this consensus, see also G. Ahlström, *op.cit.*, 1986, Th.L. Thompson, *op.cit.*, 1987, and esp. J.M. Miller, *op.cit.*, 1982 and 1986.

[77] R. de Vaux, "Method in the Study of Early Hebrew History," *Biblical and Other Studies*, ed. by J.P. Hyatt (1966) pp.15-29; *idem*, "On Right and Wrong Uses of

The long-standing debate between the schools of Albright and Alt, between the alternative interpretations of "conquest" or "settlement" as an explanation of Israel's origins, has not been as important as the common gains and the expanding basis of agreement that have been achieved by the two sides of the issues. Alt and Albright, and Noth and Bright, did not after all stand so very far apart.

De Vaux's history of 1971 was conceptually a *tour de force* of all that we have come to understand of both the history of early *Palestine* and of the origins of early Israel in terms of a synthesis of biblical and extrabiblical evidence. De Vaux brought together a lifetime of familiarity with the details of biblical archaeology critically appraised with a deep respect for an historical-critical interpretation of the biblical tradition. De Vaux's work is one of those rare achievements in biblical scholarship, accomplishing the synthesis of biblical and extrabiblical evidence that he sought. Again, few in 1971 could or did disagree with him.[78] But this is no longer true. As de Vaux's *l'Histoire* represented the achievement of biblical archaeology at its critical best, it also marked its climax. The questions raised by Albright and dealt with throughout the history of the Albright school had run their course, and yet the quest of the historical Israel remained as elusive as ever. This attempt at a synthesis of biblical and extrabiblical evidence in the historiography of ancient Israel soon entered a long period of deconstruction that still continues today.[79]

Archaeology," *Near Eastern Archaeology in the Twentieth-Century: Essays in Honor of Nelson Glueck*, ed. by J.A. Sanders (New York, 1970) pp.64-80; *idem*, *op.cit.*, 1971.

[78] See, e.g., the additions introduced into the 3rd edition of J. Bright, *History of Israel* (Philadelphia, [3]1981), esp. pp.95f. 107f. 111ff. My own analysis of the issue of historicity of the Patriarchal Narratives (*op.cit.*, 1974) in press from early in 1971, in no way dealt with the radical alterations reflected in de Vaux's 1971 *l'Histoire*.

[79] M. Weippert, *op.cit.*, 1967; Th.L. Thompson, *op.cit.*, 1974; J. Van Seters, *op.cit.*, 1975; J.H. Hayes and J.M. Miller, *op.cit.*, 1977; G. Ramsey, *op.cit.*, 1981; N.P. Lemche, *op.cit.*, 1985; G. Ahlström, *op.cit.*, 1986; J.M. Miller and J.H. Hayes, *op.cit.*, 1986; Th.L. Thompson, *op.cit.*, 1987 and the discussion of this process below in Chapter 3.

CHAPTER TWO

SOCIAL ANTHROPOLOGY AND THE HISTORY OF PALESTINE

1. *Historical Polarities*

While Albright had sought to reestablish the prehistory of Israel in its Near Eastern setting and Dalman had made considerable progress in illustrating the sociological aspects of the biblical world in terms of the anthropology of *Palestine,* much of Alt's energies were dedicated to the establishment of the historical origin and character of the periods of the judges and of the rise of the monarchy. His focus was that of integrating his understanding of biblical and extrabiblical texts and archaeology with his reconstruction of the historical, social and anthropological realities of *Palestine.* This choice of Alt's was partially determined by the form-critical and literary studies of the *religionsgeschichtliche Schule* with its general skepticism concerning the historical value of the patriarchal and Exodus narratives, as well as its widely held conviction that the literary forms of the biblical traditions had each their own definable history, which directly reflected the historical context of their emergence in Israelite history. This led Alt to major and influential investigations of several aspects of the Old Testament tradition which he saw sharply contrasting with Israel's largely Canaanite context. Where Albright had traced the various avenues of historical coherence and harmony between Israel's origin traditions and the world of the ancient Near East, Alt used contrast and polarity as his key to the discovery of Israel's prehistory.

For Alt, one of the most important clues to Israel's origins was its uniqueness, its nonconformity with what he understood as a much older Canaanite society. Through a series of form-critical studies, distinguishing Canaanite from Israelite features of the biblical texts on the basis of closeness to and distance from cuneiform tradition, Alt was able to argue that the origin of major aspects of Israelite society (most importantly its concept of deity and its legal codes) were reflected in uniquely Israelite aspects of the traditions,[1] such as "the God of the Fathers" and such apodictic laws of the Old Testament as those found in the ten commandments. Other traditions that Israel held in common with the rest of the Near East (such as the El deity and agricultural laws) were understood by Alt as having been originally "Canaanite." Understandably, albeit illegitimately, Alt gave an historical dimension to this contrast and polarity by classifying what he recognized as uniquely Israelite as belonging to Israel's origins, and what he saw as Canaanite with those aspects of society that Israel had only later adopted after its establishment in *Palestine*. These two different kinds of elements, Alt argued, had been brought together in the course of Israel's integration into the Canaanized world of the monarchy. Through a careful examination of the "Israelite" traits of the received tradition, Alt believed that much of what had originally belonged to a presettlement period of Israel's history could be reconstructed. Hence, Alt spoke of a premonarchic adherence to "the God of the Fathers" (as well as the worship of Yahweh centered on the apodictic laws of the pentateuch) as originally Israelite, in contrast to the more centralized, harmonized monotheism of the Israelite monarchy. For Alt, there was indeed an essential Israel dominant already in the premonarchic period of the judges forming a bond of unity for the tribes. It was this bond which had made them Israel during the process of settlement, in a form of "amphictyony" (or federation) of tribes. This form-critically oriented polarity not only led Alt to view the eventual Canaanization of the Israelite tribes under the united monarchy as an adulteration of the pristine purity of premonarchic Yahwism in a manner reminiscent of 1 Samuel,[2] but his entire analysis was so structured that such dichotomies

---

[1] A. Alt, "Der Gott der Väter," *KS I* (Munich, 1953) pp.1-78 ="The God of the Fathers," *Essays on Old Testament History and Religion* (Oxford, 1966) pp.3-77.

[2] N.P. Lemche, *Early Israel: Anthropological and Historical Studies on the Israelite Society Before the Monarchy* (Leiden, 1985) pp.432-435. Alt is followed in this above all by G.E. Mendenhall, "The Hebrew Conquest of Palestine," *BA* 25 (1962), pp.66-87; *idem, The Tenth Generation: The Origins of Biblical Tradition* (Baltimore, 1973); *idem,* "The Monarchy," *Interpretation* 29 (1975), pp.155-170; *idem,* "Between Theology and Archaeology," *JSOT* 7 (1978), pp.28-34; *idem,* "Ancient Israel's Hyphenated History," *Palestine in Transition: The Emergence of Ancient Israel, SWBAS* 2 (Sheffield, 1983) pp.95-103; and N.K. Gottwald, *The Tribes of Yahweh: A Sociology of the Religion of Liberated Israel 1250-1050 B.C.E.* (Maryknoll, 1979).

and oppositions inescapably distorted his perspective, built as they were on the assumption of a Canaanite-Israelite polarity.

This observation must lead to a more nuanced inquiry into Alt's Canaanite-Israelite contrast. To what extent has the importance of the differences observed been predetermined by the literary opposition of Canaanites and Israelites in Joshua and Samuel? Are Alt's observations, as he believed, confirmation of the historical reality of the polarities expressed in the tradition? In the issues of laws and concepts of the divine, the chronological differentiation (so necessary to Alt's opposition of Israelite vs. non-Israelite in legal and religiously implicated traditions) is a differentiation which Alt himself has supplied. Nothing in the texts themselves identifies one side of the polarity as either earlier or later than the other. Nor in fact can it be argued with any objectivity that any of these aspects of the tradition can be identified ethnically as peculiarly Israelite or Canaanite.[3]

Moreover, an observation based on literary form itself requires a certain distance from Alt's original conclusions. The biblical concepts of a "God of the Fathers," and of a God giving laws by command, are in their essence literary concepts observable in story traditions of the Old Testament! Because of this, it must be taken seriously that we are not first of all dealing with types of deities and laws, but rather with types of literary motifs that may or may not reflect deities or laws of a real world. If we do not have corroborative evidence from the real world that such deities and laws existed—and uniqueness was the very basis for Alt's identification of them as Israelite—then we can hardly have any form-critical or literary and interpretive grounds for using such materials for historical reconstruction. Such historical conservatism and sobriety is justified by the further observation that such literary motifs as the divine "command"—both negative and positive—and the "God of the Fathers" function admirably both as central literary elements in the multiple variant stories of Israel's constitutional law being given to Moses by God and as redactional efforts associating the patriarchal narratives with the Mosaic traditions. Chronologically, these motifs function within the literary narrative connections that the traditions

---

[3] *Mutatis mutandis*, this same argument is to be made against the Mendenhall-Gottwald polarity regarding a revolutionary purity of the time of the judges vs. the brutal centralization of the monarchy.

make, between the story time of distinct individual narratives and other origin traditions already recounted.

In 1924 and especially 1925, Alt began to develop a history of Israel's origins that survived essentially intact over a half-century.[4] Here again, the Canaanite-Israelite polarity played a central role in the development of Alt's hypothesis. I believe this polarity is both the central strength and the fatal weakness of his understanding of Israel's origins, namely, that Israel came into existence as the result of a process of gradual infiltration and sedentarization of pastoral nomads in the territories of *Palestine* that were furthest from the densely occupied agricultural zones of the lowlands.

Canaan was above all for Alt the concrete Palestinian "city-states" of the *Amarna* period and the Egyptian Empire during the Late Bronze Age, and both the chronological and socio-geographical designations are aspects of his understanding. "Presettlement Israel" on the other hand was an abstract and derivative concept, its details drawn out principally in contrast to, and through the negation of, those aspects of the tradition which he understood to be "Canaanite" in essence and origin. In polarity with "presettlement Israel," moreover, *Canaan* became a type specimen,

---

[4] A. Alt, "Ein Reich von Lydda," *ZDPV* 47 (1924), pp.169-185; *idem, Die Landnahme der Israeliten in Palästina: Reformationsprogramm der Universität Leipzig* (1925) = "The Settlement of the Israelites in Palestine," *Essays on Old Testament History and Religion* (Oxford, 1966) pp.133-169. See also *idem, Die Staatenbildung der Israeliten in Palästina*: *Reformationsprogramm der Universität Leipzig* (1930) = "The Formation of the Israelite State in Palestine," *Essays*, pp.171-237; and *idem*, "Erwägungen über die Landnahme der Israeliten in Palästina," *PJ* 35 (1939), pp.8-63. More recent studies strongly influenced by and agreeing with Alt's model have not only been such creative and detailed German studies as M. Noth, *Das System der zwölf Stämme Israels* (Göttingen, 1930); *idem, Geschichte Israels* (Stuttgart, [3]1954); M. Weippert, *Die Landnahme der israelitischen Stämme in der neueren wissenschaftlichen Diskussion*, FRLANT 92 (Göttingen, 1967); *idem*, "Semitische Nomaden des zweiten Jahrtausends. Über die *shasw* der ägyptischen Quellen," *Bb* 55 (1974), pp.265-280, 427-433; *idem*, "The Israelite 'Conquest' and the Evidence from Transjordan," in *Symposia*, ed. by F.M. Cross (Cambridge, 1979) pp.15-34; S. Herrmann, *Geschichte Israels*; H. Donner, *Geschichte des Volkes Israel und seiner Nachbarn in Grundzügen: Grundrisse zum Alten Testament: ATD* Ergänzungsreihe 4,1-2; 2 vols. (Göttingen, 1984, 1986), but also most major European and American histories of the past two decades: R. de Vaux, *L'Histoire ancienne d'Israel* I. *Des origines à l'installation en Canaan* (Paris, 1971); H. Jagersma, *A History of Israel in the Old Testament Period* (Philadelphia, 1983); N. Gottwald, *op.cit.*, 1979, B. Halpern, *The Emergence of Israel in Canaan*, SBLMS (Chico, 1983); J.A. Soggin, *A History of Israel: From the Beginnings to the Bar Kochba Revolt, AD 135* (London, 1984) and J.M. Miller, and J.H. Hayes, *A History of Ancient Israel and Judah* (Philadelphia, 1986).

no longer directly reflecting the known historical realities of the Late Bronze Age. "Canaanite" *Palestine* was the political system of interlocking city states which were by definition agricultural, monarchic and polytheist—legally, cultically and intellectually associated with the cuneiform world. "Presettlement Israel" was its opposite—a tribal culture, sheep herding and seminomadic, with personal gods and an *élan vital* that was structurally democratic.[5] The polarities that Alt used in developing his argument for the origin of Israel had been constructed from two presumably complementary dichotomies: not only that of "Canaan" vs. "Israel" but also the chronological and typological contrast between the Late Bronze and the Iron Age cultures of *Palestine*. The first of these, of course, as we noted above, was a dichotomy which the biblical tradition itself had presented to us.[6] The Late Bronze-Iron Age contrast, however, Alt developed on geographical, historical and arch- aeological grounds, within the temporal contrast of before and after Israel had become a dominant presence in *Palestine*.[7] Because of the mixed categories of Alt's polarity, the contrast that he presented was not simply descriptive, recounting typical characteristics of two known contemporary and historical groups, the Canaanites and the Israelites. Rather, Alt's "Canaanites" were known primarily through a harmony of an identification and synthesis of historical sources with a (largely independently derived) biblical ethnic concept. "Israelite" was known (if at all) only from the later historiographical accounts of its own origin traditions. The Late Bronze Period (or indeed *Palestine* of the whole of the second and third millennia)—a concept that is applicable to all of Palestine—was designated descriptively as "Canaanite" because this

---

[5] See also now N.K. Gottwald, *op.cit.*, 1979; G.E. Mendenhall, *op.cit.*, 1973; and G.A. Herion, "The Impact of Modern and Social Science Assumptions on the Reconstruction of Israelite History," *JSOT* 34 (1986), pp.3-33.

[6] A similar argument, based on Alt's Canaanite-Israelite polarity has recently been put forward by G. Ahlström, *Who Were the Israelites?* (Winona Lake, 1986). Ahlström, however, attempts to ground the polarity extra-biblically, not only with the archaeological and geographical distinctions drawn by Alt earlier, but also through the identification of the hill country of early Iron I as uniquely Israel, in contrast to a Canaan of the coastal region and central valleys, on the strength of the Israel stele of Merneptah. In this—and wholly apart from questions of method—Ahlström approaches the interpretations of Mendenhall and Gottwald.

[7] Here I again borrow the very useful concept of A. Malamat ("Die Frühgeschichte Israels: eine methodologische Studie," *Theologische Zeitschrift* 39, 1983, pp.1-16), for separating Israel's history from its prehistory.

period was in principle for Alt "pre-Israelite." The Iron Age was either understood as "Israelite" or was thought of as *Palestine* in the process of becoming Israel, the changes in the "non-Canaanite" territories of *Palestine* being identified with the emergence or the origin of Israel. In this we become aware that Alt's argumentation proceeded most emphatically as a complex typological abstraction that traced the chronological trajectories from what he had assumed to have been the radical cultural changes brought about by the settlement of disparate groups that, during this process, had come to identify themselves as "Israel." In his specific delineation of these groups, Alt emphasized a presettlement nucleus of biblical traditions that he identified through his form-critical approach to biblical narrative. This presettlement nucleus of biblical narrative formed a substantial portion of Israelite tradition that he believed had survived the integration of the early proto-Israelite tribes with what was an alien Canaanite culture.[8]

W.F. Albright[9] and many of his students[10] have applauded and generally adopted both Alt's influential interpretation of the "God of the Fathers"[11] and his amphictyony hypothesis as developed by Noth.[12] However, many of the Albright school felt that Alt's unnecessary and formal distinctions encouraged an arbitrary and negative approach to most of what they considered to be Israel's earliest prehistory, in particular the traditions of the patriarchal and Moses narratives.[13]

---

[8] This presettlement tradition is developed further in Noth's concept of *Grundlage* (M. Noth, *Überlieferungsgeschichtliche Studien* I, Halle, 1943, *passim; idem, Überlieferungsgeschichte des Pentateuch*, Stuttgart, 1948, *passim*) and is consciously taken over by N.K. Gottwald (*op.cit.*, 1979), and largely presupposed by B. Halpern (*op.cit.*, 1983). Indeed, some such argument is an essential requirement if one wishes to bridge the gap between the later biblical traditions and what are largely late second-millennium historical issues.

[9] W.F. Albright, "Albrecht Alt," *JBL* 75 (1956), pp.169–173.

[10] J. Bright, *A History of Israel* (Philadelphia, [3]1981).

[11] Developed, with major revisions, in F.M. Cross, "Yahweh and the God of the Patriarchs," *HThR* 55 (1962), pp.225–259.

[12] M. Noth, *Das System der zwölf Stämme Israels*, BWANT IV,1 (Stuttgart, 1930).

[13] It was this issue, more than any other, which separated the American and German schools of biblical studies throughout the post-World War II period until the mid-seventies. The seemingly sharp divisions in the conquest vs. settlement controversy, outlined so clearly in M. Weippert (*Die Landnahme der israelitischen Stämme in der neueren wissenschaftliche Diskussion*, FRLANT 92, Göttingen, 1967), had little more substance than the sharp polemical exchange over the quasi-fundamentalistic issue of G.E. Wright's (*Biblical*

Given Alt's form-critical approach, the presettlement period of *Palestine* was "Canaanite" not only in itself but in contrast to "Israelite." Through this complex dichotomy, historical research into the texts and archaeological remains of Bronze Age *Palestine,* and the history and culture of the rest of the ancient Near Eastern world of the second-millennium, was pursued by Alt without reference to the biblical themes that were so necessary to Albright's approach. Logically and very coherently, presettlement Israel was for Alt, by definition, extra-Palestinian! The historical and geographical setting of the patriarchs in *Palestine* was consequently understood as anachronistic and fictional, a result of post–settlement efforts to organize Palestinian Israel's cultic tradition in its new home. Alt's student Noth,[14] under the influence of Eissfeldt and Albright, attributed to the patriarchal narratives a minimal historicity: the early memory of a migration of "Proto-Aramaean"

Archaeology, London, 1957) and J. Bright's (*Early Israel in Recent History Writing,* SBTh 19, London, 1956; *idem, History of Israel*, Philadelphia, 1959) spirited and elaborate defense of Joshua's narratives about the conquest of Jericho and Ai against A. Alt ("Erwägungen über die Landnahme der Israeliten in Palästina," *PJ* 35, 1939, pp.8-63) and M. Noth's (*Geschichte Israels*, Göttingen, 1959; *idem,* "Überlieferungsgeschichtliches zur zweiten Hälfte des Josuabuches," *Alttestamentliche Studien: Friedrich Nötscher zum sechzigsten Geburtstag, 19 Juli 1950, gewidmet von Kollegen, Freunden und Schülern, BBB* 1, ed. by H. Junker and J. Botterweck, Bonn, 1950, pp.152-167) characterization of these stories as aetiological. R. de Vaux rightly rejects any substantive evaluation of this conflict ("Method in the Study of Early Hebrew History," *The Bible and Modern Scholarship*, ed. by J.P. Hyatt, Atlanta, 1966, pp.15-29). The recognition of the aetiological elements as singular motifs in larger, but nevertheless fictional, narratives should finally close this issue. Certainly today the differences between adherents of these two scholarly traditions are no longer substantial, but are limited to specific details of historical reconstruction only (B.O. Long, *The Problem of Etiological Narrative in the Old Testament, BZAW* 108, Berlin, 1968).

[14] M. Noth, *Die israelitischen Personennamen im Rahmen der gemeinsemitischen Namengebung, BWANT* 10 (Stuttgart, 1928) pp.27-30. 43; *idem, Geschichte Israels* (Göttingen, ²1954) p.117; *idem,* "Zum Problem der Ostkanaanäer," *ZA* 39 (1930), pp.214-216; "Die syrisch-palästinische Bevölkerung des zweiten Jahrtausends v.Chr. im Lichte neuer Quellen," *ZDPV* 65 (1942), pp.34f.; *idem, Die Welt des Alten Testaments, Theologische Hilfsbücher* 3 (Berlin, ⁴1962) p.213; idem, "Mari und Israel: Eine Personennamenstudie," *Geschichte und altes Testament; Beiträge zur historischen Theologie:* Festschrift A. Alt (Tübingen, 1953) pp.149f.; and esp.*idem, Die Ursprünge des alten Israel im Lichte neuer Quellen, Arbeitsgemeinschaft für Forschung des Landes Nordrhein-Westfalen,* 94 (Cologne, 1961); Th.L. Thompson, *The Historicity of the Patriarchal Narratives, BZAW* 133 (Berlin, 1974) pp.75-78; D.O. Edzard, "Mari und Aramäer," *ZA* 22 (1964), pp.142-149; M. Wagner, "Beiträge zur Aramäismenfrage im alttestamentlichen Hebräisch," *VTS* 16 (Leiden, 1967) pp.355-371.

nomadic groups into *Palestine*. These groups, known from *Mari* in the early second-millennium B.C., Noth suggested, were historically connected with migrations of semi-nomadic, Aramaean related Israelites. For Alt, however, with greater logic and theoretical consistency, only with the settlement could the history of Israel, and with it the interrelating and harmonizing of historical and biblical sources, begin.

It was this systematic and methodical exclusion of most of the then known historical texts and archaeological remains from the second-millennium B.C., and not any philosophical skepticism regarding the historical value of the pentateuch, nor any lack of confidence in the potential of archaeological research for biblical studies that distinguished Alt's research so sharply from that of his less theoretically oriented American colleague Albright, who quite clearly held no assumptions about an ethnic unity—for all its seeming necessity—of any of the preconquest aspects of ancient Israel. While Albright could argue for both the historicity of the patriarchal narratives and an historical reconstruction of the conquest based on an immigration or invasion of nomads from the desert, Alt could not. Unlike Albright, Alt was unable to separate "presettlement Israel" from his understanding of the process of settlement.

2. *The Extrabiblical Sources*

In Alt's justly famous 1925 article[15] on the settlement of the Israelites in *Palestine,* he began with the prescient statement that "as long as research continues to embrace only the history of the tribes and the people of Israel, and is based only on the relevant traditions in the Old Testament, it is extremely doubtful whether the major uncertainties can ever be resolved."[16] This has certainly been borne out in the work of M. Noth, who sought to substantiate systematically Alt's understanding of Israel's origins through an examination of the history of Israel's traditions.[17] In this study, Noth undertook a full-scale and radical revision of Wellhausen's history of the pentateuch as well as of the so-called deuteronomistic histories. Thus, he sought to make these

---

[15] A.Alt, *op.cit.*, 1925.

[16] *Ibid.*, p.135.

[17] M. Noth, *op.cit.*, 1940.

traditions historically accessible. The valid results of Noth's study are a series of negative judgments regarding questions of historicity.[18] His lasting historical contributions to Alt's program lay not so much in his biblical analysis, but rather in his detailed clarification of the "amphictyony" hypothesis[19] and in the many historical studies of detail that he pursued over many years (along with similar work by such scholars as Galling and de Vaux). The fruits of this work are reflected in his still very useful *Die Umwelt des alten Testaments,* which was aimed towards the as yet unrealized goal of a comprehensive history of *Palestine.*[20]

---

[18] M. Noth, *op.cit.,* 1962. The full implications of Noth's analysis may be glimpsed in the thorough evaluations of the biblical narratives by Miller-Hayes, *op.cit.,* 1986.

[19] M. Noth, *op.cit.,* 1930.

[20] In very recent times, many regional and ethnic studies offer considerable promise: T. Dothan, *The Philistines and their Material Culture* (New Haven, 1982); M. Weippert, *Edom* (Tübingen dissertation, 1971); S. Moscati, *I Fenici* (Milan, 1988); J. Spannuth, *Die Phönizier: Ein Nordmeervolk in Libanon* (Osnabrück, 1985); O. Loretz, *Habiru-Hebräer* (Berlin, 1984); I. Ephál, *The Ancient Arabs* (Leiden, 1982); A.H. Jones, *Bronze Age Civilization: The Philistines and Danites* (Washington, 1975); H.M. Niemann, *Die Daniter: Studien zur Geschichte eines altisraelitischen Stammes,* FRLANT 135 (Stuttgart, 1985); S. Mittmann, *Beiträge zur Siedlungs- und Territorialgeschichte des nördlichen Jordanlandes,* ADPV (Wiesbaden, 1970); M. Wüst, *Untersuchungen zu den siedlungsgeographischen Texten des alten Testaments,* BTAVO B9 (Wiesbaden, 1979); A.H. Van Zyl, *The Moabites* (Leiden, 1960); M.S. Seale, *The Desert Bible: Nomadic Tribal Culture and Old Testament Interpretation* (London, 1974); E.A. Knauf, *Ismael, ADPV* (Wiesbaden, 1985, 2nd. ed. 1989); idem, *Midian, ADPV* (1988); J.M. Miller and J.W. Pinkerton, *Archaeological Survey of the Kerak Plateau* (Atlanta, 1991). Such individual studies provide a necessary supplement to the growing number of chronologically limited surveys as those of K. Prag, "The Intermediate Early Bronze-Middle Bronze Age: an Interpretation of the Evidence from Transjordan, Syria, and Lebanon," *Levant* 6 (1974), pp.69-116; Th.L. Thompson, *The Bronze Age Settlement of Sinai and the Negev,* BTAVO 8 (Wiesbaden, 1975); idem, *The Bronze Age Settlement of Palestine,* BTAVO 34 (Wiesbaden, 1979); D.L. Esse, *Beyond Subsistence: Beth Yerah and Northern Palestine in the Early Bronze Age* (University of Chicago dissertation, 1982); R. de Miroschedji, *L'Époque pré-urbaine en Palestine,* CRB 13 (Paris, 1971); R.H. Dornemann, *The Archaeology of the Transjordan in the Bronze and Iron Ages* (Milwaukee, 1983); W.G. Dever, *The Pottery of Palestine in the Early Bronze IV/Middle Bronze I Period, ca. 2150-1950 B.C.* (Harvard dissertation, 1966); J.D. Seger, *The Pottery of Palestine at the Close of the Middle Bronze Age* (Harvard dissertation, 1965); I. Finkelstein, *The Archaeology of the Israelite Settlement* (Jerusalem, 1988). These studies also contribute substantially to the growing interest in regional approaches to the history of Israel and of Judah already anticipated in such very different works as M. Kochavi, *Judaea, Samaria, and the Golan: Archaeological Survey: 1967-1968* (Jerusalem, 1972); J.H Hayes and J.M. Miller, *Israelite and Judaean History* (Philadelphia, 1977), as well as the more comprehensive efforts

Alt's view, however, was much simpler than the more developed and very complex tradition-oriented perspective of Noth. Alt adamantly maintained that a detailed discussion of the problems surrounding the origin of Israel could emerge "only when the topographical and archaeological study of *Palestine* has succeeded in providing independent evidence to fill the gaps left by various forms of literary tradition."[21] In this, Alt is far closer to Albright than is Noth, both in his questions and in the direction of his solutions. Alt's analysis of the regional changes from the Late Bronze Age to the Iron Age of central *Palestine* (his "Territorialgeschichte") attempts to define those gaps. It is a prelude, not an alternative, to direct archaeological research. It attempts to provide an historical context which only recently has begun to be filled out by archaeological research. It is a sketch, tracing the fragments of the information we have in the search of a greater *Gestalt*, including what is yet to be discovered: the task of future archaeologists in the region of *Palestine*.[22]

In the clarity of Alt's distinction of the known from the unknown, the model that he projected for Israel's origin became programmatic for all subsequent research into Israel's origins whose central task has remained until today identical to that originally proposed by Alt: to describe in detail the socio-geographical and political changes that occurred and that created the transition from a *Palestine* dominated by the Late Bronze Canaanite city-states of the plains and valleys, to the political and military dominance of *Palestine* by Israel, a nation-state centered in the hill country at the time of the United Monarchy. In spite of the long delays in this program resulting from the divisive controversies over issues of historicity on one hand and tradition-history on the other

---

to treat the history of Israel in the context of the geography, history and archaeology of Palestine. See above all, the *Atlas of Israel* (Jerusalem, 1969), the many maps and monographs related to Palestine in the *Tübinger Atlas des vorderen Orients* (Wiesbaden, 1974-), but also the brief preliminary geographical study: *Toponomie Palestinienne: Plaine de St Jean D'Acre de Jérusalem, Publications de l'Institut Orientaliste de Louvain* (Louvain La Neuve, 1988) by Th.L. Thompson, F. Gonçalvez and J.M. Van Cangh; the popular atlas of J. Rogerson (*Atlas of Israel*, New York, 1985); the now completed comprehensive survey of archaeology in Palestine by H. Weippert, (*Palästina in vorhellenistischer Zeit, Handbuch der Archäologie, vorderasien II*, Munich, 1988); and the forthcoming survey of the history of Palestine by G. Ahlström, (*op.cit.*).

[21] A. Alt, *op.cit.*, 1925, pp.137f.

[22] *Ibid*, p.157.

between the German scholars Noth and von Rad and the Americans Bright and Wright, more recent approaches to Israel's origins have returned to Alt's programmatic essay.[23] With some considerable exceptions,[24] it is generally assumed today that our ability to write a history of Israel's origins is directly dependent on our ability to carry out a program comparable to that established by Alt in 1925. Even such scholars as Mendenhall and Gottwald, who frequently begin their discussions of Israel's origins with the claim of radical disagreement with Alt's concepts of nomadism and the autochthonous nature of early Israel, not only structure their "alternative" model within Alt's paradigm of Canaanite-Israelite polarity, but also present identical descriptions of pastoral life in ancient *Palestine* within a substantial paraphrase of Alt's understanding of the geographical origins of the people who made up

---

[23] See note 4 above.

[24] E.g., J. Dus, "Mose oder Josua? Zum Problem des Stifters der israelitischen Religion," *Archiv Orientalní* 39 (1971), pp.16-45; *idem*, "Das Stierbild von Bethel und Dan und das Problem der 'Moseschar,'" *AION* 18 (1968), pp.105-137; *idem*, "Die Ältesten Israels," *CV* 3 (1960), pp.232-242; *idem*, "Die Sufeten Israels," *Archiv Orientalní* 31 (1963), pp.444-469; *idem*, "Die altisraelitische amphiktyonische Poesie," *ZAW* 75 (1963), pp.45-54; *idem*, "Das Sesshaftwerden der nachmaligen Israeliten im Land Kanaan," *CV* 6 (1963), pp.263-275; *idem*, *Israelitische Vorfahren: Vasallen palästinischer Stadtstaaten, Europäische Hochschulschriften* (Frankfurt, 1991). See also most recently, C.H.J. de Geus, "De Richteren van Israël," *Nederlands teologisch Tijdschrift* 20 (1965), pp.81-100; *idem*, "The Importance of Archaeological Research into the Palestinian Agricultural Terraces, with an Excursus on the Hebrew Word *gbi*," *PEQ* 107 (1975), pp.65-74; *idem*, *The Tribes of Israel: An Investigation into Some of the Presuppositions of Martin Noth's Amphictyony Hypothesis, Studia Semitica Neerlandica* 18 (Assen, 1976); *idem*, "Agrarian Communities in Biblical Times: 12th to 10th Centuries B.C.E., *Recueils de la Société Jean Bodin pour l'histoire Comparatives des Institutions* 41 (1983), pp.207-237; J.A. Soggin, "The Davidic and Solomonic Kingdom," *Israelite and Judaean History*, ed. by J.H. Hayes and J.M. Miller (Philadelphia, 1977), pp.332-380; *idem*, "The History of Ancient Israel: A Study in Some Questions of Method," *Eretz Israel* 14 (1978), pp.44*-51*; *idem*, *A History of Israel* (London, 1984); N.P. Lemche, "Det revolutioneere Israel: En praesentation of en moderne forskningsretning," *Dansk theologisk Tidsskrift; idem*, "'Israel in the Period of the Judges'—The Tribal League in Recent Research," *Studia Theologica* 38 (1984), pp.1-28; *idem*, *Early Israel*, VTS 37 (Leiden, 1985); *idem*, *Ancient Israel* (Sheffield, 1988); Th.L. Thompson, "The Joseph and Moses Narratives," *Israelite and Judaean History* (1977) pp.160-166, 171-179; *idem*, "Historical Notes on 'Israel's Conquest of Palestine: A Peasants' Rebellion?'" *JSOT* 7 (1978), pp.20-27; *idem*, "The Background of the Patriarchs: A Reply to William Dever and Malcolm Clark," *JSOT* 9 (1978), pp.2-43; *idem*, *The Origin Tradition of Ancient Israel I, JSOTS* 55 (Sheffield, 1987) esp. pp.28-40; G. Garbini, *History and Ideology of Ancient Israel* (New York, 1988); G. Ahlström, *Who Were the Israelites?* (Winona Lake, 1986); *idem, op.cit.* (forthcoming).

monarchic Israel. There is today but one dominant model among Old Testament scholars for reconstructing Israel's origins: that proceeding from Alt's dichotomy of the Canaanite city-states and the Israelite nation-states.[25] What are frequently spoken of as the "conquest" and "revolt" models today are derivative variations of Alt's program. The distinctions of conquest, settlement and revolt reflect three individual scholarly emphases and evaluations of one programmatic model: that of the transition from Canaanite Late Bronze city-state to Israelite Iron Age nation-state. The structural questions asked relating to Israel's origins, and the presuppositions identifying what was being asked (even the rules by which one determines and measures the validity of potential historical descriptions) are identical. When one understands a research model as a programmatic question, one finds that Alt's formulation is widely shared, however much specific reconstructions might differ in detail. Alt's own hypothesis, for example, has substantial room for conquest traditions, and would take elements of "revolt" for granted. Bright's 1981 reconstruction differs from Noth's *Geschichte Israels* primarily in wishes and tendencies, understanding little of the conquest as dated or proven, and has much room for peaceful settlement. Gottwald's "revolt" model follows Alt's plan in detail, adding only an identification of the political and religious motivations of the new settlers (which of course, historically speaking, are unknown, and only guessed at on the basis of traditions of at least five centuries later).[26]

The importance of Alt's procedure is particularly clear now, fifty years later, when the known results of archaeology offer so much of the data that his thesis needed. Alt's method was to contrast the regions of *Palestine* of the times before and after Israel existed: quite specifically, the Late Bronze city-state system of the lowlands, which he outlined

---

[25] This perspective on the "sociological model" was first suggested to me by J.M. Miller at the 1987 SBL Annual Meeting in Boston.

[26] One might also note that Gottwald and Mendenhall rather radically disagree with each other as to the religious and ideological nature of that motivation (cf. G.E. Mendenhall, "Ancient Israel's Hyphenated History," *Palestine in Transition: The Emergence of Ancient Israel, SWBAS* 2, ed. by D.N. Freedman and D.F. Graf, Sheffield, 1983, pp.91-103). One must agree with both the aptness and accuracy of Hauser's objections (A.J. Hauser, "Israel's Conquest of Palestine: A Peasants' Rebellion," *JSOT* 7, 1978, pp.2-19; *idem*, "Response," *JSOT* 7, 1978, pp.35f.; *idem*, "The Revolutionary Origins of Ancient Israel: A Response to Gottwald [*JSOT* 7, 1978, 37-52]," *JSOT* 8, 1978, pp.46-49). Also N.P. Lemche, *op.cit.*, 1985, pp.18f.; Th.L. Thompson, *op.cit.*, 1987, pp.19f.

from the records of the Eighteenth- and Nineteenth-Dynasty Egyptian military campaigns and from the *Amarna* letters, over against the later established control of the hill country by the tribes of Israel, unified under an intertribal bond comparable to an amphictyony—an analogy that Alt drew from classical tradition. Through his comparison, Alt was able to make critical assertions regarding what brought about such a radical change, namely the process of settlement.[27]

Starting from his observations of biblical toponyms (drawn from Joshua and Judges) that the regions most commonly attributed to early Israel, especially those in the *Nablus* hills of central *Palestine*, lay entirely outside of or on the fringes of the city states, and that it was, moreover, these regions that in fact began to receive new settlement during the Iron Age period, Alt suggested that the initial entrance of the Israelite tribes could not reasonably have threatened the Canaanite states. When Alt compared Late Bronze Canaan with early Israel territorially, it became clear that whatever other changes had occurred, the most immediate and noticeable result was the emergence of new settlement in what hitherto had been sparsely inhabited regions. No complex relationship and few contiguous connections had existed between the new nation of Israel and the Canaanite territories. The conquests of cities—that Judges 1 denied anyway—was hence at best peripheral to Israel's origin, however Joshua might be read. From this vantage point, Alt's analysis presented biblical scholarship with the unshakable doubt that the initial Israelite entrance into *Palestine* had been by way of a unified invasion and conquest as suggested in Joshua's historiography. For Alt an initial conquest was both unnecessary and unexplainable. This central core of Alt's argument originated primarily from his observations regarding Egyptian texts of New Kingdom military campaigns and the biblical traditions of early Israelite settlement in the Book of Judges, and was not significantly dependent upon either his sociological and

---

[27] For this and the following, see A. Alt, *opera citata*, 1925a and 1939, but also a number of related articles of importance: *idem, op.cit.*, 1924; *idem,* "Judas Gaue unter Josua," *Kleine Schriften* II (Munich, 1953) pp.276-288; *idem,* "Das System der Stämmegrenzen im Buche Joshua," *Kleine Schriften* I (Munich, 1953) pp.193-202; *idem,* "Die asiatischen Gefahrzonen in den Ächtungstexten der 11tcn Dynastie," *ZÄS* 63 (1928), pp.39-45; *idem,* "Herren und Herrensitze Palästinas im Anfang des zweiten Jahrtausends v.Chr." *ZDPV* 64 (1941), pp.21-39; *idem,* "Die älteste Schilderung Palästinas im Lichte neuer Funde," *PJ* 37 (1941), pp.19-49; *idem,* "Die Herkunft der Hyksos in neuer Sicht," *Kleine Schriften* III (Munich, 1953) pp.72-98.

anthropological analogies of nomads from the eastern steppe or his understanding of an institution of amphictyonic union that he used in an effort to clarify and explain his model.[28]

Alt proposed that the groups that later formed Israel's tribes had lived from very early times on the fringes of the Canaanite city-states, in the hill country of *Palestine* and in the adjoining steppe zones to the South and East of the agricultural regions.[29] These disparate groups, who, according to Alt, had entered *Palestine* in different periods and had independently originated in many different ways, had lived in a pattern of subsistence analogous to that of transhumance shepherds: seasonally moving from the winter grazing lands of the steppe into the hill country and the more fertile regions of *Palestine* during the summer drought, living in a close symbiotic relationship with the distinct Canaanite population of the settled region.[30] When Alt wrote, the term "nomad" had na extensive range of meaning, and was applicable to what were recognized as several distinct patterns of living. Alt himself understood nomadism to have a wide spectrum of forms,[31] and he generally tended to categorize them into larger contrasting types. He was particularly inclined to compare forms of "transhumance pastoralism" (which he understood to belong to both the steppe and agriculturally fertile subregions of *Palestine* in a complex mix of herding and agricultural involvement, including a broad spectrum of sedentariness ranging from nomadic campsites to more permanent settlements in villages and hamlets) with the varieties of patterns of "inner-nomadism,"[32] that he understood to be found throughout *Arabia* and particularly to the various forms of "full" nomadism associated with camel herding, the caravans and with trades associated with metallurgy. Alt identified the early settlers who became Israel exclusively with the various forms of transhumance pastoralists of the Palestinian steppelands. Although G.E. Wright—in what he understood as a support of the conquest tradition

---

[28] N.P. Lemche, *op.cit.*, 1985, p.45.

[29] A. Alt, *op.cit.*, 1939, pp.139-147; G. Dalman, *Arbeit und Sitte in Palästina VI: Zeltleben, Vieh- und Milchwirtschaft, Jagd, Fischfang* (Hildesheim, 1987) pp.201ff.

[30] A. Alt, *op.cit.*, 1939, p.142: "Daß durch dieses regelmässig wiederholte und ebenso regelmässig unterbrochene Nebeneinanderleben der Sesshaften und der Nomaden mancherlei Beziehungen zwischen ihnen entstehen...*versteht sich von selbst*; aber die Gruppen bleiben dabei noch klar voneinander geschieden."

[31] A. Alt, *op.cit.*, 1925a.

[32] A. Alt, *op.cit.*, 1939, *passim*.

in opposition to Alt—favored an understanding of the origin of the Israelite tribes as land-hungry nomads from the desert sweeping over the fertile zone,[33] Alt had reserved this concept of "buin" to forms of inner-nomadism that he consequently associated with the Amelekites and Midianites of biblical traditions.[34] Very gradually—over many centuries—under a potentially wide variety of impulses, these groups settled the unoccupied agricultural zones (many of them forming new tribes wherever lands were most available) throughout the many separate geographical areas that were early Israel. In spite of their lack of territorial coherence, Alt believed—and here his thesis became severely stretched—that a unity was given to these many distinct groups through some form of intertribal religious or cultic bond, analogous to the Greek amphictyony. Only after this initial peaceful settlement, with the growth and gradual consolidation of the Israelite territories, did he understand the tribes of early Israel to have come into direct conflict with the Canaanite city-states, and only then did what were wars of expansion break out. It was in this second stage that the narratives of conquest and the wars of the judges found their historical context for Alt. Building on earlier attempts to consolidate power under a "personal union" or chieftainship, such as that of Labayu of *Shechem*, Yabin of *Hazor* and the biblical portrayal of military leaders as "judges," Alt suggested that the monarchy gradually emerged under Saul and David and was finally consolidated under Solomon.

3. *Amplifications of Alt's Settlement Hypothesis*

This hypothesis of Alt's is well known and widely used by writers on the topic today. Alt used three analogies drawn from his understanding of ancient society that enabled him to expand his model in a concrete and specific historical mode: the amphictyonic bond, the concept of city-state and the concept of transhumance nomadism. Alt's concept of tribal

---

[33] G.E. Wright, *Biblical Archaeology* (London, 1957). In Wright's reconstruction, this highly romantic image did double duty also for the hypothetical Amorite invasions of his patriarchal period; Th.L. Thompson, *op.cit.*, 1974, p.52.

[34] A. Alt, *op.cit*, 1925; also Ishmaelites: see M. Weippert, *op.cit.*, 1967 (ET: 1971), pp.44ff., 106-110. On this whole question, see now the excellent studies of E.A. Knauf, *Ishmael* (Wiesbaden, 1985, 2nd.ed. 1989); *idem*, *Midian* (Wiesbaden, 1988).

amphictyony as the bond of unity in ancient Israel has come under increasingly serious attack in recent years and can no longer be maintained with confidence on the basis of the arguments put forward by Alt and his student Noth. It is also my observation that the widespread misunderstanding in recent years of Alt's use of the central concept of city-state has grossly distorted the realities of ancient *Palestine*. Furthermore, Alt's understanding that ancient Israel emerged from the nomadic pastoralism of the Palestinian steppe has been a deeply disputed issue that is critical for any understanding of the scholarly controversies of the past thirty years.[35] For these reasons the following appraisal of these three issues must be offered before an adequate evaluation of the direction of research initiated by Alt's programmatic model can be made.

Although Alt's thesis about Israel's origin does not depend on a concept of a tribal league or "amphictyony,"[36] this concept of a twelve-tribe federation around a central shrine was built on an analogy to the early Greek amphictyony. This theory was introduced in biblical scholarship as early as Ewald[37] and was fully developed by Noth.[38] It served Alt with the unity he needed to explain the formation of a national society in the period of the judges prior to the political centralization of the monarchy of Saul, David and Solomon.[39] Noth's elaboration of this intertribal bond was, as such, a basic constituent of Alt's effort to establish the historicity of a period of the judges as a period of early Israelite history. This thesis has been supported in recent years by Weippert[40] and, in a revised form, plays a critical role in Gottwald's theories about Israel's origins in a revolt of Canaan's urban poor.[41] It has also faced devastating criticism from many directions.[42]

---

[35] G. Mendenhall, *op.cit.*, 1962; M. Weippert, *op.cit.*, 1967; C.H.J. de Geus, *op.cit.*, 1976; Th.L. Thompson, *op.cit.*, 1978a, and N.P. Lemche, *op.cit.*, 1985.

[36] With N.P. Lemche, *op.cit.*, 1985, p.41.

[37] H. Ewald, *Geschichte des Volkes Israel* I (Berlin, 1876).

[38] M. Noth, *op.cit.*, 1930.

[39] N.P. Lemche, *op.cit.*, 1985, p.45.

[40] M. Weippert, *op.cit.*, 1967, esp. pp.41, 105, 143f.

[41] *Contra* N.K. Gottwald, *op.cit.*, 1979, p.883!

[42] The most important of these have been H.M. Orlinsky, "The Tribal System of Israel and Related Groups in the Period of the Judges," *OA* 1 (1962), pp.11-20; G. Fohrer, "Altes Testament: 'Amphiktyonie' und 'Bund'?" *Studien zur alttestamentlichen Theologie und Geschichte (1949-1966), BZAW* 115 (Berlin, 1969) pp.84-119; *idem, Überlieferung und*

One of the central difficulties that scholars have faced in evaluating Alt's amphictyony hypothesis since Noth's amplification is that no common understanding or clear definition of amphictyony existed.[43] Hence, criticism and refutation of aspects of the analogy (such as the number twelve, the identity with Greek tradition and the relationship to sedentary people)[44] can be accepted without necessarily undermining the usefulness of the concept as an analogy for early Israelite unity. As sheer analogy, it is harly falsifiable. Even its link with "holy war" can be severed without requiring more than a few minor adjustments to an understanding of its historiographical function.[45] Smend's argument,

---

Geschichte des Exodus. Eine Analyse von Ex 1-15, BZAW 91 (Berlin, 1964) pp.3ff.; C.H.J. de Geus, "De Richteren van Israël," *Nederlands theologische Tijdschrift* 20 (1965), pp.81-100; *idem, The Tribes of Israel: An Investigation into Some of the Presuppositions of Martin Noth's Amphictyony Hypothesis, Studi Semitica Neerlandica* 18 (Assen, 1976), pp.193-209; G.W. Anderson, "Israel: Amphictyony:'Am; *Kahal; Edah,*" *Translating and Understanding the Old Testament: Essays in Honor of Herbert Gordon May,* ed. by H.T. Frank and W.L. Reed (Nashville, 1970) pp.142f.; R. Smend, *Jahwekrieg und Stämmebund, Erwägungen zur ältesten Geschichte Israels, FRLANT* 84 (Göttingen, 1966); *idem,* "Zur Frage der altisraelitischen Amphiktyonie," *Evangelische Theologie* 31 (1971), pp.623-630; T. Ishida, "The Leaders of the Tribal Leagues: 'Israel' in the Pre-monarchic Period," *RB* 80 (1973), pp.514-530; A.D.H. Mayes, *Israel in the Period of the Judges, Studies in Biblical Theology* 29 (Naperville, 1974), pp.15-83; *idem,* "The Period of the Judges and the Rise of the Monarchy," *Israelite and Judaean History* (1977) pp.299-308; R. de Vaux, *L'Histoire d'Israel* (Paris, 1971) pp.695-716; G. Weingreen, "The Theory of the Amphictyony in Pre-Monarchical Israel," *JANESCU* 5 (1973), pp.427-433; H. Weippert, "Das geographische System der Stämme Israel," *VT* 23 (1973), pp.76-89; K. Namiki, "Reconsideration of the Twelve-Tribe System of Israel," *AJBI* 2 (1976), pp.29-59; O. Bächli, *Amphiktyonie im Alten Testament* (Basel, 1977); N.P. Lemche, "The Greek Amphictyony—Could it be a Prototype of the Israelite Society in the Period of The Judges?" *JSOT* 4 (1977), pp.48-59; J.M. Miller, "The Israelite Occupation of Canaan," *Israelite and Judaen History* (1977) pp.269f.; C. Meyers, "Of Seasons and Soldiers: A Topographical Appraisal of the Pre-monarchical Tribes of Galilee," *BASOR* 252 (1983), pp.47-59. Gottwald constructs this sacred confederacy particularly on the basis of Joshua 24 and follows Noth in all issues except that of the term amphictyony itself. I find it very difficult to follow Gottwald's revision of his argument in *op.cit.,* 1979, p.883. On one hand he stresses Joshua 24 (a text with obvious centralizing tendencies) as a primary "historical" document for his fictional retribalization, and furthermore summarizes my brief 1978 objections to Noth, but he does not address the objections themselves. His earlier assertion (pp.86f.) that narrative formation is the primary function of the central cult is sheer fabrication and has no literary, anthropological or historical basis whatever.

[43] O. Bächli, *op.cit.,* 1977, p.5.

[44] So C.H.J. de Geus, *op.cit.*

[45] See N.K. Gottwald, *op.cit.,* 1979, pp.72ff., 86f., 207ff.; N.P. Lemche, 1985, *op.cit.,* pp.13,

however,[46] that the biblical references to a tribal league are secondary elements in the traditions relating to holy war, and Mayes's argument that the Israelite twelve-tribe structure has roots in a later perception of a Solomonic provincial system,[47] seriously undercut Noth's conclusion that the period of the judges can be understood as an historical period. This league, our sole reason for speaking of Israel at all in this period, is the bond of unity among the twelve tribes. Furthermore, the existence of a central shrine for all the groups within *Palestine* rests precariously on unsupportable assertions of a premonarchic date for such apparently deuteronomistic-style narratives as Joshua 24 and Judges 19. Finally, any social bond uniting the tribes comprising Israel in this very early period—assuming for a moment their existence as historical realities, geographically widely scattered and separated one from the other as they are assumed to have been—is difficult to imagine historically, whatever analogies might be entertained.

The fundamental weakness of the amphictyonic hypothesis is that it is only an analogy and not an historical reconstruction of early Israel based on evidence. It is in the final analysis really unimportant whether what exists in the Old Testament narratives is identical or similar to what is known to have existed in Greece or elsewhere. For all the closeness or distance between this amphictyonic analogy and ancient Israel—and that quite distant analogies can indeed be useful to historical reconstruction is an everyday experience—no analogy can replace for us the lack of evidence for any bond of unity the alleged early tribes may have had. If the traditions reflecting unity are secondary to the traditions about the monarchy, then what we know about premonarchic settlement and conquest is also by that fact knowledge that is post monarchic; hence we do not yet have grounds for establishing the existence of an Israel in premonarchic times. It appears today unlikely that such evidence will come from the biblical texts.[48] The collapse of Noth's explication of and central contribution to Alt's programmatic model for the reconstruction of Israel's origins exposes a central weakness in Alt's attempt to establish and maintain the historicity of a period of the judges. Noth, moreover, took Alt's earlier work in the direction of

---

16, 204ff.

[46] R. Smend. *op.cit.*, 1977, esp. pp.23, 26, 110f.

[47] A.D.H. Mayes, *opera citata*, esp. 1973.

[48] J.M. Miller and J.H. Hayes, *op.cit.*, 1986, pp.13f.

Traditionsgeschichte[49] and away from history and archaeology. Noth's efforts to understand the earliest of Old Testament tradition as a reflection of the time of the judges drew on Eissfeldt's attempt to see tradition as having originated in putative historical events. This permitted Noth to reconstruct history out of idealistic presuppositions and analogies.[50] In this categorical fallacy, in an effort to support what was at best an illustrative analogy of Alt's, Noth undermined the more flexible, historical and archaeological direction of Alt's 1925 article that had in fact been much closer to the work of Albright in orientation.

Noth's assumption that many of the Old Testament traditions reflected the times of the judges cannot be substantiated. Consequently, one must conclude also that the failure of Noth's efforts requires us to reemphasize that the known Israel of Alt's programmatic model is in fact not the period of the judges but the national entity of the monarchic period.[51] If some form of intertribal union in premonarchic Israel did not exist—and (though it is certainly necessary if a period of the Judges is to be used) it is extremely difficult any longer to assert that it did—then the question of unity, and the process of unification, becomes a critical factor in the question of the origin of Israel at whatever date.

The second concept relating to the structure of ancient society that Alt used is the "city-state," an important element and the starting point of his programmatic model that attempted to trace the social and political changes from Late Bronze Canaanite city-states to an Israelite nation-state of the Iron Age. Alt's understanding of the Canaanite city-state was developed in his 1924, 1925 and 1926 articles.[52] His views were based almost exclusively on his examination of Egyptian texts from the second-millennium B.C., with some supporting reference to the archaeological exploration of the time. Any reference to the biblical tradition was limited to his designation of these "city-states" as "Canaanite," in contrast to its polar opposite, "Israelite" transhumant nomadism.[53] The dialectical structure of Alt's argument unfortunately

---

[49] M. Noth, *op.cit.*, 1948.

[50] J.H. Hayes, "On Reconstructing Israelite History," *JSOT* 39 (1987), p.6.

[51] See below, and the suggestions of J.A. Soggin, *op.cit.* (1984); N.P. Lemche, *op.cit.*, 1985, pp.46–48; and esp. J.M. Miller and J.H. Hayes, 1986.

[52] A. Alt, *opera citata*, 1926; also *idem, op.cit.*, 1944.

[53] G. Ahlström (*op.cit.*, 1986) takes this presupposition of Alt's and, in a substantially altered form, makes it the central topic of an entire monograph that makes Alt's use of the

led him to understand the whole of the sedentary population of Late Bronze *Palestine* under the broad rubric of an Egypto-imperial structure of interlocking city-states that controlled the lowlands of *Palestine* and some large areas of the highlands (such as *Hazor, Shechem, Ayyalon, Gezer, Jerusalem* and others).[54] Although Alt's explicit use of the term "city-state" was generally bound by a careful use of original sources, he overextended its use and applied it to the whole of the diverse sedentary agricultural population of *Palestine.* In this excess he inappropriately exaggerated the reach of Egyptian influence and power within the region. Of course, Alt did not derive the political structure of the city-state from the Egyptian imperium itself, since this structure had long antedated the empire in Asia.[55] However, concepts such as a "system of city-states" or a "system of interlocking city-states" were either as yet unsubstantiated historically or needed to be understood in terms of support for or as a reaction to Eighteenth-Dynasty imperial interests. In either case, the implication that such a "system" existed goes far beyond what we know and what we might reasonably conclude from our sources. Although this was a central concept in Alt's program for tracing the origin of Israel, it was little examined beyond the scope of Alt's *Territorialgeschichte.*[56]

Canaanite-Israelite polarity highly problematic.

[54] This basic description of the Canaanite city-state is accepted by G. Buccellati (*Cities and Nations of Ancient Syria: An Essay on Political Institutions with Special Reference to the Israelite Kingdoms*, Rome, 1967), although one might suggest that Buccellati's views were also strongly influenced by the greater political units to the north of Palestine. F. Frick's study (*The City in Ancient Israel*, SBLDS 36, Missoula, 1977) limits itself almost entirely to the literary biblical traditions reflective of cities from a much later period, and is, unfortunately, of little help to us. His later study (*The Formation of the State in Ancient Israel*, SWBAS 4, Sheffield, 1985) is largely limited to the use of sociological analogies for what he believes Israel's early history might have been, limiting his use of archaeological evidence to the function of illustration for his sociological model. His historical model itself is not based on evidence, but is an interesting abstraction.

[55] A. Alt, *op.cit.,* 1924.

[56] A. Alt, *op.cit.,* 1939; little is added in M. Weippert, *op.cit.,* 1967, or indeed in G. Buccellati, *op.cit.,* 1967. Few of our earliest sources for the settlements of Palestine tell us much of their social structure (Th.L. Thompson, *op.cit.,* 1974, pp.113-117). Such attempts as F. Brandfon's ("Kinship, Culture and Longue Durée," *JSOT* 39, 1987, pp.30-58; and esp. *idem*, "Archaeology and the Biblical Text," BAR 14, 1988, pp.54-59) that attempt to portray Palestinian society of the Late Bronze and Iron I periods in a pattern of "socioeconomic dimorphism," based on a contrast between the hypothetical "culturally organized societies" of the Late Bronze Age and the "kin based societies" of the early Iron

Generally, Alt understands the ancient Palestinian city-state as a petty dynastic principality based on a central settlement or town, potentially with subordinate villages and settlements within its territories.[57] Extended political power was achieved through coalitions and treaties with other city-states. During the Eighteenth-Dynasty, Egyptian imperial authority maintained this political structure in a quasi-feudal direction by establishing the princes and their families as vassals of the Egyptian crown, the Egyptians maintaining a generally indirect control of the region.

In 1962, Mendenhall, basing himself primarily on E.F. Campbell's 1960 popular summary review of the *Amarna* letters in the *Biblical Archaeologist*,[58] argued that the Late-Bronze Canaanite city-state was a brutal, oppressive and largely dysfunctional political structure that "dominated the whole of *Palestine* and *Syria* at the end of the Bronze Age."[59] This was a not untypical exaggeration. Campbell, on the other hand, discussed large areas of *Palestine* which were not under city-state control. Moreover, the *Amarna* letters, which comprised the sole historical source for Mendenhall's understanding, were dated by Campbell from 1376 to 1350 B.C. rather than to the end of the Late Bronze Age, variously dated to the end of the thirteenth or to the beginning of the twelfth-century B.C. If the city-states discussed by Mendenhall were yet to survive two centuries—and many of them yet longer—one must certainly hesitate before accepting Mendenhall's

---

Age, cannot be given credence without direct evidence. Brandfon, admittedly, does discuss the "socioeconomic" meaning which he attributes to "city" in contrast to "village," but it remains unestablished and totally unclear what either of his dimorphic elements has to do with Palestine in this period. In Brandfon's articles, one notices a strong tendency to mix the ideal with history. A similar observation might be made of G.A. Herion's discussions ("The Role of Historical Narrative in Biblical Thought," *JSOT* 21, 1981, pp.25-57; *idem*, "The Impact of Modern and Social Science Assumptions on the Reconstruction of Israelite History," *JSOT* 34, 1986, pp.3-33. See now, M.G. Brett, "Literacy and Domination: G.A. Herion's Sociology of History Writing," *JSOT* 37, 1987, pp.15-40).

[57] A. Alt, "Herren und Herrensitze Palästinas im Anfang des zweiten Jahrtausends v.Chr.," *ZDPV* 64 (1941), pp.21-39; *idem*, "Die älteste Schilderung Palästinas im Lichte neuer Funde," *PJ* 37 (1941), pp.19-49.

[58] E.F. Campbell, "The Amarna Letters and the Amarna Period," *BA* 23 (1960), pp.11-15.

[59] G.E. Mendenhall, *op.cit.*, 1962, p.73.

description of them as dysfunctional![60] Mendenhall, furthermore, accepting Campbell's equation of the *'apiru* with the Hebrews,[61] understood the *'apiru* disturbance reflected in the *Amarna* texts as evidence of revolutionary activity. The *'apiru* are understood on this hypothesis not only as homeless and stateless malcontents, but as a group specifically identified in their opposition to an oppressive government structure.[62] That is, to be a Hebrew was for Mendenhall to be in a state of resistance to or withdrawal from city-state power. The rest of Mendenhall's hypothesis builds on this interpretation of the *'apiru*, seeing Israel's origin as an internal revolution of *'ibrim* (Hebrews) against corrupt city-state oppression, comparable to and to some extent an extension of what he interpreted the *Amarna* *'apiru* disturbances to have been. However, with the cohesive aid of his hypothetical "Exodus Yahwists," the thirteenth to twelfth-century *'apiru*-Hebrew revolt was (in contrast to the analogous disturbances during the *Amarna* period) successful. Mendenhall understood this revolution in religious and pacifist terms. For him the revolution was primarily internal and psychological.[63] There is of course not any echo of this sentiment in Campbell. Mendenhall repeated this theme of the Israelite spirit of revolutionary independence in his stinging repudiation (1983) of what he understood as Gottwald's misappropriation of his hypothesis in terms

---

[60] E.F. Campbell did make the common assumption (based on the complaints in the *Amarna* letters from the Palestinian leaders to *Egypt* for not fulfilling requests for military support) that *Egypt*, under a somnolent Akhenaten, was losing control of its empire. Cf. however, now, P. Bienkowski, *Jericho in the Late Bronze Age* (Westminster, 1986) pp.137-156; also *idem, op.cit.,* 1987.

[61] E.F. Campbell, *op.cit.*, 1960, p.11; on this issue see esp. M. Weippert (*op.cit.*, 1967 =ET 1971, pp.63-101) for a critical review of the *'apiru* =Hebrew =Israelite equation. In a recently published article, "Le 'origini' d'Israele progetto irrealizzabile di ricerca etnogenetica," *Rivista Biblica Italiana* 28 (1980), pp.9-31, M. Liverani strongly supports Mendendall's views. See also N.P. Lemche, *op.cit.*, 1985, p.23. O. Loretz (*op.cit.*) has a very recent comprehensive treatment of this vexing issue of the *'apiru*.

[62] G.E. Mendenhall, *op.cit.*, 1962, p.72; dependent on E. Campbell (*op.cit.,* p.15): "It seems very clear that what *Abdi-Asirta* and later his son *Aziru*, are really doing is to win over the malcontents to their side. In some cases in the *Rib Adda* correspondence, this seems to have been done simply by offering them a way out of the rather unpleasant circumstances of their lives, brought on by their loyalty to a prince who cannot feed them, and to a government which only seeks to milk the land dry."

[63] G.E. Mendenhall, *op. cit.*, 1962, p.72: "The withdrawal, not physically and geographically, but politically and subjectively of large population groups from any obligation to the existing political regimes. . . ."

of an egalitarian social uprising that had brought about a radical shift of power.[64] For Mendenhall, who is more Protestant theologian than historian, the freedom was a thoroughly religious one, and the spirit of liberty—that revolutionary Yahwism—was for him at the very heart of Israel's existence. The historicity of the Mosaic tradition and of Israel's covenant with Yahweh[65] is the core of Mendenhall's thesis. The *'apiru* uprising of the *Amarna* texts is merely the first occasion for its expression, for that revolt offers an historical analogue to the later Israel's freedom in Yahwism over against an oppressive Canaanite Ba'alism.[66] Mendenhall argued that the villages of *Canaan* became *'apiru* by choosing their religion instead of political power: "When the political empire became intolerable and unable to preserve order, they withdrew from all obligation and relationship to it, in favor of another, nonpolitical overlord whose obligations were of an entirely different and functional order. This was what being an *'apiru* meant in early Israelite times."[67] Israel was, for Mendenhall, first and foremost a "religious federation."[68] Moreover, the so-called revolt model of Mendenhall is a theological description of Israel's essence and not an historical explanation of Israel's origin. It is no more legitimate to accept it than its predecessor, Israel's own construct of *Heilsgeschichte*.[69]

Mendenhall's image of the city as corrupt and oppressive—shorn of its function as representative of Ba'alism and counterpoint to the revolutionary concept of belief in Yahweh—is taken up into Gottwald's radical revision of Mendenhall's thesis in which Israel's origin now serves rather as an idealistic form of a socialist proletarian revolution.

---

[64] N.K. Gottwald, *op.cit.*, 1983B, pp.6-8.

[65] Th.L. Thompson, *op.cit.*, 1977, pp.160-162.

[66] G.E. Mendenhall, *op.cit.*, 1973, pp.122-141.

[67] *Idem, op.cit.*, p.137.

[68] In this description of Mendenhall's arguments, I have attempted to present what I believe to be the heart of his thesis. This has been expanded (especially in his 1973 book), but has not changed significantly since his 1962 popular article. The incoherence of the historical aspects of the argument—all too obvious in my summary—has been reduced in this secondary form. For a more extensive review, N.P. Lemche, *op.cit.*, 1985, pp.1-11.

[69] "It is a faith . . . which has its justification, not in the evidence of past events; for the traditions of the past serve only as the occasion of the expression of faith, but in the assertion of a future promise. The promise itself arises out of an understanding of the present which is attributed to the past and recreates it as meaningful . . . ." (Th.L. Thompson, *op.cit.*, 1974, p.329).

In reviewing Gottwald's understanding of ancient Israel and its origin, it is important to recognize that what Gottwald says about the methodology of sociology and history is quite distinct from his hypothesis itself. The value of Gottwald's book and its associated writings is in fact entirely heuristic. It is a theological and philosophical work intended to provide contemporary theology with an alternative to the discredited biblical theology movement. That is, it deals more with the theological use of the bible by modern theologians and is neither historical nor sociological—though it frequently proposes to be both.

Following Mendenhall, Gottwald contrasts the Canaanite city-state over against a lower class or "peasant" society. In his major work on this subject, whose publication was delayed until 1979, Gottwald viewed the Canaanite city-state in terms of feudalism, with an elite aristocracy dominant over against an oppressed and indebted peasant class.[70] It is often difficult to determine both what Gottwald means by "elite" and what he means by "peasant." This confusion is greatly exacerbated by Gottwald's 1976 (written after the manuscript of the 1979 book) and 1983 articles in which he rejects the feudal paradigm so central to his 1979 work in favor of the broad Marxist concept of an "Asiatic mode of production."[71] This terminological shift, however, as Gottwald himself would certainly agree, is not merely an exercise in semantics but relates directly and fundamentally to what Gottwald understands as a sociology of ancient Israel, one of the difficulties of which is that this concept is understood as a holistic construct: each aspect of the society affecting our perception of the whole.

There are several reasons in the current debate over the history of Israel's origins for suggesting that our understanding of Late Bronze society prior to the emergence of Israel is a fundamental and useful starting point of discussion. As pointed out above, the modern scholarly discussion both begins with Alt's description of Bronze Age Canaanite

---

[70] N.K. Gottwald, *op.cit.*, 1979, p.212.

[71] N.K. Gottwald, "Early Israel and the Canaanite Socio-economic System," *Palestine in Transition* (1983) p.26; *idem*, "Two Models for the Origins of Ancient Israel: Social Revolution or Frontier Development," *The Quest for the Kingdom of God: Studies in Honor of George E. Mendenhall,* ed. by H.B. Huffmon, F.A. Spina and A.R.W. Green (Winona Lake, 1983) pp.5-24; *idem*, "Early Israel and the Asiatic Mode of Production in Canaan," *SBL Seminar Papers* 14 (1976) pp.145-154. Unfortunately, Gottwald does not grapple with this pivotal shift of his sociological perspective in the appendix to his 1979 book, which updates and revises substantial portions of the book itself.

city-state control of *Palestine,* and still understands the question of Israel's origins as answerable within Alt's programmatic model of the transference of political realities—in all their forms—from the city-states of the plains to the national states of the hills. Gottwald proposes that we accept the existence of an historical event—social revolution—as the pivot of Israel's amalgamation, bringing about the radical political shift from the Canaanite city-states to the regional states of monarchical Israel. In order to posit the historical event of a revolt for which we have no direct historical evidence whatever,[72] it is critically important that we not take for granted what the specific revolt was about. If one is to approach history in neo-Hegelian idealistic structures of polarities and societal dichotomies, one must be ever aware that neither aspect of the polarity can be understood unless both sides of the dichotomous relationship are clearly specified.

   Given this dichotomous nature of Gottwald's choice of the words "revolt" or "social revolution" to specify the historical events which gave rise to early Israel, one must conclude, without cavil, that the immensely provocative theory of an "original Israel" as an egalitarian and revolutionary society falls like a house of cards, when it is noticed that no detailed discussion of any extent is offered about the previous city-state society which ostensibly had been overturned.[73]

   Gottwald's 1979 book, *The Tribes of Yahweh,* I submit, is fatally dependent on misunderstandings of Canaanite society that he has borrowed from Mendenhall and others. This is a view of ancient Bronze Age Palestinian society that is not only in itself false but is totally incompatible with Gottwald's own 1976 and 1983 proposal of redefining this society in terms of the Marxist concept of an "Asiatic mode of production." Because of the lack of an effective terminology to describe the social realities of Bronze Age *Palestine,* great care must be used to avoid the undesirable implications that the choice of language brings to historical issues.

---

[72] J.M. Miller, *op.cit.,* 1982; *idem, op.cit.,* 1986.

[73] One finds only brief analogies (such as that on pp.212-214: N.K. Gottwald, *op.cit.,* 1979) whose application remains largely in undefined terms such as feudal, aristocracy, elite, urban classes, centralized authorities etc. My objections to this gap in Gottwald's argument are historically focussed. Gottwald's consequent descriptions of emergent Israel are gross distortions of the society of ancient Palestine.

As early as 1976, Gottwald presented a description of "the political economy of ancient Canaan" to support the core of his hypothesis that "early Israel represented a revolutionary breach in the prevailing political economy of ancient Canaan." He thereby intended to replace his earlier support for the idea of Canaan as a form of feudal society[74] that had long been disputed. In the hope of resolving this debate, which Gottwald perceived as turning on the understanding of the concept of *hupshu*,[75] he proposed the Marxist concept of "Asiatic mode of production" as a distinct type of class-society to describe ancient *Palestine*. In his description, he listed fourteen characteristics of varied importance, which I list below in an abstracted form. Gottwald's list was freely formulated, often redundant, and many of his descriptions are marred by unessential moral evaluations, which I have just as freely deleted. These characteristics of Asiatic society have their origin in a variety of articles by K. Marx and I. Engels about *China* and *India*, mostly from the 1850s, which Marx and Engels used as a counterpoint to a European capitalism that had its roots in mediaeval feudalism.

Asiatic Mode of Production[76]

1. Communal, not private ownership.
2. Cohesion and persistence of the village community.
3. Close union of agricultural work with crafts.
4. Large-scale irrigation requiring a central authority.

---

[74] *Ibid.*, p.145.

[75] M. Heltzer, "Problems of the Social History of Syria in the Late Bronze Age," *La Siria nel Tardo Bronze*, ed. by M. Liverani (Rome, 1969), pp.31-46; *idem*, "Soziale Aspekte des Heerwesens in Ugarit," *Beiträge zur sozialen Struktur des alten Vorderasien*, ed. by H. Klengel (Berlin, 1971) pp.125-131; H. Klengel, *The Rural Community in Ancient Ugarit* (Wiesbaden, 1976); *idem*, *The Internal Organization of the Kingdom of Ugarit* (Wiesbaden, 1982); *idem*, "Aziru von Amurru und seine Rolle in der Geschichte der Amarnazeit," *Mitteilungen des Institut für Orientforschung* 10 (1964), pp.57-83; *idem*, "Sesshafte und Nomaden in der alten Geschichte Mesopotamiens," *Saeculum* 17 (1966), pp.205-222; *idem*, *Geschichte Syriens im 2. Jahrtausend v.u.Z.*, Teil II: *Mittel—und Südsyrien* (Berlin, 1969); *idem*, *Zwischen Zelt und Palast: Die Begegnung von Nomaden und Sesshaften im alten Vorderasien* (Leipzig, 1972); *idem*, *Handel und Händler im alten Orient* (Vienna, 1979).

[76] In 1983, Gottwald discussed these 14 descriptive aspects less formally (N.K. Gottwald, *op.cit.*, 1983a, pp.28-30), but with no substantial change.

5. Elite social strata based on a concentration of the economic surplus in the hands of a central authority.
6. Economic dependence of towns on agriculture, and political subordination to the central authority.
7. Subsistence, not commodity production.
8. Retardation in the development of the means of production.
9. Other social groups: large landholders, merchants and bankers.
10. The village as the basic productive unit.
11. Trade oriented to the international frontier.
12. No free bourgeoisie, no free labor and no capital development.
13. Central authority related to the whole of society.
14. Some feudal aspects (however they are to be understood).

Gottwald himself recognizes that there are difficulties in taking his description of Marx's concept as descriptive of Late Bronze *Palestine*. Private ownership, for example, certainly existed, and "communal ownership" of the kind that Marx speaks of for nineteenth-century A.D. China and southern India existed neither in Late Bronze Canaan nor in Israel (no.1)! The presence and dominance of an elite social stratum (no.5) is assumed by Gottwald and exaggerated. Similarly, the significance of political subordination both in Late Bronze *Palestine* and in Marx's "Asiatic mode of production" is not as great as Gottwald believes, and agriculture is of far greater significance to the economy of the Late Bronze towns than Gottwald seems to acknowledge (no.6); for the central economic structure of the towns of Bronze Age *Palestine* is agricultural with only very limited traffic in commodities.[77] The presence of other social groups (no.9) varies substantially in different regions of *Palestine*. Gottwald's assertion of large landowners needs definition. Early Palestinian class structure seems rather oriented towards a very small bourgeoisie, some slaves and hired labor[78] (*contra* no.12). Late Bronze *Palestine* was not in the control of any central authority that related to the whole of society (no.13). Quite the contrary. Very small states were virtually autonomous and regional and a non-integrated foreign imperial system controlled aspects of the greater society, especially in regard to the military and to extra-Palestinian

---

[77] Th.L. Thompson, *The Settlement of Palestine in the Bronze Age*, BTAVO 34 (Wiesbaden, 1979) pp.66f. An assumption of subsistence agriculture is simplistic. See below Chapters 4 and 6.

[78] H. Klengel, *op.cit.*, 1982.

foreign policy, but related only marginally to the economy.[79] Given Gottwald's description of the "Asiatic mode of production," it is difficult to understand why he wishes to recommend this term as a replacement of the less inadequate concept of "quasi-feudalism," which at least has the advantage of being related to the concrete evidence for the military appropriation of lands, a *maryannu* warrior class and the dynastic leadership that we find in our texts.[80] Unlike Marx, Gottwald sees some of these descriptive characteristics as both necessary and definitive aspects of the Asiatic mode of production, especially its foundation on large-scale state-run irrigation agriculture, although unaccountably, Gottwald recognizes that such agriculture does not exist in *Palestine*.[81] Large-scale irrigation systems are indeed radically different from the forms of small-scale irrigation which were practiced in Late Bronze *Palestine*.[82] Since Gottwald (who inevitably describes all societies except that of "revolutionary Israel" in dichotomous relationships) understands the elite as the foundation of the Asiatic mode of production, he is hard pressed to explain how *Palestine* could have such a society without an agricultural economy based on such large-scale government work projects, as one readily understands to have been the case in ancient *Sumer* and Middle Bronze *Mari*, and as Marx frequently observed in regions of the *Yellow, Yangtze* and *Indus* valleys during the nineteenth-century A.D. Inconsistently for one who explicitly proposes this model of Marx's concept of primitive Asiatic society for ancient Late Bronze *Palestine*, Gottwald suggests rather that the basis of the Late Bronze economy rests not in the Asiatic mode of production at all, but rather in an ancient Egyptian imperial policy for *Palestine*, which somehow sought to "replicate the system" that existed at home. It boggles the mind to guess what kind of system would result that was an "imitation" of the large-scale state-run irrigation network[83] he seems to imagine Egypt had, in a region such as *Palestine* in which such an economic

---

[79] P. Bienkowski, *op.cit.*, 1986.

[80] Not only the letters of *Amarna* but also texts from *Byblos* and the so-called Execration Texts clearly show that dynastic forms of government had a long history in *Palestine*; Th.L. Thompson, *Historicity of the Patriarchal Narratives, BZAW* 133 (Berlin, 1974) pp.113-117.

[81] N.K. Gottwald, *op.cit.*, 1976, p.148; *idem, op.cit.*, 1983, pp.28ff.

[82] Th.L. Thompson, *op.cit.*, 1979, pp.25-29, 33-38, J.W. Rogerson, *op.cit.*, 1985, *passim*.

[83] N.K. Gottwald, *op.cit.*, pp.28-31; does Gottwald seriously propose that Egypt's economy was such?

system would be totally inapplicable. If the elite structures of Late Bronze Palestinian society had been modelled on the Egyptian empire, then they would have been independent of indigenous Palestinian economics, incompatible with Gottwald's proposed model and irrelevant to the issue of social revolution (in contrast to such other disruptive political events as rebellions and uprisings). This is not the basis Gottwald needs for his hypothesis of social revolution. The Arab revolt of 1917, for example, cannot be understood in terms of social revolution, however far-reaching its political implications.

Gottwald's understanding that the foundations of Palestinian Bronze Age society rests on "imperial politics from the Nile, the Tigris-Euphrates and Anatolia" since the Hyksos period of the Middle Bronze Age makes fiction of history. The only imperial force that had a major role in *Palestine* of the second-millennium was *Egypt*, and *Egypt* did little either to determine or to structure Palestinian society. Rather, the term "overlord," for *Egypt*'s function in *Palestine*'s economy during the New Kingdom period, is exceptionally apt. The importance of *Palestine* as a land bridge between *Egypt* and the great Asiatic empires is greatly exaggerated by Gottwald, and his concept of a "corridor effect" requires detailed documentation to be acceptable.[84] The real political structure of Palestinian society long antedated both the Egyptian and the Hittite empires and remained intact until the end of Egyptian imperial control in the early Iron Age. Even if one assumed the importance of a Hyksos overlordship in *Palestine* (and that is a formidable assumption),[85] the economic and political foundations of Palestinian society—including the construction of elite strata—are much earlier than the so-called Hyksos period, and, like the "Asiatic mode of production" elsewhere, are indigenous and rooted in the material economy of *Palestine*! The quasi-feudal, dynastic, petty principalities referred to in the literature as "city-states" go back at least to the end of the nineteenth-century B.C.[86] Not

---

[84] The *Tigris* and *Euphrates* societies never had political or economic influence of any significance in *Palestine* at this early period.

[85] J. Van Seters, *The Hyksos: A New Investigation* (New Haven, 1966); also further below, Chapter 5.

[86] We find many of the major "cities" of *Palestine* with their "princes" and other leaders mentioned in the Execration Texts (Th.L. Thompson, *op. cit.*, 1974, pp.113-117). They clearly have their economic roots in Palestinian agriculture from more than a millennium earlier (*idem, op.cit.*, 1979, pp.63f).

only did the Egyptian empire not establish Palestinian society, it hardly changed it.

Much of Gottwald's moralistic rhetoric in describing ancient "Canaanite" society is also without warrant. In general, he seems to imagine a *Palestine* where large masses of poor are oppressed by a huge and complex bureaucratic, entrepreneurial elite who rapaciously absorb most of the region's wealth and force the working class into irreversible indebtedness. Not only does this not fit the concept of Marx that he wishes to use, it does not fit what we know of the Late Bronze towns in Palestine.

The so-called revolutionary motive, according to Gottwald, is to be seen as an effort to preserve an indigenous, village, egalitarian solidarity from a form of imperialism thathad been established by the central state[87] (whether he means *Egypt* here or the city-state elite is of marginal importance). The *'apiru* are still the catalysts of revolution in Gottwald's new theory, but they now are understood as people who have been "pushed out of the security system of the family communes of village communities,"[88] an understanding of *'apiru* which is impossible to justify on the basis of ancient texts and equally impossible to imagine. The critical means of revolution is for Gottwald the ability of "the Israelite revolutionary movement (to attain) a sufficient scale of sophistication of coordination to be able to provide the basic services that central authority had claimed as its prerogative."[89] That is to say, according to Gottwald, the centralized elite had oppressed the village to such an extent that an uprising reestablished the original function of the village economy. Apart from the far more important questions of historical reality, this is not a revolution in the ordinary sense of that term, but rather a description of reactionary stability of a basic economy that had a history of nearly 3,000 years in *Palestine*.

Although Gottwald accurately recounts many aspects of the economy and society of the *Asia* that had interested Marx, many other aspects might also have been discussed. Those that Gottwald chose to deal with apply only to some of *Asia*'s societies and economies. Moreover Marx's concept, necessarily general and naive in the form in which it was developed in the 1850s and in *Das Kapital* of 1867, is an attempt to

---

[87] N.K. Gottwald, *op.cit.*, 1976, p.149; *idem, op.cit.*, 1983, pp.29-34.

[88] *Idem, op.cit.*, 1983, p.34.

[89] *Idem, op.cit.*, 1976, p.149.

distinguish the economics of Asia from those of *Europe* and especially aristocratic *England*. Marx was fascinated by the—from the perspective of *Europe*—unusual degree of independence that the agricultural economy and society of *Asia* had within the context of the equally extraordinary absolutist state forms of "oriental despotism." Marx found the distinctive characteristic of the Asiatic society in the agricultural small-scale village economy frequently described as "subsistence agriculture": an economic system in which each unit of the society—the village or small town—provides its own necessities. There is little division of labor (a critical element for Marx—of far more importance than communal property, for example), and both the means and control of production is in the hands of the producers. Typically, the elite comprises only a small handful of people (Marx speaks of a dozen in villages of some complexity). This elite is also related to the specific functions they perform. Given the subsistence nature of the economy, the village is economically independent of any greater form of imperial administration. Because of this independence, the village moreover is typically politically and socially indifferent to the empire, except insofar as such greater governmental administration occasionally impinges upon the subsistence structures of the village beyond the modest level of the surplus commodities normally produced. Marx makes an effort to describe this apoliticism of a basic subsistence agricultural society: "While the village remains entire, they care not to what power it is transferred or to what sovereign it devolves; its internal economy remains unchanged."[90] For Marx, such a society is not vulnerable to social revolution. Indeed Marx's concept of the "Asiatic mode of production" is his explanation why revolution in such an economy is there largely unthinkable, in contrast to the riper feudal-capitalistic structures of Europe: "This simplicity supplies the key to the secret of the unchangeableness of Asiatic societies, an unchangeableness in such striking contrast with the constant dissolution and refounding of Asiatic States, and the never ceasing changes of dynasty. The structure of the economical element of society remains untouched by the storm clouds of the political sky."[91] Gottwald's misrepresentation of Marx comes from his concentration on the despotic and oppressive nature of some Asiatic states. For Marx, however, despotism is neither constant nor

---

[90] K. Marx, *op.cit.*, 1952, p.175n.

[91] *Ibid.*, p.175.

unique to *Asia*. It comes and goes. It is the village which establishes the norm.

For Bronze Age *Palestine*, the term "city" is seriously misleading, and "city-state" is an immense exaggeration if we think of the normal use of such terms. The size of settlements in ancient *Palestine* was in direct proportion to their agricultural exploitation of the regions in which they were situated: a preeminent characteristic of village culture.[92] The city of ancient *Palestine* is equivalent to the modern small town; its "prince," "king," and "lords" might best be translated as "village head" (in the sense of *mukhtar*) and "elders." The term city-state used to describe the society of ancient *Palestine* refers to little more than the autonomy of a local village or village cluster from other Palestinian powers. The very largest towns rarely exceed one or two thousand people, and the average only a few hundred.[93] One could rightly think of Marx's handful of elite as typical also of the Late Bronze town, if one were to include some of the more feudal functionaries that we meet in the Late Bronze texts—such as the *Maryannu*. Moreover, the Late Bronze village and town did have slavery, free labor, capital and private ownership, all of which must be understood if we are to describe the society adequately. Nevertheless, the core of the Late Bronze Palestinian economy is quintessentially that of village subsistence agriculture. Mendenhall also states this principle, but does not seem to recognize that the "cities" of *Palestine* are themselves just such villages.[94] There is little aristocracy

---

[92] Th.L. Thompson, *op.cit.*, 1979, pp.63f.

[93] R. Gophna ("Middle Bronze Age II Palestine: Its Settlement and Population," *BASOR* 261, 1986, pp.73-90) far too generously estimates the population of Jerusalem (assumed to be the tenth-century capital of Judah) at approximately 2,000 people. Some texts report absurdly high numbers of people involved in accounts of military campaigns, and one must recognize the value of such propaganda. Most notable are the Mesha Stele, which describes the impossibly high figure of 7,000 casualties in a single morning (pointed out by S.E. Janke in personal communication) and the 101,000 captives on the Karnak inscription of the Rameses period at a time when the population of all of Palestine—at best estimates—barely exceeded that number. See also R. Gophna and J. Portugali ("Settlement and Demographic Processes in Israel's Coastal Plain from the Chalcolithic to the Middle Bronze Age," *BASOR* 269, 1981, pp.11-28), who suggest some very interesting methods for determining population size and growth on the basis of settlement patterns; also M. Broshi and R. Gophna, "The Settlements and Population of Palestine During the Early Bronze Age II-III," *BASOR* 253 (1984), pp.41-53.

[94] G.E. Mendenhall, *op.cit.*, 1962, p.73.

to speak of and little economic surplus to exploit.[95] In this regard, such language contrasting "urban" and "folk" communities[96] is grossly inappropriate.

Gottwald's tendency to blend history with abstract sociological theory is shared by J.M. Halligan in his article on the Late Bronze "peasant."[97] Halligan begins with the axiom that "Canaanite Society in the literature of the second millennium B.C.E. is reflected through the mind and interest of the royal court, its administrative personnel and the powerful upper strata of society." Such statements, of course, would make good sense if they referred to texts written by scribes of the Egyptian imperial court that controlled a population of perhaps 2,000,000 people.[98] But *Palestine* was occupied by perhaps 100 largely autonomous settlements with a total population of hardly 200,000 people. Even regionally dominant city-states such as *Shechem* or *Hazor* had only a few thousand people. The great battle of Thutmosis III against the coalition of Asiatic kings under the leadership of *Kadesh* at *Megiddo*, for example, resulted in only 340 enemy captured with 83 killed.[99] In *Palestine* we are not dealing with kings or great courts in any significant way. The resulting effort of Halligan to reinterpret the *Amarna* letters in terms of a class conflict in which scribes, merchants[100] and potters[101] became an aristocracy, is a caricature of sociological analysis. "Aristocracy" refers to the rule of what is perceived as the "best born" cr the nobility. Scribes, merchants, craftsmen and free soldiers hardly fit this term. Halligan argues rather vigorously against an understanding of Palestinian society as based on either subsistence or village based agriculture, and claims that the texts reflect rather a feudal *Palestine* ruled by "the king with his military aristocracy . . . exercising total control over the fund of power, the productivity of the people and their land."[102] Since Halligan

---

[95] *Contra* G.E. Mendenhall, *op.cit.*, 1983, p.93.

[96] G. Herion, *op.cit.*, 1981.

[97] J.M. Halligan, "The Role of the Peasant in the Amarna Period," *Palestine in Transition: The Emergence of Ancient Israel* (1983) pp.15-24.

[98] See J. Burckhardt, *The Age of Constantine the Great* (New York, 1949).

[99] *ANET*, p.237; G.I. Davies, "Megiddo in the Period of the Judges," *OTS* 24 (1986), pp.34-53.

[100] J.M. Halligan, *op.cit.*, p.16.

[101] N.K. Gottwald, *op.cit.*, 1979, p.217.

[102] It is true that he states that the texts say this of Middle Bronze Canaan (p.16), but

somehow knows that the ancient Palestinian villager was a "peasant," theories of peasants derived from a wholly different culture allow him to see Rib-Addi as a "great totalitarian dictator"[103] and, as it were out of thin air, to create "a network system of marketing" which allows him to create even further a middle-class which impoverishes his "peasant" through indebtedness. Similarly, Halligan introduces the feudal term "serf" for the ancient Palestinian slave, but then unaccountably describes him as "landless." This may or may not fit medieval Europe, but the concept "serf" (usually signifying a subject who is by definition bound to the land and therefore not in any normal sense of the term "landless") hardly applies, and, like the term "peasant," does not fit the realities of ancient *Palestine*. Halligan's definition of the Late Bronze *hupshu*[104] as "free proletarians" not only cannot adequately stand as synonymous with "peasant," but the meaning of *hupshu* cannot apply to the word "proletarian" as it is used of a stratum either of Roman society or of the laboring class of more modern times. However poor, oppressed and miserable any particular member of the *hupshu* of the Late Bronze Age might have been, he held in his dependency not only a family of several generations, but free laborers, tenant farmers, indentured servants, slaves, concubines, cattle, orchards, fields, terraces and houses! We have no knowledge of his debt. Halligan concludes his article with the claim that "it may be projected that the political turmoil witnessed in the Amarna letters did not conclude with the last datable tablet, but continued piecemeal until the unification of the land by David,"[105] without considering that the period he is projecting amounts to three and one-half centuries: ten times the length of the period of the so-called *Amarna* disturbances.

It is admittedly extremely difficult to reconstruct the history of a period for which we have little direct written evidence. Nevertheless, that is the task we have, and it simply will not do either to make up the evidence we need or to borrow it from societies of other times and of other places. This is not to say that the use of sociological analogues

---

since that is so obviously not true (the Execration texts?), he must mean eighteenth dynasty Palestine. However, the evidence he cites does not in fact relate to Palestine at all but comes from E.R. Wolf's book, *Peasants* (Englewood, 1966).

[103] J.M. Halligan, *op.cit.*, p.17.

[104] *Ibidem*, p.19.

[105] *Ibidem*, pp.22f.

does not have its place in the reconstruction of Israel's origins. It only argues against their misuse. Sound historical research is not a highly speculative discipline, but rather is based on the very conservative methodology[106] and simple hard work of distinguishing what we know from what we do not know, and of testing our syntheses and hypotheses to ensure that they respect the all-important separation of reality from unreality. It is only in this way that history, like any other of the social sciences, can be scientific, progressive and cumulative. To the extent that the social sciences are based on probability and analogy, they are also based on guesswork and prejudice. The heart of historical science (*Geisteswissenschaft*), unlike that of the natural sciences which are predictive, is the specific and unique observation of what is known.[107] When historiography functions "scientifically," it attempts to discover what did happen. When researchers go beyond the observable singular, they also goes beyond what is known and involve themselves with the theoretical and the hypothetical. When one deals with ancient history critically and where our perspective on the subject of observation is removed by millennia from the past we hope to represent, rigor in our methodology is demanded all the more.

This lack of a clear, sound methodology is at the heart of the growing number of objections raised against Gottwald's attempt to expand Alt's historical model,[108] and this lack of method is pervasive in his book: in history, in biblical criticism and in sociology and anthropology. I have pointed out the very great difficulty caused by his lack of distinction between theory and reality, between hypothesis and data; his misreading of analogies; and the confusion he adds to both ancient and modern terminology. His claims of the existence of historical data to match anthropological analogues,[109] when he knows that none exists, is quite

---

[106] Th.L. Thompson, *op.cit.*, 1974, pp.320 f.

[107] *Contra* E.A. Knauf, "From History to Interpretation," in *The Fabric of History: Text, Artifact and Israel's Past*, *JSOTS* 127, ed. by D. Edelman (Sheffield, 1991) pp.26–64.

[108] The critical review of the revolt hypothesis as put forward by Mendenhall begins, of course, with M. Weippert, *op.cit.*, 1967. In 1978, *JSOT* published a brief exchange between Gottwald, Hauser, Mendenhall, and Thompson. Since the publication of Gottwald's huge book in 1979, however, both criticism and support have grown immensely. See especially N.P. Lemche, *op.cit.*, 1985.

[109] "Most if not all, of the conditions contributory to a cohesive and effective revolutionary peasantry cited by Wolf appear to have been present in thirteenth to eleventh-century B.C.E. Canaan" (N.K. Gottwald, *op.cit.*, 1979, p.584).

extraordinary. J.M. Miller has already clearly pointed out the uncritical methodology of Gottwald's biblical criticism, primarily his inconsistent treatment of questions of historicity, his arbitrary use of tradition history, willful and very idiosyncratic exegesis of central passages (for example, Joshua 24 and the *Sinai* crossing)[110] and his total lack of any criterion for recognizing texts as relatively early or late.

The publication of N.P. Lemche's *Early Israel* presents a thorough and devastating review of Gottwald's sociological and anthropological methods. The primary thrust of Lemche's review deals with Gottwald's understanding of nomadism. Lemche makes some very important observations regarding Gottwald's distortion of our understanding of the ancient form of "city." Lemche objects strongly to the sharp separation that Gottwald and Mendenhall have made between urban culture and the countryside,[111] arguing rather for the need to understand a variety of sedentarization in the Middle East, existing within a continuum from the city dweller to the tent dwelling nomad,[112] understanding the city to be largely a conglomerate of smaller villages. He also points to the small scale of the Palestinian society in contrast to other ancient Near Eastern social structures.[113] One must question (with Lemche) whether Gottwald's understanding of the ancient city and of Near Eastern agriculture (whether ancient or modern) is not rather a construct of Gottwald's own ideology, which is anthropologically simplistic and uninformed. Gottwald's concept of peasant rebellion is as romantic as that older concept he ridicules of an eternal conflict between the desert and the sown. Evidence of discontent and conflict cannot arbitrarily be cast into a model of class warfare. Gottwald's description of ancient Palestinian city and peasant culture as "antimorphemes"[114] is totally wrongheaded, since the two are virtually identical in Palestine. Neither Gottwald nor Mendenhall has presented a description of the sedentary

---

[110] Here, I am thinking of his radical historicizing of the wilderness tradition in, *op.cit.*, 1979, pp.454f. The lack of literary comprehension is clear in his translation of the murmuring motif into "the problem of socioeconomic survival" (p.454). On Miller's critique, see J.M. Miller, *op.cit.*, 1982, pp.215f.; *idem*, 1986, pp.74-79.

[111] N.P. Lemche, *op.cit.*, 1985, p.195.

[112] Th.L. Thompson, *op.cit.*, 1978a.

[113] N.P. Lemche, *op.cit.*, 1985, p.207.

[114] N.K. Gottwald, *op.cit.*, 1979, pp.467-473.

population of Bronze Age *Palestine*,[115] and it is extremely doubtful that their allusions to it and assumptions about it can be taken seriously as informed views.[116] In this, Mendenhall, Gottwald and others have introduced a rather serious misunderstanding of the classical views of Palestinian society. In particular, they have introduced a distortion of Alt's understanding of pastoralism. Since this distortion has played a major role in the discussions about pastoralism and nomadism in the 1970s and early 1980s, it is instructive to review their position in the light of Alt's hypothesis.

In the 1962 presentation of his alternative to Alt's hypothesis, Mendenhall's thesis was conceptually oriented to an attack on Alt's understanding of nomadism. Without warrant, Mendenhall claimed that Alt's "model" had proposed that Israel originated in the sedentarization of nomadic tribes who invaded *Palestine* from outside, seized land and settled on it.[117] Mendenhall adamantly rejected what he presented as Alt's assumption that a dichotomy had existed between the small village agriculturalist and the shepherd. In rejection of this idea, Mendenhall described these two groups rather as "blood brothers."[118] In what many of his followers have come to describe as a "radically new" proposal, Mendenhall then built on this "critique" of Alt and argued that the "primary contrast of ancient times" lay rather between the city and the village, and that Israel originated in a political and subjective withdrawal "of large population groups from any obligation to the existing political regimes."[119] This pacifist "revolt," built on the rejection of what is after all not Alt but a "straw man," based on what Mendenhall describes as an interest in "social and especially cultural history,"[120] quickly became in post-1962 scholarship the "alternative" model of Israel's revolutionary origin, though its boast of presenting a "sociological" approach was empty.[121] Mendenhall pointed out correctly[122] that his

---

[115] N.P. Lemche, *op.cit.*, 1985, p.166.

[116] *Ibid.*, pp.32f., 200.

[117] G.E. Mendenhall, *op.cit.*, 1962, pp.66–72.

[118] *Idem, op.cit.*, 1983, p.17.

[119] *Idem, op.cit.*, 1962, p.72.

[120] G.E. Mendenhall, *op.cit.*, 1983, p.99.

[121] The acceptance of Mendenhall's distorted presentation of Alt begins most markedly in M. Weippert's study (*op.cit.*, 1967, esp. pp.56f., 125) which understandably misreads Mendenhall's thesis itself and esp. his "revolution" in the ordinary terms of changes in

understanding of the symbiotic relationship between farmers and pastoralists was drawn from Albright[123] and not from the more recent research of Mendenhall's student J.T. Luke. Mendenhall does not seem aware, however, that—save for their understanding of full nomadism in ancient times—Alt and Albright are substantially in agreement in their understanding of seminomadism.

Luke, in an unpublished dissertation reevaluating J.R. Kupper's study of the pastoral groups of Middle Bronze *Mari* on the *Euphrates*,[124] had argued that some preclassical nineteenth-century views on nomadism, which had understood nomadism solely in terms of marauding beduin and which understood most ancient Near Eastern Semitic groups to have originated in the desert, could no longer be maintained. The *Mari* texts referring to the Jaminites and Haneans in particular,[125] with references to both transhumance migrations, agriculture, tents and sedentary dwellings, clearly supported the classical understanding of "seminomads" that Luke saw emerging in Old Testament studies since 1945.[126] Because Kupper described these tribal groups as in the process of sedentarization at *Mari*, as having possibly originated from the steppes of *Jabal Bishri* and as violent in some of their relations with the *Mari* government, Luke caricatured Kupper's treatment as tainted with an

---

social structures and political power, while for Mendenhall this so-called revolution was an internal, theological reorientation of society's values. Weippert seems to accept Mendenhall's caricature of Alt's view of the proto-Israelites as "inner nomads" rather than as the semi-nomadic transhumance pastoralists Alt had proposed. Weippert seems to base this on a nomadic interpretation of the patriarchs—perhaps following Noth's concept of proto-Aramaeans (M. Weippert, *op.cit.*, 1967, pp.56f.).

[122] G.E. Mendenhall, *op.cit.*, 1983, p.100.

[123] W.F. Albright, *Archaeology and the Religion of Israel* (Baltimore, 1942) pp.97-99.

[124] J.R. Kupper, *op.cit.*, 1957.

[125] J.T. Luke, *op.cit.*, 1965, esp. pp.69-75.

[126] Unaccountably, Luke seems totally unaware of the German literature cited above, of Albright's treatments of 1942 and earlier, or indeed, of any of the many references cited by Kupper's study, including such indispensable works as those of G. Dossin ("Benjaminites dans les textes de Mari," *Mélanges Syriens offerts à monsieur René Dussaud: Secretaire perpetuel de l'Academie des inscriptions et belles lettres par ses amis et ses élèves; Bibliotheque archeologique et historique*, vol. 30, Paris, 1939, pp.981-996) and R. Dussaud ("Nouveaux renseignements sur la Palestine et la Syrie vers 2000 avant notre Ère," *Syria* 8, 1927, pp.216-231; *idem*, "Nouveaux textes Égyptiens d'Éxecration contre les peuples Syriens," *Syria* 21, 1940, pp.170-182).

unacceptable nineteenth-century understanding of nomadism.[127] Luke himself (like Kupper before him) otherwise describes the groups at *Mari* in the classical pattern of a symbiotic relationship of transhumance shepherding with sedentary village agriculture.[128] Luke does add one significant issue to the debate in his attack on the assumption that the origins of semites through time had derived from migrations out of the desert.[129] In spite of his vehement defense of the Amorite hypothesis for patriarchal origins,[130] which is wholly dependent on this concept of nomadic migration,[131] Luke argued against a derivation of pastoralism from the steppe or desert. In the fundamentals of his presentation, the issues are straightforward and obvious and one has no trouble or argument with Luke. The romantic concept of a direct evolutionary development from nomadism to pastoralism to the sedentary cultures is false. The domestication of sheep and goats is part of the neolithic revolution and is a development from agriculture as early as 8000–7000 B.C. (Luke: 6000–5000 B.C.). These observations are quite valid. However,

---

[127] In a much modified form, Luke repeats this in "'Your Father Was an Amorite' (Ezek 16:3, 45): An Essay on the Amorite Problem in Old Testament Traditions," *The Quest for the Kingdom of God: Studies in Honor of George E. Mendenhall*, ed. by H.B. Huffmon, F.A. Spina, and A.R.W. Green (Winona Lake, 1983) p.226. V.H. Matthews's (*op.cit.*) is more balanced and makes much of Kupper's work available to English readers.

[128] References to Luke and, indeed, Luke himself, are not always clear as to what is being described. At times, as in 1965, Luke describes two forms of society, based on a mixture of agriculture and stockraising, living in symbiosis. In other discussions, however, the element of symbiosis tends to disappear and is replaced by a harmonization of concepts as in 1983 when he speaks of "semi-nomadic-village-peasant life," as applicable to Palestine generally, thereby blurring the distinction between sedentary agricultural life and transhumance pastoralism—a distinction that had been a major gain of the anthropological research that had established the classical view of pastoralism. Luke here allows the development of a theoretical dichotomy between village life and the city, a dichotomy that is not only inapplicable to Palestine but a false understanding of social politics at Mari (N.P. Lemche, *op.cit.*, 1985, pp.12–16).

[129] For a classical description of this hypothesis, S. Moscati, *I Predecessori D'Israele, Studi orientali publicati a cura della scuola orientale IV* (Rome, 1956); *idem, The Semites in Ancient History* (Cardiff, 1959).

[130] J.T. Luke, "Abraham and the Iron Age: Reflections on the New Patriarchal Studies," *JSOT* 4 (1977), p.39.

[131] If the relationship between the patriarchal narratives and the Jaminites of Mari is not one of nomadic migrations, it is an analogous relationship only and in no way to be understood as an historical connection (Th.L. Thompson, *op.cit.*, 1974, p.88; *contra* J.T. Luke, *op.cit.*, 1983, pp.235–237).

Luke, noticing that at *Mari* some farmers were shepherds as well, illogically argued that second-millennium pastoralism was not merely symbiotically related to but an aspect of agriculture on the basis of the origin of animal domestication. When this peculiar observation was combined by Gottwald with his own related misunderstanding of Alt's position, Luke's thesis was accepted as substantially overturning Alt's "pastoral-nomadic immigration theory" of Israel's origins.[132]

Gottwald, who unaccountably accepts Luke's thesis without significant qualification, himself presents an interpretation of the relationship between transhumance pastoralists and village agriculturalists that is nearly identical to that of Alt's,[133] marking both the distinctiveness of the two economic groups and their close symbiotic interrelationship.[134] Gottwald's insistence that "the regnant pastoral nomadic model for early Israel and the sweeping historical and cultural inferences drawn from it are fundamentally in error"[135] founders in self-inflicted contradiction and illogic. His conclusion, following Luke, that pastoralism is an aspect of Palestinian village life[136] is a truism recognized by every scholar he argues with! However, it is true because of observation,[137] and does not follow logically from the Lukan premise that it originated there. It is astonishing that Gottwald and Chaney also seem to insist that forms of society are best explained in terms of their original evolution. However, the fact that the domestication of sheep and goats originated in the neolithic, agriculturally-based revolution tells us nothing either about transhumance pastoralism of the second-millennium or about questions concerning the origin of the economically distinct varieties of Semitic

---

[132] N.K. Gottwald, *op.cit.*, 1979, pp.435-463, and more emphatically pp.893f.; M.L. Chaney, "Ancient Palestinian Peasant Movements and the Formation of Premonarchic Israel," *Palestine in Transition* (1983) pp.42-44.

[133] N.K. Gottwald, *op.cit.*, 1979, pp.436-442; J.M. Miller, *op.cit.*, 1986.

[134] The position of M. Chaney (*op.cit.*, 1983, pp.42f.) is different only in that it attempts to reduce the proportion of pastoral nomads in contrast to farmers, undoubtedly to salvage the description of Gottwald's revolutionaries as indigenous. Chaney, of course, has no evidence whatever for his qualification. N.K. Gottwald, with more caution if no more evidence (*op.cit.*, 1979, pp.436f.), merely affirms a partial role of pastoral nomads in early Israel's formation.

[135] *Ibid.*, p.437.

[136] *Ibid.*, p.471.

[137] Cf. G. Dalman *et alii (opera citata)* with V.H. Matthews, *op.cit.* Also see the critique of N.P. Lemche (*op.cit.*, 1985).

groups in the Middle East. Forms of nomadism—especially hunting and food-gathering—go back, of course, to early palaeolithic times. Many thousands of years separate issues of origins from the "indigenous," sedentary, Semitic agricultural villages of the third, second and early first millennia B.C., and we have only very recently been able firmly to trace the forms of agricultural society in *Palestine* of the Late Bronze through the Early Iron Ages back to the neolithic period. We have many reasons to believe that the village life of *Palestine* of the Bronze Age is not entirely continuous with at least the earliest of the neolithic periods. Connections are only partial and fragmentary at best.[138] We do know, however, both from anthropological analogy and from written sources such as the *Mari* archives as well as from archaeological remains, that Gottwald's views of nomadism are thoroughly inadequate. Farmers from villages and towns raised sheep and goats and other livestock. Shepherds, both as individuals and as distinct groups, lived symbiotically with the more sedentary population in forms of seasonal transhumance and, in the south, in patterns of regional transmigration. They played a significant role in the economics of many of *Palestine*'s subregions, the central hill country not being among the more important of these. There was a wide spectrum of societal forms relating to nomadism associated with greater *Palestine,* including several forms of "full" or "inner" nomadism. The classical descriptions of non-urban Near Eastern society are, in their major lines and often in detail, still valid descriptions of the types of societies we are dealing with in ancient *Palestine.*

In the second half of Alt's polarity, through which he constructed his programmatic model for Israel's origins in terms of the transition from the Late Bronze Canaanite city-state to the regional states of the Iron Age, he argued that the origin of Israel was to be understood in terms of a gradual transition of transhumant pastoralists (understanding them with Noth to have been originally Aramaean or Aramaean-related)[139] to sedentary life in those areas beyond the immediate control of the city-states. Alt's hypothesis was built primarily on the basis of an analogy constructed from the observation of similar pastoralists who were

---

[138] P. Miroschedji, *L'Époque pre-urbaine en Palestine, CRB* 13 (Paris, 1971) pp.7-11, 13f., and esp., H. Weippert, *Palästina in vorhellenistischer Zeit, Handbuch der Archaeologie, Vorderasien* II/1 (Munich, 1988) pp.111-114.

[139] M. Noth, *op.cit.,* 1954, pp.117f.; also M. Weippert, *op.cit.,* 1967 (ET =1971, pp.97, 102-106).

engaged in animal husbandry and agriculture in these same regions of *Palestine* in the nineteenth and early twentieth-century A.D.—a way of life which Alt sharply distinguished from what he referred to as "full nomadism" or more clearly as "inner nomadism."[140] The discovery of the *Mari* administrative archives of the eighteenth-century B.C. gave substantial support to Alt's hypothesis, since several quasi-nomadic groups mentioned in these texts (the Jaminites, Simalites and Haneans) were understood to reflect a similar way of life and appeared not too distantly related ethnically and linguistically to the Israelites.[141] While Alt's description of these groups as "proto-Aramaeans" is excessive, and evidence is lacking for a clear historical relationship with any known analogous groups in *Palestine*,[142] the analogy to Alt's hypothesis is nevertheless useful. Were it not for the important elements of state encouragement and concerted pressure on the nomadic pastoralists towards sedentarization that were determinative factors at *Mari*, we would have a very good analogue to what Alt proposed. Although absent in Alt's reconstruction is the not yet available historical and archaeological evidence from the Late Bronze-Iron I transition[143] as well as some explanation of sufficient cause to bring about the sedentarization of transhumance pastoralist in *Palestine* at this time,[144] the description Alt offers of pastoral nomadism on the steppes bordering *Palestine* is fully consonant with the anthropological research in Alt's day and, although grossly generalized and lacking specificity, still very instructive today. It is on the basis of transhumance patterns of grazing that Alt assumes the association of his pastoralist with both the steppe and the agricultural regions of *Palestine*.[145] He argued that this long-time association had created both a common bond with the sedentary

---

[140] A.Alt, *op.cit.*, 1939, pp.141f.

[141] M. Noth (*op.cit.*) and esp. M. Weippert (*op.cit.*, 1967, p.125), who based much of his interpretation on the studies of J.R. Kupper (*Les nomades en Mesopotamie au temps des rois de Mari*, Liege, 1957) and H. Klengel, (*Benjaminiten und Hanäer zur Zeit der Könige von Mari*, University of Berlin dissertation, 1958; *idem*, "Zu einigen Problemen des altvorderasiatischen Nomadentums," *Archiv Orientalní* 30, 1962, pp.585-596). I do not see that the studies of J.T. Luke (*op.cit.*, 1965) and V. Matthews (*op.cit.*) substantially alter the views set forward by Kupper, Klengel, and Weippert before them.

[142] Th.L. Thompson, *op.cit.*, 1974, pp.58-66.

[143] See A. Alt himself, *op.cit.*, 1925.

[144] Also N.P. Lemche, *op.cit.*, 1985, pp.136ff.

[145] A. Alt, *op.cit.*, 1939 pp.142-146.

farming population and a distinctiveness which was brought about by the annual departure. The symbiosis of this relationship, established over a period of half a millennium (Alt suggests the dates for this long transition of 1500–1000 B.C.), formed a basis for sedentarization. This process explained for Alt the partly known and (at that time) partly assumed expansion of settlement in the hill country prior to the monarchy. Alt concentrates particularly on the hill country—and above all *Judaea* and *Samaria*—because of the radically different settlement patterns he noticed when the Late Bronze period was compared to the known biblical sites of the Iron Age. The economic culture of the transhumance pastoralist involved a mix of agriculture and animal husbandry, and suggested to Alt[146] that the early pastoralist gradually drifted towards an increasing dependence on agriculture.[147] Alt's understanding of the pastoral background of Israel was not substantially drawn from any supposedly nomadic background in the biblical tradition. This Alt very definitely understood to reflect a sedentary and agricultural background.[148] Rather, Alt's understanding of the early pre–Israelite pastoral groups[149] was specifically related to the realities of Palestinian topography.

Alt did not see this gradual movement from the steppe to the sedentary regions of *Palestine* as either extraordinary or unique to Israel. He understood such transitions as having occurred in different forms and at different periods throughout the history of the Middle East. Nor did he understand this proto-Israelite transition as an historically single migration.[150] In this, he referred to a wide body of anthropological literature which he felt strongly supported his own experience in

---

[146] Ibid., p.145.

[147] Citing P. Range, *Die Küstenebene Palästinas* (Frankfurt, 1922) pp.9ff.; *idem*, "Wissenschaftliche Ergebnisse einer genealogischen Forschungsreise nach Palästina in Frühjahr 1928," *ZDPV* 55 (1932), pp.42–74, here pp.53ff; *idem, Die Isthmuswüste und Palästina* (Hamburg, 1926); L. Picard and P. Solomonica, *On the Geology of the Gaza-Beersheba District* (Jerusalem, 1936); *idem,* "On the Geology of the Gaza-Beersheba District," *JPOS* 16 (1936), pp.180–223.

[148] See esp. A. Alt (*op.cit.,* 1950), in which he understands both the patriarchal (Genesis 18:10) and the wilderness tradition (Exodus 26 and Exodus 36) to reflect sedentary romanticism much more than actual historical tent dwelling cultures.

[149] A. Alt, *op.cit.,* 1925, pp.215ff.; *idem, op.cit.,* 1939, pp.139ff; *idem, op.cit.,* 1950, *passim.*

[150] A.Alt, *op.cit.,* 1939, p.140.

Palestine, and above all that of Dalman.[151] Alt's understanding of the general range of socio-economic types of groups in *Palestine* was not substantially different from that of E. Meyer,[152] who had been largely dependent on G. Schumacher[153] and Wellhausen. The strength of much of this work (particularly that based on Schumacher, Dalman and Häfeli) lies in pre–First World War anthropological research and in descriptions of societal patterns that, although chronologically far from ancient Israel, have been influenced by the same geographical and ecological contingencies as *Palestine.* They do provide substantial analogies that, when used with flexibility and care, can be quite valuable to the task of reconstructing the social and economic forms that existed at the end of the second and the beginning of the first-millennium B.C. Of course, they were also merely analogies (as Alt also was aware) and did not of themselves provide historical reconstructions.

Meyer[154] made three distinctions among tribal groups in *Palestine* that classically describe the general range of non-urban societal forms as understood by scholars until well after the end of the Second World War. Meyer understood this description as valid for all periods of Palestinian history: a) settled farmers who live in permanent houses and villages, raising grain and cattle, wine and oil; b) half-sedentary pastoralists (whom Alt refers to often as "seminomads") who live both in tents and tent villages as well as in permanent dwellings, in a pattern of transhumance grazing. They live in oases and near water sources of the steppelands, and, in the dry season, are closely associated with group a) and live in peaceful symbiosis with the agrarian villages. They understand their enemy to be the desert bedouin, not the sedentary agrarian; c) the bedouin of the desert (whom Alt refers to as the "full

---

[151] G. Dalman, *op.cit.,* esp. vol. 6, 1938. Also of great importance to Alt's understanding was A. Musil (*Arabia Petra,* vols. 1: *Moab;* 2: *Edom;* 3: *Ethnologisches Reisebericht,* Vienna, 1907f.), A. Jaussen (*Coutumes des arabes au pays de Moab,* Paris, 1903); M. Frhr. von Oppenheim, E. Bräunlich and W. Caskel (*Die Beduinen 1-3,* 1939–1952) and L. Häfeli and 'Aref el 'Aref (*Die Beduinen von Beerseba,* Luzern, 1938; idem, *Spruchweisheit und Volksleben in Palästina,* Luzern, 1939); R. Schickele, (*Die Weidewirtschaft in den Trockengebieten der Erde,* Jena, 1931); and S. Merner (*Das Nomadentum im nordwestlichen Afrika,* Berlin, 1937).

[152] E. Meyer, *Die Israeliten und ihre Nachbarstämme* (Leipzig, 1906) pp.302ff.

[153] G. Schumacher, *Tell el-Mutesellim,* vol. I (Leipzig, 1908) p.78; A. Alt, *op.cit.,* 1939, pp.142f.

[154] E. Meyer, *op.cit.,* 1906, pp.303f.

nomad" or "inner nomad"), living on animal breeding, trade, hunting and some patch cultivation.[155] Meyer, like most nineteenth- and early twentieth-century scholars, understood the origin of most Semitic groups in *Palestine* to have proceeded in an evolutionary manner from these desert beduin: not only the Israelites, but the Canaanites, the Aramaeans and the Arabs as well. He understood a basic antagonism to have existed between the beduin and the other two types of Arabs. To speak of an "eternal conflict between the desert and the sown" was at worst only an exaggeration. However, Meyer observed that to describe the inner nomad as "land-hungry" is wholly inappropriate. In known periods of nomadic conquest of the fertile zones of *Palestine* a twofold pattern of change occurred: a widespread abandonment of agriculture, land care and soil drainage systems (along with the transition of many areas to grazing) and subsequently a gradual resettlement of the area.

Following this very broad and general descriptive pattern, Alt identified the sedentary village group a) of *Palestine* with the Canaanites, the seminomadic group b) with the proto–Israelites, –Moabites, –Ammonites and –Edomites, and what he called the "inner-nomadic" group c) with the Midianites, Amalekites and Ishmaelites.[156] It is an important aspect of Alt's thesis[157] that the processes of sedentarization and Canaanitization went hand in hand, and that the social types a) and b) had become closely integrated by the end of the Bronze Age. However, the somewhat inconsequential separation that Alt allowed (and this was based on his form-critical and geographical, not his anthropological studies) was the sharp cultural division between hill country tribal groups on one hand and lowland cities on the other. This procedure was dictated for Alt by the initial chronologically oriented observations on the shift in the settlement patterns of the Late Bronze and Iron Age periods. In the synthesis of his geographical and biblical views with his social and anthropological observations, Alt unfortunately adjusted his anthropological understanding in support of a dimorphic Late Bronze Canaanite-Early Iron Israelite historical transition. This has led to many misunderstandings of his model, involving both his position regarding the close symbiotic ties as existing between the migrating pastoralist and the indigenous agricultural population, and the assumed

---

[155] A. Musil, *op.cit.*; J. Wellhausen, *op.cit.*

[156] M. Weippert, *op.cit.*, 1967, p.110; E.A. Knauf, *op.cit.*, 1989; *idem, op.cit.,* 1988, *passim.*

[157] A. Alt, *op.cit.*, 1925, *passim.*

length of the proposed process of immigration and sedentarization. It is significant that Alt's reconstruction is marginally compatible with the understanding that the settlement was indigenous to *Palestine* in so far as he had understood that the process of immigration had lasted throughout most of the Late Bronze period, and that sedentarization proceeded from the basis of fully acculturated Palestinian shepherds. Alt is very clear in distinguishing these pastoralists from the "inner nomads" of the Arabian and *Sinai* deserts. His consistent use of the analogy of pastoral nomadism implies that they were associated with the Palestinian and neighboring steppe, and (insofar as we can judge from the anthropologically derived examples available to Alt) tied to the pattern of transhumance exchange of pasturage between the steppe and the agricultural zones of *Palestine*. If one abandons the presupposition of migration from *Arabia*, Alt's hypothesis encourages one to accept his pre-Israelites as indigenous to the greater Palestinian steppe, and to describe the formation of early Israel as the amalgamation of the "Canaanite" sedentary agriculturalists of the settled region with the transhumance pastoralists, who, in the process of sedentarization, structured themselves in geographically distinctive tribal groups. There is then no clear reason that, within Alt's hypothesis, the groups that made up Israel cannot be understood historiographically as indigenous to the greater region and at the same time be easily recognized as understanding themselves as *ger* in the region. This quite minor though significant revision of Alt is substantially furthered when it is recognized that the range of the entire spectrum of nomadic and sedentary groups in *Palestine* and the adjacent steppe is both now and in history much larger than is allowed by the three classical categories, which, of course, were never intended to be exclusive.[158] The adoption of a broader spectrum-oriented description of social differences within *Palestine* would naturally reduce the emphasis on a dichotomous so-called antimorpheme between the "desert and the sown," which is such a strong tendency of classical descriptions.[159] It would further recommend that situations of

---

[158] As very strongly urged in the context of the current debate by Th.L. Thompson, *op.cit.*, 1978 and N.P. Lemche, *op.cit.*, 1985.

[159] As the classical model tended to see an unbridgeable societal rift between agriculture-pastoral groups and inner nomads, Gottwald and Mendenhall tend (as we observed above) to drive a wedge between the city and other groups. This dichotomy is irrelevant to the agricultural heartland of Bronze Age Palestine where cities, as such, did not exist. Even in Phoenicia and Philistia, where some of the towns had substantial economic functions apart

cross-social conflict be examined as discrete historical events, rather than understood as a structural, quasi-class conflict endemic to the Middle East. Such dogmatic presuppositions about the forms and events that society "must" undergo are a disservice to both history and historical anthropology.

The Mendenhall and Gottwald School's alternative description is unusable for historical reconstruction at several points:

A) an urban culture, such as we find at *Mari* and *Ugarit*, did not exist in Late Bronze *Palestine,* and the assumption of an urban-village "antimorpheme" in Late Bronze *Palestine* is meaningless.

B) Conversely, we do have reference in both second- and first-millennium texts to nomadic groups from the desert that are a threat to the sedentary population. These conflicts need to be understood as specific historical conflicts rather than as antimorphemes or class conflicts.

C) Just as nomadism in the region of *Palestine* needs a much more complex description, so too the various forms of agricultural sedentary culture are multifarious, and need to be understood as part of the wider spectrum of Near Eastern culture which extends from extreme patterns of full nomadism to town culture, and are not constructively served by the harmonizing and very distorting concept of a "village-farmer-shepherd" construct. As Lemche has clearly pointed out[160] in his discussion of this problem, we are dealing with an overlapping of two different economic, social and cultural categories: cattle raising and spatial mobility.

D) The issue of the origin of the West Semites is not an issue that can easily be settled. The debate has not been furthered by the seemingly dogmatic rejection of many texts which refer to the homeland of many groups of the second-millennium B.C. Rather, both the concept of wholesale desert origins and the concept of a totally indigenous population are to be eschewed.[161] On this issue as well it is insufficient to build a history on sociological theory alone, uninformed by direct evidence. The archaeological and epigraphic evidence relating to the

---

from agriculture and pastoralism, this dichotomy seems unjustified.

[160] N.P. Lemche, *op.cit.*, 1985, p.129; Th.L. Thompson, *opera citata*, 1978A; 1978B.

[161] Already M. Weippert, *op.cit.*, 1967, pp.102ff.

period and region involved must not only inform but direct our theories.[162]

E) Gottwald's reference to anthropological data is narrow and largely unrelated to both *Palestine* and the social forms he wishes to describe. Because of this, he is driven to use an abstract interpretive structure in lieu of evidence. Lemche[163] has suggested a much more complex and legitimate use of social scientific materials relating to forms of nomadism, which can be used with great benefit.

F) Major historical events have significant effect on patterns of society, and sociological analysis alone is inadequate for dealing with history. Such events range from political and international changes of empire and dynasties, economic changes directed to the planning and maintenance of trade, ecologically significant changes in climate, to smaller decisions of specific rulers and states to go to war, change structures and use of taxes, force sedentarization and open new lands to exploitation. It is true that such events might be expected to elicit patterned behavior and responses from the many different individuals and groups involved in such changes and events. Nevertheless, since such patterns involve many spectra of possible behavior and response, to deal with them historically one needs evidence both for the events and changes themselves and for the specific historical responses that did in fact occur.

G) Gottwald's very strange concept of "retribalization"[164] is without any sociological or anthropological parallel and seems absurd.[165] Nevertheless, Gottwald needs some such concept if he wishes to explain the process of the emergence of Israel (from what is for Gottwald a non-tribal society of Canaan) in the form of a tribally organized, egalitarian society.[166] In describing Israel (and indeed all tribal societies) as

---

[162] N.P. Lemche, *op.cit.*, 1985, p.75.

[163] *Ibid., passim.*

[164] N.K. Gottwald, *op.cit.*, 1979, pp.323-329, 465-473. On various aspects of Gottwald's concept, see also G. Herion, *op.cit.*, 1981, pp.31ff; C. Hauser, "From Alt to Anthropology: The Rise of the Israelite State," *JSOT* 36 (1986), p.7; also *idem*, "Anthropology in Historiography," *JSOT* 39 (1987), pp.15-21.

[165] See G.E. Mendenhall, *op.cit.*, 1983, p.92.

[166] Similarly, R. Brandfon, *op.cit.*, 1988, p.56, in support of N.K. Gottwald, *op.cit.*, 1979, pp.465-473. Cf. C.H.J. de Geus, *op.cit.*, p.163. N.P. Lemche (*op.cit.*, 1985, p.236) sees de Geus as distinguishing Israelites and Canaanites on the basis of the similar concept of ethnic unity.

"egalitarian," Gottwald not only confuses ideology with reality,[167] he also blurs the distinction between segmentary lineage societies (with which he would identify Israel) with acephalous societies,[168] which are not "tribal." Tribal organization is necessary for Gottwald not only because it is essential to his amphictyonic union of Israel under Yahwism of Joshua 24, but also because it is a central ingredient of his understanding of the period of the judges, so necessary to both his and Noth's revision of Alt.

H) Alt's concept of the formation of Israel's tribes on a geographical basis, subsequent to their entry into *Palestine,* is similarly adapted by Gottwald, not only in the merger of elements of both Canaanite and pastoral nomadic elements in the newly formed tribes (ultimately any difference between Gottwald and Alt here becomes one of proportion only), but also in the unifying function this tribalization serves in the greater theory. Both Alt's and Gottwald's hypotheses depend wholly and entirely on an acceptance of some substantial form of historicity for both Judges and 1 Samuel, a historicity which can no longer be taken for granted but requires detailed support. Gottwald makes no major departure from Alt on the basis of whether Israel is or is not indigenous to *Palestine* in its origin. The difference between Alt and Gottwald here is one of degree. Gottwald follows Mendenhall in his assertion, without evidence,[169] that a "Moses group" brought Yahwism from Egypt,[170] and sees them joining "retribalized" villages and pastoralists in *Palestine* to form Israel. Alt, following Noth,[171] does not deal specifically with the Mosaic tradition, but lays more stress on the contrast of Joshua with Judges. In so doing he requires a larger proportion of pastoral nomads from the steppe. Ironically, a comparison of Gottwald's thesis with Alt's suggests that Alt's reconstruction is more closely linked with anthropologically and sociologically derived analogues, and, unlike Gottwald's, largely independent of alleged "events" which can be

---

[167] Lemche, *op.cit.,* 1985, p.122; J.W. Rogerson, *op.cit.,* 1986, p.21; *idem, Anthropology and the Old Testament* (Sheffield, 1984).

[168] See J.W. Rogerson, *op.cit,* 1986, p.19.

[169] Th.L. Thompson, "The Joseph and Moses Narratives," in *Israelite and Judaean History,* ed. by J.H. Hayes and J.M. Miller (Philadelphia, 1977) pp.149-180, 210-212; also J.M. Miller and J.H. Hayes, *op.cit.,* 1986.

[170] N.K. Gottwald, *op.cit.,* 1979, p.211.

[171] M. Noth, *Das System der zwölf Stämme Israels, BWANT* IV, I (Stuttgart, 1930).

falsified by the historian. In contrast, Gottwald's vision requires acceptance of the historicality of an as yet unverified agrarian revolt as well as of the historicity of the Exodus-Wilderness stories.[172] Gottwald's thesis stands or falls on his ability to ask questions based on the belief in a preliterary tradition-history of the pentateuch, which, prior to 1975, would believably be premonarchic on the sole basis of its classification as pre-Yahwist. Since 1975, however, there is very serious doubt regarding the existence of any such preliterary historiographic source surviving from such an early period. Gottwald throughout follows Noth's pentateuchal analysis of 1948,[173] and his tradition-historical investigation makes sense as a product of 1975; but it hardly survives the revision of pentateuchal studies in the mid- to late 1970s.

Both Gottwald and Alt long before him assume without significant argument that these early Old Testament traditions reflect a period of the judges. It is however today clear that many scholars working with these texts would doubt such an assumption of historicity. They rather understand the tradition to reflect the events and perceptions of a substantially later period.

---

[172] The long delay in the publication of Gottwald's book from 1975 to 1979 has resulted in dated perspectives that Gottwald did not deal with in his revisionary essay on pp.883–916. Not least is the problem that has been brought about by the increasingly radical shift downwards in pentateuchal chronology. J. Van Seters, *Abraham in History and Tradition* (New Haven, 1975) and H.H. Schmid, *Der sogenannte Jahwist: Beobachtungen und Fragen zur Pentateuchforschung* (Zurich, 1976).

[173] N.K. Gottwald, *op.cit.*, 1979, p.72.

CHAPTER THREE

HISTORICITY AND THE DECONSTRUCTION OF BIBLICAL HISTORIOGRAPHY

1. *The Conservative Movement of Biblical Archaeology*

As we have seen in the two previous chapters, the programs of both Alt and Albright represented a decidedly conservative swing of scholarship away from the tradition of Wellhausen and the early tendencies of the "history of religions" school. This new consensus of Alt and the early Albright, which had been building prior to the Second World War, began to break up in the post-war years. Many scholars, following the lead of Albright's quest of extrabiblical evidence for Israel's origins,[1] adopted the rapidly developing understanding of biblical archaeology as a means of confirming the historicity of the biblical traditions, especially of the patriarchs, Moses and the exodus, the wilderness wanderings of the pentateuch and the conquest stories of the book of Joshua. Such generally conservative scholars as N. Glueck[2] and G.E. Wright[3] were representative of this trend.[4] Other more mainline scholars such as J. Bright[5] and R. de Vaux[6] were also strongly influential in this search for

---

[1] W.F. Albright, "The Israelite Conquest of Palestine in the Light of Archaeology," *BASOR* 74 (1939), pp.1-23.

[2] N. Glueck, *The Other Side of the Jordan* (New Haven, 1940); *idem, Rivers in the Desert* (New Haven, 1959).

[3] G.E. Wright, "The Literary and Historical Problem of Joshua X and Judges I," *JNES* 5 (1946), pp.105-114; *idem, The Old Testament Against Its Environment* (London, 1955); *idem, Biblical Archaeology* (Philadelphia, 1957); *idem, God Who Acts* (Garden City, 1962).

[4] See the review of this issue in Th.L. Thompson, *The Origin Tradition of Ancient Israel I, JSOTS* 55 (Sheffield, 1987) pp.11-15.

[5] J. Bright, *Early Israel in Recent History Writing, SBTh* 19 (London, 1956); *idem, History of Israel,* (Philadelphia, [3]1981).

[6] Esp. R. de Vaux, *Die hebräischen Patriarchen und die modernen Entdeckungen* (Stuttgart, 1959); *idem, Die Patriarchenerzählungen und die Geschichte* (Stuttgart, 1965); de Vaux's position was, of course, radically altered by 1971: *idem, l'Histoire d'Israel* (Paris, 1971); also J.A. Dugan, *Martin Noth and the History of Israel* (Brandeis dissertation, 1978) p.94.

extra-biblical confirmation of biblical historiography.[7] With the publication of Bright's *History of Israel* in 1957 and Wright's *Biblical Archaeology* in 1958, many scholars confidently spoke of the assured results of biblical archaeology for the history of early Israel: a patriarchal period well established in the extrabiblical history of the early second-millennium,[8] the authenticity of the Joseph and Moses traditions supported by our understanding of ancient *Egypt*,[9] the confirmation of the historiography of Joshua 1–12 by the excavations of major sites in *Palestine* supporting an understanding of the origins of Israel in terms of a unified conquest, and an assessment of the "historical reliability" of the period of the judges in our growing understanding of the Iron I period.

Noth and von Rad, however, found some difficulty with this direction of scholarship.[10] Their qualms lay not so much with the widespread assumption and even conviction that the earliest traditions of the Old Testament about Israel's prehistory were historically rooted in the second-millennium;[11] Rather they did not believe that non-textual archaeological discoveries were capable of confirming the biblical

---

[7] J. Bright, *op.cit.*, 1956, pp.91ff.; also J.A. Dugan, *op.cit.*, p.94.

[8] Note however, that a considerable number of scholars, above all C.H. Gordon, reflecting on the Late Bronze Nuzi texts, wished to date the patriarchal age to the fifteenth- or even the fourteenth-century ("The Patriarchal Age," *JBR* 21, 1953, pp.238-243; *idem*, "The Patriarchal Narratives," *JNES* 13, 1954, pp.56-59; *idem*, "Abraham and the Merchants of Ura," *JNES* 17, 1958, pp.28-31; *idem*, *The World of the Old Testament*, New York, 1958; *idem*, *Before the Bible*, New York, 1962; *idem*, "Hebrew Origins in the Light of Recent Discovery," *Biblical and Other Studies*, ed. by A. Altmann, Cambridge, 1963, pp.3-14; *idem*, "Abraham of Ur," *Hebrew and Semitic Studies: Essays in Honour of G.R.Driver*, ed. by D.W. Thomas and W.D. McHardy, Oxford,1963, pp.77-84).

[9] J. Vergote, *Joseph en Égypte: Genèse chap. 37–50 à la lumière des études égyptologiques récentes*, OBL 3 (Paris, 1959); K.A. Kitchen, *Ancient Orient and the Old Testament* (London, 1966). For a review of general issues, see Th.L. Thompson, "The Joseph and Moses Narratives," *Israelite and Judaean History, ed. by J.H. Hayes and J.M. Miller* (Philadelphia, 1977) pp.150-166.

[10] G. von Rad, "History and the Patriarchs," *ET* 72 (1960-1961), pp.213-216; M. Noth, "Der Beitrag der Archäologie zur Geschichte Israels," *VTS* 7 (Leiden, 1960) pp.262-282; *idem*, *Die Ursprünge des alten Israel im Lichte neuer Quellen* (Cologne, 1961).

[11] Noth himself strongly affirmed such historicity in his "Proto-Aramaean" hypothesis. M. Noth, *Die israelitischen Personennamen im Rahmen der gemeinsemitischen Namengebung* (Stuttgart, 1928) pp.27-30; *idem*, "Zum Problem des Ostkanaanäer," ZA 39 (1930), p.214; *idem*, "Die syrisch-palästinische Bevölkerung des zweiten Jahrtausends v.Chr. im Lichte neuer Quellen," *ZDPV* 65 (1942), pp.34f.; *idem*, *op.cit.*, 1961, pp.31-33.

historiographical traditions.[12] Somewhat arbitrarily and dogmatically, Noth argued that "history can only be described on the basis of literary traditions which record events and specify persons and places."[13] For this reason, he believed, the history of Israel must be approached primarily through the text of the Old Testament. It was the biblical tradition that was for Noth the primary source for the history of early Israel.[14] Archaeology could serve only a very limited and supportive role.[15]

In this rejection of any major role for biblical archaeology in the reconstruction of Israel's earliest history, Noth turned aside from that part of Alt's proposal which looked to the future of archaeology for confirmation,[16] and in doing so he undermined the conservative consensus reflected in the work of Alt and Albright. Emphatically by 1930, in his monograph on the amphictyony, Noth abandoned Alt's attempt to create a synthesis of the potential epigraphic, archaeological and biblical sources for Israel's early history in favor of an exploration of the history of the oral tradition underlying the "historical" narratives of the bible.[17]

---

[12] See the similar conviction expressed recently by G.R. Elton, *op.cit.*, 1983, p.100; and the detailed evaluations of J.M. Miller (*op.cit.*, 1986) regarding the limits of the contributions of biblical archaeology for the entire early history of Israel.

[13] M. Noth, *op.cit.*, 1960, p.42.

[14] *Ibid.*, pp.42-50; also J.A. Dugan, *op.cit.*, 1978, pp.30f.

[15] M. Noth, *ibid.*, pp.47f. J.M. Miller, in a popular essay ("Approaches to the Bible through History and Archaeology: Biblical History as a Discipline," *BA* 45, 1982, pp.211-216, esp. p.215), argues adamantly for the primacy of the biblical tradition in historical reconstructions. He points out, quite appropriately, the inadequacies of archaeological methods to either affirm or deny biblical historicity. Given these limitations, he recommends a profound skepticism towards any historical reconstruction of Israel's early history prior to the time of the Omride Dynasty, warning against a too sanguine confidence in biblical archaeology's ability to render positive historical reconstructions of what is a biblically oriented historiography.

[16] A. Alt, *Die Landnahme der Israeliten in Palästina* (Leipzig, 1925).

[17] J.A. Dugan, *op.cit.*, 1978, pp.28-49, for a convenient summary of the main ideas of Noth's work. The most important of Noth's studies for our issue are: M. Noth, *Das System der zwölf Stämme Israels* (Stuttgart, 1930); *Die Welt des alten Testaments* (Berlin, 1940, [4]1962); *idem*, *Überlieferungsgeschichtliche Studien I* (Halle, 1943); *Überlieferungsgeschichte des Pentateuch* (Stuttgart, 1948); "Das Amt des 'Richters Israels'," *Festschrift, Alfred Bertholet zum 80. Geburtstag gewidmet von Kollegen und Freunden*, ed. by W. Baumgartner et alii (Tübingen, 1950) pp.404-417; *op.cit.*, 1960; *op.cit.*, 1961.

The tradition-historical method, in tracing the primary roots of a tradition and its secondary developments, carries far more conviction in its negative conclusions than in any positive affirmations. Noth was hard pressed in his study both of the pentateuch[18] and of the so-called deuteronomistic tradition[19] to make, in his own estimation, a fully convincing case for the historicality of any of the traditions and themes that he understood made up the core of the biblical historiography. Historicity eluded Noth except in the rarest of moments, and these exceptions ironically enough related to those aspects of the traditions for which he turned to extrabiblical sources: the "proto-Aramaean" roots of the patriarchal traditions that he had related to references to West Semitic groups in the *Mari* texts;[20] the internal tribal amphictyonic union that he believed to be confirmed on the basis of a detailed socio-historical analogue with forms of ancient Greek amphictyonies;[21] and the peaceful settlement of the Israelite tribes in *Palestine* that, following Alt, he based on a synthesis of ancient Egyptian records; the evidence from excavations and surveys disclosing the absence of significant archaeological remains in the hill country of *Palestine*; and the sociological analogue of late nineteenth- and early twentieth-century transhumance pastoralists. That Noth's arguments regarding the peaceful settlement of Israel in the central hills of *Palestine* are still viable today should not distract us from the fact that this positive construction of Israel's origins is not based on the biblical traditions as primary evidence. Quite the contrary, this particular theory has developed out of and carries conviction to the extent that it adheres closely to observation of extrabiblical data, above all Egyptian geographical texts and archaeological remains in *Palestine* and views the biblical traditions only as a point of orientation and as a conceptual context. To the extent that Noth has depended on a synthesis with the biblical tradition, he has failed. Following the development of Noth's principles of tradition

---

[18] M. Noth, *op.cit.*, 1948.

[19] M. Noth, *op.cit.*, 1943. A similar evaluation of the traditio-historical method is expressed by J.M. Miller (*op.cit.*, 1982; *idem, op.cit.*, 1986). Miller himself has carried Noth's methods through to an even more devastating analysis of the biblical traditions leading to a healthy skepticism of historical reconstructions for the period of the judges and the early monarchy as well.

[20] M. Noth *op.cit.*, 1961; Th.L. Thompson, *The Historicity of the Patriarchal Narratives,* BZAW 133 (Berlin, 1974) pp.75-78.

[21] M. Noth, *op.cit.*, 1930.

history, his detailed analysis of the pentateuchal stories and of the so-called deuteronomistic history began a long process of deconstruction in biblical history that continues today. In the final analysis, one must agree with Bright that biblical historiography can only be affirmed on the basis of extrabiblical confirmation.[22] Noth's own careful tradition-historical work is the best proof that a critically acceptable history cannot be written on the basis of ancient biblical historiography. Moreover, in the few instances where Noth himself has written dependable critical history, it has been with the substantial aid and sometimes the exclusive use of extrabiblical sources.

Noth's work since 1930 moved scholarship away from the directions set by Alt and Albright. Repeating Alt's understanding of Israel's origins in his *History* and later works,[23] Noth added substantially to Alt's influence although he did not develop the argument in any lasting way. He held firmly to the classical view of history as a description of the past which can only be written "on the basis of literary traditions, which record events and specify persons and places."[24] Why this must be so, Noth never explains.[25]

In addition to his traditio-historical work, Noth inaugurated a period of fundamental critical appraisal of the efforts of scholars of the 1940s and 1950s to establish a history of Israel on the basis of a synthesis of biblical, archaeological and ancient Near Eastern data through his presidential address before the International Congress of Old Testament Studies in 1959.[26] Noth's critique was primarily aimed at the Albright school's reconstruction of Israel's prehistory. In his survey of the issues, Noth raised substantial objections to efforts at placing the patriarchal era in the Middle Bronze I, Middle Bronze II and the Late Bronze periods, and pointed out the many opinions about the patriarchs that could not be reconciled. Noth also argued that while the archaeological discoveries at *Hazor* could be understood as reflecting events similar to

---

[22] J. Bright, *op.cit.*, 1956, pp.91ff. However, the largely negative implication of this principle, as pointed out by J.M. Miller (*op.cit.*, 1982), must be underlined.

[23] Esp. M.Noth, *op.cit.*, 1961.

[24] M.Noth, *op.cit.*, 1960, p.42.

[25] Noth's historiography here as elsewhere is idealistic, with strong affinities to Hegel and Weber—certainly not "positivistic" as Dugan (*op.cit.*, 1978, p.ii) unaccountably asserts. Dugan's whole discussion is somewhat baffling, not least his description of Noth's understanding of the settlement and the Israelite amphictyony as "observable facts"!

[26] M. Noth, *op.cit.*, 1960.

those described in the biblical tradition of the conquest (Joshua
11:10–15), the same could not be said of the extensive excavations at
Jericho and *Ai*.[27] Noth's lecture began a period of reevaluation of the
alleged gains of biblical archaeology that in the 1970s and 1980s has
brought about an extensive rethinking of what since Wellhausen passed
for a history of Israel.

Work on literary analysis and tradition history of Old Testament
narrative had long since made clear the disparate origins and nature of
the traditions that were brought together as a relatively coherent whole
only by the shell of their secondary literary frameworks. The awareness
of these literary and redactional structures caused many, who, like Noth,
wished to argue on behalf of the primacy of biblical sources for Israel's
history, to appear highly skeptical and even nihilistic by the more
positivistic supporters of extrabiblical approaches.[28] The problem was
that once the acceptance of the biblical historiography had been called
into question, every historical construction that held the biblical
historiography as integral to its view of history must of necessity
collapse. This unfortunately led Noth, and many familiar with the use of
tradition history, to follow a fundamentally contradictory and
reductionist approach to Israel's earliest beginnings. On one hand he
ignored the patriarchal and exodus traditions themselves while asserting
their historical roots in the second-millennium. On the other hand, he
identified the beginning of Israel's history with its presence in the land[29]
because before that Israel was not. The conservative character of Noth's
tradition-historical effort to salvage a period of the judges was never
recognized as such. Rather, in the barrage of criticism from supporters
of a patriarchal period and an historical exodus (above all Wright), Noth
was tarred a "minimalist" and a "nihilist." Ironically, this false position
did more to establish adherence to a belief in the historicity of a period
of the judges than all of Noth's constructive efforts combined.

---

[27] *Ibid.*, pp.374f. Noth's argument that the Jericho and Ai stories are aetiological has not
survived (B.O. Long, *The Problem of Etiological Narrative in the Old Testament, BZAW* 108,
Berlin, 1968). Long's analysis, however, while not encouraging a broad sweeping
classification of the Joshua conquest narratives as aetiological, also does not permit an
evaluation of these stories as either historiographical or historical (B.O. Long, "On Finding
the Hidden Premises," *JSOT* 39, 1987, pp.10–14).

[28] Th.L. Thompson, *op.cit.*, 1974, pp.5–9.

[29] See now A. Malamat, "Die Frühgeschichte Israels: eine Methodologische Studie," *ThZ*
39 (1983), pp.1–16.

In M. Weippert's 1967 description of the then contemporary debate, three distinct positions supporting the historicity of Israel's origin traditions were clearly delineated. The focus of each was radically conservative (all adamantly affirming the historicity of the biblical historiography for the period of the judges and the united monarchy), with Noth on the far left of the spectrum.

In this pivotal study, Weippert started from the observation of the limited promise for a history of Israel's origins resulting from the breakup of a belief in biblical historiography's coherence.[30] Weippert largely limited his discussion to Alt and Albright's programs, which synthesized biblical and extrabiblical sources on the basis of analogy.[31] As many scholars do today, Weippert viewed history no longer as a direct (perhaps naive) description of events on the basis of sources, but rather as an historiographical reconstruction based on ideal models or patterns of what (on the basis of better known analogies) can or must have happened. Accordingly, he put forward three constructs of Israel's beginnings: the settlement model of Alt and Noth,[32] the conquest model of Albright, Wright and Bright,[33] and the revolt model of Mendenhall.[34] In this (of necessity harmonized) presentation, significant differences in the positions of Alt and Noth, and especially some major differences between Wright and Bright, were neglected by the form of the discussion itself, in spite of the fact that none of these scholars had understood himself as working within constructs of an historiographical model.

In this 1967 master's thesis Weippert did not seek a direct answer to the origin of Israel, but rather asked which of the accepted models of scholarship was most viable as an explanation of Israel's origins. Weippert chose Alt's approach not because it offered a thoroughly convincing and positive reconstruction of Israel's origins, but rather because it best withstood the criticisms of the opposing models (not, however, without significant problems).[35] As I have pointed out

---

[30] M. Weippert, *Die Landnahme der israelitischen Stämme in der neueren wissenschaftlichen Diskussion* (Göttingen, 1967) p.1.

[31] *Ibidem.*

[32] *Ibid.*, pp.5–46.

[33] *Ibid.*, pp.46–55.

[34] *Ibid.*, pp.55–62.

[35] *Ibid.*, pp.144f.

elsewhere,[36] the results of Weippert's review, although functioning largely as a refutation of positions of Wright and Bright, which have hardly been seriously revived since, had a much more positive effect on the acceptance of Mendenhall's revision of Alt's hypothesis. These results ironically also attracted greater scrutiny and critical appraisal to the proposals of Noth.

2. Early Alternatives to Settlement and Conquest Theories

In the 1960s and 1970s, the Israeli scholar B. Mazar wrote a series of very important articles proposing a synthesis on the origins of Israel that offered a far-reaching revision of Alt on the basis of our increased knowledge of Palestinian history and archaeology.[37] Mazar's most significant improvements on Alt's hypothesis gave new impetus and focus to questions about Israel's origins that had been largely deadlocked in the German vs. Albright school controversies reviewed by Weippert. Like Alt before him, Mazar saw the issue of Israel's emergence in terms of the transition from Late Bronze Canaan to the nation-states of the Iron Age. However, Mazar focussed on a larger context than the transition from Late Bronze Canaanite city-states of the lowlands to Iron Age Israelite hill country settlements. He rather focussed on the general changes that occurred throughout *Syro-Palestine* in the transition from the second- to the first-millennium B.C. This transition he understood from the perspective of the emergence of three new semitic peoples, each of which he believed to have developed a national state with its own culture: the Israelites, the Aramaeans and the Phoenicians.[38] Mazar begins this transition with what he understood as the collapse of the Assyrian, Hittite and Egyptian imperial hold on *Syria* and *Palestine* at the end of the thirteenth and beginning of the twelfth-century,[39] and

---

[36] Th.L. Thompson, *op.cit.*, 1987, pp.15-17.

[37] B. Mazar, "The Middle Bronze Age in Canaan," *IEJ* 18 (1968), pp.65-97; *idem*, "The Early Israelite Settlement in the Hill Country," *BASOR* 241 (1981), pp.75-85; *idem*, "The Philistines and the Rise of Israel and Tyre," *Israel Academy of Sciences and Humanities Proceedings* 1 (Jerusalem, 1964) pp.1-22. These and related articles are collected in B. Mazar, *The Early Biblical Period: Historical Studies* (Jerusalem, 1986).

[38] B. Mazar, *op.cit.*, 1964.

[39] *Idem*, p.63.

with the migrations and invasions of "sea peoples" theroughout the Mediterranean coast.

Mazar identified the early emergence of Israel with the many non-city Iron I settlements in the central hills of *Palestine*.[40] The original settlers of the hill country were associated by Mazar with this territory, as by Alt, through the assumption of a gradual process of sedentarization of transhumance shepherds.

Mazar made several significant additions to Alt's model that strengthened it and gave it new scope: a) the orientation of the transition within an ethnic history of the region (This closely tied Mazar's revision to a geographical framework, and allowed the transition to be understood as part of the fortunes of international policies and potential mass migrations); b) the integration of the questions about origins with the vastly improved knowledge of Palestinian archaeology, particularly as they relate to the new settlements of the hill country (This has provided the very specific archaeological information Alt had hoped for in 1925); c) the reference to and use of contemporary epigraphic evidence about New Kingdom nomadic groups referred to as *Shasu* (This stregthened the historical basis for Alt's immigration hypothesis by introducing a supporting argument from evidence to Alt's anthropologically and sociologically based analogy of amphictyony);[41] d) and most importantly; the refocusing of the chronological aspect of the transition. No longer was the transition understood as that of a shift from Late Bronze to Iron I (or the late thirteenth to the twelfth-century), a perception that had encouraged a narrow fixation of the question to processes of development in the initial stages of Iron I only. Mazar concentrated on the geopolitical changes between the second and first millennia and, in understanding the entirety of Iron I as a transition period, he focussed the question of Israel's origin not on a period of the judges but on the rise of the Israelite monarchy, a period in Israelite history that in the late 1960s and early 1970s stood apart from questions of origin and was undisputed in terms of historicity; e) finally, in arguing

---

[40] B. Mazar, *op.cit.*, 1981.

[41] The epigraphic evidence of the *Shasu* has been systematically collected and interpreted by R. Giveon (*Les bedouins shosou des documents égyptiens*, Leiden, 1971). Mazar's thesis was already strongly influenced by the research of Giveon and Z. Kallai (*The Tribes of Israel*, Jerusalem, 1967) and has been followed by S. Herrman (*A History of Israel in OT Times*, London, 1975, esp. pp.69-85); also, M. Weippert, "The Israelite 'Conquest' and the Evidence from Transjordan," *Symposia*, ed. by F.M. Cross (Cambridge, 1979) pp.15-34.

for a historical background of the patriarchal narratives in the period immediately preceding the monarchy (whether or not historicity be attributed to these stories), antedating their then widely assumed original written form by only a generation or two,[42] Mazar offered not only a more convincing historical evaluation of patriarchal traditions than was then generally put forward,[43] but also avoided a major weakness of the dominant theories of the Albright school that required a doubling of Israel's origins into two distinct periods that were in many ways incompatible and contradictory: an origin in the patriarchal period—whether in terms of the Amorite hypothesis of the Albright school or of the proto-Aramaean concession of M. Noth[44]—and a separate origin in the early Iron Age in terms of conquest or settlement.[45] By associating the stories of the patriarchs with the initial process of settlement, Mazar put forward very reasonable arguments that the two traditions (of the patriarchs and of Israel's settlement) reflect what was in fact a single historical process. This bold revision had its most immediate effect on evaluations of the historicity of the patriarchal period, an issue which was to dominate discussions of Israel's origins through the 1970s. Mazar's position unfortunately has had little influence outside of Israeli scholarship until most recent times.

In 1971, de Vaux published the first volume of his comprehensive study of Israel's early history.[46] He presented a reconstruction of Israel's origins on the basis of a synthesis of the biblical traditions with Palestinian archaeology and ancient Near Eastern remains, taking as his model R. Kittel's great three-volume history first published in 1888. De Vaux took great pains to integrate Israel's history with the geography, anthropology and prehistory of early *Palestine*.[47] Of necessity, much of this work is a critical summation, bringing together the current state of research. Nevertheless, de Vaux made several major departures from the

---

[42] B. Mazar, *op.cit.*, 1968; also *idem*, "The Book of Genesis," *JNES* 28 (1969), pp.73-83.

[43] *Ibid*, p.54.

[44] Th.L. Thompson, *op.cit.*, 1974, *passim*.

[45] I mention only the two most commonly discussed of Israel's alleged origin periods. Both tradition and scholarship deal with many more, most notably Israel's origin in the exodus from Egypt, in the theophany on Sinai, and in the tradition of the rise of the monarchy (Th.L. Thompson, *op.cit.*, 1977, pp.210-212; and *idem*, "History and Tradition: A Response to J.B. Geyer," *JSOT* 15, 1980, pp.57-61).

[46] R. de Vaux, *l'Histoire d'Israel I* (Paris, 1971) =*A History of Israel* (Philadelphia, 1978).

[47] *Ibid.*, 1978, pp.3-152.

views then dominant and introduced serious doubt about his own earlier published views.[48] De Vaux allowed a great deal of uncertainty in the dating of the patriarchal period.[49] Without challenging the existence of such a period directly, de Vaux's agnosticism on the question, coupled with a detailed discussion of the sources from the second-millennium, seriously undermined confidence in any specific reconstruction of that period. Similarly, de Vaux, who early in his career had made substantial contributions to the understanding of ancient Israel's social customs and practices,[50] withdrew his earlier confidence in the long held parallels between patriarchal family practices and the conditions reflected in the tables of fifteenth-century Nuzi in North Mesopotamia, pointing out that some practices were common to cuneiform law generally, others were better understood as reflecting practices close to the time of the written form of these traditions in Genesis, and yet other parallels were not entirely convincing.[51] De Vaux's brief summary marked the first major critique of the Nuzi parallels since E.A. Speiser's *Anchor Bible* commentary on *Genesis*[52] and R. Tournay's *DBS* article on Nuzi[53] had established them as *opinio communis*. Although he adamantly asserted the historicity of the patriarchal narratives, the skepticism de Vaux introduced into the consensus on this and other issues dealing with the patriarchs irrevocably undermined the nearly total acceptance of "the patriarchal period" as a definable stage of the early history of *Palestine*.

De Vaux also strongly asserted the historicity of the Joseph and Moses narratives.[54] However, his presentation of the ancient Near Eastern extrabiblical evidence for his assertion[55] does not go beyond the issue of verisimilitude.[56] The weakness of the support for historicity was glaring in a book dedicated to a comprehensive synthesis of the biblical and extrabiblical sources. Given de Vaux's great integrity and depth as

---

[48] As, e.g., in R. de Vaux, *op.cit.*, 1965.

[49] R. de Vaux, *op.cit.*, 1978, pp.256-263.

[50] R. de Vaux, *Les institutions de l'Ancien Testament*, 2 vols. (Paris, 1958) =*Ancient Israel* (New York, 1959).

[51] R. de Vaux, *op.cit.*, 1978, pp.241-256.

[52] E.A. Speiser, *Genesis, Anchor Bible*, vol.1 (Garden City, 1965).

[53] R. Tournay, "Nuzi," *DBS* 6 (Paris, 1967) cols.644-674.

[54] E.g., R. de Vaux, *op.cit.*, 1978, p.313.

[55] *Ibid.*, pp.313-320.

[56] Th.L. Thompson, *op.cit*, 1977.

a scholar, readers were led to the inevitable observation that no such evidence existed for the historicity that was claimed.

In his treatment of the period of the judges, de Vaux forcefully rejected Noth's position supporting the existence of an amphictyony in ancient Israel,[57] and accepted the historiographical problems involved in dealing with Israel in both the period of the settlement and that of the judges without any critical bond of unity which might enable premonarchic Israel to be viewed as a whole. In this he, like Mazar, oriented the discussion of Israel's origins in the direction of the monarchy, a period in which de Vaux found a stable coherent center for his nation Israel. In this radical departure from the histories of Noth and Bright, de Vaux like Alt understood the period of the judges and of the settlement as quintessentially a part of the prehistory of Israel. As a consequence of denying the existence of an "all-Israel" prior to the time of Saul, de Vaux was then free to locate many separate origins of the groups and people which made up Israel, and to extend the period of settlement and conquest over the entire second-millennium B.C.[58]

One certainly might argue that de Vaux's synthetic methodology led him to an unattainable comprehensiveness, one that would allow everything of importance to the history of ancient *Palestine* to feed into the question of Israel's origins. On the other hand, de Vaux's great complexity is thoroughly justified by the question of origins, which needs to be understood in terms of the entire corpus of early biblical tradition. Above all, when one observes the many indigenous qualities of this tradition that demand an explanation within a history of *Palestine*, such complexity of treatment is a necessity. De Vaux's weakness lies in his recurrent equivocation regarding the role of the biblical tradition in his history, and in the constriction to a confirmatory role which he forced on the extrabiblical side of his equation. Nevertheless, de Vaux's work stands as a watershed in the history of scholarship, which built on and completed the longstanding projects of biblical archaeology and the comparative methods developed by Alt and Albright. De Vaux, however, shared the circular method of reasoning, so well established in the comparative method of his colleagues, whereby texts, historical referents and hypothetical harmonies were understood and interpreted "in light of" each other, a method that encouraged a state of scholarship in which

---

[57] R. de Vaux, *op.cit.*, 1978, pp.695-716.

[58] *Ibid.*, pp.744-749.

neither biblical traditions, nor archaeological excavations nor ancient Near Eastern texts were ever examined in their own right.

3. The Systematic Critique of the Comparative Method

While Mazar and de Vaux were presenting their revisions, a number of critiques of the accepted understanding of the biblical tradition were being prepared around the issue of historicity. The first of these was a work written for an academic competition in *Copenhagen* in 1968 by H. Friis.[59] In this work, Friis critically and lucidly argued that the biblical traditions that placed the formation of the state or the "United Monarchy" under David had been the product of the exilic period. She also placed the origins of Yahwistic monotheism in the exilic period. In line with this, she understood the traditions that found the origins of Israel in *Egypt* as aetiologies. Finally, she argued that the entire complex of narrative of 2 Kings was oriented to explaining the causes of the exile to *Babylon* and must therefore have been written at some time after the deportation. Methodologically, Friis was the first to present a systematic demonstration of the necessity of developing a history of Israel independent of the Bible when she argued that questions regarding the history of David's empire have two distinct aspects. The first is an aspect of the political history of the ancient Near East in the early first-millennium. The other relates to the Old Testament traditions and belonged to a period centuries later.

This study was far ahead of its time. The author drew conclusions that most of Old Testament scholarship was not ready to draw for another decade. It existed, however, only in Danish, and the only available copies were in the library of the University of *Copenhagen*. Like many of the most promising young scholars of the late 1960s and early 1970s, Friis had no secure academic post. Unpublished until 1986, the work had little if any influence on others in the field.[60]

---

[59] H. Friis, *Die Bedingungen für die Errichtung des davidischen Reiches in Israel und seiner Umwelt*, DBAT 6 (Heidelberg, 1986). The Danish original was entitled: *Forudsaetninger i og uden for Israel for obrettelsen af Davids imperium* (typescript, Copenhagen, 1968: unseen by the present writer).

[60] B. Diebner ("Forschungsgeschichtliche Einführung," DBAT 6, 1986, pp.217-241) is certainly justified in his complaint about the professorial orientation of research and scholarship in the 1970s and early 1980s. However, this problem has hardly been confined

The first major published work on the issue of historicity, pursuing independently some of the themes laid out by Friis three years earlier, was my own study, *The Historicity of the Patriarchal Narratives.*[61] This work systematically evaluated most of the major historical reconstructions which had been put forward between 1920 and 1970 that had supported the reconstruction of a patriarchal period within the history of *Palestine* in the second-millennium B.C. Concentrating especially on a review of the long accepted *Nuzi* parallels to "patriarchal customs," and the widely held understanding of alleged migrations of nomadic "Amorites" in the early history of the second-millennium throughout *Mesopotamia*, *Palestine* and *Egypt* (the two strongest arguments put forward for the acceptance and dating of a patriarchal period), the study challenged most sustained efforts to establish the historicity of the patriarchs on the basis of extrabiblical materials. It became clear that the nature of the comparative method, as it had been practiced, had depended so heavily on circular argumentation (the understanding of the biblical text affecting and even determining the interpretation of potentially related extrabiblical materials, and the reconstruction of the extrabiblically based event, custom or tradition affecting or determining our interpretation of the biblical) that any major change in the interpretation of one part of the circle of evidence affected radically the validity of our understanding of all other parts.[62] Hence, a rejection of the *Nuzi* parallels to patriarchal customs changed not only our understanding of the biblical narratives, but also questioned our past misunderstanding of the *Nuzi* tablets and the Hurrian customs therein alleged. The rejection of the Early Bronze IV or Middle Bronze I period as the patriarchal period undermined the substantial scholarly context for understanding that period as "nomadic." Similarly, a change in the dating of the "Execration Texts" to *ca.* 1810–1770 B.C., separating them from the Early Bronze IV-Middle Beonze I period, enabled these texts to be read apart from the assumption that they derived from a period involving the incipient sedentarization of nomads. More comprehensively: separating the process of writing a history of the

---

to Germany (Th.L. Thompson, "W.F. Albright as Historian," forthcoming). It is, of course, well known that most original research is done at a sub-professorial level, and—at least in the United States—at the level of the dissertation.

[61] Th.L. Thompson. *op.cit.*, 1974.

[62] *Ibid.*, pp.52–57.

second-millennium in *Palestine* from efforts to reconstruct a prehistory of Israel based in biblical tradition—however much the issue of historicity is involved—radically altered our historical perspective and interpretation of the history of *Palestine*. The fundamental need for an independent understanding of both archaeology and the history of *Palestine* became patent. There is also a comparable need (well understood by de Vaux and Noth but generally ignored by the Albright school) for an independent understanding and evaluation of the biblical tradition as an historical source and as literature. Not least at stake is the assumption of an historiography (developed in secondary redactions of the tradition) as applicable to the whole of the tradition, as well as an understanding of the prehistory of the tradition as rooted and originating in history—an assumption nowhere justified in the texts themselves but derived rather from quite abstract assumptions about the nature and origin of folk traditions.

This book called for, and itself began, a critical revision both of our understanding of second-millennium *Palestine* and of our understanding of the nature of the biblical traditions of Genesis.[63] Since the book addressed the field on the issue of methodology, it also had an impact on those related questions regarding Israel's early history that had shared the uncritical historiographical techniques of the "Comparative Method."[64]

The most serious methodological limitation of this 1974 book is its wholesale assumption of the documentary hypothesis and the closely associated understanding of the patriarchal traditions as *Stammessage* or folk accounts of the histories of peoples. Although the work already contains some implicit distancing from the more extended uses of tradition or redaction history in its insistence that the traditions derive from the contemporary milieux of their written forms,[65] it reflected a naive adherence to the historical implications of the four-source

---

[63] On this last issue, see further Th.L. Thompson, "A New Attempt to Date the Patriarchs," *JAOS* 98 (1978), pp.76-84; *idem*, "Conflict Themes in the Jacob Narratives," *Semeia* 15 (1979), pp.5-26; and esp. *idem, op.cit.*, 1987. In the 1974 study, "positive" reconstructions were largely oriented towards quite specific historical issues in Palestinian history. More comprehensive discussions of biblical interpretation can be found in the 1987 work.

[64] See the debate between E.F. Campbell and J.M. Miller, "W.F. Albright and Historical Reconstruction," *BA* 42 (1979), pp.37-47.

[65] Th.L. Thompson, *op.cit.*, 1974, p.326.

documentary theory. This issue is significant (as is pointed out above in the discussion of Mazar's proposals) in that the assumption of the development of the pentateuch from as early as the beginning of the monarchy, as well as of the persistence of some very early oral forms of the narratives surviving through late preexilic and exilic periods, has two corollaries: the existence of a patriarchal tradition close to the time of Israel's origins, with a potential verisimilitude that might legitimately suggest a historical reference to Israel's origins, and an original core of tradition buried in the pentateuch that might understandably be misunderstood as primary, and therefore historiographically preferable to traditions that bear clear references (such as the golden calf story, or the references in Genesis 15 to *Damascus* and in Genesis 17 to *Chaldaea*) not normally understood as belonging to the prehistory of Israel. The necessary revisions in the early history of Israel consequent upon a rejection of an early date of the J and E material, whether or not some form of the documentary hypothesis is maintained, is of some consequence to any history of early Israel. Without the documentary hypothesis, or some other means of establishing an early date for many of the narratives of the pentateuch, the use of the biblical tradition of the pentateuch as an historiographic source becomes questionable.

J. Van Seters's study of the patriarchal narratives[66] concentrated most emphatically on just this issue, which had been left unexamined by me in 1974. Van Seters's book has two separate parts, both of which are significant: Part 1 is a survey of the extrabiblical evidence for an early dating of the patriarchal narratives with the resoundingly negative conclusion that the evidence that had so far been put forward was not only wholly inadequate, but suggestive of a much later date than had previously been considered.[67] Seven distinct conclusions were drawn. a) The patriarchal stories do not reflect "a nomadic presettlement phase of Israelite society" or "migratory movements" of the second-millennium B.C. b) What "nomadic details" there are are best understood in terms of the mid-first-millennium B.C. c) Archaic designations of peoples in *Palestine* reflect not the second-millennium but a much later period. d) The place-names of the patriarchal traditions reflect the history of the Israelite monarchy. e) Social customs, in any case a poor means of dating

---

[66] J. Van Seters, *Abraham in History and Tradition* (New Haven, 1975); *idem, Der Jahwist als Historiker, Theologische Studien* 134 (Zurich, 1987).

[67] *Ibid.*, p.121.

traditions, reflect a mid-first-millennium dating. f) The arguments which had been put forward for connections with the Early Bronze IV-Middle Bronze I and Middle Bronze II archaeological periods of *Palestine* are unconvincing. g) The efforts to establish a second-millennium date for Genesis 14 have not been successful.[68]

In summary, Van Seters's investigation adequately challenged "the presumption of antiquity"[69] of the patriarchal narratives. One might also add that, while Van Seters's arguments were oriented in opposition to the dominant second-millennium and especially an early second-millennium dating of the "patriarchal period," and, as such, deserving of resounding agreement and approval, his arguments also are applicable (by intention) to any attempt at an early monarchic dating of the JE sources of the tradition! Here Van Seters's arguments are more provocative than totally convincing, for there is little historiographic value in "better" or "best" analogies, when there is no clear evidence, only uncertain possibilities.[70] What I wish to emphasize as a caution in dealing with Van Seters's conclusions is that our means of dating are wholly inadequate at present. Great reserve must be practiced before claiming a known historical context for these narratives that reflect an exceedingly complex history of transmission.[71]

The first part of Van Seters's study had the primary function of clearing the way for his far-reaching revision of the documentary hypothesis in the second part of his work. The parallel roles with which Van Seters structured the two parts of his book (questions related to the history of *Palestine* and those related to the history of Israelite tradition) underline the intrinsic scholarly interrelationship of what are two quite distinct disciplines. Van Seters drew two fundamental conclusions in his study that, as they have become increasingly more acceptable, have made it extremely difficult to posit any early context for the patriarchal traditions. Most important is his conclusion that most of the narratives

---

[68] For a review of Van Seters's, see Th.L. Thompson, *op.cit.*, 1978, pp.76ff.

[69] J. Van Seters, *op.cit.*, 1975, p.122.

[70] Van Seters and I would, I believe, agree. I would no longer suggest that the traditions are from the early first-millennium. In fact, I think they are later and would argue that a very early date is not only unlikely but impossible. Nor would I insist on a late Assyrian period dating (*contra* Th.L. Thompson, *op.cit.*, 1987, pp.191-194). On this, further below, Chapter 8 and Chapter 9.

[71] Th.L. Thompson, *op.cit.*, 1987.

of Genesis were in their origin written tradition and were not based on an oral foundation. This is a contention that radically undercuts scholarly arguments that assume long periods of oral transmission, on the basis of which one might understand the narratives as having been rooted in historical events—an axiom essential to the projects of both Alt and Albright. Moreover, the historical context of the central J tradition is not monarchic, but, Van Seters has argued, belongs to the exilic and postexilic periods and reflects the events of that time. This second conclusion is a major step in Van Seters's source-critically based subsequent reconstructions of early Israelite historiography, that have had immense implications for the early history of Israel and the reconstruction of Israel's origins.[72]

I have expressed my objections to Van Seters's conclusions in detail elsewhere.[73] I do not think that we are as able as Van Seters believes to distinguish written traditions that have oral backgrounds from those which do not. However, I also do not believe that we can (because of our limited resources) reconstruct the *Redaktionsgeschichte* of our biblical traditions beyond what is clearly observable in the extant text. Departures in the history of the tradition beyond the extant text are highly speculative and largely unprovable. Although a very late preexilic or even early exilic dating for the formation of both the pentateuch and the so-called deuteronomistic history seems most likely, I do object very strongly to Van Seters's efforts to use the exilic period as an essential interpretive context for the patriarchal narratives and the pentateuch; for this historical context is derived purely from the texts interpreted, and his method consequently involves him inextricably in the kind of circular argumentation that he has so emphatically opposed in his predecessors.

The debate raised against the historicity of the patriarchs soon quickly expanded into other closely related issues. Van Seters's revision of pentateuchal chronology was followed almost immediately by the publication of H.H. Schmid's tradition historical revisions of the documentary hypothesis,[74] which also, like Van Seters's work, argued for a sixth-century date of the Yahwistic source in close association with

---

[72] J. Van Seters, *In Search of History* (New Haven, 1983).

[73] Th.L. Thompson, *op.cit., JAOS,* 1978; *idem, op.cit.,* 1987, pp.53ff.

[74] H.H. Schmid, *Der sogenannte Jahwist: Beobachtungen und Fragen zur Pentateuch-forschung* (Zurich, 1976); also *idem,* "Auf der Suche nach neuen Perspektiven für die Pentateuch-Forschung," *VTS* 32 (Leiden, 1981) pp.375-394.

the deuteronomist and the deuteronomistic traditions.[75] In 1977, R. Rendtdorff attacked the coherence of the documentary traditions themselves, arguing persuasively that in its earliest development Genesis must have stood independent of the rest of the pentateuch. Further attacks on the documentary hypothesis by E. Blum,[76] N. Whybray[77] and Thompson[78] make it extremely doubtful that the documentary hypothesis, and associated developments of tradition history, can any longer be used to defend a claim of early historiographic traditions in the extant text of the pentateuch, long antedating the latest redactions. It has also changed radically the assumption of what is early and late in Hebrew narrative.[79]

The recent chronological studies of H. Vorländer and Lemche,[80] for example, seem to require (on the basis of evidence external to the pentateuch) a dating of the Yahwist substantially later than the middle of the eighth-century B.C. The pentateuchal narratives might best be understood as common traditions of Judah only sometime after 600 B.C., closely contemporary with Ezekiel and Second Isaiah.[81] They can hardly be used as historiographical sources for any period prior to the monarchy.[82] Only very rarely can they be used for the period of the monarchy, as a significant period of historical dislocation separates the historiographical contexts that structure the biblical narratives of Genesis–2 Kings from the periods of their putative referents.

---

[75] See also H. Vorländer, *Die Entstehungszeit des jehowistischen Geschichtswerkes* (Frankfurt, 1978); M. Rose, *Deuteronomist und Jahwist: Untersuchungen zu den Berührungspunkten beider Literaturwerke* (Zurich, 1981).

[76] E. Blum, *Die Komposition der Vätergeschichte*, WMANT 57 (Neukirchen, 1984); *idem*, *Studien zur Komposition des Pentateuch*, BZAW 189 (Berlin, 1990).

[77] N. Whybray, *The Making of the Pentateuch*, JSOTS 53 (Sheffield, 1987).

[78] Th.L. Thompson, *op.cit.*, 1987. For an extensive bibliography of the recent debate see S. de Vries, «*A Review of Recent Research in the Tradition History of the Pentateuch*,» *SBL Seminar Papers* 26 (1987), pp.459-502.

[79] N.P. Lemche, *op.cit.*, 1985, pp.377f., 384f. This very complex problem cannot be dealt with extensively in this forum. The justification of this separation of disciplines I have discussed in *op.cit.*, 1987, p.39.

[80] H. Vorländer, *op.cit.*, pp.23ff., 69f., 285ff., N.P. Lemche, *op.cit.*, 1985, pp.357f.

[81] N.P. Lemche, *op.cit*, 1985, pp.324-326.

[82] So I understand Lemche's remark that "we cannot write a history of Israel which goes back before about 1000..." (*ibid.*, p.385f.).

This still ongoing tradition-historical revision of our understanding of the pentateuch has deepened the historically oriented deconstruction of biblical history, and raises a fundamental challenge to many long-held assumptions of more biblically oriented approaches to Israel's history, such as that of Noth. Noth's reconstruction of the early history of Israel had extended Alt's hypothesis in a direction that became increasingly dependent on the acceptance of an historiographically oriented history of traditions that was thought capable of reconstructing premonarchic and early monarchic times. As the publications of the mid-1970s thoroughly undermined the extrabiblical and comparative approaches to the so-called patriarchal history, three pivotal books between 1974 and 1977 fully subverted Noth's synthesis, that had been based on a history of biblical traditions supported by comparative analogies.

4. The Historicity of the Period of the Judges

In 1974, A.D.H. Mayes published his revised 1969 dissertation, and in so doing seriously threw into question the biblical basis for an acceptance of a "time of judges" as an historical period. The primary object of this book was to review the evidence put forward in favor of Noth's concept of the amphictyony, and to show that this analogy was inadequate. Mayes concluded that the tradition itself presented no positive support for the existence of an amphictyony in early Israel.[83] In the process of establishing his argument, Mayes was able to formulate a series of significant judgments that have subsequently undermined acceptance of the historicity of the narratives about judges in Old Testament scholarship. The existence of the concept of "all-Israel," so central to an acceptance of a period of judges, was related to a deuteronomistic reconstruction of earlier traditions and was not an original motif of those traditions themselves.[84] Even Joshua 2–9 (with its stories of an invasion and conquest of towns in *Benjamin*) became associated with a conquest by "all-Israel" only at a secondary stage of the tradition's development. On the basis of the bible, there had existed no central authority prior to that reflected in the Saul narratives. Nor is it implied

---

[83] A.D.H. Mayes, *Israel in the Period of the Judges*, SBTh 2/29 (London, 1974) *passim*, esp. p.83.

[84] *Ibid.*, p.5.

that the "tribes of Israel" had undertaken any communal activity involving all of Israel. Hence it is, in Mayes judgment, a serious error to continue to defend any premonarchic unifying structure for Israel. Even the song of Deborah, which plays such a central role in Mayes's own historical reconstruction, does not reflect any Israelite federation existing in the twelfth-century. Rather, Mayes would date this poem to the end of the eleventh-century and associate it with a victory in a struggle with a coalition of Canaanites and Philistines, a victory that first enabled the tribes of the central hills to join with those from the Galilee in a decisive battle for the Jezreel,[85] shortly before Israel's defeat at Aphek. Mayes's negative judgments are particularly strong here. Finally, Mayes argued that the critical bond of Israel's unity was not created by the establishment of Saul's kingdom. Rather, Mayes presupposed the existence of Israel already prior to Saul.[86] Its union was found by Mayes not in terms of a central authority, but in the gradual development of a shared worship of Yahweh. This he attempted to explain by reference to *Kadesh*, where some pre-settlement tribal groups had united around a common religious faith. Yahwism came to *Judah* through the migration of Caleb to *Hebron* from the South, and to *Shechem* and the northern tribes of later Israel through the migration of the "mid-Palestinian" tribes.

In this argument, Mayes followed the classical methods of tradition history, and because of this, his conclusions have carried great authority against Noth's hypothesis. However, while he is able to demonstrate the lack of any solid historical evidence for the amphictyony, for a very early dating of the song of Deborah and for any premonarchic unity of the Israelite tribes, his argument for a later date as "better" is largely inconsequential, and indeed is itself undermined by the same critical spector he raised against Noth. His historical reconstruction is based more on what his reading of the bible's stories would allow as fitting, rather than on evidence: any other reading must, of necessity, offer an alternative and, indeed, contradictory reconstruction. He has presented what might best be described as a *scenario* in which his historical reconstruction is not only interesting and attractive, but certain elements of the tradition arbitrarily assumed to be early such as the Song of Deborah take on a major role in the history of the origin and

---

[85] *Ibid.*, pp.94–98.
[86] *Ibid.*, p.106.

development of Israel. Following what seems to be the principle that events probably happen at the most opportune times and where they can achieve the greatest possible historical significance, Mayes presents an alternative to Noth's rightly discredited amphictyony hypothesis. His argument, however, is hardly more substantial than the impression that a new reconstruction must be somehow "superior" to a known false approach. But is it superior, or simply different? Is inner coherence a criterion for historical conviction, or is it rather a criterion which would be far better suited to good story and good philosophy, telling us more about what ought to have been and should be, rather than pointing out anything that had been in the past?

Mayes has performed an immense service in clearly detailing the lack of historical evidence for a period of judges. One must in all fairness ask for evidence for his reconstruction as well. Showing that the "all Israel" concept is late is not and cannot be understood to be the same as demonstrating that the tribes indeed once existed as independent historical realities in a period prior to Saul. Similarly, showing that the song of Deborah is to be understood as a creation of the late eleventh-century does not convince us that it in fact was. The objection is not so much that Mayes's reconstruction is hypothetical, but rather that the foundation blocks of his reconstruction are mere assertions growing out of an interpretive context, even though neither that interpretive context nor the texts interpreted have any known concrete relationship to each other in fact, other than that found in the assumption (hardly self-evident) that their association is somehow fitting. Finally, Mayes's arguments are circular, in that he is forced to presuppose that some such period of judges did indeed exist (in spite of his conclusion that no unifying structure is known) before his argument that "biblical events" best fit early or late within a premonarchic period of Israelite history can itself become convincing. Similarly, Mayes asserts[87] that "the monarchy presupposes the existence of Israel." But this is not at all true. Mayes himself has shown us that David's kingdom, if historical, was structurally a territorial state, and one must suspect that only if one understands Israel as an entity apart from the state, and preexisting that state, need one draw the conclusion that the Davidic kingdom—not of itself a national entity—presupposes Israel by its very existence.

---

[87] *Ibidem.*

If one does not presuppose the existence of a period of judges, or any such comparable period, it is no longer obvious that the existence of David's or even Saul's kingdom presupposed the existence of Israel, only that the narratives about the United Monarchy do; but that is a literary not an historical issue! This confusion in modern biblical studies has raised the question of the definition of "Israel" as one of the most critically important questions in any historical reconstruction of Israel's origins. It is doubtful that any critical history of origins can be wholly acceptable if such a pivotal question does not become clearly focussed. Simplistically put: before we can adequately discuss the origins of Israel, we have to know what "Israel" involves; for, once the traditional biblical historiographical answer has been thrown into question, we do have a significant problem in understanding our task.

Mayes makes much of the common worship and religion of *Judah* and *Samaria*. Placing Yahwism as he does as the fundamental originating cause of the ethnic nation of Israel, it is not surprising that he creates a difficulty whose solution requires the supposition that Israel's religious bond must have been established prior to the settlement. The *Kadesh* stories give him a story context, drawn from the Bible for this religious bond. However, none of the parts of Mayes's *scenario* is necessary, nor have any been shown to be historically involved in Israel's origins. Since Mayes has not demonstrated that a single text is in fact premonarchic or even probably to be dated to pre-state times, how can he presuppose that either the tradition's or Israel's involvement with Yahwism must have derived from such an early period? The question is legitimately pressed, as Mayes proposes to make Yahwism not merely an adjunct of but the originating motive factor in the existence of Israel. It is perfectly understandable that any traditions, originating from a time when Yahwism was established as the sole religion of both *Israel* and *Judah* might readily presuppose Yahwism at the very foundation of the existence of a composite "all Israel,"[88] but such an ideology does not itself offer evidence for actual history. Nor can such a concept of an "all-Israel" oriented Yahwism be shown to have existed throughout this large geographic area prior to the postexilic period! That is, Mayes asserts a common religious ground for both Israel and Judah, and he sees the religion of these two states as having developed for the same reason, to

---

[88] This is fundamental to Israel's understanding of its essence; Th.L. Thompson, *op.cit.*, 1987, pp.127f.

create their ethnicity out of their adherence to Yahwism (as the later exilic and postexilic narratives of Genesis–2 Kings have presented that development). Mayes has done this on the basis of these later historiographies, without showing that the *Kadesh* stories had been associated with both *Israel* and *Judah* (in contrast to *Judah* alone) or that these stories derive from a period antedating any Judaean hegemony over the north, or indeed any period prior to the primacy of Yahwism in either state. As such, his argumentation remains circular.

It becomes clear that the deconstructive value of Mayes's book is great, but its reconstructions are premature, and are perhaps understood best, along with Mazar's and de Vaux's works, as evocative: pointing towards a growing need for a new approach to Israel's origins. Like Mazar and de Vaux before him, Mayes largely takes for granted an historiographic tradition in the Old Testament, from at least the early monarchy, based on an even yet earlier oral tradition. As was pointed out above, this assumption has been seriously undermined since 1974, to a great extent by Mayes's own contributions.

In 1976, in the Dutch scholar C.H.J. de Geus's refutation of Noth's amphictyony hypothesis, a series of arguments were made which went well beyond the issue of whether the ancient Greek amphictyony was or was not a wholly appropriate analogue to the religious bond which held the early Israelite tribes together and led to the formation of a national consciousness. That it was an inadequate and inexact parallel had already clearly been shown.[89] De Geus sought further to challenge the concept of sedentarization as the principal explanation for Israel's origins. Here he attacked Alt's fundamental thesis.

De Geus used three approaches in his comprehensive challenge to Noth's understanding of Israel's origins. He based his conclusions on a negative historical and archaeological inquiry, which argued that no conquest could be demonstrated on archaeological grounds. He also argued that the origin of the Early West Semites (or "Amorites") should be understood as agricultural and sedentary: indigenous to *Palestine.* Finally de Geus argued[90] that the expansion of settlement in the central highlands did not give evidence of incursion from outside, but seemed rather to have been an extension of the indigenous Late Bronze and Iron Age town culture.

---

[89] See above, Chapter 2.

[90] C.H.J. de Geus, *The Tribes of Israel* (Assen, 1976) pp.165ff.

De Geus also argued, on the basis of the social structure observable in the biblical traditions, that the tribal system of Israel, which led many early scholars to suppositions about Israel's past in nomadism, is in fact relatively late in the history of Israel, and actually originated during the time of the monarchy.[91] He concluded that the traditions not only do not give evidence for an origin of Israel in nomadism outside *Palestine,* but the oldest biblical tradition has its roots in an understanding of "tribes" as geographical entities within *Palestine,* and not in any actual ethnic structure. This rather had its roots in the social structures of classes and extended families, forms of societal organization that are fully consonant with an indigenous and agrarian origin of Israel in *Palestine.*

Finally, de Geus argued on the basis of biblical texts—somewhat arbitrarily analyzed—that the biblical concept of an Israel which was not autochthonous was connected with the patriarchs. The background of the patriarchs he placed with the Amorites of the Middle Bronze Age, understood not as an incursion into *Palestine* but as an indigenous development within *Palestine* itself.[92] The unity of Israel, centered in the hill country and going back to the Middle Bronze Age, was for de Geus an ethnic unity closely associated with the Amorites.

Like Mayes's study,[93] de Geus's work was written apart from the critical reviews of the historicity of the patriarchal traditions and the radical revision of the early dating of the pentateuchal traditions. As such, the biblical and historical sides of his work were fundamentally undermined as valid historical construction, for his own study was entirely dependent on both historicity and an acceptance of the early historiography of the biblical narrative traditions. But his attack on the interpretive concept of sedentarization and the many provocative arguments he raised for the indigenous nature of early Israel were permanent contributions in the ensuing debate.[94]

---

[91] *Ibid.,* pp.69–119.

[92] *Ibid.,* esp. pp.176–181.

[93] A.D.H. Mayes, *op.cit.,* 1974; *idem,* "The Period of the Judges and the Rise of the Monarchy," *Israelite and Judaean History,* ed. by J.H. Hayes and J.M. Miller (Philadelphia, 1977) pp.285–331.

[94] N.P. Lemche, *op.cit.,* 1985, pp.73f.

With the publication in 1977 of a series of essays on Israelite history in the textbook *Israelite and Judaean History*,[95] the deconstructive shift in Old Testament historical studies, begun in the early and mid-1970s, received sharp focus. Over half of this large volume dealt with the biblical traditions and historical periods leading up to the united monarchy. These contributions revealed the consensus that little to nothing was known about Israel's origins, that it was highly unlikely that extrabiblical materials would add greatly to our knowledge of Israel's prehistory, and that the biblical tradition is at best an inadequate source for historical knowledge. The range of disagreements in both methods and conclusions among the authors of this handbook, however, clearly demonstrated that this consensus could not be understood as the opinion of any single school, but rather that it represented a movement already widely entertained in the field.

The fact that presuppositions regarding both the biblical texts and the extrabiblical sources varied considerably, and that the various authors of the textbook's chapters were frequently in sharp disagreement regarding specific conclusions and approaches to the problems of Israel's history, underlined the strength of the negative evaluation of any traditional history along the lines that had been proposed by Albright and Alt.

Of the seven authors who contributed to the discussion of Israel's prehistory, three (Miller, Mayes and M. Clark) developed a positive, though tentative, historical reconstruction almost solely on the basis of analyses rooted in the tradition-history of biblical historiography. Three (Thompson, D. Irvin and A. Soggin) distanced themselves sharply from tradition-history, and questioned the appropriateness of viewing the biblical narratives as historiographical traditions, preferring much more the categories of traditional stories and other types of imaginative literature. Five of the articles dealt explicitly with archaeological and extrabiblical sources for these periods (W.G. Dever, Thompson, Miller, Mayes and Soggin), and all were very skeptical of past syntheses of the biblical and extrabiblical sources. Only Dever attempted a synthetic correlation of archaeological discoveries and biblical tradition, in an effort to defend the historicity of the patriarchal period.[96] Most[97]

---

[95] *Op.cit.*, ed. by J.H. Hayes and J.M. Miller (Philadelphia, 1977).

[96] W.G. Dever, "The Patriarchal Traditions," *Israelite and Judaean History*, ed. by J.H. Hayes and J.M. Miller (Philadelphia, 1977) pp.102-119.

[97] M. Clark, "The Patriarchal Traditions," *ibid.*, pp. 142-148; J.M. Miller, "The Israelite

attempted a tentative biblically-based history of the period with which they dealt, while Thompson[98] asserted that there is no historiographical value for a prehistory of Israel to be found in the biblical tradition.

J.M. Miller's article on Israel's occupation of the land is the most directly pertinent to our discussion of origins, and the one which took as its starting point the need for reconstructing Israel's origins apart from simple questions of historicity and apart from the use of archaeological and historical data merely to confirm or reject the biblical historiographies which are based on much later redactional frameworks. After a clear and precise survey[99] of both the written and the archaeological sources (the most complete and comprehensive since Weippert's 1967 review), Miller suggested three tentative conclusions which sharply and accurately focussed the issues of concern on historical and archaeological research from 1967 until today: a) "The oldest strata of the conquest traditions and the narratives of the book of Judges associate the tribes of Israel primarily with the mountainous regions..."; i.e., this was the core of their settlement. Only after the establishment of the monarchy, Miller argued, was Israelite domination extended throughout the lowlands of *Palestine* and central and northern Transjordan. This observation has become an important common denominator in the understanding of what early premonarchic "proto-Israel" has been in many of those studies of the following decade, in which the central hill country settlement of Iron I has been understood to be virtually identical with Israel. Only Ahlström has (subtly) distanced himself from this opinion. b) "Since the tribes had their own individual origins and had entered Palestine under different circumstances—indeed, since the tribalization itself occurred to some degree after settlement in the land—it is not possible to assign a specific date to the Israelite occupation." Here Miller has not only raised anew Alt's view of the origins as lasting an extended period of time, he has also implicitly cast doubt on the concentration of scholarship on the Late Bronze-Iron Age transition, and encourages us to view all of Iron I as a transition period, potentially prior to Israel. He brings the discussion of origins greater

---

Occupation of Canaan," *ibid.,* pp.279-284; A.D.H. Mayes, *op.cit.,*1977, pp.308-331; J.A. Soggin, *op.cit.,* 1977, pp.343-380.

[98] Th.L. Thompson, "The Joseph and Moses Narratives: The Narratives about the Origin of Israel," *op.cit.,* 1977, pp.210-212.

[99] J.M. Miller, *op.cit.,*1977, pp.213-284.

clarity with his restriction of Saul's monarchy to the hills of Ephraim, and with his questioning of the historicity of the stories about the United Monarchy in his *A History of Israel and Judah* of 1986. 3) "Only occasional glimpses of the early histories of the individual tribes can be attained from the biblical materials."[100] This last conclusion of Miller's has incipiently carried discussion of Israel's origins away from the need to deal with "all Israel" in our historical reconstructions, and has encouraged discussions of regional and geographic studies. Israel of the twelve tribes, embracing all of *Palestine,* was a product of a period no earlier than the monarchy and perhaps belongs to an even later period. Miller's summary study is not only the most thorough to date; it has also had immense influence. Without question the issues he formulated in 1977 have dominated research through the 1980s, and have been critical to a number of significant works of this decade.[101]

What can be described as the rising tide of literary studies of Old Testament narrative[102] in the 1970s such as D.M. Gunn's study of David[103] and J.P. Fokkelman's extensive study of the Jacob and Samuel stories,[104] added immeasurably to the growing disassociation of biblical narrative and history, but the negative thrust of the deconstruction of biblical history was at its greatest in the publication and reviews of the Hayes-Miller textbook of 1977. Four years later, G.W. Ramsey, echoing the perspectives of de Vaux, Thompson and Miller, published a popular but detailed summary of this movement and its effect on biblical studies.[105] The inconclusiveness of any positive reconstruction of the history of Israel's origins at that time was apparent through every page of this admirable statement regarding the state of scholarship. What was not history had become very clear. In fact the distinction in Old Testament studies between what we know about Israel's past and what we don't know might be understood as having been a newly won insight,

---

[100] Quotations from J.M. Miller, *op.cit.,* 1977, pp.279-282.

[101] See below, Chapter 4.

[102] Begun by W. Richter, *Traditionsgeschichtliche Untersuchungen zum Richterbuch, BBB* (Bonn, 1968).

[103] D.M. Gunn, *The Story of David* (Sheffield, 1976); also *idem, The Fate of King Saul, JSOTS* 14 (Sheffield, 1980).

[104] J.P. Fokkelman, *Narrative Art in Genesis* (Assen, 1975); *idem, Narrative Art and Poetry in the Book of Samuel* (Assen, 1981).

[105] G.W. Ramsey, *The Quest for the Historical Israel* (London, 1981) esp., pp.90-98. Ramsey also reviews the hypotheses of Mendenhall and Gottwald.

however discouraging it might have then appeared. Even the methods and sources available for a constructive historiography of early Israel were clearer than ever before. Nevertheless, the effort towards such a new historiography had not yet been taken, and a brief hiatus in research set in that was to last from the publication of the Hayes-Miller volume in 1977 to the appearance of Soggin's *History* in 1984. Five reasons might be used to explain this hiatus: a) a strong, almost virulent reaction against the traditional historical orientation of Old Testament studies, especially in Old Testament narrative studies; b) the emergence of a bitter reaction in biblical archaeology against subordination to or close association with biblical studies in protest to the excessive concentration on issues of synthesis with biblical studies for the sake of maintaining historicity; c) the outbreak of a far-reaching, complex revision of and debate over the documentary hypothesis in the mid- to late 1970s, continuing today, which is of major importance to our understanding of tradition history and consequently to issues about the historical relevance of the biblical narratives; d) the publication of Gottwald's *Tribes of Yahweh*,[106] which dislocated much of historical research into an alternative sociological and anthropological approach to historical questions; and finally, e) the continued concentration of the mainstream of historical scholarship on the methods of tradition- and redaction-history, in spite of a paralyzing uncertainty about both their legitimacy and adequacy.

5. The Search for a New Paradigm for the History of Israel

During the past five years or so, an immense surge of publication[107] on Israel's origins has occurred. A significant group of these studies are marked by a conscious distancing of their assumptions from both the

---

[106] N.K. Gottwald, *The Tribes of Yahweh* (Maryknoll, 1979).

[107] J.A. Soggin, *A History of Israel* (Philadelphia, 1984); N.P. Lemche, *Early Israel*, VTS 37 (Leiden, 1985); D.C. Hopkins, *The Highlands of Canaan*, SWABAS 3 (Sheffield, 1985); G. Ahlström, *Who Were the Israelites?* (Winona Lake, 1986); J.M. Miller and J.H. Hayes, *A History of Ancient Israel and Judah* (Philadelphia, 1986); O. Borowski, *Agriculture in Iron Age Israel* (Winona Lake, 1987); R.B. Coote and K.W. Whitelam, *The Emergence of Early Israel in Historical Perspective*, SWABAS 5 (Sheffield, 1987); I. Finkelstein, *The Archaeology of the Israelite Settlement* (Jerusalem, 1988).

conquest[108] and the revolt[109] models for Israel's origin, and most can be understood as either supporting Alt's settlement hypothesis[110] or offering a variant of Alt's reconstruction. The differences among these scholars in methods and conclusions are considerable, and one can hardly claim that there is today anything like a consensus in the field. Nevertheless, there is much common ground.

Unlike most earlier studies of Israel's origins, these do not start with a review of the pros and cons of the three classical alternative explanations from the past generation: the conquest, the settlement, and the revolt models for Israel's origins. Rather, all take as their point of departure the historiographical crisis created by the rapid deconstruction of "biblical history," which culminated in the Hayes-Miller textbook volume *Israelite and Judean History* of 1977.[111] The historiography of

---

[108] Most thoroughly developed in J. Bright, A History of Israel, (Philadelphia, 1983); also A. Malamat "Die Frühgeschichte Israels: Eine methodologische Studie," *ThZ* 39 (1983), pp.1-16. For critiques, see M. Weippert, *op.cit.,* 1967; J.M. Miller, *op.cit.,* 1977, pp.213-284.

[109] G.E. Mendenhall, *The Tenth Generation* (Baltimore, 1973); N.K. Gottwald, *The Tribes of Yahweh: A Sociology of the Religion of Liberated Israel* (New York, 1979); D.N. Freedman and D.F. Graf, *Palestine in Transition: The Emergence of Ancient Israel, SWBAS* 2 (Sheffield, 1983); for critiques, see A. Hauser, "Israel's Conquest of Palestine: A Peasants' Rebellion?," *JSOT* 7 (1978), pp.2-19; *idem,* "Response to Thompson and Mendenhall," *JSOT* 7 (1978), pp.35-36; Th.L. Thompson, "Historical Notes on Israel's Conquest of Palestine: A Peasants' Rebellion?" *JSOT* 7 (1978), pp.20-27; *idem, The Origin Tradition of Ancient Israel I, JSOTS* 55 (Sheffield, 1987) pp.17-20; B. Halpern, *The Emergence of Israel in Canaan* (Chico, 1983); and esp. the devastating sociologically based critique of N.P. Lemche, *op.cit.,* 1985.

[110] Classically formulated in A. Alt, "Die Landnahme der Israeliten in Palästina," *Kleine Schriften I*, pp.89-125; *idem,* "Erwägungen über die Landnahme der Israeliten in Palastina," *Kleine Schriften I*, pp.126-175; M. Noth, *The History of Israel* (New York, ²1960); M. Weippert, *op.cit.,* 1967; and R. de Vaux, *op.cit.,* 1971; most recently supported by V. Fritz, "Die Kulturhistorische Bedeutung der früheisenzeitlichen Siedlung auf der Hirbet el-Msas und das Problem der Landnahme," *ZDPV* 96 (1980), pp.121-135; *idem,* "The Israelite Conquest in the Light of Recent Excavations at Khirbet el-Meshash," *BASOR* 241 (1981), pp.61-73; *idem,* "The Conquest in the Light of Archaeology," *Proceedings of the Eighth World Congress of Jewish Studies* (Jerusalem, 1982), pp.15-22; V. Fritz and A. Kempinski, *Ergebnisse der Ausgrabungen auf der Hirbet el-Msas (Tel Masos) 1972-1975* (Wiesbaden, 1983); B. Halpern, *op.cit.,* 1983; Z. Kallai, *Historical Geography of the Bible* (Jerusalem, 1986); H. Donner, *Geschichte des Volkes Israel und seiner Nachbarn in Grundzügen I-II* (Göttingen, 1984-1986).

[111] Op.cit.; especially W.G. Dever, Th.L. Thompson, J.M. Miller, A.D.H. Mayes and J.A. Soggin, *opera citata.* These issues also receive summary treatment in G.W. Ramsey, *op.cit.* Certainly G. Garbini, *History and Ideology in Ancient Israel* (London, 1988) belongs to this

the tribal conquest of the Book of Joshua is nowhere understood in these reviews as a viable historical understanding of Israel's origins,[112] and most ignore any such reconstruction without discussion.

The revolt hypothesis, on the other hand, still receives considerable attention. Lemche subjected the revolt hypothesis to a sustained and devastating attack.[113] Not only did Lemche object to the commonplace, arbitrary and uncritical use of biblical and historical materials, he made his strongest criticisms against Mendenhall and Gottwald's use of sociology and anthropology, and in particular their understanding of shepherds, farmers and city dwellers in the Middle East. A yet more recent major work, I. Finkelstein's *The Archaeology of the Israelite Settlement,*[114] closes this peculiarly ill-conceived and uncritical chapter of Old Testament historiography by pointing out, as Miller had done in his 1977 article, that there is no support for the revolt hypothesis from the archaeological evidence of early Iron Age settlements in the hill country of *Palestine,* the very groups which Gottwald and Mendenhall would see as revolutionaries.

Alt's thesis of a peaceful settlement of nomadic steppe dwellers is the only one of the classical hypotheses which has survived in this recent literature, but it too is being given significant revision today. These recent studies, since the mid-1980s, take a new direction which today seems most promising and takes us away from an historiography based on the fragile syntheses of biblical and archaeological research that had been overly dependent on issues of historicity and a biblical perspective, in the direction of an independently conceived history of Israel's origins. To fulfill this potential, the goal of research into Israel's origins can no

---

movement of deconstruction. While Garbini's skepticism regarding an early historiography for ancient Israel must be commended, his methodology is idiosyncratic. Of greater use is his earlier, important work, *I Fenici: Storia e Religioni* (Naples, 1980).

[112] For a brief discussion of the history of these issues up to Soggin, see the summary in Th.L. Thompson, *op.cit.,* 1987, pp.11-40.

[113] N.P. Lemche, *op.cit.,* 1985, pp.80-395; for earlier critiques of the "revolt" hypothesis, M. Weippert, *op.cit.,* 1967; A. Hauser, *op.cit.,* pp.2-19; *idem, op.cit.,* pp.35f.; Th.L. Thompson, *op.cit.,* 1978, pp.20-27; *idem, op.cit.,* 1987, pp.16-20; B. Halpern, *op.cit.,* esp. pp.49ff., 81ff.; and G.E. Mendenhall, "Ancient Israel's Hyphenated History," *Palestine in Transition,* ed. by D.N. Freedman and D.F. Graf, pp.91-103. An important summary article supporting the "revolt model" is that of M.L. Chaney, "Ancient Palestinian Peasant Movements and the Formulation of Premonarchic Israel" in *idem,* pp.39-90.

[114] I. Finkelstein, *op.cit.,* esp. pp.306-314.

longer be some point within the "history of Israel," where historical-critical research might acceptably meet or harmonize with biblical historiography, at which point our research into Israel's prehistory might be seen to support and establish—however critically—what is finally only a bible history. Rather, our goal must be to write a history of Israel which is methodologically apart from the late Judaean historiography about its past. Whether elements within the history of Genesis–2 Kings have survived within folk tradition from early events within Israel's actual past can only be established if we first have a history within which the folk narratives can be compared and find a context, but that basic historical reconstruction must be formed independently of that to which it might render a context. This new perspective is a significant departure from Alt's understanding of his task.

Although Alt understood the original transhumant migration to have extended throughout the Late Bronze Age, and the period of settlement to have extended throughout a period of judges and to have culminated in the period of the United Monarchy, he also saw his interpretation as establishing the historicity of a period of judges, and understood the early history of Israel as beginning with that period.

It is on this issue of the synthesis of historical data and biblical historiography that the greatest revisions are now sought and on which the debates over historicity of the 1970s have been most deeply felt. The theses of J. Van Seters and the present writer rejecting the historicity of the patriarchal narratives[115] are accepted by these writers. Moreover, an acceptance of the lateness of the extant biblical tradition and the radical questioning of the historicity of the traditions about Moses, Joshua and judges also seem now to be in the center of contemporary discussions.

6. The United Monarchy and the Origin of Israel

Soggin and Miller[116] both begin their histories of Israel on the basis of biblical criticism with the United Monarchy and find in the rise of the monarchy a sufficient coherence of historical political forces to create what might be understood as the Israel of history. Both stress the issues

---

[115] Th.L. Thompson, op.cit., 1974; J. Van Seters, op.cit., 1975.

[116] J.A. Soggin, op.cit., 1984; J.M. Miller and J.H. Hayes, op.cit., 1986.

of historicity, Soggin indeed seeing the period of the United Monarchy in the biblical tradition as a demarcating watershed between an historiographically dependable history and the legendary prehistory of the biblical traditions leading up to the monarchy,[17] while the Miller-Hayes history, in presenting a more detailed critical review of the early traditions and the issues of historicity and plausibility, considers the book of Judges to reflect an "authentic tradition" about Israel's origins. Miller is more thorough and consistent in his historical-critical methodology than Soggin, and radically questions the historiographical value of the biblical story about the united monarchy[18] on the same grounds of literary and form criticism on which he had dealt with with the traditions of the patriarchs, Moses, Joshua and judges. For example, Miller locates the stories of the judges within an understanding of early Israel's settlement in the central hills of *Palestine*. Indeed, in this he is both dependent on the biblical tradition and critical of it, on the grounds of plausibility and tradition-history as well as on grounds of a hoped-for synthesis with historical and archaeological information. Miller is among the first to limit Saul's kingdom to the central hills of *Ephraim* and to support the ahistorical and literary character of the biblical traditions about the rise of the monarchy as made immensely clear in the recent literary studies of Gunn and Fokkelman.[19]

While both Soggin and Miller see the monarchy of Saul and David as central to issues of the origins of Israel, both clearly indicate marked ambivalence about the united monarchy, in both its origin and nature, and stress the divided monarchies' separation and the independence of *Judah* and *Israel* as essential and structural characteristics of these two nations. Soggin makes this point in his opening remarks about the David stories,[20] and Miller-Hayes, as mentioned above, clearly underline this independence and distinctiveness in the title of their work itself. In this, they mark the artificiality of the concepts of a "united monarchy" and an "all Israel" at this very early period and see in the union of these

---

[17] Th.L. Thompson, *op.cit.*, 1987, pp.30f.

[18] E.g., J.M. Miller, *op.cit.*, 1986, p.200.

[19] D.M. Gunn, *op.cit.*, 1978; *idem*, *op.cit.*, 1980; J.P. Fokkelman, *op.cit.*, 1981. The specific issue of historicity of the United Monarchy traditions was briefly raised by the present writer in "The Narratives about the Origins of Israel," *op.cit.*, 1977, pp.210-212, and in "History and Tradition: A Response to J.B. Geyer," *JSOT* 15 (1980), pp.57-61.

[20] J.A. Soggin, *op.cit.*, 1984, pp.40f.

states a quasi-imperialist expansion by the southern kingdom. This historicizing revision by both Soggin and Miller marks what I see as an understandable but nonetheless significant departure from their otherwise commendable critical reading of the biblical tradition. Their efforts at reconstruction of a united monarchy no longer proceed from or are based in what we know. They are rather centered in a wish to salvage a substantial element of the tradition, namely, a greater-Israel ruled by David and Solomon. Critically speaking, once the specters of literary form and historicity have been raised, there is no as yet discernible characteristic within the biblical traditions alone by which the historicity of any major segment can be ascertained. The character of the narratives themselves is not historical, and historicity—even historical relevance—cannot be assumed of them. "External evidence"[121] is no longer a luxury but a necessity, and without it we simply cannot write a history of Israel.

Both Soggin and Miller speak of the biblical tradition as the "primary source" for their histories, however undependable they have judged it, marking their adherence to Alt's tradition of historical criticism, as well as to Noth's critique[122] of a misuse of biblical archaeology that has often occurred through a variety of fanciful reconstructions of early Israelite history and origins.[123] Indeed, Miller has often argued orally (and one may assume Soggin's concurrence) that a history of Israel's origins can only be written from the perspective of an historical-critical evaluation of the biblical traditions on the *prima facie* basis that it is from the biblical tradition alone that we understand what Israel is and take the measure of the history we wish to write. In this, Miller is unquestionably correct. Nevertheless, Miller has also demonstrated that this biblical tradition must be our entry to an understanding of what Israel was that we wish to reconstruct historically. It is however decidedly a "secondary" source for the historical reconstruction itself. The issue of whether a history of Israel can be written at all must indeed take central stage in all future discussions. Both Soggin and Miller are decidedly skeptical of our abilities today to say anything about Israel's origins.

---

[121] M. Noth, "Der Beitrag der Archäologie zur Geschichte Israels," *VTS* 7 (1960) pp.262–282.

[122] *Ibidem.*

[123] Th.L. Thompson, *op.cit.*, 1974; J.M. Miller, *op.cit.*, 1977.

The conclusion of Miller and Soggin, that there is little that can be learned from the bible about Israel's origins in history, but they concentrate on only one of several potential sources for that history: that which derives from late Judaean tradition. Other sources are also available, some of which are clearly more germane to a modern history than folk traditions, several centuries removed from the events. There are many good reasons for concluding, on the strength of these two scholars, that a major step forward has been taken in contemporary biblical historiography, in that a heretofore centrally used source for the early history of Israel (the historiographical perspectives and the reconstructions of the Genesis–2 Kings traditions) can now be seen as both inappropriate and of limited use to the task of writing a history of Israel's origins.

This is not to deny all historical relevance and historicity to this biblically derived historiographical body of literature, elements of which may indeed prove useful. Nor do I wish to imply that some of the perhaps historically more viable traditions are themselves made of whole cloth. Of particular importance are the traditions dealing with the Assyrian conquest of *Samaria* and with events that led up to the fall of *Jerusalem*. I wish, rather, to stress the need for corroborating historical evidence, either in sources independent of the specific tradition, or, minimally, from a context contemporary with the tradition's formation. For example, the traditions of dynastic succession, insofar as they can be reconstructed, and perhaps also some of the regnal year accounts of the monarchies of *Israel* and *Judah*, appear to be usable historiographical accounts (albeit secondarily dependent on their earlier sources. As long as one remembers that such historicity hardly applies to those aspects of the traditions about Saul, David and Solomon that mark them indelibly as legends of dynastic founders and of rulers of a golden age. Similarly, the tradition fragments about Israelite kings prior to Omri, falling as they do outside a fixed dynastic structure, have a weak claim to historicity. Also questionable is any connection between a kingdom of Saul and the historically more verifiable Omride dynasty.[124]

The success of the movement challenging historicity represents the growing departure of mainstream Old Testament historical research from such earlier more conservative approaches as those represented by S.

---

[124] For a new treatment of dynastic chronologies, see the forthcoming study of J.H. Hayes (in press).

Hermann's *Geschichte Israels*[125] or John Bright's *History of Israel*.[126] It is not only Soggin's and Miller's dismissal of the historicity of the biblical traditions with reference to a premonarchic period in Israel's history (neither is wholehearted in this), nor their insistence that a history of Israel as such must begin with the monarchy (both, and especially Miller, are skeptical about the historicity of many of the biblical narratives about the united monarchy) that marks this change. Much more important is the shift in historical-critical perspective that finds expression in their work. This has changed the foundations on which the history of Israel is written today.

I have used the term "deconstruction" to describe the process that has brought about this change to emphasize the fact that it is not just that the conclusions of historians about Israel's early history have become increasingly critical, but rather that the methodology itself that has governed the historiography of scholars dealing with the history of Israel during the last decade and a half has altered. So magnificent work as de Vaux's *l'Histoire ancienne d'Israel*[127] is no longer viable, not simply because its conclusions are wrong but far more because its questions are wrong. It is no longer apparent that he has written about the origins of the historical Israel. In fact, he has not: he speaks of Israel only in respect to the plausibility and potential historical relevance of Israel's traditions and their many possible external referents. That is a task, however sophisticated, of biblical exegesis and interpretation; it is not the same as writing history. Moreover, while questions of historicity and judgments of historical relevance and association are fundamental to the historian's task of evaluating potential literary sources, they are critical questions that are largely negative in their thrust. They do not render history; they prepare the ground for it.

7. The Synthesis of Syro-Palestinian Archaeology

D. Edelman, in her dissertation, limits Saul's kingdom, as Miller had, to the hills of *Ephraim* and *Manasseh*, and attempts to relate this kingdom directly to the new early Iron I settlements there, offering rather

---

[125] S. Herrmann, *A History of Israel in Old Testament Times* (London, [2]1981).

[126] J. Bright, *A History of Israel* (Philadelphia, [3]1981).

[127] R. de Vaux, *The Early History of Israel* (London, 1978).

archaeological support for Ahlström's reading of the Merneptah stele.[128] Ahlström's 1982 study of early Israelite religion likewise renders historical support to this understanding of the name "Israel." More important than whether this thesis is provable by itself is the usefulness of Ahlström's hypothesis in the more complex picture of a history of *Palestine,* as well as the promise it holds for an understanding of both the bible and Israelite religion within such a history of *Palestine.*[129] Like Lemche's 1985 work, Ahlström's stresses the non-ethnic indigenous nature of early Israel. Ahlström's and Edelman's work can be understood as a much needed complement to Lemche's.[130] As in Lemche's work, the issue of exactly where the early Israelite settlers came from is explored but in no way settled, except in the general designation of them as indigenous to *Palestine* and indistinguishable from "Canaanites."

D. Edelman's thesis, that the monarchy developed out of the sedentarization of the central hills during the Iron I period, has its roots in the archaeological research done since Y. Aharoni's dissertation of 1957 on his surveys in the *Galilee,* and is particularly strongly focussed on the work of M. Kochavi and I. Finkelstein in the central hills.[131] The competence with which she deals with many of the issues of historiography and historicity make this work particularly useful for illustrating both the benefits and the pitfalls of reconstructions of the early history of *Palestine* on the basis of a synthesis of archaeological evidence and biblical tradition. In the explication of her hypothesis of an early Saulide monarchy, not only are some (perhaps primary) episodes of the biblical tradition isolated, but her historical reconstruction, resting on the possible historical reality of some such analogous political structure—limited to the central highlands, as J.M. Miller had long argued[132]—is well developed and persuasive. Since archaeological data,

---

[128] D. Edelman, *The Rise of the Israelite State under Saul* (University of Chicago dissertation, 1987).

[129] G. Ahlström, *op.cit.* in press.

[130] Without enthusiasm, Ahlström also cites the work of Mendenhall with approval (pp.6f.), understanding the early hill country settlers as "withdrawing" rather than as rebelling from Canaanite society. Ahlström's work is written independently of Lemche's major study (cf., however, p.8 n.20, where he cites Lemche's earlier critiques of the revolution hypothesis), but is nevertheless at one with it.

[131] See below, Chapter 4.

[132] J.M. Miller, *op.cit.,* 1977, esp. pp.213-245.

however, and especially evidence from surveys, can be reconstructed politically and chronologically in a variety of ways, and are notoriously difficult to circumscribe geographically, synthetic aguments are at best plausible—what is often confused with historical "probability." Edelman's argument depends on our ability to maintain a close association between Iron I *Ephraim* and the Israel of tradition. In spite of the sophistication of her archaeologically oriented discussion, the ultimate validity of her synthesis stands or falls on the much simpler issues of historiography and historicity.[133]

Some of the difficulties I find in seeing with Edelman an early monarchy of Saul in the developing sedentarization of Iron I Ephraim are the following: a)If one follows, as Edelman generally does, the recent late datings of 1–2 Samuel, there exists a three to four century gap, including a period of dislocation of the population of *Palestine*, between the biblical tradition and the reconstructed events to which the "primary" traditions supposedly refer. Considerations of dynastic tradition make this weakness particularly awkward. The continuity necessary to this thesis, between a hypothetical kingship of Saul and the dynastic development of the state of *Samaria*, and through both of them with the "Israel" of the extant biblical tradition, is a continuity which is supported by a fictional, or at least fictionalized, continuity with the legendary[134] Davidic dynasty of a neighboring state. b) In spite of her concurrence with Ahlström in rejecting the Canaanite-Israelite ethnic distinction, Edelman does not escape the assumed equation (developed especially by Israeli scholars from Aharoni to Finkelstein) between the Iron I settlements of the central hills and the origin of the state which

---

[133] Edelman's interesting methodological advances are well worth noting, since they involve an acceptance of many of the new developments in Syro-Palestinian archaeology, and esp. the historically significant survey studies of the central hills. In her discussion of methodology ("Doing History in Biblical Studies," *The Fabric of History*, ed. by D. Edelman, *JSOTS* 127, Sheffield, 1991, pp.13-25), she stresses the importance of distinct analyses of literary and artifactual evidence. Nevertheless, she maintains the primary quality of the biblical tradition for historical interpretation, and, following tradition history's understanding of biblical narratives as rooted in memories of past events, tends to accept the historicity of any given tradition on the basis of verisimilitude and plausibility, as well as the appropriateness of the tradition within the historical reconstruction. Methodologically she is very close to the work of Soggin and Miller, except that she has a greater confidence in the usefulness of archaeological research in historical reconstruction.

[134] I am thinking here, among other things, of the well-worn numerical motif of 40 for the number of kings from Saul to the Judaean exile.

in much later periods is known by both tradition and international politics as *Israel,* with its capital in the city of *Samaria.*[135] This equation, even with objections to any overly simplistic identification of the Iron I settlements before Saul as "Israelite," is open to an unwarranted double association: that of Saul with the political structures of the Iron I settlements, and that of Saul's chieftainship with the state of *Samaria.* Both of these derive from a hardly independent selection of "primary" biblical traditions. c) The doubts raised by these observations are intensified when we further notice that we lack any direct evidence for the (surely necessary) process of regional centralization in the central hills prior to the foundation of *Samaria* during Iron II. d) To assert, as Edelman does, the existence of an historical political entity, "Israel," as early as Iron I (however small a "chieftainship" or "kingship" that might be) creates enormous difficulties in establishing political continuity. These difficulties are twofold: continuity with the state of *Samaria* of the Assyrian period and unity with the early settlements of other regions (such as with those of the *Jezreel* and the Upper *Galilee*) and especially with the Iron II sedentarization of *Judah.* However judiciously these associations might be expressed, they remain in the realm of assertion. To relate, further, a hypothetical Davidic chieftainship with the *Hebron* and northern *Negev* does not lighten the problems of political continuity, however much it may help bypass issues of historicity with arguments of comprehensiveness bolstered by plausibility.

   The greatest problem with all such synthetic reconstructions raises the paramount issue of modern historiography of ancient Israel: the effervescent relationship between biblical literature and historical research. One cannot but question any alleged "reliable pool of information." Reminiscent of the Albright school's syntheses of the 1950s and 1960s, the concept of a state or chieftainship of either Saul or

---

[135] B. Mazar, *Canaan and Israel* (Jerusalem, 1974); *idem, op.cit.,* 1981, pp.75-85; Y. Aharoni, *The Settlement of the Israelite Tribes in Upper Galilee* (Jerusalem, 1957); *idem,* "New Aspects of the Israelite Occupation in the North," *Near Eastern Archaeology in the Twentieth Century: Essays in Honor of Nelson Glueck,* ed. by J.A. Sanders (Garden City, 1970) pp.254-265; *idem,* "Nothing Early and Nothing Late: Rewriting Israel's Conquest," *BA* 39 (1976), pp.55-67; M. Kochavi, "The Period of the Israelite Settlement," in *The History of Eretz Israel, II: Israel and Judah in the biblical Period,* I. Ephal (ed.), (Jerusalem, 1984) pp.19-84; *idem,* "The Land of Israel in the 13th-12th Centuries B.C.E.: Historical Conclusions from Archaeological Data," *Eleventh Archaeological Conference in Israel* (Jerusalem, 1985) p.16; I. Finkelstein, *op.cit.*

David is an unhistorical hybrid, and bears little resemblance to either the Israel we know from tradition or any historical realities potentially derived from archaeology. Historical reconstructions are based on research, not theoretical models. They must be related to established evidence if they are to be historically viable. History is *Wissenschaft*, not metaphysics. When historicity cannot be granted to the biblical traditions as a whole, nor to specifically defined parts of the tradition, we must not be tempted to adopt a perspective which is derived from that theoretically comprehensive whole, or from any segment of it whose historicity will not stand on its own. Such anachronistic reconstructions as that Saul's kingdom was a precursor of the Davidic monarchy, or that it had its roots in the divinely rejected northern hills, are not supported by evidence. If this is so, what benefit do we derive historically in attributing any observable political centralization of the central hills during Iron I to Saul?

8. *Ideology and Biblical Historiography*

The issue is neither the lack of evidence nor whether our history will be thick or thin. The central issue is the nature of the historical questions themselves. These no longer ask whether biblical historiography can be critically reconstructed, but rather how to describe the origins and development of the Israel that we know from tradition. Such a history cannot be derived directly from the Bible itself, but must understand that tradition as the endpoint of an historical trajectory. This change in perspective has greatly influenced recent archaeologically and geographically oriented research into the origins of Israel in the central hill country.[136] In spite of dependence on Alt's foundational work,[137] and in spite of the assumption that Israel existed from the time of the united monarchy, the basis of critical evaluations lies apart from the biblical tradition, in the epigraphical, archaeological and regional history

---

[136] D.C. Hopkins, *The Highlands of Canaan* (Sheffield, 1985); N.P. Lemche, *Early Israel*, *VTS* 37 (Leiden, 1985); R.B. Coote and K.W. Whitelam, *The Emergence of Israel* (Sheffield, 1987); and esp., I. Finkelstein, *op.cit.*

[137] Esp. A. Alt, *op.cit.*, 1925, pp.135-169; *idem*, "Die Staatenbildung der Israeliten in Palästina," *Kleine Schriften II* (Munich, 1964) pp.1-65; *idem*, "Erwägungen über die Landnahme der Israeliten in Palästina," *PJB* 35 (1939), pp.8-63.

of *Palestine.* Therein lies the history of Israel's origin—culminating, not beginning, in Israel's tradition.

G. Garbini's recent popular work reflects this change of perspective, and attempts to support and justify it.[138] Garbini's work makes no effort to deal with the issues comprehensively. His book is first of all a collection of originally independent essays written in the course of the 1980s and deals with several quite disparate topics. Although published in 1986 (revised ET: 1988), its point of departure is that of the late 1970s and early 1980s. Moreover, it is self-consciously the work of a Semitist concerned with philological and historical details that point to and largely determine, but do not themselves comprise, historical synthesis. Nevertheless, the issues Garbini raises effectively carry the discussion of Israel's origins beyond the works of Soggin and Miller, and emphasize the methodological need for new departures in the development of a modern historiography of Israel's origins. One may be strongly tempted to argue with Garbini's provocative and acerbic account of recent biblical scholarship from Noth to Hayes-Miller of 1977,[139] and with his (at times) idiosyncratic interpretation of biblical tradition, especially in regard to what he refers to as "ideological" motivations of the later redactional frameworks in which a variety of independent sources have been integrated. Nevertheless, the essential relevance of Garbini's approach cannot but be acknowledged: a reappraisal of Israel's earliest history must be undertaken apart from a theologically motivated defense of a biblically derived historiography.

Garbini's case for an historiography of ancient Israel independent of the biblical tradition is not objectionable. Not only is there no evidence for any biblical period prior to the time of the monarchy, but there is also no basis—other than theoretical—that could support the traditional chronology. In dealing with the putative earlier periods, Garbini is refreshingly consistent, not only in his rejection of a patriarchal period but also in his recognition, for example, that we have no evidence that judges ever existed, and no convincing evidence of a conquest.

---

[138] G. Garbini, *op.cit.* A work based on similar assumptions that comes to different conclusions, is N.P. Lemche, *Ancient Israel* (Sheffield, 1988).

[139] M. Noth, *A History of Israel* (Philadelphia, 1950); J.H. Hayes and J.M. Miller, *op.cit.,* 1977.

Garbini claims not to consider any tradition of the bible historically reliable unless it has been confirmed elsewhere.[140] Basing himself on observations which allow for a description of the tenth-century B.C. as a period of settlement and of consolidation of Phoenician material culture in *Palestine,* and judging from the general improbability of any strong interregional state at this time, Garbini does offer a reduced history of David and Solomon.[141] However, he is emphatically aware that even that does not have the substance of reliable history, but lies at best in the realm of possibility.

The most important benefits of Garbini's essays lie in the clearer focus he gives to the extreme fragility of our modern historiography of Israel even when addressed to the post-Davidic periods. His reassessment of the reign of Omri, his disassociation of the Shoshenk campaign from biblical chronology, his observations on the epigraphic evidence for the so-called Hebrew language as distinct from Phoenician (which suggests a southern orientation postdating the onset of the Assyrian period)[142] and his awareness of the distortions implicit in 2 Kings's all too comprehensive assessment of a Josianic reform—all serve to reduce our confidence in translating any of the biblical traditions relating to pre-exilic times directly into history.

Garbini's deconstruction of biblical history is not limited to the assured observations of Soggin and Miller that the United Monarchy period was created in story during what he calls the "exilic" and "post-exilic" periods as a Golden Age, comparable to Arthur's England. Rather, he argues that all of early Israel's history needs to be understood as an artificial construct, shaped by motivations long postdating any known evidence of events. A real history of Israel for Garbini begins with the fragments of information we have of Omri's dynasty and the limited epigraphic remains from the eighth to sixth centuries B.C. Nor does Garbini find a secure watershed within biblical tradition for a dependable historiography after what he understands as "the exile"; for the putative accounts of Israelite history during the Persian period are themselves dependent on ideological fictions deriving from periods long postdating the events they only purportedly recount. Critical historical reconstruction for Garbini must begin apart from them and largely

---

[140] G. Garbini, *op.cit.,* p.16.

[141] *Ibid.,* p.32.

[142] *Ibid.,* p.19.

independent of them—even down to the hellenistic period. While Garbini's deconstructive work is most provocative and exciting, it should not distract us from the detailed positive attempts he makes towards a modern reconstruction of Israel's history, many of which need to be considered seriously in any comprehensive treatment. I select three essays—that on Abraham, that on Ezra, and that on Israelite religion—to illustrate what I believe are some of the most critical issues.

In his treatment of the Abraham traditions,[143] Garbini follows the conclusions of Van Seters and myself[144] that the received tradition reflects the sixth-century Babylonian exile, and more specifically can be placed in the reign of Nabonidus. He also follows me against Van Seters in arguing that, in placing Hebrew origins with Abraham in Ur of the Chaldees, the tradition implies the existence of stories about Abraham, whether written or oral, that antedate the exile. Garbini goes further, in arguing for a southern context for the Abraham stories, and in contrasting the role that Abraham plays as the ultimate ancestor of all Israel with that of the patriarch Israel who is the direct eponym of the northern state, and whose narrative tradition was supplanted by the identification of Israel with the stories of the hero Jacob and his twelve sons, reflecting ancestral traditions with a much wider geographical range in *Palestine*. The long acknowledged independence of the Jacob cycle from the Abraham traditions is now observable in the secondary and fragile linkage doubling Abraham with Isaac and—I might add—Ishmael with Esau. The ultimate origin of the ancestral hero Abraham, Garbini suggests, is the eponym of the tribal group referred to as *Raham* in a thirteenth-century inscription of Sethos I from *Beth Shan*.[145] The context for the amalgamation of tradition whereby the southern Abraham tradition took pre-eminence over Israel and Jacob lies in a Judaean post-exilic understanding of themselves as the political and cultural heirs of their northern neighbors,[146] a process which with justice might be seen to have begun as early as the reign of Hezekiah, but almost certainly by the time of Josiah.

---

[143] *Ibid.*, pp.76–86.

[144] J. Van Seters, *op.cit.*, 1975; Th.L. Thompson, *op.cit.*, 1974.

[145] Originally suggested by M. Liverani, "Un ipotesi sul' nome di Abramo," *Henoch* I (1979), pp.9–18.

[146] G. Garbini, *op.cit.*, p.82.

There are some difficulties of detail with Garbini's reconstruction that prevent a wholehearted affirmation. The association of the thirteenth-century *Raham* with a "southern" Abraham tradition of the seventh- to sixth-century, apart from the historicistic implications of Garbini's adoption of this alleged parallel,[147] reflects more than a passing gap in evidence. This gap is both geographical and chronological. The geographical gap is all the more important if one wishes to assert, with Garbini, the independence of the cultural and political history of *Judah* from the North. Similarly, the chronological gap of over five centuries is almost unbridgeable if *Judah*'s involvement in the north began only with Hezekiah! Moreover, the growing conviction among scholars that the Abraham stories are relatively late products of tradition, in contrast to, for example, the Jacob stories[148] and the Moses traditions,[149] is an aspect of the perspective on the patriarchal narratives which forms Garbini's point of departure, and Garbini would be hard pressed to propose an adequate historical cultural linkage. Garbini's efforts to maintain a southern provenience for the Abraham stories is perhaps, after all, questionable—little more than a holdover from efforts to define the sources of the documentary hypothesis geographically by ignoring Abraham's association with the central hills in the itinerary of the "wandering" tradition. Finally, the lucidity of Garbini's contrast of the Abraham with the Jacob traditions is marred by the geographic complexity of the Jacob traditions.[150] Jacob's association with *Shechem* cannot be entirely explained by assumptions regarding the displacement of the patriarch Israel, and an understanding of the patriarch as uniquely southern is hypothetical. The methodology pursued by Garbini that arbitrarily focuses on some aspects of the traditions as original simply because they have acquired, in the process accumulation of tradition, a greater weight, must be questioned. A similar criticism must also be made of his treatment of the ten commandment theophanies of the Mosaic tradition. That they are now

---

[147] Garbini's efforts here evoke Y. Aharoni's earlier attempt to find an historical reference to Abraham in the place name of the Shoshenk list: *p3 hqr ibrm*, which, however, at least has the virtue of geographical appropriateness. Y. Aharoni, "Excavations at Tell Beersheba," *BA* 35 (1972), pp.111-127; here p.115.

[148] H. Vorländer, *op.cit.*, 1978.

[149] Already K.Galling, *Die Erwählungstraditionen Israels* (Berlin, 1928).

[150] Garbini follows de Vaux here: *op.cit.*, 1978, pp.169-175; G. Garbini, *op.cit.*, p.81.

dominant tells us nothing of the history of tradition-building. That the Abraham and Jacob stories developed a focus oriented to southern *Palestine* may reflect nothing more than the perspective of some of their later tradents; for few of the stories of the patriarchs—or indeed of Moses—bear geographical markings that are indigenous to the stories.

Apart from the Abraham wandering narrative and the exodus itineraries, geographical location is most commonly a characteristic either of the narrative chain or of closing aetiologies, clearly separable even when not separated from the mainline stories. Some of the stories that are geographically fixed reflect toponymic variation within the larger tradition—*Haran-Ur, Gerar-Egypt,* the wilderness of *Shur*-wilderness of *Beersheva* and *Padan Aram-Aram Naharaim*; others do not easily lend themselves to Garbini's Judaean ideology (e.g., *Damascus of Genesis 15*). Some narratives, furthermore, bring Abraham from the south (e.g., Genesis 14) only secondarily, as a by-product of the accumulation of traditions. The old folkloric theory of *Ortsgebundenheit* is, I believe, peculiarly ill-suited to a discussion of the Abraham narratives. However much such stories might have become attached to localities and regions, these localities are not demonstrably indigenous to the extent that we can define places or regions of origin. In this Garbini confuses the world of the tradition's tradents with actual origins. In his discussion of the Abraham stories generally, Garbini is strongest when he draws attention to the tradition's complexity, weakest when he attempts a synthetic harmony through efforts at tradition history by means of a hypothetical ideology.

Garbini's treatment of the Ezra tradition is perhaps the most provocative of the many contributions of this book. Because of Garbini's interest in the ideological function of the biblical traditions, his arguments for the fictional nature of the book of Ezra take central focus. His dating of the work to 159 B.C. and his attempt to identify Ezra's "law" with the "Temple Scroll" are subordinate to this. Since much of this argument is an attempt to historicize as sectarian conflict the founding of *Qumran*, with the aid of the Damascus Document and fragments of information about the high priest Alcimus and his liturgical reform, we are left at the mercy of eisegetical efforts that identify such worthies as the "teacher of righteousness" and the "wicked priest" with historical personages. Garbini's identification of Ezra as a fictional Alcimus is clever, but unconvincing. The less precise arguments he makes for a late dating of the Book of Ezra on one hand and the greater antiquity of 1 Esdras on the other, which are comparable to his earlier discussion of the relationship between Chronicles and Kings, are of greater value because of his understanding of their relationship as ideologically independent variants rather than as directly dependent traditions. However, such a perspective makes a precise determination of the specific *Vorlage* of tradition, whether oral or written, impossible, and any association between content and context bewildering. The use of such materials for an historical reconstruction of the late Persian period is wholly precluded, and we are on no firmer ground than when using 2 Kings and Chronicles for a reconstruction of the history of the states of ancient *Judah* and *Israel*.

I find it difficult to evaluate Garbini's contribution to the history of the origin and development of Yahwism.[151] His primary conclusion is that the worship of Yahweh is to be described as an indigenous development within Phoenician-Canaanite religions. The exclusive Yahwism of the Old Testament is understood as a product of a Jerusalemite priestly class of Garbini's post-exilic period that, through a fiction of origins, grounds its faith as extra-Palestinian and understands that faith as inimical to the Phoenician cultic traditions of the indigenous population. These conclusions go far in creating a synthetic framework for understanding much of the biblical tradition and of the epigraphic and archaeological evidence from *Palestine*. However, there are difficulties of severe oversimplification on both sides of Garbini's synthesis. From the biblical side, his presentation of "Hebrew religion" from "the Old Testament as a whole"[152] creates a straw man, on the basis of which Garbini can argue for the existence of an ideology that strongly reflects what is in fact a fictional composite: "biblical monotheism." This concept has generally been assumed of the tradition by a long history of Jewish and Christian interpretation. His emphasis on an "exile," a critical evolutionary watershed and a period of radical transformation, lends itself well to the support of this mainline interpretation. This enables Garbini to identify the social class of a post-exilic *Jerusalem* priesthood as the creative force behind this revision. However, the "exile" is not immediately translatable as an historical period within the history of Israel. It is an ideological concept of Israel's self-understanding. Only our almost total ignorance has allowed us to

---

[151] *Ibid.,* pp.52–65.

[152] *Ibid.,* pp.52f.

assume its pivotal place in history. We base this, however, on its literary and theological centrality, a centrality that it has been given by those great Persian- and early hellenistic-period philosophers who were the writers of the biblical texts and their commentaries.

We need to ask more specifically what the role of the exile in fact was: in the real past as well as in the perceived past of those who formed and accepted the tradition and in the created past that grew from the tradition itself. For instance, did an "exilic period" have a significant role in the formation of the so-called post-exilic period at any time prior to the late Persian period's comprehensive consolidation of the tradition? This is an important question because it was this assumed wholeness of the tradition that gave the concept of exile the ability to empower Israel with a sense of new beginnings, and for the first time render for the people of *Palestine* a self-understanding as one people. Without this later and fictive ideology, the exile itself disappears from history as a significant period in Israel's formation. Without it, Jews who actually lived in Babylon play no more intrinsic role than those from *Nineveh* or *Elephantine*. Indeed, one must also ask whether the concept "return" is historically significant as event! Or was the self-definition in terms of "exiles returning" both synchronous and synonymous with their self-understanding as Jews and therefore "the remnant of Israel"? It is in this kind of a context, I think, that Lemche's suggestion that we "erase the exile"[53] has powerful heuristic implications for a critical history of *Palestine* and ancient Israel.

Garbini nowhere argues a case for the ideological or cultural unity of the various traditions that comprise his view of the "Old Testament as a whole" at such an early period, and his own work in the history of the formation of the tradition argues rather vehemently against the existence of so early a core of orthodoxy, whether in origin priestly, prophetic or proto-rabbinic. One must wonder whether Garbini, in his enthusiasm for identifying specific religio-politically motivated ideologies as factors in the creation of biblical tradition, has not presented us with an anachronistic view of the Old Testament and placed it in the minds of a *Jerusalem* priesthood. Such a view did not exist or cannot be shown to have existed (like the priests themselves) prior to the second temple period, and perhaps not before the hellenistic period. However much cultic centrism might be associated with the *Jerusalem* priesthood

---

[53] Personal communication.

consonant with the Josiah of Chronicles and 1 Ezdras, the creative *Sitz im Leben* of such distinctive religious themes as an inautochthonous Yahwism, henotheistic exclusivity and universal monotheism cannot be so radically delineated, though one might well claim that both an exilic concept and the Jerusalem priesthood played important formative roles in the development of both. What Garbini refers to as "Yahwistic monotheism" is not an historically established datum of Israelite religion, expressive of the "Old Testament as a whole,"[54] though it commonly appears as a *theologoumenon* in Old Testament scholarship.

"Yahwistic monotheism" (as if true monotheism needed such a determinative) is historically derivative of these three quite distinctive orientations, and is better understood as an ideological product of a modern theological perception of the "Old Testament as a whole" than as an understanding of the traditions themselves. For example, Zechariah 14:5, late as it is, is still an acceptable product of a henotheistic perception and worldview. Similarly, Deuteronomy 32:8f. LXX, as thoroughly Yahwistic as Deuteronomy and the LXX are, subordinates Yahweh to Elohim as his son. This Garbini unaccountably argues is comparable to what occurs in the Baal Cycle of *Ugarit* and suggests for Yahweh a role comparable to the gods of other nations in his effort to offer an analogy to Yahweh's role with Israel.[55] However, if these texts were read within the "Old Testament as a whole," the Yahwism of Deuteronomy and Zachariah must be understood as identifiable, if not entirely synonymous, with Garbini's Jewish monotheism. This, of course, Garbini is not claiming, and I do not think it unfair to suggest that the anachronism he has introduced here is unintentional.

It is unfortunate that this also hides an important aspect of the tradition that might be of great importance in understanding the historical development of early Persian period inclusive monotheism. There are many texts in the bible that reflect various degrees of polytheism, henotheism and syncretism. Some of these, such as in 2 Kings, but unlike those in Zechariah 14 and Deuteronomy 32, understand individuals and groups—even Israel as a whole—to be practicing and promoting religious beliefs that are inimical to the religious perceptions of the author. Other texts, however, suggest that

---

[54] G. Garbini, *op.cit.*, pp.52f.
[55] *Ibid.*, p.56.

the perceptions of the authors themselves imply a polytheistic, henotheistic or syncretistic worldview. These texts reflect the perceptions of the tradents of the received tradition. Here no passage clarifies this issue better than that of Leviticus 16: 6-11, on Azazel, a desert deity subordinate to Yahweh.

The presence of such texts, as well as those of Zechariah and Deuteronomy, begs explanation. It is extremely difficult to argue that such texts are "fragments of the past"—that is, no longer conscious remnants from the past that the tradition has inadvertently included in spite of an effort to present an "ideal of a religious reform . . . bent to the sole purpose of showing the truth of a particular religious vision . . . ."[156] It is abundantly clear that many of these texts are themselves bent on "showing the truth of a particular religious vision," and that such religious perspectives continued to be acceptable to subsequent collectors and redactors. The pluralism of religious perspectives reflected in the Old Testament is apparent not only in the earliest stages of an only supposedly past "mythology" and folklore, but lies at the very heart of the collective tradition, and this, I submit, is a fully conscious choice of the late Persian period editors. No part can serve legitimately as an interpretive matrix for the whole bible. In this early period there is no comprehensive tradition to give such wholeness that the traditions themselves could be judged and "corrected." That historical passage in the evolution of religion belongs more properly to the use to which the traditions were put, once normative status was achieved.

In describing what he calls the "pre-exilic" Israelite-Phoenician cult that the "post-exilic" priesthood adamantly opposed, Garbini creates a context in which the polemical tradition of Israelite religion might be judged realistic. However, Garbini also dehistoricizes both the extrabiblical evidence of the religious practices in *Palestine* during the Assyrian period and the religious conflicts that are related in the biblical texts as meaningful in the later world of their tradents. The religious pluralism implicit in the prophetic tradition's attack on syncretism was long ago recognized by such scholars as Ahlström.[157] The more recent archaeological and epigraphic evidence of such pluralism in *Palestine*

---

[156] *Ibid.*, p.61.

[157] G.W. Ahlström, *Aspects of Syncretism in Israelite Religion* (Lund, 1963); *idem, An Archaeological Picture of Iron Age Religions in Ancient Palestine, Studia Orientalia* 55,3 (Helsinki, 1984).

does not so much confirm the existence of an Israelite syncretism as present us with historical data with which we might understand the development of monotheism in *Palestine*. With the awareness of such pluralism we come to understand how many in *Palestine,* understanding themselves as a remnant of ancient Israel and identifying themselves with ancestors—understood to have suffered deportation and exile—reflected on their tradition in terms of a lapse into syncretism. To identify the ideology motivating the biblical text, as Garbini has attempted to do, does not in itself translate that text historically; for the text does not only speak to an ideological motive in a description of a real past. It also creates a vision of that past, and it is this figment that it addresses as its primary referent and from which it develops an *ethnos*.

It is not relevant whether that vision is historically accurate. It is not even essential that we affirm the historicity of a contemporary existent "Israel" other than as a literary process in history through which this vision is achieved. The text presents us with a window into the intellectual world of the authors and tradents of the tradition's history, and enable us to understand how they understood their past. In only a limited and very distorted way, however, does it let us glimpse the real world of the author's present. Literature is not readily transposed into a history of either its referent or its context.[158] While Garbini has much to say about ideology in Persian period Palestinian literature, the sources he uses as the primary basis of his reconstruction render little history as such.

An independent history of the people and the religious ideas reflected in the Bible must be created on yet other grounds. Ideology is only one of the motivations in the formation of literature, and it is questionably a dominant one. Certainly those ideologies that played a role are neither so transparent nor so obvious that we are permitted to understand the history of the so-called second temple period in *Palestine* as simply the mirrored reflection of our biblical texts. Rather, we first need an independently derived history before we can adequately discern the nature and context of the ideologies that are implicit in the text.

---

[158] Th.L. Thompson, "Text, Context, and Referent in Israelite Historiography," *The Fabric of History, JSOTS* 127, ed. by D. Edelman (Sheffield, 1991), pp.65-92. See further below, Chapter 8.

CHAPTER FOUR

NEW DEPARTURES TOWARDS AN INDEPENDENT HISTORY OF ISRAEL

I. An Anthropological Revision of Alt's Settlement Hypothesis

In writing an independent history of ancient Israel, we must consider three different types of direct evidence[1] from primary sources for the historical reconstruction of early Israel: a) archaeological excavations and their analysis, the classification and interpretation of archaeologically derived *realia* and archaeological surveys and the settlement patterns of ancient *Palestine* understood regionally and geographically; b) the wealth of ancient written remains directly and indirectly related to ancient *Palestine*: the people, its neighbors, its economy, religious and political structures, mode of life and known events; and c) the biblical traditions that reflect explicitly and implicitly the world in which they are formed and which portray that understanding of Israel whose origin we are seeking.[2]

This last source is, of course, of use when we consider the origin of a specifically Israelite religion and tradition. The text often renders direct circumstantial witness to Israel's history at the time of that specific tradition's formation and transmission. Distinctions must necessarily be made, however, as to what the biblical account knows as reality and what it knows as tradition. For example, there is a narrative world of difference between peoples it knows from its own real world of politics and diplomacy, such as *Ammon, Moab, Edom, Midian, Aram*, the Philistines, Phoenicians, the Egyptians and Assyrians, and those it knows from tradition, such as the Horites, Hivites, Girgashites, Perizites,

---

[1] What follows should be read in the light of Th.L. Thompson, "The Background of the Patriarchs," *JSOT* 9 (1978), pp.7f.; *idem*, "History and Tradition," *JSOT* 15 (1980), pp.57-61; and esp. *idem, The Origin Tradition of Ancient Israel I, JSOTS* 55 (Sheffield, 1987) pp.36-40.

[2] Th.L. Thompson, "Text, Context, and Referent in Israelite Historiography," *The Fabric of History*, ed. by D. Edelman (Sheffield, 1991); and *idem*, "Historiography: Israelite," *Anchor Bible Dictionary*, ed. by D.N. Freedman, forthcoming.

indeed, even the Canaanites, Midianites, Amorites and Hebrews; or of places of tradition such as *Eden, Aram Naharaim, Gerar, Goshen, Sodom, Gomorrah* and *Salem*—even perhaps *Har Sinai*, over against places actually known by the tradents, such as *Jerusalem, Gezer, Megiddo, Jericho* and *Ai.*

Much that was hitherto considered obvious are indeed problematic. For instance, are the tribes of Israel "real" or "traditional" within the world of the biblical tradition's formation? *Sitz im Leben* has both historical context and syntax. For the fifth- to third-century Judaean traditionist, are the twelve tribes of Israel—indeed is "Israel"—past or present reality? And, if past, to what extent is that a known past? Are they realities of the present based on and interpreted by traditions of the past? Or are they traditions of the past made present for present ideological purposes, or perhaps for a future goal? Or are they idealistic: projections of wishes and hopes without reference to any existent reality, past or present?

Of indirect value for the historical reconstruction of Israel's past—but nevertheless providing primary data—are sources that relate to the reconstructible physical world of ancient Israel: Palestinian geography, knowledge of the history and cultures of the ancient world; and especially information regarding the people and events most closely related to the development of Israel.[3] Rendering secondary and indirect evidence for Israel's origins is a growing body of research involving historical and modern anthropological studies that offers potential analogies to the ancient peoples of Palestine, as well as sociological studies that can be used to illustrate the changing structures of the ancient societies existing in *Palestine* of the first-millennium. With such secondary and indirect analogies and sources, however, it is of course ever necessary to recognize their chronological and geographical distance from the historical realities we are trying to describe. Anthropological and sociological studies offer us analogies for what Israel might have been, that is, models and forms for a history of Israel, but not substance. The closeness of such analogies is of first importance methodologically,

---

[3] The bibliography on these issues is immense and cannot be treated here. See most recently the various publications associated with the *Tübinger Atlas des vorderen Orients*; also some of the creative maps of J. Rogerson. *Atlas of the Bible* (Oxford, 1985); also M. Weippert, *Edom* (Tübingen dissertation, 1971); E.A. Knauf, *Ismael, ADPV* (Wiesbaden, 1989); N.P. Lemche, *Ancient Israel* (Sheffield, 1988); and esp. H. Weippert, *Palästina in vorhellenistischer Zeit: Handbuch der Archäologie* (Munich, 1988).

and analogues from the Middle East and especially from the same regions of *Palestine* and, if possible, from a period close to the time of Israel's origins must be sought. Minimally, one must offer the *caveat* that both the extent and the appropriateness of any analogy must be examined in every case, and its limitations included in evaluation.

Regarding this critical issue, N.P. Lemche's *Early Israel* is important. Of particular value is Lemche's departure from a "models" approach to historical anthropology and the lucid and erudite manner in which he displays anthropological data not as forms and laws to be accepted or rejected, but rather as elements of a spectrum of possibilities which enables us to structure our much more specific and significantly different historical data. Lemche's book does not attempt to offer us a solution to the questions of Israel's origins, as much as it opens a means by which one might enter the labyrinth of the anthropological and sociological worlds relevant to ancient *Palestine*. The richness of Lemche's work cannot be overestimated. Moreover, while Lemche's critical command of sociological and anthropological literature relating to nomads is impressive.[4] This work is also the first sustained attempt since A. Alt's seminal essay in 1925 that has suggested an historical account of Israel's origins apart from the bible's own view of its past. Lemche's review deals with many of the relevant issues and should command respect.[5] In fact, as Miller-Hayes, *A History of Israel and Judah*, marks the culmination of a long tradition of critical revisions of biblical historiography,[6] Lemche's book, published just briefly before the Miller-Hayes volume, marks a distinct departure from that scholarly tradition in the direction of an independent historiography of Israel.

The more recent studies of Coote and Whitelam and Finkelstein[7] are also based on extrabiblical texts and on the archaeology and settlement patterns of Palestine. But both of these works—whatever might be said of their use of archaeologically derived data and their historical

---

[4] A recent sound study of one aspect of greater Palestine's nomadic past is the critical, detailed and refreshingly clear monograph of E.A. Knauf, *op.cit.*, 1989. See also his *Midian, ADPV* (Wiesbaden, 1988) pp.9-13.

[5] N.P. Lemche, *op.cit.*, 1985, pp.306-435; see also the less sustained study in *idem, Ancient Israel* (Sheffield, 1988).

[6] P.R. Davies and D.M. Gunn "A History of Ancient Israel and Judah: A Discussion of Miller-Hayes (1986)," *JSOT* 39 (1987), pp.3-63.

[7] R.B. Coote and K.W. Whitelam, *op.cit.*, 1986; I. Finkelstein, *op.cit.*, 1988.

reconstructions—presuppose the Israel of the biblical traditions, and, like M. Noth and J.A. Soggin before them, seek the Israel of biblical tradition within an historical and geographical context pre-determined by the much later biblical historiographical framework. This is clearest and most specific in their identification (with Alt) of originating Israel in the Iron I settlements of the central hill countries, particularly in contrast to both the lowland population on one hand, and a Late Bronze chronological horizon on the other. G. Ahlström, however,[8] like Lemche, raises serious objections both to the Canaanite-Israelite and the Late Bronze-Iron I dichotomies of Alt's reconstruction.

Lemche's book is only a start to such a new historiography. In his opening discussion of a history of Israel's origins,[9] Lemche argues against Mendenhall and Gottwald's unverified and unverifiable assumption that substantial blocks of tradition were datable to a period of judges. He asks rather: "In what phase of the history of Israel did the concept of a common prehistory for the entire Israelite people emerge as a guideline for historical writing in the Old Testament?"[10] Basing himself on a review of current scholarship's chronology of Old Testament literature, and building on the studies of H. Vorländer[11] and recent critics and revisionists of the documentary hypothesis,[12] Lemche has come to the conclusion that "on no account were the basic preconditions present for the emergence of the concept of Israel as a unity before the period of the monarchy," and further, "on no account could the concept of a united Israel have resulted in pan-Israelite historical writing before the time of the exile."[13] Lemche's positions are

---

[8] G. Ahlström, *Who Were the Israelites?* (Winona Lake, 1986).

[9] N.P. Lemche, *op.cit.,* pp.326-385.

[10] *Ibid.*, p.384.

[11] H. Vorländer, *Die Entstehungszeit des jehowistischen Geschichtswerkes, Europäische Hochschulschriften* 23/109 (Frankfurt, 1978).

[12] See J. Van Seters, *Abraham in History and Tradition* (New Haven, 1975); R. Rendtorff, *Das Überlieferungsgeschichtliches Problem des Pentateuch, BZAW* 147 (Berlin, 1977); also H.H. Schmid, *Der sogenannte Jahwist: Beobachtungen und Fragen zur Pentateuchforschung* (Zurich, 1976); as well as M. Rose, *Deuteronomist und Jahwist: Untersuchungen zu den Beruhrungspunkten beider Literaturwerke, AThANT* 67 (Zurich, 1981); E. Blum, *Die Komposition der Vätergeschichte, WMANT* 57 (1984); N. Whybray, *The Making of the Pentateuch, JSOTS* 53 (Sheffield, 1987); Th.L. Thompson, *The Origin Tradition of Ancient Israel I, JSOTS* 55 (Sheffield, 1987).

[13] N.P. Lemche, *op.cit.,* p.384.

certainly well argued, however one might eventually need to adjust them. The biblical tradition does not and cannot supply us with a factual basis for the existence in history of a "united monarchy." This is a motif, a literary concept that shares in the "all-Israel" tradition that is a creation of the late redactions of disparate traditional materials that are first brought together in their final redaction. And, if only for the sake of historiographical integrity (however disorienting this may first appear), one ought not presuppose the existence of a united monarchy in fact, without first having either corroborating evidence—which indeed fails—or, minimally, a sustained historical and form-critical evaluation of the received tradition that strongly supports both the historiography and the historicity of the narratives about Israel's "golden age."

This methodological issue must be stressed here, as it is the collapse of just such argumentation that Lemche thoroughly chronicles in the pages prior to his conclusions.[14] On the other hand, I am not as convinced as Lemche that the entirety of the pentateuchal and the deuteronomistic tradition must of necessity fall into the exilic and postexilic periods. Only a firm belief in at least a revisionist's view of the documentary hypothesis and similar theories regarding the so-called deuteronomistic history could lead one to such global conclusions.[15] While a relatively late date for many of these collective traditions seems appropriate and necessary, any date subsequent to the fall of *Samaria* in 720 B.C. is theoretically possible and periods close to the reigns of Hezekiah or Josiah seem viable for some of the narratives.[16]

I would not, however, wish my quibble on this relatively minor issue of tradition-history to obscure a wholehearted concurrence with Lemche's methods and conclusions, epitomized succinctly in the

---

[14] *Ibid.,* pp.357-384.

[15] As, for example, the positions taken by J. Van Seters (*op.cit.,* 1975; *idem, In Search of History: Historiography in the Ancient World and the Origins of Biblical History,* New Haven, 1983) and H. H. Schmid (*op.cit.,* 1976). For some recent alternatives to the documentary theory which, if accepted, would seriously undermine this conclusion of Lemche's, R. Rendtdorff, *op.cit.,* 1977; E. Blum, *op.cit.,* 1984; Th.L. Thompson, *op.cit.,* 1987; and R.N. Whybray, *op.cit.,* 1987. Following some of the observations of E.A. Knauf concerning historical context and referents (*opera citata,* 1988, 1989), I think one must clearly distinguish the traditions themselves from the traditions as collected and transmitted. Nevertheless, the logic of Lemche's arguments for a Hellenistic dating is unassalable (see also chapter VIII, note 10).

[16] I.W. Provan, *Hezekiah and the Book of Kings,* BZAW 172 (Berlin, 1988) pp.114-130.

principle he has formulated at the close of his study: "I propose that we decline to be led by the biblical account and instead regard it, like other legendary materials, as formally ahistorical; that is, as a source which only exceptionally can be verified by other information."[17]

Lemche presents as an alternative to the biblical historiography a review of the transition from Late Bronze to Iron Age *Palestine* on the basis of archaeological sources. In this aspect of his approach it is clear that Lemche follows the broad procedural lines drawn by Alt in 1925, namely, the well known thesis that by contrasting the changes that occur in *Palestine* between the Late Bronze and the Iron Ages, a historical trajectory can be drawn from the Late Bronze Canaanite city-state culture to the Iron Age Israelite nation-state. Lemche's analysis is restricted both by the then limited availability of archaeological surveys—especially relating to the Iron Age—and by the inadequate differentiation that has plagued Palestinian archaeology between the sub-periods within the Late Bronze and Iron Ages.

Lemche improves on this situation through a judicious review of excavated sites. His Bronze Age settlement patterns are, however, largely limited to the broad review offered by this writer in 1979.[18] Unfortunately the present understanding of Late Bronze Settlement patterns has only slightly improved since this summarizing study, the research for which was done in the early 1970s. This improvement has come mostly in the Transjordan, as Lemche notes. The current reconstruction of the Iron Age on the other hand is much improved over anything that had been available to Lemche.

Lemche's understanding of the transition from the Late Bronze to the Iron Age, like Miller's similar discussion,[19] reflects the growing awareness in archaeological circles of the many cultural continuities (in spite of differences in settlement patterns) between the Late Bronze and Iron Age periods in Palestine. Lemche accurately observes that the common distinction between Canaanite and Israelite culture is not justified in the received archaeological record. This lead him also to the historical conclusion, shared by a growing number of scholars, that Israel

---

[17] N.P. Lemche, *op.cit.*, p.415.

[18] Th.L. Thompson, *The Settlement of Palestine in the Bronze Age*, *BTAVO* 34 (Wiesbaden, 1979).

[19] J.M. Miller, *op.cit.*, 1977, pp.218ff.

had been indigenous to *Palestine*.[20] This, in itself, is not as major a departure from Alt as one might be led to believe when reading him through the eyes of Noth, since the transhumance shepherds that Alt had proposed as his model for the proto-Israelites, had lived in the steppe zones and hill country of *Palestine* from as early as the beginning of the Late Bronze Age.[21]

Lemche's conclusion that there is nothing intrinsically "Canaanite" about the Bronze Age nor "Israelite" about the subsequent Iron Age—an observation which also has broad validity in the eyes of Soggin and Miller, and especially Ahlström—points out quite emphatically that we do not find in Alt's dichotomies a method directing us to the question of Israel's origin. It is this understanding, already present in his 1985 study, that drives many of the developments of Lemche's 1991 book.[22] This observation is already implicit in Miller's greater skepticism about our ability to define that origin on the basis of any of the mainstream biblical traditions. Soggin's unsubstantiated assertion that the history of Israel begins with Saul and David's monarchy, in spite of Miller's *caveat*, both short-circuits the historiographical process, and itself shares the fictive quality of those earlier assertions which had begun that history with the patriarchal narratives. Soggin sees the stories about the united monarchy as marking a transition in biblical narrative between the historically undependable biblical folklore prior to the stories of Saul and David and the truly historiographic and dependable traditions of the monarchy.[23] Lemche, on the other hand, clearly argues for the necessity of extrabiblical confirmation and evidence before the biblical traditions can provide us with an adequate basis for reconstructing the history of Israel.

---

[20] E.g. J.A. Callaway, "A New Perspective on the Hill Country Settlement of Canaan in Iron Age I," *Palestine in the Bronze and Iron Ages: Papers in Honour of Olga Tufnell*, ed. by J.N. Tubb (London, 1985) pp.31-49; L.E. Stager, "The Archaeology of the Family in Ancient Israel," *BASOR* 260 (1985), pp.1-35.

[21] A. Alt, "Die Landnahme der Israeliten in Palästina," *Kleine Schriften I* (1925) pp.115-125. I. Finkelstein (*op.cit.*, 1988), arguing within the same spectrum of ideas, indeed, points to the Middle Bronze II occupation of this hill country for the ultimate origin of these pastoralists, marking the potential compatibility of Alt's program with the concept of the indigenous character of Israel's origins. However, see further below, chapters 6 and 7.

[22] N.P. Lemche, *The Canaanites and Their Land* (Sheffield, 1991).

[23] See the review of this position in Th.L. Thompson, *op.cit.*, 1987, pp.30-32.

This issue becomes particularly clear in examining the way that Lemche has dealt with the prehistory of the monarchy, especially his treatment of the Late Bronze *'apiru* and the early Iron I period "Philistines." Lemche's decision to speculate on the *'apiru* as potentially informing the origins of Israel is self-consciously hypothetical: an idea awaiting evidence.[24] It is a revision of an interpretation of the *Amarna 'apiru* recently reasserted by M. Liverani[25] that the *'apiru* were originally a disaffected underclass, refugees of Egyptian imperial oppression, who had fled to the hill country to live off brigandage and banditry against the overland trade routes. They are seen to have eventually settled the hill country in the post *Amarna* period, and to have formed—under pressure from the Philistine Pentapolis—political structures of lineages and clans that later became Israel under the centralizing fictions of tribal associations. These changes connect the *'apiru* we meet in the *Amarna* letters with the early Iron Age sedentarization of the hill country that Lemche suggests may have formed the core of a population that at a much later date developed a narrative tradition that frequently identifies Israelites with the seemingly ethnic biblical term *'ibrim*. Important to this interpretation is the effort to explain not only the historical development of the *'apiru-'ibrim*, but also the semantic shift from a social class of *'apiru* to the gentilic *'ibrim* which we find in the bible. The objections to any reconstruction based on an *'apiru = 'ibrim* identification are many.[26] Loretz, who is very critical of historians efforts to associate *'apiru* with Hebrews, points out the categorical mistake of these efforts to explicate the origins of Israel with this association. His devastating critique is both simple and straightforward: We have no historical evidence to associate

---

[24] This is neither dependent on a necessary historical association with *'ibrim* or with any later biblical tradition. That Lemche does not depend on such associations is very clear in his 1991 book (N.P. Lemche, *The Canaanites and Their Land,* Sheffield, 1991). It is unfortunate that this work was unavailable to me until the very final stages of this study.

[25] M. Liverani, Review of R. De Vaux, *l'Histoire ancienne d'Israel I-II*, in *OA* 15 (1976), pp.145-159; also, N.P. Lemche, "'Hebrew' as a National Name for Israel," *StTh* 33 (1979), pp.1-23; *idem*, "'Hebraeerne': Myths over habiru—hebraeerproblemet," *DTT* 43 (1980), pp.153-190. See, already J. Bottéro, *Le Problème des Habiru à la 4e Rencontre assyriologique internationale* (Paris, 1954) and M. Weippert, *Die Landnahme der israelitischen Stämme in der neueren wissenschaftlichen Diskussion* (Göttingen, 1967).

[26] For a very thorough review of this problem, see now O. Loretz, *Habiru-Hebräer: Eine sozio-linguistische Studie über die Herkunft des Gentiliziums 'ibri vom Appelativum Habiru, BZAW* 160 (Berlin, 1984), esp. pp.229-232, 271-275; also M. Weippert, *op.cit.,* 1967.

the fourteenth-century *Amarna* letters and the *'apiru* mentioned in them with the origins of Israel. Whatever linguistic associations there may be between these radically different terms, we have no reason to see this philological issue as in any way related to the historical origins of Israel. Not least important is the argument fostered by Lemche's critique of Gottwald's *Tribes of Yahweh*, namely, that the largely exilic and postexilic tradition takes its written form only centuries after the essential social structures of Iron Age *Palestine* had been established, throwing into doubt ˙any *ad hoc* use of these traditions for a reconstruction of premonarchic times.[27] The issue is not merely the length of time involved, but the extent of the social transformation that took place, separating the very different worlds of the premonarchic and postexilic worlds. Lemche has given us substantial *a priori* reasons to doubt that the fifth to third-century literary world can be translated in such a way as to give us insight into the real social world of fourteenth to tenth-century *Palestine*. With Loretz and Lemche,[28] we might add that we have even less hope of reading in these biblical texts any reflection of the Late Bronze *Amarna* period, given the radical social transformations of the Late Bronze-Iron Age transition.[29]

For none of the literary traditions about Hebrews would Lemche argue historicity. Hardly the Abraham, Joseph, Moses, and David stories! But without such historicity, where might one, following Lemche, find premonarchic roots in the biblical tradition about *'ibrim*? Even if the *'apiru* = *'ibrim* equation were granted, and that is a very formidable equation,[30] all we could conclude from this is that by the postexilic period this term had undergone a substantial semantic shift and had taken on a dominant quasi-ethnic signification, and was used at times as a synonym for the gentilic "Israel," which term itself had undergone considerable change over centuries. The lack of evidence for historical continuity between the *Amarna* letters and the biblical tradition prevents historians, in the light of Lemche's and Liverani's work, from

---

[27] This does not detract from the value of Lemche's and Liverani's efforts to understand the *'apiru* as part of the early history of highland Palestine and their suggestion of a possible transvaluation of the term *'apiru* to *'ibrim* over the course of a millennium.

[28] O. Loretz, *op.cit.*

[29] See below, Chapter VI.

[30] O. Loretz, *op.cit.*, pp.235-248; also pp.14f.

understanding the term *'ibrim* apart from the literary world in which it has its context.

Essential to Lemche's understanding of the social realities of Late Bronze *Palestine* is his perception of the Egyptian empire's role as oppressive and exploitative, conducive to both the impoverishment and the dislocation of the Palestinian population. This not only contradicts the little evidence we have of the tax structures of the Late Bronze Syro-Palestinian city-states,[31] but recent evaluations of the economic effects of the Egyptian empire in the region indicate that the presence of Egyptian imperial authority helped to stabilize many of the towns in the central valleys and the coastal plain during the disruptions of the latter part of the Late Bronze Age and early Iron I, enabling some regions to maintain a level of prosperity, when so much of *Palestine* faced economic disintegration. It is hence difficult to see the *'apiru* phenomenon as a direct reaction to Egyptian imperial policy or as a movement leading to the sedentarization of the central hills in an effort to "escape" the oppression of government. Moreover, the evidence of *'apiru* banditry in the *Amarna* letters comes from a time considerably earlier than any significant breakdown of the Late Bronze town structures, and centuries earlier than any substantial withdrawal of Egyptian interests in *Palestine*. This makes it difficult to accept that the *'apiru* disturbances were caused by either city-state political collapse or the weakness of Egyptian power in the area. The association of the *Amarna* *'apiru* with new settlement is particularly specious, as the settlement patterns of the central hills during the *Amarna* period are uniquely marked by a gap in such settlement![32] One might, indeed, consider the possibility that the *'apiru* disturbances themselves may have been a significant factor during the *Amarna* period preventing settlement in this region which could only with difficulty be policed by the regnant city-states or by imperial troops. For this, at least, we have evidence.[33]

---

[31] See above Chapter II and below Chapter VI.

[32] Th.L. Thompson, *The Settlement of Palestine in the Bronze Age*, BTAVO 34 (Wiesbaden, 1979) pp.45ff.

[33] The bibliography here is enormous. I still find J. Bottero, (*op.cit.*, 1953) extremely helpful; for more complete references, O. Loretz, *op.cit.* esp. p.57. For translations of the Amarna tablets, J.A. Knudtzon, *Die El-Amarna Tafeln* (Leipzig, 1915), and A. Rainey, *El Amarna Tablets 359-379, AOAT* 8 (Neukirchen, 1978).

Lemche's assumption that these brigands, having removed themselves to the sanctuary of the central hills, survived by plundering the trade routes runs into topographic and historical difficulties. During the second-millennium, overland trade proceeded along the coastal plain, largely bypassing the central hills (reaching *Jerusalem,* for example, by way of the *Ayyalon* Valley, not the Judaean highlands). Most trade was still seaborne. An association of overland trade routes with transients, nevertheless, is supported by evidence from this period, but that is found along the North *Sinai* coastal strip.[34] Furthermore, international trade seems to have been considerably disrupted throughout the whole of the eastern Mediterranean world, ca. 1200 B.C., just at the time that Lemche would see the *'apiru* ambushing caravans in the highlands. One need hardly more than mention the economic and demographic difficulties involved in assuming such large numbers of *'Apiru*, as are mentioned in the *Amarna* letters and as Lemche needs for the extensive highland settlement of Iron I, in terms of outlawry. Not even nineteenth-century *Sicily* had the prosperity to support so many thieves.

Lemche's suggestion that this name may have survived in the biblical traditions in the form *'ibrim* is very appropriate and marks this problem as a purely literary and linguistic issue, and stands apart from questions of historical continuity of the population. One finds a similar problem with Lemche's related argument that the process of political amalgamation of the central hill country settlements is to be understood in terms of a reaction of the independent hill country settlers to growing Philistine political ambitions during the eleventh-century. The continuity of the *peleset* of the Egyptian texts and the archaeological remains of the early Iron I period along the Palestinian coast with the Philistines of the biblical tradition and of Assyrian records is understood in quasi-ethnic terms: as a continuity of a people, and not first of all as a continuity in a name and within the parameters of etymology and texts. In this case, the continuity, in fact, is assumed and not argued. For Lemche, as for most historians of early *Palestine*[35] the Philistines of biblical tradition are the historical people, living in the southern and central coastal plains of *Palestine,* who played a major role in the historical developments of the early Iron Age in *Palestine:* not only as successors to Egyptian power

---

[34] Th.L. Thompson, *The Settlement of Sinai and the Negev in the Bronze Age, BTAVO* 8 (Wiesbaden, 1975), pp.9-13.

[35] Now, most recently, G. Ahlström, *The Early History of Palestine,* forthcoming.

during Iron I, but also in the context of a political and military polarity
with the emerging statehood of the United Monarchy. In accord with the
narratives of the Books of Samuel, most modern historiography of
Israel's origins, early Israel's opposition to Philistine hegemony is
commonly understood as the *raison d'etre* of Saul and David's kingdoms,
and is a central aspect of the nearly unanimous opinion of scholars that
the central hill country of *Palestine* is not merely the heartland of the
Israel of biblical tradition, but also the historical geographical context of
its origination. This perception of the history of the Philistines justifies
for many the relegation to secondary status (historically and traditio-
historically) of not only the entire "Philistine" plain, but the coastal
plain of *Acco,* the *Jezreel,* the whole of the *Galilee* and the *Jordan* Valley.
This is methodologically disturbing as essential aspects of this "history"
are critically dependent on the historicity of traditions otherwise known
to be largely legendary and late. Again we are faced with a many
centuries long break in the chain of evidence between the Egyptian texts
and the archaeological evidence on one hand and the Assyrian records
and biblical tradition on the other. The archaeological evidence,
moreover, is substantially tainted, as its alleged coherence rests almost
solely on biblical traditions.[36] The history of analogous and largely
contemporaneous toponyms in *Palestine* should lend caution to efforts
to historicize biblical referents to Philistines on the basis of the
historical *Peleset (prst)* of the early Iron Age. Among the "Sea Peoples"
who migrated to *Palestine* in the wake of the Mycenaean collapse were
the *Dananu (dnyn)*. They, however, survive in the history of *Palestine*
neither ethnically nor material culturally, but only in their name. Any
toponymic similarities with the later biblical traditions tribe of *"Dan"*
might well have given credence to the legend about a translation of the
tribe of *Dan* from its "original" homeland to the region in Northern
Galilee in the *Jordan* Rift which was attributed to the time of *Dan* in the
tradition. Even the meaning of the biblically ubiquitous name *"Canaan"*
that in historical texts originally refers to the Bronze Age territory (and
derivatively, the population) of *Palestine,* and in some texts (most
notably the Merneptah stele) seems restricted to the lowlands, is rather
radically transposed centuries later in the biblical tradition where it is

---

[36] Compare T. Dothan, *The Philistines and Their Material Culture* (Jerusalem, 1982), and
the more cautious treatment of H. Weippert, *Die Archäologie Palästina in vorhellenistischer
Zeit* (Munich, 1988).

used most frequently to designate a legendary ethnic population of pre-Israelite *Palestine,* which is perceived in some texts as a variant of "Amorite" and even "Jebusite." That such a group ever had an historical coherence which we normally associate with ethnicity is hardly likely. Nevertheless, the name survives in transmuted form as that of a people in biblical tradition. The name "Israel" itself might be so understood. Etymologically, it is unquestionably a gentilic.[37] Nevertheless, the first attested reference to this name in the Merneptah inscription of the late thirteenth-century might conceivably understand it as the name of a region, in polarity with the clearly geographical name: *Canaan.*[38] G. Ahlström, in presenting this thesis, had further argued that the name "Israel" had been first used to refer to a political entity when Saul's kingdom (involving, for Ahlström, only the hill country north of *Jerusalem)* was established. The name *"Judah"* that had also originally been a territorial name had, at this time, its proper northern correlate not in "Israel" but in the regional designator: *"Ephraim."* The mountain regions of *"Judah"* and *"Ephraim"* hence had been understood in Ahlström's revision of the "United Monarchy" as subregions of a larger territorial entity called "Israel," which represented the whole of the central hills. Objections to the traditio-historical assumptions involved in Ahlström's understanding of the biblical term "Israel" are quite formidable. Such assumptions are hardly to be taken for granted. Equally difficult is Ahlström's effort to establish a correspondence between the

---

[37] See E.A. Knauf's review of Ahlström's book in *JNES* 49 (1990), pp.81-83. This objection is not simply based on the hieroglyph sign for "people" in the Merneptah stele itself, which, as Ahlström correctly points out may be interpreted variously, but rather on the function of this type of name which is confirmed by the syntactic use of the name "Israel" in other contexts. J. Holtyzer, *A search for Method: A Study in the Syntactic Use of the H-Locale in Classical Hebrew, Studies in Semitic Languages and Linguistics* 12, Leiden, 1981, p.241 n688. On the other hand, against Knauf (*op.cit.,* p.82, and *Ismael, ADPV,* Wiesbaden, 1989, p.38 n170) one might agree with Ahlström (*op.cit.,* p.7) that in names such as Israel (and Ishmael), formed by an epithet + *'el,* the divine name *El* is to be understood, rather than the common noun "God," in contrast to those names where the element *'el* occurs in conjunction with a divine name. Only rarely, and usually in conjunction with or by reference to another deity other than *El,* do the words *'el-'elohim* and their variants clearly and unequivocally carry a generic signification. Following Knauf, I would find Genesis 33:20's *'el 'elohe yisra'el* as the best prooftext for identifying the name of the god *El* in the name Israel.

[38] G. Ahlström, *Who Were the Israelites?* (Winona Lake, 1986). Ahlström's hypothesis is based on the assumption of a poetical chiasm. This is attractive, but implausible.

Egyptian late thirteenth-century use of this term and biblical usage. However, Ahlström does not only offer a disputable interpretation of the Merneptah stele, he also argues very clearly that the biblical identification of the term "Israel" in theological terms as the people of Yahweh was a very late development, which allowed the name "Israel" to be preempted by the southern kingdom of *Judah* some time after the fall of *Samaria,* and to be ultimately used as a term referring to the cultic community of an all Israel, with strong exclusionistic tendencies in the postexilic period.[39]

However the disputed issue regarding the Merneptah stele might resolve itself, *Israel* is clearly the name of a state in the Assyrian period, with its capital at *Samaria.* In the yet later, largely postexilic biblical tradition, not only does this signification survive in the tradition, but, independently, the name "Israel" is used both as the name of an eponymic ancestor, and of the whole people of *Palestine,* reflecting the claim of a common ethnicity in the religious ideology of the survivors of the state of *Judah.*

The semantic transformations of the originally geographic toponyms of *Judah, Ephraim, Benjamin, Gilead,* and *Issachar* similarly undermine Lemche's efforts to historicize the biblical traditions about the Philistines. The Aegean associations of aspects of the material culture of coastal *Palestine* during Iron I are in no way to be denied. They certainly reflect the historical reality of incursions into the region from the Aegean. However, that the "Philistines" are to be understood as representing a foreign population intrusive to *Palestine* must certainly be denied. The influence from the Aegean is only partial, and, on the basis of known evidence, largely peripheral and superficial. In language, religion, and material objects—even in the earliest forms of so-called Philistine pottery—the culture of the central coastal region is markedly native to *Palestine.* It might be described well as Aegean influenced, but wholly semitized and acculturated to *Palestine.* From its very roots it is the heir to the Late Bronze coastal towns, and for a short period it may have been the political successor to the Egyptians. However, that a cultural political unity was formed in *Philistia* during the Iron I period

---

[39] Ahlström's discussion should be read together with his important earlier study: *Administration and National Religion in Ancient Palestine* (Leiden, 1982) as well as the extremely able dissertation of D. Edelman on the monarchy of Saul: *The Rise of the Israelite State under Saul* (University of Chicago, 1987).

is no more likely here than in any other region of *Palestine*. Rather, anything like Philistine ethnicity is far better understood as an aspect of the regional orientation of *Palestine* that developed during the Iron II period, a product of the political structures directly and indirectly forced on *Palestine* by the Assyrian Empire's interests in the region. The inautochthonous origin of the Assyrian period's Philistines, along with their putative origins in *Caphtor* is as much a fiction created by the biblical tradition as the comparable origin of *Judah* itself. Both *Judah* and the Philistines are cultural entities indigenous to *Palestine*, ultimately derivative of the culture and population of the Bronze Age, which, in the course of the Iron II period was distinguished into regional proto-ethnic groups in the form of petty states under the demands of an external empire.[40]

2. *Agriculture in the Central Hills*

These issues regarding the associations of both Israel and biblical traditions with historical reconstructions is also at stake in two other recent works that deal with the agriculture of the early Iron Age hill country settlements. The first of these, published in 1985, is the dissertation of D. Hopkins on the ecology and early agriculture of the hill country of *Palestine*.[41] Hopkins's book is partially based on and supplements the dissertation of O. Borowski.[42] Both books share the common assumption that their studies deal directly with Israel's origin because they deal with early Iron Age settlement in the Palestinian hill country. This assumption is both understandable and common among recent scholars since Y. Aharoni's dissertation on the then newly discovered largely one period settlements in the Galilean hills.[43] Methodologically, however, this assumption is worrisome, not only because Hopkins, Borowski, and others assume *a priori* a specific resolution of the problem of Israel's origin before that issue has been in

---

[40] On this, see below Chapter VII.

[41] D.C. Hopkins, *The Highlands of Canaan*, SWBAS 3 (Sheffield, 1985).

[42] O. Borowski, *Agriculture in Iron Age Israel* (Winona Lake, 1987).

[43] Y. Aharoni, *The Settlement of the Israelite Tribes in Upper Galilee*, (PhD Jerusalem, 1957); "Galilee, Upper," *EAEHL*, vol. I, pp.74f, 82-89; "Nothing Early, Nothing Late: Rewriting Israel's Conquest," *BA* 39 (1976), pp.55-76.

fact resolved, but also because they then understand conclusions drawn from this procedure as evidence and justification of their hypothesis! Hopkins, whose historical methodology is more consistent than Borowski's, limits his inquiry to the highland region, but his assumption that this early Iron Age settlement is in fact "Israelite" settlement[44] is nowhere defended or in any way supported, although it appears seriously anachronistic.[45] Apart from such problems, these two very solid monographs on agriculture provide a wealth of information, important not only for issues relating to the Iron Age settlement of *Palestine,* but also to an understanding of the central role that agriculture played in *Palestine*'s economy, and therefore in the formation of Israel in the course of the transformations of *Palestine* during the Iron Age.

There are significant differences between the two studies. Hopkins's work has two parts: the first is a study of the agricultural ecology of the Palestinian highlands,[46] and the second is a very innovative, if methodologically undisciplined, research into possible "agricultural objectives and strategies,"[47] associated with the initial agricultural settlement of the hill country, leading up to an original and exciting discussion of "risk spreading" and "risk reduction" as determinative factors of the highland economy that Hopkins believes formed a significant basis for the Israelite polity.[48] Hopkins's central thesis is well argued, and insofar as it relates to the history of agriculture (however much one might of necessity adjust details in the argument), convincing. Borowski's study, on the other hand discusses the agriculture of the hill country more from a technological perspective in the tradition of Forbes

---

[44] D. Hopkins, *op.cit., e.g.,* p.265.

[45] This growing anachronistic assumption is also shared by Coote and Whitelam and I. Finkelstein (further below). Coote and Whitelam, indeed, take this unsupported identification of Israel's origins so much for granted that they force their uncritical assumption onto a quotation which had been consciously formulated to avoid just this assumption. R.B. Coote and K.W. Whitelam, *The Emergence of Early Israel in Historical Perspective,* SWBAS 5 (Sheffield, 1987) p.75, quoting Th.L. Thompson, "Historical Notes on 'Israel's Conquest of Palestine: A Peasant's Rebellion,'" *JSOT* 7 (1978), p.25. Finkelstein, on the other hand, is fully aware of the anachronistic quality of this assumption (I. Finkelstein, *op.cit.,* pp.27f.), but nevertheless unaccountably chooses to restrict his study to its parameters.

[46] D. Hopkins, *op.cit.,* pp.25-170.

[47] *Ibid.,* pp.171-261.

[48] *Ibid.,* pp.265-275.

or Dalman,[49] with detailed discussions of land usage and tenure;[50] field work;[51] types of crops;[52] and issues of fertility and crop destruction.[53] Given the encyclopedic nature of his study, Borowski's brief chapter, entitled "Conclusion" is wholly unnecessary and mars the work as a whole, offering little more than an unsupported and summary statement about some very interesting issues which Borowski considers important. Here, Borowski, with enthusiastic if misguided nationalism, tries to identify whatever was innovative in Palestinian agriculture during the Iron Age with "Israelite" inventiveness: most importantly, terracing, which "enabled occupation" of the hill country,[54] also, deforestation, runoff agriculture, innovations in water storage, iron tools, crop rotation, fertilizing, fallowing, the invention of the "beam oil press," and innovative storage facilities.[55]

Hopkins, on the other hand, inheriting this assumed time frame which takes for granted an identity between the emergence of Israel and the emergence of early Iron I highland agriculture, rejects such a constellation of agricultural advances as having been causative in the settlement process, and apparently perceives such an effort as a misbalanced "focus on technology."[56] In this critique, however, that adds no new information to the discussion, Hopkins misunderstands Borowski and others, who are not so chronologically oriented as he in their discussions of the origins of Iron Age hill country agriculture. They rather deal with these technological issues structurally, arguing that such technological elements are indeed fundamental to this settlement process, taking a position parallel and complementary to Hopkins's own discussion of the "dynamics" of highland agriculture and its "struggle for subsistence,"[57] a dynamic and a struggle which were effective largely thanks to just such long term, innovative, technological advances if not

---

[49] R.J. Forbes, *Studies in Ancient Technologies*, 9 vols. (Leiden, 1964ff.); G. Dalman, *Arbeit u. Sitte in Palästina*, 8 vols (Paderborn, 1940ff.).

[50] O. Borowski, *op.cit.*, pp.15-44.

[51] *Ibid.*, pp.45-84.

[52] *Ibid.*, pp.85-140.

[53] *Ibid.*, pp.141-162.

[54] *Ibid.*, pp.163f.

[55] *Ibidem.*

[56] D. Hopkins, *op.cit.*, pp.22-24.

[57] *Ibid.*, p.24.

inventions of Palestinian agriculture, developments which are indeed born out by the archaeological record![58] Hopkins's polemic against such technological innovations and their explanatory potential for new settlement is misdirected. A widening use over time of most of these technological advances enable the very processes of "risk reduction" and "risk spreading" which Hopkins puts forward as alternative explanations. While it is true that no "single innovation in agricultural technology" is the "key for explaining the transformation of the settlement map,"[59] it is also true that no one whom Hopkins refers to in his notes claims that there exists any such single innovation, nor do any of these scholars see a constellation of such technological innovation as adequately "explanatory" of the settlement change. Nor are Hopkins's "subsistence strategies" in themselves explanatory, and they are even less able to explain the difficulties of agriculture in the hill country if one sees them as somehow independent of such technological innovations. Hopkins's conclusions are in fact most questionable when they follow upon his devaluation of the importance of technology.[60]

Some of the important innovative technologies which enabled settlement in the highlands are as follows: A) Forest clearing, whether by fire or axe, though gradual, is nonetheless an essential ingredient in the diversification of economy, as well as in the interrelationship of an expanding population with an expanding region of settlement, so necessary to both the mass and continuity of population which became involved in subsequent historical political developments in the hill country. B) The "hewing of cisterns" is, as far as we can say today, "among the prerequisites for highland settlement," in many subregions of central *Palestine,* which solves a very real need for water. Of course, as with most human needs, this need for water was also open to a variety of technological solutions: hewn cisterns, slaked lime cisterns, closeness

---

[58] *Contra* Hopkins, *ibid.,* pp.265f.

[59] *Ibid.,* p.267.

[60] It is methodologically false in history writing to isolate any single element, whether of material advancement or social strategy, as being of itself "explanatory." It is even worse to assume that because they are not fully and independently explanatory they are irrelevant. It is also a mistake to mark one point in time as a point of origin for a people when the conjoining of many factors—each with its own history—is involved in the formation of a people, an economy and a culture. Hopkins's attempt to separate Israel's origins from factors of technological development, in an effort to find an all explanatory key, acts as an argument against his own thesis.

to springs, wells, and the use of *pithoi* for water storage.[61] That the hewing of cisterns is not universal in all settlements of the highlands does not reduce its importance in those settlements where it does play a pivotal role. C) I find it difficult to agree with Hopkins that the use of Iron is unimportant,[62] though I would agree that it is hardly a *sine qua non* of hill country agriculture. Its widespread use in the hill country from the tenth-century on does correspond to a major expansion of settlement into the hill country's most difficult terrain, as well as to the later expansion during Iron II into the more arid areas of the Judaean Hills where poorer soils pertain. Very possibly, the increased use of iron does correspond with an augmented construction of terracing and forest clearing, enabling especially southern highlanders of the Iron II period and other settlers of marginal areas to take the increased risks involved in extending their regions of exploitation. D) Similarly, terracing is not a factor at all sites, but it is a prerequisite in some regions where settlement expands from as early as 1050 B.C. (in the western sector of the central hills). There is good reason to believe that terracing becomes standard practice in most regions by the eighth-century. Its necessary interrelationship with horticulture links it with oil, wine, and fruit production, which form the foundations of the agricultural economy throughout large areas of the highlands, and hence, like forest clearing, terracing is of immediate relevance to questions of the origin of the highland settlements. Hopkins, unfortunately, does not adequately discuss either chronology or regional differences within the highlands. E) Finally, the extensive use of grain storage silos and *pithoi* as a buffer against famine created a more stable environment in an area where rainfall patterns are extremely undependable.[63] Hopkins is partially correct, however. These technological innovations are not of themselves explanatory. They reflect rather the survival techniques of these early settlements.

Hopkins's introduction of such concepts as "risk spreading" and "risk reduction" is immensely useful in understanding the development and stability of hill country agriculture, and especially some of the anomalies in the settlement patterns. It is certainly one of the most important contributions of Hopkins's study, though I would welcome greater clarity

---

[61] I. Finkelstein, *op.cit.*, 1988.

[62] D. Hopkins, *op.cit.*, p.265.

[63] See also *ibid.*, p.268.

in the distinctive function of each technique. Similarly, Hopkins's designation of the extended family[64] as a context for risk sharing is of great interest, but he offers little evidence and little reason for our knowing how the family actually functioned in this capacity, and one is left to wonder whether this is perhaps only a fashionable sociologism. His use of later biblical traditions as aids in his discussion of subsistence strategies[65] is questionable at best. His assumption of the historicity of the "sabbatical year," and his understanding of it as a device for the "simulation of a crisis of crop failure," enforcing an "elasticity of agricultural production and promoting social cohesion" are difficult to take seriously. Hardly a "simulation," the transregional practice of a sabbatical year, if ever put into effect, would create quite real famine and nullify the essential risk reduction techniques of food storage which we know were used. It is exceedingly difficult to see the sabbatical year as an early Israelite form of *Ramadan*.

3. *Sociology and the Rise of the Monarchy*

Hopkins's portrayal of the rise of the monarchy as opposed to the basic Israelite "village based subsistence objectives" is not only exegetically and historically uncritical, but such a disruption in the agriculture of the highlands at the onset of the monarchy (or at the close of the eleventh-century) is hardly supported by the "ample evidence" Hopkins claims.[66] I select this particular issue for discussion because it is critical to Hopkins's entire understanding of highland agriculture in relation to his view of the emergence of Israel. Like Alt and Gottwald before him (and indeed like the redactor of I Samuel), Hopkins does not see the monarchy as creating the nation Israel so much as bringing about a fall from grace.

Hopkins sees the monarchy as having been responsible for a twofold change in agricultural production: A) First of all, he sees the monarchy as having been the effective cause in the development of such cash crops as oil, wine, and cereals for the purpose of taxation and trade. That is, Hopkins sees the development of an agricultural regime that follows the

---

[64] The *Mishpaha*; C.H.J. de Geus, *The Tribes of Israel* (Amsterdam, 1976) pp.133ff.

[65] D. Hopkins, *op.cit.*, pp.273f.

[66] *Ibid.*, pp.274f.

typical pattern of a Mediterranean economy in *Palestine*'s hill country both as an innovative creation of the monarchy, and as having had an origin which was separate from the period of Israel's emergence. He also sees this Mediterranean form of agricultural economy as having been inimical to the "village based subsistence objectives of risk spreading and optimizing labor through the diversification of subsistence means."[67] B) Secondly, largely in conflict with "the realities of the variable environment of highland subsistence," he sees the very early monarchy to have created new agricultural systems, distinct from those of Iron I.[68] What those systems actually were is left to further study, though their function is identified as having been created to enhance "specialization and regularity."[69]

That Hopkins has any, let alone "ample," evidence for such changes within this early period of settlement is doubtful. Rather, this purely hypothetical discussion about the monarchy's effect on Palestinian highland agriculture illustrates a major danger in the careless and uncritical use of sociological "theory" when dealing with the social structure and economy of early Israel. Hopkins assumes many things we do not know. We do not know that these settlements are "Israelite"; we also do not know whether the biblical tradition of centuries later is directly applicable to an understanding of these Iron I sites. Hopkins, himself, gives substantial arguments which make such assertions gratuitous. Finally, and much more importantly, we do not know whether we are dealing with a form of subsistence agriculture, an assumption upon which Hopkins's entire book depends, although it is nowhere justified or supported by evidence. Unfortunately, Hopkins neglects describing or defining this, for him, pivotal concept of subsistence agriculture, which he contrasts to the equally undescribed and undefined Bronze Age and lowland agriculture, as well as to what Hopkins thinks of as later economic forms of the monarchy. Subsistence farming, in simplest terms, is a sociologically distinct form of agricultural production which enables a self sufficiency and independence of villages, hamlets, and homesteads. It also has an adverse effect on inter-village and transregional relationships, since these are extraneous infringements on a subsistence economy. Hopkins's insistence on this particular form

---

[67] *Ibid.*, p.275.

[68] *Ibidem*.

[69] *Ibidem*.

of agriculture as characteristic of hill country farming—in spite of all its clarifying abilities for biblical history—needs justification through sustained argument. Though I believe, and have often argued myself,[70] that subsistence farming was in widespread use throughout much of *Palestine* during the Bronze Age (and especially in the Early Bronze I and the Early Bronze IV-Middle Bronze I transition periods), it was hardly universal at any time. As Hopkins rightly points out: cereals, wine, and oils are cash crops. Minimally, they reflect some agricultural specialization and some regional trade. The "surplus" of subsistence farming, on the other hand, requires neither specialization nor centralization in production or marketing. The diversification and professionalization of agriculture required for the development of such cash crops, have not been developments fostered by centralized political forces such as monarchies alone, howevermuch such complex economic levels of society may have promoted centralizing tendencies in political power, and however much their preexistence may have been a requirement for monarchy to develop. They have, nevertheless always been essential characteristics of any Mediterranean type of economy, as they have always been necessary for any substantial settlement in the less optimal regions of *Palestine*'s hill country. That is, there are *a priori* reasons to suspect that Palestinian highland village agriculture during Iron I was unlikely to have been a form of subsistence agriculture.[71]

Hopkins's assertion that it was taxation that was the major cause of sweeping changes in hill country agriculture during the transition to the monarchy not only makes unsubstantiated assumptions that initial and earliest settlement had been the creation somehow of isolated and independent individuals—an assumption of major proportions given the widespread and relatively rapid nature of such settlement[72]—but also implies that this taxation by the hypothetical early Israelite monarchs was so oppressive and burdensome that survival required a massive transformation of the entire economy throughout the hill country away from subsistence agriculture. That any monarchy had such power ever,

---

E.g., Th.L. Thompson, *op.cit.*, 1979; *idem*, "The Background of the Patriarchs: A Reply to William Dever and Malcolm Clark," *JSOT* 9 (1978), pp.2-43.

[71] Below, in Chapter VI, I discuss some evidence that it in fact was not, and could not have been a form of subsistence agriculture.

[72] Even if we could assume with Coote and Whitelam an almost frenetic fertility rate among villages!

anywhere, is certainly open to dispute. That premonarchic Iron Age *Palestine* was free of taxation is moreover unknown, although any consistent and enforced policy of taxation during the Iron Age is unlikely before the Assyrian period. What we do know is that in the city-state of Ugarit on the North Syrian coast at the end of the Late Bronze Period (and in the eyes of this new sociological school of American Old Testament research, nothing is more oppressive than a Canaanite city-state monarch, or more "Canaanite" than Ugarit!) taxation on crop yield was (by today's standards) a modest 10%,[73] which, while large enough to complain about, was hardly sufficient to create any major economic dislocation. Although the extent of taxation in the kingdoms of Israel and Judah is largely unknown, the system of tithing—a form of taxation set at 10% as well—is known from the much later biblical tradition. Methodologically speaking, this unfortunate effort to develop theoretical reconstructions of early Israelite history on the basis of arbitrary and unfounded assumptions concerning ancient societies and economies, without a concerted effort to build a body of evidence, lends itself far too readily to the creation of imaginary historical scenarios with no more justification than the rhetoric used to sustain them.[74]

While Hopkins's work is marred by unsupported assumptions of sociological generalizations, a yet more recent book by R. Coote and K. Whitelam carries this methodology even further.[75] At first promising, particularly because of its emphasis on the fluidity of shifts in the Palestinian economy between village oriented agriculture and less sedentary pastoralism, it is ultimately a disappointing work, both because

---

[73] B.R. Foster, "Agriculture and accountability in Ancient Mesopotamia," *The Origins of Cities in Dry-Farming Syria and Mesopotamia in the Third Millennium B.C.*, ed. by H. Wiess (Guilford, 1986) p.116; M. Liverani, "Economia delle fattorie palatine ugaritiche," *Dialoghi di Archeologia* 1 (1979), pp.70ff.

[74] J.M. Miller describes this method as the "Ham and Eggs" method of historiography: "If we had some eggs, we could have ham and eggs, if we had some ham." Numerous articles on economics and taxation in the ancient orient have been published over the past twenty years in the *JESHO* series. See also on Ugarit the very important publications of M. Heltzer, esp. his: *The Rural Community in Ancient Ugarit* (Wiesbaden, 1976): and *idem, The Internal Organization of the Kingdom of Ugarit* (Wiesbaden, 1982).

[75] R.B. Coote and K.W. Whitelam, *The Emergence of Israel in Historical Perspective* (Sheffield, 1986); also their article: "The Emergence of Israel: Social Transformation and State Formation Following the Decline in Late Bronze Age Trade," *Social Scientific Criticism of the Hebrew Bible and its Social World: The Israelite Monarchy, Semeia* 37 (1986) pp.107–147.

it neglects the historical contexts for such shifts which are so marked in both the Early Bronze IV-Middle Bronze I and the Iron I transition periods, and because it isolates one aspect of these economic changes as peculiarly causative. I would like to choose two issues which are central to Coote and Whitelam's work that might help to illustrate what I see as substantial problems in accepting their hypothesis that the rise and fall of international trade are an exceptional key to understanding Israel's origins. These remarks are apart from objections to the unargued assumption, which they share with so many, that the beginnings of Israel are somehow reflected in the changes and dislocations of the transition between Late Bronze and Early Iron I in *Palestine.* Nor do these remarks deal with the complex assumption (whose seeming contradiction should at least have given pause) that Israel is both indigenous to *Palestine* and inseparably connected with the fortunes of the new Early Iron Age settlers of the central hill country but not with contemporary developments in the lowland so-called Canaanite population.[76]

A) Coote and Whitelam ask the very difficult but significant question: "Did bedouin exist in *Palestine* prior to the emergence of Israel?"[77] Their answer to this question is largely based on secondary research, particularly on their reading of M.B. Rowton's concept of "enclosed nomadism"[78] as well as on the dissertations of J.T. Luke and V. Matthew on nomadic forms reflected in the Mari texts.[79] Unfortunately, they do not use the much more relevant and intellectually more sophisticated sociological and historical anthropological studies of M. and H. Weippert, N.P. Lemche and E.A. Knauf.[80] This topic of

---

[76] Evidence for the indigenous qualities of the central hill settlers is extensive (see below, *passim*), but rooted in the early, often cited observations of J. Callaway, that the cultural remains of these settlements are not sufficiently distinctive to support an identification of them as a separate ethnic entity: J.A. Callaway, "New Evidence on the Conquest of Ai," *JBL* 87(1968), pp.312-320; *idem*, "Village Subsistence at Ai and Raddana in Iron Age I," *The Answers Lie Below*, ed. by H.O. Thompson (Lanham, 1984) pp.51-66; *idem*, "A New Perspective on the Hill Country Settlement of Canaan in Iron Age I," *Palestine in the Bronze and Iron Ages*, ed. by J.N. Tubb (London, 1985) pp.31-49.

[77] R.B. Coote and K.W. Whitelam, *op.cit,* p.101.

[78] M.B. Rowton, "Enclosed Nomadism," *JESHO* 17 (1974), pp.1-30.

[79] J.T. Luke, *Pastoralism and Politics in the Mari Period,* (University of Michigan dissertation, 1965); V. Matthews, Pastoral Nomadism in the Mari Kingdom (Cambridge, 1978).

[80] M. Weippert, *Edom* (Tübingen dissertation, 1971); N.P. Lemche, *op.cit.,* 1985; *idem*, "Det Revolutionaere Israel. En Praesention af en Moderne Forskningsretning," *Dansk*

nomadism is admittedly difficult, if only because of the extremely limited and fragmented state of the evidence for nomadism in the ancient world. The attempt to see the many forms of Palestinian nomadism as subsumed under such a rubric as "enclosed nomadism" is hardly more helpful than the commonly repeated observation of Luke's that animal husbandry was developed originally from agriculture. We have long had overwhelming evidence of many forms of nomadism in *Palestine* during the Bronze and Early Iron Ages.[81] Not even *Mari* fits this abstract ideal of "enclosed nomadism." The Suteans were hardly such, and the Yaminites only marginally so. It is suspected that the Haneans seem to fit this model only because the content of this abstract concept is drawn from texts referring to the Haneans. Finally, the description of nomads at *Mari* can indeed be used analogously with biblical interpretation (as long ago recommended by Kupper, Klengel, and M. Weippert[82]) insofar

---

Teologisk Tidsskrift 45 (1982), pp.16-39; *idem*, "Israel in the Period of the Judges—The Tribal League in Recent Research," *Studia Theologica* 38 (1984), pp.1-28; E.A. Knauf, *op.cit.,* 1989; *idem*, "Midianites and Ishmaelites" in J.F.A. Sawyer and D.J.A. Clines (eds.) *Midian, Moab, and Edom, JSOTS* 24 (Sheffield, 1983) pp.147-162; *idem, op.cit.,* 1988; H. Weippert, *op.cit.,* 1988.

[81] Coote and Whitelam's interpretation of my understanding of nomadism (R.B. Coote and K.W. Whitelam, *op.cit.,* p.104) is blatant nonsense. What they assert as my understanding is at times a caricature of my published views, and at times a total misrepresentation. There is a radical topographical difference between the Great Syrian Steppe (which impinges directly on the potentially arable Euphrates Valley) and the Palestinian Steppelands (which are separated from the central agricultural regions of Palestine). I thought everyone knew that. This is a very significant reason for assuming that forms of nomadism may be different. There is no single norm for nomadic societies, enclosed or otherwise, and Palestinian culture reflects many such forms that are quite distinct and separate from Palestinian town and village life. I not only do not see Palestinian nomadism as "some ideal absolute," but the only significant point of the one very brief article which Coote and Whitelam cite (Th.L. Thompson, "Historical Notes on Israel's Conquest of Palestine: A Peasants' Rebellion," *JSOT* 7, 1978, pp.20-27) is that there are very many forms of nomadism existing along a spectrum between the absolutely nomadic and the absolutely sedentary, with a variety of interaction. What Coote and Whitelam have partially understood is that I do deny a close analogy between nomadism at Mari and nomadism in Palestine, a position that I set out originally in 1974 (*op.cit.*) and expand with examples and details in 1978. Specific forms of ancient Palestinian nomadism are further suggested in 1975 (Th.L. Thompson, *The Settlement of Sinai and the Negev in the Bronze Age, BTAVO 8*, Wiesbaden, 1975, *passim*), and again in a long article of 1978, (*op.cit.*) as well as in 1979 (*op.cit.,* pp.3ff.).

[82] J.R. Kupper, *Les nomades en Mesopotamie au temps de Mari* (Liege, 1957); H. Klengel, *Benjaminiten und Hanäer zur Zeit der Könige von Mari* (Berlin dissertation, 1958); M.

as it reflects an understanding of pastoral groups in the process of sedentarization, and I see no substantial reason to deny that such sedentarization was an ongoing process among many pastoral groups in the territory of *Mari* in the seventeenth-century B.C. I believe that such an analogy is even more directly relevant to the process of Iron I sedentarization east of the Jordan, a position which I think is in partial agreement with Coote and Whitelam.

B) Central to Coote and Whitelam's understanding of Israel's origins is the idea that initial highland and steppe settlement at the beginning of the Iron Age came as a result of the collapse of Late Bronze Age trade, and that a revival of trade later in Iron I "caught the crest of the trade growth that eventually led to the formation of an Israelite State under David and Solomon."[83] They state the governing principle that "the focus of settlement shifts to the highland or steppeland villages at times of decline or collapse in interregional urban trade, as a means of risk reduction when an agricultural pastoral subsistence economy offers the greatest hope of survival away from the more vulnerable lowlands. The emergence of Israel appears to fit this . . . pattern."[84]

Many things must be said against any such interpretation:

1) It is simply false that "the focus of settlement shifts to the highland or steppeland villages." These regions do have many new sites, but the majority of the population still lives in the lowlands and valleys, and the new sites in the hills are small, initially few, and fragile.

2) It is not obvious that this new settlement comes out of any Late Bronze collapse in trade.[85] Not only is the chronological sequence unsound, but many other factors are also involved, including the role of the Egyptian empire in support of trade, the role of Palestinian city-states, new technologies, and political and economic stability in the hill country.

3) New settlement is not restricted to the highlands and steppe, but is found also on the coastal plain and in the *Jezreel,* dating from the Late Bronze period and extending into the Iron Age.[86]

4) Hill country and steppeland settlement does not occur at one time only, is not simply progressive, and substantially depends on

---

Weippert, *op.cit.,* 1967, pp.106, 110; Th.L. Thompson, *op.cit.,* 1974, pp.87f.

[83] R.B. Coote and K.W. Whitelam, *op.cit.,* p.75.

[84] *Ibidem.*

[85] So also I. Finkelstein, *op.cit.,* 1988.

[86] *Ibid.;* further, below, Chapter VI.

4) Hill country and steppeland settlement does not occur at one time only, is not simply progressive, and substantially depends on interregional trade.[87] As "expansion," the history of new settlement in each region seems to be independent and has its own chronological setting, dated from the Late Bronze Age to well into the Iron II period, suggesting that the correlation of the new settlement with the Late Bronze-Early Iron Age trade collapse is partly coincidental and not entirely causative.

5) Coote and Whitelam choose the Early Bronze IV-Middle Bronze I transition period as an instructive analogue to the collapse of the Late Bronze and the settlement of the hills in Early Iron, as it illustrates their sociologically based generality that settlement patterns shift from the lowlands to the highlands and steppe at times of decline or collapse.[88] However, their analogue fails, because the pattern of settlement after the Early Bronze collapse is substantially different from that of Iron I. The hill and steppe regions of western *Palestine* are strikingly empty of significant settlement during Early Bronze IV-Middle Bronze I. Although Coote and Whitelam are probably quite right in describing the changes of settlement patterns during this period as an indigenous development (and are surely correct that they are not the result of Amorite migration),[89] the settlement patterns are otherwise not really comparable to the Late Bronze-Early Iron changes in their geographical displacement. In contrast to both the Early Bronze and the Middle Bronze II periods, when the Cisjordan hill country hosts a substantial population, the Early Bronze IV-Middle Bronze I period resembles much more the gap in settlement of the Late Bronze period than it does the new settlement of Iron I.[90] Some aspects of the Early Bronze-Middle Bronze transition in Western *Palestine* can be compared to the Middle Bronze IIC-Late Bronze transition which follows the widespread

---

[87] See below, Chapter VI.

[88] R.B. Coote and K.W. Whitelam, *op.cit.*, p.74.

[89] Th.L. Thompson, *op.cit.*, 1974; but not K. Prag, *op.cit.*, 1974; *idem, op.cit.*, 1984.

[90] Compare Th.L. Thompson, "Palästina in der Übergangszeit der Frühbronze-Mittelbronzezeit," *Tübinger Atlas Des vorderen Orients*, map B II 11b (Wiesbaden, 1978) with *idem*, "Palästina in der Frühbronzezeit," *ibid., B II 11a; idem*, "Palästina in der Mittelbronzezeit," ibid., B II 11c (1980); *idem*, Palästina in der Spätbronzezeit," *ibid.*, B II 11d. H. Weippert's comparison of the Late Bronze-Early Iron transition period with Early Bronze IV-Middle Bronze I is much more apt than that offered by Coote and Whitelam; further, see below and in Chapter V.

collapse of Middle Bronze II hill country agriculture. On the other hand, the Early Bronze IV-Middle Bronze I settlements of the *Negev* and the Transjordanian highland settlement are unique to this period. Analogies with other periods of settlement in this region, such as the Chalcolithic or Iron II periods, because they are a part of the larger spectrum of such shifting settlement patterns, are also unhelpful in that they illustrate the variable quality of what are after all discrete historical responses to unique situations of economic stress.

6) Although we lack evidence to distinguish the ethnicity of the highland settlements from contemporary settlements in the lowlands, and undoubtedly we must see the period of the early Iron Age as a significantly indigenous development, we do not have evidence yet[91] that these changes are to be explained exclusively in terms of a transference of population from the lowlands to the highlands. There are some reasons to argue that the origins of the Iron I highland population can not be reduced to any single factor.[92]

7) Coote and Whitelam's assumptions about the differences between the lowland and highland economies are not sound. Such an assertion that "an agricultural pastoral subsistence economy offers the greatest hope of survival away from the more vulnerable lowlands" is unacceptable for several reasons: They nowhere clarify the nature of the vulnerability of the lowland sedentary population, nor do they show that specifically in Early Iron I, the lowlands are particularly in danger, so that the vulnerability of lowland agriculture might be understood as a significant factor in the process of the regional settlement in the highlands. My understanding of the lowland settlements of this period is that most are unfortified,[93] which I believe might be seen as an apparent indication that military danger is not excessive. Furthermore, the lowland economies are also agricultural and pastoral with some regional commitments to horticulture, and in terms of agricultural potential are less vulnerable than the central highlands. The highland economy, during Iron I is hardly to be understood as involving more of a subsistence type of farming than that of the lowlands. The broad geographic spread of many aspects of the material culture of Iron I

---

[91] *Pacem*, Callaway, *opera citata*.

[92] I. Finkelstein, *op.cit.*, 1988; H. Weippert, *op.cit.*, 1988; further below, Chapters VI and VII.

[93] H. Weippert, ibidem.

suggests that, in spite of the relative regionalization of *Palestine* during this period, regional and interregional trade in both the lowlands and the highlands is minimally maintained. The collapse is markedly in the realm of international not regional trade. One would never claim that international trade was responsible for the very existence of lowland settlements, however much it may be seen to contribute to prosperity. The existence of these villages and towns is rather clearly related to the agricultural potential of the regions in which they are found.[94] Trade collapse may have deepened the Iron I economic depression, and it may have hastened the departure from the towns, but this identifies the collapse of international trade as a contributing factor in the dislocations of this period, not its principle cause.

8) Nor can the rapid expansion of the highland population be seen as the direct result of a rise of international trade as Coote and Whitelam have suggested. Such trade is hardly significant until Iron II. The growing population, however, did have a substantial surge late in Iron I which seems to have continued throughout the early part of Iron II. This can be directly associated with the concomitant expansion of horticulture and terracing in the region. That is, it can be associated with regional and interregional trade. International trade is only clearly reestablished in Iron II, as a result both of a prosperous economy and of the centralization of political powers. Coote and Whitelam are fully 150–200 years too early in giving a major role to international trade in hill country economics.

9) The rise of a limited kingship or chieftainship in the region of the central hills, as for example, Miller and Edelman describe,[95] seems possible at the end of Iron I or at the beginning of Iron II. However, such a small political unit as might be posited in the hills of *Ephraim* at this early period seems wholly independent of any expansion of international trade. At least I know of no evidence for any such trade, and Coote and Whitelam's assertion that international trade is the causative factor in the rise of the monarchy remains baffling.

10) Finally, the dramatic rise of population in the hills towards the very end of Iron I and in early Iron II, because of its relationship to horticulture and terracing, requires an assumption of substantial stability in the region. Coote and Whitelam's assumption—shared by many—of

---

[94] Th.L. Thompson, *op.cit.*, 1979.

[95] D. Edelman, *op.cit.*, 1987; J.M. Miller, *op.cit.*, 1977; *idem*, *op.cit.*, 1986.

an intense conflict and open warfare of the Israelites with the Philistines at this early date is an unverified assumption based on the historically anachronistic retrojection of much later biblical traditions.

In the opening chapter of Coote and Whitelam's book, the authors had proposed to write a new form of history of Israel largely independent of biblical traditions, based on historical geography and the patterns of settlement in *Palestine* as reflected in recent developments in Palestinian archaeology.[96] They sought to interpret the data provided by archaeology in order "to throw light on the settlement history, demography, and economic and political relationships."[97] In the actual production of the book, however, the settlement patterns and the historical, economic, and political relationships are assumed at the outset. Archaeology and historical geography are used, when they are used at all, as merely illustrative of sociological, anthropological, and ecological patterns that are drawn largely from outside of *Palestine* and apart from historical evidence.

Coote and Whitelam do not move the discussion of Israel's origin significantly beyond the discussion of Alt's similar descriptions of the radical changes of settlement patterns during the Late Bronze-Early Iron transition. The issue of whether the ultimate origin of the hill country settlers lies apart from *Palestine* is not as great as it at first might appear, since Alt himself had suggested that the original migrational patterns of many of his transhumance pastoralists who settled down during the Iron Age was first established as early as the Middle Bronze-Late Bronze transition, when great areas of the hill country lay empty of permanent settlement. H. Weippert, presenting much the same data that Coote and Whitelam have used as a basis for their book, has offered a synthesis which is both more accurately detailed and more healthily independent of any single all explaining cause. Of particular interest are her discussions of "submycenaean Palestinian" pottery, of the hill country's pillared houses, as well as her clear designation of the whole of Iron I as a transition period between the Late Bronze and Iron II.[98] Coote and Whitelam's suggestion, shared by H. Weippert, Finkelstein, and Esse, that the process of periodic collapse and resettlement was a

---

[96] R.B. Coote and K.W. Whitelam, *op.cit.*, pp.18f.

[97] *Ibidem.*

[98] H. Weippert in a lecture at St. Georgen, Frankfurt on November 16, 1985; see now *idem, op.cit.,* 1988.

recurrent process endemic to the more marginal regions of *Palestine,* is, in spite of an urgent need for refinement, a concept of substantial importance, and must certainly continue to play a future role in discussions of both new settlements and nomadism. It can not, however, serve as the sole explanation of the source of the highland settlers of Iron I and II, and should not be understood as an alternative to other explanations, but rather is to be seen as a structural context for interpreting the specific historical causes of the new Iron I and Iron II ethnic formations throughout *Palestine.*[99] Connections of some of the highland settlements with the established towns of both the hills and the lowlands needs yet to be clearly traced. Moreover, there is sufficiently substantial reason to believe that there was, in addition to the indigenous populations of greater *Palestine,* considerable influx of new population elements into Palestine between the end of Middle Bronze IIC and mid-Iron II: from the Aegean, from *Syria* and *Anatolia,* and from the West Semitic and Arab related groups to the East and to the South of *Palestine.*

In a recent joint article,[100] members of the Madaba Plains Project have focussed on what they describe as "cycles of intensification and abatement in settlement and land use."[101] In such terms, comparisons between the Middle Bronze IIC-Iron II and the Early Bronze II–III-Middle Bronze II transitions can proceed much more clearly and more satisfactorily, as these broader cycles of land use can be viewed analogously. This more complex and comprehensive understanding also supports the similar thesis of S. Richards, which proposes what she refers to as a "systemic perspective of urban collapse, decline, and regeneration" for an understanding of the Early Bronze IV transition at *Khirbet Iskander,*[102] rather than seeing such transitions, as Coote and Whitelam and Finkelstein have, as simple shifts from sedentary agriculture to pastoral nomadism. Such structural arguments allow more complex descriptions of change over time in both transregional and subregional contexts. At Khirbet Iskander, for example, it is not so much

---

[99] See my discussion below in Chapter VII.

[100] L. Geraty *et alii,* "Madaba Plains Project: A Preliminary Report of the 1987 Season at *Tell el-'Umeiri* and Vicinity," *BASOR,* Supplement 26 (1990), pp.59–88.

[101] *Ibid.,* p.59.

[102] S. Richards, "The 1987 Expedition to Khirbet Iskander and its Vicinity: Fourth Preliminary Report," *BASOR* Supplement 26 (1990), pp.33–58; quotation from p.56.

a change in specialization from farming to pastoralism that has occurred,[103] as it is a systemic adaptation to climatic, demographic, technological, and other change.

4. Archaeology and an Independent History of Israel

Alt had pointed to the new field of archaeological exploration and excavation as early as 1925 as the (as yet inadequate) primary source necessary to put the history of Israel's origins onto a sound footing.[104] Recurrently since Alt's paradigmatic study, historians have echoed this frustration, as it has become clearer how enormous and complex was the demand that Alt's thesis made on the field.[105] Finkelstein's English edition and revision of his 1986 work: *The Archaeology of the Israelite Settlement*[106] finally fills this gap with a survey of archaeological remains relevant to Israel's origins which is breathtaking in its scope as well as sound and critical in its argumentation. Finkelstein's book offers a new perspective, which, I believe, radically changes our approach to the field of Israel's origins. We now have a well presented, synthetic account of the archaeological remains of the early Iron Age that opens this period to historical research, wholly independent of the hitherto dominant issues of biblical historiography and historicity. Finkelstein's survey makes it abundantly clear that the conquest theory is dead. Moreover, several footnotes have been added to Lemche's obituary of the "revolt model." Certainly the extent to which Finkelstein's study revises Alt's settlement model will be debated in the reviews.

Of central importance today for research into the issue of Israelite origins, is the question whether the new highland settlements of the Iron Age are in any way related to the lowland, so-called Canaanite, towns. What becomes so refreshingly clear is Finkelstein's perspective, which

---

[103] As W.G. Dever has argued: "New Vistas on the EB IV ('MB I') Horizon in Syria-Palestine," *BASOR* 237 (1980), pp.35–64; *idem* (with R. Cohen), "Preliminary Report of the Third and Final Season of the Central Negev Highlands Project," *BASOR* 243 (1981), pp.57–77.

[104] A. Alt, *op.cit*, 1925.

[105] As early as M. Noth, *Die Ursprünge des alten Israel im Lichte neuer Quellen,* (Cologne, 1961).

[106] I. Finkelstein, *op.cit.,* 1988.

contrasts the remains of hill country settlements with the contemporary
Iron Age settlements of the lowlands, marking each type as reflecting
regionally distinctive economic units, rather than more simplistically and
typically as chronologically successive entities.

While Finkelstein's publication does provide much of the
archaeological data asked for by Alt, and presents it in an easily
accessible form, his work is only indirectly related to Alt's questions and
methods. Finkelstein himself argues for an alternative to Alt's thesis,
taking as his starting point a perspective which was Alt's conclusion;
namely, the hypothesis that the Iron Age settlement of the hill country
was quintessentially Israelite settlement. This very central hypothesis
from Alt's earlier work plays the role of a postulate in Finkelstein's
argument, disarmingly put forward as a necessary procedural assumption,
allowing questions of origin to be asked of the archaeological record
through a perhaps questionable understanding of these new settlements
as a single historical entity in complex flux. For example, Finkelstein's
request that we accept those highland settlements which later become
Israel as in themselves Israelite, in contrast to the cities and towns of the
lowlands, is only acceptable if one already assumes his postulate! Not
only does Finkelstein believe, in contrast, for example, to Ahlström,[107]
that his proto-Israelites are significantly distinct historically from the
contemporary lowlanders or Canaanites, but this (for Finkelstein) very
important contrast becomes tenuous, when one reflects that the *Jezreel*
and much of the coastal plain also later "became" Israelite. Not only can
these and other regions not be excluded from a discussion of the origins
of emerging Israel but a political economic unity embracing both the
central hills and the *Galilee* is difficult to imagine without the *Jezreel*,
and only an assumption which would insist upon the biblical
historiography's necessary ethnic distinction between Israelites and
contemporary Canaanites could exclude the population of the *Jezreel*
from any workable reconstruction of a greater *Israel*, extending beyond
the hills of *Ephraim*. Yet, the new Iron I settlements in this region are
specifically excluded from "Israel" by Finkelstein. Similar, but with even
less logic and consistency, is Finkelstein's distinction between settlements
which are Gibeonite and those which he would see as Israelite in the
traditionally Benjaminite territories. This fundamental principle which
guides Finkelstein's identification of early Israel would become wholly

---

[107] G. Ahlström, *op.cit.*, 1986; *idem*, *op.cit.*, forthcoming.

arbitrary and self contradictory if one were also to argue—as I suspect Finkelstein ultimately does—that those wholly new settlements which became Israel at the inception of the monarchy are the ones which are to be classified as "Israelite settlements" in the "prehistory" of the settlement period—since, as we shall notice below, many large sections of the hill country, which Finkelstein posits as "Israelite," hardly fit this criterion. Moreover, Finkelstein asserts *a priori*, on the apparent basis of unexamined later biblical traditions, that Israel's origins are to be found uniquely in specific clusters of new settlements of the central hills and the *Galilee.* Certainly the patterns of settlement which he does examine are of paramount importance, but we have no reason to claim that either the hill country population, or the new settlers of that region are uniquely to be identified with emerging Israel. In evaluating Finkelstein's study, the issue of the identification of what is to be included under the concept of Israel within any given chronological horizon, becomes most critical, for Finkelstein's own criterion seems wholly arbitrary. One is even driven to question the confidence of Finkelstein's title for his book: *The Archaeology of the Israelite Settlement.* Is he not rather and perhaps better dealing with the archaeology of the early Iron Age settlements of central *Palestine,* leaving for others the question of Israel's origin? What Finkelstein describes of these new settlements, however, might be mistaken as vicariously answering the question of Israel's origins. The circularity of Finkelstein's argument easily escapes the unwary reader.

Finkelstein departs from Alt's hypothesis of transhumance pastoralists in arguing for an indigenous origin of the highland settlers, relating them not so much to the contemporary lowland (or "Canaanite") towns as to a prior highland settlement, which had collapsed in Middle Bronze IIC and had been transformed into a pastoral nomadic population, living in the uplands and the steppe areas integral to them in a relation of symbiosis with the limited Late Bronze sedentary elements of the region. He further presents a carefully argued chronology for the development of the highland settlements in three stages between 1200 and 1000 B.C., directly leading to the "United Monarchy" of Iron II. It might be noted that the nature of his survey data and the inadequacies of pottery chronology mark Finkelstein's three stages as perhaps more uncertain than we would wish. Nevertheless, Finkelstein makes substantial progress here. Finkelstein's study confirms much of Miller's reconstruction and works very well with Soggin's history,[108] as well as with the studies of Lemche, Ahlström, Edelman, and the technical aspects of Borowski's study,[109] and could be synthesized with them profitably with only minor adjustments. It is substantially at odds, however, with Coote and Whitelam's, and Hopkins's work,[110] though Hopkins's development of the techniques of highland agriculture—particularly the issues of "risk spreading" and "risk reduction"—could profit greatly from the concreteness of Finkelstein's "data base," and indeed, Coote and Whitelam deal more with the issues surrounding the collapse of Late Bronze and the rise of the monarchy, taking for granted many of the issues of the settlement process itself. The Miller-Hayes history could be well used to correct Finkelstein's relatively limited efforts at biblical interpretation, and with its greater critical historical ability, would help to overcome the few, yet formidable faults of Finkelstein's excessively biblically oriented historical reconstruction of Israel's beginnings.

Finkelstein's work is above all else a very honest book; that is, he presents a clear and detailed picture of the information and archaeological data on which he bases his interpretations, and he leads the reader through his argument from data to hypothesis to conclusion, with the happy result that—however much any individual might wish to debate the specific steps along the way—his book remains an elemental source book and an ever welcome approach to a very difficult complex of historiographical issues.

As such, Finkelstein's book is a landmark in biblical archaeological research, now finally moving out of the historiographical crisis over the history of Israel's origins which has dominated the field for the past 15 years.[111] His book establishes a firm foundation for all of us to begin building an accurate, detailed, and methodologically sound history of Israel. I believe Finkelstein's work has made it abundantly and unequivocally clear that it is no longer legitimate to write a history of Israel and its origins apart from the archaeological record, even though archaeological surveys and excavations leave us with substantial uncertainties, not the least of which are the difficulties of identifying

---

[108] J.M. Miller and J.H. Hayes, op.cit., 1986; J.A. Soggin, op.cit., 1984.

[109] N.P. Lemche, op.cit., 1985; idem, op.cit., 1988; G. Ahlström, op.cit., 1986, idem, op.cit., forthcoming; D. Edelman, op.cit., 1988; and A. Borowski, op.cit., 1987.

[110] R.B. Coote and G.W. Whitelam, op.cit., 1987; G. Hopkins, op.cit., 1985.

[111] Th.L. Thompson, op.cit., 1987, pp.11-40.

ethnicity, and the even greater uncertainties of a pottery oriented chronology that is founded on a basis more biblical than historical.[112] It is important to stress that this book has demonstrated that we must and can use primary historical evidence in writing a history of Israel. Historical criticism of the bible, as well as anthropology and sociology, are all important to the history of Israel, and broad syntheses of data and interpretive hypotheses are needed. Indeed, an interpretive context for our work is as necessary as ever. However, the nature of the historical discipline as one which is descriptive is demonstrated by Finkelstein's seminal study.[113] Basing himself on some of the most successful work of Israeli, American, and German scholarship,[114] Finkelstein presents a new departure in the study of Israel's earliest origins.

Nevertheless, there are a number of issues of method which cause major concern in a reading of Finkelstein's book. They are issues which

---

[112] I am referring here not only to the general penchant to date specific archaeological strata at major sites on the basis of stories about battles and military campaigns in the deuteronomistic traditions, but also to such problems as the unwarranted use of the Merneptah stele's reference to "Israel," and of the use of the stories of the United Monarchy to date the transitions between Late Bronze and Iron I and between Iron I and Iron II. Only very recently are such mainstays of archaeological chronology as the so-called Solomonic gates of Gezer, Megiddo and Hazor receiving independent critical evaluation.

[113] *Contra* E.A. Knauf, "From History to Interpretation," *The Fabric of History*, ed. by D. Edelman (Sheffield, 1991) pp.26-64.

[114] Esp. Y. Aharoni, *The Settlement of the Israelite Tribes in Upper Galilee* (Hebrew University dissertation, 1957); *idem*, "New Aspects of the Israelite Occupation in the North," ed. by J.A. Sanders, in *Near Eastern Archaeology in the Twentieth Century* (New York, 1970) pp.254-265; J.A. Callaway and R.E. Cooley, "A Salvage Excavation at Raddana in Bireh" *BASOR* 201 (1971), pp.9-19; J.A. Callaway, "Excavating Ai (et-Tell): 1964-1972" *BA* 39 (1976), pp.18-30; *idem*, "Village Subsistence at Ai and Raddana in Iron Age I," *The Answers Lie Below: Essays in Honor of Lawrence Edward Toombs*, ed. by H.O. Thompson (Lanham, 1984) pp.51-66; *idem*, "A New Perspective on the Hill Country Settlement of Canaan in the Iron Age I," *Palestine in the Bronze and Iron Ages: Papers in Honour of Olga Tufnell*, ed. by J.N. Tubb (London, 1985) pp.31-49; M. Kochavi, *Judaea, Samaria, and the Golan Archaeological Survey 1967-1968* (Jerusalem, 1972); V. Fritz and A. Kempinski, *Ergebnisse der Ausgrabungen auf der Hirbet el-Msas (Tel Masos) 1972-1975* (Wiesbaden, 1983); A. Mazar, "Giloh: An Early Israelite Settlement Site Near Jerusalem," *IEJ* 31 (1981), pp.1-36; I. Finkelstein, *'Izbet Sartah An Early Iron Age Site near Rosh Ha'ayin, Israel, BAR* 299 (Jerusalem, 1986); *idem*, "Excavations at Shiloh 1981-1984" *Tel Aviv* 12 (1985), pp.123-180; Z. Gal, "Ramat Issachar" *Tel Aviv* 12 (1985), pp.123-180; *idem, Ramat Issachar* (Tel Aviv, 1980); *idem, The Lower Galilee in the Iron Age* (Tel Aviv University dissertation, 1982).

are also critically at stake in the Hopkins, Ahlström, Coote and Whitelam, and Miller-Hayes histories. Five of them seem to me to be both substantial and pivotal in understanding the history of Israel's origins and will be discussed in greater detail in Chapters 5-7 below. A) The use of the concept of subsistence agriculture as a description of the economy of the early I settlements in the central hills functioned as a domain assumption of both Hopkins's and Coote and Whitelam's work. It also has considerably affected Lemche's and Finkelstein's understanding of the nature of early Israel. B) The "ethnic" identification of the terms "Israelite" and "Canaanite," so common in contemporary scholarship, forms a structural foundation for Finkelstein's work, and needs to be seriously reexamined in the light of the objections raised by G. Ahlström, H. Weippert, and especially N.P. Lemche.[115] C) The far reaching and historiographically very productive development of regional histories, which has played such an important role in Finkelstein's study of the settlement patterns of the central hills, not only needs to be integrated with other historical data, but needs to be applied to the whole of greater *Palestine*. D) The validity of the new benchmark of the "United Monarchy," towards which most scholars since J.A. Soggin have directed their investigations into Israel's origins, and from which most assume today that Israel's history proper can begin in terms of Saul's rise to power in the central hills or of David's consolidation of territories in an effort at centralization, needs to be examined not only in terms of the historicity of the appropriate biblical traditions but in view of its historical warrant and the principle of falsifiability. E) The pivotal and most critical issue of dispute about the autochthonous or indigenous quality of Israel's origins needs further explication in a more comprehensive discussion of the historical and archaeological evidence. Finkelstein's arguments, which trace the origins of the early Iron I highland settlements to a steppeland pastoralism that had its ultimate roots in the displaced population of Middle Bronze IIC, adds substantially to the discussions of Alt, Coote and Whitelam, Esse and H. Weippert. The issue, however, is far from resolved but needs to be integrated both with data from the whole of *Palestine* and with other information relating to the dislocation and transferences of population

---

[115] G. Ahlström, *op.cit.*, 1986; *idem, op.cit.,* forthcoming; H. Weippert, *op.cit.*, 1988; N.P. Lemche, "Who Were the Canaanites?," Lecture at Marquette University, Dec. 5, 1990; *The Canaanites and Their Land* (Sheffield, 1991).

in the region from Middle Bronze IIC to the reestablishment of stability in the course of Iron II.

This review of scholarly literature, I believe, finds an appropriate close with reference to two recent major works in the field: H. Weippert's *Die Archäologie Palästina in vorhellennistischer Zeit*[116] and G. Ahlström's *The Early History of Palestine.*[117] Both works are comprehensive syntheses of the antiquities of *Palestine*, and both present an overview from the Stone Age to the Hellenistic period. Both are clearly and critically written and establish rather formidable standards for historical work in our discipline. Weippert's study offers a surprisingly well condensed summary of most of the sites, excavations and surveys that are significant to the history of *Palestine*. Although hundreds of critical issues are raised throughout, the book is marked by two critical perspectives rarely engaged in books of this magnitude. Weippert recurrently reminds the reader that the concept of *Palestine* as a single coherent region is misleading. Not only does an archaeological understanding of the territory demand constant reference beyond its borders and an awareness that no single archaeological issue is either uniquely or specifically Palestinian, but she also makes it refreshingly clear that *Palestine* itself is profoundly divided into separate and distinct subregions and that within greater *Palestine* we have a number of independent evolutions of material traditions. This is so much the case, that the custom of archaeological discussion that assumes homogenous spectra and direct linear developments of material forms is fundamentally distorting. The second critical perspective that rewards the reader of this work is one that is closely associated; namely, her understanding of chronology. In reading through this study, one becomes painfully aware of the extreme fragility of Syro-Palestinian archaeology's absolute datings—not merely those that are based on an only presumably well anchored Egyptian chronology, but also and particularly those that, linked as they are to a much later, literarily motivated and artificial biblical chronology, have truly very few referents to historical reality at all. The archaeological chronology that is derivative of such thinking provides—by whimsy—little that is of use. Few scholars are as aware of this as is Weippert. It is not so much that she counsels caution when field archaeologists assign destructions to the time of a Deborah or a

---

[116] H. Weippert, *op.cit.,* 1988.

[117] G. Ahlström, *op.cit.,* forthcoming.

David, or when administrative buildings and fortifications are made over to a Solomon. Rather she raises the more serious question as to whether this kind of language and thought belong to the field of archaeology at all. Weippert directs the reader's attention both to the accumulated archaeological data that have been uncovered during the past century, and to the fundamentals of historical interpretation of archaeological remains. It is a rare treat when a book on Palestinian archaeology is written by a good historian.

These two perspectives: geographical regionalism and chronological ambivalence and fragility, are clearly brought together in her discussions of relative chronology. Of particular interest is her treatment of evolutionary developments thought to be contemporary, especially during major periods of transition such as that between Late Bronze and Iron I, or between Iron I and Iron II. Weippert presents a principle for consideration that must ever be a concern to any involved in historical questions that have reference to more than a single subregion within *Palestine*. She refers to this principle as that of the *"Gleichzeitigkeit der Ungleichzeitigen"* (the "contemporaneity of what is not contemporary"). It is a principle based on common sense. At times of rapid change in the heartland, regions at a distance or on the periphery will accept developments and change in technology and material goods at a different pace and hence often in a different evolutionary order than that of the creative center. In *Palestine* this issue is compounded by the existence of multiple creative centers. The implications of this for archaeological theory are serious. For example, the many evolutionary and transregional typological studies of artifacts, pottery, and palaeography, so popular in the late 1960s and in the early 1970s are rendered almost totally dysfunctional,[118] and urges us to attend more intelligently to both the chronological and historical implications of the new directions and interest being taken in regional archaeologies.

Ahlström's *History of Early Palestine,* like Weippert's synthesis, also lays stress on the regional differences within *Palestine*. What distinguishes it from so many of the earlier histories is not simply its regional orientation, but its ability to work historically—when dealing with Israel—apart from biblical historiography. This has given the study the flexibility to entertain historical approaches that are far less dependent on issues of historicity than are, for instance, the works of

---

[118] One must certainly here think of the inscriptions from *Tell Khuweilifeh*.

Coote and Whitelam and Finkelstein. Ahlström clearly demonstrates the potential of a "secular" history. Nevertheless, like most other recent histories, once Ahlström enters the period of the monarchy (whether he is dealing with the "United Monarchy" of David and Solomon, the separate states of *Judah* and *Israel,* or with conflicts with the Philistines and other neighbors) his history becomes more conventional. The issues about historicity and efforts to create a coherent synthesis of extrabiblical literature with biblical narrative increasingly dominate. Although the critical quality of this discussion is consistently high, frequently offering valuable correctives to biblical historiography, the validity of the biblical historiography continues to be the issue that takes central stage. What in the biblical tradition remains plausible and possible after critical reflection consequently finds a substantial place in this history.

Two recent monographs make additional specific contributions to this new direction of historical research. E.A. Knauf, in his study of the Ishmael traditions[119] clearly establishes the rootedness of some of the Genesis Ishmael tradition in the Assyrian period, by identifying the gentilics of this tradition with Arab tribes that existed between the ninth and seventh centuries B.C. Not only does his respect for an *ad quem* dating of the referents of this tradition set his work apart from comparable efforts of the Albright school, but his concentration on the historical context of the tradition referent, without thereby assuming the historicity of the biblical narrative itself, allows for a critical sensitivity to narrative forms that departs wholly from any form of historicism. In a yet more recent study, Knauf argues similarly that the historical referents of the Shem and Ham genealogies of Genesis 10 are geographical and gentilic entities of the ninth to seventh-century Assyrian and Egyptian empires.[120]

In these discussions, Knauf has made the important and necessary shift from the question of historicity to the historiographically more important questions about the context and milieu out of which the stories and their referents derive. This method of analysis promises to be particularly valuable in identifying specific traditions or tradition elements (in either written or oral form) as having their origins in a period prior to and considerably earlier than their contexts in biblical

---

[119] E.A. Knauf, *op.cit.,* 1989.
[120] E.A. Knauf, unpublished lecture read in Heidelberg: June, 1991.

narration. In this, Knauf raises the issue of the historicality of biblical narrative: that delicate and difficult to delineate relationship that texts have to their contexts.[121] Knauf remains within the classical tradition of critical biblical scholarship, and understands Old Testament narrative in a manner not far from that of Van Seters and Garbini,[122] in that he sees it as a form of creative historiography, expressing the ideologies, perspectives and distortions of its writers, and reflecting the historical and political worlds and conflicts of its origins and transmission. With Van Seters and Garbini, Knauf understands the narrative world of the bible as a refraction of a specific and potentially identifiable real world. However, this is neither patent nor implicit from Knauf's analysis, and his argument that it is appropriate to understand the narratives in this manner is not furthered by pointing out the plausibility of such historiography by translating the text in terms of its received context.

The question of whether biblical narrative is in fact historiographical is finally clearly raised by N.P. Lemche in his recent study of the "Canaanites."[123] Lemche was led to this question by his conclusion that the biblical tradition's understanding of "Canaanite" did not refer to any ethnicity of the real world of Israel's past or of any historical-politically defined contemporary entity. Not only does this lead Lemche to question the appropriateness of our use of modern concepts of ethnic groups and nations when attempting to understand the bible, but it has also drawn him to ask whether the bible seeks to view the world of the real past at all or tries to do something altogether different. Although Lemche's understanding of the function of biblical narrative and tradition collection, stressing its character as an ideological refraction of the Persian period is similar to that of Knauf and Garbini,[124] his characterization of the tradition as "story" carries the issues of reference substantially further than a discussion of historiography can. It is not so

---

[121] For a preliminary review of this issue, see Th.L. Thompson, "Text, Context, and Referent in Israelite Historiography," *The Fabric of History*, ed. by D. Edelman (Sheffield, 1991) pp.65–92.

[122] J. Van Seters, *Abraham in History and Tradition* (New Haven, 1975); *idem, In Search of History* (New Haven, 1983); G. Garbini, *op.cit.,*

[123] N.P. Lemche, *op.cit.,* 1991, pp.151ff; also, independently, Th.L. Thompson, "Historiography: Israelite," *ABD*, forthcoming.

[124] One might also refer to an article by B. Lang: "The Yahweh Alone Movement and the Making of Jewish Monotheism," *Monotheism and the Prophetic Minority* (Sheffield, 1983) pp.13–59.

much merely ideological tendentiousness that distinguishes fictional stories and tales from historiography. Historiography is a subgenre of narrative literature, and, even in the ancient world, distinguishes itself from other narrative genres by its intention to give a representation of what was perceived or traditionally held to be the real world of the past. The worlds of biblical traditions are, however, neither those of the real past, nor of its contemporary world's politics and cant. They are rather worlds of story and fragmented tradition past, worlds from which theology and self understanding—with their future orientations—spring. In terms of genre, the biblical traditions are rather origin traditions than historiography. In this, Lemche's deceptively little book offers a major contribution to discussions of biblical genres.

The validity of Alt's program to understand the origins of Israel in terms of a transition from a Canaanite Late Bronze *Palestine* dominated by the lowland city-states, to that of an Israelite nation-state in the Iron I central highlands, as a framework for a history of Israel constructed independently of biblical historiography has been seriously challenged on many fronts. The following chapters will undertake a revision of Alt's paradigm on the basis of which we might be more able to understand the emergence of the people of *Palestine,* its economies, its languages, and its political and economic organizations, leading to the development of an *ethnos* that we might ultimately identify as the historical foundation of the "Israel" of biblical tradition.[125] It is hoped that the foregoing survey of literature, while neither complete nor wholly adequate, has helped to demonstrate what I believe to be the potential which exists in the research of contemporary scholarship to understand the complex historical process by which the Israel we know from the bible acquired a dominant presence in the history of *Palestine.* Scholarship of the past twenty five years[126] has not only grown exponentially; it has also created a basis from which a critical history of Israel can develop independently of biblical scholarship. Recent publications show clearly that a history of Israel's origins can now be written, in a relatively

---

[125] This proposed revision has much in common with the remark of W.G. Dever when he writes: "It is evident that we can recover its (i.e., the Bible's) original use as historical commentary in the oriental world of the first-millennium B.C., only if we can put the text back into its original context. And that is precisely the use that archaeology can make." *Recent Archaeological Discoveries and Biblical Research* (Seattle, 1990) p.11.

[126] Esp. since the publication of M. Weippert, *op.cit.,* 1967.

objective, descriptive manner, once issues relating to the historicity and relevance of later biblical tradition are bracketed. Of the three models for Israel's origins that have traditionally been put forward: conquest, revolt, or peaceful settlement, both the conquest and revolt models[127] seem completely out of place in any descriptive analysis of settlements and settlement patterns of Bronze and Iron Age *Palestine,* and Alt's settlement model needs profound revision.

Our growing ability to reconstruct a detailed history of Israelite origins makes it increasingly necessary to abandon the use of biblical historiography as a viable source of our own history writing. Such reconstructions are without legitimate historical foundation. We must be ready to radically alter and consciously distance ourselves from all presuppositions that have been imposed on us by the biblical account. Such a task will undoubtedly be disorienting and has unforeseeable consequences; for when the foundations of historiography undergo such radical transformation, everything indeed for a time can appear questionable—even (and the implications of this are hardly yet understood) the very chronology of our archaeology that has played such a central role in the present historiographical revolution. Our long range goal of reconstructing a sound and critical history of Israel and of its origins within the context of the historical geography of *Palestine* is not one which will be reached quickly or easily—nor should it be otherwise.

Each of us works with our own questions and within our own complex of issues, and each of us contributes to the greater task—which is that of an entire field of research. No single work will provide us with the answer of Israel's origins or its history; we rather together establish an understanding and a context within which our discipline might write a history of Israel. In this task we are building a foundation for a new history of Israel. In the work of establishing a vast factual base upon

---

[127] The conquest model can no longer be supported for the following reasons: many sites were not occupied at the end of the Late Bronze Age; many Late Bronze sites were abandoned towards the end of the period, but not destroyed; many Late Bronze sites continued during Iron I, and those Late Bronze sites that did show destruction were either subsequently unoccupied for a long period after the destruction or were immediately reoccupied by the same population. For a critique of the revolt model, N.P. Lemche, *op.cit.,* 1985, and above, Chapter 2. Finkelstein's interpretation is wholly incompatible with the revolt model as he does not allow for any substantial direct connection between the new Iron I highland settlement and the lowland populations—a relationship that is essential to Mendenhall and Gottwald's theories.

which our work might proceed confidently, the task of interpreting such data accurately is of immense importance. The works which have been reviewed above have all offered major and significant contributions which will occupy us for some years to come.

In such an environment, whether one of us is correct or mistaken on any given issue is only briefly of importance. What we are building is a comprehensive alternative view of ancient Israel, wherein not only our interpretation but also the object of our interpretation must be established and given foundation, and this in a context in which the presuppositions of our research are themselves collapsing. Some of us will bring new data to our research; others present new interpretive hypotheses; yet others will challenge the presuppositions upon which the whole has been constructed. In the process, much humility will be learned. Our field is no longer in crisis and can remain productive as long as the revolution it is now undergoing is kept clearly in mind.

CHAPTER FIVE

THE ORIGINS OF THE POPULATION AND SETTLEMENTS OF THE WEST SEMITES OF GREATER PALESTINE

1. *The Origin of the Semites in the "Green Sahara"*[1]

Thanks to Old Kingdom texts from the south of our region and those of *Ebla* from the North, we have little doubt that a West Semitic population was firmly established in *Palestine* and in the whole of the South Levant since at least the late Early Bronze period. Continuities of the material culture and settlement patterns throughout the early third-millennium are particularly instructive, and suggest the probability that the origins of this population as a whole must certainly have extended minimally from the beginning of the Early Bronze II period, and possibly even as early as the Late Chalcolithic.[2]

Certainly, it seems increasingly difficult to clearly define a break in the cultural continuity of the Palestinian population as a whole prior to the gaps in the archaeological records from the late fifth and fourth millennia (absolute chronology: ca. 4500–3500 B.C.), and even then it seems somewhat arbitrary to argue for a massive incursion of a completely new population and a displacement of the indigenous neolithic agriculturalists and shepherds, when more conservative interpretations are open to us.[3]

---

[1] The following is highly speculative. A detailed study of the large body of relevant data and literature is urgently needed. It is hoped that this brief review, sketched here in the form of an introduction to the historical question of Israel's origins, will provoke just such a study.

[2] Continuities in material culture and in settlement at individual sites, let alone historical continuities, are notoriously difficult to establish prior to the Early Bronze Age because of the fragmented nature of archaeological remains from these early periods. Nevertheless, the comprehensive discussions of P.R. Miroschedji (*l'Epoque pre-urbaine en Palestine, CRB*, Paris, 1971) and most recently of H. Weippert (*Die Archäologie Palästina in vorhel-lenistischer Zeit*, Munich, 1988) summarize well current understanding.

[3] Part of this difficulty certainly derives from the atmosphere of general disfavor that "nomadic invasion" theories find themselves increasingly subject to in interpretive models in prehistoric reconstructions. See my brief discussion of this in the review of Miroschedji:

Recent studies in comparative linguistics, together with our increasing knowledge of the history of Quaternary climatic changes, suggest significant alterations in our understanding of the changes and fluctuations of the population of *Syria-Palestine* from what was commonly held 30 years ago as, for example by S. Moscati who supported the long held view that the Proto-Semites formed a unified people, indigenous to *Arabia*, who had, in successive migrations, moved from the desert to the periphery, forming the semitic cultures of *Mesopotamia, Syria,* and *Palestine* of the fertile crescent with their languages over time.[4] By 1969, however, Moscati expressed serious doubts that the Arabic verbal structure was indeed archaic and recognized that this observation undermined his assumptions of Proto-Semitic as closer to Arabic than for example Accadian, Ugaritic and Old South Arabian.[5] O. Rössler's earlier theories attacking the independence of the Semitic languages on the basis of affinities recognized between the Accadian and Berber languages,[6] gained much support during the 1960s, most importantly in the classificatory study of I.M. Diakonoff[7] that opened the way for comparative linguistic studies of Semitic with the so-called Hamitic branches of the Afro-Asiatic language family; namely, Egyptian-Coptic, Berber-Lybian, Cushite, and Chad. This encouraged the study of the antecedents of the historically later Semitic languages in the context of a history of the whole of what is understood as the Afro-Asiatic linguistic family.[8] The essential lexicographical basis for these comparative studies was firmly established in the pivotal studies of P. Fronzaroli in the late 1960s, in which he worked out in convincing detail a history of Semitic isoglosses.[9] In an even earlier study, Fronzaroli had

---

ZDPV 90 (1974), pp.60f.

[4] S. Moscati, *The Semites in Ancient History* (Cardiff, 1959) pp.28-36.

[5] S. Moscati *et alii, An Introduction to the Comparative Grammar of the Semitic Languages* (Wiesbaden, 1969) p.16.

[6] O.Rössler, "Verbalbau und Verbalflexion in den semitohamitischen Sprachen," *ZDMG* 100 (1950), pp.461-514; *idem* "Der semitische Charakter der lybischen Sprache," *ZA* 50 (1952), pp.121-150; *idem,* "Ghain im Ugaritischem," *ZA* 54 (1961), pp.158-172; *idem,* "Eine bisher unbekannte Tempusform im Althebräischen," *ZDMG* 111 (1961), pp.445-451; also S. Moscati, *op.cit.,* 1969, pp.16f.

[7] I.M. Diakonoff, *Semito-Hamitic Languages* (Moscow, 1965).

[8] Paraphrasing I.M. Diakonoff, *ibid,* p.105.

[9] P. Fronzaroli, "Studi sul lessico commune semitico" I-VI, *Academia Nazionale dei Lincei, Rendiconti della classe di scienze morali, Storiche e Filologiche,* Series 8, vols. 19-20.

already argued on the basis of prehistoric archaeology that the homeland of the Semites had been not the Arabian desert but the agricultural heartland of *Syria-Palestine* itself.[10] Using the Semitic "protolexikon" established by Fronzaroli as a point of departure, Tyloch (while not accepting Fronzaroli's theory of Syro-Palestinian origins) strongly confirmed his understanding of the origin of the Semites as "a sedentary people to whom agriculture was well known."[11] One of the main strengths of this new direction in comparative linguistics was its historical orientation and its recognition of the necessity of linking linguistic theory to the archaeological records in terms of ethno-archaeological history.[12]

Because of the ties of this new perspective in historical linguistics to archaeology and the specific historical languages of the comparison, it was able to understand Proto-Semitic (and proto-Afroasiatic as well) as involving an historical rather than a purely theoretical concept. Burney underlined the necessity of recognizing an overlapping but nevertheless independent development and spread of genetic, linguistic, and material cultural aspects of the population,[13] and Fronzaroli stressed that proto-Semitic must indeed be understood as an historical language. It existed,

---

23. 24 (1964-1969).

[10] P. Fronzaroli, "Le origini dei Semiti come Problema Storico," *Accademia Nazionale dei Lincei Rendiconti della Classe di scienze Morali, Storiche e Filologiche* 15 (1960) pp.123-144; also, O. Rössler, "Das Ägyptische als semitische Sprache," *Christentum am Roten Meer*, ed. by F. Altheim and R. Stiehl (Berlin, 1971) pp.263-326, and W. Tyloch, "The Evidence of the Proto-Lexikon for the Cultural Background of the Semitic Peoples," *Hamito-Semitica*, ed by J. and T. Bynon (The Hague, 1975) p.55. Some of the implications of this shift of orientation to Palestine as the matrix of the Semitic diffusion for biblical studies have been drawn out by E.A. Knauf's *Midian, ADPV* (Wiesbaden, 1988) and *idem, Ismael, ADPV*, 2nd. ed. (Wiesbaden, 1989).

[11] W. Tyloch, *op.cit.*, pp.59f. This understanding of agriculture in the protolexikon includes the wholly sedentary forms of horticulture and viniculture as well as some of the less sedentary forms of grain agriculture and animal husbandry.

[12] Already by G. Widengren in his review of S. Moscati, *Le antiche Divinita Semitiche* (1958), in *JSS* 5 (1960), pp.397-410, and very strongly argued by C.B.M. Burney, "The Archaeological Context of the Hamitic Languages in N. Africa," *Hamito Semitica*, pp.495-506; B.J. Isserlin, "Some Aspects of the Present State of Hamito-Semitic Studies," *ibid.*, pp.479-485, as well as by P. Fronzaroli, *ibid.*, pp.50f.

[13] C.B.M. Burney, *op.cit.*, p.495.

and needs to be understood as a linguistically differentiating continuum prior to the separation of Accadian.[14]

In 1981, basing himself on the proto-lexikon of Fronzaroli, Diakonoff attempted a schematic history of the origin of the Semitic languages out of proto-Afroasiatic in migrations from North *Africa* between the sixth and fourth millennia consequent upon the desiccation of the *Sahara*.[15] The original dissolution of the Afroasiatic dialects into families Diakonoff places between the ninth–seventh millennia prior to the expansion of the North African dunes.[16] In the mid 1980s, P. Behrens suggested a major correction of Diakonoff's reconstruction, arguing against his placing the origin of the Afroasiatic languages in the "Green *Sahara*," recommending rather the *Kordofan-Darfur* region of the *Sudan* at some time prior to 6000 B.C., when he suggests the Berber language moved into the *Sahara* before the expansion of the desert closed North *Africa* from the "proto-Berber" languages of the Southeast.[17] Behren's correction of Diakonoff is particularly attractive as it resolves the problem of isolated Berber languages both North and South of the *Sahara*. It is, however, dependent upon the accuracy of the reconstruction of the progress of the *Sahara*'s desiccation and does not seem to offer as adequate an understanding of the development of the other Afro-Asiatic languages in the North.

In the early stages of the post glacial Holocene (ca. 9000–7000/6500 B.C.), global sea levels rose considerably and a warmer and wetter climate with longer winters and summer monsoon rains pertained generally.[18]

---

[14] P. Fronzaroli, *op.cit.*, pp. 50f.

[15] I.M. Diakonoff, "Earliest Semites in Asia," *Altorientalische Forschungen* 8 (1981), pp.23–74.

[16] *Ibid.*, pp.27f.

[17] P. Behrens, "Wanderbewegungen und Sprache der frühen Saharanischen Viehzüchter," *Sprache und Geschichte in Afrika* 6 (1984-1985), pp.135-216, esp. p.208.

[18] A wholly satisfactory synthesis of climatological conditions during the holocene is still problematic, and only the most general understanding is offered here: E. Galili and M. Weinstein-Evron, "Pre-History and Palaeoenvironments of Submerged Sites along the Carmel Coast of Israel," *Paléorient* 11 (1985), pp.37-52, here pp.49-51; D.O. Henry, "The Pre-History and Paléoenvironments of Jordan; An Overview," *Paléorient* 12 (1986), pp.5-26, esp. p.20; A. Horowitz, *The Quaternary of Israel* (New York, 1979) pp.343f.; A.D. Crown, "Toward a Reconstruction of the Climate of Palestine 8000 B.C.-0 B.C.," *JNES* 31 (1972), pp.312-330, esp. pp.320f. 329; H.H. Lamb, "Reconstruction of the Course of Postglacial Climate over the World," *Climatic Change in Later Pre-History*, ed. by A.F. Harding (Edinburgh, 1982) pp.11-32, esp. p.27-30; and from a quite different perspective: B.

During the seventh-millennium B.C., the temperatures continued to rise, but the climate grew gradually drier. Archaeologically, this corresponds with the agricultural sedentarization of the North African neolithic and the pre-pottery neolithic B of *Palestine (Jericho)* and *Jordan (Beidha)*. Around 6000 B.C. or shortly before, a regression of the seas and an extremely dry period set in, extending into the early fourth-millennium[19] and lasting perhaps as late as 3500 B.C., with the height of the drought being reached around 4000 B.C. In North *Africa* this drought brought about the gradual desiccation of the *Sahara* and the expansion of sand dunes across the entire region and particularly into the Lybian desert, cutting off and isolating the proto-Egyptians in the East from the Berber dialects in the far West. It must have been during this long period of drought of 6000–4000 B.C. (following Diakonoff),[20] that the cross cultural transfer of the Afrosemitic languages occurred, with migrations Eastward into *Egypt* and northwards into *Syria-Palestine.*[21] How early this transfer began is uncertain. The gradual movement of Semitic peoples into *Syria-Palestine* may be understood to have begun anytime in the course of the drought, and might be considered to have lasted throughout this period, though in the early centuries of the drought movement across the Egyptian Delta (at this time a region of marshland and lakes) seems unlikely for shepherds and farmers. A route across the *Nile* and up the *Wadi Hamamat* is far more plausible if one sets the transference early. A late date, closer to 4000 B.C. is particularly appropriate for explaining the isolation of proto-Egyptian, because the lowering of the water table in the Delta and the lessening of the *Nile*

Brentjes, "Zu den Ursachen der Herausbildung zu Domestikation in Vorderasien," *Paléorient* 1 (1973), pp.207-211, and W. Nützel, "The Climatic Changes of Mesopotamia and Bordering Areas ca 14000-2000 B.C.," *Sumer* 32 (1976), pp.11-24. On the fluctuations of Sea Levels, see especially: A. Ronen, "Late Quaternary Sea Levels inferred from Coastal Stratigraphy and Archaeology in Israel," *Quaternary Coastlines and Marine Archaeology*, ed. by P.M. Masters and N.C. Flemming (London, 1983) pp.121-134; Y. Sneh and M. Klein, "Holocene Sea Level Changes at the Coast of Dor" *Science* 226 (1984), pp.831f., and the early article of N.C. Flemming, "Mediterranean Sea-Level Changes," *Science* (1968), pp.51-55.

[19] A. Horowitz, E. Galili, W. Nützel, A.D. Crown, H.H. Lamb: *opera citata*; H.A. McClure, *The Arabian Peninsula and Prehistoric Populations* (Miami, 1971); C.K. Pearse, "Grazing in the Middle East," *Journal of Range Management* 24,1 (1966), pp.13-16; A.M. Khazanov, *Nomads and the Outside World* (Cambridge, 1983) esp. pp.90-95.

[20] I.M. Diakonoff, *op.cit.*, 1981.

[21] *Ibid.*; B. Brentjes, *op.cit.*, p.208.

floods at the height of the drought would have opened up large areas of the Delta and the *Nile* Valley to agriculture,[22] while at the same time *Egypt* would have grown more isolated from the West because of the growth of the Lybian sand dunes (optimal growth: ca. 4000 B.C.). The corresponding desiccation of the *Negev, Sinai* and Eastern desert of *Egypt* would also likely have broken sustained contact with Afro-Asiatic groups into *Syria-Palestine,* allowing the development of the Egyptian language independent from Semitic, now (5000–4000 B.C.) geographically located in *Syria-Palestine.*[23] It must also have been during this period (the height of the period of extreme aridity: ca. 4000 B.C.) that West Semitic separated from the North Central Semitic dialects which moved into *Mesopotamia,* coming into contact with Sumerian during the course of the fourth-millennium. The following subpluvial phase in *Syria-Palestine* lasting from 3500 to approximately 2350 B.C. (developing the intensive agriculture of the Early Bronze Age) also led, in the course of the intense sedentarization of the region, to the linguistic isolation and individualization of the early North Central Semitic dialects that we find in our late third and second millennia texts.[24] This process of language change in *Palestine* and *Syria* during the Late Neolithic and early Chalcolithic periods should probably not be understood either in terms of any massive invasion or of a dislocation of the indigenous population. By the Neolithic period the genetic mix in *Palestine* is already complex, and no known significant change is introduced during this transition to the Chalcolithic period. Moreover the level of material cultural existence of the indigenous population with villages and towns of considerable size and a social structure far surpassing anything that might be expected in

---

[22] For a similar phenomenon occurring in lower Mesopotamia, H.J. Nissen, *The Early History of the Ancient Near East* (Chicago, 1988) pp.55f.

[23] The frequently noticed West Semitic influence in early Egyptian (Th.L. Thompson, *The Historicity of the Patriarchal Narratives,* Berlin, 1974) should perhaps best be understood in the context of a return of Semites across the Negev and Sinai during the subpluvial Chalcolithic-Early Bronze occupation of the Sinai, when many areas were amenable to grazing and some dry agriculture, rather than to the period of the sixth and fifth millennia at the time of the Afroasiatic linguistic dissimulation. Evidence for this can be drawn from the archaeological surveys of the Sinai which indicate a considerable semi-sedentary population in the Sinai from the Chalcolithic-Early Bronze I and the Early Bronze II Periods (For a summary review of these surveys, Th.L. Thompson, *The Settlement of the Sinai and the Negev in the Bronze Age, BTAVO* 8, Wiesbaden, 1975, *passim.*

[24] Most notably Eblaite, Amorite, and Ugaritic.

Africa, makes it very difficult to view *Syria-Palestine* as vulnerable to what must have been the very small number of Semitic agriculturalists and shepherds who moved into the region from North *Africa* in the course of these two millennia. Rather, the indigenous population remained; the change was linguistic and gradual. In a process of acculturation and as a result of sedentarization and integration (perhaps after the dissimilation of Accadian eastwards into *Mesopotamia),* Proto-West Semitic became first a second language and—with the intensification of sedentarization in the Late Chalcolithic and Early Bronze Ages[25]—developed into the dominant, and eventually exclusive, dialects of the indigenous populations of *Syria* and *Palestine,* at a time considerably earlier than *Ebla.*

2. *The Early Bronze Age and the Development of a Mediterranean Economy*

However speculative such reconstructions may be, they clearly suggest that the indigenous population of Palestine has not substantially changed since the neolithic period. In the course of the sixth- to fourth-millennium B.C., it became Semitic (linguistically understood) and, during the course of the Early Bronze Age established a pattern of settlement and economy[26] that was characteristic of the region until at least the Assyrian period.

The basic pattern of Palestinian agriculture, involving forms of grain agriculture, horticulture, viniculture and animal husbandry was established during the Late Chalcolithic and expanded during the Early Bronze Age, when the extent of the regional expansion of agriculture reached a degree unsurpassed before the Iron Age II period. Supporting this expanse of agricultural regional displacement, considerable rise in population, and intensification of sedentarization characterizing the Mediterranean mode of agriculture, was a significant climatic change in the region beginning as early as 3500 B.C. and lasting until approximately 2350 B.C., during which extended period considerably higher rainfalls and

---

[25] Th.L. Thompson, *The Settlement of Palestine in the Bronze Age, BTAVO* 34 (Wiesbaden, 1979); P. Miroschedji, *op.cit.*; H. Weippert, *op.cit.*

[26] Th.L. Thompson, *ibid.,* p.64.

cooler temperatures pertained throughout most of our region.[27] In the
early part of this agriculturally optimal period, the sea level and water
table continued to fall,[28] large areas of swamp and marshland dried up
and opened rich usable fields to agriculture for the first time.[29] The
opening of the *Beisan* area and the north central *Jordan* Valley to
agriculture, with the subsidence of Lake *Beisan* to the present contours
of the Sea of *Galilee* and the drying up of the marshlands of the
Chalcolithic period, permitted the development of a region that was
perhaps, through most of the Bronze Age, one of the most densely
occupied regions of *Palestine*.[30] Concurrently, a considerable extent of
marsh must have closed to agriculture much of the lower *Jezreel* and the
low lying coastal plain East of the sand dunes prior to the fourth-
millennium, which gradually became available to agriculture only in the
course of the Chalcolithic period.[31] The Chalcolithic and Early Bronze
agricultural expansion also brought about substantial deforestation as
large areas were opened to olive production and other forms of
horticulture and viniculture.[32]

This period of agricultural stability and expansion, which with its
intensive sedentarization had undoubtedly established some regional
diversification in the early West Semitic languages and had also led to
the establishment of some considerable political structures, has led many

---

[27] B. Brentjes, *op.cit.*, p.208; E. Galili and M. Weinstein-Evron, *op.cit*, pp.49; V.M. Fargo
and K.G. O'Connell, "Four Seasons of Excavation at Tell el Hesi," *BA* 41 (1978),
pp.165-182, esp. p.180; A.D. Crown, *op.cit.*, pp.321 ff; J.L. Bintliff, "Climatic Change,
Archaeology, and Quaternary Science in the Eastern Mediterranean Region," in A.F.
Harding, *op.cit.*, p.147; K.W. Butzer "Environment and Human Ecology in Egypt during
Predynastic and Early Dynastic Times," *Bulletin de la Société de Géographie d'Égypte* 32
(1959), p.65; P. Behrens, *op.cit.*, p.148.

[28] E. Galili and M. Weinstein-Evron, *ibid.*, pp.49-51, M. Inbar and D. Sivan, "Paleo-Urban
Development of the Quaternary Environmental Changes in the Akko Area," *Paléorient* 9
(1983), pp.85-91, esp. pp.89f.

[29] F.L. Kaucky and R.H. Smith, "Lake Beisan and the Prehistoric Settlement of the
Northern Jordan Valley," *Paléorient* 12 (1986), pp.27-36, esp. pp.32f.

[30] Th.L. Thompson, *op.cit.*, 1979, pp.25-29.

[31] For a brief discussion of the relationship of potential Early Bronze settlement of these
lowlands to problems of drainage, *ibid*, pp.33f. and pp.57-60.

[32] U. Baruch, "The Late Holocene Vegetational History of the Kinneret," *Paléorient* 12
(1986), pp.37-48; A. Horowitz, "Preliminary Polynological Indications as to the Climate of
Israel during the last 6000 Years," *Paléorient* 2 (1974), pp.407-414; *idem, The Quaternary
of Israel* (New York, 1979) p.343.

scholars to speak of an "urbanization" of *Palestine* during the Early Bronze Period. While such an understanding might well fit some of the larger sites of *Syria* (above all *Tell Mardikh-Ebla*) the lack of clear regional hegemony, the primary orientation of even the very largest settlements towards agriculture, the absence of considerable luxury goods and of writing—that mainstay of city bureaucracy—make it difficult to assume that any of the larger towns (and some were considerable) had achieved any greater complexity than that necessary for regional trade, mutual defense and the maintenance of cult. Whether one ought to speak in terms of petty kingships, chieftainships or more simply headmen is perhaps, lacking texts, a moot point.[33] C.S. Steele has argued for a form of paramount chieftainship as a framework for understanding the integration of regional settlements in *Palestine* in terms of core periphery relationships. Much of her argument seems important to an understanding of Early Bronze *Palestine,* however much it may seem necessary to reject the relatively small amount of trade (with *Egypt* and its concomitant political ties) as critical to the Palestinian economy.[34] One need not go outside of *Palestine* and *Syria* to explain either the prosperity or the complexity of *Palestine*'s thoroughly agricultural population at this time. Specialized trades, cash crops (above all horticulture and herding, but also grains), luxury goods, (above all metals), regional and interregional trade (an important aspect of any complex Mediterranean agriculture), in addition to a small priestly, political and perhaps military "elite," existed and can easily be understood to have maintained themselves substantially in terms of the inner economy and society of *Palestine.* International trade existed and it introduced some wealth and some foreign influences, but these were marginal to the survival and maintenance of what was an indigenous economy.

Similarly, we do not need to look to a breakdown in international trade to explain the collapse of prosperity during the last third of the third-millennium. Understanding *Palestine* as a land bridge between *Egypt in the South* and *Syria-Anatolia* to the North and *Mesopotamia* to the Northeast may be significant in understanding the value *Palestine* had for other states of other regions—though during the Bronze Age it

---

[33] C.S. Steele, *Early Bronze Age Socio-political Organization in Southwestern Jordan* (MA Thesis, State University of New York,1983) esp. pp.99-107.

[34] *Ibid.*, pp.101f.

was hardly ever anything more than a land bridge. This geopolitically strategic location had little positive effect on *Palestine*'s economy that had ever been almost entirely self sufficient and was largely unaffected by the international trade that passed through its borders. It is hardly believable that the breakdowns of international trade both at the end of the Early Bronze and at the end of the Late Bronze periods could have of themselves brought about significant and widespread deleterious effects on the Palestinian economy as to create wholesale dislocations throughout the region, and especially in so many subregions (such as the hill country and the Northern *Negev*) that were both far from and only marginally affected by the trade routes at the height of their activity. *Palestine* has never been seriously integrated into the "higher" literate civilizations of *Mesopotamia, Egypt* or even *Syria*. The collapse of the Early Bronze prosperity in *Palestine* during the late third-millennium, introducing the Early Bronze IV-Middle Bronze I transition period was not brought about by an international monetary and trade depression, somehow created by the political chaos of *Egypt*'s First Intermediate Period, any more than it was caused by recurrent invasions and pillaging of nomadic Amorites.[35] Rather, as the Early Bronze prosperity was based in an indigenous agricultural prosperity, one marked by an intensification of sedentarization throughout the Mediterranean farming zones in a "trimorphic" pursuit of intensive and grain agriculture, animal husbandry and especially a major expansion of horticulture, so the great depression of Early Bronze IV needs also to be seen as the result of an internal and agricultural recession[36] that the population of *Palestine* survived only through a widespread and extensive transformation that shifted the population away from the more sedentary modes of the Mediterranean economy. This was most thorough in the marginal periphery and in ecologically fragile subregions such as the Judaean hills, the *Arad* basin, and the southern coastal plain, where the dislocation of the agricultural population was nearly total.[37] The roots of the disaster that overcame the Early Bronze Age in *Palestine* lie within the period itself, in its large towns and villages and its prolific population. The

---

[35] Th.L.Thompson, *op.cit.*, 1974, pp.118-177.

[36] Th.L. Thompson, "The Background of the Patriarchs: A Reply to William Dever and Malcolm Clark," *JSOT* 9 (1978), pp.2-43, esp. pp.26-28; *idem*, "Palestinian Pastoralism and Israel's Origins," *SJOT* 6 (1992), pp.1-13.

[37] Further see below, Chapter VII.

prosperity of Early Bronze II is not just a counterpoint to the poverty of Early Bronze IV-Middle Bronze I it is perhaps one of its ultimate causes.[38]

3. *The Early Bronze IV-Middle Bronze I Transition and Desedentarization*

In ca. 2400–2350 the Chalcolithic and Early Bronze subpluvial climatic phase abruptly came to an end and was succeeded by an excessively hot arid period of drought that lasted until about 1950 B.C. The shorter winters and longer, hotter summers, the lowering of the water table, the reduction of rainfall, and—in *Egypt*—the recurrent insufficiency of the *Nile* floods brought about an agricultural collapse of disastrous proportions, comparable to but much shorter than that of the fifth-millennium.[39]

During this drought the agricultural population of the lowland plains and valleys fell sharply.[40] The manner in which the population adjusted to the climatic changes differed markedly from region to region. The major towns of water rich *Syria* and *Lebanon* remain stable throughout this period. On the fringes of the agricultural zones of *Syria*, and especially into the Syrian steppe, there seems to be an increase in herding with an admixture of some grain agriculture, especially in the better climate zones of the uplands such as *Jabal Bishri*. A variety of Mesopotamian cuneiform documents suggest some gradual movement from this region eastwards and partial immigration of West Semites into North Mesopotamia and even further into the South.[41]

---

[38] Quoting with minor change Th.L. Thompson, *op.cit.*, 1978, p.26.

[39] W. Nützel, "The Climatic Changes of Mesopotamia and Border Areas 14000-2000 B.C.," *Sumer* 32 (1976), p.21; H. Ritter-Kaplan, "The Impact of Drought on Third Millennium BCE Culture on the Basis of Excavations in the Tel Aviv Exhibition Grounds," *EI* 17 (1983), pp.333-338; B. Bell, "The Dark Ages in Ancient History I: The First Dark Age in Egypt," *JNES* 75 (1971), pp.1-26, esp. p.24; A.D. Crown, *op.cit.*, 1971, esp. pp.321-324; D. Neer and K.O. Emery, *The Dead Sea Depositional Processes and Environments of Evaporites* (Jerusalem, 1967); K.W. Butzer, *op.cit.*, 1959, esp. pp.70f.; A.F. Harding, "Introduction: Climatic Change and Archaeology," in *Climatic Change in Later Pre-History*, ed. by A.F. Harding (Edinburgh, 1982) pp.1-10, esp. p.9; M. Magny, "Atlantic and Sub-Boreal: Dampness and Dryness" in *ibid.*, esp. pp.34-47; I. Shennan, "Problems of Correlating Flandrian Sea Level Changes and Climate," in *ibid.*, p.52.

[40] R. Gophna and M. Broshee, *op.cit.*

[41] Th.L. Thompson, *op.cit.*, 1974., pp.67-78.

In *Palestine,* the population of most of the major towns of the lowland valleys survived, but most of these settlements are noticeably limited to the areas along the flood plains of the major wadis and rivers (as in such areas of abundant water resources as the *Beth Shan* and northern *Jordan* valleys) and their size is substantially reduced.[42] This form of settlement dispersion is found primarily in the central and northern coastal plain, the *Jezreel,* and the *Jordan* Valley. In the central hills, the impact on sedentary agriculture is even more marked. In the hills of *Samaria* and the *Wadi Fari'a,* most settlements seem restricted to areas where there are permanent water resources. Moreover many of the Early Bronze locations in the western, more horticultural areas of the central hills are abandoned. This agrees well with the notable collapse of olive horticulture around the *Galilee* at this time noted by Baruch,[43] and Horowitz.[44] The agricultural areas in the central and Eastern zones are maintained, perhaps indicating an inability to maintain horticulture and a greater emphasis on grains and herding. In the climatic fringe areas of the hill country—and most noticeably in *Judah*—most permanent sedentary agriculture seems to have been abandoned, as also seems to have occurred along the southern coast of the Mediterranean and in the *Beersheva* and *Arad* Basins. Unlike this fringe area of South *Palestine,* which in the Early Bronze Age had provided a solid support of grazing to the farmers of the region, but which was now given up to the steppe and desert, much of the northern slopes of the central *Negev* during Early Bronze IV-Middle Bronze I was given over to transhumance grazing and some more permanent agriculture.[45] The situation in the *Transjordan* is comparable with most of the agricultural sites that survived the drought having been found

---

[42] An adequate comprehensive view of the history and settlement of this period still does not exist. One might use K. Prag's comprehensive article of 1974 with some profit ("The Intermediate Early Bronze-Middle bronze Age: An Interpretation of the Evidence from Transjordan, Syria and Lebanon," *Levant* 6, 1974, pp.69-116). The reader might be referred to the articles of S. Richards ("The Early Bronze Age: The Rise and Collapse of Urbanism," *BA,* 1987, pp.22-43) and of W.G. Dever ("From the End of the Early Bronze Age to the Beginning of the Middle Bronze Age," *Biblical Archaeology Today,* ed. by J. Aviram, Jerusalem, 1985, pp.113-35) for recent bibliography. The 1988 ASOR lectures of S. Richards, I. Finkelstein and G. Palumbo fairly represent current evaluation of the period.

[43] U. Baruch, *op.cit.,* p.45.

[44] A. Horowitz, *op.cit.,* 1974, esp. pp.407-411.

[45] Th.L. Thompson, *op.cit.,* 1975.

along the fringe, the steppe and desert to the East and away from the rugged more horticultural amenable regions of the West, suggesting that there was a substantial but nevertheless partial agricultural collapse that forced the settlers to abandon the unterraced slopes of the west and to concentrate more on grains and grazing.

The sharp drop in the size of the population should not be ignored, and a shift over to more viable economies of grazing undoubtedly led to some migration away from the region of *Palestine* as it had in *Syria* (confirmed by cuneiform sources). The small villages, hamlets, and campsites of the southern Transjordanian fringe, and especially of the central *Negev*,[46] might best be understood as evidence of a considerable movement of West Semitic groups away from *Palestine*. That is, while the basic West Semitic population was able to maintain its stability in the agricultural heartland of *Syria*, Northern *Palestine* and the *Transjordan* (albeit in much reduced numbers) by means of significant adjustments to the more arid climate, the agriculturally peripheral[47] regions became radically destabilized, forcing many groups into a semi-sedentary economy of grain agriculture and herding, many of whom were forced across the steppelands of the *Transjordan* and into *Arabia*. During the course of the Early Bronze IV-Middle Bronze I period a linguistic continuum between *Palestine* and *Arabia* was maintained, although a dependable chronology for this continuum must remain uncertain, dependent as it is on the notoriously undependable Palestinian pottery typology.[48]

With the end of the arid climatic episode around 1950 B.C., a brief humid period ensued that lasted until about 1700 B.C.,[49] resulting in an expansion of the population and the resedentarization of much of the Palestinian periphery, including large areas of the Judaean hills during the Palestinian Middle Bronze II period. With the renewed orientation towards village agriculture, the marginal settlements of the Central *Negev*, the *Sinai* and the southern *Transjordan* were abandoned, leading

---

[46] Possibly, with Dever, to be understood as seasonally tied to the marginal sites in the Judaean hills.

[47] At least at the level of Bronze Age technology.

[48] W.C. Overstreet *et alii, The Wadi al-Jubah Archaeological Project,* vol. IV (Washington, 1988), esp. pp.474f.

[49] A.D. Crown, *op.cit.,* 1972, pp.322, 329; D. Neer and K.O. Emery, *op.cit.,* and A.F. Harding, *op.cit.,* 1982, p.9.

to the linguistic isolation of the south peripheral Semitic linguistic groups of the South and East (the forerunners of Arabic) from the now long established West Semitic dialects of *Syria-Palestine* reflected in the Eblaite, Amorite, proto-Canaanite and Ugaritic of our third- and second-millennium texts.[50]

Over the past twenty years, the development of an historical perspective of the prehistory and early history of *Palestine* has increasingly concentrated on three periods of transition about which we knew very little in the early sixties. These periods are commonly referred to as "dark ages": 1) The period between the neolithic and the post Ghazzulian or late Chalcolithic (roughly 5000–3500 B.C.); 2) The period of Early Bronze IV-Middle Bronze I from the end of Early Bronze II-III to the establishment of the Middle Bronze Age (ca. 2400–1950 B.C.); and 3) the transition from Late Bronze II to the Iron Age proper (thirteenth to the tenth-century B.C.)

These major gaps in our understanding of the history of *Palestine* were handled in the 1950s and 1960s with the help of widely accepted theories about population destruction, migrations and especially the archaeologically always ephemeral (and therefore attractive) theories of nomadic incursions. For the latter two periods, cuneiform studies, Egyptology and biblical studies were readily synthesized with what meager archaeological information we had, creating an understanding of radical disruption, population change and transition to the better known periods of the Early Bronze so-called city-states, the Hyksos "empire" and the Israelite monarchies respectively. This orientation of the interpretation of the "dark ages" as preparatory to the subsequent better known periods is important to notice, since it was really these later periods that were the known anchor and focus of interest. The interpretation of the "dark ages" as supplying a population base for succeeding "cultures" marked the dark ages functionally as transition periods, and historical-critically without a substance of their own. The concept of invading nomads served to explain the end of the preceding period by wiping the slate of *Palestine* historically clean, and by introducing the succeeding period by recreating a population that can be given meaning as an historical culture; i.e., by definition, one that we

---

[50] For the association of the Early Bronze IV-Middle Bronze I *Negev* sites with *Arabia*, I am indebted to personal communication with E.A. Knauf; *idem, Midian, ADPV* (Wiesbaden, 1988).

know, thus enabling us an unhindered progression from the Neolithic to the Early, the Middle and Late Bronze, and finally into the Iron Age.

While our understanding of all three of our prehistoric Palestinian dark ages have profoundly changed over the past two decades, the transition period between the great Early Bronze and Middle Bronze civilizations appears most amenable to historiography today. As this period has been examined in its own right, the rapid change of understanding that has come about has been immense. As our ability to create cultural coherence out of the data from the transition period itself has increased, we have suddenly become able to separate our historical questions about the collapse of the Early Bronze culture from those entirely distinct questions (separated by half a millennium) that are related to the rise of the later Middle Bronze cultural horizon.

The process towards this historicization and periodization of the Early Bronze IV-Middle Bronze I transition has been an interesting one, requiring the jettisoning of historical fictions about the period itself and of significant distortions about the Early Bronze and the Middle Bronze periods as well. It has also been a process involving significant advances in our historical methods related to prehistoric periods that have moved us much closer to a coherent understanding of the socio-political evolution and fluctuation within the agricultural economy of Bronze Age *Palestine* from about the middle of the fourth-millennium to about the ninth-century B.C., when *Palestine* found itself on the threshold of the Assyrian Empire, where history proper finds both its literary and political roots.

Over millennia of the occupation of Palestine, the geographic spread of the population has expanded and has shrunk; the size of the population as a whole has varied greatly; the proportions between town, village and steppe dwellers has fluctuated widely; towns, village and individual regions have at times suffered abandonment and overpopulation. Nevertheless, these changes and fluctuations have been variations in the fortune of what has clearly been a single population holding together a complex but common cultural and chronological thread through time. In *Palestine,* economic, political and historical disruptions and dislocations are commonplace in a landscape that has never known an indigenous transregional statehood save in an unrealized eschatological future; the population itself, however, reflects an astonishing constant.[51]

The disintegration of the *idée fixe* of a wave of land hungry nomads welling out of *Arabia* to overrun the Levant can already be noticed (ironically enough) in G.E. Wright's analysis of the Early Bronze pottery forms that linked the ceramic repertoire of this period unshakably with some of the most central and durable motifs of the Early Bronze pottery traditions,[52] an observation, both thorough and irrefutable in its presentation, that stands diametrically contradicting the assumptions both of a nomadic destruction of the Early Bronze culture and of the foreign origin of its successor in the Early Bronze IV-Middle Bronze I period.

It is perhaps educational to note that some of the strongest primary adherents to the nomadic Amorite hypothesis (such as Wright) were themselves responsible for pointing out some of the fundamental contradictions to the theory that were eventually to lead to its total dismissal. So, N. Glueck, whose early surface explorations along the Transjordan plateau and the southern *Negev* desert had been so influential in the early descriptions of the Early Bronze IV-Middle Bronze I culture as uniquely steppe oriented and unlike the rest of the Bronze Age agricultural settlements of *Palestine,* was also one of the few major scholars writing on this period in the forties and fifties who had insisted on the sedentary quality of at least the *Transjordan* settlements.[53] K. Kenyon, perhaps the most adamant and coherent advocate of an interpretation of an Early Bronze IV-Middle Bronze I nomadic settlement in terms of an Amorite invasion, had, in her major excavations at the unique oasis site of *Jericho,* sharply separated this period from both the preceding and succeeding periods, so much so as to require a doubling of the Amorite hypothesis to explain both a change from the Early Bronze and an equally radical change to the Middle Bronze.[54] Her understanding of the period as a unique "Intermediate Period" however, encouraged an approach to this period (for all the peculiar summary descriptions of it as a transitional dark age) as a cultural period in its own right and on its own terms, apart

---

[51] See below, Chapter VII.

[52] G.E. Wright, *The Pottery of the Early Bronze Age* (Cambridge, 1938).

[53] N. Glueck, *The Other Side of the Jordan* (New Haven, 1959).

[54] K. Kenyon, *Amorites and Canaanites* Oxford, 1967).

from the Early Bronze II and Middle Bronze II periods. This eventually led to a challenge of both the invasion and the nomadic aspects of her own interpretation in the excavations of her student K. Prag who demonstrated many of the indigenous, sedentary and agricultural qualities of the period in her publications in the mid-seventies.[55]

Finally, it was G.E. Wright's student, W.G. Dever, one of the last major scholars working with this period to give up the nomadic Amorite hypothesis, who, in his analysis of Middle Bronze I pottery forms marking out a variety of regional cultural families, in which he tried to explain the chronological progression and process of the hypothesized Amorite invasion,[56] finally integrated his teacher's observations about the close relationship of this pottery with the Early Bronze forms with much of the archaeological evidence for economic and social structures.[57] This ultimately decisively undermined the assumptions of an external invasion. Finally, Dever's research and excavations in the *Negev* led him to accept the at least partially sedentary quality of much of this period.[58] More significantly, however, his observations of the specifically regional demarcation in his pottery studies makes the necessity of looking at this culture in *Palestine* as a conglomerate of separate and distinct regional developments adamantly clear, and points to yet another significant feature of Palestinian prehistory. *Palestine* has best been described as a "heartland of villages" because of the local regional factors that have determined the quality and form of the society.

---

[55] K. Prag, *op.cit.*, 1974.

[56] W.G. Dever, *op.cit.*, 1966.

[57] *Ibidem.*

[58] On the development in Dever's interpretation, consult the following: W.G. Dever, "The EB IV-MB I Horizon in Transjordan and Southern Palestine," *BASOR* 210 (1973), pp.37-63; *idem*, "New Vistas on the EB IV ('MB I') Horizon in Syria-Palestine," *BASOR* 237 (1980), pp.35-64; *idem*, "Be'er Resisim—A Late Third Millennium B.C.E. Settlement," *Qadmoniot* 16 (1983), pp.52-57; *idem*, "From the End of the Early Bronze to the Beginning of the Middle Bronze," *BAT* (Jerusalem, 1985) pp.13-35; *idem*, "Village Planning at Be'er Resisim and Socio-Economic Structures in EB IV Palestine," *EI* 18 (1985), pp.18-28. The studies of G. Edelstein and E. Eisenberg ("Emeq Refaim," *Excavations and Surveys in Israel*, 3, 1984, pp.51f.; *idem*, "Emeq Refaim," *ibid.*, 1985, pp.54-56) and L.K. Horwitz ("Sedentism in the Early Bronze IV: A Faunal Perspective," *BASOR* 275, 1989, pp.15-25) underscore the clearly sedentary quality of many of the settlements of this period. Th.L. Thompson, *op.cit.*, 1974, pp.144-171; and more recently, I. Finkelstein, "Further Observations on the Socio-Demographic Structure of the Intermediate Bronze Age," *Levant* 21 (1989), pp.129-140.

Any assumptions of a transregional history of *Palestine* prior to the onset of the imperial age in the ninth-century Assyrian domination are hardly any longer acceptable.

When we try today to put together a coherent understanding of the Early Bronze IV-Middle Bronze I period in Palestine, a descriptive approach to the culture of the region shows great promise. The indigenous nature of the population now appears unquestionable, both because of the increasingly obvious Early Bronze roots of the material culture shown in the pottery, the tools, the architecture, the burial practices and even the patterns of settlements in many areas, but also because of the widespread recognition of the indigenous West Semitic character of the earlier Early Bronze culture. The hypothesis of an Amorite invasion from the Syrian steppe, from *Arabia* or from *Mesopotamia* no longer explains anything. The basis of the economy in *Palestine* is also now recognized as lying in a combination of agriculture with a major admixture in sheep and goatherding, with settlement in the major valleys and agricultural regions concentrating in villages and semi-permanent hamlets, and with transhumant pastoralism dominating the steppe regions such as the central *Negev* highlands. Although the extreme diversity in the form of regional settlement discourages the identification of any single form of economy as typical for the whole of *Palestine,* the assumption of nomadism as a dominant form must be abandoned in favor of these much more complicated descriptions.

The older scenario of invading nomads as the cause of the massive and sudden destruction of Early Bronze towns and villages has given way to more ecologically and climatically oriented explanations for the gradual collapse of the Early Bronze civilization. This has been greatly helped by our ability to identify a subpluvial phase in Middle Eastern climate from about 3500 to 2350 B.C. that supported the major advances of agriculture and population growth of the Early Bronze period. This subpluvial phase was followed by a period of severe drought affecting *Palestine* from about 2350 to approximately 1950 B.C., comprising the period of Early Bronze IV-Middle Bronze I and corresponding closely to the First Intermediate of Egypt. In the agriculturally marginal regions of *Palestine,* this led to a situation of severe overpopulation and dislocation of the Mediterranean form of agriculture throughout most regions, leading both to a sharp drop in the population and to an increasing dependence on the more drought resistent economies of grain agriculture and herding with a widening spread of the population into the normally thinly populated steppe regions in the Transjordan and the central Negev. The heavier rainfall areas of Lebanon and coastal Syria (unlike most areas of *Palestine)* were able to maintain the traditional forms of Mediterranean town and village agriculture. The continuity of settlement in Syria and Lebanon throughout this period and into the Middle bronze Age proper then allows for an explanation of a transition to the Middle Bronze culture in terms of a technological cultural diffusion from the north into more marginal *Palestine.*[59]

The Early Bronze IV-Middle Bronze I settlements of southern Transjordan and the Central Negev are to be understood not as the harbingers of semi-sedentary or semi-nomadic settlement in *Palestine* proper coming out of Arabia, but rather as a movement eastwards away from *Palestine* into Arabia at some period prior to the full establishment of the Middle Bronze culture in *Palestine,* and as ultimately responsible for the Semiticization of Arabia.

Our limited knowledge of prehistoric *Palestine* has given us a myopic view of historic process and change in early *Palestine,* centered on those cultural periods we know best: the Early Bronze II, the Middle Bronze II, the Late Bronze II and the Iron II periods. In a similar vein, historiography has concentrated on those major towns that have rendered extensive stratigraphic development during these well known periods. The paradigms of development and evolution and the confirmed observations of transregional cultural change (which we learned to understand from these prosperous coherent periods) have been used all too long as interpretive models for both the regional and chronological gaps in our knowledge.

The longevity and prosperity of the great tells of *Palestine,* with their continuous stratified remains in Early Bronze II, Middle Bronze II, Late Bronze II and Iron II can no longer profitably be understood as the norm for the late prehistory of *Palestine.* They are only part of the picture. The all Palestinian cultural continuity that they display (along with their prosperity) reflects unique episodes of political stability, supporting an interregional and international trade in which the agricultural heartland of *Palestine* took a small share in the great early civilizations of Mesopotamia and *Egypt.* However, *Palestine* itself has never been able to maintain such a high culture in its own right. Even the view of the great tells of the agricultural heartland during their

---

[59] See below, section 4.

peaks of prosperity that sees them as so-called city-states, is a wrenching distortion of the realities found through excavation. Village scrub farmers, living in villages, hamlets and small market towns of a few thousand people at best, are all they ever were, with only fragments of high culture derivative of the Egyptian and Syrian civilizations. Those towns that were able to maintain contact with the greater world during the Early Bronze II, Middle Bronze II, Late Bronze II and Iron II periods do display patterns of cultural development and processes that permit descriptions of an historical progress firmly anchored to relative and absolute chronologies, allowing for those transregional and international correlations that are the focus of histories of the ancient world, centered on evolutionary and developmental themes. However, the rest of *Palestine,* and the rest of Palestinian prehistory–especially the so-called dark ages—cannot be integrated into such histories on the basis of what are thoroughly transregional and international developments, that quite simply did not significantly transform them. For these regions (and for greater *Palestine* during these lesser historical periods) it is not chronological process or evolution that provides us with a workable historical framework, but it is rather an increased focus on broad periodization (coupled with an examination of regionally defined and limited cultural change) that can open the way for a more accurate understanding of *Palestine*'s history. The great tells of Early Bronze II and Middle Bronze II provide us with fixed chronological benchmarks, but the historical cultural distance between those benchmarks cannot be traversed with a traceable line of transition, whether cultural or chronological. The lack of coherence and continuity in stratigraphy (both in the region as a whole and on individual sites) are not so much a failure of information as it is rather one of the factors that demands understanding and interpretation!

The Early Bronze IV-Middle Bronze I period of *Palestine* is neither simply a transitional process between the Early and Middle Bronze Ages of Palestine, nor is it a univocal concept representing a single trans-Palestinian culture. It is first of all a chronological time span (ca. 2350 B.C. to 1950 B.C.) during which a wide spectrum of largely regionally restricted ecological, economic and cultural changes and events occurred, marking in each region, severally, a great agricultural depression with many different modes of survival undertaken by the population of *Palestine* as a whole. Many died; many left; many changed their economic modes of their lives; many stayed on in such impoverished conditions as to lose many of the cultural and technological abilities of their ancestors. The explanations of transition, however, both from the Early Bronze and to the Middle Bronze lie largely outside the population of *Palestine* itself and are international and ecological in nature.

Finally, historical descriptions of the internal cultural development within the Early Bronze IV-Middle Bronze I period of *Palestine,* and to a pervasive extent within the entire pre-Assyrian history of the region as a whole, might gain in clarity if we can learn to avoid a too great dependence on models of linear chronological developments that are transregional in nature, and if we take more seriously the ecological and geographic fragmentation of *Palestine* into many distinct and largely isolated cultural subregions. Those changes that developed in the central *Negev* highlands hardly affected the cultural procession occurring on the Transjordanian plateau, and that itself had little echo in the *Beth Shan* Valley near the Sea of *Galilee,* and even less in the uplands of central *Palestine* or along the culturally more volatile Mediterranean coast. Each region had its own internal history of development and change, which indeed did overlapwith that of its neighbors, but which nevertheless maintained its own continuity and economic integrity. Only rarely and incompletely in pre-Assyrian *Palestine* did a transregional power influence these disparate regions to such an extent that they marched together along a cultural continuum.

It may help us a bit in this confusing process of making history out of prehistory if we entertain for a moment the seeming contradiction of a German concept introduced into Palestinian archaeology in the handbook on Pre-Hellenistic Palestinian archaeology recently published by H. Weippert. This idea may help us to grapple with greater dexterity the plethora of contradictions in which all historians of *Palestine* become enmeshed whenever they deal with chronology, both relative and absolute. The problem of chronology and chronological development is not a side issue of little importance. It rather lies at the heart of nearly every difficult problem and nearly every sharp divergence of opinion we face in the field today. The problem of interpretation that Weippert focuses on is conceptualized by her as the problem of the "*Gleichzeitigkeit des Ungleichzeitigen*"; that is, the "contemporaneity of what is not contemporaneous." The problem is one of both the chronological dispersion of cultural developmental patterns throughout the many regions of *Palestine,* as well as the related problem of the regional dislocations in the more localized processes of cultural transmission and diffusion. The issues are less contradictory but no less problematic if we use examples to clarify. Settlements that show the classical cultural pattern known as Early Bronze III may be and at times are contemporaneous with some settlements of the so-called earlier Early Bronze II period, and this even when the Early Bronze III settlement shows a development from and continuity with a truly earlier Early Bronze II occupation of the same site. Early Bronze IV settlements may succeed without a lapse in occupation from Early Bronze II settlements, while elsewhere in *Palestine* Early Bronze III cultures dominate. Similarly Early Bronze IV A, B or C settlements may be contemporaneous even when the designation of these periods as successive has been hard won through stratigraphic or detailed ceramic studies. It has long been recognized by many scholars that much of Middle Bronze IIA is contemporaneous with Early Bronze IV-Middle Bronze I,[60] and we have no evidence whatever that the cultural developmental processes from Early Bronze III A and B, Early Bronze IV A, B and C, and Middle Bronze IIA are steps that are in fact followed within even a single region of *Palestine,* and, moreover, we know that we have a lack of correlation between regions, as well as some evidence to suggest that regions in the Northern *Jordan* Valley and perhaps the *Jezreel* have what we might describe as a faster chronological clock than what might be found in more isolated regions such as the highlands or the Transjordanian plateau. It is time to accept the necessity of a much more complicated chronological history of *Palestine* than we are used to dealing with. We need to question our confidence in a sweeping comprehensive and linear history of the Early Bronze IV-Middle Bronze I Period, that can understand *Palestine* as a country so overrun with steppe dwelling nomads of the desert that the agricultural heartland of *Palestine* lay abandoned at the same time that the ecologically more difficult *Transjordan* plateau and the central *Negev* steppelands found a dense population of agriculturalists and shepherds.[61] The way out of such anomalies should proceed through increased attention to regional histories of the many discrete cultures that the agricultural exploitation of *Palestine* left behind in the millennia

---

[60] E.g., A.Kempinski, *The Rise of an Urban Culture, Israel Ethnographic Society Studies* 4 (Jerusalem, 1978).

[61] Th.L. Thompson, "The Settlement of Early Bronze IV-Middle Bronze I in Jordan," *Annual of the Department of Antiquities in Jordan* (1974), pp.57-71.

long process of becoming a heartland of villages: the domaine, not of kings and emperors, but of scrub farmers and shepherds.

4. Middle Bronze II and Early State Development

It is in the prosperity of the Middle Bronze II period that *Palestine* first gives clear unequivocal evidence of sedentary state forms, at least in the lowlands and in a handful of towns in the larger intramontane Valleys of the central hills and the lower *Galilee* such as *Shechem* and *Hazor*. In Egyptian texts, most notably the "Execration Texts" (ca. 1810–1770 B.C.),[62] personal dynastic leadership of local princes and chieftains seems well established in several possible forms. If a continuity of political structures is assumed with the much later *Amarna* period (and it seems safe to conclude that the Egyptian Empire did not radically alter the indigenous political structure), large areas of *Palestine* followed the forms of city-state government that had been long established in *Syria* and *Lebanon*, and included even in *Palestine* some portion of military and political elite, however small. The major fortifications protecting most larger towns, as well as the pottery typology and the character of the material culture, generally underscore *Palestine*'s place on the southern fringe of the political and cultural world of greater *Syria*. Not that the heavily fortified Palestinian towns apart from Hazor ever approached the size and power of their northern contemporaries. We do not know the effect of their power beyond their immediate environs,[63] and their size need not require a function beyond that of subregional centers for crafts, markets and local defense. If one can use a sociologically derived systemic model to describe *Palestine* of the early second-millennium, one might profitably use that of a complex chieftainship,[64] with a central town, possible secondary fortified villages and a periphery of small hamlets, with the interrelationships between the core and the periphery largely restricted to an agriculturally delimited subregion.[65] The many small villages and hamlets that have been found

---

[62] Th.L. Thompson, *op.cit.*, 1974, pp.98–117.

[63] Hazor is a notable exception among Palestine's towns and is known in Mari texts as a regional power. A. Malamat, "The Head of All These Kingdoms," *JBL* 79 (1960), pp.12–19.

[64] C.S. Steele, *op.cit.*, 1983, pp.83ff.

[65] The best examples of this might be Hazor (A. Malamat, *ibid.*) and Shechem (E.F.

well beyond the immediate peripheries of larger settlements, however, are best understood as economically independent and self sufficient entities, at least to the extent that they display subsistence forms of agriculture that are regionally oriented. Settlements that are dominated by cash crop industries such as herding, and olive and wine production of necessity involve larger political frameworks fostering an inner-regional trade network. Although some forms of subordination and pyramiding of power through family alliances, economic specializations, trade and military hegemony over larger regions must have developed, such coalitions, however hierarchical, do not seem, except for a few exceptions such as *Hazor,* to have been institutionalized in any form of larger regional statehood. Even as late as the period of the Egyptian empire, when the Egyptians maintained a military hold on the region in competition with the Hittites to the north, local political structures were hardly bureaucratically advanced beyond a primitive form of oriental despotism of little consequence to the broader social or political economy, and one must think of the "kings" and the councils of these city-states at best as village headmen, chieftains and landowners, dependent more on their own personal influence and wealth in land than on any civil bureaucracy or class structure for their power.[66]

The well known story of Sinuhe is particularly instructive in this regard,[67] as, apart from a reference to *Byblos,* this fictional story portrays the whole of the land of Upper *Retenu* (i.e. *Palestine*) as a land of farmers and shepherds, whose "prince" is not the king of any great city or small empire, but resembles rather a clannish or tribal chieftain. Even the town oriented *Amarna* letters of the Late Bronze Age[68] do not envisage any considerable bureaucracy, but rather small, largely independent petty chieftainships, able to be protected (and controlled) by very small numbers of soldiers.

Campbell, "The Shechem Area Survey," *BASOR* 190, 1968, pp.19–41). One might also point to the northern coastal towns of *Acco* and *Achziv* (M.W. Prausnitz, "Acho, Plain of"; *idem,* "Achziv," *EAEHL I,* Jerusalem, 1975, pp.23–30).

[66] The *Amarna* letters related to Labaya of *Shechem* offer a wonderful illustration of just such a "chieftainship."

[67] Dated to the end of the reign of Sesostris I. For text, K. Galling, *Textbuch zur Geschichte Israels,* 2nd. ed. (Tübingen, 1968) pp.1–12.

[68] J. Knudtzon, *Die El-Amarna Tafeln I-II* (Berlin, 1964) *passim*; esp. those referring to *Shechem* and *Jerusalem.*

In spite of the relative prosperity of the Middle Bronze II period, it is, I believe, surely a mistake to expand the Kamose Stele's reference to the fifteenth dynasty's Apophis as a "Prince of *Retenu*" into a thesis of a Hyksos empire in southern *Palestine*,[69] let alone to see this as supporting an understanding of the so-called Hyksos rule of Egypt as a southern extension of a Palestinian empire! A. Kempinski's suggestion of a fifteenth dynasty Egyptian empire, centered in southern *Palestine* and the Delta, in competition for control of the southern Levant with the kingdom of *Aleppo* in *Syria,* as an immediate predecessor of the eighteenth dynasty's imperial control of *Palestine* in competition with the Hittites[70] too readily translates linguistic, cultural and trade relationships into direct political and military control. Whatever the significance of 18th dynasty propaganda against its predecessors in Egypt, the West Semitic linguistic connections between *Palestine* and Egypt hardly need such an imperial explanation. The fifteenth dynasty's base of political power was wholly Egyptian, albeit oriented to the Egyptian delta,[71] and the caricature of some of its rulers as "foreign" (*hq3 h3 s.wt*) is little more than a reflex of the eighteenth dynasty's Theban proclivity to exclude the Delta's Semites from their understanding of what they felt was truly Egyptian. This "foreign" hegemony of the fifteenth and sixteenth dynasty over *Egypt* that had reduced "*Egypt*" to a region sandwiched between the territories of the Asiatics from *Avaris* in the north to that of the black Africans in the South.[72] The *Nile* is Asiatic as far as *Cusae* (25 miles south of *Hermopolis*) and the Delta or upper Egypt is also referred to as "the land of the Asiatics."[73] This so-call Asiatic dominance was overthrown when *Thebes* reasserted its control over *Egypt* and drove the "Asiatics" ('*3mw*) from *Egypt* under Ahmose I. The connections between this defeat of *Avaris* at the hands of the founders of the eighteenth dynasty and the establishment of the Egyptian empire in *Asia* is at best a distant one, Thutmosis I's campaign

---

[69] J. von Beckerath, *Untersuchungen zur politischen Geschichte der zweiten Zwischenzeit in Ägypten, ÄgF* 23 (1964), pp.146f.

[70] A. Kempinski, *op.cit.* pp.197-224, esp. pp.210f.

[71] J. Von Beckerath, *op.cit.*, J. Van Seters, *The Hyksos*, (New Haven, 1966).

[72] *ANET*, pp.232f., 554ff. Less tendentiously, this latter text refers to Egypt being divided between three powers.

[73] *Ibid.*, p.232.

into *Retenu* being more than a generation distant from Ahmose I's conquest of *Avaris* and *Sharuhen*.[74]

The three year compaign after the fall of *Avaris* against *Sharuhen*[75] has led many scholars to look for this site in southern *Palestine* on the strength of a much later reference to a *Sharuhen* in Joshua 15:6, and to identify it with either *Tell el Fârah* South or more recently with *Tell el-Ajjul*. The Egyptian text, however, seems to imply that the fighting took place not in *Retenu* at all but in a region in or close to the *Nile* delta. There is indeed considerable evidence of Egyptian influence in the south of *Palestine* and at the site of *Tell el-Ajjul* from the period of the Second Intermediate.[76] However, the extent of influence and the quantity of Egyptian material remains (including finds of royal seals) hardly matches the comparable finds along the trade routes of *Palestine* from the earlier twelfth dynasty.[77] To assume a direct Egyptian military and political control on the basis of such limited evidence when close trade relations offer an adequate explanation seems unwarranted.[78] Wherever the *Sharuhen* of the Egyptian texts might be located,[79] the battles for *Avaris* and *Sharuhen* seem militarily much more oriented towards an eighteenth dynasty policy of consolidation of Egyptian territory under the authority of *Thebes*, which had also included campaigns into territories to the south of *Thebes* under Ahmose I, Amenhotep I, and Thutmosis I. Only after *Thebes* had established political control and acquired a monopoly of power throughout the whole of *Egypt*, did the eighteenth dynasty under Thutmosis III, a century after Ahmose I, develop ambitions for an empire in *Palestine*. That some of the fifteenth and sixteenth dynasty pharaohs bore West Semitic names is only to be expected, given the prevalence of West Semitic speaking peoples in the Delta since at least the Old Kingdom and probably since predynastic times, as well as Egyptian economic involvements in the copper and turquoise mines of the *Sinai* and the apparently indigenous nature of West Semitic groups

---

[74] See the text from the tomb of the soldier Ahmose: *ibid.*, p.233.

[75] *Ibid.*, p.233, line 15.

[76] J. Von Beckerath, *op.cit.* and A. Kempinski, *op.cit.*

[77] R. Giveon, *The Impact of Egypt on Canaan*, OBO 20 (Göttingen 1978) pp.73-80.

[78] *Contra* R. Giveon, *ibidem*.

[79] Possible analogies for the existence of settlements, bearing identical names in both *Egypt* and *Palestine*, are found by reference to *Succoth* (Genesis 33:17 and Exodus 13:20) and *Goshen* (Genesis 47:6 and Joshua 10:41).

not only in the Delta but in *Egypt*'s Eastern desert.[80] Similarly, the many religious and cultural ties that existed between *Egypt* and *Palestine* hardly gives warrant to assumptions of political unity, since we are dealing with close neighbors, both of whom have extensive symbiotic ties with non sedentary Semitic speaking peoples traversing the Arabian Steppe, the *Negev, Sinai,* and the Eastern desert of *Egypt.*[81] In fact, given the geographical contiguity of the regions, cultural discontinuity can be expected only in extraordinary times (such as that of the great drought at the end of the Neolithic period). Direct evidence of a substantial material continuity between *Palestine* and the Delta is abundant from the Late Chalcolithic through the Byzantine period, whether or not there were existing political and military connections or separations by borders. The importance of trade and other forms of communication and exchange between *Egypt* and *Palestine* is well supported in the archaeological levels and is particularly marked during the twelfth dynasty and the Second Intermediate period on both the Egyptian and the Asiatic sides of the *Sinai.* Following the collapse of Egyptian-Palestinian trade lasting throughout the great drought of the First Intermediate (Early Bronze IV-Middle Bronze I) period, overland trade is clearly reestablished during the twelfth dynasty[82] and continues throughout the rest of the Bronze Age until at least the reign of Ramses

---

[80] Th.L. Thompson, *op.cit.*, 1974, pp.142f.

[81] The roles of the deserts and steppelands that lay between the agricultural lands of *Egypt* and *Palestine*, supporting a spectrum of symbiotic economic forms, has a rich and growing literature. I. Finkelstein (op.cit., 1979) for a discussion and bibliography of some of the more important anthropological and archaeological issues; P.E. Newberry, *Beni-Hasan I-IV* (London, 1893ff.); A.H. Gardiner, T.E. Peet and J. Cerny, *The Inscriptions of Sinai I-II* (London, 1952-55); and especially a number of valuable interpretive articles by R. Giveon, "Le Temple d'Hathor à Serabit el-Khadem," *Archealogia* 44 (1972), pp.64-69; *idem,* "Investigations in the Egyptian Mining Centres in Sinai," *Tel Aviv* 1 (1974), pp.100-108; *idem, op.cit.,* 1978, pp.51-72, as well as his popular work: *The Stones of Sinai Speak* (Tokyo, 1978), and his important monograph: *Le Bèdouin Shosou des documents ègyptiens* (Leiden, 1971); also, E.A. Knauf, *op.cit.,* 1988, pp.42ff. Much new information, especially on communications between the two regions, can also be drawn from several Israeli archaeological expeditions: B. Rothenberg *Timna* (London, 1972); I. Beit-Arieh and R. Gophna, "The Early Bronze Age II Settlement at 'Ein el Qudeirat (1980-1981)," *Tel Aviv* 8 (1981), pp.128-135; R. Cohen, *The Settlement of the Central Negev* (Hebrew University dissertation, 1986); E.D. Oren, "The Overland Route between Egypt and Canaan in the Early Bronze Age," *IEJ* 23 (1973), pp.198-205; Th.L. Thompson, *The Settlement of Sinai and the Negev in the Bronze Age, BTAVO* 8 (Wiesbaden, 1975) esp. pp.9-13.

[82] The excavations at Tell el-Ajjul: W.M. Petrie, *Ancient Gaza I-IV* (London, 1931-1934).

VI. Trade between *Palestine* and *Egypt* during the Middle Bronze period is not a phenomenon that can be appropriately explained either by an hypothesis of a Syro-Palestinian Asiatic rule in *Egypt* or one of an Egyptian empire in *Asia*. Rather, the evidence of close cooperation and mutual exchange of many types is no more than we should expect from the natural business of neighbors with significantly diverse and contrasting economies. Certainly not all of these interchanges reflect good relations, support and mutual beneficence. Quite the contrary! Some of them, indeed, in the form of confrontation and antagonism expressed or implied, underscore the necessity of seeing these two regions as politically and militarily separate. For example, the great wall built by Amenenes I, and apparently maintained throughout at least the twelfth dynasty, was built at great cost in order to protect *Egypt* from marauding Asiatic *st.tyw* and *hryws'* as well as to control access and immigration into *Egypt* by Asiatics. Such a physical barrier clearly marks a frontier to the East of the Egyptian delta[83] and speaks very strongly against Kempinski and Giveon's claim of twelfth dynasty imperial control of Southern *Palestine*. One needs more than small punitive expeditions, and royal representatives for purposes of trade before speaking of empire. If *Palestine*'s prosperity and stability during the two most significant phases of the Middle Bronze period were dependent on a South Palestinian Asiatic empire, then the situation in both *Palestine* and *Egypt,* following the overthrow of the so-called Hyksos, would certainly appear anomalous. The reign of Ahmose I, and the war against both the delta and the southern part of *Egypt* that ensued, does not mark any radical shift in these regions in either settlement patterns or material cultural development. Moreover, the practice of Palestinian Archaeologists of marking the date of the transition from the Middle Bronze to Late Bronze with the hegemony of Ahmose has not a single significant argument to support it, except that of an undifferentiated wish to harmonize Palestinian ceramic typologies and stratigraphic sequences from major Palestinian sites with a presumably superior chronology based on Egyptian dynastic changes. Such Palestinian chronologies, however, are only truly strengthened when they stand independently and coherently on their own chronological footing. This pertains, unfortunately, neither in Palestinian ceramic typologies, which at this time have only the most general coherence within the context of

---

[83] Th.L. Thompson, *op.cit.*, 1974, pp.123–133.

a relative chronology, nor, indeed, in linked stratigraphic sequences, which are frequently dependent solely on the assumptions of ceramic chronology or even less dependable artifactual and architectural analogies. This admittedly pessimistic picture is perhaps particularly pertinent to this Middle Bronze-Late Bronze transition where the synchronisms between *Egypt* and *Palestine* have been both long standing and arbitrary. Kempinski's pertinent suggestions of separating Palestinian chronology from Egyptian politics entirely, which would result in substantially raising the date for the beginning of Late Bronze I to ca. 1600 B.C., has much to recommend it,[84] allowing as it does for an overlap between the final years of the Second Intermediate in Egypt and the beginning of Late Bronze I in *Palestine*.

During the Middle Bronze II period, Egypt's influence in *Palestine* is found at most major sites in the southern half of *Palestine*. This is not the situation, however, throughout the whole of the Palestinian region. In the northern lowland areas, and especially along the coastal strip, many aspects of the material culture of the Middle Bronze Age indicate that the most dominant foreign influences that are identifiable stem from *Syria* and *Anatolia* and had done so for a considerable time. This is strongly marked already in the earliest formation of the Middle Bronze IIA ceramic repertoire and continues through the *Mari* period.[85] In fact, the parallels are so clear that many early discussions of this period had understood the Middle Bronze II population itself to have migrated from the North, bringing an already long established Syrian culture into *Palestine* with them by way of *Byblos*. The interpretation of K. Kenyon, which was dominant through the sixties, had understood the earlier Early Bronze IV-Middle Bronze I transition period to have been a period in *Palestine* that had come about by way of a massive migration or invasion of West Semitic "Amorites" from the Syrian steppe.[86] She understood the transition to the Middle Bronze Age proper to have occurred as a result of population movements of "Canaanites" from the northern coast near *Byblos* south and southeastward into *Palestine*.[87] In

---

[84] A. Kempinski, *op.cit.*, p.223.

[85] The excellent charts representing this early trade in P. Gerstenblith, *The Levant at the Beginning of the Middle Bronze Age, ASORDS* 5 (Winona Lake, 1983) p.17, as well as an excellent summary discussion of the Anatolian and Mari texts relating to trade on pp.7-21.

[86] See above all K. Kenyon, *Amorites and Canaanites* (Oxford, 1966).

[87] *Ibid.*, pp.58ff.

his dissertation and subsequent early publications, William Dever,[88] maintained this concept of "Amorite" invasions as explaining the anomalies of both the Early Bronze IV-Middle Bronze I transition period as well as the succeeding Middle Bronze Age. By the mid-1970's, however, perhaps influenced by growing objections to Kenyon's hypothesis,[89] Dever reasserted his teacher's G.E. Wright's understanding of an indigenous Early Bronze IV pottery repertoire[90] that had argued for a cultural continuity with the previous Early Bronze period, and argued for the substantially indigenous quality of the Early Bronze IV-Middle Bronze I material remains,[91] while attempting to maintain the connections with "Amorite" invasions with the peculiar assertion that although both "waves of 'Amorites'" came from the same steppeland region, those responsible for Early Bronze IV had come from a "seminomadic culture" and had (therefore?) brought no distinctive culture with them, adopting rather that of *Palestine,* while the second migration (that responsible for the onset of the Middle Bronze Age) had already been "partly or wholly urbanized" before its entrance.[92] Without attempting to explain "urbanization" on the Syrian steppe or to offer a cause for such a migration of sedentary groups, Dever nevertheless moved decisively away from Kenyon's dominant interpretation, and by 1982[93] had clearly joined a growing consensus that not only rejected an "Amorite" invasion theory for Early Bronze IV-Middle Bronze I but understood it to have been both substantially

---

[88] W.G. Dever, *op.cit.,* 1966; *idem,* "The People of Palestine in the Middle Bronze Period," *HThR* 64 (1971), pp.197-226.

[89] A. Haldar, *Who Were the Amorites?* (Leiden, 1971); M. Liverani, "The Amorites," *Peoples of Old Testament Times,* ed. by D.J. Wiseman (Oxford, 1973), pp.100-133; Th.L. Thompson, *op.cit.,* 1974, pp.67-97.

[90] G.E. Wright, *op.cit.,* 1938.

[91] W.G. Dever, "The Beginning of the Middle Bronze Age in Syria-Palestine," *Magnalia Dei: The Mighty Acts of God,* ed. by F.M. Cross *et alii* (Garden City, 1976) pp.3-38. This was supported by the historical arguments of A. Haldar, *op.cit.,* M. Liverani, *op.cit.,* 1973; and Th.L. Thompson, *op.cit.,* 1974, pp.144-171.

[92] W.G. Dever, *op.cit.,* 1976, p.15.

[93] W.G. Dever and R. Cohen, "Preliminary Report of the Pilot Season of the 'Central Negev Highlands Project'," *BASOR* 232 (1978), pp.29-45; *idem,* "Preliminary Report of the Second Season of the 'Central Negev Highlands Project'," *BASOR* 236 (1979), pp.41-60; *idem,* "Preliminary Report of the Third and Final Season of the 'Central Negev Highlands Project'," *BASOR* 243 (1981), pp.57-77; R. Cohen, *op.cit.,* 1986.

indigenous and sedentary.[94] A strong mixture of pastoralism as an important aspect of the Early Bronze IV-Middle Bronze I economy is recognized by this new consensus, and this is generally understood to have been of a transhumance pattern in at least the *Negev* region.[95]

The minor dispute that still exists among scholars regarding the transition from the Early Bronze IV-Middle Bronze I period to the Middle Bronze period proper, with P. Gerstenblith and J. Tubbs[96] explaining the changes in the Middle Bronze II pottery repertoire as the result of technological development and as reflecting resurgence of trade with *Syria,* and Dever still understanding this revival of the sedentary lowland culture as in some way associated with "Amorite" migrations, is hardly any longer significant. Dever's excessive dependence on pottery typology as an indicator of historical and ethnic change in *Palestine* seems inadequate, and we have no reason to follow him here. Gerstenblith's comprehensive treatment adequately closes this debate. There seems today little reason to dispute the continuity of the Early Bronze and Middle Bronze civilizations. Both the Early Bronze IV-

---

[94] K. Prag, "The Intermediate Early Bronze-Middle Bronze Age: An Interpretation of the Evidence from Transjordan, Syria, and Lebanon," *Levant* 6 (1974), pp.69-116; *idem*, "Continuity and Migration in the South Levant in the Late Third Millennium: A Review of T.L. Thompson's and Some Other Views," *PEQ* 116 (1984), pp.58-68; Th.L. Thompson, *loc.cit.*, 1974; *idem*, "The Background of the Patriarchs and the Origin of Israel: A Reply to William Dever and Malcolm Clark," *JSOT* 9 (1978), pp.2-43; *idem, op.cit,* 1979, pp.64f.; D. Esse, *Beyond Subsistence: Beth Yerah and Northern Palestine in the Early Bronze Age* (University of Chicago dissertation, 1982) esp. pp.342-368; P. Gerstenblith, *op.cit.,* 1983, esp. the summary on pp.123-126; J. Rogerson, *Atlas of Israel* (London, 1985); S. Richard, "Toward a Consensus of Opinion on the End of the Early Bronze Age in Palestine-Transjordan," *BASOR* 237 (1984), pp.5-34; *idem*, "From the End of the Early Bronze Age to the Beginning of the Middle Bronze," in *BAT* (1985), pp.113-135; *idem*, "The Early Bronze Age: The Rise and Collapse of Urbanism," *BA* 50 (1987), pp.22-43.

[95] Th.L. Thompson, *op.cit.,* 1975; *idem*, "Palestinian Pastoralism and Israel's Origins," *SJOT* 6 (1992), pp.1-13; I. Finkelstein, *op.cit.,* 1989. An "urban" quality for the Early Bronze IV transition period is to my knowledge nowhere apparent, and the period has never been so described (*pacem* Dever!). I find Dever's insistence in (W.G. Dever, *op.cit.,* 1982) that he disagrees with my understanding of the sedentary and indigenous qualities of this entire period thoroughly puzzling. The acrimony he introduces into the discussion is particularly baffling as his interpretation of the period appears largely derivative of the analyses of G.E. Wright, K. Prag, myself, and others. Some rarely cited but important and well balanced discussions that express this new consensus are D. Esse's Chicago dissertation (*op.cit.,* pp.342ff.) and H. Weippert's new encyclopedia of archaeology (*op.cit., passim*).

[96] P. Gerstenblith, *op.cit.,* pp.23-87; J. Tubb, "The MB IIA Period in Palestine: Its Relationship with Syria and its Origin," *Levant* 15 (1983), pp.49-62.

Middle Bronze I and Middle Bronze IIA periods seem best explained in terms of their indigenous Palestinian qualities. One might understand the radically changing patterns of settlement and demographics in terms of the internal subsistence strategies of *Palestine,* periodically shifting from a Mediterranean type of economy, centered on the cash crops of cereals, oil, fruits, wine and herding, to more limited regionally oriented economies, involving even periodic collapses and shifts of economic dependence towards a dominance of grain agriculture and pastoral pursuits.[97]

Because of the cash crop orientation of a Mediterranean economy, such a comprehensive perspective of the economic patterns of settlement in *Palestine* draws attention to both international and interregional relationships as a significant component of prosperity throughout *Palestine.* These had impact on our understanding of the development and stability of towns and cities (especially along the major trade routes) as well as of regional and interregional political changes. The strong associations of the early Middle Bronze pottery with sites in *Syria* give extensive evidence of a close and dependent relationship of at least northern *Palestine* on trade with more prosperous *Syria.* It is particularly in terms of the development of the Bronze industry in *Palestine* (which requires the importation of tin) that all of the technological innovations of the Middle Bronze Age, including those of pottery, architecture and fortifications find their context in the trade networks of *Mesopotamia,*[98] eventually fostering the development of towns and "city-state" political forms. By the Middle Bronze II period, *Palestine* had taken an integral place within this international trade network, and continued to take part in the intellectual and cultural development of the cuneiform world throughout the remainder of the Bronze Age, even subsequent to *Palestine*'s conquest by Thutmosis III and its political and military subordination to the Egyptian empire during the Late Bronze Age.

The universally recognized prosperity of the Middle Bronze Age in *Palestine* (parallelled in *Egypt* with the rise of the twelfth dynasty that developed trade relations with *Byblos* and along the coastal region of southern and central *Palestine* and into the *Jezreel*) reflected a growing southern extension of Syro-Mesopotamian culture throughout most of the southern Levant. This prosperity led to an increase of population

---

[97] See above, Chapter V, section 1; and below, Chapter VII.

[98] P. Gerstenblith, *op.cit., passim* (well summarized on p.125).

marked by both the development of large fortified towns throughout the lowlands and to an extensive spread of small sedentary villages and hamlets throughout the most favorable agricultural areas of the land. Not only the more richly watered regions of the lowlands were affected by this growth, but substantial numbers of settlements were scattered throughout the upland valleys as well, and some evidence exists of at least seasonal occupation of the more arid small steppelands of the eastern slopes of the Palestinian hills and of the fringes of the great Syrian desert.[99] This surge of population and the prosperity that supported it seem to have lasted for some three centuries (until ca. 1600 B.C.). While the rise of foreign influences and international trade relations closely corresponds to this growth and prosperity (and certainly furthered them and marked the character of the material culture of the period), neither trade nor military involvement from outside seem sufficient in themselves to have caused these changes. Nor, as we have argued above, does there seem any significant evidence for a substantial influx of population form outside *Palestine* in the form of Early West Semite or "Amorite" migrations, whether or not they had derived from a sedentary or from a nomadic background.[100] Before a migratory explanatory cause can be seriously entertained for the development of Middle Bronze II *Palestine,* movements out of the agricultural areas of *Syria* and *Lebanon,* or migrations resulting from a massive overpopulation of the Syrian steppelands (e.g. in the region of *Jabal Bishri*) need to be manifest. Rather, the return to prosperity and a rapid population growth throughout *Syria* and *Lebanon* are everywhere apparent.[101] The steppelands on the fringe of the Great Syrian desert also seem to be developing an unprecedented prosperity, reflected in the *Mari* texts in the growth of extensive steppeland tribal systems living in symbiosis with the sedentary societies of the agricultural zones along the

---

[99] R. Gonen, "Urban Canaan in the Late Bronze Period," *BASOR* 253 (1984), pp.61-73, esp. pp.63-65. A valuable bibliography is given on pp.71-73.

[100] Following, e.g., either W.G. Dever (*op.cit.*) or K. Kenyon (*op.cit.*).

[101] A. Kuschke, S. Mittmann and U. Müller, *Archäologischer Survey in der nördlichen Biqaʿ, Herbst 1972: Report on a Prehistoric Survey in the Biqaʿ* (by I. Azoury), *BTAVO* 11 (Wiesbaden, 1976); K.C. Simpson, *Settlement Patterns on the Margins of Mesopotamia: Stability and Change along the Middle Euphrates, Syria* (University of Arizona dissertation, 1983) esp. pp.439-444.

Euphrates from at least the eighteenth-century B.C.[102] That is, the evidence throughout the Levant is of unprecedented expansion during the Middle Bronze period in sharp contrast to the depression, conflict and dislocation that seem to have marked the drought periods of the sixth–fifth millennia and of the end of the third-millennium.

A primary cause of the changes in the economy and settlement patterns in *Palestine* during the Middle Bronze period was the radical changes in climate and the chain of effects that followed. These seem to have pertained throughout the Levant. There is considerable evidence today for understanding a positive climatic change after ca. 2100–2000 B.C. with a rainfall regime somewhat wetter than today's norm obtaining in *Palestine* from approximately 1900–1700 B.C.[103] that corresponds with evidence in *Egypt* for higher than normal *Nile* floods from ca. 1840–1770 B.C.[104] From the sixteenth-century B.C., however, the climate of *Palestine* was much drier, approximately the same as today or perhaps slightly more arid. While these fluctuations in climate are relatively moderate, their effects on the economy of *Palestine* and on patterns of agricultural exploitation in a region so close to the limits of the Mediterranean zone can be great, demarcating periods of prosperity and expansion of land use as well as of famine and the abandonment of marginal lands. Two examples of such climatically oriented shifts in economy and settlement might be drawn: A) The pattern of olive exploitation indicates that Middle Bronze II production is considerably expanded and maintained throughout the northern part of *Palestine* during this period, in sharp

---

[102] J.R. Kupper, *Les Nomades en Mesopotamie au temps des rois de Mari*, *Bibliothèque de la Faculté de Philosophie et Lettres de l'Université de Liège*, 182 (Liège, 1967); M. Klengel, *Benjaminiten und Hanäer zur Zeit der Könige von Mari* (Berlin dissertation, 1958); idem, "Zu einigen Problemen des altvorderasiatischen Nomadentums," *ArOr* 30 (1962), pp.585–596.

[103] A.D. Crown, "Toward a Reconstruction of the Climate of Palestine 8000 B.C.–0 B.C.," *JNES* 31 (1972), pp.312–330; also R.W. Fairbridge, "An 8000-yr Paleoclimatic Record of the 'Double-Hale' 45-yr Solar Cycle," *Nature* 268 (1977), p.415; *idem*, "Effects of Holocene Climatic Change," *Quartenary Research* 6 (1976), pp.532–538, esp. the table on p.533; G. Einsele *et alii*, "Sea Level Fluctuation During the Past 6000 yr at the Coast of Mauritania," *Quartenary Research* 4 (1974), pp.282–289.

[104] In contrast to a period of low Nilotic flooding from ca. 2250–1950 B.C.; K.W. Butzer, "Pleistocene History of the Nile Valley in Egypt and Lower Nubia," *The Sahara and the Nile*, ed. by M. Williams and H. Faure (Rotterdam, 1980) pp.253–280, here p.278; following B. Bell, "Climate and the History of Egypt: The Middle Kingdom," *American Journal of Archaeology* 79 (1975), pp.223–269.

contrast to an apparent drop in production during the Late Bronze period.[105] B) The settlement patterns of the sites of the 'Iron hills, where settlements are extensive during the Middle Bronze period, indicate that the typically sharp summertime drop in the water table in this region (which, even in the best of years, has led to the seasonal failure of wells and springs) apparently created a barrier to settlement during the substantially drier Late Bronze period.[106]

5. The Late Bronze Period: Economic Stress and Regional Collapse

Perhaps the most extensive changes in the history of the transition from the Middle to the Late Bronze Age in *Palestine* occur in the changes of settlement patterns. These changes correspond well with a gradual warming trend and a shift towards drier conditions from about 1600 that continued until about 1300 B.C., or slightly later. In contrast to the extensive geographic spread of agriculture during the Middle Bronze into many marginal areas along the fringe of the Mediterranean climatic zone (most noticeably along the southern coastal strip, the central and Judaean highlands, and the *Shephelah*), the climatically poorer Late Bronze period resulted in a marked destabilization of farming in these marginal regions. This created significant gaps of occupation that lasted throughout most of the Late Bronze Age in scores of the marginal subregions of *Palestine*. This dislocation and abandonment is most marked in the central hills. This destabilization and marginal collapse is commonly associated with the end of Middle Bronze IIC. In terms of historical causation, it is important to recognize that this process of change began already long before the establishment (in the course of the fifteenth-century) of Egyptian eighteenth dynasty military hegemony over the Palestinian coastal plain and central lowland valleys. *Egypt*'s imperial thrust into *Palestine* was not punitive, but was related to *Egypt*'s attempts to establish and maintain overland trade routes with *Mesopotamia* and

---

[105] N. Lipschitz, "Olives in Ancient Israel in View of Dendroarchaeological Investigations," *Olive Oil in Antiquity*, ed. by M. Heltzer and D. Eitam (Jerusalem, 1988) pp.139-145; idem, "Overview of the Dendrochronological and Dendroarchaeological Research in Israel," *Dendrochronologia* 4 (1986), pp.37-58.

[106] Th.L. Thompson, *op.cit.*, 1979, pp.43-45.

Syria.[107] This establishment of an Egyptian imperial presence in *Palestine* was not at the cost of the prosperity or security of the lowland settlements. It is particularly difficult to identify this long term deterioration of the general prosperity of *Palestine* with either *Egypt* or the region's inclusion into the Egyptian "empire." Rather, the already existent internal economic stress and partial collapse seems to have led to a comparable and pervasive military weakness throughout the region, certainly creating by the fifteenth-century a situation in which *Palestine* was particularly vulnerable to any attack from outside and hence ripe for domination by an ambitious and resurgent Egypt. Militarily, there was little in *Palestine* that would incline the Egyptians to resist the temptation, and the growing consolidation of the Hittites further northward might indeed have precipitated just such a takeover. It should be stressed here that the often cited geopolitical and trade centered economic role of *Palestine* as the indispensable "land bridge" between the stronger and more advanced civilizations of *Egypt, Anatolia* and *Syria* is a role that *Palestine* first began to play only as a consequence of the Egyptian conquest. It is a role that is uniquely structured by imperial designs, not one that ought to be viewed ahistorically and as somehow intrinsic to *Palestine.* The vast majority of earlier trade between *Egypt* and the greater states of *Asia* did not move overland at all but proceeded by sea by way of the Phoenician and Syrian coasts. Southern *Palestine* was a peripheral market for *Egypt* and of interest primarily because of *Egypt*'s metallurgy and mining interests in the *Sinai.* Interests in its lumber, olive oil and wine had only begun to be explored. Northern *Palestine* lay rather on the fringes of the cuneiform world of *Syria* and *Mesopotamia.*[108] *Palestine*'s increased direct involvement in

---

[107] The assumption of an Egyptian conquest of the whole of Palestine in the mid-sixteenth-century, while frequently still maintained (So J.M. Weinstein, "The Egyptian Empire in Palestine: A Reassessment," *BASOR* 241, 1981, pp.1–28), apart from issues of evidence, does not make sense either militarily or economically, and certainly does not explain the desertion of so many sites and subregions of Palestine. Especially troublesome is the steady decrease in the wealth and material culture of the lowlands during the early part of the Late Bronze period in contrast to the relative prosperity resulting from the Egyptian involvement in southern Palestine during the thirteenth-century (N. Na'aman, "Economic Aspects of the Egyptian Occupation of Canaan," *IEJ* 31, 1981, pp.172–185, esp. p.185; R. Gonen, *op.cit.,* 1984 p.63).

[108] See the studies and explorations along the *Via Maris* by E. Oren (*op.cit.*) and the evidence he gathers demonstrating the extensive exploration of this trade route only subsequent to the establishment of the empire in *Asia.* Evidence for the use of this route

international trade during the early part of Late Bronze II and the region's increased political vassalage to *Egypt* probably affected economic stability positively, although it does not seem to have resulted in any sustained economic expansion until the fourteenth and thirteenth centuries, during which the occupation of the major tells of *Palestine* increased sharply.[109] The revival of the lowlands during the *Amarna* period from the Middle Bronze-Late Bronze transition's economic and demographic depression underlines the positive impact of the Egyptian presence during Late Bronze II, and argues strongly for viewing the reduced population of this period as relatively prosperous in the history of *Palestine*. The widespread views among biblical scholars who understand the larger towns of the *Amarna* period as having been in a state of internal disintegration and intercity strife under an only nominal control of a somnolent Egyptian empire needs considerable revision.[110] It seems particularly unlikely that Egyptian power had had any contact whatever with the marginal areas of the Palestinian highlands during the sixteenth-century, where Bronze Age settlement patterns suggest the most radical dislocations to have occurred.[111]

Once the Middle Bronze-Late Bronze transition has been separated from the end of the so-called Hyksos rule in *Egypt* and from the eighteenth dynasty's imperial aspirations, a clearly definable external

---

for trade prior to the empire period is limited and occasional.

[109] R. Gonen, *op.cit.* pp.63-65.

[110] This trend in biblical studies usually refers to the *Amarna* Period disturbances, with reference to political conflict and fighting discussed in a number of the *Amarna* letters. This view has been generally supported by such influential scholars as W.F. Albright (*The Archaeology of Palestine*, 1949, pp.100ff.) and K. Kenyon ("Palestine in the Time of the Eighteenth Dynasty," *CAH* vol 2,1, London, 1971, pp.526-566), and has recently been give new impetus in biblical scholarship by N.K. Gottwald (*The Tribes of Yahweh*, New York, 1979) and in historical studies generally by S. Ahituv ("Economic Factors in the Egyptian Conquest of Palestine," *IEJ* 28, 1978, pp.93-105), and seems to be supported by R. Gonen (*op.cit.* p.70). N. Na'aman (*op.cit.*), J.M. Weinstein (*op.cit.*, 1981), and G. Ahlström (*op.cit.*, forthcoming), on the other hand, seem to argue for an extensive revision of our understanding of the Egyptian empire in Palestine, involving a much more critical perspective on the *Amarna* tablets.

[111] The tendentious function of many of the *Amarna* letters (namely, to get money, supplies, troops, or moral support from the Egyptians) should cause us to hesitate before we read them as direct reflections of reality. Authorities in the best of times feel harassed by enemies and brigands. When they shout loudly as they have in the Amarna letters, we are not warranted on the strength of these shouts alone to conclude that the sky was falling, only that they wished to convince someone that such disaster was imminent.

cause becomes extremely difficult to identify for these changes in settlement patterns, particularly because of the regional nature of the dislocations that mark the shift from a Middle Bronze to a Late Bronze horizon. In many areas, and especially in those in which *Egypt* did take interest in the course of the imperial period, substantial continuity is patent and the changes involve what might generally be described as an extensive economic depression and decline, with the larger towns playing an increasingly significant role. In other regions the change is marked by collapse and abandonment of regional agriculture, and apparently the more isolated a region was the more extreme were the effects on the local economy. Our interpretation of these changes suffers for lack of adequate chronological criteria that might serve the whole of *Palestine*. We have every reason to believe that this long transition from Middle Bronze IIC to Late Bronze II did not occur everywhere at the same time.[112]

The departure from the many discrete and isolated small agricultural villages and hamlets of the Middle Bronze hill country, corresponding to clearly defined but relative chronological changes in the archaeological records of stratified sites that survived the transition, marks a distinctive pattern (in spite of a potentially erratic diffusion of material culture) of diminishing agricultural activity and reduction of population, consequent upon the breakup of the stability and prosperity that were characteristic of the Middle Bronze Age in all regions of *Palestine*. In the agriculturally sensitive Judaean uplands, for example, the collapse, of the sedentary population's hold on the region was near total. This collapse brought about a considerably extended wilderness period that did not end until new settlement of the Iron II period was established more than a half-millennium later. A similar though by far more limited disaster affected the *Galilee,* the central hills, the southern coast, large areas of the *Transjordan* and most other marginal regions in *Palestine*. Neither international politics nor trade were fundamental to these changes and had little influence in their onset. The causes, rather, seem to have been indigenous to *Palestine* and in their roots economic and agricultural in nature. That those regions most severely affected were the same areas that had been desedentarized during the much more severe drought of the late third-millennium B.C. seems significantly to point towards climatic factors and drought as the efficient cause of the

---

[112] A. Kempinski, *op.cit.*

Middle Bronze IIC collapse as well as towards the inability of the Late Bronze sedentary population to regain control of these ecologically fragile areas of *Palestine*.

As we have already mentioned, lowland settlement, although sorely stressed and impoverished, is at least regionally maintained throughout the Late Bronze Age, with a number of the larger tells of the lowlands and greater intermontane valleys giving evidence of substantial continuity with the Middle Bronze Age.[113] The Late Bronze towns are, however, considerably smaller and materially poorer, and most are probably unfortified,[114] perhaps as a result of an Egyptian imperial policy that may have found it more efficient to deal with unfortified vassal states than with potentially contentious rebellions. The Egyptian presence in *Palestine* continues through the onset of Iron I until at least the reign of Ramses VI, when the Egyptians apparently withdrew from the *Jezreel*. On the strength of the *Amarna* tablets, it seems justified to suggest that this presence did not lead to direct Egyptian rule of the Palestinian territories, but rather supported indigenous dynastic rule centered in the larger towns through forms of vassalage with the aid of Egyptian troops and communications with the Egyptian court. The base of power of these town rulers, although strengthened by their alliance with Egypt, seems to have been entirely local and regionally limited, oriented economically to land ownership and politically to family alliances. When that economic foundation weakened, as it did precipitately at the end of the thirteenth and the beginning of the twelfth centuries, established political strength also began to disintegrate. Neither the Egyptian presence nor the ultimate withdrawal of Egyptian power from the area under the Ramesside pharaohs was the cause of such decline and impoverishment. Rather the Egyptian presence delayed the collapse, and withdrawal was itself a response to the economic deterioration that overtook not only *Palestine* but the whole of the Western Mediterranean world. Viewed historiographically in terms of *"la longue durée*," the presence of Egyptian troops and the maintenance of the international trade and agricultural economy they promoted, together with the political cohesiveness that supported the local dynastic rule of the towns, enabled the sedentary population of the most fertile regions of *Palestine*

---

[113] See especially the very fine summation of R. Gonen, "Urban Canaan in the Late Bronze Period," *BASOR* 253 (1984), pp.61-73.

[114] *Ibid.; contra* Th.L. Thompson, *op.cit.*, 1979, pp.66f.

to survive a long and serious economic depression at a significant level of stability and culture throughout most of the Late Bronze Age, at a time when the population of less favored regions had been entirely dislocated.

Apart from the territories immediately under the political control of the major towns, large areas of the central highlands and of *Judaea* (exclusive of the immediate areas surrounding such towns as *Hazor, Shechem,* and *Jerusalem*) underwent a transition away from sedentary agriculture to distinct marginal economies during the post Middle Bronze IIC period. In fact, throughout *Palestine,* settlement in outlying villages and hamlets is almost entirely absent during most of the succeeding Late Bronze Age.[115] Given the extremely long period following this desedentarization and the large territories involved, one might expect to find a furthering of differentiation in the population and the gradual development of groups and subcultures to reflect a distinctive ethnicity. Direct evidence for the emergence of such groups in the marginal regions of Late Bronze *Palestine* prior to a new process of sedentarization in these regions that begins only at the very end of the Late Bronze period, is extremely limited. Direct archaeological evidence for any of the various forms of nomadic pastoralism is absent. However, in the best of circumstances such evidence is rare. We do have nevertheless some limited textual evidence in Egyptian texts of the period, most notably from the *Amarna* archives. R. Giveon and O. Loretz have recently produced excellent studies of a large number of texts that refer to non sedentary groups of *'apiru* and *Shasw* associated with the upland and steppe regions of *Palestine.*[116] The appelative *'apiru* (particularly in the texts of *Amarna*) is used to refer to acts of (or to bands of) brigands, and seems to refer to the social status of groups in conflict with some of the Late Bronze rulers. It is, however, not used as the name of any specific ethnic group in *Palestine.*[117] Rather, the texts refer to people who, because of poverty or other personal disaster, had been relegated to the fringes of society, had lost normal status and

---

[115] *Ibidem.*

[116] R. Giveon, *op.cit.*; O. Loretz, *op.cit.*

[117] O. Loretz, *ibid.*, pp.195-248; M. Weippert, *op.cit.*, 1967, pp.68-71. The potential connection with the much later postexilic biblical term *'ibrim,* with its ethnic connotations, seems at best a linguistic one relating to etymology, and does not imply any historical continuity: Loretz, *op.cit.*, pp.247f. 270f.

lived as vagabonds, surviving as hired laborers, mercenaries and robbers. They were neither farmers nor pastoralists, nor distinctively nomadic or sedentary, but lived apart from the ordinary patterns and norms of society. The threat that they posed for the established Late Bronze social order reflects something of the depth of the economic depression and the inability of the sedentary population to assert control over the marginal lands beyond the immediate agricultural zones.[118] The term *Shasw* (probably related to the cuneiform name *Sutu*) on the other hand, refers to West Semitic groups who lived over a wide geographical area including the *Transjordan*, the fringes of the Arabian desert, the *Sinai*, as well as some of the marginal areas of *Palestine*. This extensive spread of the *Shasw* and their frequent association with pastoralism, suggest that they might reasonably be identified as steppe dwellers, occupying the grasslands and marginal agricultural areas of the Levant from the periphery of the *Euphrates* Valley to the Eastern desert of *Egypt*. Neither Egyptian nor cuneiform texts of the second-millennium are particularly clear in the specific identification of ethnicities, and the references to *Shasw* and *Sutu* include a number of distinct ethno-linguistic and tribally differentiated units. Giveon seems clearly to have shown that they are West Semitic, and closely related linguistically, and perhaps historically, to the peoples of the first-millennium who established a tier of ethno-regional states in the *Transjordan*.[119] In contrast to the *'apiru* underclass of the *Amarna* tablets, the *Shasw* do not seem to directly derive from, or have been immediately indigenous to, the agricultural heartland of Late Bronze *Palestine*, but seem rather indigenous to the larger marginal areas bordering *Palestine*. Whether many of their numbers had been originally created as a result of the destabilization of the Middle Bronze economy and ultimately reflect the population displaced then as Finkelstein and others have suggested,[120] or whether,

---

[118] J. Bottero's studies of the *'Apiru* are indispensable: *Le Probleme des Habiru, Cahiers de la sociètè asiatique* 12 (Paris, 1954); *idem*, "Habiru," *RLA* 4 (1972) pp.14-27; *idem*, "Entre Nomades et Sèdentaires: les Habiru," *DHA* 6 (1980) pp.201-213; *idem*, "Les Habiru, les nomades et les sedentaires," *NSP* (1981) pp.89-107; also: "Eastern Society Before the Middle of the 2nd Millennium B.C.," *Oikumene* 3 (1982), pp.7-100, esp. pp.55f. 96ff.

[119] R. Giveon, *op.cit.*

[120] I. Finkelstein, *The Archaeology of the Israelite Settlement* (Jerusalem, 1988); also R.B. Coote and K.W. Whitelam, *The Emergence of Israel in Canaan* (Sheffield, 1987); H. Weippert, *op.cit.*

as I believe more likely, the origins of such nomadic groups ultimately relate to even earlier periods in the development of marginal economies in the steppelands that are reflected in archaeological remains from the Chalcolithic, Early Bronze II and Early Bronze IV-Middle Bronze I periods, is as yet difficult to determine with any precision, since continuity in the occupation of the steppe during this more than two millennia period is not yet verified.[121] The existence of pastoralism along the Palestinian periphery, developing social structures largely independent of the agriculturalist sedentary population, may go back to as early as the Neolithic period, when the grasslands of the steppe and indeed even large areas of inner *Arabia* were capable of supporting a considerable pastoral population prior to the onset of drought conditions in the fifth-millennium.[122] Continuity in material culture, when that is known at all, proceeds only by reference to the sedentary populations. The wide varieties of known economies (in mining, metal working, trade, pastoralism, grain agriculture, horticulture in oases, hunting, etc.), while they demonstrate the potential of these marginal areas to support significant population in a large spectrum of forms from nomadism to sedentary, also speak for such a potential diversity of peoples with both regional and chronological distinctiveness that it seems highly arbitrary to identify any specific contributive factor in the growth of non sedentary social structures as causative and originative. Certainly, if, at the end of the Middle Bronze IIC, a drought had created severe stress on and dislocation of the highland agricultural population and that of the smaller villages and hamlets of the whole of *Palestine,* we should also expect that the southern and eastern grasslands, and indeed the entire Levantine steppe region, would have suffered an even greater depression, if for no other reasons than the greater vulnerability to drought and the greater fragility of their economies. While one might rightly suggest a broader diversification of the agricultural economy into more drought resistent subsistent strategies such as pastoralism, one might also expect that steppe dwellers, and primarily the transhumance pastoralists among them, would make more permanent incursions into

---

[121] See below, Chapter 7.

[122] A.M. Khazanov, *Nomads and the Outside World* (Cambridge, 1984) pp.99f.; also, H.A. McClure, *The Arabian Peninsula and Prehistoric Populations* (Miami, 1971); C.K. Pearse, "Grazing in the Middle East," *Journal of Range Management* 24 (1966), pp.13–16; E.A. Knauf, "Beduin and Beduin States," *ABD*, forthcoming.

the woodlands and hill country of central *Palestine* and *Judaea* in response to the abandonment of these territories by agriculturalists. Frequent changes in the patterns of land use—what might be described as desedentarization—occurred in more recent historical times, affecting not only the hill country but many lowland areas as well. All known periods have involved some incursion from the steppe.[123] It seems wholly inadequate to understand such population shifts as entirely indigenous to a single subregion. One must also include in the discussion not only the Mediterranean zones of *Palestine* proper but the much more expansive steppelands on its borders. Given the immense chronological gap in sedentary exploitation of the central hills and the many subregions of lowland *Palestine* extending not only over most of the Late Bronze period, but, in some regions lasting well into the Iron II period, efforts to identify the dislocated populations of Middle Bronze IIC with movements towards resedentarization at the end of the Late Bronze Period, during Iron I and at the beginning of Iron II, lack adequate justification. That some such pastoral and nomadic groups, indigenous to greater *Palestine,* formed part of the population that is reflected in the ethnic and regional diversity of Iron Age *Palestine* seems no longer questionable. That other population factors were also involved is equally patent.

---

[123] W.-D. Hütteroth, *Palästina und Transjordanien im 16. Jahrhundert, BTAVO* 33 (Wiesbaden, 1978) *passim*; Th.L. Thompson, F.J. Gonçalves and J.M. Van Cangh, *Toponomie Palestinienne: Plaine de St Jean D'Acre et Corridor de Jérusalem, Publications de L'Institut Orientaliste de Louvain* (Louvain-La-Neuve, 1988).

CHAPTER SIX

THE LATE BRONZE-IRON AGE TRANSITION

1. The Collapse of Late Bronze Civilization in the Western Mediterranean

From the period of approximately 1200 to 1000 B.C. (which was a tumultuous two-century long period that witnessed many radical changes throughout the territories bordering on the eastern Mediterranean) there is abundant evidence in support of a long period of drought and recurrent famine that capped the long economic and political decline of the Late Bronze Age. The extensive deterioration of the Mediterranean basin shoreline is closely correlated with a global climatic change. In contrast to the dominant climatic regime after 1000 B.C., a Sub-Atlantic period of aridity, with an approximately 20% decrease in rainfall and rising temperatures from 2.0°–3.0° C. above normal, had become particularly acute around 1200 B.C. During the early first-millennium, a cooler, wetter climate returned to most of *Europe*[1] and rainfall patterns in the Near East again reached a level comparable to that of modern times.[2] At the close of the Late Bronze period (around 1200 B.C.), a sharp increase in aridity took place throughout the Near East.[3] This period of aridity is closely analogous to a similar but less intensive drought that struck *Palestine* during the latter part of the third-century A.D., which had been partially responsible for a severe socio-economic deterioration that overwhelmed this part of the Roman empire.[4]

---

[1] A.F. Harding, "Introduction: Climatic Change and Archaeology," *Climatic Change in Later Prehistory*, ed. by A.F. Harding (Edinburgh, 1982) pp.1-10, esp. p.9.

[2] N. Shehadeh, "The Climate of Jordan in the Past and Present," *SHAJ* II (Amman, 1985) pp.25-37, esp. pp.26f.

[3] W. Nützel, "The Climatic Changes of Mesopotamia and Border Areas," *Sumer* 32 (1976), pp.11-24, esp. p.21; D.L. Donley, *Analysis of the Winter Climatic Pattern at the Time of the Mycenaean Decline* (University of Wisconsin dissertation, 1971) p.131; also, J. Neuman and S. Parpola, "Climatic Change and Eleventh–Tenth Century Eclipse of Assyria and Babylonia," *JNES* 46 (1987), pp.161-182.

[4] D. Sperber, "Drought, Famine and Pestilence in Amoraic Palestine," *JESHO* 17 (1974), pp.272-298.

The effects of even minor droughts on marginal areas that lie close to the border of aridity have often been disastrous. Whereas in better watered regions the effects of drought appear only in terms of a scarcity in food supply, in regions such as southern and eastern *Palestine* (located as they are on the border of aridity demarcating agricultural from steppelands) even relatively minor fluctuations of climate, when maintained or recurrent over years, can result in serious ecological and economic dislocation with radical political and social consequences. Desiccation becomes particularly marked in areas where irrigation is not employed.[5] Although downward trends in rainfall fluctuations have a particularly harsh impact on steppe and marginal zones such as the southern coastal plain, the *Beersheva* Basin and the Judaean hills, prime agricultural areas such as the central riverain valleys or upland regions of typically very high rainfall patterns display a greater resistance to such droughts, and consequently display a greater stability in settlement. In a year of severe aridity when rainfall in the Upper *Galilee* drops 15–20% below the norm, the reduced precipitation is still adequate to support most forms of dry agriculture, albeit at lower levels of productivity. However, the same weather cycle may lower rainfall in the *Beersheva* Basin by as much as 50% or more, drying up grasslands and, if the drought persist over years, transforming agricultural land to steppe and steppelands to desert. In truly arid and steppe regions (where pastoralism is a more dominant aspect of the economy) the population is most severely affected by drought when its severity and duration cause both a lowering of the water table and a reduced availability of grasslands, inevitably leading to overgrazing and subsequent severe erosion, creating ecological deterioration from which the region may take centuries to recover.[6]

Even in those more stable regions that normally support a form of Mediterranean economy, a change in the rainfall patterns, when extended over a lengthy period can cause long standing, radical changes in vegetation; for example, a study of wood charcoals from archaeological sites in the highland area just north of the *Negev* indicates a shift from predominantly Mediterranean to Saharan vegetation forms. This change in types of vegetation corresponds to the transition from the

---

[5] A.D. Crown, "Toward a Reconstruction of the Climate of Palestine: 8000 B.C. to 0 B.C.," *JNES* 31 (1972), pp.312–330, esp. pp.313ff.

[6] *Ibid.*, pp.115ff.

end of the Late Bronze to the Iron I period.[7] In other areas, where irrigation agriculture is supported or where rainfall is normally abundant, the onset of a period of severe aridity can be particularly disruptive and ultimately effect long term survival, because of a lack of indigenous drought resistent types of vegetation in the immediate area.[8] Both water and wind erosion also dramatically increase with drought conditions.

Human adaptation to drought (which can be either constructive or destructive to the environment) also affects the agricultural economy by opening new areas to settlement and closing or reducing settlement in others. In a recent article on the Iron I settlements in the region of *Manasseh,*[9] A. Zertal argued well that many of these sites became open to agriculture as a result specifically of the use of collared rim *pithoi* for water storage, an adaptation to drought conditions that had far reaching consequences for the sedentarization of many areas of the central highlands. In the *Shephelah,* however, which lies closer to the border of aridity, a very moderate incursion of agricultural settlement in areas away from the major *wadis* during Iron I seems to have precipitated a major deterioration of the natural habitat that resulted in the irreversible deforestation of the hilly regions and brought about the onset of severe erosion. It is possible that this deterioration was caused by extensive herding.[10] In contrast to the Late Bronze period and to the early part of Iron I, when olive trees were abundant in many of the marginal areas of *Palestine,*[11] the extremely long duration of the

---

[7] C 14 dates of ca. 3150 BP: J.L. Bintiiff, "Climatic Change, Archaeology, and Quaternary Science in the Eastern Mediterranean Region," *Climatic Change in Later Prehistory,* ed. by A.F. Harding (Edinburgh, 1982) pp.143-161, here p.147.

[8] Such factors might well be considered in efforts to explain the extensive collapse of Early Bronze agriculture, consequent upon a shift from subpluvial to drought conditions. See Th.L. Thompson, "The Background of the Patriarchs: A Reply to William Dever and Malcolm Clark," *JSOT* 9 (1978), pp.2-43.

[9] A. Zertal, "The Water Factor During the Israelite Settlement in Canaan," *Society and Economy in the Eastern Mediterranean, Orientalia Lovaniensia Analecta* 23, ed. by M. Heltzer and E. Lipinski (Leuven, 1988) pp.341-352.

[10] J.D. Currid, "The Deforestation of the Foothills of Palestine," *PEQ* 116 (1984), pp.1-11.

[11] V.M. Fargo and K.G. O'Connell, "Five Seasons of Excavation at Tell el-Hesi," *BA* 41 (1978), pp.165-182, esp. p.180; W. Van Zeist, "Past and Present Environment of the Jordan Valley," *SHAJ* II (1985) pp.199-204; N. Lipschitz, "Olives in Ancient Israel in View of Dendroarchaeological Investigations," *Olive Oil in Antiquity,* ed. by M. Heltzer and D.

drought sharply decreased the presence of olives in these regions sometime before the end of Iron I.[12]

The clearest evidence for the existence of extended drought from ca. 1250 to 1050 B.C. is found in indications of a severe drop in sea level that corresponded to the end of the thirteenth and the beginning of the twelfth-century.[13] Although sediments from the *Dead Sea* do not give evidence corresponding to this Sea level change during the Late Bronze-Iron Age transition,[14] the measurement of patterns of *Dead Sea* fluctuations "may be largely insensitive to any but the most drastic periods of change."[15] In contrast, ocean levels correspond closely to change in both temperature and rainfall patterns.[16]

In 1966, R. Carpenter first proposed a global climatic change as the cause of the Mycenaean decline and collapse that closed the Late Bronze Age in the Aegean.[17] In reviewing this hypothesis, P. Ålin confirms the ability of Carpenter's theory to explain the widespread deterioration of the regional culture,[18] but concludes that the hypothesis fails to explain the fire destructions so evident in excavations.[19] The dissertation of

---

Eitam (Haifa, 1988) pp.139-142.

[12] *Ibid.*, p.141.

[13] The bibliography relating to sea changes worldwide is immense. H. Ritter-Kaplan, "The impact of drought on Third Millennium BCE Cultures on the Basis of Excavations in the Tel Aviv Exhibition Grounds," *EI* 17 (1983), pp.333-338, esp. p.8; also, J. Laheyrie, "Sea Level Variations and the Birth of the Egyptian Civilization," *Radiocarbon Dating*, ed. by R. Berger and H. Suess (Berkeley, 1979) pp.32-35; R.W. Fairbridge, "Shellfish Eating Preceramic Indians in Coastal Brazil," *Science* 191 (1976), pp.353-359, esp. p.358; R.W. Fairbridge and C. Hillaire-Marcel, "An 8000 Year Palaeoclimatic Record of the 'Double Hale' 45 Year Cycle," *Nature* 268 (1977), p.415.

[14] D. Neev and K.O. Emery, *The Dead Sea Depositional Processes and Environments of Evaporites* (Jerusalem, 1967); cited by A.D. Crown, *op.cit.*, p.325.

[15] *Ibid.*, p.321.

[16] I. Shannon, "Problems of Correlating Flandrian Sea Level Changes and Climate," *Climatic Change in Later Prehistory*, ed. by A.F. Harding (Edinburgh, 1982) pp.52-67, esp. pp.52 and 63.

[17] R. Carpenter, *Discontinuity in Greek Civilization* (Cambridge, 1966); more recently C.G. Thomas (*The Earliest Civilizations*, Washington D.C., 1982, pp.61ff.) who relates this more generally to widespread cultural changes throughout the western Mediterranean.

[18] P. Ålin, "Mycenaean Decline—Some Problems and Thoughts," *Greece and the Eastern Mediterranean in Ancient History and Prehistory*, ed. by K.H. Hinzl (Berlin, 1977) pp.31-39. For a general overview of the Mycenaean decline, see above all, F. Schachermeyer, *Die Agäische Frühzeit*, vol. 4: *Griechenland im Zeitalter der Wanderungen* (Vienna, 1982).

[19] P. Ålin, *ibid.*, p.39.

D.L. Donley confirmed that the existence of a climatic change (dated to approximately 1200 B.C.) that had brought about drought conditions as posited by Carpenter for Mycenae, was synchronous throughout the hemisphere.[20] Stiebing placed the peak of this drought between 1200–1190 B.C. and related it to references to drought and famine in the Hittite Empire mentioned in Egyptian texts involving grain sent to *Anatolia* from *Ugarit* during the reign of Merneptah.[21] Finally, in a very fine dissertation, F.R. Dupont[22] has argued very persuasively that the civilization of *Ugarit,* although greatly weakened by the effects of the drought that had seriously depressed the entire region, had been destroyed neither by the drought itself nor by the invasions of "Sea Peoples" coming from the Mycenaean region. Rather, long standing drought conditions had brought about such widespread impoverishment at Ugarit, and a consequent weakening of the political structures,[23] that the population of *Ugarit* was prevented from rebuilding after the city had been destroyed by earthquake in 1182 B.C. This suggested reconstruction of Dupont is particularly attractive in that it clearly indicates that climatic change alone—in such a well watered prime agricultural region as *Ugarit*—was only one of the factors in bringing about the end of this complex society. The drought was responsible for the diminished capacity of *Ugarit*'s society to rebuild once the destruction had occurred, but it did not itself cause the destruction. In addition to the climatic shift (and here the analogy to *Mycenae* is apt), yet other specifically historical

---

[20] D.L. Donley, *Analysis of the Winter Climatic Patterns at the Time of the Mycenaean Decline* (University of Wisconsin dissertation, 1971) pp.127–134.

[21] H. Stiebing, "The End of the Mycenaean Age," *BA* 43 (1980), pp.7–21. Further, *idem, Out of the Desert? Archaeology and the Exodus-Conquest Narratives* (Buffalo, 1989), especially regarding evidence for droughts from Near Eastern contemporary texts. One might also profitably consult the articles of J. Brinkman, "Settlement Surveys and Documentary: Regional Variations and Secular Trends," *JNES* 43 (1984), pp.175–179; and J. Neuman and S. Parpola, *op.cit.*, which refer to the contemporaneous drought in Southern Mesopotamia.

[22] F.R. Dupont, *The Late History of Ugarit* (Hebrew Union College dissertation, 1987).

[23] See the very perceptive article by M. Liverani, "Economia delle fattorie palatine ugaritiche," *Dialoghi di Archeologia* 1 (1979), pp.57–72, esp. pp.67, 70ff. For further background on the economic structures of Ugarit; also: M. Heltzer, *The Rural Community in Ancient Ugarit* (Wiesbaden, 1976); *idem, The Internal Organization of the Kingdom of Ugarit* (Wiesbaden, 1982). Certainly the likelihood of widespread rebellion under such severe conditions of stress should be given considerable weight.

events caused the destructions of the Late Bronze towns, and these must be sought in each distinct subregion of the Mediterranean basin.[24]

Whether by earthquake, fire, military force, rebellion or the collapse of the economic and political structures, many of the Late Bronze towns were destroyed during the course of the thirteenth and twelfth centuries in the primary agricultural regions of *Palestine*. Some, like *Hazor*, were resettled in much impoverished conditions with a substantial alteration of political structures. Some were abandoned, and still others like *Megiddo* maintained their occupation and survived throughout this difficult period of transition. It is in this context of significant deterioration of the agricultural heartland of *Palestine* that we begin to find new settlements occurring both in the well watered lowland regions and major highland valleys, but also in some of the marginal, previously more sparsely occupied subregions of *Palestine*, as the population sought an ever larger area of subsistence in face of the falling productivity. The earliest of such new settlements seem to have been concentrated in the coastal plain, and are found along the trade routes.[25] Within the Late Bronze cultural continuum, a combination of a sharp reduction in the size of larger towns and a fourfold increase[26] in the number of smaller settlements within the coastal plain represents an overall drop in population and a dispersal (apparently in response to the inability of the larger towns to support their populations) into smaller, economically more viable, agricultural units. By the twelfth-century (corresponding to the development of Iron I pottery forms) a similar pattern of change occurred in the *Jezreel* and *Beth Shan* valleys. The dispersal of the population into more marginal areas seems to have progressed, involving not only the lowlands but also spreading into the isolated regions of the *Galilee* and the hills of *Ephraim* as well. The drastic changes in the occupation of these highland regions ultimately led to the long term evolution of social, political and cultural entities: away from the control of the town centers, leading to a gradual development of regionally

---

[24] Some significant progress has been made in distinguishing destructions which were "man-made" from those which had "natural" causes, especially in regard to the Mycenaean collapse (P. Ålin, *op. cit.*), and one might hope for further success in establishing such causes in the future.

[25] R. Gonen, *op. cit.*, p.66.

[26] *Ibidem.*

organized society, a development that would eventually transform the political structures of *Syria-Palestine*.

2. The Central Hills of Ephraim and Manasseh

As described in Chapter 4 above, Zertal's and Finkelstein's regional studies of the early settlement of *Ephraim* and *Manasseh*[27] attempt to give an account of Israel's origins geographically in terms of the settlement patterns of the central hills. Fundamental to their argument is the chronologically oriented settlement sequence that they establish. Finkelstein has refined what Zertal originally argued: that the process of initial sedentarization along the eastern steppe fringe of the central highlands during Iron I indicates a gradual sedentarization of semi-nomads that ultimately developed into a region wide occupation of the hills on the basis of subsistence agriculture. According to Zertal and Finkelstein, this process involved a chronologically defined "shift from cereal to olive orchard and vineyard production."[28]

Echoing the earlier proposals of Albrecht Alt,[29] Coote and Whitelam have developed a supporting argument for Zertal's and Finkelstein's hypothesis of the origin of the central highland settlements

---

[27] A. Zertal, *Arubbath, Hepher, and the Third Solomonic District* (University of Tel Aviv dissertation, 1986); I. Finkelstein, *The Archaeology of the Israelite Settlement*, (Jerusalem, 1988); for a review of Finkelstein, G. Ahlström, *op.cit.*, forthcoming, Chapter VII; also A. Rainey's review of *Biblical Archaeology Today* (Jerusalem, 1985) in *BASOR* 273 (1989), pp.87-95 and that of C. Edens, *AJA* 93 (1989), pp.289-292.

[28] C. Edens, *ibid.*, p.290.

[29] See above chapter IV; A. Rainey strongly supports these proposals in *op.cit.* 1989, as does Edens with caution. The general process of sedentarization might well be elaborated—in the context of drought conditions—by such studies as that of J.E. Rafferty, "The Archaeological Record on Sedentariness: Recognition, Development and Implications," *Advances in Archaeological Method and Theory*, vol. 8, ed. by M.B. Schiffer (Orlando, 1985) pp.113-156. For a recent update on the unfortunately largely aimless continental discussion, see A. Lemaire, "Deux origines d'Israel: la montagne d'Ephraim et le territoire de Manassé," *La Protohistoire d'Israel*, ed. by E.-M. Laperrousaz (Paris, 1990); J. Soggin, *Einführung in die Geschichte Israels und Judas* (Darmstadt, 1991). Neither Lemaire nor Soggin deal substantially with the archaeological and sociological directions in which Finkelstein (*op.cit.*, 1988) and N.P. Lemche (*op.cit.*, 1985) have turned the field as a whole. Nor do they engage issues of evidence and warrant.

from indigenous Palestinian steppe dwellers and pastoralists.[30] Similarly, studies on early highland agriculture by D. Hopkins and L. Stager strongly illustrate the efforts of Zertal and Finkelstein to define what they understand as a subsistence economy in the Iron I central hills.[31] Both Zertal and Finkelstein (somewhat inadequately) attempt to explain the origin of these settlements solely in terms of the resedentarization of seminomadic pastoralists originally deriving from the Middle Bronze IIC period. This is partially the result of a too narrow focusing on the highlands alone. Even more questionable is their seemingly arbitrary selection of the steppe fringe settlements in the eastern sector of the highlands as the earliest of the early Iron I settlements, not to mention their assumption (on the basis of site quantification alone) that settlement expansion moved from the fringe to the agriculturally richer areas of the central zone.

However dissimilar the settlement at 'Izbet Sarta may be, G. Ahlström reminds us that as a result of Finkelstein's own excavation on the site, we have one of the very earliest of these highland settlements that, both in terms of geography and material culture, can be closely associated with the settlement of Aphek, which lies on the edge of the coastal plain.[32] With Ahlström, I find Finkelstein's argument that *Aphek* was already destroyed by the time of the foundation of 'Izbet Sartah unconvincing. *Aphek* is known to have survived at least until 1230 B.C.[33] Much of the 'Izbet Sartah pottery shows clear Late Bronze derivation, with parallels not only from *Aphek* but also from *Beth Shan* VI and Late Mycenaean IIIB. Moreover, 'Izbet Sartah did not survive into the

---

[30] For a revision of Finkelstein's views on the ethnicity of Iron I Israel, now: I. Finkelstein, "The Emergence of Israel in Canaan: Consensus, Mainstream and Dispute," *SJOT* 1,2 (1991), pp.47-59, esp. pp.50ff. and 56.

[31] D. Hopkins, *The Highlands of Canaan* (Sheffield, 1985); L.E. Stager, "The Archaeology of the Family in Ancient Israel," *BASOR* 260 (1985), pp.1-35. This interpretation is also supported by C.H.J. de Geus, *De Israelitische Stad* (Kampen, 1983) pp.236-238; also R.B. Coote, "Settlement Change in Early Iron Age Palestine," *Early Israelite Agriculture: Reviews of David C. Hopkins's Book The Highlands of Canaan*, ed. by O.S. Labianca and D.C. Hopkins (Berrien Springs, 1988) pp.17-27. Subsistence types of agriculture distinguish themselves from agricultural forms that are based in market economies, as well as from a variety of symbiotic or dimorphic forms. The production of specialized industries or "cash crops" are indicative of non-subsistence agriculture.

[32] G. Ahlström, *op.cit.,* forthcoming, Chapter VII.

[33] Following G. Ahlström, *ibid.,* based on the chronology of I. Singer, "Takuheinu and Haya: Two Governors in the Ugarit Letter from Tel Aphek," *Tel Aviv* 10 (1983), pp.3-25.

following Iron II period. Both its origin and its demise fall within the disturbance marked transition period.

The first Iron Age settlement at *et-Tell* (dated by its most recent excavator to Iron IA, with some expansion and remodeling at the beginning of Iron IB: ca. 1220–1125 and 1125–1050 B.C. respectively) followed a very similar pattern.[34] Although interpretation of the archaeological remains of *et-Tell* has frequently been overwhelmed by attempts to associate these levels and destructions with Joshua's story of *'Ai*, as well as by efforts to identify the ethnic allegiance of the villagers of this ancient settlement,[35] there seems little warrant from the excavations either to affirm the historicity of Joshua 7–8. or to identify the ethnicity of *Ai's* inhabitants.[36] An agricultural background for the settlers of *et-Tell* is strongly suggested by the use of terracing and rock cut cisterns (with filter traps and settling basins) associated with individual dwelling units.[37] Moreover, the pottery associations relate readily to the regional traditions reflected in the final Late Bronze level of nearby *Beitin*. Unquestionably, Callaway's efforts to associate this settlement with the sedentary, agricultural population of *Palestine* from the Bronze Age, seem fully justified. It is important to note, however, that the question of whether *et-Tell* of Iron I is to be identified as "Israelite" or "Canaanite" ("Hivite") does not effect its clear association (like *'Izbet Sartah*) with indigenous agriculturalists.

Finkelstein himself departs from Zertal and makes a significant distinction between the settlements of *Manasseh* and those of *Ephraim*.[38] The distinction is largely based on ecological grounds, and extends into questions of settlement history as well. Unlike *Ephraim* (and in contrast to the near abandonment of *Ephraim)* *Manasseh* possessed well watered and fertile valleys that supported a considerable Late Bronze population. Consistent with this, Finkelstein argues for a continuity of *Manasseh's* Iron I settlements from the Late Bronze Age

---

[34] J.A. Callaway, "New Evidence on the Conquest of 'Ai," *JBL* 87 (1968), pp.312–320; *idem*, *The Early Bronze Age Citadel and Lower City at Ai (Et-Tell)* (Cambridge, 1980).

[35] J.A. Callaway, *op.cit.*, 1968; *idem*, "Excavating Ai (Et-Tell): 1964–1972," *BA* 39 (1976), pp.18–30; and the criticism of Z. Zevit, "Archaeological and Literary Stratigraphy in Joshua 7–8," *BASOR* 251 (1983), pp.23–35.

[36] A. Kuschke, "Hiwwiter in Ha-'Ai?" *Wort und Wahrheit, AOAT* 18, ed. by H. Rösel (Neukirchen, 1973) pp.115–119.

[37] J.A. Callaway, *op.cit.* 1976, pp.29f.

[38] I. Finkelstein, *op.cit.*, 1988, pp.89–91.

and a growth of new settlement in this region out of the indigenous sedentary population of *Palestine*. This, I believe, is an accurate revision of Zertal. However, it nonetheless raises rather serious difficulties for Finkelstein's own hypothesis regarding both *Ephraim* and the central hills as a whole. If the demarcation between Canaanite and Israelite ethnicity can be so substantially relaxed as Finkelstein does for *Manasseh*, then what reasonable grounds does Finkelstein have to maintain it elsewhere, particularly in neighboring *Ephraim*? Moreover, if Zertal's *Manasseh* was settled during Iron I by originally sedentary agriculturalists, then how were these pioneering farmers—and there were considerable numbers of them—kept out of the agriculturally most viable regions of *Ephraim*? Is not *Manasseh* one of the more obvious potential sources for *Ephraim*'s new settlers?

Not only do we need to deal with the issues of the ethnicity and economic background of the earliest Iron Age highland settlers, but when we turn to the excavations of Iron Age *Seilun*, the core of Finkelstein's early chronology, through which he is able to reconstruct a specific direction of settlement from East to West, must be questioned.[39] In so far as the Iron I collared rim store jar (the almost sole basis for pottery chronology during Iron I) is found throughout all phases of this period here and throughout *Ephraim* and *Manasseh*, it is clear that Finkelstein's efforts to date this settlement to the second half of the twelfth-century rather than to the end of the thirteenth-century were not based on criteria of ceramic chronology. Rather, he interpreted the architectural structures of *Seilun* as "public buildings" from a perspective which (in this argument) already assumed that seminomadic pastoral groups had previously established a central cultic shrine there. In this way, he was able to disassociate the alleged cultic installation from the sedentary agricultural settlement at *Seilun*, to which it, however, clearly belongs. Moreover, his perception of the site as cultic does not rest entirely on the remains from the Iron I period, but ultimately depends on the former presence of a Late Bronze II temple that had performed what was understood as a comparable function on

---

[39] M.-L. Buhl and S. Holm-Nielsen, *Shiloh* (Copenhagen, 1969); I. Finkelstein, "Shiloh 1981," *IEJ* 32 (1982), pp.148-150; *idem*, "Shiloh 1982," *IEJ* 33 (1983), pp.123-126; *idem*, "Shiloh Yields Some, But Not All, of its Secrets," *BAR* 12 (1986), pp.22-41; *idem*, 1988, pp.205-234; also, the very judicious discussion in D.G. Schley, *Shiloh: A Biblical City in Tradition and History*, JSOTS 63 (Sheffield, 1989) esp.pp.65-99.

that site. In describing the fragility of Finkelstein's argument, D.G. Schley[40] notes that the discussions of the cultic shrine intrinsically undermine the equation that Iron I = Israelite settlement. Apart from equivocal interpretation concerning the economic functions of the inhabitants, and in spite of a gap in site occupation, what the evidence of *Seilun* does show is that this settlement also reflects continuity with the earlier Bronze Age occupation of the region.

Two other major sites in the central hills, *Beitin* and *Tell Balatah*, are important in understanding the nature of the highland settlement in this region. The reports of the *Beitin* excavations[41] are particularly difficult to evaluate critically. The Late Bronze II town had been destroyed by fire and reoccupied shortly thereafter. This early Iron I occupation was much smaller and considerably impoverished. Its architecture and pottery (compared by the excavators to *Tell Beit Mirsim* B1) apparently show little immediate continuity with the previous Late Bronze II town. The two earliest phases of Iron I, dated to the end of the thirteenth and twelfth centuries, were also destroyed by fire, and the settlement does not show a stability of occupation until Phase 3 (or possibly phase 4) when the village began to expand and became a major town in the Iron II period. The fire destructions of the Late Bronze II and earliest Iron Age levels reflect a period of continued disturbance, comparable to what we find elsewhere both in the central hills and throughout most of the regions of *Palestine* and the whole of the western Mediterranean. This evidence does not support, however, the hypothesis put forward by Finkelstein of an extended period of peaceful sedentarization of pastoralists. Rather, the continued disturbances of the lowlands are also mirrored in the highlands.

Thanks to the very careful excavations undertaken by ASOR from 1956 to 1969, the site of ancient *Shechem (Tell Balatah),* gives us a very clear picture of the changes that overtook the highland population at least in this always very important region of the northern central hills.[42]

---

[40] *Ibid.*, p.79.

[41] J.L. Kelso, *The Excavations of Bethel, AASOR* 39 (1968).

[42] For a discussion of the excavations at *Tell Balatah*, see especially G.E. Wright, *Shechem, The Biography of a Biblical City* (New York, 1965); E.F. Campbell, "The Shechem Area Survey," *BASOR* 190 (1968), pp.19-41; *idem*, "Tribal League Shrines in Amman and Shechem," *BA* 32 (1969), pp.104-116; I. Finkelstein, *op.cit.,* 1988, pp.81f; L.E. Toombs, "Shechem: Problems of the Early Israelite Era," *Symposia*, ed. by F.M. Cross (Cambridge, 1979) pp.69-83. Unfortunately, the final excavation reports of this very important site have

Late Bronze II *Balatah* was destroyed at the end of the fourteenth or early in the thirteenth-century, and the resettlement (considerably impoverished and much smaller) continued occupation of this very rich agricultural region through the Iron I period. The material and ceramic remains show considerable continuity with the Late Bronze period and, at least in the earliest phases of Iron I, this pattern of major disturbances and new settlements at an economically depressed level is fully comparable to what occurs during this same period in the lowlands.[43] As in *Seilun* and *Beitin*, the Iron I occupation of *Shechem* ends in a great fire. Regional occupation, however, continues throughout the Iron I period. In this, the highland settlements of Iron I are hardly unique.

At nearby *al-Burnat* on the slopes of Mount *Ebal*, a site with a large enclosure wall and considerable evidence of agricultural activity, was excavated by the University of *Haifa*. The excavations uncovered occupation in two phases (dated to the reigns of Ramses II or III) from the end of the thirteenth-century through the twelfth-century. This site also displayed elements of continuity between the end of Late Bronze II and the earliest phases of Iron I. In spite of radical dislocations in material culture, alterations of settlement patterns and changing economic structures of the highland population during this very long transition period, the almost universal tendency of archaeologists and historians to mark too sharp a break between the Late Bronze and the Iron Age seems entirely unwarranted, driven more by the need to find an historical context for Israel than by legitimate historiographical concerns related to evidence.

Nevertheless, while Zertal and Finkelstein's arguments for supporting their hypothesis that the new Iron Age settlers are resedentarizing pastoralists, and their contention that the very earliest of these settlements lie along the Eastern steppe fringe of the highlands, are fragile and debatable at best, they are not, especially when sharply limited to *Ephraim*, entirely refutable. Indeed, a pastoral element among the early settlers of this region, at least of a transhumant variety, is a given.[44]

---

not yet been published.

[43] R.S. Boraas, "Iron IA Ceramic at Tell Balatah: A Preliminary Examination," *The Archaeology of Jordan and Other Studies* (Berrien Springs, 1986) pp.249-263.

[44] J.A. Callaway, *op.cit.,* 1976. See further below, Chapter VII.

The structure of Finkelstein's analysis of settlement patterns, which forms the basis for his interpretation of the settlement process as a progressive movement from the eastern steppe to the western slopes and from pastoralism to horticulture, rests on a false and untenable assumption that the new economy that the Iron Age I highlanders pursued was that of "subsistence agriculture" rather than a market economy. This problem affects our understanding not only of the chronological process of settlement but also of the interregional relationships that existed between contemporary settlements, the associations of the highland settlements with both highland and lowland trade, and the long process of the gradual unification of the hill country settlement with its slow development of an economic basis conducive to centralization.

The now well established discussion concerning the interplay between Palestinian village agriculture and animal husbandry has already crucially challenged any too automatic acceptance of the Palestinian highland economy as a form of "subsistence agriculture," and the attempt to use a bipolar concept such as "village-pastoral subsistence farming" (as Hopkins does) does not solve the issue, but rather directs our attention to the weaknesses of any such assumption. Herding economies do not exist on their own, nor do economies based on horticulture, and economies based on symbiosis (of whatever description) are by definition not "subsistence" economies established in independence. They are rather mixed market based economies, necessarily tied to barter, trade and economic interdependence. This understanding is even more important in relationship to those regions that border on large steppe zones, where the likelihood of ethnic and linguistic distinctiveness becomes a correlative factor of separate economic options, where one must speak of trade relations between such as the *fellahin* and the *beduin* (*mutatis mutandis* for early periods). It is also premature to jump to an assumption of "dimorphism" as an adequate economic description of the highland settlements without having clear evidence that that is in fact what we are dealing with. That dimorphic economies perhaps existed in the Middle Bronze Age along the upper *Euphrates*[45] does not really help our understanding of the very different geographical regions of

---

[45] J.T. Luke, *Pastoralism and Politics in the Mari Period* (University of Michigan dissertation, 1965); M.B. Rowton, "The Topological Factor in the Hapiru Problem," *Assyriological Studies* 16 (1965), pp.375-387.

Palestine of another time.[46] Both space and time have a way of changing economic and sociological realities.

Finkelstein has argued that we do have archaeological grounds to suppose that there existed at least a mixed economy of herding and grain agriculture in the territory of *Ephraim* during Iron I, and that this form of economy is particularly clear in the earliest part of the settlement period. Finkelstein, indeed, does not see the archaeologically based ·settlement patterns to imply dimorphism. He rather suggests that the patterns of settlement indicate a regional process and direction of new settlement development in the highlands. This has led him to the conclusion that the settlers, though clearly indigenous to greater *Palestine,* had come from a nomadic and herding environment, beginning settlement first along the eastern desert fringe, the central range and along part of the northern slopes.[47]   He argues that the settlers gradually moved westward, developing a major expansion of settlement in the foothills and along the southern slopes by the end of Iron I. The *floruit* of the settlement of these regions came during Iron II.

Finkelstein bases this interpretation on an alleged statistical curve of both settlement and population rising from East to West: from the fringe to the center of the highlands and to the more rugged slopes to the West and Southwest. He understands this transition as a development in the economy from one that had been dominated by herding and grain agriculture, to a later economy dominated by the traditional Mediterranean mix of grains, oil, fruits, nuts and wine. Most importantly, Finkelstein draws the pivotal historical conclusion that this curve in the settlement process of Iron I *Ephraim* should be understood as evidence that settlement began not through an initial introduction of terracing, but rather along the unterraced desert fringe, the north central range and the *Bethel* plateau. The settlers are to be understood, accordingly, not as primarily agriculturalists from the lowlands and Late Bronze settled areas of *Palestine,* but rather as pastoralists. They were at home on the steppeland: sedentarizing nomads, who only subsequently

---

[46] W.G. Dever, "The Patriarchal Traditions" in J.H. Hayes and J.M. Miller (eds.) *Israelite and Judaean History*, (Philadelphia, 1977) pp.70-119; also Th.L. Thompson, "The Background of the Patriarchs: A Reply to William Dever and Malcolm Clark," *JSOT* 9 (1978), pp.2-43. One must here strongly support N.P. Lemche's concept of a "socio-economic continuum," and should not arbitrarily exclude the involvement of the many surviving lowland towns as markets for the highland's cash crops (*op.cit.,* 1985).

[47] I. Finkelstein, *op.cit.,* pp.185ff.

and gradually introduced terracing and horticulture to the highlands.[48] In this, Finkelstein presents a picture strongly resembling the hypothesis of Alt, disagreeing with him only as to the ultimate origin of these pastoralists. The addition of a seemingly greater chronological sophistication in Finkelstein's study of settlement patterns with his use of excavated sites, would be, if it were not quite so highly speculative, a tremendous improvement over previous studies, and would lend, if provable, a great deal more credence to this hypothesis. Nevertheless, like Hopkins's arguments (which had, however, been based on earlier and now intrinsically dated studies of settlement patterns in the hill country), Finkelstein's hypothesis, in so far as it relates to the origins of the settlers, is tied to a number of other far less likely assumptions. That the highlands' earliest settlements were primarily largely independent hamlets and villages based in what he understands as a subsistence economy, is among the most important of these premises.[49]

Finkelstein's observations concerning the subregional economic differences among the regionally, markedly distinct hills of *Ephraim* are important and convincing, and must be part of any substantial comprehensive explanation of the area's settlement patterns. The region that Finkelstein defines as the desert fringe (the eastern steppeland forming the eastern border of the central highland range) is an arid region dominated by pastoralism and some grain agriculture. The primary agricultural zone of the highlands of *Ephraim* he circumscribes to the central range and the northern region of the western slopes, supporting a mixture of grain and field crops supplemented by some grazing and some horticulture. Finkelstein's observations that the rugged southern slopes, with few water resources, are for the most part unsuitable for general agriculture and (because of woodlands) are also unsuited to grazing, set these subregions apart from the northern slopes and central range, and mark it as a region with the economic potential of a dominance in horticulture (olives, grapes, and a variety of fruits and

---

[48] Mostly after 1050 B.C.; pp.198ff. These arguments of Finkelstein's are repeated with moderate expansion in his "The Emergence of the Monarchy in Israel: The Environmental and Socio-Economic Aspects," *JSOT* 44 (1989), pp.43-74.

[49] J.B. Davis, *Hill Country Village Subsistence in the Period of the Judges* (Southern Baptist Theological Seminary dissertation, 1984) pp.146ff., and especially pp.176f. Davis argues for a type of evolutionary development from "subsistence" to a trade economy that seems to suggest that trade is based more on issues of expansion and surplus than on specialization and distribution.

nuts). It is also a region in which agriculture is primarily dependent on terracing.

The population of all of the subregions of the hills of *Ephraim* expanded considerably over the course of Iron I. Along the desert fringe and in the central range, the population doubled in size,[50] while on the western slopes (both North and South) and in the foothills, where the total population was considerably smaller, the population increased from 2 1/2 to 5 times. This very possibly reflects an initially slower settlement process in this area due to the ecological problems related to limited water resources, land clearing and terrace building. Once a core of settlement in each subregion was well established by the end of Iron I, ecological capacity seems to have determined settlement growth and population increase. There was relatively little growth and increase of settlement along the desert fringe and in the south central regions.[51] Large increases occurred in the agriculturally more amenable north central range and along the northern slopes. The settlement of the southwestern slopes and the foothills showed an equally dramatic increase, possibly reflecting the growing importance of oil and wine as cash crops that fed into the revival of international trade during the Iron II period.

The chronology Finkelstein uses allows him to sketch an evolutionary development from the early Iron I settlement along the marginal desert fringe to that along the southern slopes in Iron II. This has encouraged the conclusions that the pattern of initial settlement reflects a settlement by pastoralists in the process of sedentarization, and that the later increase in settlement of the southern slopes and foothills reflects the centralizing, ultimately royal support for trade by the United Monarchy in Iron II. Both interpretations draw on assumed historical contexts (nomadic pastoralism and the United Monarchy) whose relationships to the archaeological reconstructions of the settlement patterns are neither immediate nor obvious. The interpretation of the earliest of the Iron I sites attempts to read the archaeological record in the light of an hypothesis of a recurrent cycle in *Palestine* of sedentary collapse and resettlement, involving substantial demographic shifts from a dominance of intensive agriculture and horticulture (Middle Bronze II) to a

---

[50] *Ibid.*, p.194.

[51] *Ibid.*, p.188.

dominance of grain agriculture and pastoralism (Early Iron I).[52] The context for the interpretation of the Iron II sites in the southwestern zone is based on the assumed influence on settlement by the United Monarchy, which not only presupposes the biblical historiography about a "United Monarchy," but also the political and economic assumption that the monarchy's centralization initiated trade.[53] The benefit of such contextual assumptions is great, as they attempt to integrate the changes in the central hills with contemporary changes, not only in *Palestine* but in the greater international world of commerce, in which the production of oil and wine in *Palestine* had a significant place. The difficulty is a methodological one: the assumption that the initiating cause of settlement expansion lies apart from the settlers' own subsistence strategies. The development of cash crops (and the oil, wine and lumber of the central hills are important cash crops, valuable both within the Palestinian markets and to external trading partners) is far more the cause of *Palestine*'s reentry into the world of international trade (and the subsequent development of centralization in this region) than an effect of these.

Finkelstein's interpretation of Iron I is partly due to an interpretative distortion of his statistics. Of the three subregions discussed by Finkelstein, the desert fringe area during early Iron I has the most stable population, though the specific *loci* of the settlements vary considerably. The aridity of the climate marks this area as a predominantly cereal raising region. The form of subsistence is likely mixed with an economy of herding. The increase of the population in Iron II is very moderate.[54]

---

[52] For the background of this hypothesis, one should look to the very perceptive interpretation of settlement patterns by D.L. Esse in his dissertation, *Beyond Subsistence: Beth Yerah and Northern Palestine in the Early Bronze Age* (University of Chicago dissertation, 1982). Comparable patterns or cycles of change have been suggested by R.B. Coote and K.W. Whitelam, *The Emergence of Early Israel in Historical Perspective* (Sheffield, 1987) and H. Weippert, *Die Archäologie Palästina in vorhellenistischer Zeit* (Munich, 1988). Other literature related to this hypothesis can be found in the discussions of L. Geraty *et alii* ("Madeba Plains Project: A Preliminary Report of the 1987 Season at Tell el-Umeiri and Vicinity," *BASOR* supplement 26, 1990, pp.33-58), S. Richards ("The 1987 Expedition to Khirbet Iskander and its Vicinity: Fourth Preliminary Report," *BASOR* supplement 26, 1990, pp.33-58), and E.A. Knauf ("Bedouin and Bedouin States," *Anchor Bible Dictionary*, ed. by D.N. Freedman, forthcoming). For a revision of this hypothesis, Th.L. Thompson, "Palestinian Pastoralism and Israel's Origins," *SJOT* 6 (1992), pp.1-13.

[53] Similar arguments are put forward by R.B. Coote and K.W. Whitelam, *op.cit.*

[54] *Contra* Finkelstein's conclusion on p.197, where he unaccountably states that the Iron

Moreover, if one considers economic needs not in subsistence categories as Finkelstein has done, but rather in terms of both the economic bearing capacity of a given subregion (here the very limited capacity of the desert fringe), and the economic needs of the greater region as a whole for the products produced by the sub-area, the growth ratio of the desert fringe area does not markedly signal a substantial change of economy either within this subregion or within the central hills generally from early Iron I to Iron II. Rather, the stability of this subregion suggests continuity in the economy between early Iron I and II.

The north central hills area finds early settlement focussed on fertile interior valleys, where a prosperous mixed agriculture can be supported. Many of the newer settlements expand the regional occupation beyond these valleys into areas where grains and goats would be likely to form a proportionately greater part of the economy. A similar pattern of expansion is noticed in the new Iron II settlements of the northern slopes region and in the foothills area that have a greater proportion of grazing than any region other than the desert fringe zone.

When the economy of the whole of the central hills is considered, we notice that grain producing and livestock producing areas expand proportionately to the rise in population of the entire region. Horticulture, on the other hand, involves a clearly disproportionate increase—especially during Iron II—and this increase is most marked, as Finkelstein has observed, when the southern slopes are studied. This undoubtedly reflects the necessity of greater stability and labor investment in terraced based agriculture. Since these horticultural areas in the central hills are hardly capable of supporting a mixed or subsistence agriculture, but are rather oriented to the development of cash crops, such as nuts and fruits, wine and oil, their development necessarily involves regional trade. Their disproportionate expansion in the Iron II period suggests an even greater economic development of extra-regional trade, and with that an involvement in increasing centralization. This partially supports Finkelstein's argument.[55]

II population actually decreased. It is, of course, extremely difficult to estimate the size of the fringe area's population during Iron I. Because many of these sites are very small and ephemeral, we can hardly be certain that they are all contemporary, and we may indeed have a greater growth with the more permanent Iron II hamlets than is at first apparent.

[55] More recently: I. Finkelstein, "The Emergence of the Monarchy in Israel: The Environmental and Socio-Economic Aspects," *JSOT* 44 (1989), pp.43-74; esp. pp.55ff. Finkelstein presents a substantially similar picture for the latter part of Iron I in which he

However, this expansive growth in horticulture and terracing continued a technology already in place in the very earliest settlements of Iron I. The increase in economic capacity during Iron II inherits its efficient cause from its predecessor. This suggests both trade (at least within the central hills) and a modicum of symbiosis and centralization from the very earliest periods of settlement.

On the basis of these subregional observations, I would suggest that we try to understand the economic background of the early Iron I settlement patterns in terms of a region wide economy involving markets and exchange of goods, rather than on the basis of individual sites or of subregions. It is not justified to assume that the marginal areas such as the desert fringe, the foothills and the southern slopes—especially during the earliest Iron I settlement period—were based on a subsistence economy. Only some small areas of the intramontane valleys seem capable of that. The desert fringe, with an economic regime dominated by sheep and goat herding and a grain agriculture primarily used in a role supporting and supplementing grazing, is not a likely candidate for subsistence living anymore than is the livestock producing areas of the foothills. It is far better, I believe, to suggest that these regions supplied the greater population with meat, wool and dairy products, forming not a subsistence economy, but an interdependent or symbiotic relationship with the central region. Similarly, the terrace oriented, horticultural settlements of the southern slopes should not be understood in terms of subsistence farming either, but are better seen (as such settlements are understood throughout the history of *Palestine*) as producers of specialized "cash crops," living in dependence on the greater population within the larger region.

Rather than assuming an economy of subsistence agriculture in the central highlands of *Palestine*,[56] one understands agriculture in this region by adopting categories such as "risk spreading" and "risk reduction" as Hopkins has proposed.[57] It is hardly an anomaly to find early Iron I sites "nestled in both marginal and quite favorable

---

sees intra-regional trade economy developing on the basis of cash crops, which formed an essential economic basis for inter-regional cooperation, trade and ultimately patterns of centralization.

[56] As I. Finkelstein (*ibid.*) D. Hopkins (*op.cit.*) and others have.

[57] D. Hopkins, *op.cit.*, pp.267ff.

locations."[58] Even less should we argue that the early exploitation of grains and animal husbandry suggests a nomadic or pastoral background or pre-history for our settlers.[59] Rather, from its earliest period, settlement in the central hills seems to have involved a threefold economy, each of which experienced the dominance of "cash crops," and hence also allowed an essential role for bartering and regionally or extra-regionally oriented trade; namely, animal husbandry on the eastern fringe, grain agriculture and field crops in the central heartland, and horticulture along the rugged southwestern slopes. Such territorially delimited interrelated agriculture reflects a form of economy that has dominated most regions of the Mediterranean world from at least the Late Chalcolithic period to the present. This cultural concept of a "Mediterranean economy" is far preferable to that of an unspecified and unrealistic "subsistence agriculture."

The Mediterranean form of economy goes further to explain the data of Finkelstein's settlement patterns than does his explanation of an evolutionary direction of development from a pastoral economy of the eastern borders to the terrace dependent horticulture of the West. The limited number of more ephemeral outlying settlements along the desert fringe and western slopes might well be understood as secondary and as economically related to an almost equal number of sites in the central range. Population growth led to a more rapid and greater intensification of settlement in the ecologically more favorable central zone than in either the pastoral or the horticultural zones. Any true sense of population explosion towards the limits of the agriculturally inviting north central range and northern slopes is hardly involved before the onset of Iron II.

A chronologically oriented migration of settlement from East to West is also dubious. It is not clear that all of the settlements of the desert fringe area, of the foothills and of the southern slopes, existed as year around permanent villages. Initially, transhumance patterns may have obtained with permanent settlement occurring in the major villages. Only over time and as the result of an expansion of population and agricultural intensification, might we expect sedentary stability in these marginal zones. Social patterns explored by N.P. Lemche and C.H.J. de

---

[58] *Ibid.*, p.268.

[59] So I. Finkelstein, *op.cit.*

Geus[60] such as of the extended family and clan lend themselves well to such interdependent and complementary economies.

In the Early Iron Age, the best areas of all three of the ecologically distinctive zones of the central hills is occupied. It seems possible that during the initial period of settlement in this region all three economic forms had been exploited (at times seasonally) by the same families in patterns of both transhumance pastoralism and transhumance agriculture. Such a scenario would provide a social context for the marginal and less permanent sites involved in the earliest settlement patterns both along the eastern steppe and on the rugged western slopes. As the population grew in the course of Iron I, these more transient settlements would have stabilized into permanent villages. During Iron II, with the expansion of trade beyond the immediate region of the hill country, a greater orientation of the economy towards specialization could be expected to have developed as hill country agriculture became increasingly dominated by interregional and eventually international interests, rather than being limited merely to that of a subsistence balance of the central hills alone. It is noteworthy that, because of the need for interdependence in the larger economy, the establishment of permanent settlement along the desert fringe and in the horticultural zone would have created, along with the growing population of the entire area, an increasingly stable economic base which is, of course, a *sine qua non* for the development of both extra-regional trade and nascent statehood. This supports the conclusion that emerging centralizing political structures, rather than bringing about radical changes in the economic and social structures of the region, themselves grew out of and supported the intrinsically expansive commitment to a Mediterranean economy. The frequently observed uncertainty[61] about the extent of terracing prior to Iron II is well founded. It is unlikely that we can assume a population in those regions that had been dependent upon terracing any greater than what Finkelstein has already suggested,[62] nor indeed a total population beyond 10,000 for all the hills of *Ephraim* during Iron I. Certainly even that number seems

---

[60] N.P. Lemche, *Early Israel*, VTS (Leiden, 1985).

[61] See the excellent discussion by D. Hopkins, *op.cit.*: pp.268ff.

[62] *Ibid.*, p.194; also his clear description of the geographical range of Ephraim in *op.cit.*, 1989, pp.59ff.

seriously inflated.[63] It is not before the Iron II period that the settlement of the central hills reached its *floruit*, and it is first in this period that one can comfortably entertain an expansion of political and military interests beyond the central highlands themselves.[64]

The increase in the settlement of the central highlands during the Iron I period can hardly be explained as a natural growth of the Late Bronze population of this highland region alone.[65] Nor can the increase and continued spread of the agricultural exploitation of the highlands during Iron II be explained in terms of indigenous growth. Moreover, the ongoing instability and poverty of the settlement during Iron I does not encourage us to see this period as the result of an expansive prosperity. Rather, the whole of the Iron I period should be seen as an extended period of transition from the Late Bronze age to the Iron Age II period, with recovery and prosperity first beginning about 1050 B.C. The origins of some of these new settlers of both Iron I and Iron II must be sought outside the central hill country itself and the cause of the prosperity of the Iron II expansion needs to be identified. Evidence of cultural continuity with the Late Bronze sites of the lowlands and a number of towns of the highlands that survived the depression following Middle Bronze II C, especially in the *Manasseh* area, suggests that substantial numbers of the new settlers either came from or were tied through markets to the indigenous agricultural population of *Palestine,* although the evidence hardly allows us to be more specific.[66] The process of deforestation and the establishment of a stable Mediterranean economy of intensive agriculture, herding, grains and horticulture allowed for a steady internal expansion of the population that was accelerated by the increased establishment of terracing, first in Iron I at such sites as

---

[63] The calculation of population of the villages of the Iron I period in the central hills is rightly calculated on the density of the number of rooms within a definable area, which figure is, of course, based on excavated sites. The unknown factors relating to open spaces within the site, animal enclosures, etc. are likely to reduce the *per dunam* population in the smallest of our settlements, very few of which are excavated.

[64] In the Israeli surveys of Ephraim, some 190 sites are presented for the Iron II period, in contrast to 115 sites during Iron I and only 5 in the Late Bronze period: M. Kochavi, *Judaea Samaria and the Golan* (Jerusalem, 1972).

[65] L. Stager, "The Archaeology of the Family in Ancient Israel," *BASOR* 260 (1985), pp.3ff.

[66] G. Ahlström, *op.cit.*, forthcoming, chapter VII.

Raddana and *et-Tell*,[67] and then over many large areas during Iron II. That some of these new settlers derived from a process of sedentarization of pastoral nomads from the Palestinian steppelands also seems possible. Although direct evidence for such sedentarization is lacking in the central hills as early as Iron I, a close symbiotic relationship between agriculturalists and pastoralists in these highlands is to be expected and would establish at least an economic basis for such sedentarization, if not a sufficient cause.[68]

It seems unlikely that the radical transformation implied in the sedentarization of pastoral groups that had hitherto been nomadic or transhumant would have occurred without some quite specific necessitating cause. The suggestion of Finkelstein of a resedentarization of the population that had been originally displaced by the Middle Bronze II C collapse of highland agriculture, while attractive because of its efforts to maintain both an indigenous and a pastoral origin for Israel, relates at best to an increase in pastoralism in the Late Bronze period, but says nothing to the process of resedentarization fully three centuries later. A rather serious anomaly in Finkelstein's historical account substantially reduces the explanatory potential of his suggestion. The issues concerning cycles of desedentarization and sedentarization in *Palestine* do not support the integrity or continuity of any specific regionally bound population group within *Palestine* let alone within such a small region as *Ephraim,* nor do they make more substantial any given group's potential to preserve agricultural technology and sedentary forms of identity over extensive reaches of time. We are rather dealing with problems of quite substantial change in both the forms of economic exploitation and the social structures that support identity in groups. Desedentarization and sedentarization involve not only subsistence strategies, but the disintegration and formation of specific forms of societies. The desedentarization brought about by the disastrous regional collapses of the Middle Bronze IIC period led to a displacement and restructuring of the population involved. Pastoralists of greater *Palestine* at the end of the Late Bronze Age, to any extent that they might be derivative from the sedentary agriculturalists of the Middle Bronze central hills, survived the dislocation from village farming through a successful adaptation to other societal forms that are divergent from

---

[67] L. Stager, *op.cit.*, pp.5ff.

[68] Th.L. Thompson, *op.cit.*, 1992, and further below, Chapter VII.

sedentary agriculture. Moreover, the changes reflected in the Late Bronze-Iron I transition are changes brought about in response to drought and economic disintegration. They are in no way to be understood in terms of the return to prosperity that Finkelstein and others assert. Thus to speak of the early Iron I settlement as primarily the result of a process of resedentarization begs explanation; for the essential questions related to the transition period remain unanswered.

It is unlikely that large numbers of nomadic pastoralists would have exploited this region if for no other reason than that the optimal natural grazing areas are quite limited here, and are found primarily along the eastern slopes of the hills. The western sectors of the central highlands during the Late Bronze Age could have supported pastoralism in the small intramontane valleys to the extent that they were not dominated by forest lands. Such pastoralists would, however, have existed in limited numbers. Moreover, once the immigrant sedentary agricultural population from the lowlands had stabilized throughout the region, the pastoralists would have been threatened by displacement and given a limited tolerance in forms of transhumance that would symbiotically support the agricultural economy. Economic and political pressure on nomadic pastoral groups to sedentarize might also then be expected. References to such independent pastoral groups in the *Amarna* tablets and other New Kingdom Egyptian texts in this region gives reason to accept their presence here and to assume that they were affected by the stress of the Late Bronze-Iron II transition as well. With the onset of drought at the close of the Bronze Age, pressure on the pastoralists to move away from the steppe and into the better watered highlands on a permanent basis would also have pertained, and would have supported a shift in subsistence strategies away from transhumant patterns and towards the more stable forms of possession and control that are characteristic of sedentary land based economies and that support a gradual adaptation to agriculture. Evidence of increments to the central highland population from areas to the north of *Palestine* is extremely limited.[69] It is also unlikely that migrations of people from the Aegean and *Anatolia* had directly penetrated the highlands in any significant way. Nevertheless, the dislocation of much of the coastal Late Bronze population, in response to the drought as well as to the incursions from

---

[69] Cf., however, the discussion on the "Bull Site" by G. Ahlström, *op.cit.*, forthcoming, chapter VII.

the northern Mediterranean rim, may well have been responsible for some of the growth in Iron I new settlements in the highlands as the displaced population of the coastal plain moved into the more marginal lands of the hills.

3. The Galilee and Carmel Hills

The early settlements of the large highland region of the *Galilee,* west and northwest of Lake *Tiberias* was first brought into the discussion of Israel's origins by the surface explorations of Y. Aharoni in the mid-fifties.[70] Initially, Aharoni had attributed a number of the Early Bronze Age sites of the region to the Late Bronze period. Because he had also found some Late Bronze sherds at several Iron I sites in his survey of the lower *Galilee,* he dated the beginning of new settlement in the hills of *Galilee* to the final phases of the Late Bronze, sometime in the course of the thirteenth-century. Aharoni's interpretation of these sites and their dating was also closely associated with his chronology for the excavated strata XIII and XII at *Hazor.*[71] More recent surveys of this region have been undertaken by Z. Gal and, in the area along the Lebanese border, by R. Frankel and I. Finkelstein.[72] Reconstructions of the historical transition in this area differ greatly. To some extent these variations of interpretation are due to competing efforts to relate and harmonize the archaeological studies either in a reconstruction of Joshua's conquest following Albright or of the Book of Judges's peaceful settlement in support of Alt's hypothesis.

---

[70] Y. Aharoni, *The Settlement of the Israelite Tribes in Upper Galilee* (Hebrew University dissertation, 1957).

[71] Y. Aharoni, "Nothing Early and Nothing Late: Rewriting Israel's Conquest," *BA* 39 (1976), pp.55-76, over against Y. Yadin, *Hazor* (London, 1972).

[72] Z. Gal, "Tel Rechesh and Tel Qarnei Hittin," Eretz Israel 15 (1981) pp.213-221; *idem, Ramat Issachar* (Tel Aviv, 1980); *idem,* "The Settlement of Issachar: Some New Observations," *Tel Aviv* 9 (1982), pp.79-86; *idem, The Lower Galilee in the Iron Age* (University of Tel Aviv dissertation, 1982); *idem,* "The Late Bronze Age in Galilee: A Reassessment," *BASOR* 272 (1988), pp.79-84; R. Frankel, "The Galilee in the Late Bronze and Iron Age," *The Land of the Galilee,* ed. by A. Schmueli (Haifa, 1984); *idem, The History of the Processing of Wine and Oil in Galilee in the Period of the Bible, the Mishnah, and the Talmud* (University of Tel Aviv dissertation, 1984); I. Finkelstein, *op. cit.,* 1988, pp.94-110.

The occupation of the *Galilee* during the Late Bronze Age was limited to a small number of widely scattered sites over this very large region. In the upper *Galilee,* only five of the major tells show occupation: *Tel Rosh, al-Hirbah, Kedesh, Hazor,* and *Tel Dan (Tell el-Qadi),* three of which are associated with the *Hula* Basin. Similarly, throughout most of the Lower *Galilee,* Late Bronze settlements are found only at a small number of tells in the very fertile regions in and near the *Sahl Battuf (Biq'at Beit Netofah).* On Mount *Carmel,* no Late Bronze sites have yet been found, and only in the lower hill of the *Carmel* Range do we come across two small, Late Bronze settlements, one of which has been found in the *Nahal Tut* valley. The other is situated some five kilometers to the South, just north of the agriculturally rich *Nahal Tanninim.* We find an extensive spread of settlement in only two unique subregions of the Lower *Galilee*: along the broad plateau of *Ramat Yissakhar* overlooking the *Beth Shan* Valley from the North, and in the low, rolling foothills along the northwestern edge of the *Jezreel* between the valley and *Nahal Sippori.* Apart from *Tel Rosh* and *al-Hirba* in the far north, the Late Bronze occupation of the *Galilee* is clearly oriented, as elsewhere in *Palestine,* to the well watered and agriculturally richest and most viable regions.

The only major sites that have been excavated in the whole of the *Galilee* are *Hazor* (some fifteen kilometers north of the Sea of *Galilee*) and *Tel Dan* (on the northern rim of the *Hula* Basin). Any immediate historical reconstruction of the Late Bronze-Iron II transition period in this region substantially rests on a comparison of the settlement history of these two sites. Happily, excavations have given us considerable information. By extension, the information from these excavations could conceivably provide a basis for interpreting the settlement patterns of the larger region known to us from surface exploration. Unfortunately, however, the site of *Hazor* does not seem to have been occupied continuously through the very long transition from Late Bronze II until Iron II. Furthermore, disputes about the chronology of *Hazor's* strata make it extremely difficult to use this site confidently as a standard for both the upland sites and for those along the northern rim of the *Jezreel.*[73] Moreover, the relative isolation of both *Tel Dan* and *Hazor*

---

[73] Of course, the failure of the excavators of Hazor to publish an adequate commentary on the excavations of this critical site (Y. Yadin, *Hazor I, III-IV,* Jerusalem 1958, 1961) has hampered historical interpretation for decades. The recently published text volume for

from most of the sites of the *Galilee* creates some hesitation in accepting these excavations too comprehensively as an interpretive matrix for the surveys, since historical connections between *Dan* and *Hazor* and the rest of the *Galilee* are neither immediate nor obvious.

Following Yadin's popular account of the excavations at *Hazor*,[74] the final Late Bronze level of occupation (Stratum XIII-Ia) shows considerable signs of impoverishment when compared with the earlier strata. Then, the Late Bronze site in both the lower city and on the acropolis was abandoned and signs of the destruction of Stratum XIII-Ia by fire is almost everywhere obvious. The date of the site's abandonment is usually given at 1230 B.C. on the basis of Mycenaean pottery. The date for the destruction of *Hazor* could be placed even earlier if we were to follow Tufnell and Finkelstein,[75] who place it in the first half of the thirteenth-century. The acropolis of *Hazor* is reoccupied during Iron I (Stratum XII). The pottery of this stratum is now dated by Finkelstein to the very end of the twelfth or the beginning of the eleventh-century.[76] This suggests a gap in occupation at *Hazor* of more than a century and a half. In this earliest Iron Age level of Stratum XII, the settlement seems extremely limited. Large numbers of storage pits have been uncovered, and there is little evidence of any substantial architectural structures. It is in Stratum XI (dated to the eleventh-century) that we have the first clear evidence of the development of an Iron Age town. This town occupation then continued throughout the course of the later Iron Age strata at *Hazor*.

The existence of a break in the continuity of the settlement history of *Hazor* at the end of the Late Bronze period is undisputed and seems indisputable on the basis of comparisons of *Hazor*'s Late Bronze pottery.[77] The length of that break, however, is uncertain. The close correspondence of the earliest Iron Age pottery from the pits of *Hazor* Stratum XII with the Iron Age pottery from the sites in the *Galilee* from both Aharoni's and later surveys clearly suggests that if there is any historical connection between the sites from the surveys and the tell at

---

Hazor III–IV (unseen by the writer) may fill this need.

[74] Y. Yadin, *op.cit.*, 1972, pp.108ff.

[75] O. Tufnell, "Reviews and Notices: Hazor II," *PEQ* 93 (1961), pp.94-98; I. Finkelstein, *op.cit.*, 1988, pp.100f.

[76] I. Finkelstein, *ibid.*, p.101.

[77] O. Tufnell, *op.cit.*

Hazor, it is with the new Iron I resettlement of Stratum XII. It is highly unlikely that there was any direct historical connection between the massive fire destructions of *Hazor* XIII and either the new Iron I settlements of the *Galilee* or indeed *Hazor*'s resettlement. In fact, if Finkelstein's chronology were to be followed, it would be necessary to conclude that the entire region of the *Galilee* had experienced a more than century-long hiatus in its agricultural settlement.

As unlikely as this is, it would accord with Finkelstein's chronological hypothesis for the beginning of the Iron Age here. However, Finkelstein's dating of *Hazor* XII to ca. 1100 B.C. does not seem related so much to an analysis of the pottery assemblages of either *Hazor* XII or the comparable pottery from other sites in the *Galilee* region as it does to his efforts to establish transregional correlations of the early Iron Age settlements in the *Galilee* to those of the *Ephraim-Manasseh* highlands. These unlikely correlations, involving rather substantial unargued assumptions, are an extension of Finkelstein's efforts to interpret the highland Iron I settlements as separate from the demise of the Late Bronze culture. If Finkelstein were successful in this separation of the Iron I settlements from the Late Bronze, his argument that the settlement of Iron I resulted from a process of sedentarization by pastoralists on previously abandoned lands would become thereby more plausible.[78]

Finkelstein's argument that *Hazor* XII's cooking pots are of a later type than that generally found at the earliest Iron I sites (where a continuity with the Late Bronze cooking pot tradition is apparent) is not in itself sufficient cause to lower Stratum XII's date to as late as 1100 B.C. It is, moreover, possible to date some of the central highland's earliest Iron I sites to the late thirteenth-century if we do not follow Finkelstein's low chronology too rigidly. Finkelstein himself has repeatedly argued[79] that Iron I pottery assemblages are remarkably regionally oriented. If this is true, such transregional ceramic association

---

[78] I. Finkelstein, *op. cit.*, pp.270ff. 299ff. 322f. In this effort, Finkelstein, for instance, is willing to understand the collared rim store jar found at Late Bronze *Aphek* as having derived from the Iron I hill country settlements (p.283), in spite of what is for him the troublesome flexibility this brings to his Iron I pottery chronology. Finkelstein excludes *Aphek*'s influence in the hill country settlements, in spite of many of the pottery continuities that are observable in the repertoire at *Aphek* and from the highland settlements generally, and particularly those from nearby *Izbet Sartah*.

[79] *Ibid.*, pp.270f.

(as Finkelstein's low dating of *Hazor* XII requires) must bring with it a rather substantial ± chronological factor.

The pottery from the pits of *Hazor* XII, and from the early Iron I sites of the *Galilee* generally, is substantially different from the pottery of the central hills; so different that we can hardly share Finkelstein's confidence in evaluating either *Hazor* or the *Galilee* on the basis of a pottery chronology from the central hills. Indeed, Finkelstein's ceramic and chronological arguments seem highly dependent on poorly supported, and largely unargued, ethno-historical assumptions that assert the priority of the central hills in the diffusion of Iron I highland culture. His argument is fundamentally circular, illustrated rather than supported by the archaeological evidence. In fact, the collared rim store jar (the hallmark of the pottery of the central hills during Iron I) is extremely rare in the *Galilee* (*Tel Dan*). As Finkelstein, himself, notes, it is the "Galilean" *pithoi* that dominate the assemblages of *Hazor* XII. This pottery type is a direct descendent of *Hazor* XIII's Late Bronze forms, and is found not only here but throughout the Iron I sites of the *Galilee*. This can be understood as substantial pottery evidence against Finkelstein's gap in settlement and for a continuity with both the indigenous culture and population. The other form of *pithoi* commonly found in the surveys of the region is of the "Tyrian" type (*Tel Dan*, stratum VI). The presence of this type indicates a continuous Phoenician and coastal influence throughout the region during this early transitional period. Such influence from the coast had been characteristic of the Late Bronze settlements of the *Galilee* as well.

The association of the pottery of the Upper *Galilee* with *Phoenicia* and the northern Palestinian coast (rather than with either *Samaria* or *Judaea*) is important historically. Material culture and economic associations, like language and religious associations, geographical proximity and societal forms, are among our most important criteria for determining ethnicity. The material cultural divergence of the *Galilee* region from the central and southern hill country settlements of the Iron Age is also supported by observations of the Upper *Galilee*'s independence in technological developments associated with olive production. The use of screw presses in the manufacture of olive oil throughout the *Galilee* marks a sharp contrast in the economic associations of this region with those of the southern hill country of

Judaea and the *Shephelah* where "direct frame" presses were used![80] The material culture of the Upper *Galilee* was also distinct and separate from that of the foothill regions of the Lower *Galilee* to the South, which was more closely associated with that of the *Jezreel.* Cultural links in the Upper Galilean highlands point neither to the Lower *Galilee* nor to the central highlands but rather to the Phoenician coast to the West and to the uplands of *Lebanon* to the North. The Iron I settlements of the Upper *Galilee* are best understood as having developed an economically insignificant Phoenician hinterland.

The pottery remains and structural characteristics of *Hazor* Stratum XII are similar to those of *Tel Dan* stratum VI, excavated by A. Biran.[81] Moreover, the Late Bronze stratum of *Hazor* XIII also clearly parallels the limited excavated remains of *Tel Dan*'s Late Bronze stratum VII, whose destruction is dated to the very beginning of the twelfth-century B.C.[82] Stratum VI, at *Dan*, however, shows no gap in the occupation from stratum VII,[83] in striking contrast to the stratum following *Hazor* XIII.[84] The subsequent developments at *Hazor* from strata XII-XI are again paralleled in *Dan* strata VI-V. The close association of the material remains of these two major tells suggests a coherent and integrated region wide pattern of settlement and therefore recommends the development of an interrelated historical reconstruction.

Assuming such an interrelated development of the region, the evidence for dating the transition from *Dan* VII to VI in the early twelfth-century would require a date for *Hazor* XII to the early twelfth-century as well.[85] This would then allow for a 30+ year gap at *Hazor*,

---

[80] R. Frankel, "Oil Presses in Western Galilee and the Judaea: A Comparison," *Olive Oil in Antiquity*, ed. by M. Heltzer and D. Eitam, (Haifa, 1988) pp.63-73; *idem, The History of the Processing of Wine and Oil in the Period of the Bible, the Mishna, and the Talmud* (University of Tel Aviv dissertation, 1984).

[81] A. Biran, "Tel Dan," *BA* 37 (1974), pp.26-51; *idem*, "Notes and News: Tel Dan," *IEJ* 26 (1976), pp.54f; *idem*, "Tell Dan—Five Years Later," *BA* 43 (1980), pp.168-182; *idem*, "Die Wiederentdeckung der alten Stadt Dan," *Antike Welt* 15 (1984), pp.27-38; also, H.M. Niemann, *Die Daniten* (Göttingen, 1985) pp.261f.

[82] A. Biran, *op.cit.*, 1974, p.35, and esp. *idem*, "The Collared Rim Jars and the Settlement of the Tribe of Dan," *Recent Excavations in Israel: Studies in Iron Age Archaeology*, ed. by S. Gitin and W.G. Dever (Winona Lake, 1989) pp.71-97, esp. pp.79f.

[83] A. Biran, *op.cit.*; H.M. Niemann, *op.cit.*

[84] Y. Yadin, *Hazor* (London, 1972) p.254.

[85] I. Finkelstein's efforts to lower *Dan*'s dates to ca. 1100 B.C. to accord with his low date

without any significant hiatus regionally. For the eastern *Galilee* generally, a transition from the Late Bronze to Iron I in ca. 1200 should then be expected.

Architectural remains from the early Iron I settlements are extremely limited at both *Tel Dan* and *Hazor*. Salvage excavations at the three sites of *Sasa*, *Har Adir*, and *Horvat 'Avot* have uncovered some building structures. At *Adir* a casemate fortification has been uncovered. Efforts that have attempted to see *Hazor* XII as a nomadic or pastoralist encampment[86] are misleadingly attractive. They offer a means of historically understanding aspects of a settlement that are puzzling and of which we have only fragmentary remains. Certainly, the many examples from throughout *Palestine* of extremely limited or impoverished settlements at numerous Early Iron I sites is indeed a central issue in understanding this transition from the Late Bronze to the Iron Age and we need to ask specifically whether the recurrence of ephemeral and impoverished remains in the very earliest strata of Iron I really should be taken as indicative of either a pastoral orientation of the economy or of a nomadic past of the population as is so commonly suggested in the secondary historical and archaeological literature.[87] Widespread impoverishment is not in itself evidence that the settlers originally came from a pastoralist economy or a nomadic form of subsistence prior to their settlement at *Hazor* or elsewhere. Several far from legitimate correlations have been assumed in this dominant interpretation: not only the association of poverty with nomadism and pastoralism, but also the relationship of pastoralism with nomadism itself. In fact, these sites do not give us any evidence of the economy or forms of society that the new settlers had had prior to their immigration into the region, but only evidence of the economy and form of society that they pursued subsequent to the time of their settlement. At *Hazor*—however impoverished the settlement may have been—these immigrants are

---

for Hazor (*op.cit.,* 1988, pp.108–110) ignores the continuity of settlement at *Dan* between Strata VII and VI.

[86] Y. Yadin, "The Transition from a Semi-Nomadic to a Sedentary Society in the Twelfth Century B.C.E.," *Symposia,* ed. by F.M. Cross (Cambridge, 1979) pp.57–70; S. Geva, "The Settlement Pattern of Hazor Stratum XII," *Eretz Israel* 17 (1984), pp.158–161.

[87] A similar assumption concerning the limited remains of Early Bronze IV settlements had been a centerpiece of the "Amorite Hypothesis." Th.L. Thompson, *The Historicity of the Patriarchal Narratives, BZAW* 133 (1974) pp.144–171.

sedentary, and their economic orientation is decidedly agricultural. At *Dan* we have no reason to assume that there are immigrants at all.[88]

The possibility needs yet to be explored whether the poverty itself may not have been a substantial causative factor propelling immigration into the highlands of *Galilee*. One need not turn with Finkelstein to the Iron I settlements of the central highlands for an exploration of the Late Bronze-Iron Age transition in the Eastern Galilee. The correlations between *Hazor* and *Dan* are themselves extremely instructive. The Late Bronze town of *Hazor* XIII comes to an end as *Ugarit* had in a massive destruction and fire. Also like their counterparts in *Ugarit*, the occupants of Stratum XIII at *Hazor* were unable to rebuild and continue at the site after the destruction. Indeed, the gap at the site indicates that their land was not forcibly taken from them by enemy (and in the best of times *Hazor* was a prosperous city) but rather it had been abandoned. While there are a wide spectrum of possible causes that could have led to such a radical dislocation of a considerable population, neither invasion nor entrepreneurial expansion are likely to have been among them. Indeed, the inability of the population to rebuild does not demand but does suggest severe stress, poverty and political disruption. The contemporary level at neighboring *Tel Dan* (Stratum VII) is not abandoned. However, the extreme poverty of *Dan* VII allows us the interpretation that the population of *Dan* "held on" and survived a crisis similar to that suffered of *Hazor*. *Dan* VI neither indicates a revival of prosperity nor a new population, but rather only the survival of the agricultural population under continued stress, a return to expansion and prosperity beginning first in Stratum VI-V. Consistent with this, *Hazor* XII indicates a settlement of the site contemporary to *Dan* VI, and the material remains suggest a resettlement of an agricultural population living in severe poverty under continued stress until Stratum XII-XI, sometime late in the eleventh-century. With the onset of Iron II, the expansion and return to intense sedentarization is irreversible and the region as a whole undergoes a new cycle of prosperity.

In the Upper *Galilee,* some handful of Iron I sites reported by Gal had also been occupied (along with *Tel Rosh* and *al-Hirbah*) during the Late Bronze Age. An even larger number of such sites found on the

---

[88] Grain storage pits and *pithoi* are characteristic of and form the bulk of the earliest remains that have survived. Neither of these types of artifacts have ever been associated with any known nomadic or non-agricultural site.

Issachar plateau above the *Beth Shan* Valley had been occupied in the Late Bronze period. At least four sites with occupation in both the Late Bronze and in Iron I have been found in the Lower *Galilee* in the region just to the north of *Nazareth*. Finkelstein has certainly correctly noted that the Late Bronze and Iron I pottery at these settlements should not be understood as necessarily marking a common occupation history at all the sites.[89] However, such a possibility should not be ignored solely on the basis of an assumed discontinuity between the Late Bronze and Iron Age populations. These are not spring fed sites, and a cause for this apparent pattern of settlement other than regional continuity of the population is not obvious. Confidence in such continuity is supported by the coherence of material cultural remains by way of *Phoenicia* in both the Late Bronze and Iron Age periods. Uncertainty about such continuity stems from two sources: a) the very large geographical area and the widely scattered sites involved, and b) the prior ideologically and religiously motivated commitment of both historians and archaeologists to identify the Iron Age with Israel and the Late Bronze sites with an ethnically distinct Canaan. The occurrence of settlement at a large number of sites on the geographically confined and coherent *Issachar* plateau in each of the Late Bronze, Iron I and Iron II periods, however, suggests a continuity of both site and regional occupation in at least this region, whatever our prejudgments of historical issues.[90]

The Upper *Galilee* was a very large, considerably depopulated, rugged highland region during both the Late Bronze and the Iron I periods. Substantial settlement did not occur until Iron II was well established. At whatever time we date that development (perhaps as late as the end of the tenth or the ninth-century), the necessary question to be asked is no longer whether there had been a change in the ethnicity of the area as a whole. It is whether we have evidence of any coherent society (i.e., ethnicity) in the process of formation in the *Galilee* at all. We should also ask whether there are any identifiable bonds of association with

---

[89] I. Finkelstein, *op.cit.*, pp.95-97.

[90] *Contra* Z. Gal, who unaccountably argues for an ethnic change from "Canaanite" to "Israelite" in the transition from Iron I to Iron II (Z. Gal, *Ramat Issachar*, Tel Aviv, 1980). There is even less evidence for the assertion of such a population dislocation at the Iron I-II transition than for Finkelstein's similar arguments about the Late Bronze-Iron I transition. Of course, both Gal's and Finkelstein's conclusions regarding ethnicity require a break in development and a change from "Canaanite" to "Israelite." Such a break in continuity not only is not indicated, it seems wholly unlikely and improbable.

other less isolated regions. Neither question directs us towards the central hills. If there is not, after all, a shift or transference of associations in the Western Upper *Galilee* away from the Phoenician coast from the Late Bronze period through the Iron II period, and if the associations of the Eastern *Galilee* in fact vary between connections with *Phoenicia,* with the *Jezreel,* and northeastward with *Aram* and Northern *Mesopotamia,* what archaeological or historical reasons do we have for accepting an association with the central highlands or with an Israel seeking definition? If the region of the Upper *Galilee* is ever to be associated with Israel historically, we cannot take such an association for granted. Geographically, such an association is not to be expected. Archaeologically, our limited evidence argues against it. Socio-politically, the domination of the *Galilee* would require considerable resources within a context of both an imperial worldview and a willingness to accept very small returns without foreseeable gains.

An area of the lower *Galilee* that is extremely instructive for the history of the transition from Late Bronze to Iron II is the small area of foothills on the northwestern edge of the *Jezreel* surrounding *Qiryat Tiv'on*.[91] A large number of sites have been found in this area from the Late Bronze Age. Most of these suggest continuous occupation from earlier periods. These settlements lie between the *Nahal Qishon* and the foothills that rise between *Bet She'arim* and *Qiryat Tiv'on*. On every one of these sites, there is evidence of very early Iron I occupation. North and East of *Qiryat Tiv'on*, however, where five Late Bronze settlements have been found in agriculturally less favorable locations, no occupation has been identified from the Iron I period. One is led to conclude both that the agricultural exploitation of the region as a whole probably had been continuous from the Late Bronze period, and that many individual sites in the agriculturally more marginal sectors had been abandoned for reasons that were endemic and specific to this area!

Furthermore, the surface surveys report that all but one of the Iron I sites in the region around *Qiryat Tiv'on* showed evidence of some occupation in the subsequent Iron II period. For this reason, a claim for a regional stability of the population can easily be made in spite of the discontinuity of the occupation on individual sites in the northern and eastern sectors. In the more marginal area of the hill country bordering

---

[91] Surveyed by I. Raban, "Nahalal," *Survey of Israel* (Jerusalem, 1981) Pal. grid Sq. 17–23, maps 2 and 3.

this small region, seven new sites show evidence of occupation during Iron II. This suggests that there was an expansion of the indigenous valley population northwards into the Lower *Galilee* once the drought of Iron I had closed. In this very limited region, where settlement patterns are analogous to the *Issachar* plateau, several issues become clear: a) There is a clearly continuous occupation of the region from the Late Bronze period through Iron Age II; b) The continuity of the occupation is agricultural; c) These new highland settlements have their origins in the lowland valleys; d) Continuity of settlement is regionally oriented—not to individual sites; and e) the proliferation of new settlement into the highlands has at least two distinct causes: a severe dislocation of the sedentary population at the end of the Late Bronze period or very early in Iron I, and an expansive growth and prosperity after the onset of Iron II.

A similar, and perhaps even more dramatic pattern of settlement growth during Iron II (in contrast to an extremely restricted Late Bronze-Iron I occupation) is characteristic also of the *'Iron* hills and supports revision of our interpretation.[92] These surveys in the Lower *Galilee* and the hills surrounding the *Jezreel,* suggest unequivocally that Finkelstein's concentration (first of all on new sites in the highlands and secondly on Iron I sites alone) introduces not only a severe limitation to the discussion, but distorts our perception of both the origins and cause of new settlement. Moreover, it blinds us to the extent of the period of transition that, very clearly in the Lower *Galilee,* emphatically involved the onset of the Iron II period even more than that of Iron I.

A revision of Finkelstein's analysis clearly requires us to look at many of those areas of *Palestine* that do not have so obvious a biblical claim for an association with Israel's earliest origins as do the regions of *Ephraim, Manasseh, Judah* and the *Galilee.* Not only is the phenomenon of new Iron Age settlement not confined to the highlands or to the Iron I period, the origins of those new highlanders do not seem to direct us to any common source, however proto-ethnically they are perceived. The causes that drove the highland settlement in fact is not confined to the highland regions alone. Rather, they involve changes that occurred over an extended period of some four centuries and left traces that have been found throughout all of the regions of greater *Palestine.* It also needs to

---

[92] Surveyed by A. Olami "Daliya," *Survey of Israel*, (Jerusalem, 1981) Pal. grid sq. 15-22, maps 2 and 3.

be observed at this point that there is no legitimate historical reason whatever that these changes in settlement patterns, or indeed the Bronze Age-Iron Age transition, have any direct relationship to the issues surrounding Israel's origins.

4. The Lowland Valleys

The *Jezreel* Valley is economically the most stable agricultural region of *Palestine*. Blessed with a mild climate, abundant groundwater and adequate rainfall, especially in the western part of the valley where deep rich alluvial and brown grumusols predominate, agricultural production has made this large central lowland the breadbasket of northern *Palestine*. The higher ground and the rolling hills of the extreme northeastern and southeastern corners of the valley has suffered severe erosion, beginning when deforestation first occurred early in the Bronze Age. Here also, relatively immature protogrumusols predominate in some areas.[93] The infrequent springs and relative aridity (ca. 400 mm.) in these two subregions contribute to their lesser suitability for agriculture. Nevertheless, they do produce stable grazing lands that contribute substantially to the economy of the valley as a whole. In contrast, the high water table, abundant springs and very flat terrain (a gradient of less than 0.2%) of the central and western valley (while requiring regular maintenance of the drainage systems to control flooding and salinity) have helped maintain the stability of agriculture there even during drought years. The poor natural drainage of the southwestern and northwestern rims of the valley has at times created conditions of extensive swampland in these areas whenever drainage has not been actively fostered.

Such necessary maintenance of extensive drainage systems, especially along the *Nahal Qishon*, was undoubtedly a significant and efficient cause for intersite regional political organization. Moreover, the importance of the *Jezreel* Valley for interregional and international trade routes is unparalleled in *Palestine*, connecting as the *Jezreel* does the central coastal region, the Phoenician coast, the *Jordan* Rift, the Central Hills, and the Lower *Galilee*. The *Jezreel* held a pivotal role,

---

[93] Th.L. Thompson, *The Settlement of Palestine in the Bronze Age, BTAVO* 34 (Wiesbaden, 1979) pp.33-35.

economically, politically and militarily, and was recurrently influenced by a wide range of interests from the exterior.[94]

Modern archaeological research in the area of the *Jezreel* Valley is long standing, and there have been extensive excavations at several of the great tells of the region, most notably at *Tel Yoqneam, Tell Ta'anek, Megiddo* and *Beth Shan*.[95] Excavations at two lesser sites (*Tel Qiri*[96] in the Western *Jezreel,* and *Tel Yin'am*[97] in the nearby *Yavneel* Valley, some 8 km south of *Tiberias*) also give considerable information that helps us understand the nature of the smaller agricultural villages from Iron I and Iron II that have been found throughout the *Jezreel, Beth Shan* and Central *Jordan* Valleys. Archaeological surveys have also added much new data, particularly helping us determine the diffusion of settlement both within the *Jezreel* Valley itself and in the hills of its immediate periphery.[98]

---

[94] In Egyptian imperial interests the Jezreel was second in importance only to the southern coast, and Egypt maintained its presence in the valley at least until the end of the twelfth-century. See esp., J.M. Weinstein, "The Egyptian Empire in Palestine: A Reassessment," *BASOR* 241 (1981), pp.17-28; S. Ahituv, "Economic Factors in the Egyptian Conquest of Canaan," *IEJ* 28 (1978), pp.93-105; N. Na'aman, "Economic Aspects of the Egyptian Occupation of Canaan," *IEJ* 31 (1981), pp.177-180; *idem,* "The Political History of Eretz Israel in the Time of the Nineteenth and Twentieth Dynasties," *The History of Eretz Israel*, vol. I, ed. by I. Eph'al (Jerusalem, 1982) pp.241-251; *idem,* "Pharaonic Lands in the Jezreel Valley in the Late Bronze Age," *Society and Economy in the Eastern Mediterranean*, ed. by M. Helzer and E. Lipinski (Leuven, 1988) pp.177-185. An awareness of the economic interests of the Egyptians in the Jezreel itself has created significant revisions of many earlier views. W.H. Shea, "The Conquests of Sharuhen and Megiddo Reconsidered," *IEJ* 29 (1979), pp.1-5.

[95] For *Megiddo's* bibliography, *EAEHL III*, p.856, and the very judicious review by G.I. Davies, "Megiddo in the Period of the Judges," *Crises and Perspectives, Oudtestamentisches Studien* 24 (Leiden, 1986) pp.34-53. For *Beth Shan, EAEHL I*, p.229; Th.L. Thompson, "Beth-Sean," *Biblisches Reallexikon*, ed. by K. Galling (Tübingen, 1977) pp.46f.; for *Tell Ta'anek, EAEHL III*, pp.1138-1147; Th.L. Thompson, "Thaanach," *BRL*, pp.342-344; W. Rast, *Taanach II* (1978); for *Tel Yoqneam*, esp. M.L. Hunt, *The Iron Age Pottery of the Yoqneam Regional Project* (University of California, Berkeley dissertation, 1985).

[96] A. Ben-Tor, "Tell Qiri: A Look at Village Life," *BA* 42 (1979), pp.105-113; M.L. Hunt, *op.cit.*

[97] H. Liebowitz, "Excavations at Tel Yin'am: the 1976 and 1977 Seasons: Preliminary Report," *BASOR* 243 (1981), pp.79-94.

[98] Here, not only the *Survey of Israel (op.cit.)*, but also the extensive surveys of N. Zori in the eastern sectors of the valley are of immense importance. (See especially his *An Archaeological Survey of the Beth Shan Valley* (Jerusalem, 1962) and his *The Land of Issachar Archaeological Survey* (Jerusalem, 1977). A beginning of a comprehensive review

The *Chicago* Oriental Institute's early excavations at *Megiddo* have created considerable confusion over the years because of their inadequate definition of *loci*. This confusion has prevented a clear association of the pottery to archaeological strata and has led to a great deal of uncertainty about *Megiddo*'s chronology. *Megiddo*'s fundamental importance to the political history of the Valley and of *Palestine* as a whole added fuel to the debate. However, the more recent excavations at *Ta'anach* to the East and at *Yoqneam* to the West (along with its villages at *Tel Qasis* and *Tel Qiri*) have improved our situation for understanding the history of the valley immensely.[99] The similarity and continuity of local regional pottery, which had been seemingly hopelessly obscured by past concentration on *Megiddo*'s more abundant supplies of better decorated wares, has been demonstrated at all of these sites.[100] *Megiddo*'s unique role as an Egyptian administrative center during the Late Bronze-Iron I transition is reflected in these more unusual pottery types. *Megiddo*'s most typical pottery, however, reflects a continuity and stability of the population within both the *Megiddo* region and at the site itself. A comparison of the common wares with that of its neighbors mark the continuity of the population in spite of the considerable architectural changes that reflect significant political and economic transformation at Megiddo.

Megiddo Stratum VIIB (generally dated to the end of the thirteenth-century, and perhaps lasting into the very beginning of the twelfth-century)[101] continued the prosperity of the Late Bronze occupation of the site. Some of the regional wares found in this stratum indicate that this level spans the onset of Iron I in the *Jezreel*.[102] Stratum VIIA marks a stage of considerable rebuilding of the palace and of temple 2048, but very few changes in the plans of the buildings have been noticed, and there is no indication of any change in the function of the

---

of archaeological remains in the Jezreel can be found in the dissertation of M.L. Hunt (*op.cit.*). Any convincing integration of the archaeological remains with historical records is, however, yet in the future.

[99] M.L. Hunt, *ibid.*, p.192.

[100] *Ibid.*, pp.181–184.

[101] G.I. Davies, *op.cit.*, p.36.

[102] These are similar to pottery found at *Tel Qiri*, stratum IX: M.L. Hunt, *op.cit.*, p.182 *et passim*; also: A. Ben-Tor, *op.cit.*, pp.105–113.

city as an administrative center.[103] Mycenaean and Cypriote pottery no longer seem to have been imported during this period. This reflects the general cessation of such imports throughout the southern Levant, and also supports the general consensus of a widespread collapse of trade in the western Mediterranean during the twelfth-century.

The continuity of the administrative buildings and of the temple in Stratum VIIA, and the probable association with this stratum of two cartouches of Ramses III (1184–1153 B.C.), and a bronze statue base with inscriptions that link it with Ramses VI (1142–1135 B.C.),[104] suggest that the town remained under Egyptian control until at least 1140–1130 B.C. The survival of Egyptian administrative control in the *Jezreel* Valley (here at *Megiddo* and at *Beth Shan* in the East) is of considerable historical importance in understanding the Iron I settlements of these central lowland valleys. The control and distribution of lands associated with villages and towns at considerable distance from the administrative centers is reflected in a Late Bronze letter from *Tell Taanach*.[105] N. Na'aman discusses this text in relationship to references to Egyptian administration in several of the *Amarna* letters.[106] The administrative character of most of the excavated areas of *Megiddo* in the early Iron Age strata, suggests a regional control of the various settlements of the *Jezreel* during early Iron I, linking the towns with the new Iron I settlements of the valley and supporting the conclusion that there was an association between these new settlements and the Egyptian economic administrations centered at *Megiddo* and *Beth Shan*. The analysis of the common pottery of the *Yoqneam* Regional Project by M.L. Hunt[107] confirms this view of continuity and coherence in the agricultural economy of the *Jezreel* during the transition from the Late Bronze to the Iron Ages. An association of the economy and the political structures of *Taanach* can also be suggested in spite of the drastic change in settlement form there, from that of a considerable

---

[103] Following G.I. Davies, *op.cit.*, pp.36f. The "thick layer of debris" so important to Y. Aharoni and Y. Yadin (*EAEHL*, p.847) hardly negates the many signs of continuity between these two strata.

[104] G.I. Davies, *op.cit.*, pp.37f.; Y. Yadin, *op.cit.*, pp.847f.

[105] A.E. Glock, "Texts and Archaeology at Tell Ta'annek," *Berytus* 31 (1983), pp.58–63.

[106] N. Na'aman, "Pharaonic Lands in the Jezreel Valley in the Late Bronze Age," Society and Economy in the Eastern Mediterranean ca. 1500–1000 B.C., ed by M. Heltzer and E Lipinski (Leuven, 1988) pp.177–185.

[107] M.L. Hunt, *op.cit.*, especially, pp.181ff.

town to a simple unfortified village, with a gap in occupation on the site and a smooth transition of pottery forms from Iron I through the tenth-century.[108]

The transition from Stratum VII to VIB at *Megiddo* should similarly be understood in this regional context. Stratum VII at *Megiddo* ends in considerable destruction. This destruction may well mark the end of Egyptian control throughout the region, ca. 1130 B.C. The buildings of Stratum VIB, moreover, do not continue those of Stratum VII at all. They also reflect a considerable decline in the prosperity of the site.[109] Indeed, some suggest a gap in the occupation at this point.[110] *Megiddo* of Stratum VIB might be described as a relatively poor, unfortified village, and stands in sharp contrast to the administrative center of Stratum VII. However, one should not assume too quickly that these differences reflect any significant ethnic change in the population.[111] As at *Taanach*, the changes at *Megiddo*, reflected in the transition from Stratum VII to VIB, profoundly affected the pattern of settlement and involved a transformation in both political and economic structures. Unquestionably, a radical transformation of the economy occurred. Nevertheless, the regional continuity of the population is reflected in the continuity of the pottery from Stratum VII to VIB at *Megiddo*, a continuity that is also observable at *Tell Taanach* and *Tel Qiri*.[112] *Megiddo*'s Stratum VIB might best be understood as a transition period of impoverished survival after the Egyptian administrative center of

---

[108] W. Rast, *Taanach I* (New Haven, 1978); M. L. Hunt, *op.cit.*, pp.178ff; also on Taanach generally: A.E. Glock, "Taanach," *EAEHL* III, pp.1138-1147.

[109] Y. Yadin, "Megiddo," *EAEHL*, pp.850f; also, G.I. Davies, *op.cit.*, pp.36ff.

[110] W. Rast, *op.cit.*, Table 2; already, W.F. Albright, *The Archaeology of Palestine* (London, 1949) pp.117f.; cf., however, G.I. Davies, *op.cit.*, pp.40f.

[111] So Y. Yadin, *ibid*.

[112] M.L. Hunt, *op.cit.*, pp.203f. For an analogy to this ceramic continuity in the lowlands, one might profitably refer to the excavations at *Tall an-Na'am (Tel Yin'am)* on the western rim of the *Yavneel* Valley. Here a metallurgical site from the Late Bronze II period (Stratum VIB) shows pottery forms found elsewhere in both Late Bronze II and Iron I levels. The Iron I level continues some of these (as well as some Late Bronze forms) with early twelfth-century forms at *Megiddo* and *Ta'anach*. Nothing in the archaeological record suggests a break between *Tel Yin'am* VIB and VIA and there is no evidence that there had been either destruction or abandonment. It seems necessary to assume that there was continuity here (as elsewhere in the lowlands) between the Late Bronze and the Iron Age sedentary populations of the site. H. Liebowitz, "Excavations at Tel Yin'am:the 1976 and 1977 Seasons: Preliminary Report," *BASOR* 243 (1981), pp.79-94.

Stratum VII had been destroyed, and prior to the resurgence of *Megiddo* as a regional administrative center in Stratum VIA that continued through the eleventh-century. A similar period of impoverished reorganization is found in Stratum VB following the catastrophic destruction of VIA. The dates for these destructions are unknown. Attempts to identify this latter transition to a hypothetical Davidic conquest and subsequent Israelite settlement cannot be confirmed without evidence.[113] The recurrent pattern, however, of impoverished resettlement and even gaps in occupation following major destructions, might well be explained as direct results of such major disasters, whatever their immediate cause. One need not think of the resettling population as either newcomers or Israelites.[114]

There has been only limited excavation of the sites in the Beth Shan Valley to the east of the Jezreel and along the Jordan southwards to the *Dead Sea*. On the east bank of the *Jordan,* the major exceptions to this are the sites of *Tell as-Saidiyeh*[115] (excavated by J.B. Pritchard) and *Tell Deir 'Alla* (dug by H.J. Franken).[116] Iron I levels were not reached on the mound of *Tell as-Saidiyeh*. In the adjacent Late Bronze and early Iron I cemetery, Pritchard notes a considerable impoverishment of the Iron I burials. At *Deir 'Alla*, a Late Bronze shrine was excavated. This building was destroyed by earthquake early in the twelfth-century. Subsequent to the destruction (during Iron I), the site was occupied by what Franken describes as a "winter encampment," with a mixed economy of agriculture and pastoralism. During Iron II, the settlement expanded and developed as a walled village.[117]

Several surveys report considerable remains from the Iron I period in both the *Beth Shan* Valley[118] and in the Rift Valley on both sides of

---

[113] On this, T. Dothan, *The Philistines and their Material Culture* (1982) pp.291f.

[114] The tentative argument put forward by G.I. Davies that Stratum VIA had been Philistine, and was ultimately destroyed by David on the grounds that "Megiddo was certainly in Israelite hands by the time of Solomon" (p.47) is based entirely on an effort to harmonize 2 Samuel and 1 Kings with the excavation reports. His archaeological warrant for this, however, is limited to the so-called Philistine pottery of Stratum VIA.

[115] J.B. Pritchard, *The Cemetery at Tell es Sa'ideyeh* (Philadelphia, 1980).

[116] H.J. Franken, *Excavations at Tell Deir 'Alla* I (Leiden, 1969); *idem,* "Deir 'Alla," *EAEHL* I, pp.321-324.

[117] Franken speaks of this as a new settlement.

[118] N. Zori, "An Archaeological Survey of the Beth-Shean Valley," *The Beth Shan Valley* (1962).

the *Jordan*.[119] The accuracy of the pottery attributions of these many
sites is very mixed. Finkelstein suggests that some of the sites in the
Jordan Valley are likely to have been seasonal occupations of
pastoralists. This is probably true. Nevertheless, the contrast of site
frequency during Iron I with the Late Bronze sites known from the
region, suggest that the *Jordan,* and especially the *Beth Shan* Valley, had
been affected by the climatic stress of the Late Bronze-Iron Age
transition in a way comparable to what led to the economic dislocations
and disruptions of the *Jezreel.* The population spread over a much larger
area of exploitation than was settled in the Late Bronze period. Many
new small villages, encampments, or hamlets were established, and a
sedentary population first achieved stability and prosperity during the
Iron II period. The site of *Beth Shan* itself, it should be remembered,
had a history of continuous settlement from the Chalcolithic Period.
Evidence of Egyptian influence in the town parallels that of *Megiddo*,
and there seems to have been continuous occupation on the site at least
until the end of Stratum VI (Late Bronze-Iron I), and probably until the
end of Stratum V (Iron I-II). It is in Stratum IV (Iron II) that the
settlement seems to have been built on an altered plan and the temple
area no longer was in use.

The sketchiness of Finkelstein's treatment of the lowland valleys, and
particularly that of the *Jezreel,* underlines his biblically based confidence
that the archaeological remains from the Late Bronze-Iron I transition
in these regions are only peripheral to issues of the early "Israelite"
settlement that is the focus of his work. Three arbitrary premises seem
to underlie this methodological decision: 1) Finkelstein's understanding
of "Israelite" in this early pre-state period is confined to those territories
that he understands (with historical-critical inconsequence) to have
subsequently formed Saul's kingdom in ca. 1000 B.C. He determined the
boundaries of the territory of Israel through a moderately critical reading
of 1 Samuel (which he assumes to be an historical work), strongly
influenced by a harmonization with the Books of Joshua and Judges (of
whose historicity he is curiously more skeptical).[120] 2) Perhaps
influenced by the common Israeli anachronistic terminology designating
the archaeological period of the "Iron Age" as the "Israelite period,"
and the Bronze Age as belonging to "Canaanites," Finkelstein further

---

[119] On this, I Finkelstein, *op. cit.* pp.111f. for a convenient summary.
[120] I. Finkelstein, *op.cit.,* 1988, pp.27f.

assumed "early Israelite" to be defined by that part of the population of
Palestine that is in the process of settling down.[121] 3) He, moreover,
maintained the *a priori* historical opinion that (in contrast to the central
highlands) there had been no Israelite settlement in the *Jezreel* before
the tenth-century B.C.[122] This allowed him to examine the early Iron I
process of settlement of the lowlands, insulated from any larger
chronological or geographical contexts that might suggest an association
with the highland sedentarization. This led him to the unfortunately
predetermined conclusion that the key to and the origins of the Iron I
process of sedentarization should be sought exclusively in the highlands.
This he divorced from the "Late Bronze Canaanite" highlanders, whose
occupation of the hills continued into the early Iron Age, in accord with
the needs of his argument. While Finkelstein's archaeological
thoroughness remains strong and impressive, his historical logic is weak
and circular.

Finkelstein's obvious intellectual dependence on the basic results of
Alt's 1925 programmatic essay that had established on the basis of a
synthesis of Egyptian campaign records with a biblically oriented
Territorialgeschichte, rigid ethno-political dichotomies between the
highlands and the lowlands, between the Late Bronze period and the
Iron Age, and between the so-called Canaanites and Israelites, renders
the conclusions of Finkelstein's entire enterprise suspect. However,
Finkelstein's own very solid archaeological research undermines the
usefulness of these dichotomies by exposing again and again the
arbitrarily limiting and restrictive role of his historical reconstruction.
One must conclude that it is not the archaeological evidence after all,
but rather this predetermined biblically oriented perspective that has
guided (and distorted) Finkelstein's historiography. If one puts Alt's
framework aside, the archaeological data perceived comprehensively
leads one in decidedly different directions. It is necessary to understand
the process of the Iron I settlement of the highlands within the larger
geographical context of changes throughout *Palestine*, as well as in the
broader chronological context of the historical and archaeological
transition beginning already in the deterioration of Late Bronze II and
lasting until the establishment of a new stability in the settlement and
the dominantly agricultural exploitation of *Palestine* during Iron II. This

---

[121] *Ibidem.*

[122] *Ibid.,* p.28.

needs to be done prior to the expansion of our discussion to issues of historical, political and ethnic transitions between the second and first millennia B.C., as well as to the much more difficult issues of the origins of Israel. These separate problems have their own independent integrity and significance, and must be dealt with with objectivity and without prejudgment.

The importance of separating our historiographical analysis from a dependence on biblical historiography and historicity is nowhere more apparent than in reviewing the archaeologically oriented Late Bronze-Iron Age transition in the Lowland valleys, especially in the *Jezreel*. No other single region of *Palestine* has played such a pivotal role in the military, political and economic history of *Palestine* since the Early Bronze Age than has the *Jezreel* with its eastern extension into the plain of *Beth Shan*. Because of its agricultural richness and the comparative stability of its considerable population, the *Jezreel* Valley is marked as the primary region for establishing and maintaining the geographical contiguity that has always been necessary for assuming any significant political or ethnic unity in northern *Palestine*.

The central highlands, on the other hand, form a distinctively self enclosed region. Historically, they had acquired a modest political unity and centralization through the prosperity and dominance of the few larger intramontane valley towns, of which the Middle Bronze and *Amarna* period hegemony of *Shechem* is the best example. For any transregional expansion of the limited political power of the central highlands towards the northern towns of the *Jezreel,* the intensively more populated and always politically significant *Jezreel* must of necessity be neutralized. However, the central highlands are not naturally centralized (and hence any unified political thrust from the central highlands should not be assumed) prior to the rise of *Samaria* in Iron II. Moreover, no basis of union between the central highlands and the geographically distant upper *Galilee* is known to have existed except that derived from a very selective and tendentious reading of the centuries later biblical tradition that asserts a unity of Israel originating already in the *Sinai,* prior to any settlement in *Palestine*. Any historiography of the origins of Israel that takes its starting point apart from the biblical historiography must of necessity also entertain the possibility of an alternative process of unification.[123] The Iron I settlement of the central highlands cannot be understood as "Israelite," and that designation be also extended to contemporary settlements in the *Galilee*, without understanding the *Jezreel* as part of the equation. It simply will not do to bypass the history of Iron I in the *Jezreel* as irrelevant, and to depend on the legendary prowess of a David to neutralize the lowlands two centuries too late.

As already noted, the early Iron I settlements in the Upper *Galilee* can hardly be seen as part of the process of the sedentarization of the central hills, even if some of these sites can be associated with the Iron I towns of *Hazor* and *Dan*. The new settlements of the Upper *Galilee* appear as fragmented pockets of settlement, with a material culture sharply distinct from that of the central highlands and oriented much more obviously to the towns along the Phoenician coast. The problem is even more immediate when we address ourselves to such smaller geographic units as that of the Lower *Galilee* region to the West of *Nazareth*, of the *Issachar* Plateau or of the *'Iron* hills: areas which cannot be ignored if we are to understand the Late Bronze-Iron Age transition period in *Palestine*. Finkelstein's dependence on the primacy of the process of settlement in *Ephraim* and *Manasseh* for Israel's origins is an argument *pars pro toto* and thus cannot be maintained. On the basis of settlement patterns, the above discussed settlements in the region of the Lower *Galilee* (along the northwestern edge of the *Jezreel* in the vicinity of *Qiryat Tiv'on*) reflect (comparable to the new sites of the *Galilee* in their relationship with *Phoenicia*) a continuum[124] with the Late Bronze Age, and are to be associated with the occupation of the *Jezreel* itself rather than with either the Upper *Galilee* or the Central Highlands. On the basis of chronological process, the settlements of *Issachar* and of the

---

[123] The necessity of some principle of unity such as the no longer viable amphictyony hypothesis (above, chapter II; also N.P. Lemche, "On Sociology and the History of Israel: A Reply to Eckhardt Otto—and Some Further Considerations," *BN* 21 (1983), pp.48-58; *idem*, "Israel in the Period of the Judges—The Tribal League in Recent Research," *Studia Theologica* 38 (1984), pp.1-28) in order to discuss any transregional concept of "Israel," as Finkelstein puts forward, is obvious in discussions relating to the Jezreel. Prior to the development of secondary state structures, it is extremely difficult to posit social or ethnic unities among sedentary agriculturalists that go beyond immediate geographical and economic boundaries. As Finkelstein himself suggests, to assume ethnic or lineage associations between such geographically distant and distinct regions is methodologically perverse. Moreover, even Finkelstein now admits (*op.cit.*, 1991-1992) that there could not have been an Israel before the late eleventh-century.

[124] As pointed out by N.P. Lemche (personal communication).

Iron hills, with their most significant rise of new settlement after the onset of Iron II, are also better associated with the patterns of settlement of the lowland valleys than with those of the Central Highlands.

If the direction of this hypothesis is defensible, then it is necessary to reformulate our questions regarding the specific significance of the new wave of settlement of the Iron I and Iron II periods in both the regions of the lowlands and elsewhere in *Palestine*. Moreover, even when such new villages might be understood in ethno-historical categories, it cannot yet be as "Israel" that they can be understood; for such an understanding is indubitably the product of a tradition that did not yet exist, and this is true whatever the historicity of the various units of that tradition might be. While the trajectory of our historiography must lead to the "Israel" of this biblical tradition, for that is the perspective from which we come to know Israel, the development of our historiography must proceed apart from it and be directed toward it.

5. *The Coastal Plain*

The effect of the extended drought of ca. 1200 B.C. was particularly severe on the coastal plain. The widespread impoverishment that it brought in its wake all along the Mediterranean coast from the Aegean eastwards was devastating and had revolutionary potential. For example, *Ugarit*'s inability to rebuild after the destruction of 1182 B.C. ended the centralized political control of an entire region that resulted in it becoming vulnerable to the disintegrating forces incumbent in political and economic collapse as well as famine. South of *Ugarit*, the dislocations caused by drought and the influx of migrants—especially from the north—following the collapse of *Mycenae* brought the entire Phoenician coast that stretched from the northernmost city of *Tell Sukas* to *Acco* in the south[125] under far-reaching social stress and change.

---

[125] S. Moscati, "Territory and Settlements," *The Phoenicians*, ed. by S. Moscati (Milan, 1988) pp.26f. One should also include within Phoenician territory not only the western part of the Upper Galilee, but also the entire "Plain of Acco" to the Carmel range. This is suggested by the excavations at *Tell Abu Hawam*, and is certainly clear as a result of the digging at *Tell Keisan* by the *Ecole Biblique* (J. Briend and J.-B. Humbert, *Tell Keisan, 1971-1976: Une Cité phenicienne en Galilée*, Paris, 1980; J. Balensi, "Tell Keisan, Lémoin original de l'apparition du 'Mycenien IIC 1a', au Proche Orient," *RB* 88 (1981), pp.399-401.

However, for a variety of reasons, the major Phoenician cities survived the initial onslaught of the drought without widespread collapse. The relative geographical isolation of these towns along the morphologically fragmented Lebanese coast had always rendered these towns a political independence and economic autonomy lacking to larger and more coherent regions. This led the cities to develop self sufficient political and material resources for survival. In fact, in the long run, although some of the southern sites such as *Tel Akko* and *Tell Keisan* reflect considerable disturbance,[126] the various Phoenician coastal city-states—especially *Tyre* and *Sidon*—gained considerably from the political and economic changes that occurred elsewhere in *Palestine*.[127]

Unlike Ugarit to the North, which in 1200 B.C. was on the fringe of the Egyptian empire and within the orbit of the collapsing Hittite world,[128] the Phoenician cities, and especially *Byblos, Tyre* and *Sidon* were (at least at the very beginning of the transition period) still firmly within the Egyptian sphere of trade and, although most likely politically independent of *Egypt*, benefited by the stability that these trade relations brought, as had the more dependent towns of the *Jezreel*, and especially those along the southern coast of *Palestine* and in the *Shephelah*.[129] The collapse of *Ugarit* in fact removed a dominant competitor from the eastern Mediterranean Sea trade, encouraging the Phoenician ports, as *Egypt* withdrew from its involvement in the overseas trade routes, to fill the vacuum in sea trade left by the great powers. During the early twelfth-century, the only outside competitor for Phoenician controlled resources was that of the relatively minor regional state of *Amurru*, which competed with the coastal cities for control of their Galilean

---

[126] M. Dothan, "Akko: Interim Excavation Report: First Season 1973-4," *BASOR* 224 (1976), pp.1-48; J. Briend and J.-B. Humbert, *op. cit.*

[127] For the early history of the Phoenician coast, above all S. Moscati, *et alii, op.cit.*, especially the articles: S. Moscati, "Who Were the Phoenicians?," pp.24f.; S.F. Bondi, "The Origins in the East," pp.28-35; *idem*, "The Course of History:, pp.38-45. Also of value is H.-H. Bernhardt, *Der alte Libanon* (Munich, 1976).

[128] On the chronology for the collapse of the Hittite empire, see now especially I. Singer, "Dating the End of the Hittite Empire," *Hethitica* 8 (1987), pp.413-421.

[129] See further, below. Even in association with the Egyptian empire during Late Bronze proper, the towns of *Palestine* with their dynastic kinglets, and especially those of *Phoenicia*, were rarely wholly subordinate "creatures" of the empire, but at most allies and vassals, involved with *Egypt* in a very flexible association that at times bordered on independence (See above, chapter 5).

Hinterland.[130] However, this was only a passing, if recurrent threat, as the center of the economy of the coastal cities was oriented not eastward towards agriculture but westward, towards commerce and the sea, and their relationships with the Galilean settlements were more symbiotic than simply exploitative.

By 1100 B.C., the Egyptians had withdrawn from *Palestine* and Egyptian influence over trade and the timber industry had all but disappeared.[131] It is also at this time that the Assyrian Tiglathpileser I makes his first expedition to the coast in search of timber. His annals claim tribute from *Aradus, Byblos*, and *Sidon*.[132] This campaign of Tiglathpileser I began a relationship between the northern Palestinian coastal cities and the Assyrian empire that (through policies of coercion and cooperation and led by the tenth-century maritime expansion of the city-states and a near monopoly of trade in the eastern Mediterranean) rendered the Phoenician cities an extended period of prosperity and political stability.[133]

The Phoenician coastal cities did not form either a political or a national unity. Many aspects of their culture prevented this, not least being Assyrian political interests. The separations and distinctiveness of the Phoenician city-states begin already in the geographical displacement of the cities.[134] Although all are set along the Mediterranean coast, either on off shore islands or promontories jutting into the sea, and are situated on the narrow coastal strip of *Lebanon* between the sea and the mountains, the coastal strip is not itself continuous or easily unified, but is broken both by westward flowing streams draining the mountains to the East and by promontories that reach the sea and hinder north-south communications along the plain. Moreover, the physical setting of the cities on islands and peninsulas along the coast helped protect their independence from both foreign and local competitors. Finally, the entrepreneurial nature of overseas commerce at this time fostered an

---

[130] S.F. Bondi, *op.cit.*, p.341.

[131] The eleventh-century story of Wen Amon's visit to *Byblos* illustrates the independence of the prince of Byblos; *ANET*,pp.25-29; S.F. Bondi, *op.cit.*, pp.38f.

[132] S.F. Bondi, *ibid.*; *ANET* pp.282-284.

[133] The direct military involvement of the Assyrians into Phoenician affairs is clearly present by the ninth-century in the campaigns of Asshurnasirpal II (833-859 B.C.) and Shalmaneser III (858-824 B.C.); S.F. Bondi, *op.cit.*, p.41.

[134] S. Moscati, *op.cit.*, 1988, pp.24f. 26f.

autonomy of the cities that can well be compared with that enjoyed by the Italian commercial trade centers of more than two millennia later.

Further south, in the plain of *Sharon*, the Late Bronze-Iron I transition has traditionally been associated with the arrival of the "*Tjekker*"[135] who are mentioned as the inhabitants of *Dor* in the eleventh-century Egyptian text of *Wen-Amon*. However, in the recent excavations at *Dor*[136] a new port installation and landing stage was discovered datable to the thirteenth-century. The ashlar stone work associated with this installation is unique in *Palestine*, and can be associated with similar structures found elsewhere in the Aegean.[137] It is very clear that, as Ahlström points out, the planners of this reconstruction of the harbor were immigrants from elsewhere in the Mediterranean. If these are the *Tjekker-Sekel* they seem to have worked within the established local economy and culture of the Late Bronze Age, supporting and adding to it. New technical innovations brought about long term improvements in the maritime industry.[138] As at some sites further south, the archaeological evidence suggests that the new immigrants at *Dor* did not bring about a radical change and destructive displacement of the population of the coast. Rather, the immigrants seem to have been peacefully integrated into the indigenous coastal population. Similarly, M. Dothan's excavations at *Acco*[139] suggest that after the destruction of the city by Ramses III the population reestablished its occupation of the site on a lesser scale without fortifications. Some of the industrial installations indicate the settlement of immigrants from the West: either from *Cilicia* or the Aegean. Dothan

---

[135] Or *Sekel*, following A. Rainey, "Toponymic Problems," *Tel Aviv* 9 (1982), pp.130-136.

[136] G. Foerster, "Dor" *EAEHL I*, pp.334f; *idem.*, "Recent Archaeological Research in Israel," *International Journal of Nautical Archaeology* 10 (1981), pp.297-305, 12 (1983), pp.229-238; *idem.*, "The Ancient Harbors of Israel in Biblical Times," *Harbor Archaeology*, ed. by A Raban (Oxford, 1985) pp.23-27; A. Raban, "The Harbor of the Sea Peoples at Dor," *BA* 50 (1987), pp.118-126; *idem.*, "The Constructive Maritime Role of the Sea Peoples in the Levant," *Society and Economy in the Eastern Mediterranean*, ed. by M. Heltzer and E. Lipinski (Leiden, 1988) pp.261-294; K. Raveh, "A Concise Nautical History of Dor-Tantura," *International Journal of Nautical Archaeology* 13 (1984), pp.223-241; A. Raban and E. Galili, "Recent Maritime Archeological Research in Israel," *IJNA* 14 (1985), pp.332-349.

[137] See further on this, G. Ahlström, *op.cit.*, forthcoming, Chapter VI.

[138] A. Raban, *op.cit.*, 1988.

[139] M. Dothan, *op.cit.*

reasonably suggests that these settlers be understood as the *Sherden*. However, the *Sherden* already formed a part of Ramses II's army in the battle of *Qadesh*,[140] and might be expected to be already substantially acculturated to the region prior to the destruction. So also the substantial Late Bronze seaport town of *Jaffa* was (as far as we can tell from the archaeological finds) succeeded by a large unfortified village (much in the manner of the *Sharon*'s *Tel Zeror* and *Tell Burgata*). It apparently did not recover from the drought-driven economic depression until at least the onset of Iron II.[141] That little "Philistine" ware has been found at *Jaffa*, as pointed out by Ahlström,[142] does not indicate that immigrants from the West were unknown there. After all, the occurrence and non-occurrence of such pottery is not indicative of the ethnicity of the inhabitants. Moreover, nearby *Tel Qasile*, which had established both a port on the *Yarkon* River and a temple complex, displays many signs of ties with either *Cilicia* or the Aegean.[143] Large amounts of so-called Philistine bichrome ware were found together both with imports from *Egypt* and local Palestinian ware comparable to that found at *Jaffa*.[144] Ahlström's suggestion that the port of *Jaffa* may have been transferred to *Qasile*[145] is a reasonable one and, if confirmed, would suggest that the occurrence of "Philistine" ware certainly does not identify ethnicity at all. It rather marks at most the extent to which a settlement had been integrated into the economic network of the region. That is, it is a sign of economic and trade associations.

The *Sharon* is unfortunately not well known archaeologically. The alluvial strip that runs along the eastern portion of the coastal plain has been subject to intensive agriculture over centuries. In brief and limited surveys, a few sites occupied in the Late Bronze II and Iron I periods have been identified to the west of the alluvial strip.[146] At both

---

[140] *ANET*, pp.255ff. (courtesy of N.P. Lemche, personal communication).

[141] J. Kaplan, "Jaffa (Joppa)," *EAEHL II*, pp.532-541.

[142] G. Ahlström, *op.cit.*, Chapter VI.

[143] B. Maisler (Mazar), "The Excavations at Tell Qasile: Preliminary Report," *IEJ* 1 (1950-51), pp.61-76, 125-140 and 194-218.

[144] B. Mazar, "A Philistine Temple at Tell Qasile" *BA* 36 (1973), pp.42-48; *idem*, "Excavations at Tell Qasile," *BA* 40 (1977), pp.81-87.

[145] G. Ahlström, *op.cit.*, forthcoming, Chapter VI.

[146] Reported in an abstract by R. Gophna and M. Kochavi, "An Archaeological Survey of the Plain of Sharon," *IEJ* 16 (1966), pp.143-144; also I. Finkelstein, *op. cit.*, 1988, pp.91f. who also refers to Y. Porath, S. Dor and S. Applebaum, *The History and Archaeology of*

excavated sites, the transition from the Late Bronze period to that of early Iron I follows a familiar pattern. Late Bronze town life seems to come to an end and is succeeded by an extremely impoverished and ephemeral layer consisting primarily of pits used for silos, with pottery continuing the Late Bronze traditions. The Iron I sites in the survey appear to have been newly settled small hamlets or campsites. The town settlement of *Tel Zeror* was revived later during Iron I (eleventh-century) with the construction of a citadel, a casemate fortification wall and a number of well built houses. Much "Philistine" pottery marks this town as both contemporary to and associated with *Tel Dor* as well with the sites to the south of *Tel Zeror*.

On the basis of the very limited reports of the excavation at *Dor*, it is uncertain whether this settlement underwent a period of severe economic depression and population dislocation at the onset of Iron I, or whether it followed rather a more stable pattern comparable to the Phoenician cities to the North. The suggestion that the brief early Iron I pit strata at *Tel Zeror* and *Tell Burgata* are to be identified as Israelite, succeeded by Philistine occupation as first put forward by Kochavi and Gophna, and cited with approval by Finkelstein,[147] seems arbitrary. Not only does it seem to give both the storage silos and the later "Philistine" pottery the value of ethnic markers, it ignores the clear elements of continuity (most notably in the pottery of both the Late Bronze-Iron Ia and the Iron Ia-Ib transitions) involving only a very small population. A similar continuity is represented at all sites of the *Sharon*. *Tel Dor* witnesses to the immigration of people from the West as early as the thirteenth-century. The transition to the earliest Iron I levels at both *Zeror* and *Burgata* reflect impoverishment, dislocations and abandonment. The new settlements of the Iron I period reflect an effort of the sedentary population to adopt to the impoverishment of the towns by opening new lands to cultivation. The reestablishment of *Tel Zeror* as a town during the eleventh-century does not so much indicate the arrival of a new people as rather the gradual restabilization of the population in this region.

Emeq-Hefer (Tel Aviv, 1985)[unseen by this author]. Two of these surveyed sites have been excavated: *Tel Zeror*, 20km South of *Tel Dor* (K. Ohata, *Tel Zeror* I-III, Tokyo, 1966-75) and *Tell Burgata* (R. Gophna and M. Kochavi, *op. cit.*).

[147] *Ibid.*, p.92.

The settlement pattern of the Late Bronze-Iron II transition which we find in the *Sharon* is repeated, with some significant variation, in the coastal plain further to the South. This area is commonly known as the Philistine plain, and reconstructions of the historical transitions during the thirteenth to the tenth-century are commonly keyed to the history of such a people in the region. However, the last two decades have brought about major changes in our understanding both of the origins of the so-called Philistines and of the nature and extent of Egyptian presence in the region. Much of the historical understanding of this region and of the interpretation of the archaeological reports depend directly on the interpretive value given to Philistine pottery and our understanding of it as an ethnic identifier. Happily, historians have made great progress on this in recent years. As early as 1963, Ruth Amiran pointed out the complex character of the so-called Philistine ware and classified the "Philistine" repertoire as a hybrid with some forms, decorative patterns and pottery building techniques, both borrowed and derivative from "Mycenaean" traditions.[148] As I. Singer has pointed out, the designation "Mycenaean" is to be understood topologically, but not as signifying a specific place of origin; for such pottery has been found in several localities of the Aegean and all along the coast of *Cilicia*.[149] However, the pottery itself was clearly made in *Palestine* and continued many traditions of both form and decoration related to Iron I indigenous wares and derivative of Palestinian Late Bronze pottery. In his 1979 study of pottery from *Tell el Far'ah* South, T.L. McClellan pointed out that there was not a clear correlation between the Philistine pottery and either the arrival of the Philistines in *Palestine* or their presence there.[150] In a long series of publications, T. Dothan has convincingly clarified the relationship between the "Philistine" ware and

---

[148] R. Amiran, *Ancient Pottery of the Holy Land* (Jerusalem, 1969) pp.266f; also G. Ahlström, *op.cit.*, forthcoming, Chapter VI.

[149] I. Singer, "The Origin of the Sea Peoples and Their Settlement on the Coast of Canaan," *Society and Economy in the Eastern Mediterranean*, ed. by M. Heltzer and E. Lipinski (Leuven, 1988) pp.239-250, esp. p.244.

[150] T.L. McClellan, "Chronology of the 'Philistine' Burials at Tell el-Far'ah (South)," *Journal of Field Archaeology* 6 (1979), pp.57-73. On the pottery, Sir F. Petrie, *Beth-Pelet* I (London, 1930) pp.7ff. See also J. Waldbaum, "Philistine Tombs at Tell Fara and their Aegean Prototypes," *AJA* 70 (1966), pp.331-340; W.H. Stiebing, "Another Look at the Origins of the Philistine Tombs at Tell el-Far'ah (S)," *AJA* 74 (1970), pp.139-143; and especially G. Ahlström, *op. cit.*, forthcoming, Chapter VI.

Mycenaean IIIC 1b pottery, understanding it as a Palestinian extension of a "Mycenaean" imported tradition of pottery making. Mycenaean IIC 1 pottery imports had been identified by V. Hankey at *Beth Shan*.[151] T. Dothan identified a monochrome Mycenaean IIIC ware at *Ashdod* which she suggested was derivative of the type identified by Hankey and which could be understood as what she calls a "missing link" between directly imported ware and the Palestinian tradition of "Philistine pottery."[152] Similar local production of Mycenaean ware has been found on *Cyprus*.[153] That this Mycenaean IIC 1b ware was locally made was decisively proven by neutron activation analysis for *Ashdod* in 1971[154] and confirmed for similar pottery from *Tel Miqne*.[155]

It is particularly on the basis of the associations and mutual confirmation of the finds at *Tel Ashdod* and *Tel Miqne* that Dothan was able to convincingly outline her understanding of the origins of the indigenous "Philistine" ware as derivative from and rooted in a transplanted Mycenaean pottery tradition carried out in *Cyprus, Syria,* coastal *Palestine* and elsewhere.[156] The Mycenaean IIIC 1B pottery at *Tel Miqne* appears first in Stratum VII in the context of a newly fortified settlement following the destruction of the Late Bronze city of Stratum VIIIA. In Stratum VII not only does Mycenaean IIIC 1B pottery appear

---

[151] V. Hankey, "Mycenaean Pottery in the Middle East," *BSA* 62 (1967), pp.127-128.

[152] T. Dothan, "Philistine Material Culture and Its Mycenaean Affinities," *The Mycenaeans in the Eastern Mediterranean* (Nicosia, 1973) pp.187f. For the pottery from *Ashdod*, M. Dothan and D.N. Freedman, *Ashdod I, Atiqot VII* (Jerusalem, 1967); M. Dothan, *Ashdod II-III, Atiqot IX-X* (Jerusalem, 1971) Stratum XIIIB, *passim*.

[153] T. Dothan, "The Arrival of the Sea Peoples: Cultural Diversity in Early Iron Age Canaan," *Recent Excavations in Israel: Studies in Iron Age Technology*, ed. by S. Gitin and W.G. Dever (Winona Lake, 1989) pp.1-15, here p.5.

[154] F. Asaro, I. Perlman and M. Dothan, "An Introductory Study of Mycenaean IIIC:1 Ware from Tel Ashdod," *Archaeometry* 13 (1971), pp.169-175.

[155] T. Dothan, *op.cit.*, 1989, p.12 n2; *idem*, "Aspects of Egyptian and Philistine Presence in Canaan During the Late Bronze-Early Iron Ages," *The Land of Israel: Cross-Roads of Civilizations*, ed. by E. Lipinski (Leuven, 1985) pp.55-75, esp. p.69.

[156] For further literature on *Tel Ashdod* and the origins of Philistine Pottery T. Dothan, *The Philistines and their Material Culture* (Jerusalem, 1982) pp.289-296; *idem.*, "The Philistines Reconsidered," *Biblical Archaeology Today* (Jerusalem, 1985) pp.165-176. For the *Tel Miqne* pottery, see esp. T. Dothan and S. Gitin, "Notes and News: Tell Miqne (Ekron)," *IEJ* 32 (1982), pp.150-153; 33 (1983), pp.128f.; 35 (1985), pp.67-71; 36 (1986), pp.104-107; J. Gunneweg *et alii*, "On The Origin of Pottery from Tel Miqne-Ekron," *BASOR* 264 (1986), pp.3-16.

for the first time, but imports cease to be found on the site. In Stratum VI, Dothan identifies a distinctive style of Mycenaean IIIC 1B which she describes as "Elaborate Style" in contrast to the "Simple Style" of Stratum VII.[57] It is contemporaneous with and in connection to this later "Elaborate Style" that Dothan sees the emergence of "Philistine" bichrome ware whose *floruit* comes in Stratum V and which extends through Stratum IV.[58] However, Dothan wishes to date the emergence of the "Elaborate Style," "early in the reign of Ramses III" and as "connected with the first historically recorded appearance of the Philistines." Both of these historical associations are arbitrary, however necessary they may be to understanding the bichrome ware as an indicator of Philistine ethnicity. Dothan seems to press the evidence unduly in stressing the prior occurrence of the "Simple Style" of Mycenaean IIIC 1b solely on the stratigraphic evidence of Tel Miqne. In doing so, she marks both a chronological distinction between this style of Mycenaean pottery and Philistine ware, and an historical distinction of major proportions, understanding the "Simple Style" as originating in a distinct migration from that which led to the development of the "Elaborate Style," which, solely on the basis of contemporaneity with the bichrome ware she had identified with the Philistines and dated post Ramses III. Similarly, other scholars associate the onset of the Philistines in the second quarter of the twelfth-century (i.e., post Ramses III), and characterize it by the appearance of both the Monochrome IIIC 1b and the closely contemporary bichrome ware.[59]

There are several weaknesses in the arguments and historical interpretations of both Dothan and her opponents:

A) First, the references to Ramses III's conflict with the *Peleset* and the *Djekker* in the Harris papyrus and in the reliefs from *Medinet Habu* do not give us a dating *a quo* in Ramses III's eighth year for the arrival of these people in *Palestine*. Such texts should not be used for a dating of either the Mycenaean IIIC 1b wares or the "bichrome" pottery, let

---

[57] Following B. Kling, "Comments on the Mycenaean IIIC:1b Pottery from Kitian Areas I and II," *Kitian V* (Nicosia, 1985) pp.38-56.

[58] T. Dothan, *op.cit.*, 1989, pp.7f.

[59] I. Singer, *op.cit.* 1988, pp.240f, basing himself especially on A. Mazar, "The Emergence of the Philistine Material Culture," *IEJ* 35 (1985), pp.95-107 and L. Stager, "Merenptah, Israel and Sea Peoples: New Light on an Old Relief," *Eretz Israel* 18 (1985), pp.56-64; also I. Singer, "The Beginning of Philistine Settlement in Canaan and the Northern Boundary of Philistia," *Tel Aviv* 12 (1985), pp.109-122.

they serve as a foundation for stratigraphic chronology. We already have some reason for seeing the influence of western immigrants at sites on the coast both in early Iron I levels and Late Bronze levels. The sea raids on the northern coast of *Syria*, at *Ugarit* and along the Cilician coast in the thirteenth-century are also clear evidence that the migrations into the eastern Mediterranean region had begun already long before the reign of Ramses III.[160] The "Sea Peoples" first clearly come in conflict with *Egypt* in the reign of Merneptah, among whom both the *Sherden* and the *Tjekker (Sekel)* are mentioned.[161] Ramses III's claims of victory and total conquest of these groups should not be interpreted as the specific cause of the Sea Peoples' immigration to the Palestinian coast, even though these are the earliest references to the *Peleset*.[162] First of all, the concept of total victory needs to be moderated by references indicating that the Egyptians allowed these people to settle in Egyptian territory to be fed and clothed. In fact, they were not repelled from *Egypt* in Ramses III's eighth year and forced to attack a more vulnerable Palestinian coast. It is difficult to wholeheartedly see them as invaders against whom *Egypt* needs Ramses's ruthless military as protection. Some are portrayed on Ramses's victory portrayal bringing oxcarts, heaped with family goods. Moreover, it may even be doubted that these people attacked *Egypt* itself at this time. At least the overland migrations may not have reached any further than southern *Palestine*. The reference to Ramses III's line of defense in the "land of *Djati*" *(Palestine)* suggests that these Sea Peoples are already in *Palestine* before moving on to Egypt. That they may have been there for some time is indicated by *Medinet Habu*'s reference to the *Peleset* as "hidden in their towns."[163] These texts can support the general interpretation that the immigration of Sea peoples (including the *Peleset*,

---

[160] For a clear summary of these texts, G. Ahlström, *op.cit.*, forthcoming, Chapter VI.

[161] L. Stager, *op.cit.*, 1985, p.60.

[162] For a clear discussion of this and the following with a full bibliography, esp. G. Ahlström, *op.cit.*, forthcoming, Chapter VI, which is today one of the most critical and comprehensive treatments of the Philistines in Palestine available. For a brief summary of the Egyptian texts dealing with the "Sea Peoples," see B.L. Beck, *The International Role of the Philistines during the Biblical Period* (Southern Baptist Theological Seminary dissertation, 1980) pp.41-66.

[163] G. Ahlström (*ibid.*) refers to a text dated four years later in which the Egyptians claim to have overthrown "the land of the *Peleset*" (That is—already!—Palestine).

Djekker, Sherden and *Dananu*) into the Palestinian coastal area antedates Ramses III and began already sometime in the thirteenth-century.

B) Apart from the reliefs of *Medinet Habu*, there are many indications to suggest both that we are dealing with a peaceful immigration, not an invasion, and that we should interpret this in terms of a gradual integration of newcomers into a relatively stable population rather than in terms of a displacement of people. Not only does the Egyptian presence not seem threatened during the Late Bronze-Early Iron Age transition throughout the lowlands from *Gazza* to *Beth Shan*[164], but the building of the port at *Tel Dor,* the reconstruction of *Akko* after Ramses III's punitive campaign there, and the settlement at *Ashdod*'s *Tel Mor* all confirm a peaceful interaction between Egyptians, immigrants and the indigenous population. The destruction of Late Bronze cities, such as those at *Ashkelon, Ashdod* and *Tel Zeror* cannot be identified with a destructive invasion.[165]

C) While the importance of transitional links such as the "Simple" and "Elaborate" styles of Mycenaean IIIC ıb ware can hardly be overstressed, because they establish the essential rootedness of bichrome ware in the Mycenaean pottery traditions, the associations of these pottery types and traditions (as at *Tel Ashdod* and *Tel Miqne*) show that the bichrome ware is not itself reflective of specifically immigrant potters. Imported techniques are used in both the "simple" and "elaborate" Mycenaean IIIC ıb styles, but they are on this very basis best understood in contrast to the bichrome pottery. The so-called Philistine pottery is clearly derivative and reflects a development that stylistically lies already at some distance from the work of immigrant potters who had worked within alien, imported Mycenaean traditions. Although the bichrome pottery reflects roots in Mycenaean tradition, it also just as clearly reflects a substantial departure from it and a wholehearted integration with indigenous Palestinian pottery traditions, reflecting both contemporary ceramic traditions of *Palestine* and roots in *Palestine*'s Late Bronze traditions. "Philistine" pottery does not simply

---

[164] On this, further, below. Also M. Dothan, "Archaeological Evidence for Movements of the Early 'Sea Peoples' in Canaan," *Recent Excavations in Israel: Studies in Iron Age Archaeology,* ed. by S. Gitin and W.G. Dever (Winona Lake, 1989) pp.59-70.

[165] On *Tel Zeror,* see above, on *Ashdod* and *Ashkelon,* A. Rainey, "The Identification of Philistine Gath," *Eretz Israel* 12 (1975), pp.63-76. Mycenaean IIIC ıB pottery and so called Philistine ware occurs only in later strata.

reflect Philistine people. Nor is there any justification for seeing these potters themselves as immigrants or as descendants of immigrants, how ever much that may reflect the personal history of some of them. Rather, this pottery reflects a synthesis of ceramic traditions of more than one population group, giving evidence for the rapid acculteration of the "Sea Peoples" into the indigenous coastal population. The arcane pottery indicates the integration of two distinct ceramic traditions. One cannot identify the ethnicity of even the potter, let alone that of the settlements in which the pottery is found.

D) The close association of the *Peleset* with the "Sea People's" migrations and their integration into the population of the Palestinian coast is, like that of the *Sherden, Dananu, Tjekker (Sekel)* and other groups, confirmed on both textual and archaeological grounds. The direct identification of the *Peleset*, however, and even less any other of these groups such as the *Tjekker* or *Sherden*, with the "Philistines" of either the Assyrian or biblical traditions, does not follow so immediately.[166] Nor are we justified on the basis of these centuries later traditions to speak of any specific ethnic entity controlling the southern Palestinian coast during the last quarter of the second-millennium, let alone can we legitimately use a pottery type as a viable means of defining the territorial extent of political power and influence. Although the name *Peleset* survives in the later term Philistine, much as the name *Dananu* is continued in the biblical name *Dan*[167] and *Sherden* in the name *Sardinia*, the specific historical signification of the names *Peleset* and Philistine are decidedly separate and distinct.[168]

---

[166] Certainly we cannot follow Dothan in using the term Philistine as a gentilic, synonymous with "Sea Peoples."

[167] *Contra* R.D. Barnett, "The Sea Peoples," *Cambridge Ancient History* (Cambridge, 1975) pp.359-378.

[168] See above, Chapter 4. The association with the name of the *Dananu* is seriously disputed by H.M. Niemann, *Die Daniten: Studien zur Geschichte eines altisraelititschen Stammes, FRLANT* 135 (Göttingen, 1985) pp.273-291. The more than half-millennium gaps between the names of the "Sea Peoples" and comparable names in biblical tradition is such that historical continuities are surely untraceable with any conviction. Indeed, even the association of nomenclature is hardly provable. Nevertheless, Niemann's historicistic reading of the biblical tradition does not really address the issue of names, but only potential associations of peoples. See further below on this and the whole issue of the survival of names over centuries; also, E.A. Knauf's review of Niemann in *ZDPV* 101-102 (1986), pp.183-187.

The word Philistine is not used for the immigrants to *Palestine* from the Aegean or *Cilicia*, nor is it used to describe any of the disruptive elements of the late Egyptian empire, but rather it is used at a much later date as the name of the people of the southern coastal plain and as a gentilic related to the population of the city-states of *Philistia*. The population of the Palestinian coastal plains was of mixed origins, dominantly west Semitic and indigenous to *Palestine* in their material culture, language, and religion.[169] The term "Philistine" refers primarily to a geographical reality. In biblical narrative it achieves a fictional ethnicity specifically as the central antagonist to the emergence of the "people" Israel in the stories of Judges and 1–2 Samuel. The Philistines do not exist as a people apart from the biblical tradition's late ethnocentric perspective. References in the Assyrian texts to *Pi-liš-te*, like thosecomparable references to *Ia-u-di*,[170] are geographical as opposed to ethnic references[171]

E) G.E. Wright's assumption that the immigrating "Sea Peoples" established themselves on the Palestinian coast in the form of mercenary colonies, where they became the surrogates and successors of Egyptian power in *Palestine*,[172] needs major revision today because of our clearer understanding of Egypt's role in this region during the twelfth-century.[173] As previously noted, the pottery itself indicates the integration of the "Sea Peoples" into the local population, not a displacement or establishment of a new ethnicity. The spread of bichrome to the *Jezreel*, the *Jordan* Valley and elsewhere in *Palestine* does not reflect the expanding power of a new belligerent entity in *Palestine*, but much more modestly only the continued functioning of the

---

[169] E. Paltiel, "Ethnicity and the State in the Kingdom of Ugarit," *Abr-Nahrain* 19 (1980), pp.43-58. The recent article of G. Garbini ("Philistine Seals" *Biblical Archaeology Today*, Jerusalem, 1985, pp.443-448) for example, which classifies Palestinian seals in "ethnic" terms (Hebrew, Phoenician, Aramaic, Ammonite, Moabite, and Edomite) and identifies a specifically Philistine group of seals seriously confuses distinct linguistic and geographical criteria, which do not specifically translate into ethnicity.

[170] *ANET*, p.287.

[171] *Contra* S. Gitin and T. Dothan, "The Rise and Fall of Ekron of the Philistines: Recent Excavations at an Urban Border Site," *BA* 50 (1987), pp.197-222, esp. p.214.

[172] G.E. Wright, "Fresh Evidence for the Philistine Story," *BA* 29 (1966), pp.70-86.

[173] Part of this understanding of the Philistine role in Palestine is based on the false association of bichrome pottery with Philistine presence, especially at such pro-Egyptian sites as *Beth Shan*.

Egyptian trade network in the lowlands. The political structures of the major towns on the southern coast continue a tradition that had been in place at least since the Middle Bronze Age and is typical of the entire Palestinian coast. The changes that occur along the coast during the twelfth and eleventh-century, although clearly marked by an Aegean and Anatolian derived influx to the population, are changes driven by the region wide, drought driven, economic collapse of both agriculture and trade.

The relatively rapid recovery of the coastal towns, in contrast to so much of the rest of *Palestine,* is best attributable to Egyptian imperial efforts to maintain control of the Palestinian lowlands and the overland trade route that crossed the Northern *Sinai.* It is because of this trade route that the southern coast of *Palestine* provided *Egypt's* primary focus. In attending not only to the elements of change in the Late Bronze-Iron Age transition (e.g., the disruptions of Late Bronze town life, dislocations of population and immigration), but also to those elements that mark stability and continuity during this transition period, our historical understanding of the period improves rather substantially.

When Thutmosis III established the Egyptian empire in *Palestine* and Syria (1482 B.C.), he established a number of military and administrative centers.[174] The central administrative center for southern *Palestine* was at *Gazza.* This system brought considerable stability to *Palestine,* especially in the southern coastal plain and in those Palestinian lowlands that were of greatest strategic and economic importance to the Egyptians. The *Amarna* period, rather than having been a period witnessing the disruption and deterioration of the Egyptian control of *Palestine,* is far more accurately understood as a period of relative peace and stability, ushering in a significant period of prosperity in *Palestine* (the latter part of Late Bronze IIA), a prosperity not seen since the Middle Bronze IIB period.[175] Egyptian commerce and military traffic to and from *Palestine* moved across the North *Sinai* coast throughout the New Kingdom period. Over a decade since 1972, E. Oren conducted a

---

[174] S. Ahituv, *op.cit., 1978, here, pp.94f.* M. Weinstein, "The Egyptian Empire in Palestine: A Reassessment," *BASOR* 241 (1981), pp.1-28, here p.12; also N. Na'aman, *The Political Disposition and Historical Development of Eretz-Israel According to the Amarna Letters* (University of Tel Aviv dissertation, 1975); E. Owen, "Governors' Residencies' in Canaan under the New Kingdom: A Case Study in Egyptian Administration," *Journal of the Society for the Study of Egyptian Antiquities* 14 (1985), pp.37-56.

[175] J.M. Weinstein, *op.cit.,* pp.15-17.

series of explorations and excavations of the coast that discovered nearly eighty sites along this route. This substantial trade route reflects the importance that *Egypt* gave to *Palestine,* and especially to the southern coastal area during the nineteenth and twentieth Dynasties.[176] It was in this period (the thirteenth and twelfth centuries) that Egyptian policy towards the trade routes and the control of Southern *Palestine* changed considerably.

The Egyptians entered into a three fold direction of affairs in *Palestine* that reached its climax under Ramses III,[177] developing what I. Singer describes as a thorough "Egyptianization" of Southern *Palestine.*[178] This three fold Egyptian policy involved aggressive military interventions, the direct integration of Egyptians into the economy and politics of the trade routes and towns and an active administrative control of the lowlands. The military policy of the Nineteenth Dynasty Pharaohs (and especially Seti I, Ramses II, and Merneptah) corresponds chronologically with the ecological and agricultural deterioration of the western Mediterranean in the course of the thirteenth-century. This policy was directed to control incursions of the Hittites southwards, to localize revolts against Egyptian rule within *Palestine* and to reduce or eliminate raids of the *Shasu* against the southern coast. Unlike the earlier punitive campaigns of the eighteenth dynasty, Egyptian military efforts involved military occupation and the garrisoning of troops at strategic administrative centers.[179] It is in the context of this policy that Merneptah's campaign against *Palestine* (1208 B.C.), recorded in the "Israel" Stele, is to be understood.[180] The towns of *Ashkelon, Gezer,* and *Yeno'am* are attacked. The names *Hatti, Canaan,* and *Hurru* are all general geographical terms, usually used for *Syria-Palestine* or its inhabitants. Only the name *"Israel,"* identical to that of the centuries

---

[176] E. Oren, "The 'Ways of Horus' in North Sinai," *Egypt, Israel, Sinai: Archaeological and Historical Relationships in the Biblical Period,* ed. by A. Rainey (Tel Aviv, 1987) pp.69-119.

[177] J.M. Weinstein, *op.cit.,* pp.17ff.; I. Singer, "Merneptah's Campaign to Canaan and the Egyptian Occupation of the Southern Coastal Plain of Palestine in the Ramesside Period," *BASOR* 269 (1988), pp.1-10; further, E. Oren, *op.cit.,* 1985; O. Goldwasser, "Hieratic Inscriptions from Tel Sera in Southern Canaan," *Tel Aviv* 11 (1984), pp.77-93; and D. Ussishkin, "Levels VII and VI at Tel Lachish and the End of the Late Bronze Age in Canaan," *Palestine in the Bronze Age,* ed. by J.N. Tubb (London, 1985) pp.213-230.

[178] I. Singer, *op.cit.,* p.1.

[179] M. Weinstein, *op.cit.,* 1981, pp.17f.

[180] *ANET,* pp.376-378.

later highland state of "Israel" and the *"Israel"* of the Bible, presents
serious difficulties in interpretation. It has been recently read by L.
Stager[181] as paired with the name *"Hurru,"* and by G. Ahlström and D.
Edelman[182] as a geographic term used in chiasmic parallel with *Canaan*
to signify a considerable segment of *Palestine* or of its population. While
neither interpretation is impossible, both seem forced. The Egyptian text
describes *"Israel"* as a people who are defeated by Merneptah. F.
Yurco's recent reinterpretation of the battle scenes at *Karnak* (previously
attributed to Ramses II) as portraying this campaign of Merneptah,[183]
observes that the Egyptian artists picture *"Israel"* in the same manner
as they do the inhabitants of *Ashkelon, Gezer,* and *Yeno'am.* If, as is
likely, Yurco is to be followed here—and Stager and Ahlström-Edelman
cite him with guarded approval—one must perhaps then accept that four
enemies had been the focus of Merneptah's campaign and that *Hatti,*
Canaan, and *Hurru* are not to be understood with the specificity that the
three towns and the people *"Israel"* are given. Both Stager's and
Ahlström-Edelman's interpretations are driven by the desire to support
a perception of historicity of some aspect of the biblical "Israel." Stager
does this by associating the stele with an impossibly high dating of the
"Song of Deborah" in Judges 5.[184] In a more complex argument,
Ahlström and Edelman argue for an association of a primarily
geographical term with not yet existent Iron I settlers of *Ephraim,* who
are ultimately called "Israel" and who, according to Ahlström and
Edelman, ultimately formed the regional core of Saul's chieftainship and
of the "United Monarchy" of biblical "Israel." The function of this
argument for Ahlström and Edelman is to support their understanding
of the indigenous nature of the biblical Israel. Both they and Stager,
however, assert far more than we know or can reasonably conclude. The
group "Israel" defeated by Merneptah are neither Stager's "Israel" of
Judges 5, nor Ahlström and Edelman's "Israel" of the highlands of
Ephraim. They are rather a very specific group among the population of
Palestine which bears a name that occurs here for the first time that at

---

[181] L. Stager, "Merenptah, Israel, and Sea Peoples: New Light on an Old Relief," *Eretz
Israel* 18 (1985), pp.56*-64*.

[182] G. Ahlström and D. Edelman, "Merneptah's Israel," *JNES* 44 (1985), pp.59-61.

[183] F. Yurco, "Merenptah's Palestinian Campaign," *Society for the Study of Egyptian
Antiquities Journal* 8 (1978), p.70.

[184] *Ibid.*, p.61.

a much later stage in *Palestine*'s history bears a substantially different signification.

It is primarily in the remains of the nineteenth dynasty that Egyptian involvement in the civilian economy and life of *Palestine* becomes most apparent. Evidence for this is of course most abundant at those sites where the Egyptian occupation was concentrated. Weinstein argues well for a considerable amount of locally produced Egyptian pottery employed for domestic purposes,[185] and he notes occurrences of such pottery at *Beth Shan, Tell el-Far'ah, Deir el-Balah, Tell esh-Shari'a, Tell Mor, Megiddo, Lachish, Beth Shemesh, Gezer, Ashdod, Tell Deir 'Alla*, and *Tell es-Sa'idiyeh*. While the pottery confirms the presence of Egyptian potters in *Palestine*, architectural features in temples at *Beth Shan, Lachish*, and *Shechem* indicate a much broader range of Egyptian craftsmen active in *Palestine*.[186] Also some inscriptions suggest the possible presence of Egyptian temples, or temples dedicated to Egyptian deities, at *Gazza, Ashkelon*, and *Aphek*.[187] The Temples at the mining sites of *Timna* and *Serabit al-Khadim*[188] suggest that the use of such religious centers was neither confined to nor intended for the use of Egyptians alone. They are rather indicative of Egyptian influence among the indigenous populations working and living in the area.[189] The extent of this Egyptianization of the population of the southern coast comes from the excavations of *Haruba* by E. Oren and of *Deir el-Balah* by T. Dothan.[190] At *Haruba* an intact Egyptian potter's workshop was uncovered that had produced pottery modelled on Egyptian types. The skeletal remains at the fort of *Haruba* indicate that the majority of the population at the Egyptian fort was indigenous to *Sinai* or *Palestine*.[191] Similarly, at *Deir el-Balah* near *Gazza*, T. Dothan uncovered New Kingdom burials in anthropoid coffins in which the skeletal evidence

---

[185] M. Weinstein, *op.cit.*, 1981, pp.21f.

[186] *Ibid.*, p.19.

[187] *Ibid.*, pp.19f.

[188] *Ibidem.*

[189] On Timna, B. Rothenberg, *Timna* (London, 1972); and esp. I. Beit-Arieh, "Canaanites and Egyptians at Serabit el-Khadim," *Egypt, Israel, Sinai*, ed by A. Rainey (Tel Aviv, 1987) pp.57-67.

[190] E. Oren, *op.cit.*, pp.93-110.

[191] *Ibid.*, pp.93ff.

clearly indicates the indigenous Palestinian nature of the officials of this administrative center.[192]

The focus of Egyptian presence in the *Shephelah* and Southern Coast of *Palestine,* and the source of both the Egyptianization of the region and of the long term stability that this region enjoyed,[193] was the direct rule established here through the construction of a number of Egyptian administrative centers.[194] Apart from the central administrative and military center at *Gazza,* fortresses or administrative buildings were constructed by the Egyptians in the South. M. Weinstein lists *Tell el-'Ajjul*'s "Palace IV," *Tell el-Far'ah*'s "Residency," *Tell esh-Shari'a*'s public buildings of Strata X-IX, *Tel Mor*'s "Citadel" of Strata VIII-VII and the "*Migdol*" of Strata VI-V, and the "Government House" at *Aphek.*[195] To this, one might add the public building at *Tell Hesi* excavated by Bliss and dated by Oren to the end of the Late Bronze Age.[196] Administrative texts inscribed in hieratic have been found at both *Tell esh-Shari'a (Tel Sera')* and *Lachish,*[197] and there can be little doubt that *Lachish* also formed an Egyptian administrative center, as perhaps did *Tell Jemmeh.*

Most scholars now put the withdrawal of Egyptian presence in *Palestine* in the third quarter of the twelfth-century with Ramses VI (1141-1134 B.C.) or slightly later[198]. Oren concludes that the evidence from the Northern *Sinai* and elsewhere clearly shows that *Egypt* had maintained a strong presence in *Canaan* through the reign of Seti II and Queen Twosret.[199] This, I believe, should be extended through the reign of Ramses III (1151 B.C.) when Egyptian building activity is still

---

[192] *Ibid.,* pp.107f.; T. Dothan, "Anthropoid Clay Coffins from a Late Bronze Age Cemetery near Deir el-Balah: Preliminary Report II," *IEJ* 23 (1973), pp.129-146; *idem, Excavations at the Cemetery of Deir el-Balah,* Qedem 10 (Jerusalem, 1979).

[193] *Contra* S. Ahituv, *op.cit.,* 1978, and J.M. Weinstein, *op.cit.,* 1981, p.22.

[194] See on this esp. E. Oren, *op.cit.,* 1985.

[195] J.M. Weinstein, *op.cit.,* p.18.

[196] E. Oren, *op.cit.,* 1985.

[197] *Ibid.,* p.107; O. Goldwasser, "The Lachish Hieratic Bowl Once Again," *Tel Aviv* 9 (1982), pp.137f.; *idem,* "Hieratic Inscriptions from Tel Sera' in Southern Canaan," *Tel Aviv* 11 (1984), pp.77-93.

[198] So, M. Weinstein, *op.cit.,* p.23.

[199] E. Oren, *op.cit.,* 1987, p.111; also pp.94ff and his discussion of the chronology of phase II at Haruba.

strong.[200] The immediate cause of the Egyptian withdrawal from *Palestine,* which, in a very brief period of time after Ramses II's reign, reversed a policy that had been maintained for a century or longer, is still uncertain.[201] Civil war in *Egypt* is certainly a possible explanation. Any threat or the reality of civil war at home would have made it much more difficult for *Egypt* to maintain such an expensive administration abroad. The situation would be all the more difficult if the economic and social structures of *Palestine,* and with it *Palestine*'s agricultural production of grain, wine and oil had continued to deteriorate, reducing and perhaps eliminating a return to the Egyptians' investment.[202] One can certainly suggest that the nineteenth and early twentieth dynasties' efforts to stabilize *Palestine* and to maintain the overland trade route were motivated by the desire to secure a source of cheap agricultural produce, which the inflation, necessarily associated with the extended drought of ca. 1200 B.C., had made extremely difficult.

6. *The Shephelah and the Northern Negev*

To the East of the coastal plain, the lower hills of the *Shephelah* give witness to an extensive continuity of settlement (coupled with a pattern of economic deterioration and substantial dislocation) between the latest of the Late Bronze and the earliest of the Iron I settlements.[203] Most of our information for this region comes from excavations, especially those at *Tell Beit Mirsim, Tell ed-Duwer* and *Beth Shemesh,* as well as from *Gezer* and *Tell Huwellifah* on the edge of the *Shephelah.*

---

[200] I. Singer, *op.cit.*, 1988, p.6.

[201] J. Cerny, "Egypt: From the Death of Ramses III to the End of the Twenty-First Dynasty," *Cambridge Ancient History* (Cambridge, 1975) pp.606–657, here pp.612f.

[202] Basing himself on the studies of J.J. Janssen (*Commodity Prices from the Ramesside Period: An Economic Study of the Village of Necropolis Workmen at Thebes*, Leiden, 1975) and J. Cerny ("Fluctuations in Grain Prices during the Twentieth Egyptian Dynasty," *Archiv Orientalni* 6, 1934, pp.173–178) Weinstein notes (M. Weinstein, *op.cit.,* p.23) that grain prices in Egypt reached a peak in the mid-twentieth dynasty; that is, during the collapse and dislocation of much of Palestine's agricultural lowlands, but prior to any clearly marked recovery.

[203] A.F. Rainey offers a sound historico-geographical review of the *Shephelah*: "The Biblical Shephelah of Judah," *BASOR* 251 (1983), pp.1–22.

Substantial stress on the Late Bronze population had begun already in th late fourteenth-century with the destruction of Stratum IXB at *Tell Huwellifah* that was succeeded by what J. Seger describes as a "modest squatters' occupation," partially reusing the structures of IXB.[204] Stratum VIII gives evidence of a "large storage complex"[205] found in all the excavated areas of the site. This stratum shows limited occupation during the thirteenth-century that continued through Iron I (Stratum VII).[206] The Iron II levels show a significant expansion of the use of the site through the end of the eighth-century. A survey of the region immediately surrounding the tell confirms the initial results of the excavations on the tell. The most important early activity on the site occurred in the Early Bronze and Iron II periods of occupation.[207] Similarly, Greenberg's reevaluation of the excavations at *Tell Beit Mirsim*[208] indicates continuity between Albright's Stratum C (Late Bronze Age) and his Strata B1-2 (Iron I),[209] in the form of a significantly impoverished resettlement continuing the ceramic tradition of the Late Bronze period, with particularly close parallels to *Tell ed-Duwer*. Again, at *Tell Beit Mirsim*, as at *Tell Huwellifah*, a resurgence of occupation is most marked during Iron II. Stratum B2 shows some "Philistine" pottery on the site, but the quantity seems insufficient to the excavators to suggest any ethnic or political affiliation of the inhabitants with "sea peoples."[210] A similar picture is seen at *Beth Shemesh*, if Wright is to be followed in his argument that the storage pits or silos cutting into the Late Bronze Stratum IVB showed pottery comparable to *Tell Beit Mirsim* B1 and are to be dated later than Stratum IVB.[211] The continuity of the Late Bronze population (in an extremely

---

[204] J.D. Seger, "Investigations at Tell Halif, Israel," *BASOR* 252 (1983), pp.1-23; here p.4.

[205] *Ibidem.*

[206] *Ibid.*, pp.6-10.

[207] *Ibid.*, p.21.

[208] R. Greenberg, "New Light on the Early Iron Age at Tell Beit Mirsim," *BASOR* 265 (1987), pp.55-80.

[209] W.F. Albright, *The Excavations at Tell Beit Mirsim III: The Iron Age, AASOR* 21 and 22 (1943).

[210] So also, I. Finkelstein, *op.cit.*, 1988, pp.54f. The presence of such "Philistine" pottery, of course, directly reflects not ethnicity or hegemony but the influence of potters or trade from the neighboring coastal plain where such pottery is abundant.

[211] G.E. Wright, "Beth-Shemesh," *EAEHL I*, pp.248-253; also E. Grant and G.E. Wright, *Ain Shems Excavation V* (Haverford, 1939).

diminished and impoverished form) is confirmed at *Beth-Shemesh* as well. This occurs prior to a major expansion of settlement on the site during the Iron II period. As with other excavated sites in the region, the pottery assemblages of the earliest Iron I finds at *Beth Shemesh* appear to have been indigenous to at least the region as a whole, and to have developed prior to any Philistine sherds. At *Lachish (Tell ed-Duwer)*, which is in this region a pivotal site for interpretation, the recent excavations by D. Ussishkin show that the Late Bronze occupation continued into the twelfth-century until the time of Ramses III, after which the site was abandoned for a considerable length of time.[212] Again, it is early in Iron II that *Lachish* became a town of considerable proportions, with major fortifications and a large population. At *Gezer*, on the northwestern rim overlooking the *Shephelah*, we find a destruction at the end of the Late Bronze Age that results in a gap of occupation, after which Philistine sherds are found.[213] *Gezer* VIII (tenth-century) indicates a major expansion of this site comparable to that of *Lachish* V.

Surveys of the *Shephelah* are not yet available, but Finkelstein reports that there is as yet no clear evidence of new Iron I villages in the region.[214] If this is indeed a sound description, the archaeological investigations seem to indicate a steep depression of the Late Bronze agricultural economy from as early as the beginning of the thirteenth-century, a partial abandonment of the region during the early phases of Iron I, and a vigorous process of resettlement early in Iron II. This suggests a pattern of agricultural response to stress and change in this region similar to what took place in *Benjamin* and the more prosperous parts of *Judah*. Such response seems appropriately understood as an adaptation to substantial changes in climate. New accretions to the population from outside seem to have been the product more of a general transregional expansion of agriculture throughout the hill country during Iron II than of events limited to the *Shephelah*. Sources of the increased population to the *Shephelah* early in Iron II are likely

---

[212] D. Ussishkin, "Excavations at Tel Lachish 1978–1983: Second Preliminary Report," *Tel Aviv* 10 (1983), pp.97–175; *idem*, "Lachish: Key to the Israelite Conquest of Canaan?" *BAR* 13 (1987), pp.18–39.

[213] W.G. Dever, "Gezer," *EAEHL II*, pp. 428–443; *idem*, *Gezer I* (Jerusalem, 1970); *idem*, *Gezer II* (Jerusalem, 1974).

[214] I. Finkelstein, *op.cit.*, 1988, p.55.

to have been both the steppe regions to the south and the southern coastal areas to the west. The population growth at this time seems clearly to exceed any possible natural growth of the *Shephelah's* indigenous population. The combination of Late Bronze collapse with marginal resettlement suggests a long period of economic dislocation that must have lasted almost the entire period of drought from 1300 to 1000, in a region that is known historically to be particularly vulnerable to climatic change.[215] Any theories based on concepts of conquest, invasion, or displacement seem, on the other hand, to be ruled out specifically because of the severe centuries long lag in the eventual resettlement of the region.

A substantially different pattern of settlement occurs, however, in the large steppelands of the Northern *Negev*. To date, no settlement from the Late Bronze period has been found in the *Beersheva* Basin.[216] Settlement begins here from the very end of the thirteenth-century or the beginning of the twelfth.[217] The interpretation of the Iron I settlement in this region is strongly disputed. While disagreement has centered on the issue of whether the site of *Khirbet el-Meshash* is to be understood as an "Israelite" settlement derivative from highland settlement and representative of early Iron I settlement in the region generally,[218] the issues under dispute touch upon questions about absolute chronology, contemporaneity and interregional association, as

---

[215] Th.L. Thompson, *op.cit.,* 1979, *passim.*

[216] *Ibid.*; I. Finkelstein, *op.cit.,* p.41.

[217] I. Finkelstein, *Ibid.*; V. Fritz, "Erwägungen zur Siedlungsgeschichte des Negeb in der Eisen I Zeit (1200-1000 v. Chr.) im Lichte der Ausgrabungen auf der Hirbet el-Msas," *ZDPV* 93 (1975), pp.30-45, here p.30.

[218] The excavation and interpretation of *Khirbet el-Meshash* was directed by Y. Aharoni, V. Fritz, and A. Kempinski. Y. Aharoni, "The Settlement of the Tribes in the Negev: A New Picture," *Ariel* 41 (1976), pp.3-19; *idem.,* "The Negev During the Israelite Period," *The Land of the Negev,* ed. by A. Schmueli and Y. Grados (Tel Aviv, 1979) pp.209-225; V. Fritz, "Bestimmung und Herkunft des Pfeilerhauses in Israel," *ZDPV* 93 (1977), pp.30-45; *idem.,* "Die Kulturhistorische Bedeutung der früheisenzeitlichen Siedlung auf der Hirbet el-Msas und das Problem der Landnahme," *ZDPV* 96 (1980), pp.121-135; *idem.,* "The Israelite 'Conquest' in the Light of Recent Excavations at Khirbet el-Meshash," *BASOR* 241 (1981), pp.61-73; *idem.,* "Conquest or Settlement? The Early Iron Age in Palestine," *BA* 50 (1987), pp.84-100; V. Fritz and A Kempinski, *Ergebnisse der Ausgrabungen auf der Hirbet el-Msas (Tel Masos) I-III* (Wiesbaden, 1983); A. Kempinski, "Tel Masos," *Expedition* 20 (1978), pp.29-37; A. Kempinski *et alii,* "Excavations at Tel Masos 1972, 1974, 1975," *Eretz Israel* 15 (1981), pp.154-180.

well as on the identification of ethnicity and the origin and evolutionary development of the so-called Israelite house.[219] V. Fritz, in particular, has used his excavations at *Khirbet el-Meshash* to develop an interpretation of Israelite settlement for all of *Palestine*. The objections raised by Finkelstein[220] are well founded. It is exceedingly difficult to convincingly explain Israelite origins on a basis that almost entirely rests on an understanding of what is after all an exceedingly unique site, whose most striking characteristics distinguish it quite sharply from so many other early Iron I settlements. On the other hand, Finkelstein goes too far[221] in dismissing *Khirbet el-Meshash* from his analysis of Israel's origins, by disassociating his explanation of the site from that of the other sites in the *Beersheva* Basin. The distinctiveness of the town that was established at *Khirbet el-Meshash* is uniquely attributable to its geographical situation on the border where *Palestine*'s steppe meets the agricultural zone.

Certainly the architectural innovation, developed over the course of two centuries in *Palestine* referred to as the "pillared" or "four room" house, is difficult to associate with the broad roomed tent as argued by Finkelstein, Fritz, and others, except abstractly. This innovation in house structures during Iron I rests substantially on remarkably sophisticated advancements in building techniques that simplified wall construction considerably, and is hardly to be understood as based on any symbolic number of rooms or any supposedly anachronistic adherence to tent poles.[222] Similar to the use and distribution of collared rim store jars, the early Iron I broad room pillared houses are geographically and

---

[219] N. Na'aman early disputed the identification of *Khirbet el-Meshash* with biblical *Hormah*: "The Inheritance of the Sons of Simeon," *ZDPV* 96 (1980), pp.136-152. The inconsequence of the ethnic identity of the site was demonstrated by M. Kochavi, "The Conquest and the Settlement," *Et-Mol* 7 (1982), pp.3-5. The issue of the ethnicity of the inhabitants of *Khirbet el-Meshash* has played a central role in objections raised against Aharoni's, Kempinski's and especially Fritz's interpretation (esp. Z. Herzog, *Beer-Sheba II: The Early Iron Age Settlements*, Tel Aviv, 1984; C.H.J. de Geus, *De Israelitische Stad*, Kampen, 1984; G. Ahlström, "The Early Iron Age Settlers at Hirbet el-Msas:, *ZDPV* 100, 1984, pp.35-52; and I. Finkelstein, *op.cit.*, pp.37-47.) and has done serious harm to a growing clarification of both *Khirbet el-Meshash* and the region.

[220] I. Finkelstein, *op.cit.*, pp.45f. More recently, V. Fritz reasserts his argument substantially unchanged: "Die Landnahme der israelitischen Stämme in Kanaan," *ZDPV* 106 (1990), pp.63-77.

[221] *Ibid.*, pp.46ff.

[222] T. Staubli, *Das Image der Nomaden* (Göttingen, 1991) p.215.

contextually consistent (in both economic and ecological terms) with the hill country region in which they are most commonly found. As the *pithoi* had served for both grain and water storage in the fissured limestone of the central highlands, so this type of house construction is particularly suitable for an agricultural people with a heavy commitment to livestock, and can reasonably be considered indigenous only in an area with an adequate geological context for the cutting of such large monoliths; that is in the hills or in areas with easy access to limestone deposits. Not only are nomads at any time unlikely innovators in the building trades, and the *Beersheva* Basin an unlikely region for the origination of houses built from these materials, but that Fritz can understand the variety of floor plans of houses at *Tell Esdar* and at *Khirbet el-Meshash* in terms of a typology derived from tents is entirely inconsequential to either the question of the origin or the evolution of these buildings. Fritz' typology[223] associates aspects of these structures that are functionally distinctive. It does not account for either the changes or developments of both materials and construction techniques, and hence must be seen as largely irrelevant to the questions of origin and evolution that he poses. Moreover, his typology is expressive of a considerable spectrum of variants in form. That this variety is found within a single site and exists within the same archaeological strata marks Fritz's evolutionary interpretation as significantly arbitrary. This arbitrariness is additionally underlined when one considers some limited evidence of the existence of such structures beyond both highland *Palestine* and the traditionally perceived "Israelite" regions. One must also consider the archaeological and architectural indications that the development of the "pillared house" had begun already prior to the onset of Iron I; that is, earlier than the initial settlement at *Khirbet el-Meshash*.[224]

---

[223] V. Fritz, *op.cit.*, 1977; *idem.*, *op.cit.*, 1981, esp. pp.65f.

[224] For an extensive treatment of the considerable literature on four room houses in Palestine, I. Finkelstein, *op.cit.*, pp.254-258; also, more recently, *idem.*, "Arabian Trade and Socio-Political Conditions in the Negev in the Twelfth-Eleventh Centuries, B.C.E.," *JNES* 47 (1988), pp.241-252, esp. pp.241-245. For a discussion of some of the "extra-Israelite" and Late Bronze evidence, G.L. Klein and A. Mazar, "Three Seasons of Excavations at Tel Batash-Biblical Timnah," *BASOR* 248 (1982), pp.1-36, esp. pp.10ff; A. Mazar, "The Israelite Settlement in Canaan in the Light of Archaeological Excavations," *Biblical Archaeology Today* (Jerusalem, 1985) pp.61-71, esp. pp.67f; G. Ahlström, "The Early Iron Age Settlers at Hirbet el-Msas (Tel Masos)," *ZDPV* 100 (1984), pp.35-52, esp. pp.45f.

On the other hand, Fritz' and Kempinski's interpretation of Iron I *Khirbet el-Meshash* as a settlement reflecting a symbiosis between the indigenous sedentary population of *Palestine* (with associations both with the southern coastal plain and the Egyptian occupation of the coastal strip) and the nomadic shepherds of the steppe, with a considerable impact on the development of trade with the *Arabah* and Northwest *Arabia,* has both great interpretive value and is also congenially appropriate to *Khirbet el-Meshash's* geographical and archaeological context.[225] The uniqueness and importance of *Khirbet el-Meshash* is closely associated with its geographical setting: on the banks of the *Wadi Ghazza (Nahal Besor),* along the trade route connecting the *Arabah* with the coastal plain. Possessing easy access to an abundant source of water a few meters below the surface, *Khirbet el-Meshash* sits close to the juncture of two ecologically distinct zones: the agriculturally dominant Mediterranean zone and the pastorally oriented great northern Sinai steppe. The earliest stratum on the site reflects the same type of dislocation and poverty among the settlers that we find in almost every early Iron I new settlement elsewhere in *Palestine.* Moreover, the pottery of this stratum is clearly derivative of the Late Bronze period and is closely associated with that of *Palestine's* southern coast.[226] *Khirbet el-Meshash's* water needs were amply supplied by a large number of wells. In the second half of the twelfth-century, the settlement developed into a considerable town: one of the largest in *Palestine* during this period. Public buildings with clear Egyptian associations indicate both political and economic ties with the coast. Sherds of so-called Edomite ware suggest trade relations with the *Arabah.* The very large proportion of bones from beef cattle also suggest a markedly Mediterranean zone economy in contrast to that of the sheep- and goat-herding of the steppe. Fritz' and Kempinski's efforts to see this as a market town existing in symbiosis with the pastoralism dominant in the steppe certainly seems confirmed. Indeed such symbiotic association appears to have been the very *raison d'être* for the settlement. Undoubtedly, some of the settlers derived from forms of pastoralism. However, this type of symbiotic settlement is derivative of agricultural *Palestine.* It is market-

---

[225] V. Fritz, *opera citata,* 1975; 1981; 1987; A. Kempinski, "Baal-Perazim and the Scholarly Controversy on the Israelite Settlement," *Qadmoniot* 14 (1981), pp.63f.; *contra* I. Finkelstein, *op.cit.,* 1988, pp.41-47.

[226] The absence of collared rim store jars indicates only the lack of need for such vessels.

oriented and integrally sedentary, forming a bridge between the desert and the sown. Every indication suggests that we are dealing with an outpost of the southern coastal plain.

Although there seems to be considerable uncertainty about pottery chronology, those who wish to see *Khirbet el-Meshash* as "Israelite," date Stratum IIb along with other sites of the region such as *Khirbet 'Ar'ara, Khirbet Gazze, Khirbet el-Garra, Tell el-Milh* and possibly even *Tell 'Arad* and *Tell es-Seba*[227] to the early Iron I period. Other scholars, such as Finkelstein and Herzog, would delay the "Israelite" settlement to the end of the twelfth and even to the eleventh-century, and consequently (Sic!) date the other sites of the plain accordingly. It need hardly be said that the lack of hard evidence for chronologies within Iron I is so pervasivein today's research that historical reconstruction is vulnerable to both the influence of fashions in interpretation and the whims of any excavation's director. A relatively early date for *Khirbet el-Meshash* is supported both by a clearly discernible Late Bronze tradition and numerous associations with coastal sites. The other sites of the *Beersheva* Basin that may possibly have been contemporary were extremely small settlements, and their expansion and development lagged behind *Khirbet el-Meshash* until late in Iron I; that is, late in the eleventh-century.[228] Such a late chronology for these sites is based on recent arbitrary tendencies to place the onset of the Iron Age—whatever such a concept signifies—in the mid-twelfth-century, and is not entirely consistent with the early dating given to *Khirbet el-Meshash* by Fritz.

Aware of the uncertainties in our chronology and terminology (!), it might be argued that the symbiotic market culture of *Khirbet el-Meshash* dominated what was primarily an expansive steppe pastoral region at least until the settlement of *Beersheva* took on a comparable and competitive role in the second half of the eleventh-century B.C. Prior to that time, the very sparsely sedentarized *Beersheva* Basin had a mixed population, derivative of both displaced farmers from the southern coast and pastoralists from the steppe.

With the onset of Iron II, significant changes occur. The town at *Khirbet el-Meshash*, Stratum I, no longer continues its public buildings and no longer appears to have maintained the symbiotic center it had

---

[227] So V. Fritz, *op.cit.*, 1975, pp.32f.

[228] Beginning with *Beersheva* VIII (which is dated from 1025-1000 B.C.), Z. Herzog, *op.cit.*, p.67. The very meager remains of *Beersheva* IX are dated from 1150-1050 B.C.

supported in Stratum II.[229] Rather, a diminished settlement continues until about the mid-ninth-century. Contemporary with this stratum, major forts were established at *'Arad*,[230] *Beersheva*[231] and *Tel Malhata*. Military installations or forts were also built at *Khirbet Rabud* in the *Shephelah*[232] and at *Kadesh Barnea* and several sites in the central *Negev*.[233] Comparable to the seventh-century military installations at *Khirbet Abu Tabaq, Khirbet es-Samrah*, and *Khirbet el-Maqari* in the *Judaean Desert*,[234] the sites in the central *Negev* included small agricultural hamlets pursuing forms of desert agriculture.[235] Indeed there was in the early Iron II period a considerable number of such settlements, with *Kadesh Barnea* apparently the most important of them.[236] These hamlets and military installations clearly involve the sedentarization of nomads in these regions. One might also associate the major expansion of settlement in the *Beersheva* Basin (and the newly established forts there) with such efforts at sedentarization. The sedentarization of the Northern *Negev*—as *Palestine* returned to normal climate conditions—effectively eliminated the unique economic foundations on which *Khirbet el-Meshash* had been established, and the entire region was opened to the mixed form of economy that P. Briant

---

[229] V. Fritz, *op.cit.*, 1981, p.69.

[230] M. Aharoni, "The Pottery of Strata 12-11 of the Iron Age Citadel at Arad," *Eretz Israel* 15 (1981), pp.181-204; Z. Herzog, *et alii*, "The Israelite Fortress at Arad," *BASOR* 254 (1984), pp.1-34.

[231] Z. Herzog, *op.cit.*, p.79.

[232] M. Kochavi, "Khirbet Rabud =Debir," *Tel Aviv* 1 (1974), pp.2-33.

[233] Y. Aharoni, "Forerunners of the Limes: Iron Age Fortresses in the Negev," *IEJ* 17 (1967), pp.1-17; M. Dothan, "The Fortress at Kadesh-Barnea," *IEJ* 15 (1965), pp.134-151; B. Rothenberg, *Negeb* (Ramat-Gan, 1967); C. Meyers, "Kadesh-Barnea: Judah's Last Outpost" *BA* 39 (1976), pp.148-151; Z. Meshel, "Horvat Ritma: An Iron Age Fortress in the Negev Highlands," *Tel Aviv* 4 (1977), pp.110-135; and especially, R. Cohen, "The Iron Age Fortresses in the Central Negev," *BASOR* 236 (1980), pp.61-79, and *idem.*, "Excavations at Kadesh Barnea 1976-1978," BA 44 (1981), pp.93-107.

[234] L. Stager, "Farming in the Judaean Desert during the Iron Age," *BASOR* 221 (1976), pp.145-158.

[235] P. Mayerson, *The Ancient Agricultural Regime of Nessana and the Central Negeb* (London, 1960) and M. Evenari *et alii*, *The Negev* (Cambridge, 1971); M. Kochavi, *The Settlement of the Negev in the Middle Bronze (Canaanite) I Age* (Hebrew Univeristy dissertation, 1967); Th.L. Thompson, *The Settlement of Sinai and the Negev in the Bronze Age BTAVO* 8 (Wiesbaden, 1975).

[236] R. Cohen, *opera citata*, 1980; 1981.

aptly refers to as "agropastoralism,"[237] an economic form that comes to dominate not only the Northern *Negev* but also most of the Judaean highlands. The para-military policing of the southern Palestinian steppelands, represented by these settlements and forts, reflect a very active and assertive policy of the agricultural sector of southern *Palestine* that aimed both to protect and encourage new settlement and to control and regulate the movement of pastoral groups and transhumance nomads across the southern frontier.[238]

Certainly the interests of the growing towns in the Northern *Negev* and the established settlements of the western coastal plain and the *Shephelah* were considerably furthered by the increased security of these regions as they supported the new trade routes connecting the Palestinian coast with *Arabia*.[239] In connection with the return to normal climatic conditions with the concomitant rise in prosperity throughout the southern Levant, one might well relate the control and sedentarization of the Central and Northern *Negev* to both the increase of settlement in the *Shephelah* during early Iron II, and to the onset of intensive sedentarization throughout the Judaean highlands. That is, the origins of the population of both the Northern *Negev* and the Judaean highlands seem best explained as the result of the active involvement of the sedentary population in the control of the nomadic sector, encouraging, supporting and forcing sedentarization.[240]

Following sedentarization, one might expect a village population in the Judaean highlands to gradually adapt from a mixed economy of grains, field crops and pastoralism towards an increasing dominance of a more characteristic Mediterranean economy, with its typical substantial investments in the cash crops of olives, oil, grapes and wine, consequent upon the gradual construction of terracing. As the population was integrated into a Mediterranean economy, it was also thereby integrated into the regional trade networks, which in turn must have attracted the

---

[237] P. Briant, *Etats et pasteurs au Moyen-Orient ancien* (Cambridge, 1982) esp. pp.9-56 and 237.

[238] See the Assyrian period texts in *ANET*, pp.653f. that refer to 'he policing of the eastern frontier with the speciifc purpose of establishing "peace of mind" for the sedentary population (reference is courtesy of S.E. Janke, personal communication).

[239] E. A. Knauf, *Midian, ADPV* (wiesbaden, 1988) pp.91-96.

[240] For a general introduction to the population shifts between agricultural and pastoral sectors, Th.L. Thompson, op.cit., 1992.

interest and investments and the continued political and military involvement of the towns.

7. Benjamin and Judah

The patterns of settlement in the highland regions of *Benjamin* and *Judah* during the Late Bronze-Iron II transition are substantially different chronologically, topologically and in origin from those of the central highlands of *Ephraim* and *Manasseh.* They also require quite different historical explanations. The saddle between the hills of *Ephraim* and *Judah* south of *Beitin* and north from *Jerusalem* is, if the surveys of Z. Kallai are acceptable, one of the better known regions of *Palestine.* Archaeological surveys indicate that during the Late Bronze period the Judaean hills between *Jerusalem* and *Hebron* were nearly entirely abandoned, with significant settlement found only at *Jerusalem, Khirbet Rabud* and possibly at *Beth Zur.*[241] Occupation of these sites continued in the Iron I period. Few new Iron I sites, however, have been found in the area. Most of these have been found near the watershed along the eastern edge of the Judaean desert.[242]

Judging from the excavations of the larger sites and of *Giloh* (a small Iron I site southwest of *Jerusalem*), the pottery of the few Iron I settlements indicates significant continuity with the Late Bronze[243] occupation of the region. The excavations at *Khirbet Rabud* suggest a possible continuity of settlement from the end of the Late Bronze period into Iron I,[244] perhaps similar to the settlement at *Beth Zur* and even *Hebron.*[245] An association of these new very small Iron I sites along the margin of the more agriculturally viable regions with pastoralism is very attractive, whether or not this historical process is to be understood as

---

[241] M. Kochavi, *op.cit.,* 1972; Th.L. Thompson, *op.cit.,* 1979; L. Stager, *Ancient Agriculture in the Judaean Desert* (Harvard dissertation, 1975); C.H.J. de Geus, *op.cit.,* 1984; I. Finkelstein, *op.cit.,* 1988, pp.47-53.

[242] I. Finkelstein, *ibid.,* p.52; S. Mittmann *et alii, op.cit.,* forthcoming.

[243] A. Mazar, "Giloh: An Early Israelite Settlement Site near Jerusalem," *IEJ* 31 (1981), pp.1-36; here pp.18-31.

[244] M. Kochavi, "Khirbet Rabud =Debir," *Tel Aviv* 1 (1974), pp.2-33.

[245] On *Beth-Zur,* O. Sellers, *The 1957 Excavations at Beth Zur, AASOR* 38 (1968); on *Hebron,* P. Hammond, "Hebron: Chronique Archaeologique," *RB* 72 (1965), pp.267-270 and most recently: *Hadashot Archeologiot* 85 (1984); *idem,* 88 (1986).

a development from the larger sites of the area in a response to drought by widening their area of occupation through animal husbandry. To understand these settlements with Finkelstein as the result of an initial sedentarization of previously nomadic pastoralists, is, while possible, more difficult. A sufficient cause for the sedentarization of pastoralists on such marginal lands is not apparent. In the course of Iron II, however, the settlement of the Judaean highlands expanded dramatically, especially in the latter part of Iron II,[246] when a substantial Iron Age occupation of the Judaean highlands occurs for the first time. This rapid expansion of settlement in the course of Iron II hardly brought with it any significant displacement of the aboriginal population in the area. Quite to the contrary, the material culture of the Iron IIA and Iron IIB occupation is obviously indigenous to the region and is continuous with the settlement from both Iron I and the yet earlier Late Bronze traditions. The new growth in settlement during Iron II throughout the Judaean highlands is best understood to have resulted from both the gradual and direct increase of the Late Bronze-Iron I population of southern *Palestine,* as well as from a substantial immigration from outside *Palestine*'s southern agricultural zone, adding thereby to the limited indigenous population.[247]

The general geographical disposition of the Judaean highlands with its eastern border in the *Judaean Desert* and its southern in the expansive steppelands of the *Beersheva* Basin and in the southern coastal steppe to the Southwest, places the settlements of the region in a natural symbiotic relationship with pastoralists along the southern rim of agricultural *Palestine.* Direct evidence of such forms of symbiosis during Iron I comes from both the above discussed *Khirbet al-Meshash* in the *Beersheva* Basin and *Tell Jemmeh* in the southern coastal plain. The fact that agriculture in the climatically vulnerable Judaean hills has typically involved a substantial commitment to animal husbandry as a means of reducing the impact of the region's endemic vulnerability to drought, marks this territory as open to processes of sedentarization in whatever periods the climate encourages agriculture, as it did in *Palestine* from 1000 to ca. 700 B.C. (i.e., during the Iron II period).

---

[246] M. Kochavi, *op.cit.,* 1972, p.85, and *passim.* S. Mittmann *et alii, Tübinger Atlas des vorderen Orients* (forthcoming).

[247] The sites of the Judaean desert, originally classified by Kochavi (followed by Stager) as Iron I may well be Iron II: So I. Finkelstein, *op.cit.,* 1988, p.53.

Judea's openness and vulnerability to the larger steppelands that border it on three sides, the marginal nature of its agriculture, its ecological fragility, its high risk of precipitate deforestation, and the greater dominance of sheep and goat herding in its Mediterranean economy following upon the sedentarization of the Iron II period, as well as the increased stability of the sedentary population of the whole of *Palestine* during the Iron II period, all suggest that the greater portion of the new population influx into the Judaean highlands during the Iron II period had derived from the substantial pastoral groups of the steppelands who had been, over time, closely associated with the *Shasu* of the south and southeast, and with the desert dwellers of the South. The sedentarization of *Judaea*, hence, proceeded in a manner more analogous to that of *Edom* than to the history of settlement in the central hills.[248]

It is also during Iron II, and especially in the ninth-century, that the primary agricultural regions of greater *Palestine* had increasingly developed significantly centralized regional forms of government (e.g. *Phoenicia, Philistia, Israel, Aram, Ammon, Moab* and *Edom*) and that *Arab* controlled overland trade began to make a major economic impact in the emerging capitals of these states. These two factors undoubtedly led to efforts on the part of the dominant agriculturalists to control the freedom of the transhumant pastoralists, if only to police this important new adjunct to the economy. The development of systems of forts in the steppe of both the Northern *Negev* and in the *Transjordan*[249] give clear evidence of such efforts. The historical implications are as clear and as direct as the evidence. The cause that brought about the shift of the population of the Judean hills from the transhumant pastoralism of the Late Bronze and Iron I periods to a Mediterranean form of sedentary agriculture is to be ascribed to a forced sedentarization policy, instigated through the expanding political power of the towns of the Northern *Negev*, the *Shephelah* and of the southern coast of *Palestine*.

The great expansion of settlement in *Judaea* during the course of Iron II also corresponds chronologically well with the *floruit* of new settlement in the central hills to the north, and the controlled centralization of political power in *Samaria*. The confluence of these elements suggests that it was only later, in the course of this Iron II

---

[248] M. Weippert, *op.cit.*, 1979; E.A. Knauf, *op.cit.*, 1988.

[249] Th.L. Thompson, *op.cit.*, 1992.

period, that the demographic basis for the Iron Age regional hegemony of *Jerusalem* first developed as the expanding cash crop economies of herding and horticulture drew the Judaean highlands into an increasing dependence on the major trade centers for their markets. Efforts to control these trade goods, in turn, encouraged *Jerusalem* to compete with the southern towns of the Judaean region: most immediately with *Hebron* and the large towns of the *Shephelah,* such as *Lachish,* as the central market for the southern highlands. An extension of *Jerusalem*'s political influence southwards in an effort to expand its *Hinterland* beyond the *Ayyalon* Valley and the *Jerusalem* saddle, is not clearly supported by the excavations of *Jerusalem* and the archaeological surveys of the Judaean hills at any period earlier than the seventh-century B.C. and perhaps not before the middle of the seventh-century, when the population of *Jerusalem* explodes, develops the structures and capacity of a city for the first time, and, following the destruction of *Lachish* by the Assyrians, *Shephelah* agriculture becomes oriented towards several new smaller towns close to the Judaean watershed and within easy access of now populous *Jerusalem*[250]. Chronologically, we can expect that the political development of *Jerusalem* as a regional state, controlling the Judaean highlands, lagged substantially behind the consolidation of the central highlands further north. *Jerusalem* itself, of course, seems to have maintained its influence over the *Ayyalon* Valley through the Late Bronze–Iron II transition.[251] Unlike the development of new state formation in the central highlands, the development of the regional highland state of *Judah* reflects a development along a political spectrum more like that of the expanding power of a city-state, attempting to impose its control over a region imperialistically, in competition with the less viable centers that lay on the periphery of the highlands as had *Lachish* and *Hebron*. *Samaria* may well be understood as Late Bronze *Shechem*'s successor, but, unlike *Shechem, Samaria* was created as a product of the centralization of complex regional associations that extended throughout the central highlands. In this, *Samaria* was the capital city for an entire region. The basis of power in *Jerusalem,* in contrast, never great before well into the seventh-century, was indigenous to the city itself. The state of *Judah* was created as the

---

[250] M. Kochavi, *op.cit.,* 1972.

[251] S. Mittmann *et alii, op.cit.,* forthcoming.

highlands were subjected to the extension of *Jerusalem*'s power, which, however, was extraneous to the highlands.

The most significant historical question arising from the coherence of the settlement patterns in the *Shephelah*, is the relationship of the major towns of the region in early Iron II both to *Jerusalem* and to the emerging village agriculture of the highlands of *Judah*. That several substantial regional towns were established early in the development of Iron II, especially at *Lachish* and *Gezer* but also at other sites, encourages our understanding of these towns as vitally independent of both *Jerusalem* and *Hebron*, competing with *Jerusalem* in a struggle for the economic control of the emerging highland villages and hamlets. It seems likely that many of these new villages were created as satellites of the already established larger towns. The relationships of the towns of the *Shephelah* to *Jerusalem* then, like that of *Hebron*, lay along a spectrum of conflict from hegemony to subordination, rather than one of shared evolution, given the indispensibly independent and competitive economic and political structures of each. To the extent that *Jerusalem* successfully consolidated power over the highlands—and there is little warrant for supposing that it did—it had to deal with the multi-focal economic orientation of the greater region. Politically, this suggests a strong tendency in *Judah*, in contrast to the more centralized regional state structures of the central highlands, to a polycentric subordination, in varieties of vassalage, with a high potential for fragmentation and the development of several independent polities emanating from its subregional centers, each with their independent economic interests. *Jerusalem*'s dominance over the Judaean highlands (to say nothing of control over the Northern *Negev* or the *Shephelah*, both of which boasted towns easily comparable and perhaps superior to *Jerusalem*) seems best dated at the earliest from the destruction of *Lachish* at the turn of the century.[252]

---

[252] It is, I think, significant that *Lachish* is not rebuilt. Rather Jerusalem begins to expand greatly, and this expansion in size and influence is likely to have occurred in association with the similar expansion of the town of *Ekron*, in association with Assyria's rationalization of its trade in oil, with Jerusalem as the market town funneling the olive production through the *Ayyalon* Valley to the presses at *Ekron* and the caravans that brought the oil northwards along the coastal route.

8. *The Transjordan*

In comparison to western *Palestine,* the region of the *Transjordan* is poorly known through archaeology.[253] However, some of the best and most recent work in the *Transjordan* has approached the antiquities of the area from a regional perspective that seeks to integrate both surface explorations and excavations.[254] Moreover, the association of Transjordanian archaeological studies with biblical and ancient Near Eastern studies has for the most part reflected a far higher critical standard than generally has pertained in studies of western *Palestine.*[255]

---

[253] R. Dornemann, *The Archaeology of Transjordan in the Bronze and Iron Ages* (Milwaukee, 1983); *idem,* "The Beginning of the Iron Age in Transjordan," *SHAJ* I (Amman, 1982) pp.135-140; K. Nashef, "Ausgrabungen, Forschungsreisen, Geländebegehungen: Jordanien (1980-1982)," *AfO* 29-30 (1983-1984), pp.241-292; *idem,* "Ausgrabungen, Forschungsreisen, Geländebegehungen: Jordanien II," *AfO 33* (1986), pp. 148-308; L.T. Geraty and L.A. Willis, "Archaeological Research in Transjordan," *The Archaeology of Jordan and Other Studies,* ed. by L.T. Geraty and L.G. Herr (Berrien Springs, 1986) pp. 3-72; J.A. Sauer, "Prospects for Archaeology in Jordan and Syria," *BA* 45 (1982), pp.73-84.

[254] Above all the very promising project led by P.E. McGovern at *Hirbet Umm ed-Dananir* (P.E. McGovern, *The Late Bronze and Early Iron Ages of Central Transjordan, UMM* 65 (Philadelphia, 1986); *idem,* "Baq'ah Valley Project - Survey and Excavation," *Archaeology of Jordan* II, 1, ed. by D. Homès-Fredericq and J.B. Hennessy (Amman, 1989) pp.25-44; *idem,* "Central Transjordan in the Late Bronze and Early Iron Ages: An Alternative Hypothesis of Socio-Economic Transformation and Collapse," *SHAJ* 3 (Amman, 1987) pp.267-274.

[255] One thinks above all of several fine studies in German; e.g., S. Mittmann, *Beiträge zur Siedlungs- und Territorialgeschichte des nördlichen Ostjordanlandes, ADPV* (Wiesbaden, 1970); *idem, Deuteronomium 1, 1-6, 3: Literarkritisch und Traditionsgeschichtlich Untersucht, BZAW* 139 (Berlin, 1975); M. Weippert, *Edom: Studien und Materialien zur Geschichte der Edomiter auf Grund schriftlicher und archäologischer Quellen* (Tübingen dissertation, 1971); *idem,* "The Israelite 'Conquest' and the Evidence from Transjordan," *Symposia,* ed. F.M. Cross (Cambridge, 1979) pp.15-34; idem, "Edom und Israel," *TRE* 9 (1982), pp.291-299; M. Wüst, *Untersuchungen zu den Siedlungsgeographischen Texten des Alten Testaments I: Ostjordanland, BTAVO* 9 (Wiesbaden, 1975); E.A. Knauf, *Ismael: Untersuchungen zur Geschichte Palästinas und Nordarabiens im 1 Jahrtausend vChr, ADPV* (Wiesbaden, 2nd ed., 1989); U. Hübner, *Die Kultur und Religion eines transjordanischen Volkes im 1. Jahrtausend* (Heidelberg dissertation, 1991). S. Timm, *Moab zwischen den Mächten: Studien zu historischen Denkmälern und Texten, ÄAT* 17 (Wiesbaden, 1989). One should also mention here the Moab survey project of J.M. Miller (J.M. Miller and J.W. Pinkerton, *Archaeological Survey of the Kerak Plateau* (Atlanta, 1991). Contrast, however a number of recent works that reintroduce considerable confusion into our contemporary understanding of ancient Transjordan: J.A. Sauer, "Ammon, Moab, and Edom," *Biblical*

Because of this research, it seems quite possible to make some general
conclusions about the *Transjordan* that might be understood by way of
a contemporary analogy to the better known regions of western *Palestine*.

Gilead, or the area of the Northern *Transjordan* that lies between the
Wadi Zerqa and the *Yarmuk*, has three distinct geographical regions: the
Ajlun, *Jerash* and the Plain of *Irbid*, all of which have had some survey
work in recent years.[256] S. Mittmann's survey of the *Ajlun* and *Irbid*
regions substantially corrects and fills out the earlier survey of N.
Glueck.[257] As one might expect, most of the Late Bronze sedentary
population (12 of 15 sites) had been settled in the agriculturally rich,
well watered plain of *Irbid*. The rugged hills of the *Ajlun*, however, found
little settlement during this period. In this, the settlement pattern during
the Late Bronze Age might be seen as comparable to the settlement
pattern of the central hills of Western *Palestine*. At the present stage of
our understanding, the transition from Late Bronze to Iron I in the *Irbid*
region seems to have witnessed a moderately greater stability than that
in the highlands of Western *Palestine*. Most of the Late Bronze sites
continued their occupation, though perhaps in diminished circumstances.
In addition, some twenty new small settlements extend the area of
exploitation throughout most of the *Irbid* plain. In the *Ajlun* region,
Mittmann lists nearly forty new sites—mostly very small and with limited
remains. This radical contrast compares rather closely with the pattern
of settlement in *Ephraim*. The more moderate changes on the plain of
Irbid might be compared profitably to *Manasseh*. In the transition to
Iron II, we find in the *Irbid* region what might be described as a
continuity and intensification of settlement, reflecting considerable

---

Archaeology Today, ed. by J. Amitai (Jerusalem, 1985) pp.206-214; *idem*, "Transjordan in
the Bronze and Iron Ages: A Critique of Glueck's Synthesis," *BASOR* 263 (1986), pp.1-26;
R.G. Boling, *The Early Biblical Community in Transjordan*, *SWBAS* 6 (Sheffield, 1988); G.
Reinhold, *Die Beziehungen Altisraels zu den aramäischen Staaten in der israelitisch judäischen
Königszeit* (Frankfurt, 1989).

[256] C. Steuernagel, "Der 'Adschlun nach den Aufzeichnungen von G. Schumacher," *ZDPV*
47 (1924), pp.191-240; *idem*, 48 (1925), pp.1-144. 201-392; *idem*, 49 (1926), pp.1-167.
273-303; N. Glueck, *Explorations in Eastern Palestine* IV, *AASOR* 25-28 (New Haven,
1951); S. Mittmann, *op.cit.*, 1970; J.W. Hanbury-Tenison, "The Jerash Region Survey,
1984," *ADAJ* 31 (1987), pp.129-158; and A. Leonard, "The Jarash-Tell el-Husn Highway
Survey," *ADAJ* 31 (1987), pp.343-390.

[257] On the general history of the region, see now the very early but nonetheless careful
study of M. Ottosson (*Gilead: Tradition and History*, Lund, 1969). Unfortunately,
Mittmann's study (*op.cit.*, 1970) was not available to Ottosson.

stability and growth. In the *Ajlun*, following the drought driven expansion of territorial exploitation throughout the hills in Iron I, the Iron II settlement is again comparable to the patterns of the Western highlands of *Ephraim*. We find that the number of sites in the area is contracted, with the population centering itself in larger villages in ecological areas that support extensive terracing and which are more accessible to water resources. The continuity of settlement from the Late Bronze Age through the Iron II period is equally signified in the pottery typology and in its evolution. The pottery displays both an indigenous and a regional development with foreign influences almost entirely disappearing at the onset of the Iron Age. While certainty is not yet possible without extensive excavation, a description of the transition from Late Bronze to Iron I as impoverished and economically depressed, with a considerably higher portion of marginal settlements and a proportionately greater influence of steppe dwellers, seems justified. There seems, however, little support for understanding a displacement of population whether in terms of an Israelite conquest or settlement, or in terms of an Aramaean migration. Rather, we seem to have a radical transformation of the settlement occupation of Northern *Transjordan*, but a transformation that is both indigenous and regional in nature, taking part in the greater region's cultural and economic dislocation and eventually followed by a widespread recovery in Iron II.[258]

In the region of ancient *Ammon*, generally defined by the territory between the *Wadi Zerqa* and the *Wadi el-Mujib*,[259] we are dealing with a very complex area in which the majority of the population of the *Transjordan* lived. The region of the central *Transjordan* plateau is dominated by the region around *Amman*. However, in the northwestern portion of the region of *Ammon*—the *Baq'ah* Valley is dominated by *Khirbet Umm ed-Dananir*. The *Buqe'a* centers on *Tell Safut*, the eastern sector of *Ammon* on *Sahab*, the south on *Tell el 'Umeiri*, and *Tell Hesban*

---

[258] R. Dornemann, "The Beginning of the Iron Age in Transjordan," *SHAJ* I (Amman, 1982) pp.135-140.

[259] The term *Ammon* is understood here as neither a political-historical nor an ethnic specific designation, but is uded only in its geographical signification. *Heshban*, for instance, although north of the *Wadi al-Hasa*, was never part of the state of *Ammon*. U. Hübner, *op.cit.,* p.149.

forms the center of the region around *Wadi Hesban*.[260] Research projects in two areas are particularly useful for understanding the transition from the Late Bronze to the Iron Age: that involving the excavations at *Tell Hesban* and surveys in the surrounding area, and the *Baq'ah* Valley project with its excavation at *Khirbet Umm ed-Dananir*. The occupation of *Tell Hesban* begins during Iron I, increases and expands late in Iron I, and reaches its *floruit* in the late eighth or seventh-century.[261] The survey of the surrounding region suggests a similar pattern of intensification in the pattern of settlement.[262] The Late Bronze period sees only very limited settlement at four sites. During Iron I, there are a total of 28 sites, with the majority of these occurring late in the period.[263] Early in Iron I, settlement is exceedingly sparse and begins to expand in the late eleventh or tenth-century.[264] This still awaits a systematic critical evaluation on the basis of Transjordanian regional studies. It is in Iron II, and especially in Iron IIc (late eighth to seventh-century B.C.) that the region around *Hesban* turns to the intensive forms of sedentarization that are typical of Mediterranean agriculture, with as many as 59 settlements reported.[265]

---

[260] *Ibidem*.

[261] S.H. Horn and R.S. Boraas, "The First Campaign at Tell Hesban: 1968," *AUSS* 7 (1969), pp.97-239; *idem*, "The Second Campaign at Tell Hesban: 1971," *AUSS* 11 (1973), pp.1-144; *idem*, "The Third Campaign at Tell Hesban: 1973," *AUSS* 13 (1975), pp.101-247; R.S. Boraas and L.T. Geraty, "The Fourth Campaign at Tell Hesban: 1974," *AUSS* 14 (1976), pp.1-216; *idem*, "The Fifth Campaign at Tell Hesban: 1976," *AUSS* 16 (1978), pp.1-303.

[262] See especially, O.S. LaBianca, *Sedentarization and Nomadization: Food System Cycles at Hesban and Vicinity in Transjordan* (Brandeis dissertation, 1987) pp.231f.

[263] There is some difficulty in comparing this with surveys in Western Palestine, since in Transjordan Iron I terminology usually includes the whole of the tenth-century pottery repertoire, which in Western Palestine is commonly classified as Iron IIa.

[264] J.A. Sauer, *Heshban Pottery, 1971: A Preliminary Report on the Pottery from the 1971 Excavations at Tell Hesban, Andrews University Monographs* 7 (Berrien Springs, 1973).

[265] Again, differentiation among the sites is particularly difficult, and only the most general conclusions can be accepted with confidence due to the unfortunately somewhat theoretical and ideologically oriented analyses used by the Hesban team. R. Ibach, "Archaeological Survey of the Hesban Region," *AUSS* 14 (1976), pp.119-126; *idem*, "Expanded Archaeological Survey of the Hesban Region," *AUSS* 16 (1978), pp.201-213; L.T. Geraty and O.S. LaBianca, "The Local Environment and Human Food Producing Strategies in Jordan: The Case of Tell Hesban and its Surrounding Region," *SHAJ* II (Amman, 1985) pp.323-330.

The *Hesban* region lies directly on the border of aridity. The shifts in settlement patterns from the Late Bronze to the Iron II periods seem particularly affected by shifts in subsistence strategies from pastoralism to intensive farming and horticulture, and follows a pattern in response to the changing climate that is remarkably similar to that of the Judaean highlands. While the revival of trade and political stability during the Assyrian period certainly supported an intensification of sedentary agriculture, the causes of the shifts in forms of subsistence from Late Bronze to Iron II seem far more to be associated with climate and ecology than directly with either trade or political developments.[266] While O. LaBianca'a study asks some very important questions of archaeology, the highly abstract level of his historico-sociological approach makes most of his conclusions rather irrelevant for a regional study of the *Hesban* area. For instance, he leans heavily on Muhly's rather general study of the development of Iron technology, but fatally ignores the *Baq'ah* Valley studies relevant to the introduction of Iron in this region of the *Transjordan*. His surprisingly uncritical biblical analysis, coupled with a neglect of other regional studies in the *Transjordan*, finds the *Hesban* region somewhat romantically surrounded by hostile nations, including the Amorites, Moabites, Edomites and Israel.[267]

When we turn to the *Baq'ah* Valley project, however, we find an analysis (although limited and as yet incomplete) that is extremely helpful in sketching the history of this transition in the *Transjordan*. The conclusions from this project are also fully consonant with much of the data recovered from the *Hesban* survey and excavations. Although only very limited Late Bronze remains were uncovered at *Umm ed-Dananir*, the excavators were able to establish five criteria (large burial deposits, the use of bread and emmer wheats, large cattle, the pathologies of arthritis and dental caries, and an environmental setting of fertile fields and perennial springs: all of which are characteristics of a sedentary agricultural population) to form a substantial hypotheses for the existence of a town.[268] A very large burial cave from Iron Ia shows a

---

[266] *Contra* O. LaBianca, *op.cit.*, 1987, pp.220–234.

[267] *Ibid.*, pp.223f.

[268] P.E. McGovern, *The Late Bronze and Early Iron Ages of Central Transjordan: The Baq'ah Valley Project, 1977-1981*, *University Museum Monograph* 65 (Philadelphia, 1986) pp.336f.

continuity of this town into the Iron Age. Indeed the methodology used by this project has created the ability to show clear continuities in culture and technology throughout the Late Bronze-Iron II transition.[269] The coherent picture made possible by these surveys includes a period of depression and impoverishment at the end of the Late Bronze Age, a dispersal of the population over the countryside early in Iron I, followed by a gradual recovery and intensification of sedentarization late in Iron I and the maintenance of an expansion and flourishing of intensive agriculture during Iron II. P.E. McGovern also finds a considerable symbiotic involvement of agriculturalists with transhumant pastoralists that encouraged increasing sedentarization.[270] Again in the reconstruction that is possible for the region, the population of the Iron Age shows considerable continuity with that of the Bronze Age. Economic collapse led to rapid desendetarization, and a considerable period of agricultural stress was followed by a recovery that developed a prosperous, sedentary agricultural society during Iron II (approx. eighth to sixth-century). U. Hübner, in his dissertation on the Ammonites of the first-millennium, describes this transition in economic terms: The collapse of the East Mediterranean and Near Eastern economy brought about the end of the indigenous city-state system of the central Transjordanian plateau. The economic depression that resulted involved a collapse in trade, which ultimately brought an end to the high culture of the Late Bronze Age. The population of the region maintained its continuity in the region (albeit on a lower economic level) by orienting itself to a village agriculture, living symbiotically with the pastoralists of the steppe. This transition took place without significant participation of major armies or influences from outside the region. The so-called Aramaean migration has neither epigraphic nor archaeological warrant. Rather, the population of the *Ammon* plateau seems to have been thoroughly indigenous and (surviving this period of extreme climatic and economic stress) developed a complex state society only after a long development, flourishing from the eighth to the sixth-century B.C.[271] This independently derived description that Hübner

---

[269] *Ibid.*, pp.338f. McGovern here sketches six lines of continuity: pottery, metals, silicate, cemetery usage and forms, occupation, and basis of subsistence.

[270] *Ibid*, pp.338-341; also *idem*, "Environmental Constraints for Human Settlement in the Baq'ah Valley," *SHAJ* II (Amman, 1985) pp.141-148, esp. p.147.

[271] Partially paraphrased from U. Hübner, *op.cit.*, pp.178-180.

draws for the Ammonites can be used *mutatis mutandis* for every marginal region of *Palestine*.

Until recently, modern archaeological work in the region of *Moab* has been extremely limited.[272] In 1978, however, J.M. Miller led a survey of the region between the *Wadi Mujib* and the *Wadi el Hasa*, which has set consistently high standards in its methods of research, and now in its publications.[273] During the first two seasons, the survey explored central *Moab*, and in the third season southern *Moab* was investigated. The Plateau lies close to the margin of aridity and has a broad variability of average rainfall from as little as 100mm to as much as 500mm a year. Similarly, while *terra rosa* soils predominate, large areas of very shallow grumusols are found. The area also supports very good grazing land. Sedentary agricultural settlements were generally very small villages adjacent to a stable water source and within walking distance from arable lands[274]. Productive dry farming in wheat and barley and a strong admixture of pastoralism can be expected in the areas in which settlements have been found, with fruit, olives and vineyards along the escarpment above the Dead Sea and on the terraces above the *Wadi el-Hasa*.[275] Miller suggests a very close symbiotic association between village farmers and pastoral nomads in the area. Miller also points out the very strong role that governments played in the expansion of agriculture and (one might add) in the sedentarization of nomads. In summarizing Miller's survey for the Late Bronze-Iron II transition, one notices that the continuity of settlement between the Middle and Late Bronze is quite marked (71%).[276] In the transition to Iron I, however, the total number of sites are substantially reduced (62%). 58 percent of the Iron I sites had also been occupied in the Late Bronze period, so that a continuity of the population is indicated. The shift in the settlement pattern indicates economic disruption and

---

[272] W.F. Albright, "The Archaeological Results of an Expedition to Moab and the Dead Sea," *BASOR* 14 (1924), pp.1-12; N. Glueck, *Explorations in Eastern Palestine* I, *AASOR* XIV (Cambridge, 1934) pp.1-113; J.M. Miller, "Recent Archaeological Developments Relevant to Ancient Moab," *SHAJ* II (1982) pp.169-173.

[273] J.M. Miller, "Archaeological Survey of Central Moab: 1978," *BASOR* 234 (1979), pp.43-52 and esp. J.M. Miller, *op.cit.,* 1991. For a discussion of the texts from Moab, S. Timm, *op.cit.,* 1989.

[274] Th.L. Thompson, *op.cit.,* 1979, *passim.*

[275] J.M. Miller, *op.cit.,* 1991, pp.6ff.

[276] For data and statistics, *ibid.,* pp.547ff.

indigenous collapse. The Iron II sites indicate a substantial continuity of settlement at the Iron I settlements (65%), with a major expansion of both the size and total number of sites, clearly indicating a return to prosperity. Miller's survey in *Moab* demonstrate that the settlement pattern of *Moab*, like those elsewhere in the *Transjordan*, follows the pattern of an indigenous continuation of the Late Bronze-Early Iron I settlements, suffering from severe depression and instability during Iron I, and finally developing a progressive and strong recovery in Iron II. The archaeological finds here and throughout the *Transjordan* substantially confirm the patterns of ecological stress and recovery that were suggested by the archaeological remains throughout the *Cisjordan*.

CHAPTER SEVEN

ISRAEL AND ETHNICITY IN PALESTINE

1. *Palestine's Diversity*

Finkelstein's argument that the Iron I settlement of *Ephraim* originated in the previous hill country agricultural population of a supposedly desedentarized and pastoralized Middle Bronze IIC economy is disputed in this study in favor of a more complex view. The positions put forth by Stager, Ibrahim, Lemche, Ahlström, Callaway, and Coote and Whitelam,[1] which link the material culture of much of Iron and Late Bronze Age *Palestine,* appear quite substantial. I acknowledge the distinctiveness of the *Ephraim* hill country settlements noted by Finkelstein. This is a quite unique geographically delimited situation, however, that reflects the specific regional and functional variations of what had developed, *mutatis mutandis,* throughout the many subregions of *Palestine.* For example, the distinctiveness between the pottery traditions of Late Bronze and Iron I occupations seems far less marked on sites in areas such as the *Shephelah,* the hills of *Benjamin,* and the valleys of the *Jezreel* and *Hazor,* where a greater continuity of settlement within these regions or at specific sites had pertained. In the central hills, the demands of a distinct geographical setting, the consequent variant forms of agriculture and of village and transhumant pastoralism, and the spatial and perhaps chronological dislocations inherent to new settlement in what was at this period a frontier region, are such that greater innovation in material cultural forms can be expected than is

---

[1] N.P. Lemche, *Early Israel* (Leiden, 1985); G. Ahlström, *Who Were the Israelites?* (Winona Lake, 1986); *idem, The History of Ancient Palestine from the Palaeolithic Period to Alexander's Conquest* (in press); J.A. Callaway, "Village Subsistence at Ai and Raddana," *The Answers Lie Below,* ed. by H.O. Thompson (Lanham, 1984) pp.51-66; *idem,* "A New Perspective on the Hill Country Settlement of Canaan in Iron Age I," *Palestine in the Bronze and Iron Ages,* ed. by J.N. Tubb (London, 1985) pp.31-49; R.B. Coote and K.W. Whitelam, *The Emergence of Early Israel* (Sheffield, 1987); L. Stager, "The Archaeology of the Family in Ancient Israel," *BASOR* 260 (1985), pp.1-35; M. Ibrahim, "The Collared-rim Jar of the Early Iron Age," *Archaeology in the Levant,* ed. by P. Parr and R. Mooney (London, 1978) pp.116-126.

observable within areas and sites that were able to maintain a Late Bronze II-Iron I continuity. The Bronze Age-Iron Age transition is marked throughout greater *Palestine* in regionally characteristic ways. The well watered lowland valleys within the Mediterranean climatic zone, for example, typically display a pattern which suggests that this sector of *Palestine* suffered a loss of many small villages and hamlets at the beginning of the Late Bronze Age, while the diminished population consolidated itself in the larger towns.[2] The transition to the early Iron Ages seems to have been marked by a deepening economic depression, by destructions, and by widespread dispersal of the lowland population over a broader area, in a larger number of much smaller settlements that display many clear indications of continuity in material culture with the towns.

The uplands of this Mediterranean zone, however, are marked by their own distinctive response to climatic stress. Here we find a region wide collapse and abandonment of sedentary village agriculture through the course of the Late Bronze Age,[3] and a complex of new small village settlement during Iron I in the central hills, with a delay of settlement in many of the more marginal regions such as the *Carmel* range and the *Issachar* plateau until Iron II.[4] As one might expect, in those areas where there were regional gaps in occupation over a considerable period of time, the new Iron Age settlement took on a more distinctive character, especially in those aspects of the material culture that reflect new subsistence strategies.

On the border of the Mediterranean climatic zone of *Palestine,* where sedentary agricultural villages generally have had a greater orientation to the steppelands of the South and Southeast, the dislocation of the Bronze-Iron Age transition was even more marked. Region wide abandonment of sedentary agriculture was more extensive, and the

---

[2] Th.L. Thompson, *The Settlement of Palestine in the Bronze Age*, BTAVO 34 (Wiesbaden, 1979) *passim.*

[3] *Ibidem.*

[4] See not only I. Finkelstein (*The Archaeology of the Israelite Settlement* (Jerusalem, 1988) but also M. Kochavi, *Jerusalem, Samaria and the Golan* (Jerusalem, 1972) and S. Mittmann *et alii,* "Palästina: Israel und Juda in der Königszeit und Siedlungen der Eisenzeit (ca.1200–550 v.Chr.)," *TAVO* Karte B IV 6 (forthcoming). I would like to thank Professor Mittmann and Dozent Dr. G. Schmitt and the Biblisch-Archäolgisches Institut of the University of Tübingen for allowing me access to these maps and their data files in the summer of 1990.

eventual resettlement of the more marginal regions lagged considerably behind sedentarization in the North. Nevertheless, in Southern *Palestine* (as in the North) greater material coherence between Late Bronze II and Iron I strata is observable on any given site or in any given region that had been able to maintain a Bronze-Iron Age continuum. This is true without respect to whether we are dealing with a supposedly proto-Israelite region or what are often assumed to have been non-Israelite regions, such as the Southern *Transjordan*, the *Shephelah*, or the coastal plain. Continuity is most marked in areas of greater Egyptian influence.

Given such general observations, greater caution needs to be introduced into our discussion before we associate developments in settlement forms and economies, or innovations in physical remains, with changes in ethnicity. Such factors are not ethnic markers, howevermuch they may provide the material cultural foundation for ethnic formation.

Whatever the distance between the town of *Aphek*, nestled on the edge of the coastal plain and the small village of *'Izbet Sarta*, on the western edge of the highlands,[5] both the geographical context and the different forms of economic activities of these two settlements are reflected in respectively quite different regional ecologies and subsistence responses. Such factors are far more determinative of variance in material culture than either distance, ethno-political separateness, or a brief span in time.

Finkelstein's suggestion of the origins of at least some of *Ephraim*'s Iron I settlements in pastoralism, and particularly his discussion of a nomadic population developing from the Middle Bronze IIC hill country's response to economic depression, attempts to answer some very important questions.[6] The possible correlation of this suggestion with many Egyptian epigraphic sources referring to non-sedentary groups in *Palestine* during the Late Bronze Age adds to the attractiveness of the hypothesis.[7] Moreover, the stability of the sedentary population in the

---

[5] An issue of pivotal importance for Finkelstein's reconstruction: I. Finkelstein, *op.cit.*, 1988, pp.31ff.

[6] *Ibid.*, esp. pp.339ff. Related concepts have been put forward in several recent works: R.B. Coote and K.W. Whitelam, *op.cit.*; H. Weippert, *Palästina in vorhellenistischer Zeit* (Munich, 1988); R. Geraty *et.alii*, "Madaba Plains Project: A Preliminary Report of the 1987 Season at Tell el-Umeiri and Vicinity," *BASOR* supplement #26 (1990), pp.33-58; Th.L. Thompson, "Palestinian Pastoralism and Israel's Origins," *SJOT* (1992), pp.1-13.

[7] Here reference must be made primarily to the *'apiru* (J. Bottéro, *Le Problèm des Habiru à la Rencontre d'assyrilogique internationale* (Paris, 1954) and the *Shasu* (R. Giveon, *Les*

lowlands at the end of Late Bronze and throughout Iron I is hardly so great as to explain all or even most of what must be understood as a considerable population expansion that occurred throughout *Palestine* by the end of the eighth century B.C. One legitimately looks for increments to the indigenous sedentary population. However, Finkelstein's suggestion, also shared by Coote and Whitelam and H. Weippert,[8] cannot stand on its own and needs development and detail, as it lends itself immediately far more to an explanation of what happened to the Middle Bronze IIC population of this region (that is, to a clarification of a process in desedentarization) than it does to a process of resedentarization some four centuries later. One cannot maintain a continuity of ethnicity here between agriculturalists, pastoralists and the new Iron I population if the Egyptian *Amarna* and other New Kingdom texts relating to *Shasu* and *'apiru* (and neither can be understood as an "ethnic" group) are to be integrated into the theory. Nor can one readily assume a continuity of regional tenure on the part of the descendants of the Middle Bronze population through such a large expanse of time.[9] Rather, one must ask anew the question of the process of formation of ethnicity during the Late Bronze and Iron Age not only in the central highlands but in *Palestine* as a whole.[10]

A fully adequate description of the Late Bronze-Iron Age transition is elusive. For example, some new settlement occurs already in the thirteenth century, most notably along the southern coastal strip[11] in the form of small dispersed hamlets. We need not only ask whether these new settlements reflect an indigenous expansion of population or

---

Bedouins shosou des documents égyptiens. Documenta et Monumenta Orientis antiqui 18 (Leiden, 1971). W.A. Ward's arguments ("The Shasu 'Bedouin': Notes on a Recent Publication," *JESHO* 15, 1972, pp.35-60, esp. pp.52ff.) that with the *Shasu* we are essentially dealing with a social or economic group rather than an ethnic one is a rather important correction of Giveon. That this term was primarily used by the Egyptians to refer to groups in greater Palestine who were indigenous steppe dwellers or, within Palestine proper, transhumant pastoralists, seems very likely (*Ibid.*, pp.51-59). Giveon's argument that they are immigrants with a tribal ethnic unity seems rather unlikely.

[8] R.B. Coote and K.W. Whitelam, *op.cit.*; H. Weippert, *op.cit.*

[9] Cf., further, below.

[10] A substantial beginning of this line of questioning is found in G. Ahlström's *op.cit.*, 1986, but especially in the recent publication of N.P. Lemche: *The Canaanites and Their Land* (Sheffield, 1991).

[11] R. Gonen, *op.cit.*

an influx of immigrants. That implies the almost indefensible assumption that these new settlements give evidence of a growth in population, with the highly improbable corollary that such new settlement (and especially those of Iron I) reflect recovery and a return to prosperity.[12] Rather, a far more adequate explanation is that these new settlements do not suggest either growth or prosperity at all prior to the Iron II period. The first stage of change was a process of desedentarization or dislocation that was the result of a shift of subsistence strategies in reaction to a new period of aridity that had destabilized the entire sedentary population and had forced a substantial migration away from the larger Late Bronze towns.

Coote and Whitelam, in developing an argument similar to Finkelstein's, suggest that the "normal" economic flux of settlement in *Palestine* involved changes during periods of trade disruption and depression along a spectrum from the fully sedentary in the lowlands to a pastoral mode in fringe areas. They point to the Early Bronze IV-Middle Bronze I transition period as a close analogy to the Late Bronze-Early Iron transition. Our knowledge of the Early-Middle Bronze transition is, however, quite uncertain, and the actual state and extent of such an indigenous nomadic pastoralism at the onset of Iron I is still largely unclear, and needs to be explored further. Other important additional sources for the origin of the Israelites are the well attested migrations of "sea peoples," who played a substantial role in the formation of early Israel, as has often been suggested with reference to the name of the tribe of *Dan*. Unfortunately, the later biblical traditions of conflicts with the Philistines have encouraged a dissipation of efforts to define the process through which the Aegean and coastal Anatolian immigrants had been absorbed into the general population of *Palestine*. The onomastics of the Late Bronze period also suggest at least some very minimal influx or influence of peoples from Hurrian and Hittite regions, but even names do not imply ethnicity. Moreover, the extension of the settlement process into the tenth–eighth centuries, reaching a *floruit* close to the time of state emergence, must also allow for substantial infiltration of non-sedentary people from the fringe and

---

[12] Cf., above, Chapter VI. A good popular summary of many of these issues within the perspective of traditional historiography is conveniently found in the excellent book of W.H. Stiebing, *Out of the Desert?* (Buffalo, 1989). Note his very useful chronological table of climatic stress in Palestine on p.193.

especially from the steppe zones, among whom *Shasu* and *Sutu* must undoubtedly play a significant role alongside that of *'apiru*. The process of integration of these several distinctive origins, along with the development of proto-ethnic divisions in *Palestine* in the forms of secondary states in the Assyrian period, need yet to be traced. However, we cannot assume that they existed as early as the Iron I period—even in the more stable coastal region and lowland valleys.

Given the geographical exposure of *Palestine* to migration from the North, the South, and the sea, and given the international dislocations that occurred throughout *Palestine* and the whole of the eastern Mediterranean world at the turn of the millennia, the populations of not only the city-states on the coasts of *Phoenicia* and *Philistia*,[13] but also those areas where eventually the regional states of *Israel* and *Judah* emerged in the hill country during the Iron II period of the ninth and eighth centuries, must have involved more than just the indigenous population of *Palestine* and its steppe. These regions—including the central hills—must have absorbed many displaced groups immigrating into *Palestine* from the outside. Ethnic unity is an unlikely factor in historical reconstructions of the early formation of any of these states. Even the term "proto-ethnic" is first appropriate for the political units that from the ninth century on respond to the expansion of the Assyrian empire west and southwestward.

It seems all the more necessary to point out that historians have not established a continuity between the "group" called "*Israel*" that Merneptah claims to have destroyed and the proto-ethnic population of the ninth century political state of *Samaria* that is known to us in both biblical and extrabiblical texts as "*Israel*." Moreover, it is not really an anomaly that the Egyptian report of Shoshenk's late tenth century campaign directed against the major towns and trade routes of *Palestine*

---

[13] The formation of the various states of *Philistia* remain extremely unclear (Cf., above, Chapter VI) although there are many indications that several of these cities in the Assyrian period reflect (like *Lachish, Gezer, Megiddo* and *Beth Shan* of the Iron I period) a political structure that survived the Bronze Age collapse. The cities of *Phoenicia*, on the other hand, especially *Byblos*, quite clearly show that continuity. The collapse of the Bronze Age polity, while bringing disaster and hardship to the area as a whole, marked a transition to an independence that eventually inaugurated (by the turn of the millennia) rapid expansion and creation of commercial empires. For a sound summary, S. Moscati, "Who Were the Phoenicians?," *The Phoenicians*, ed. by S. Moscati (New York, 1988) pp.24f., and *idem*, "Territory and Settlements," *ibid*, pp.26f.

does not reflect a *Palestine* under the imperial control of *Jerusalem*. Neither *Judah* nor *Israel*, and neither *Jerusalem* nor any viable capital of the central hills invite Shoshenk's attention in his efforts to enforce *Palestine*'s political and economic subordination to Egypt. *Jerusalem* is a small highland town at the time, and the existence of an *Israel* or a *Judah* at such an early date is unsupported by what is known of *Palestine* of the time. The evidence drawn from the archaeological and textual data we have certainly argues against the assertion of any transregional political structures in the highlands, and precludes any coherent sense of a unity of the population during the Iron I or early Iron II periods, prior to the building of *Samaria*.

F.R. Brandfon's 1983 dissertation[14] offers a comprehensive survey of the archaeological remains of *Palestine* that serves well as a larger context for I. Finkelstein's historical and archaeological review of the new Iron I settlements in the central hills of *Ephraim* and *Menasseh*.[15] Brandfon traces the growing tendency of most field archaeologists today to revise the chronology and stratigraphy of the Late Bronze-Iron I transition[16] to show a considerable period of overlap for the end of the Late Bronze II repertoire and the beginning of new settlements in several regions of *Palestine*, with the end of Late Bronze II correlating well with the final stages of the Egyptian presence in the *Jezreel* in the reign of Ramses VI; that is, after the mid-twelfth century. The earliest traces of the Iron Age, however, are associated with the occupation of the new villages, which Brandfon argues begins "in every region" prior to the destruction of the Late Bronze towns.[17]

The difficulties involved in correlating the stratigraphy of the excavated larger towns with the for the most part only surveyed new settlements are perhaps more intractable than Brandfon allows. Yet, his central contention that the emergence of new settlement needs to be understood as a widespread phenomenon, not subsequent but contemporary to the deterioration of the Late Bronze culture, seems to be a significant and valid rereading of the archaeological data that is supported by Zertal and Finkelstein's more detailed studies of the

---

[14] F.R. Brandfon, *The Beginning of the Iron Age in Palestine* (University of Pennsylvania dissertation, 1983).

[15] I. Finkelstein, *op.cit.*

[16] F.R. Brandfon, *op.cit.*, Part I.

[17] *Ibid*, pp.418f.

central hills. Prior to some of the most significant Late Bronze II destructions at *Megiddo, Ashdod, Gezer, Beth-Shan, Tel Mor, Jaffa,* and *Tell Abu Hawam* that mark the beginning of the end of the Late Bronze period in *Palestine,* the process of the settlement of early Iron Age villages had already in some regions begun.[18] The post destruction rebuilding of these towns indicate an impoverished continuity of the Late Bronze occupation into the twelfth century.[19] The early twelfth century saw further destructions, most notably at *Tell Beit Mirsim* and *Hazor,* but several important lowland sites such as *Megiddo, Ashdod, Beth Shan,* and possibly *Gezer* in the foothills along the coastal plain, continue into the middle of the twelfth century and are clearly contemporaneous with the earliest Iron I settlements in these regions. However this transition is to be understood historically, both the destructions and the process of resettlement, both the collapse of a town centered and the emergence of an at first dispersed and then village centered economy, are correlative responses to a crisis that affected the population of *Palestine* as a whole. These changes are best understood in complementary rather than polar terms, and are in many ways analogous to the earlier shift from the diversified town and village economy of Middle Bronze II C to that of the almost exclusively town based economy of Late Bronze agriculture.[20]

That Sub-Mycenaean III C pottery is now increasingly recognized as the result of an indigenous Palestinian development under marked Aegean influence, also suggests that whatever the immediate causes of the Late Bronze-Iron I transition, the disruption and dislocation resulting from a major migration of "sea peoples" from *Anatolia* and the Aegean cannot be understood as entirely accurate. The migrations were not wholly responsible for the disruptions, but must be seen as only one of the components of a transition and dislocation of settlement that affected the whole of the eastern Mediterranean, including all of *Palestine,* bringing about the final stages of Late Bronze II until a new stability of settlement was established sometime during Iron I.[21] The

---

[18] *Ibid.*, pp.416f. This is on the basis of a chronology tied to Mycenaean imports, i.e. prior to ca. 1210-1190 B.C.

[19] *Ibid.*, and "chart 13."

[20] Th.L. Thompson, *op.cit.*, 1979.

[21] Brandfon's suggestion that we might understand the initial cause of this transition in terms of the aftermath of the battle of Qadesh in the first quarter of the thirteenth century,

destruction of towns may well be explained by the immediate events of war and the impoverishment it brings. These destructions may also have been caused by earthquake, fire, or pestilence. The radical impoverishment of the entire society—stretching beyond the borders of any single region—coupled with an increasing inability of the society to rebuild and restructure itself within towns after such disasters, however, can only with great difficulty be explained by reference to singular events or passing fortune. As these radical dislocations among the population are typically marked by an extensive transition to new socio-economic forms they are not to be explained in terms of secondary (and at times peripheral) political and economic causes such as Egyptian imperial policy or the collapse of international trade. The foundations of the Palestinian economy were indigenous and agricultural in essence, and its collapse was brought about by the failure of that agricultural foundation. In fact, Egyptian presence, and the trade that that presence helped maintain brought with it a small measure of stability during the twelfth century in the primary regions of Egyptian interests: the *Jezreel* and *Beth Shan* valleys and the southern coastal plain. The inability of the Late Bronze towns (which comprised nearly the whole of the sedentary population) to maintain themselves agriculturally, led to their frequent destruction and impoverishment, their recurrent abandonment, and the dispersal of their populations into more viable forms of economic subsistence in smaller units by creating villages and hamlets over an increasingly larger acreage, pressing the frontiers of more marginal lands and regions, increasing their reliance on the more drought resistant

---

appears inadequate as a comprehensive explanation of events that occurred over the next two centuries in Palestine, howevermuch one might suggest that this battle affected both the sphere of Hittite influence and Egypt's long-range imperial policies. The widespread disruption of international trade (one of the hallmarks of the Late Bronze II-Iron Age I contrasts) does not simply affect Palestine's ties with Syria and Anatolia, but reflects a phenomenon manifest throughout the whole of the eastern Mediterranean seaboard and that lasts for at least two centuries. This involves a region wide collapse of Late Bronze civilization. Moreover, Egyptian influence in Palestine continues dominant for yet another century. The absence of trade and luxury goods in the earliest Iron Age settlements, corresponds more with the general impoverishment throughout this part of the world, which impoverishment itself seems to have been the cause of trade collapse, rather than its result. Brandfon's attribution of the Hittite famine to the Qadesh battle not only ignores chronology, but also fails to take account of the widespread evidence we have for both drought and famine affecting not Qadesh alone but the whole of the Mediterranean world at the onset of the Late Bronze-Iron Age transition.

forms of agriculture and husbandry, especially of sheep and goat herding and grain agriculture, and—along the coastal plain—of fishing.

One of the great barriers to understanding the history of *Palestine* is the lack of any natural unity of the region as a whole. *Palestine,* in its earliest periods, is an artificial concept at best, and neither a cultural nor a political one. Even geographically, it has ever been sharply divided into many different regions, separated from each other by formidable physical and socio-political barriers. If we are today to turn effectively to a socially based, archaeologically oriented, history of *Palestine,* this differentiation in *Palestine*'s physical and human geography needs more serious attention. The new settlement process associated with the onset of the Iron Age in *Palestine* is decidedly different in each of the many, quite distinct regions of *Palestine.* New settlement is not limited to the central hills of *Ephraim* and *Manasseh,* which had been the focus of Finkelstein's study. Nor does it of itself answer the question of Israel's origins. Iron I settlements in the *Galilee,* the Coastal Plain, the *Shephelah,* the *Beersheva* Basin, the *Jezreel,* and especially those through the *Transjordan,* are comparable to those in the highlands, and raise very serious problems to any arbitrary identification of the settlements of the central hills as "Israelite."

2. *Israelites and Canaanites*

Both the terms *"Israel"* and *"Canaan"* are known to us from historical records and from the Bible, and each have variant referents.[22] It has become exceedingly misleading to speak of the term "Israelite" in an archaeological context of Iron I *Palestine.* From the perspective of the archaeological remains from Iron I, one can hardly use "Israelite" both for the new settlements of *Ephraim* and *Manasseh,* and for those of the *Galilee.* The settlements in the *Galilee* must be understood as substantially separate and distinct from those found in the central hills. Apart from this very problematic use of the term *"Israel"* for the central hills of *Ephraim,* the designation ill fits any region of *Palestine* prior to Iron II and, even then, it can not be used with any confidence apart from

---

[22] Th.L. Thompson, *op.cit.,* 1987, pp.39f.; and G. Ahlström, *op.cit.,* 1986. See now also, N.P. Lemche, *op.cit.,* 1991.

the regional state called "*Israel*" whose capital was *Samaria*.[23] References to the Merneptah stele are not really helpful. This text renders for us only the earliest known usage of the name "*Israel*." This gentilic in Merneptah's list, however, does not correspond with the usage of the name in reference to the Assyrian period state of that name, to the clan of *shr'l* of the *Samaria* Ostraca[24] or to any biblical use of the term. One cannot thus affirm the existence of the *Israel* of the Bible solely on the strength of the *Israel* stele.[25]

The term "Canaanite" is badly used by most everyone in archaeology and ancient Near Eastern studies today.[26] *Aphek* and *Megiddo* are no more "Canaanite" than are, for that matter, *Bethel*, or *'Isbet Sarta* "Israelite." The term "Canaanite" as it is used in biblical archaeology today as a gentilic, has its roots in the anti-Ba'alist, early post-exilic, Old Testament origin traditions. It is the polar opposite of "Israelite" and, in Iron I, even more inappropriate. It is objectionable to define "Canaanite" as the city-state culture of the plains and major valleys. That is not only arbitrary in its limitations, but assumes a politico-ethnic unity and substance that simply does not correspond with any reality we know, even during the Bronze Age. Not only is the term "*Canaan*" a geographic name and unknown as a gentilic at this early date, but the associated description of *Palestine*'s lowlands as dominated by city-states during Iron I is ludicrous. Decentralized village agriculture, horticulture, and animal husbandry is dominant throughout *Palestine*. The sharp boundaries, which the use of the terms "Canaanite" and "Israelite" make possible, are wholly unwarranted and inapplicable.

If the distinction between Canaanite and Israelite cannot be made when we speak of the variant cultural traditions of Iron I, have we really sufficient grounds for seeing this period as uniquely the period of emergent Israel? Is the question of Israel's origin a question about events of the Late Bronze-Iron I transition, or is that transition rather only one among many factors relating to the prehistory of people some of whose descendants later formed part of Israel? Certainly the surveys

---

[23] D. Edelman and G. Ahlström, *op.cit.*, 1985.

[24] A. Lemaire, "Excursus II: Le Clan D'Aprill et Israël, les Origines de la Confederation Israélite," *Inscriptions Hebraiques Tome I: Les Ostraca* (Paris, 1977) pp.283-286.

[25] As, for instance, L.E. Stager, "Merneptah, Israel, and Sea Peoples: New Light on an old Relief," *Eretz Israel* 18 (1985) pp.*56-*64.

[26] N.P. Lemche, *op.cit.*, 1991.

of Iron Age I settlement patterns do not render Israel for us historically, for even in *Samaria*'s central hills, the wave of new settlement does not crest until well into the Iron II period, when it becomes difficult to understand the process of Israel's origins in terms of the newness of settlement alone.

According to both biblical and scholarly tradition, the "United Monarchy" was established by Saul in approximately 1020 B.C., continued through the reign of David and David's son Solomon, and developed into what might well be described as the "golden age" of Israel. According to this tradition, after a considerable period of growth in wealth, territorial conquest, and influence, this "United Kingdom" of Israel was broken into two separate, independent kingdoms, that of *Judah* in the south (continuing under the Davidic dynasty until *Jerusalem*'s fall in 586) and that of *Israel* in the north (which, after a succession of kingships in *Penuel* and *Tirzah*, was finally firmly established under the dynasty of Omri at *Samaria* in the early ninth century). Although plagued with dynastic struggles, *Samaria* remained its capital until the kingdom was swallowed up by the Assyrian empire in 720 B.C. Such is the tradition.

Given the relatively consistent picture of a well established core of settlement in the hill country of *Samaria* and in the *Jezreel* during Iron I, along with a process of settlement that did not reach its *floruit* until Iron II is well established, one might do well to suggest that no kingdom of *Israel* yet existed. There is, moreover, little basis for affirming the existence a kingdom of *Judah* in the South. Not until well after the time that tradition marks out for the "United Monarchy" was the population of *Judah* sufficiently stable to support a comprehensive regional political entity. This must have occurred at the earliest sometime during the course of the ninth century. The eventual settlement of the Judaean highlands is hardly to be explained merely as an extension of the Iron I settlements in *Ephraim*. The beginning of Iron I in *Palestine* is not a reflex of prosperity, sedentarization, and growth. Rather, when the whole of *Palestine* is considered, early Iron I and the beginning of new settlement was a period of great instability and transition. By the Iron II period, however, the situation in *Palestine* had radically altered and the proliferation of new settlements during this period had a substantially different cause from that of the centuries earlier onset of Iron I. There is no evidence that enables us to connect historically the archaeological evidence of Iron I settlement in *Ephraim* with the much later Iron II Judaean highland sedentarization. Nor can we argue that these later settlements are in any way dependent on or derivative of the north. The agricultural occupation of these two substantially different types of regions, separated as they are by significant ecological differences and removed as they are by centuries, demand different explanations.

The Omride dynasty, established in *Samaria*, was certainly historical, but the Omrides were hardly the successors of a Saulide monarchy. Certainly by the early ninth century, with the construction of *Samaria*, there is sufficient archaeological justification for speaking of an historical Israel in terms of the State of *Israel*. Prior to that period (lacking both historical verification and dynastic succession), it seems doubtful that one can speak of Israel in political terms. Any assumption of a "United Monarchy" as a factor in the origins of Israel, must appear far fetched, and one perhaps is best occupied in seeing the "United Monarchy"—along with other traditions relating to a unified "original" *qol yisra'el*—as a much later effort of *Jerusalem* to adopt Israel's traditions as its own.[27]

Arguments that have been brought forward by numerous scholars, such as L. Stager,[28] M. Ibrahim,[29] N.P. Lemche,[30] G. Ahlström,[31] J.A. Callaway,[32] and R.B. Coote and K.W. Whitelam,[33] linking the material culture of much of the Iron Age highland settlements with indigenous Iron and Late Bronze Age *Palestine,* appear quite substantial, and I am unwilling to see the distinctiveness of the hill country settlements noted by Finkelstein as more than regional and functional variations of responses to events that affected the whole of *Palestine*.

---

[27] Cf., Th.L. Thompson, "Text, Context, and Referent in Israelite Historiography," *The Fabric of History: Text, Artifact and Israel's Past,* ed. by D. Edelman (Sheffield, 1991) pp.65-92.

[28] L. Stager, "The Archaeology of the Family in Ancient Israel," *BASOR* 260 (1985), pp.1-35.

[29] M. Ibrahim, "The Collared-rim Jar of the Early Iron Age," *Archaeology in the Levant,* ed. by P. Parr and R. Mooney (London, 1978) pp.116-126.

[30] N.P. Lemche, *op.cit.,* 1985.

[31] G. Ahlström, *op.cit.,* 1986.

[32] J.A. Callaway, *«The Significance of the Iron Age Village at 'Ai (et-Tell),»* Proceedings of the Fifth World Congress of Jewish Studies *(Jerusalem, 1969) pp.56-61.*

[33] R.B. Coote and K.W. Whitelam, *op.cit.*

This distinctiveness seems far less marked in areas—such as the *Shephelah*, the settlements north of *Jerusalem*, and those in the *Hazor* region—where a greater continuity of settlement pertains. Whatever the distance between *Aphek* and *Isbet Sarta*, the economic activities of these two settlements on the edge of the central highlands are quite different. Because of this, one must also expect similar differences in their material cultures. This, however, does not speak to the issue of ethnicity at all. The diversity of the settlements in the central hills seem satisfactorily explained as the result of different subsistence strategies of the indigenous agricultural and pastoral people of *Palestine*. They were firmly established during Iron I and expanded rapidly as prosperity returned with the better climate of Iron II with the support of a trade economy centered in the horticultural sector of the economy.

The origin of the population of the southern highlands, however, developed not only later, but were much more likely to have been linked to a sedentarization process from steppe pastoralism, with a chronological horizon in the late tenth and ninth centuries. Regional histories of the origin of the people of *Palestine* who ultimately become identified as "Israel," based on an understanding derived from geography and archaeology, separate themselves rather substantially from historiographical views that have been based on Israel's origin traditions.[34] In fact the two are incompatible. The origin traditions, formed within the context of an already existing conception of Israel, are not implicitly or directly oriented towards questions of history, but rather deal with questions surrounding the meaning and significance of Israel, which has a future orientation that functions as the matrix of the tradition.[35]

Historical questions of the origin of Israel are specifically oriented to the real past of the people who came to identify themselves as such, and is limited by what we know and can reconstruct of that past. Fundamental to an understanding of the historical question of Israel's origins is the recognition that the question refers to the origin of the people themselves and their settlements which later biblical tradition came to understand as Israel. Such a question is simplistic and

---

[34] A similar argument from the perspective of the tradition is asserted in Th.L. Thompson, *The Origin Tradition of Ancient Israel* I (Sheffield, 1987).

[35] Th.L. Thompson, *The Historicity of the Patriarchal Narratives*, *BZAW* 133 (Berlin, 1974) Chapter XIIB.

straightforward. It is also indisputably reflected by historical archaeological research and open to very concrete descriptive answers. The initial settlement of the central hill country of *Palestine* (which significant aspects of the tradition understood as the heartland of ancient Israel) is certainly pivotal in any hope for accommodation with traditional historiographies. However, the origin of the people and settlements of regions other than the central hills are essential as well, as they too form part of the fundamental core of the Israel of tradition. Furthermore, as it becomes increasingly clear in the history of the settlement of *Palestine* that the occupation and exploitation of different regions developed separate and distinct processes through history, any questions about the emergence of Israel take on the character not only of research into the historical development of these separate regions but also of an analysis of the process of their political, cultural, and ethnic consolidation and unification, letting alone for a different context the issue of the development of the unity as an ideology and a tradition about a real Israel. Nevertheless, because of the ideological, traditional and literary quality of the biblical conception of Israel, the identity of this perception with an historical reality of Israel apart from the text is hardly to be assumed.[36]

A discussion about the origin of the people and settlements of what was to become the Israel of tradition can not *a priori* begin with a discussion of the transition from the Late Bronze to the Iron Age. The settlement of some of the regions of *Palestine* betray an apparent locally determined continuity of settlement long predating the Bronze-Iron Age transition, and other of the regions (associated with Israel by the tradition) are not settled until centuries later, including such pivotal regions as *Issachar* and the Judaean highlands. There is no obvious imperative (even in terms of biblical historiography) to understand the "core" of ancient Israelite settlement as co-terminal with the Iron I settlements. Nor is there any obvious reason to equate the earliest manifestations of that settlement, with Israel's beginnings. However, if our biblical traditions are an historical refraction of a real past, Israel's origin as a people needs to be associated with the unification and integration of the central highland with the lowland valleys, the Judaean highlands, the Judean coast, the *Shephelah*, the *Galilee*, *Gilead* in *Transjordan,* and the southern steppelands, and this never occurred in

---

[36] Th.L. Thompson, *op.cit.,* 1991.

history prior to the Persian period at the very earliest. The history of Israel's origins is then to be found in the development of such unities for the regions of *Palestine* and the identification of that resultant, coherent whole with the "Israel of tradition." The origins of Israel's people lie inextricably with the origins and histories of these apparently distinct regional settlements. In this observation, the search for the origins of Israel merges with the history of *Palestine*. They are indeed confluent.

3. *The Mediterranean Economy of Greater Palestine*

The questions of Israel's origins within the history of *Palestine*, in trying to identify the context within which Israel achieves a unification emerging as a dominant presence in *Palestine* can hardly restrict its focus to Iron I. Rather, it is in the Iron II period, and especially Iron IIB-C (the Assyrian period of the ninth—seventh centuries) that the subregional demographic displacement of *Palestine*'s population (coinciding with the development of secondary state structures by coherent regional entities in the context of Assyrian interests in *Palestine*) first clearly takes on a socio-political character that was supportive of early forms of ethnicity. In exploring the early development of states and proto-ethnic groups in a region such as *Palestine*, it is important to be aware that centralizing and integrating tendencies linked to a rise in prosperity, an expansion of population, a resurgence in regional and international trade, and the military organization of subregional powers, are not immediately open to simple linear evolutionary growth, even in a situation (as pertained from the late twelfth to the late tenth century) in which the collapse of the Hittite and especially the Egyptian empire left a power vacuum in the region. Quite the contrary! The economic structures indigenous to *Palestine* were essentially centrifugal, inimical to both political and proto-ethnic consolidation beyond the boundaries of very small geographically defined sub-units. The collapse of international trade and the ultimate withdrawal of Egyptian forces in the region placed the few remaining towns of the twelfth century in jeopardy. Those towns that were primarily commercial trade centers faced a devastating economic depression from which they would take more than a century to recover. Others, more linked to agricultural production and distribution, struggled with the instabilities and dislocations of the extended drought and famine, from which they did not begin to recover until the mid-eleventh century. Few of these cities could likely have looked beyond their own borders for economic expansion and growth.

Moreover, the economies of the commercial cities, built as they were on a pluralized and multi-linguistic diversity, were not conducive to the development of the kind of unifying *ethos* that might support conceptions of common purpose and destiny that are typical of ethnic formation except within their immediate borders. Even in the cities of the central and southern coasts of *Palestine,* the scholarly assumptions of a Philistine organized inheritance of Egyptian power depends far too heavily on much later biblical tales. Not only do they ignore the economic problems of agriculture at the time, and do not adequately consider the economic dislocations following the long deterioration and then collapse of the overland trade routes,[37] they take for granted a harmonized biblical view of ethnic unity. What we know of the region historically, however, requires that we consider not only the considerable diversity of the indigenous population, but also recognize the very wide range of distinct groups among the immigrant population.[38] Both pottery, material remains, and Egyptian texts suggest that the process of amalgamation lasted well beyond a century. Rather than a new form of centralized political power of an essentially alien nature, indigenous structures of competing city-states are what emerge during Iron II. Judging from our earliest Assyrian texts relating to this region, the assertion of Assyrian power is not directed against the capitals of a Philistine people, but rather against the independent city-states of *Ashkelon, Gazza, et alii.*

The resurgence of city-state forms of government both here and along the Phoenician coast in the first millennium, moreover, suggests that, in these regions at least, distinctions in the population based on isolating economic structures such as small village agriculture and transhumance and steppe pastoralism continue the polarities endemic to symbiotic associations. Whatever we might be able to say about the rise of commercial and military power in the regions of *Phoenicia* and *Philistia* in early Iron II and the beginning of the Assyrian period, the

---

[37] One must here reflect that the eventual successors of the Egyptians in control of the overland coastal trade route were not the Philistines, but the Arabs, even when during Iron II the cities of Palestine's southern coast achieved considerable political power.

[38] G. Ahlström, *op.cit.,* 1986.

populations of these regions do not reflect the homogeneity and common purpose one might legitimately associate with the use of Gentilics such as Phoenician and Philistine. Geography, economy, and the indigenous political structures based on the polarities of clans and towns,[39] create a social and historical context that is seriously inimical to the formation of common ethnic structures.

The dominant economic strategies that persisted over centuries in *Palestine* were centrifugal not centralizing. The indigenous central powers of *Palestine,* such as *Tyre, Hazor, Megiddo, Gezer, Lachish, Beersheva, Ashkelon, Gazza, Tell el-Meshash, Jerusalem,* and *Shechem,* had their primary basis of power in the narrow economic associations of their local regions. The emergence of transregional authorities such as *Jerusalem's* assertion of interests beyond the *Ayyalon* Valley and the *Jerusalem* saddle to include the length of the Judaean highlands, and potentially the northern *Negev* and the *Shephelah,* and *Samaria's* apparent amalgamation of the very diverse central highlands and the extension of their interests and influence into the agriculturally rich and densely populated *Jezreel* and northern *Jordan* valleys, potentially extending this influence to the sea in the west and to the *Transjordan* in the East, demand historical explanation for these expansions are glaring anomalies in the history of *Palestine.* Understanding must go well beyond (though it may include) the emergence of powerful individuals with sharp swords. The biblical "historiography" centered in the wars with Philistines as the amalgam of nation building, and depending on the integrity of charismatic leadership, such as that of Saul and David, lies at the very heart of great literature. It, however, explains nothing historically. Lacking any obvious need for *Lebensraum* and lacking any intrinsic basis for conflict between these regions, one is left only with a scenario, not an explanation, and even such a scenario of necessity presupposes the internal sub-regional unity and external polarity that the situation of conflict supposedly created. It seems fair to conclude that Alt's question concerning the emergence of regional states centered in the Palestinian highlands has not been answered in the archaeological discoveries relating to the collapse of Late Bronze and the transition to Iron I. Geographical, anthropological, and archaeological studies, nevertheless, do clarify the process of regional state formation once we move beyond the chronological limits that Alt set.

---

[39] N.P. Lemche, *Early Israel, VTS* (Leiden, 1985).

From as early as the Late Chalcolithic, if not indeed already from that initial sedentarization in the neolithic revolution of agriculture and animal domestication, the occupants of *Palestine,* living in that perennial "heartland of villages,"[40] were occupied in what might be schematically described as a threefold pattern of settlement, strongly correlated in their geographic displacement to the economic potential of their environment:[41] 1) architecturally planned and unplanned small towns[42] mostly dominating the central, well watered lowlands and intramontane valleys or along major trade routes, maintained through a broad mixture of economies (including interregional and regional trade[43]), crafts of various sorts (especially construction, pottery making, cloth production,

---

[40] G. Falconer, 1987, as cited by E.A. Knauf, unpublished SBL paper: 1987.

[41] The relationship between the geographic displacement of sedentary villages, hamlets, and towns to the environmental potential for economic exploitation was the focus of the earlier studies: Th.L. Thompson, *The Settlement of Sinai and the Negev in the Bronze Age,* *BTAVO* 8 (Wiesbaden, 1975); *idem, op.cit.,* 1979. For a very instructive illustration of some of the fluctuations in population and in the patterns of settlement, the recent article of R. Gophna and J. Portugali, "Settlement and Demographic Processes in Israel's Coastal Plain from the Chalcolithic to the Middle Bronze Age," *BASOR* 269 (1988), pp.11-28. The extreme demographic fluctuations outlined by Gophna and Portugali should be mitigated through a less distinct demarcation of the Bronze and early Iron Age periodizations that have been derived through pottery forms.

[42] I use the term "small towns" here decidedly. The usage of terms such as "city" and the associated concepts of urban and urban elite are, for early Palestinian settlements, misleading as, e.g., S. Richards, "The Early Bronze Age: The Rise and Collapse of Urbanism," *BA* 50 (1987), pp.22-42; also recently H.M. Niemann, *Stadt, Land, und Herrschaft,* (Habilitation, U. of Rostock, 1990) in contrast to C.H.J. de Geus, de israelitische Stad (Gorkum, 1987). Aside from a small handful of sites such as Early Bronze III's *Beth Yerah (=Khirbet Kerak)* and Middle Bronze II's *Hazor (=Tell el-Qadi),* the size of Palestine's towns was exceedingly small prior to 7th century *Jerusalem.* It is not until the Hellenistic period that some of the lowland towns take on the character of urbanism with a substantial elite class. For a clearer sociological perspective than generally pertains in studies on Palestine, see the excellent articles of J. Sapin, "La géographie Humaine de la Syrie-Palestine au Deuxième millénaire avant J.C. comme Voie de Recherche Historique" I-III, *JESHO* 24 (1981), pp.1-62; *idem,* 25 (1982), pp.1-49. 113-186; M.A. Zeder, "Understanding Urban Process through the study of Specialized Subsistence Economy in the Near East," *Journal of Anthropological Archaeology* 7 (1988), pp.1-55. Even in the hierarchically organized "cities" of the Amarna period claims about a significant class of elites are excessive and misleading.

[43] Here I would include not only such port towns as *Acco,* and overland trade centers like *Gazza,* but also towns that live symbiotically with the steppe such as *Khirbet el-Meshash, Beersheva, Ashkelon, Hebron, Jericho,* and even *Beth Shan.*

and metal working), religion and its public manifestations in cult, a basic Mediterranean type of agriculture of grains and garden vegetables, with a horticulture of grapes, olives, and fruits dependent on the different regional ecologies, and with a geographically determined variable mix of animal husbandry in sheep and goats, beef cattle, pigs and poultry. 2) Villages within the Mediterranean climatic zone, with a variety of clusters of unfortified family oriented housing and outlying individual homesteads and hamlets, whose agriculture shows a broad range between dominant cash crops of horticulture, grain agriculture, and animal husbandry, dependent on specific local subregional ecologies. These villages usually display some minor crafts, especially those of pottery, oil, wine, and cloth production as well as regionally based agricultural specializations, particularly those of horticulture and pastoralism. 3) Villages, hamlets and campsites of variable sizes in the steppe zones of *Palestine* found primarily to the East and South of the Mediterranean climatic zones, with an economy largely dominated by pastoralism, with a strong admixture of cereal agricultural, and in some regions—most notably in the *Negev* and the steppe zones of the southern coast—periodically supported by involvement of the mining and metallurgy industries of the desert regions of the *Sinai*, as well as the international overland trade routes from *Egypt* and, at least by the Late Bronze or Early Iron Age, from *Arabia*.[44] One must also consider not only camel breeding and caravaneering, but also the sub-economies of raiding, smuggling, and mercenary activities peculiarly endemic to less sedentary populations,[45] from which undoubtedly arises the sedentary

---

[44] The complexity of the nomadic-pastoral spectrum of economic activity should not be underestimated (Th.L. Thompson, "Historical Notes on Israel's Conquest of Palestine: A Peasant Rebellion," *JSOT* 7 (1978), pp.20-27; but already T. Ashkenazi, *Tribus Semi-Nomades de la Palestine du Nord* (Paris, 1938).

[45] The remarkably sharp distinction popular among sociologically oriented biblical scholars between predominantly camel breeding and trade oriented Arab bedouin on one hand, and the predominantly sheep and goat herding pastoralists of the steppe on the other, is largely due to the classification of the latter as "enclosed nomadism" (M.B. Rowton, "Economic and Political Factors in Ancient Nomadism," *Nomads and Sedentary Peoples*, ed. by J.S. Castillo, El Colegio de México, 1981, pp.25-36; *idem*, "Enclosed Nomadism," *JESHO* 17, 1974, pp.1-30; also V. Matthews, *Pastoralism Nomadism in the Mari Kingdom*, ASOR Dissertation Series 3, Cambridge, 1978; *idem*, "The Mari Texts and Enclosed Nomadism," typescript of SBL paper, Anaheim, 1990.) This distinction introduces severe distortions into the discussion since most frequently the descriptions of "enclosed nomadism" are drawn from the study of the texts from *Mari*, from a time prior to the domestication of camels.

population's frequently expressed perception of nomadic pastoralists as "belligerent."[46] This complex continuum that existed in antiquity cannot be used to ignore aspects of full nomadism as simply a modern anachronism.[47] Questions regarding the "beduinization" of the marginal lands of greater *Palestine*, the *Sinai*, and *Arabia* are profitably pursued by E.A. Knauf through categories of successive epochs: "pre-beduin" (third and second millennium B.C.); "proto-beduin" (tenth to sixth century B.C.); "early beduin" (fifth century B.C. to third century A.D.); and "full beduin," which continues into modern times.[48] Camel domestication reaches back at least to the second half of the third millennium,[49] and camel caravans are involved in trade in *Palestine* from the Late Bronze period at the latest.[50] The time frame for Knauf's "pre-beduin" needs to be pushed back to at least the fourth millennium, B.C. We have evidence for such nomadism in the *Sinai*, existing at a great distance from *Palestine*, and subsisting on Metallurgy, some pastoralism, hunting, and limited patch agriculture. We also know of

---

Not only were there many forms of nomadism at this time that need to be included under the rubric "enclosed," and many of whom were desert dwellers, but once the Arab bedouin came to dominate the deserts of *Arabia, Sinai*, and the *Sahara*, this brought about radical transformations in most other forms of nomadism, especially among the steppe dwellers, most of whom were pastoralists. This trans-chronological distinction between "closed" and "open" nomadism is thoroughly misleading and often false. On related issues A.S. Gilbert, "Modern Nomads and Prehistoric Pastoralists: The Limits of Analogy," *JANES* 6 (1974), pp.53-71. On the onset of Arab influence on greater Palestine, P. Wapnish, "Camel Caravans and Camel Pastoralists at Tell Jemmeh," *JANES* 13 (1981), pp.101-121; P. Wapnish and B. Hesse, "The Contribution and Organization of Pastoral Systems," *Early Israelite Agriculture*, ed. by O.S. LaBianca (1989) pp.29-41.

[46] S.T. Parker, "Peasants, Pastoralists, and Pax Romana: A Different View," *BASOR* 265 (1987), pp.35-51; *contra* E.B. Banning, "Peasants, Pastoralists, and Pax Romana: Mutualism in the Highlands of Jordan," *BASOR* 261 (1986), pp.25-50. D.F. Graf, "The Saracens and the Defense of the Arabian Frontier," *BASOR* 229 (1978), pp.1-26; and, most perceptively, N.P. Lemche, *op.cit., 1985, p.133n.*

[47] As does J. Tracy Luke, *Pastoralism and Politics in the Mari Period* (University of Michigan dissertation, 1965) *passim.*

[48] E.A. Knauf, *Ismael, ADPV* (2nd ed., Wiesbaden, 1989) pp.136-138, clarifying his earlier discussion from 1985 on pp.40-45.

[49] See the very clear discussion of this issue by E.A. Knauf, *Midian, ADPV* (Wiesbaden, 1988) pp.9-15.

[50] P. Wapnish, *op.cit.*, 1981, pp.101-121; E.A. Knauf, *op.cit.*, 1988, pp.9f; *idem*, "Supplementa Ismaelitica," *BN* 40(1987), p.20; *idem, op.cit.*, 1989, p.138.

other groups related to the North *Sinai* trade route in both the Chalcolithic-Early Bronze I and the Early Bronze II periods.[51] Nor can we see even these early periods as the earliest in which nomadic forms occur in greater *Palestine*. We have every reason to assume that hunter-gathering societies had continued to exist apart from the agricultural heartland in the periods following the neolithic revolution. Moreover, although it is highly likely that sheep and goat domestication did in fact develop as one facet of the complex Mediterranean agricultural economy, the great Syrian steppe and its extensions along the eastern and southern flanks of *Palestine* is fully capable of developing a pastoral population that is only marginally and symbiotically related to the sedentary peoples of the fertile crescent. Certainly with the expansion of the *Sahara* from 6000–4,000 B.C., pastoralists had moved into the region of greater Palestine. While the subpluvial prosperity of the late forth and third millennia brought about an intense sedentarization throughout the Middle East, it also brought prosperity to the nomadic sectors of the economy. Knauf clearly distinguishes pastoralism, nomadism, and transhumant patterns of survival and, in doing so, creates considerable potential for furthering our understanding of the development of proto-ethnic population groups that existed along the fringe of *Palestine*.[52]

The interrelationships of the three forms of occupation in the Mediterranean economy of *Palestine* reflect a marginal symbiosis along the peripheries of what were quite discrete, but not wholly independent, regionally determined, occupation patterns. They were sufficiently distinct in both geographic location and *modus vivendi* to give rise to and, once established, maintain historically significant and economically based "quasi-ethnic" divisions in greater *Palestine* (comparable to the *medini, fellahin* and *beduin* distinctions of the medieval and early modern Middle East). While the demarcation of specific identifiable ethnicity in any given region of *Palestine* is necessarily dependent on either textual references to and epigraphic evidence for distinctly separate groups on one hand, or on a variety of speculations relating to the development of

---

[51] Th.L. Thompson, *op.cit.,* 1975, pp.29f.

[52] E.A. Knauf, "Bedouin and Bedouin States," *ABD* forthcoming. For some of the complexities of ethnic relationships and divergence across the sedentary-nomadic spectrum, K.A. Kamp and N. Yoffee, "Ethnicity in Ancient Western Asia during the Early Second Millennium B.C.: Archaeological Assessments and Ethnoarchaeological Perspectives," *BASOR* 237 (1980), pp.85–104.

West Semitic languages on the other. Such evidence, where available, rather consistently suggests the kind of distinctiveness that we can describe as ethnic differentiation of the many groups within *Palestine,* from at least the close of the Early Bronze Age, and possible earlier. The questions of this study, oriented as they are to the emergence of Israel as a dominant group within *Palestine* needs to consider the historical processes of group formation in *Palestine* over time. This issue offers an entrance into the more specifically historical problems surrounding the emergence of regional states, which played a substantial part in the biblical view of Israel, and hence in the development of Israel's self understanding as a people.

Finkelstein's suggestion that the origins of Israel are to be traced to indigenous Palestinian pastoralism—and particularly to the nomadic population that developed from the Middle Bronze IIC economic depression in the central hill country[53]—is well argued, correlating both archaeological settlement patterns and several collections of Egyptian texts that refer to non-sedentary groups who are known to have been involved in this subregion of *Palestine.* Certainly one needs to argue that the indigenous population of greater *Palestine* has never been limited to the more stable sedentary agriculturally dominant population, and the absence of village dominance in the highlands throughout the Late Bronze Age must encourage us to consider the nomadic and transhumant aspects of Palestinian pastoralism and patch agriculture[54]. Coote and Whitelam also develop an argument comparable to Finkelstein's, suggesting that the "normal" economic flux of settlement in *Palestine* typically involves changes along a spectrum from the fully sedentary to a pastoral mode in fringe areas and in periods of trade disruption and depression. They point to the Early Bronze IV-Middle Bronze I transition period as a close parallel to the economic shifts that occurred during Late Bronze-Early Iron I transition. Indigenous forms of nomadism in Late Bronze and Early Iron Age *Palestine* are in this argument an important factor in the discussion of Israel's origins. This is an essentially sound interpretation. This long transition period, in which most of the social and economic structures of *Palestine* broke down under stress, the population of *Palestine* experienced a radical

---

[53] Above, Chapter IV.

[54] Th.L. Thompson, "Palestinian Pastoralism and Israel's Origins," *SJOT* 6 (1992), pp.1-13.

transformation. Given the geographical exposure of *Palestine* to the steppe, and given the severe international dislocations that occurred throughout the Mediterranean world at the turn of the millennia, the regional states of *Israel* and *Judah* that eventually emerged during Iron II as part of the new order of the Assyrian empire, undoubtedly included in their originating sedentarization many different groups from the indigenous sedentary populations seeking refuge and alternatives to the deterioration and economic collapse of the lowlands and intermontane valleys of *Palestine,* but they also absorbed many of the displaced pastoralists and steppe dwellers from the even more severely depressed highlands and fringe areas to the South and East of the agricultural heartland, and without question the many groups of foreign refugees as well that had been dislocated from their homelands and had migrated into *Palestine* from many parts of the eastern Mediterranean basin.

In considering the originating components of the Assyrian period states of *Israel* and *Judah,* we need to look beyond just the desedentarized highland agriculturalists of the Middle Bronze IIC period. Pastoralism and nomadism have always played a significant role in the population of greater *Palestine* and had been part of the indigenous population long before the late Middle Bronze period. The continuity of the agricultural portion of *Palestine*'s population, since the Late Chalcolithic period's farmers established village settlements throughout the lowlands of *Palestine* and many of the agriculturally most amenable highland regions, is beyond dispute apart from the archaeologically difficult to determine transition periods, where radical historical change took place. The continuity of settlement in the Bronze Age is particularly marked. The description of the long period of transition between the Early Bronze II-III period and Middle Bronze II has been much in dispute among archaeologists and historians for some time. Nevertheless, a general consensus has recently been reached in our understanding of the collapse of the Early Bronze towns and of the onset of the Early Bronze IV-Middle Bronze I transition period. Prolonged drought, a collapse in international trade, and concomitant political and military disturbances, brought about what perhaps is best described as a radical shift in subsistence strategies, away from the cultivation of the trade oriented cash crops of the Mediterranean economy towards a substantially less sedentary economy of grain agriculture and pastoralism.[55] Earlier explanations of the Early Bronze IV-Middle Bronze I transition period, as a period of West Semitic "Amorites" from the Syrian steppe,[56] have generally been abandoned by most scholars.[57] The substantial indigenous and even sedentary quality of this period is now nowhere disputed.[58] The mixture of pastoralism in the economy is recognized as an important aspect of the Early Bronze IV-Middle Bronze I economy, recognized to be of a transhumance pattern in at least the Negev region.[59] On the other hand, the town character, typical of much of the Early Bronze II settlement is now, in this transition period, nowhere apparent.[60] Some dispute still exists regarding the transition from the Early Bronze IV-Middle Bronze I period to the Middle Bronze period proper, with Gerstenblith and Tubbs explaining the changes in the Middle Bronze II pottery repertoire as the result of technological development and as reflecting resurgence of trade with Syria, while Dever still understands this revival of the sedentary lowland culture as the result of migrations. Dever's excessive dependence on pottery typology as an indicator of historical and ethnic change in *Palestine* seems, however, inadequate, and we have insufficient reason to follow him here. One might, then, look to

---

[55] A well balanced discussion of this transition can be found in D. Esse, *Beyond Subsistence: Beth Yerah and Northern Palestine in the Early Bronze Age* (U. of Chicago diss. 1982), especially pp.342-386.

[56] Especially K. Kenyon, *Amorites and Canaanites* (London, 1966); W.G. Dever, *The Pottery of Palestine in the Early Bronze IV-Middle Bronze I Period, ca. 2150-1850 B.C.* (Harvard diss. 1966); *idem,* "The People of Palestine in the Middle Bronze Period," *HThR* 64 (1971), pp.197-226.

[57] Th.L. Thompson, *op.cit.,* 1974; *idem,* "The Background of the Patriarchs and the Origins of Israel," *JSOT* 9 (1978), pp.2-43; *idem, op.cit.,* 1979; J. Rogerson, *op.cit.,* 1985; D. Esse, *op.cit.,* 1982; J. Tubbs, *op.cit.,* 1985; K. Prag, *op.cit.,* 1984; S. Richards, "From the End of the Early Bronze Age to the Beginning of the Middle Bronze Age," *BAT* (Jerusalem, 1985) pp.113-135. Dever's insistence that he disagrees with my 1974 position is at best puzzling.

[58] Independently discussed in M. Liverani, "The Amorites," *Peoples of Old Testament Times,* ed. by D.J. Wiseman (Oxford, 1973) pp.100-133; Th.L. Thompson, *op.cit.,* 1974,, pp.144-171; and K. Prag, "The Intermediate Early Bronze-Middle Bronze Age: An Interpretation of the Evidence from Transjordan, Syria, and Lebanon," *Levant* 6 (1974), pp.69-116.

[59] Th.L. Thompson, *op.cit.,* 1975; and especially W.G. Dever and R. Cohen, *op.cit.,* 1982.

[60] *Pacem* W.G. Dever, *ibid.* As far as I am aware, this has never been used as a description of this period.

the radically changing patterns of settlement between Early Bronze II and Middle Bronze II in support of an understanding of the greater economy of *Palestine* as periodically shifting from a region wide, trade dominated Mediterranean economy, centered on the cash crops of cereals, oil, fruits, wine, and herding, to more limited regionally oriented strategies—involving the periodic regional collapse of large towns, and a resulting shift of economic dependence towards a dominance of grain agriculture and pastoral pursuits.[61] This comprehensive economic perspective forms a basis for understanding changes within *Palestine*'s settlement patterns as a response to indigenous developments. However, the whole of greater *Palestine* must be considered in these transitions.

The restricted focus of Finkelstein's study, chronologically limited as it is to the settlements of Iron I, and geographically limited to the central highlands, brings with it the dangers of myopia.[62] We cannot legitimately limit our analysis to either this region or this period without begging the very question of Israel's origins that Hopkins' and Finkelstein's studies set out to illustrate. We also need to examine the many regional differences throughout *Palestine* with their variety of responses to climatic, demographic, and technological change.[63] Finkelstein's suggestion that we understand the gap of settlement in the central highlands during the Late Bronze period[64] in terms of the desedentarization of the Middle Bronze IIC population and the resedentarization of the Iron I period is essentially sound. However, it is also misleading. We need not think in terms of a single spectrum with the population of *Palestine* moving to and from sedentary agriculture and nomadic pastoralism through linear time. Nomadism and sedentarism are also concomitant and contemporary responses to subsistence challenges in any given region at any period. In the context of the

---

[61] Th.L. Thompson, *op.cit.*, 1978, pp.2-43.

[62] Indeed, the study of L. Geraty *et alii*, ("Madeba Plains Project: A Preliminary Report of the 1987 Season at Tell el-Umeri and Vicinity," *BASOR* Supplement 26, 1990, pp.59-88) and S. Richards ("The 1987 Expedition to Khirbet Iskander and its Vicinity: Fourth Preliminary Report," *BASOR* Supplement 26, 1990, pp.33-58) make it very clear that we are dealing here with cycles of town "collapse, decline, and regeneration" (*Ibid.*, p.56) and "cycles of intensification and abatement of land use" (Geraty *et alii*, *op.cit.*, p.59) which are neither limited to Iron I nor to the central hills of Western Palestine.

[63] For a preliminary version of this and the following, Th.L. Thompson, *op.cit.*, 1992.

[64] M. Kochavi, *op.cit.*, 1972 and Th.L. Thompson, *op.cit.*, 1979, *passim*.

collapse of Middle Bronze IIC, the process of desedentarization corresponds to a concentration of the Late Bronze population—away from village agriculture—in the larger towns. The abandonment of agricultural in many areas of the highlands would bring with it some reforestation, and the concurrent rise of pastoralism and nomadism would lead to both an increase in the already existent population of the steppe and an expansion of the steppe in climatically marginal zones—most notably in the Judaean hills. Nothing that we know of the Late Bronze period either confines the former Middle Bronze IIC highland population to the central hills or supports any assumption of a direct continuity of those population groups with the process of "resedentarization" in Iron I. In fact the initial process of settlement in early Iron I in the hills of *Ephraim* and *Manasseh*, suggest that it was a subregional economic interchange, specifically of the early Iron I period, that had established the political foundation in extended families and clans, which ultimately underlay the political development of statehood in the region, rather than any earlier existent forms of ethnicity.[65] If a proto-ethnicity can be ascribed to the region at all, it seems rather to have been an aspect of the centralizing process that led to the building of *Samaria* than of any indigenous unity of the population.

Nor does Finkelstein's concept adequately either oppose the many arguments that have been raised supporting the indigenous nature of the Iron I highland settlements by Mendenhall, Gottwald, Callaway, and others or provide an alternative to Alt's paradigm.[66] Rather, it functions as a middle ground between these reconstructions, providing a context for the nomadic or pastoral component involved in the process of the Iron I settlement. It is not an alternative to an understanding of the impetus for settlement originating in the lowland agricultural collapse, but rather adds a pastoral and nomadic component to those changes. Certainly, it raises the question of the impact of the Mycenaean drought, with its displacement of populations, on the indigenous nomadic sector of the Palestinian population. That one gains thereby an adequate explanation for sedentarization of this sector of the population, however, is not immediate, as pastoralism is an alternative mode of subsistence, and, like agriculture, has a tendency to expand with a return to favorable conditions, not sedentarize. What Finkelstein's hypothesis does suggest,

---

[65] Above, Chapter VI.

[66] Above, Chapter III.

however, is that at the transition from the Late Bronze period to Iron
I we are dealing (in the highlands and the lowlands) not with empty
spaces, but—at   least   in   the   well   watered,   most   viable
subregions—pasturelands, with a population substantially in place, and
potentially competitive (in a period of a deteriorating ecology) with
efforts at agricultural sedentarization. It was not a return to prosperity,
but the increased desiccation of grasslands in the greater steppe regions
during the Mycenaean drought that pressed pastoralists increasingly to
shift their subsistence strategies towards the more intensive land use of
agriculture. The concurrent incursion of dislocated agricultural
lowlanders into the highlands acted to force compromise over the
deteriorating resources throughout the whole of greater *Palestine*.
Similarly, the collapse of towns and their monopolistic defenses, together
with the expansion of subsistence agriculture over ever larger areas of
the lowlands, invited the incursions of pastoralists and nomads into these
regions, creating conflict, but also compromise and accommodation.
While the Late Bronze Age reflected a bi-polar symbiosis between town
agriculture and forms of pastoralism, the economic shifts forced on all
sectors of the economy, transformed the bulk of the population before
the second half of the eleventh century into a rather complex mix of
small village agriculture, transhumant agriculture and herding, and
steppe pastoralism.[67] Stabilization of the population, however, did not
occur until the post drought return to favorable conditions in the latter
half of the eleventh century.[68] Recovery is most marked throughout the
lowlands, and one must certainly understand any revival of trade as
associated with the increasing strength of the towns throughout the
lowlands.

The early settlement of the central highlands had established patterns
of both transhumant pastoralism (centered in grain agriculture and
herding) and transhumant agriculture (focused in intensive agriculture
and terrace dependent horticulture) across three, regionally distinct,
ecological zones of steppeland, intermontane *terra rosa*, and rugged

---

[67] "Steppe" in this period is understood as including the greater portion of the Judaean
highlands, the less watered regions of the southern coast, and substantial portions of the
central *Jordan* Valley and the *Wadi el-Fari'a*.

[68] Agreeing here with Finkelstein's distinctions in Iron I; above, Chapter IV and Chapter
VI, *passim*.

western slopes.[69] The last phase of Iron I and the onset of the sedentarization of the Judaean highlands occurred only after the consolidation and stabilization of the Late 11th century and the return to prosperity throughout *Palestine*. Simultaneous with the expansion of terracing along the rugged western slopes of the central hills, and the related increase of trade in the region, settlement begins to expand in many other of the empty regions of *Palestine*. Following the recession of the climatic border between the Mediterranean and steppe zones southwards as ecological conditions improved, small villages began to transform the Judaean highlands. By this time, *Lachish* had recovered along with the rest of the *Shephelah*, and the dimorphic society of *Khirbet el-Meshash* had given way to a growing population in the northern *Negev*, centered in such towns as *Beersheva* and *Arad*. The population of these regions increased manifold. Two factors seem to have been involved in the sedentarization of the Judaean highlands: the political and military monopoly of the towns in southern *Palestine*, and the development of an economy, increasingly dominated by the return of international trade to the region, that was shifting from pastoralism to horticulture. While it is as yet impossible to reconstruct the shifts in the balance of political power between the northern *Negev* (and perhaps *Hebron*), the major towns of the *Shephelah*, and the ultimate winner in this struggle: *Jerusalem* in the north, one might suggest some of the demographic and economic components of this struggle.

In the tenth and early ninth centuries the highlands of *Judah* witnessed a transition from an economy and population largely restricted to pastoralism and stepped nomadism to one of village agriculture with dominants in pastoralism and horticulture. The subsequent two centuries experience a rapid and substantial growth in population that ultimately transformed it into the heartland of *Judah* with *Jerusalem* as its political head. Climatic conditions were favorable to this transition. The creation of forts in both the Judaean desert and the northern *Negev* are difficult to explain merely in terms of the economic exploitation of the specific places in which these forts are found. That they took the form of paramilitary settlements along the borders of aridity, suggests an association with efforts of the sedentary population centers (e.g.

---

[69] Above, Chapter VI; also, I. Finkelstein, *op.cit.*, pp.184-200; S. Mittmann *et alii*, "Palästina: Israel und Juda in der Königszeit und Siedlungen der Eisenzeit (ca. 1200-550 v.Chr.)," *TAVO* Karte B IV 6 (forthcoming: courtesy of S. Mittmann and G. Schmitt).

Beersheva, Arad, Tell Jemma, Lachish, Tell el-Khuwelifa, and *Hebron*) to stabilize the region for agriculture. The forts can be understood as evidence of attempts by the agricultural sectors of the population to force the sedentarization of the pastoral-nomadic sector of the population. The shift to intensive forms of agriculture created, along with its prosperity, a dependence on a growing inter-regional and international trade network of markets, in which the primary cash crops of *Palestine* (oil, wine, meat, and at least initially lumber) played a significant role.

The towns of the northern *Negev* probably continued their function as markets for the steppe that they had inherited from the earlier settlement at *Khirbet el-Meshash*. However, as the sedentary agricultural population of the *Beersheva* basin grew during Iron II, these towns increasingly took on the character of other market towns of *Palestine*. One might well understand a gradual transition in this region from an economy dominated in Iron I by nomadic pastoralists living in symbiosis with a small number of market towns, to a broadly mixed economy in Iron II, substantially sedentary, heavily committed to grain agriculture and animal husbandry, with a mixed population of recently sedentarized nomads and the long established sedentary population from the settlements of Iron I, living in the major towns with a few small villages in those limited areas of the steppe where the water table rises close to the surface of the plain.

In the Judaean highlands to the north of the plain, *Hebron*, which, although never very large, had maintained some continuity through the Late Bronze and Iron I periods (perhaps like *Khirbet el-Meshash* of the Iron I period) as an outpost of *Palestine*'s sedentary population, supplying a conduit for goods to and from the steppe. During Iron II, contemporary with the sedentarization of the Judaean highland, *Hebron* grew as an agricultural market town because of its easy access for the population that spread along the highland ridge north of *Hebron*. In terms of geography, *Hebron* was a natural and readily accessible market for the new settlements of the ridge. The region of the southern *Shephelah* also played a significant role in this transition. The extent to which the *Shephelah* directed the pacification[70] and sedentarization of

---

[70] Above, Chapter VI. The paramilitary nature of the "forts" of the Judaean desert and the northern and central Negev, from *Arad* to *Kadesh Barnea*, like those of the Transjordan in the region of *Amman*, with some analogies to the Roman *limes* of later Transjordan,

these two rather large regions of former steppelands of the Judaean highlands and the *Beersheva* Basin, must have been great. Not only had the population of the towns of the *Shephelah*, such as *Lachish* and *Tell Khuwelifa*, survived the Iron I transition, but, as prosperity returned to the *Shephelah* and as the population began to expand outward forming small pockets of agricultural villages throughout the southern foothills, the *Shephelah* developed the character of a region of transition or buffer zone between the lower coastal plain (that was controlled by the great trade centers of the west such as *Eqron, Ashkelon,* and *Gazza*) and the highland steppe. The economy that gradually developed in the highlands, centered in the cash crops of oil and herding, required markets, which the established towns of the lower hills could supply as a competitive hedge against *Hebron*'s potential dominance. The sedentarization of the former steppelands, however, brought more than commercial advantage and potentially new lands to the town centers of the *Shephelah*. It also brought security. As the border of aridity receded to the edge of the Judaean desert in the East and to the highlands of the central *Negev* in the south, the stabilization of the population within these regions also expanded the frontiers of Mediterranean agriculture (and the vulnerability that went with that) eastwards and southwards, rendering the prosperity of the growing economy of the *Shephelah* secure within the agricultural heartland of southern *Palestine*.

It is unlikely, in this early period of settlement during the final decades of Iron I and the early part of the Iron II period, that any single regional center in southern *Palestine* had held sufficient power or density of population to dominate other established centers of population. The expansion of the frontier and the rapid growth of population speaks to a considerable period of stability and prosperity, to economic competition, but not to substantial conflict over scarce resources. *Jerusalem* lay at the northern extreme of the Judaean ridge. Historically, it had functioned throughout the Bronze Age as a politically dominant center of commerce and trade for the many small and agriculturally stable towns of the *Jerusalem* saddle. Its interests in the trade routes from the coastal plain oriented its political interest westward by way of the *Ayyalon* Valley, for which it functioned as a most important market town. Although by early Iron II the agricultural and trade centered economy of *Jerusalem* and its *Hinterland* had long survived the

---

seems more than adequate to justify the use of this term.

disruptions and dislocations of the Mycenaean drought, and had fully
participated in the return to prosperity and growth, it was not a very
large town, and was by no stretch of the imagination yet a city. Its
relative isolation protected its independence in a period absent of any
great political power in *Palestine*. This same isolation restricted its power
and political influence largely to its own region, and the small subregions
contiguous to it. The limited excavations in *Jerusalem* confirm this
picture of a small provincial commercial center, substantially removed
from the international trade routes and their centers of power.[71]

Jerusalem's eventual reorientation of its interests southwards into
Judaea followed from an expansion of commercial and trade ambitions
rather than from other military or political purposes; for trade, and
specifically regional trade, was the heart and center of its economy. Its
agricultural interests expanded far more into the *Ayyalon* Valley, with its
rich and well watered bottomlands, and the many fertile agricultural
pockets of the *Jerusalem* Saddle to the north of the city. Certainly,
Jerusalem's interests would have drawn it to support the sedentarization
of the highland ridge, but, at least initially, in the interests of security in
an effort to push back the frontiers of the steppe, than from the less
pressing need for new farmlands or other commercial advantage.
Jerusalem's eventual expansion of political power into *Judaea* followed
rather than preceded the sedentarization of the highlands. Once the
settlement of the Judaean ridge had been established in the course of
Iron II, the increase of its production in oil and herding developed the
region as a major source for trade goods that supplied the markets of
Hebron, the towns of the *Shephelah*, and of *Jerusalem*. This led *Jerusalem*
into direct competition with *Gezer, Lachish, Hebron* and the other
markets of the southern hills, eventually leading (most likely by the
middle of the ninth century) to an effort at the direct political
domination of the uncentralized Judaean highland villages. This move
towards increasing centralization and the consolidation of commercial
interests required the subordination of the commercial centers of
Jerusalem's competitors. This move towards a monopoly of agricultural
production ultimately threatened the autonomy of the towns of the
northern *Negev*. Without essentially changing the commercial and

---

[71] E. Jamieson Drake, *Scribes and Schools in Monarchic Judah* (Duke University diss.,
1988), = *Scribes and Schools in Monarchic Judah: A Socio-Archaeological Approach*
(Sheffield, 1991).

economic foundations of the society in the region, *Jerusalem* was able to establish a network of interdependent relationships within the region that served to secure and support Jerusalem's prosperity and hegemony. However, there are reasons to doubt that the political structures of the region were radically altered. It was not until the last quarter of the eighth century and especially in the second half of the seventh, that *Jerusalem* began to take on some of the trappings of a dominant regional state power.[72] The size of the city of *Jerusalem* began to grow in the closing decades of the eighth century, following on the Assyrian takeover in the north and *Jerusalem* taking its subordinate role on the edge of the Assyrian orbit. However, it was not until Assyria's move against the south at the end of the eighth century, the destruction of *Lachish*, and the Assyrian rationalization of the coastal trade around the oil processing center of *Eqron,* that *Jerusalem* begins to take on both the size and the character of a regional capital. The radically altered political situation in greater *Palestine,* and the need to absorb a considerable influx of refugees to its population transformed *Jerusalem* from a small provincial, agriculturally based regional state, comparable to *Moab* and *Edom* in *Transjordan,* into a stratified society, with a dominant elite[73] (and perhaps a temple supporting a state cult),[74] in the form of a buffer state lying between two major imperial powers: *Egypt* to the South and *Assyria* to the North. These changes, and the radical alteration of the

---

[72] D. Jamieson-Drake, *op.cit.*, 1988, esp. pp.217ff; also E.A. Knauf, "The Migration of the Script and the Formation of the State in South Arabia," *PSAS* 19 (1989), pp.79-91; *idem,* "From History to Interpretation," (forthcoming); Y. Shiloh's discussion ("The Material Culture of Judah and Jerusalem in Iron Age II: Origins and influences," in E. Lipinski, *op.cit.*, pp.113-147), is misleading throughout, based entirely as it is on a biblically determined interpretation of his excavations.

[73] The dissertation of E. Jamieson-Drake (*ibid.*) clearly outlines the archaeological conditions for positing an urban elite in *Jerusalem* no earlier than the late 8th century, the establishment of a bureaucratic center with ties to a priestly and scribal class. He also clearly shows that it is first from this period that we can expect not only the formation of a state bureaucracy but also the formation of schools and the support of literacy that were a necessary prerequisite for the creation of state archives and intellectually oriented literary traditions. It is also from this period that we first find evidence in *Jerusalem* for what might be described as a trade in luxury goods .

[74] Archaeological evidence for a temple or state cult in *Jerusalem* of this time is as yet lacking. Nevertheless, the development of other elite and state structures suggest the existence of such a temple as likely. That it was a temple of Yahweh and destroyed by the Babylonians is possible, though difficult to demonstrate and not wholly free from objection.

political map of *Palestine,* brought—at least for *Jerusalem's* new
elite—considerable growth in wealth and prestige as a component of the
sometimes violent but always precarious role that *Jerusalem* played out
in the course of the following century.[75] This growth in the wealth and
prosperity of its elite, as *Jerusalem* became increasingly involved in the
international politics of trade, ultimately led *Jerusalem* into direct
confrontation with the Assyrian army and its final destruction and
dismemberment by the Babylonians. Attacks by the Assyrians and
Babylonians on *Jerusalem* and the whole of *Judah* and the Northern
Negev destroyed not only *Jerusalem,* but most of its major towns. The
devastation itself brought to southern *Palestine* a physical
impoverishment and economic depression that ravaged the region.
Assyrian and Babylonian military and political policies of administration
systematically destroyed the region's infrastructure and brought about
the collapse of the entire society.

4. *Population Coherence and Proto-Ethnicity*

The process of new settlement during Iron I and II in the highlands
of Cisjordan suggests substantial differences in the origins of the
population. While people of the central highlands originated from the
indigenous Late Bronze highland towns, a drought dislocated portion of
the Palestinian population of the lowlands, indigenous non-sedentary
groups already in the region, transhumant pastoralists from the steppe
and possibly some of the immigrants who had originally come from
coastal *Syria, Anatolia,* and the Aegean, the highland population of the
Judaean ridge was much more homogeneous, not only coming much
later in the Iron Age but deriving primarily from the sedentarization of

---

[75] There is growing speculations about *Jerusalem's* role in the north, with and without
Assyrian support, after *Samaria's* fall. Much of this is fostered by efforts either to
historicize the traditions about Hezekiah and Josiah in II Kings, or to understand Judah's
interests in Israelite traditions as having originated in historical claims on the territory
already in a pre-exilic period. Certainly the Assyrian administration of this province was
neither so direct or thorough as to easily fill the power vacuum left by *Samaria's* fall,
especially in those regions where geography is not conducive to centralized control.
Nevertheless, *Judah's* uneasy subordination to *Assyria's* power in the region hardly leads one
to be entirely convinced that *Assyria* would acquiesce to any expansive ambitions on
Jerusalem's part over what was Assyrian territory.

steppe pastoralists and a trade oriented expansion of agriculture from the *Shephelah*.

The population of the regional states of *Judah* and *Israel* of the period of Assyrian domination is even more, not less diverse. Again, *Judah*'s population under state rule included the indigenous population of the *Shephelah* with roots in the Bronze Age, some admixture from the southern coast of *Philistia*, the mixed population of steppe dwellers, town tradesmen, and Arabs associated with the overland trade of the Northern *Negev*, as well as the long standing indigenous population of the *Jerusalem* saddle and the *Ayyalon* Valley, and the multi-cultural population of *Jerusalem*. *Judah*'s population, however, maintained a greater homogeneity among its people because of its greater isolation and independence from *Assyria*. Nevertheless, the essential city-state structure of its political system maintained an isolation of the population of the capital from the city's expanding *Hinterland* to the South. The growth of population that followed the fall of *Samaria* and *Lachish* undoubtedly increased the separation of *Jerusalem*'s elite from the marginal agriculturalists and shepherds of highland *Judah*.

By the time of or shortly after the building of *Samaria*, the population of the central highlands, in spite of the extreme diversity of its origins, must have been considerably integrated. The lack of dominance of town structures, both the common character and the inter-related economics of an essentially agricultural population, and the general isolation of the core of the population from the international trade routes and other extra-regional influences, all fostered economic integration and political unity in the area. The nature of the political structures of the regionally based state created in *Samaria* suggests that this integration had been already established at the onset of state forms. This early ninth century *Israel* of the central highlands had developed a political, economic, and ethnic coherence comparable to some of the new Iron Age states of the *Transjordan* such as *Aram, Ammon, Moab*, and, in the eighth century, *Edom*. With the expansion of *Samaria* beyond the central hills, the highland state quickly became involved with the long standing indigenous populations of the Phoenician coast, the *Jezreel* and the Transjordan. However, there is little reason to believe that any significant integration of the population resulted, beyond limited relationships related to trade, the military, and the political elite. One can expect little integration of the core of *Israel*'s population with these subject territories that were only temporarily held by *Samaria* in competition with *Tyre, Damascus*, and *Moab*. Nevertheless, the influence of *Israel* and of its competitors on these territories must have been considerable.

The recognition of the distinctiveness of the highland regions of *Israel* and *Judah* from the rest of *Palestine* finds some limited support from West Semitic linguistics. As geography, economics, and the process of sedentarization are the most fundamental factors causing ethnic differentiation in these regions, language is the single most apparent and distinctive ethnic marker. The linguistic differentiations and affiliations of Palestinian languages and dialects of the first millennium are complex. The effects of sedentarization on the formation of the language diffusion of Proto-Semitic into major linguistic communities, reflected in every epigraphic discovery of the Bronze Age in *Syria-Palestine*,[76] continues in the fragmentation of language groups of the first millennium. There have been clarifying attempts to distinguish Biblical Hebrew (with its significant morphological distortion)[77] from the Hebrew of the first millennium B.C., as well as efforts to separate the Hebrew of biblical tradition from the extensive linguistic diversity in the languages of the epigraphic finds.[78] This distinguishes the language of the biblical texts as an artificial literary construct (a *Bildungsprache*) of the Persian Period.[79] Knauf, for example, places the foundations of this literary construct from the destruction of the Judaean state in 586 B.C. He, however, does not see it as the result of a single coherent construction, but one that can be traced from a consonantal text of the middle of the first millennium B.C., with roots in "Judaean." of the eighth–sixth

---

[76] The bibliography is both too large and too diverse to be profitably cited here. Certainly the *Amarna* corpus, with its considerable geographical diversity is most promising. The syntactical study of J.L. Hayes (*Dialectical Variation in the Syntax of Coordination and Subordination in Western Accadian of the El-Amarna Period*, UCLA dissertation, 1984), for example, establishes substantial differences of syntax in the letters from *Gezer, Ashkelon, Amurru* and *Alashiya*. (See the fine summation in *ibid.*, pp.320ff.) complementing the long established differences in the language affected in the letters from *Byblos, Gezer*, and *Jerusalem*.

[77] W. Gross, *Verbform und Funktion: Wayyiqtol für die Gegenwart?*, *Alttestamentliche Studien* 1 (St. Otilien, 1976).

[78] See the very helpful study of E. Ullendorf, *Is Biblical Hebrew a Language?*, *Studies in Semitic Languages and Civilizations*, (Wiesbaden, 1971); and especially that of E.A. Knauf, "War 'Biblisch-Hebräisch' eine Sprache?," *Zeitschrift für Althebräistik* 3 (1990), pp.11-23.

[79] *Ibidem.*

century B.C., to its Massoretic vocalization of the mid-first millennium A.D.[80] Unfortunately, a number of monographs of the 1980's, dealing with West Semitic epigraphic finds but strongly influenced by biblical studies, have brought a great deal of confusion and distortion into the discussion, failing to distinguish not only the geographical provenience of texts from evidence of the language of a given geographical region,[81] but also harmonizing such basic distinctions in Semitic studies as that between a "language." and a "dialect,." in an effort to preserve a close tie between "Israelite." and "Judaean,." as well as an Aramaic orientation of the East Canaanite languages. This is done under the aegis of the leveling assertion of a dialect continuum between "Canaanite." and "Aramaic.."[82] Still others would preserve a biblically derived historiographical perspective of Hebrew as a *Mischsprache* of the monarchic period, with roots in the pre-monarchic period of settlement.[83] Such insouciance in the methodological principles of the field as a whole has led some scholars to preserve without the slightest challenge the often too mechanical and naive processes of an earlier generation's analysis.[84] While I am reluctant to assume a complete

---

[80] *Ibid.*, p.21.

[81] So K.P. Jackson, *The Ammonite Language of the Iron Age, HSM* 27 (Chico, 1983); W.E. Aufrecht, "The Ammorite Language of the Iron Age,." *BASOR* 266 (1987), pp.85-95.

[82] Most notoriously in W.R. Garr, *Dialect Geography of Syria Palestine, 1000-586 B.C.E.* (Philadelphia, 1985); See the devastating review by E.A. Knauf and S. Maani, "On the Phonemes of Fringe Canaanite,." *Ugarit-Forschungen* 19 (1987), pp.91-94.

[83] This seems to be the perception of a wide range of scholars, such as P.K. McCarter, "The Balaam Texts from Deir 'Alla: The First Combination,." *BASOR* 239 (1980), pp.49-60; S.A. Kaufman, "The Aramaic Texts from Deir 'Alla,." *BASOR* 239 (1980), pp.71-74; L. Herr, "The Formal Scripts of Iron Age Transjordan,." *BASOR* 238 (1980), pp.21-34. This analysis becomes almost opaque in B.S.J. Isserlin (."The Israelite Conquest of Canaan: A Comparative Review of the Arguments Applicable,." *PEQ* 115, 1983, pp.85-94) and especially in the article of G.E. Mendenhall, "Ancient Israel's Hyphenated History,." *Palestine in Transition: The Emergence of Ancient Israel*, ed. by D.N. Freedman and D.F. Graf (Sheffield, 1983) pp.91-103.

[84] I am thinking here of J.A. Hackett's methodical but unproductive analysis of the morphology and lexicology of the Deir 'Alla Balaam text (."The Dialect of the Plaster Text from Tell Deir 'Alla,." *Orientalia* 53, 1984, pp.57-65; *idem, The Balaam Text from Deir' Alla, HSM* 31, Chico, 1984), as well as the theologically tendentious statistical analysis of J. Tigay (*You Shall Have No Other Gods: Israelite Religion in the Light of Hebrew Inscriptions, HSS* 31, Atlanta, 1986). One might also refer to the chronological confusion in this field exemplified by the epigraphic studies of L.G. Herr (The Scripts of Ancient

identity of language differentiation with geography and early state forms, the importance of language to the development of ethnicity and "national." identity is paramount. Whatever the limitations of our current analysis of the languages of greater *Palestine* of the first millennium, the function of language in creating the unity and homogeneity of the region's emerging ethnicity cannot easily be dismissed.[85] The conclusions of B. Halpern[86] persuasively encourage us to a sensitivity to geography, topology and sociology in our assessment of our early language groupings. Bearing in mind the *caveat* that the present stage of scholarship in historical linguistics is insufficiently independent of arguments from related disciplines, Knauf's differentiation of the "Canaanite." language family into "West Canaanite." (Phoenician, Israelite, and Judaean) and "East Canaanite." (Ammorite, Moabite, and Edomite) has much to offer.[87] When Knauf's further distinctions between these languages and the literary language of biblical Hebrew,[88] as well as that between a core Canaanite (represented by Phoenician and the dialects of Israelite) and "Fringe Canaanite." (Judaean, Ammorite, Moabite, and Edomite),[89] are maintained, the potential for using epigraphic materials (in support of conclusions drawn independently from historical, economic and geographical arguments) for understanding the development of proto-ethnic groups in *Palestine* of the Assyrian period is substantially enhanced. In this, Knauf's distinctions require that the transition between the proto-ethnic populations of the Assyrian periods Israelite (eighth century) and Judaean (eighth–sixth century) be traced through the biblical Hebrew of Genesis–2 Kings with its roots in eighth–sixth century Judaean to the third century's middle Hebrew of such as

---

Northwest Semitic Seals, Missoula, 1978).

[85] *Contra* D.I. Block, *The Foundations of National Identity: A Study in Ancient Northwest Semitic Perceptions* (University of Liverpool diss., 1981). Throughout this dissertation, and especially in his discussion of genealogies, Block confuses both ideology and aetiology with history.

[86] B. Halpern, "Dialect Distribution in Canaan and the Deir Alla Inscriptions,." *Working With No Data*, ed. by D.M. Golomb (Winona Lake, 1987) pp.119-139; here, p.139.

[87] E.A. Knauf, *op.cit.*, 1990.

[88] *Ibidem.*

[89] E.A. Knauf and S. Maani, *op.cit.*

Qohelet.[90] This remains essentially an historical question, relating directly to issues of the continuity of the population of *Palestine*, which in the course of the Persian period, came to identify itself, not so directly with the Judaeans of the eighth–sixth century as with the nation "Israel." of the composite tradition.

5. *The Destruction of Israel and Judah: Imperial Policies of Population Transportation*

The historical process or trajectory from the proto-ethnic entities of the Assyrian period's *Israel* and *Judah* to that of the Israel of tradition is neither direct nor simple, and cannot adequately be described with the concepts of either continued assimilation or survival. The term "proto-ethnic,." rather than "early ethnic." or the like, is particularly appropriate for these state entities since the historical developments within *Palestine* over nearly four centuries are strongly marked more by population dislocations than by continuity. A unity of the population of the highland state of *Samaria* with the populations of the lowlands and other regions of greater *Palestine* that the kings of *Samaria* attempted to control was never accomplished. *Assyria* intervened decisively and irrevocably, and, as it incorporated the former state of *Israel* into the province of *Samaria*, through which it controlled many of the territories *Israel* had coveted, and subordinated the whole under provincial authority, *Assyria* also systematically destroyed the coherence of the population which had given the region its strength. *Judah*, whose proto-ethnicity lay far more in the relative homogeneity of the population of the Judaean highlands and the Northern *Negev* than it had in the state form imposed on it from *Jerusalem*, fared better. Though it survived the ultimate decapitation of *Jerusalem* by the Babylonian army, it lost with *Jerusalem* both its economic and its historical moorings.

The imperial policies and practices of population control,[91] and specifically the policies of deportation and resettlement introduced by *Assyria*'s army and civil administration, were not uniquely Assyrian. They had formed a central aspect of imperial warfare in ancient *Egypt*,

---

[90] E.A. Knauf, *op.cit.*, 1990, p.21.

[91] S. Timm, *Die Dynastie Omri* (Göttingen, 1982).

Babylon, and the Hittite world since early in the second millennium.[92] They are also found as a pillar of Babylonian and Persian imperial policy long after *Assyria*'s collapse. Under *Assyria*, however, these policies were much more complex and varied, and had immense consequences on subject lands in every corner of the empire. Policies toward subject peoples do not seem to have rested solely on a pragmatic *ad hoc Realpolitik*. They were also based on ideological perspectives related to what might be better understood with the help of the analogy of "Right of Conquest," tempered by theologically based concepts of the royal duties of the king in his role as servant of the God Ashshur. As shepherd of nations and peoples, the Assyrian king's goal was to exemplify mercy, and to bring all peoples of the four corners of the world under the universal authority of Ashshur.[93] Assyrian policy is also based on an ideology that the defeated have no rights. They are rather seen as the booty of the king.[94] While one must emphatically agree with Saggs that 1 Samuel 15 epitomizes the ancient Near Eastern ideology of "Right of Conquest," one must not confuse a form of ethnographic ideology with actual historic polity. The context of Assyrian ideology was centered in the theology of empire, of which the biblical tradition has historical experience only from the perspective of subject.[95] Saggs understanding of the egalitarianism of Assyrian policy in terms of ethnicity needs to be adjusted both by the exploitative character of the

---

[92] W. Helck, *Die Beziehungen Ägyptens zu vorderasien im 3. und 2. Jahrtausend* (Wiesbaden, 1962) esp. pp.359-390; I.J. Gelb, *Prisoners* (Chicago, 1966); and J.B. Pritchard, *ANET, passim*, esp. pp.248, 260f., 303ff., 318 and 530. The following discussion is heavily indebted to the excellent studies of B. Oded (*Mass Deportation and Deportees in the Neo-Assyrian Empire*, Wiesbaden, 1979), S.A. Irvine (*Isaiah, Ahaz, and the Syro-Ephraimitic Crisis, SBLDS* 123, Atlanta, 1990, S. Timm (*op.cit.*), and W.T. Pitard (*Ancient Damascus, A Historical Study of the Syrian City-State from Earliest Times until Its Fall to the Assyrians in 732 B.C.E.*, Winona Lake, 1987).

[93] This ideological perspective is captured by H.W.F. Saggs (."Assyrian Prisoners of War and the Right to Live," *Archiv für Orientforschung* 19, 1982, pp.85-93). The distinction Saggs draws between theory and practice exemplified by biblical texts, however, hardly justifies his contrast between an assumed Israelite ethnocentricity and an Assyrian ambience of pluralism. Rather, Saggs makes a categorical error, confusing the retroactive ideological expression of *Haram* with historical policy.

[94] B. Oded, *op.cit.*, p.28.

[95] One might profitably contrast the ideology of texts such as 1 Samuel 15, which have their referent to a lost past, to such as Ezra 1:2ff, which understand Yahweh as an inclusive universal deity, with referents to the beneficence of empire.

Assyrian administration over the provinces and subject peoples and by the destructive components of its population policies. While in early Egyptian texts, the capture of slaves, the creation of *corvée* labor for Egyptian work projects, military conscription, and a variety of punitive goals, might be seen as significant administrative aims of empire, the economic policies of the Egyptian empire maintained and supported the indigenous social and economic structures of its subject peoples. In *Assyria*, however, the system, especially as organized from the time of Tiglath Pileser III's rule, lay at the very foundation and nature of empire.[96] While the texts, in which many of the decisions related to these policies are recorded, are clearly propagandistic, they are nonetheless also clearly transparent and expressive of Assyrian intentions. The effects of such policies on subject territories follow almost of necessity from the character of the policies and the intensity of their application.

B. Oded, in his extensive study of Assyrian policies of mass deportation, outlines two distinct different patterns in the Assyrian policies of population control: a) Although less than half of the 157 extant Assyrian texts that relate large scale population transference, indicate the area to which the populations are being transferred, some 85% of these are one way deportations to the cities of *Assyria*, especially *Assur, Calah, Nineveh,* and *Dur Sarrukin*[97] b) Other deportations displaced people from one part of the empire and resettled them in other regions from which there had been deportations.[98] They also transferred populations from one area and resettled them in a variety of different locals.[99]

The extent of the deportations is difficult to determine with accuracy. The geographic extent of the regions affected by these policies reached

---

[96] B. Oded, *op.cit.*, p.19.

[97] *Ibid.*, pp.28ff. It is, however, not clear (as Oded points out) that these people were all settled in the central cities themselves.

[98] *Ibid.*, p.29. Oded refers to Tiglath Pileser III's destruction of *Nikkur*, his rebuilding of the city, and his settlement of the city by new people from other conquered territories. Also Sargon II deported people from *Ashdod* and resettled peoples from elsewhere in the empire and from *Arabia*. Sargon also sent deportees from *Hamath* to Assyria and resettled in *Hamath* people from both *Karalla* and *Assyria*.

[99] *Ibid.*, p.30. Oded cites ND 2634 where 6000 prisoners are sent to 105 different settlements. Similarly, people from *Samaria* were deported to *Assyria, Media*, and Northern *Syria*. The region was resettled by groups from Northern *Syria, Babylon, Elam*, and *Arabia*. *ANET*, pp.284, 286 and Ezra 4:1f., 9f.

across the whole of the ancient Near East from *Elam* and the *Persian Gulf* to the *Taurus* mountains and the Phoenician coast, and southwards into *Egypt*. Even limiting our understanding to the texts that have survived, as Oded has in his study, we have clear knowledge of over 150 acts of population transference from the Neo-Assyrian period alone. From Babylonian records we have records of 36 acts of deportation.[100] Moreover, of the 157 known Assyrian period cases, many of them refer to deportations from entire regions such as the texts relating to *Ammuru* and *Judah*. It is impossible to estimate realistically the actual number of people involved in these dislocations. While many of our texts speak of total populations being transported, there are also indications that this is a stereotypical exaggeration. Similarly, in some 13 of the 43 texts in which the population is enumerated, more than 30,000 people are mentioned as affected by each deportation, including the deportation from Babylon of 208,000 people by Sennacherib.[101] However, even discounting such surely impossible numbers, one must consider a figure high in the hundreds of thousands as a reasonable total of all those affected by such Assyrian policies, and a number well exceeding a million has a great deal of evidence to support it.

Oded outlines a number of reasons that influenced the Assyrians in undertaking such an intense transformation of the empire's population structure.[102] The goals of these policies were extremely diverse. Deportation was used as a punishment for resistance or rebellion. It was used to eliminate both actual rivals and the potential for resistance and insurrection. The policies of resettlement established groups within the subject populations who were dependent on and therefore loyal to Assyrian power. Much of the policy was oriented to military conscription, to the control of political leaders and of the intelligentsia, the development of an economic monopoly of craftsmen and skilled laborers, the support of *corvée* labor and the limited slave trade. Some new settlements were created for strategic purposes, including a considerable number of paramilitary border settlements. Some populations were transferred in an effort to restore and rebuild

---

[100] *Ibid.*, esp. pp.19f. 22ff. Oded also notes that *Media* suffered 18 known deportations, *Elam* 13, and *Manna* 12.

[101] *Ibid.*, pp.20f.

[102] *Ibid.*, pp.41ff.

conquered cities, and to repopulate abandoned or empty lands.[103] One might also add the goals of the control and sedentarization of unruly nomads, associated with the support of vassal states. In *Palestine,* one must not only think here of the *Arab* tribal groups who were settled in the region of *Samaria,* but also of Sennacherib's subjugation of Hezekiah, the deportation of the population of "46 of his strong cities,." numbering 200,150 (sic!), and the division of the Judaean *Hinterland* among the kings of *Ashdod, Ekron,* and *Gazza* who, as vassals of *Assyria,* were supported in their struggle against *Jerusalem.*[104] This subjugation of Hezekiah, creating *Jerusalem* as a vassal state of *Assyria* marked a period of reduced political power, but nevertheless an extended time of considerable prosperity for *Jerusalem* that lasts through much of the seventh century.[105] The association of deportation with support of vassal states is also apparent in the campaigns of Tiglath Pileser III (744–727) in northern *Palestine.*[106] While the historical progression of these undated texts is uncertain, the Assyrians were organizing the territories that had formerly belonged to Rezin of *Damascus,* along the northern rim of *Samaria,* including the *Jaulan, Gilead,* and the *Galilee* under the direct control of the empire.[107] S.A. Irvine argues[108] that texts ND 4301 and 4305 (if Hoshea's name can be restored in line 10) not only relate the establishment of the border of *Assyria* along *Bit*

---

[103] *Ibid.,* pp.62ff.

[104] *ANET,* pp.287f.

[105] D. Jamieson-Drake, *Scribes and Schools in Monarchic Judah* (Sheffield, 1991), but especially S.W. Bulbach, *Judah in the Reign of Manasseh as Evidenced in Texts During the Neo-Assyrian Period and in the Archaeology of the Iron Age* (New York U. diss, 1981). Also see M. Broshi, "The Expansion of Jerusalem in the Reigns of Hezekiah and Manasseh,." *IEJ* 24 (1974), pp.21-29. For a limited review of the archaeological data, Y. Shiloh, *Excavations at the City of David I: 1978-1982,* Qedem 19 (Jerusalem, 1984); idem, "The Material Culture of Judah and Jerusalem in the Iron Age II: Origins and Influences,." *The Land of Israel: Crossroads of Civilization,* ed. E. Lipinski (Leuven, 1985); idem, "Judah and Jerusalem in Eighth-Sixth Centuries B.C.E.,." *Recent Excavations in Israel: Studies in Iron Age Archaeology,* ed. by S. Gitin and W.G. Dever (Winona Lake, 1989) pp.97-105.

[106] *ANET,* pp.282-4.

[107] H. Tadmor, "The Southern Border of Aram,." *IEJ* 12 (1962), pp.114-122; S.A. Irvine, *op.cit.,* pp.56-69; for the general context of this discussion, M. Cogan, *Imperialism and Religion: Assyria, Judah and Israel in the 8th and 7th Centuries B.C.E.,* SBLMS 19 (Missoula, 1974).

[108] S.A. Irvine, *op.cit.,* pp.56-62.

Humri's (*Samaria*'s) northern rim and a substantial conflict with *Tyre*, but also the appointment of Hoshea as king of *Samaria* in Pekah's place.[109] However, Irvine here seems to harmonize this too closely with text III R10, 2 that refers to the inclusion of *Aram*'s territories within the border of *Assyria*, and in lines 15–19 reads,

> The Land of Beth Omri...the entirety of his people [together with their possessions] to Assyria I led away. Pekah their king they deposed and Hoshea [for king]-ship over them I appointed.[110]

Lines 1–9 of ND 4301–4305 do not seem to imply that *Bit Humri* is involved in this campaign. The struggle is rather on *Samaria*'s border. Even if line 10 does in fact speak of Hoshea (.".....Hoshea as king over them I set...."), it need not be understood to refer to *Israel*. The context rather suggests that it is the territories of Hiram of *Tyre* over which Hoshea is appointed.[111] *Beth Hazael, Tyre,* and *Bit Humri* obviously share borders. If lines 5–8 of text III R10, 2 do refer to *Gal'aza* and *Abil* [xxx] (=*Abil-Akka*)[112], then not only did the former territory of Rezin of *Damascus* include the *Gilead, Acco,* and most likely much of the *Galilee,* but this text could be read, as it is dated subsequent to ND 4301–4305, to imply that Hoshea, who is appointed as king over *Samaria* in III R10, 2 had previously been given Tyrean territory along the northern border of *Samaria,* i.e. the *Jezreel,*[113] and that with Hoshea's appointment as king of *Samaria, Israel* (for the first time?) gains, with Assyrian support, undisputed claim over the *Jezreel* (with the territories of *Acco,* the *Galilee,* and the *Gilead* lying within *Assyria*'s borders). Certainly, this would supply a context for *Assyria*'s attack on *Samaria,* and the deportation of its people in support of the Assyrian vassal Hoshea.[114] The conjunction of the town of *Samaria,* overthrowing Pekah, and the subsequent betrayal and deportation of the population,

---

[109] *Ibid.*, p.58f.

[110] *Ibid.*, p.63.

[111] One might note here the confusion of the successions from Menahem to Hoshea in 2 Kings 15–17 as well as that Pekah seems to have been the ruler of *Gilead* prior to his rule in *Samaria*.

[112] As H. Tadmor has argued, *op.cit.*

[113] Isaiah 1:4–5.

[114] *Contra* Irvine, *op.cit.*, p.68 who suggests that Tiglath Pileser had not yet invaded Israel.

is in no way at variance with Assyrian policies. It is, however, one of the aspects of siege negotiation. This, of course, is delightfully played out in story form in 2 Kings 18–19's tale of Sennacherib's humiliation by Yahweh. What is interesting here is that the king of *Assyria*'s speech to the people of *Jerusalem* promises that if the people revolt, he will reward them with deportation.

This aspect of Assyrian deportation policy—to create loyalty and support of the population both against rulers opposing Assyrian policy and for Assyrian rule in the conditions of their resettlement—however cynical it may appear and have been, was nevertheless most effective. Deportation is presented in some of our texts not as punitive at all but as an alternative to punishment for resistance against *Assyria*'s power.[115] Indeed, some of our texts go so far as to present the Assyrians as acting on behalf of the people, promoting their interests, and protecting the people, saving them from the oppression of their rulers. The deportees not only received land and prosperity from the Assyrians upon resettlement, but also were given support and protection against the indigenous population, who, of course saw them as intruders and usurpers. Oded summarizes this well:

> ...the exiled communities played a role very similar to that of the Assyrian garrisons stationed in all parts of the Assyrian empire, or to that of Assyrian citizens who were settled in conquered countries either as city dwellers, farmers, or officials. This explains the favorable treatment the deportees generally enjoyed, and the great concern shown by the Assyrian rulers for their welfare.[116]

Even in Assyria's great cities, the deportees served as a dependable influence against unrest or rebellion.[117] Indeed, this was one of the more significant reasons that they were brought to the great Assyrian cities in such large numbers.

---

[115] Again, the story at the walls of *Jerusalem*, captures this brilliantly: "Make peace with me, surrender to me, and every one of you will eat the fruit of his own vine and of his own fig tree, and drink the water of his own cistern until I come to deport you to a country like your own, a land of corn and good wine, a land of bread and vineyards, a land of oil and of honey, so that you may not die but live.

[116] B. Oded, *op.cit.*, p.47.

[117] *Ibid.*, p.48.

The economic and civil importance of resettlement policies to the cities of *Assyria* is well illustrated by the literary text of Ashurnasirpal II, relating to the building of the new capital in *Calah*.[118] The similarities of this account to the text of the Idrimi statue of the fifteenth century King of *Alalakh* are striking, and give witness to both the longevity and the international character of such policies.[119] As Idrimi—styling himself as the "servant of Adad."—had used Hittite prisoners to build his palace at *Alalakh* and had forced the sedentarization of the Suteans to rebuild towns, so Ashurnasirpal II, "the high priest of Ashshur." and "shepherd of all mortals,." not only consolidates his empire through conquests and the taking of hostages, but also in his rebuilding of his capital, transfers the conquered peoples (of whom he claims personal ownership) and resettles them in *Calah*. With their labor, he digs irrigation canals to irrigate and open new agricultural areas and plant orchards in the *Tigris* Valley. He builds for the first time temples to Ninurta and Enlil and rebuilds storehouses and palaces throughout his territory. In summation, he "added land to the land of *Assyria*, many people to its people.."[120]

Imperial policies of population transference or deportation do not end with the collapse of the Assyrian empire in the last quarter of the seventh century. The number of texts available to us, however, from both the Neo-Babylonian and Persian military campaigns, is not only much smaller but also substantially different. Moreover, the ideological *Tendenz* of the few texts we have relating to population transferences is much more clearly propagandistic. Some of the most important are not written for administrative purposes or to gain the support of the army or people of Babylon and Persia, but are rather addressed to the subject peoples, and are written with the transparent purpose of encouraging their acceptance of the radical changes brought about by the changes of empire, first to the Babylonian and then to the Persian administration. Both the Babylonians and the Persians fell heir to an already established Assyrian empire. Their long term goals consequently were far more oriented towards the creation of loyalty and support among the individual subject groups and peoples of their complex empires, than

---

[118] *ANET*, pp.558–560.

[119] For the Idrimi inscription, *ANET*, pp.557f.

[120] *ANET*, pp.275f.

towards conquest. Hence, the propagandistic function of these texts is primary.

Two pairs of stelae, possibly originating in the early Persian period and modeled on Babylonian texts, probably originating in the temple of Sin in *Harran*, recount Nabonidus' construction of the temple.[121] Both present Nabonidus as the obedient servant of Sin, the king of all the Gods who reside in heaven. Nabonidus acts under the direct instruction of Sin to build the temple Ehulkul in *Harran*, to bring about the return of Sin to the city, and to rebuild the past greatness of *Harran*. Nabonidus then claims to have brought people from *Babylon*, Upper *Syria*, and from as far away as the borders of *Egypt* ("all those whom Sin, the king of the gods, had entrusted to me . . . ."), and, after completing the construction brought "Sin, Ningal, Nirsku, and Sadernunna from *Babylon* to *Harran*. In these texts, Nabonidus is presented as returning the God Sin to the provincial city of *Harran* and restoring that city to its former, and hence appropriate, status. While there is no claim that the transported populations, some of whom are from *Babylon*, are returning (his description of them as "entrusted." to him marking them as deportees), both the "renewal." of the Sin cult and the renewal of the city, make it very clear that we are dealing with the creation of a new society, which is ideologically understood as an act of restoration. The texts are addressed not to *Babylon* but to a new society in *Harran*, whose center is the temple of Sin and whose servant is the emperor Nabonidus. In such a text, we gain an entry into how the imperial administration wanted the deportees and the receiving populations to understand the changes enacted: the deportees as the means of restoration, and the indigenous populations as the recipients of benefice, all under the auspices of not a new God, but one who is "truly." and "originally." the god of *Harran*, and the god of the whole world as well.

An earlier "messianic." Babylonian text is found in the *Wadi Brisa* inscription.[122] Here, Nebuchadnezer II (605–562 B.C.) presents himself as restoring the security of *Lebanon*'s villages, freeing the country from "foreign." (i.e., non-Babylonian) oppression. The language is particularly informative. He "led back to their settlements...collected and

---

[121] One pair alleges to be a final testament of Nabonidus' mother (*ANET*, pp.560–562); the other presents itself as the dedicatory stela of the temple by Nabonidus himself (*ANET*, pp.562ff).

[122] *ANET*, p.307.

reinstalled." the people. Here, unequivocally the theme of "return." is
a central ideological concept of the Babylonian policy of deportation and
resettlement. Similarly, the Babylonian chronicle's account of the fall of
Nineveh at the hands of a Babylonian and Mandaean coalition,[123] refers
to the destruction of the city ("into ruin hills") and massive deportation,
as well as some possible resettlement of deportees from *Rusapu*.[124]
Throughout Nabopolassar's campaign against *Assyria*, the Medes and the
Babylonians continued the deportations of both populations and gods.

An interesting shift in imperial ideology can be seen in the
inscription on a basalt stele dated to the reign of Nabonidus.[125] Here
again the Babylonian king is portrayed in the messianic role of restorer
of the gods, and as permitting the return of exiles. But not only is
deportation couched in the language of "resettlement." under the
instruction and guidance of Marduk, but here Babylonian responsibility
for the destruction of Assyrian cults is specifically denied. Rather, blame
for such barbarous deeds is given to their former allies, "the king of the
Manda hordes.." The Babylonians take the high ground as champions of
the population of the former Assyrian empire, restoring the cities and
rebuilding the former temples that Marduk "had put into his
(Niriglissar's) hands. . . ." Among those "resettled" are 2850 prisoners
from *Hume* who are dedicated by the king as temple servants.[126]

Such ideological efforts, however, are perfected by the Persians. The
good Nabonidus, the darling of his mother's piety to Sin, the king of all
gods, the restorer of both religions and populations forgotten during the
deprivations of *Assyria*, is now looked at from the perspective of a much
more effective (i.e., later) propaganda machine, a propaganda that still
largely determines our understanding of Persian imperial policy.[127] The
text of 2 Chron 36:22f and Ezra 1:1–11 identifies the Persian deity *elohe
shamayim*, whom Cyrus "restores," as the long neglected indigenous
Palestinian deity *Yahweh*. Chronicles sees Cyrus as having been given all

---

[123] *ANET*, pp.303-305.

[124] *Ibid.* Here, however, the text is damaged.

[125] *ANET*, p.309.

[126] Tablet IX: *ANET*, p.311.

[127] Here I am transposing an insight originally expressed about biblical tradition by H.W.
Saggs, *op.cit.* The biblical traditions to which Saggs refers are reflections of Persian policy.

the kingdoms of the world by the supreme deity who, in accordance with Jeremiah's prophecies, orders him to *build* his temple in *Jerusalem* (as Nabonidus had built a temple to Sin in *Harran* following his own direct communications from Sin). Ezra ɪ portrays Cyrus as rebuilding the temple and restoring what the Assyrians had taken away. Moreover, Ezra stresses the indigenous character of *Yahweh* as "the God of *Israel*." (So, similarly, Nabonidus' mother).

In the victory account of the destruction of *Babylon* at the hands of the Persians,[128] the Babylonian king, Nabonidus, is described, no longer as the servant of the gods of *Babylon*, but as one who had allowed the festivals and services of the temple to be neglected. Nabonidus is further portrayed as the brutal agent of massacre of his own population. In contrast, Cyrus and Cambyses restored religious rites and were welcomed by the people of *Babylon*. The Persians impose only peace, and the gods all return to their proper places. The most important of the Persian texts, however, that relates to the transferral of populations across the empire, is the Cyrus cylinder.[129] It is propaganda. The now deposed ruler of *Babylon* had destroyed the integrity of religion. Instead of real gods, only replicas were worshipped, and the rituals, offerings, and prayers were all wrong. Even the worship of Marduk was perverted. He ruined the people with constant *corvée* work. Settlements were in ruins, and the whole population "had become like dead . . . ." The gods had been carried off to *Babylon* and now abandoned the city. Marduk, however, in his mercy, searched for an appropriate ruler, and finally called Cyrus, who, after becoming the ruler of the whole world, always tried "to treat according to justice the black headed whom he (Marduk) has made him conquer.." It was because of Cyrus' goodness and upright heart that Marduk had ordered him to march on *Babylon*. Cyrus, of course, who possessed Marduk as his true friend, did not use weapons. He did not need to, but was welcomed as one who had helped the people "come to life from death . . . ." Cyrus is king of *Sumer* and *Akkad* because both the gods and the people want him as their ruler. Cyrus then claims in this text to have abolished *corvée* labor and (interestingly) also credits himself with having rebuilt the slums. Both Cyrus and his often mentioned "many" troops were in *Babylon* on a mission of peace. The whole world welcomed Cyrus' accession to power,

---

[128] *ANET*, pp.306f.

[129] *ANET*, pp.315f.

as he is portrayed as having busied himself in restoring both gods and peoples to their proper places where they can be happy.[130]

The Persian texts present Cyrus as understanding the restoration of peoples and gods as the primary function of empire: a literary if not entirely historical policy that was continued under his successors Xerxes and Darius II.[131] Under Darius, the Persians, in their effort to bring about close administrative control of the empire by Persian officials, who, in their administration, were forced to deal with diverse legal traditions throughout the empire, began to centralize and rationalize the legal and economic structures through which the Persians governed. They did this by enforcing the "king's law." by "the favor of Ahura Mazda." in terms of a "restoration." of the traditional legal customs of the subject peoples. The "Demotic Chronicle." claims that in 519 B.C., Darius ordered the codification of the legal traditions of *Egypt*: "The law of the Pharaoh, of the temples, and of the people.."[132] Following this policy, Persian legal codes were mandated throughout the empire in the form of restorations of indigenous tradition.[133] The Persians were not necessarily creating a form of home rule through these measures. Rather they were creating a tightly structured, centralized administration, interpreted through propaganda as home rule, and using indigenous traditions extensively to curry local support.

The effectiveness of all of these Persian policies of persuasion is perhaps nowhere better illustrated than in the biblical traditions that relate to a return of the exiles from *Babylon*, under the direct order from Cyrus as inspired by Yahweh, with instructions to restore the temple cult of Yahweh in *Jerusalem*. One can also not neglect the law code promulgated under the auspices of the Persian administration by Ezra. The delay in temple construction to a period long postdating Cyrus should not cast doubt on the historicity of the decree itself.[134]

---

[130] My favorite phrase here is the heart-catching, "ducks and doves."

[131] *ANET*, p.317.

[132] L.V. Hensley, *The Official Persian Documents in the Book of Ezra* (University of Liverpool diss., 1977) p.196.

[133] *Ibid.*, p.197.

[134] L.V. Hensley (*op.cit.*) raises substantial form critical arguments for understanding the Ezra "documents." and the decree as authentic. Moreover, a recognition of the documents as essentially administrative acts of public relations, i.e., propaganda, supports rather than undermines their authenticity. That the decrees were not carried out with dispatch, affects

Similarly, the correspondence relating to Artaxerxes and Darius in Ezra 4–6 reflect no more than the administrative difficulties endemic to policies introducing new population elements and central cults into a region and an established population with long standing autonomous functions and associations. The tensions and conflict reflect only some of the unpleasant reactions to be expected of the intrusive nature of Persian relocation policies on the regional populations that had been structured by the prior Assyrian and Babylonian polity. To these people, both the policy of a centralized cult, imposing a legal and economic restructuring under a resurgent *Jerusalem*, would not help but be understood as a threat to the established order, and this is exactly what is protested in the account of Ezra.

---

only our understanding of Persian intentions, not of their declared policies. That the Persian period deportees understood themselves as returning to their land or origin speaks to the effectiveness of such decrees, supporting not negating that effectiveness.

CHAPTER EIGHT

ISRAEL'S TRADITION: THE FORMATION OF ETHNICITY[1]

1. *The Literary Nature and Historicity of the Tradition*

In efforts to reconstruct historically the origins of Israel and its earliest beginnings, questions concerning the historicity of the biblical tradition are of singular importance.[2] That evidence from extrabiblical sources (both from texts and archaeology) are far more supportive of the historicity of an Israel of *Samaria* than the Israel of tradition is both an interesting and significant factor for historical reconstruction, since, from the perspective and ideology of the tradition as a whole, the Israel of *Samaria* is an illegitimate and false "Israel." Indeed, the Israel of tradition is asserted as a self understanding of those who perceive themselves as survivors and as a remnant of Israel based on the affirmation of an historical continuity with the no longer existent state of *Judah*, with a focus on *Jerusalem*. An understanding of the coherence of the biblical tradition, as arising out first within intellectual milieu of the Persian period, causes great difficulty in affirming the historicity of

---

[1] A systematic and comprehensive treatment of the complex relationship between a history of Israel and its traditions goes well beyond the limits of this book, though it is a project that sorely needs doing. Nevertheless, the close relationship between this attempt to reconstruct the prehistory and early origins of Israel and our current understanding of the biblical tradition requires that the issue be addressed. At the risk of considerable redundancy and repetitiveness, I present the following discussion on the complex interrelatedness of the issues of literary genre, historicity, biblical chronology, historiography, historical context and implicit and intentional referents in the following four essays. In their composition, they are largely independent of each other and have their origin in papers that I have written in the course of this book's production. Indeed earlier forms of the last two have been published elsewhere, and the substantial revisions introduced here reflect the changes in my perspective that this work has engendered.

[2] On the issues of historical "origins," esp. M. Liverani, "Le 'Origine' d'Israele progetto irrelizzabile di ricerca etnogetica," *Rivista Biblica Italiana* 28 (1980), pp.9-31.

the Israel of tradition at all, and suggests rather that in dealing with this concept, the perspective of the tradition suggests we are involved with an entity that is both intellectually and literarily an entirely new creation beginning in the late Persian period's transforming revisions and collections of tradition. The recurrent and unifying theme of the composite of tradition that extends from Genesis to 2 Kings, as well as that of its tradition variant in 1–2 Chronicles,[3] is one that needs little introduction. The concept of origin is dominant to the reader of the Bible.[4]

From the point of view of narrative content and narrative theme, the issue of origin, cause or beginnings dominates the biblical narrative from Genesis to 2 Samuel. The central plots of these books and their major parts relate to origin, answering in one way or another how Israel and its world came to be. Genesis itself is a coherent aetiology of how Israel's world, in its political, ethnic and physical aspects, came into existence.[5] Also the great blocks of tradition which we find in Exodus, Numbers and Leviticus collect variations of traditions that play on the theme or relate to: the origin of Israel as a nation, Israel's chosenness by Yahweh, the origin of such central ideological concepts and institutions as the passover, the Torah, the priestly cast, the legendary ark and its sanctuary, and the contract that Israel's God had once forged with Israel at and as its foundation. Deuteronomy reiterates many of these origin themes as it recounts in three great speeches of Moses the terms of Israel's covenant with Yahweh and the legitimacy of their possession of the land of *Canaan*.

Origin traditions, however, do not stop with the Pentateuch though they are most clear and explicit there. Joshua and Judges relate Israel's

---

[3] P. Welten, *Geschichte und Geschichtsdarstellung in den Chronikbüchern*, WMANT 42 (Neukirchen, 1973); H.G.M. Williamson, *Israel in the Book of Chronicles* (Cambridge, 1977).

[4] In this and the following, I am strongly influenced by H. Cancik (*Mythische und Historische Wahrheit*, SBS 48, Stuttgart, 1970; *idem., Grundzüge der Hethitischen und alttestamentlichen Geschichtsschreibung, ADPV*, Wiesbaden, 1976). But see also: H. Schulte, *Die Entstehung der Geschichtsschreibung im Alten Israel*, BZAW 128 (Berlin, 1972); R. Schmitt, *Abschied der Heilsgeschichte?*, Europäische Hochschulschriften 195 (Frankfurt, 1982); J. Van Seters, *In Search of History* (Yale, 1983); A. Lemaire, *Les Écoles et la Formation de la Bible dans l'Ancien Israël*, Orbis Biblicus et Orientalis 39 (Göttingen, 1981); G.W. Trompf, *op.cit.*, and G. Garbini, *History and Ideology in Ancient Israel* (London, 1988).

[5] Th.L. Thompson, *The Origin Tradition of Ancient Israel* I, JSOTS 55 (Sheffield, 1987).

foundation in narratives of conquest and settlement with such clarity of verse that many modern historians are single mindedly attracted to these traditions as it were towards historical memories of a nation's earliest beginnings. This unquestionably concurs with the biblical tradition's own themes and intentionality; for it is in these stories that Israel's foundation as a nation in possession of its land and the orientation of its ethnic and tribal relationships at the very foundation of its emerging politics are formed. It is in the books of Samuel that these themes are brought to maturity in the traditions about the origin of the ill fated monarchy and the survival of Israel's self understanding as a nation under God: an account indeed of the origin of its own destruction, whose history is so inexorably related in the books of 1 and 2 Kings.

The order of the progression of the greater tradition, however, is not so closely thematic and logical. In a continuous reading, one frequently notes a lack of continuity in narration. A significant dissonance is also marked at the junctures of the great blocks of tradition that make up the story of Israel's origins. Most noticeably are those awkward bridges between the traditions of the patriarchs and that of Joseph and especially between the Joseph narrative and the story of Israel's enslavement in *Egypt*.[6] Such dissonance is also clearly and jarringly apparent in the transition from the story of the origin of the Torah in Exodus 16–23 and the several variable add on traditions of the extended wandering stories that follow in the narrations of Exodus and Numbers. The essential independence of Leviticus and Deuteronomy is a hallmark of the documentary hypothesis.[7] A similar dissonance of plot and theme can be noticed in the transition from Joshua to Judges and then to Samuel. This disorientation of narrative plot and theme are not simply evidence that we are dealing with a complex of several traditions. That is evident enough on other grounds and need not be argued at this point. It has been argued already with great justification[8] that these clear breaks in the tradition make it exceedingly difficult to assume or support the assumption of continuous strands of pre-existent traditions that bridge such gaps, as the traditional understanding of the documentary hypothesis has done. Indeed one might well argue that the

---

[6] R. Rendtorff, *Das überlieferungsgeschichtliche Problem des Pentateuch*, BZAW 147 (Berlin, 1977).

[7] J. Wellhausen, *Prolegomena zur Geschichte Israels* (Halle, 1886).

[8] Most notably by R. Rendtdorff, *op.cit.;* also Th.L. Thompson, *op.cit.,* 1987.

creation of just such bridges of continuity has been the primary function of this literary theory that has influenced scholars now for more than a century; for the tradition alone does not render such continuity.

There is also a more direct conclusion to be drawn from our observation of such breaks in the narrative development: The formation of the pentateuch and the narrative development beyond the pentateuch down to the end of 2 Kings has a unity which is not and cannot be assumed to be based on either coherent plot development or expansion of narrative theme as has been maintained both by supporters of the documentary hypothesis and by anti-Wellhausen critics who assert a unity of the pentateuchal narrative.[9] Rather, the coherence of the pentateuch and of the so-called deuteronomistic accounts leading up to the narration of 2 Kings is based neither on plot development nor on theme. The order of progression in these narrative traditions is rather much more simply, and one might say, expectedly, an aspect of their association within a collection from the perspective of antiquarians and traditionists of a time no earlier than the Persian period, and possibly as late as the Hellenistic period.[10] That is, the association of successive literary units renders a perception of chronology whether or not that chronology is intrinsic to the work as collected. This is an order and a

---

[9] As e.g., N. Whybray, *The Making of the Pentateuch, JSOTS* 54 (Sheffield, 1987).

[10] N.P. Lemche (*The Canaanites and Their Land*, Sheffield, 1991) makes a very strong case for looking to the Hellenistic period as the central period of formation of the Hebrew bible. Certainly, sound methodology requires that we must look to the mid-second-century as the earliest possible date for the extant form of the pentateuch (Th.L. Thompson, *op.cit.*, 1974, p.10), and such a late date is confirmed by the variant chronologies of the LXX and the Samaritan Pentateuch. Indeed, the formation of the Hebrew Bible and the LXX may well be coterminal. Certainly, the reference to a collection of books in 2 Maccabees 2:14 is to be preferred to the legend referred to in 2 Maccabees 2:13, if for no other reason than that 2:14 refers to the collection of 2:13 having been lost in the wars. However, in this we are dealing with a *terminus ad quem*. For a *terminus a quo*, our earliest possible date for the onset of the process of tradition collection must be placed with the formation of the Jewish people and their identification of themselves as "Israel"; that is, hardly earlier than the construction of the temple, whenever that occurred. My Persian period date stands or falls with the dating of Ezra 4, 5 and 7. The issue of Greek influence does not, however, lock us into the Hellenistic period. Not only do we know precious little about late Persian period literature, but *Palestine*, on the Mediterranean fringe of the Persian world, comes into contact with the Aegean world at least from the onset of hostilities between the Greek city-states and *Persia*. The extreme parameters of our chronology then might be seen to lie between the mid-fifth to the mid-second centuries and, methodologically, we must argue from the known late date to possible early dates.

structure, however, which the biblical redaction has drawn from the tradition itself. The pentateuch is dominated at its outset by the genealogical framework of an aetiology that comprises the whole of Genesis as *Toledoth*." Building its chronological progression on that structure, the "pentateuchal–deuteronomistic" tradition moves forward by means of the succession of great leaders. Adam, Cain, Noah, Abraham, Jacob, Joseph, Moses, Joshua, and the succession of judges from Judah to Samuel succeeded by Saul, David and Solomon, and continuing through 2 Kings by means of a harmony of dynastic lists or traditions.

This hero oriented historiographic progression is of its very essence a secondary, imposed structure that orders, interprets and gives meaning to the successive narratives of the tradition. By collecting traditions about each hero in turn, discrete narratives of mixed origin, context and theme are brought together within what becomes implicitly a chronological framework that makes them both contingent and consecutive: relationships which do not pertain apart from this secondary context. Similarly, this progressive order results in a tradition that is presented through a series of thematic duplication and parallelism as tradition variants collect around individual heroes, or, having been associated with different heroes, find themselves at home in discrete stages of Israel's origin. Yet other narrative variants expand the tradition as they become harmonized through a developing perception of periods or stages in Israel's past. Some of the more obvious are: the time of the patriarchs, the enslavement in *Egypt*, the Exodus, the wandering in the wilderness and the giving of the law, the entrance into the land, the conquest and settlement, the succession of judges, the wars with the Philistines, the rise of the United Monarchy and the wars of succession.

However, chronological ordering does not itself create historiography, which rather relates to the intentions of narrators and redactors. The reading of the text as a progressive narration makes it even clearer that these developing external structures are wholly secondary, most frequently the result of placement alone and only occasionally altering the narration itself. A given narrative unit's placement within the succession, and its order within a perceived reference in time, are for the most part adamantly irrelevant to the structures of plot and theme that belong integrally to the traditions that are collected. Rather, one finds

---

" Th.L. Thompson, *op.cit.*, 1987, pp.167–172.

that the received text proceeds on two levels of narration: one on the level of the unit itself, and the other on the level of redaction. Any effort of the reader to integrate these two distinct acts of narration either destroys the integrity of the plot line independently supported in successive narrative units, or creates narrative discord in the redactive narration. This characteristic of the tradition is so marked in some parts of our text that one must seriously doubt whether they were ever intended to be read as an integrated whole.[12] Again one is driven to the necessity of distinguishing this process of tradition collection from forms of historiography.[13]

One of the results of the imposition of this secondary structure on the origin traditions is a thematic displacement of some of our narratives that, in their present chronological context, may at first appear dislocated. So, for example, Genesis 17, with its narrative discussion of circumcision, and Exodus 12, with its instructions regarding passover, relate aetiologies of basic social customs. They introduce themes which are otherwise at home in the "wilderness" traditions. Their present place in the tradition is derived from their editorial placement: Genesis 17 as a pivotal and interpretive narrative in the "biography" of Abraham, and Exodus 12 within the aetiological context of the Exodus narrative. Similarly, stories with conquest themes are found in traditions apart from the collective conquest structures of Joshua and Judges. Most notable are the stories of the destruction of *Shechem* in Genesis 35 and of the Amalekites in Exodus 18. These have attained their canonical positions because of their association with the patriarchs and Moses respectively. One might also suspect a similar disorientation in the story of the conquest of Og and Bashan in Numbers (given its received context within the wilderness wanderings) consequent upon the inclusion of Deuteronomy and the geographically oriented stories about the preparations for the conquest of *Palestine* in the editorial transition from wilderness to conquest traditions.

This imposition of the structures of successive heroes and successive originating periods has not been thorough nor has it been consistent. Most jarring is the entirely incoherent placement of the patriarch Judah

---

[12] Two of the clearest examples of this are found in Genesis 18-21 and Exodus 3-6.

[13] Here, one might profitably compare these difficulties in biblical tradition with Philo of Byblos: H.W. Attridge and R.A. Oden, *Philo of Byblos: The Phoenician History, CBQMS* 9 (Washington, 1981).

as the first of the judges and the story of the conquest of his homeland with the help of his brothers. Not so jarring, but nonetheless significant, is the role that Joshua plays in the wilderness narratives of Exodus and Numbers prior to his succession to Moses's role of leadership. In this example, harmony has been facilitated by Joshua's role in the Torah theophanies. Similar disorientation of narrative, where the necessary harmonizations have not been wholly successful, are found where the themes of conquest, of the wars against the Philistines, and of succession are ordered within the periodical framework of the conquest, the judges and the monarchy.

Such difficulties of narration are not surprising when one considers the immensity of the collectors' task. They sought not only to order the traditions as successive events understood as the past of the people of the whole of "Israel" unified under one leader, they also sought to include in that succession of events numerous variant accounts of similar or comparable traditions. The range of such variant traditions is very great. All, of necessity, interfere with the perception of narrative succession:

A) *Tale Variants.* Many individual tales demonstrate the existence of minor variations of pre-existent, multiple recountings, reflected in variant endings, motifs or episodes within the received tale. So, for example, such interesting discrepancies as the use of the divine name Yahweh in an aetiology of the name Ishmael in Genesis 21 might well be explained on the supposition of multiple tale variants. When the variant readings are as extensive as we find in the flood story of Genesis 6–9, the existence of story variants is virtually certain and observable in detail. Similar observations can be made of such extended narratives as the Jacob-Esau conflict story when one notices the striking variant reasons for Jacob's departure from home. In this narrative, it is apparent that the variant telling of the story departs significantly from the mainline story. The mainline story has Esau seeking to murder Jacob. The variant has Jacob sent away by his parents to find the "proper" wife. Similar but less radical divergences are also found in the narration of Jacob's return, where three or more variations of telling are discernible. I would classify these anomalies of narration as story or tale variants, because it seems apparent that the ancient collector or redactor saw them as related to each other and basically as telling the same tale, and the collector or the composite tradition presented them in the form of a single tale with variant possibilities of recital.

B) *Functional Variants.* A second form of narrative variant is indicated where separable and distinct narrations are understood by the tradition as comparable, with the result that they are narrated successively in the tradition and given a functionally equivalent role in the greater narrative. Two very clear examples of this type are: The conjunction of the Tower of Babel story with the Shem, Ham and Japheth genealogy[14] as two distinct narrations, fulfilling the same tradition function: the aetiology of human society's spread over the earth. The second example is the conjunction of five distinct genealogies or genealogical type lists of Esau in Genesis 36:9–43. Functional variants are extremely common in biblical literature, and particularly apparent in Genesis. The relationship between such variant narratives reflects editorial techniques rather than the origin or the original signification of the discrete tales in question. Prior to this secondary context they must be assumed to have been unrelated.

C) *Tradition variants.* A third form of variant might be best referred to as a tradition variant. This type is comparable to the tale variants discussed above, in that the respective variant units of the tradition reflect a relationship that is essential and indigenous to the tradition formation. Here we encounter tellings of intrinsically the same traditions. They are distinct from type A) in that here there is no apparent awareness, in both their transmission and development, that any greater relationship exists between the variants than that of a functional equivalency. Most striking are the variants of the Torah theophanies within Exodus 19–40 and Numbers, as well as those variants associated with each other through inclusion at a tertiary level such as the "cultic" and "legal" collections of Leviticus and Deuteronomy.[15]

D) *Variant Traditions.* To be sharply distinguished from tradition variants (in which a common traditional core can be discerned) are those extremely important cases of variant traditions which result from pseudo-historiographical assumptions, whereby a narrative account comes to be understood as an account of distinct events or as a chronologically arranged series of events. From a literary point of view these are not at all, properly speaking, variants. Rather they are quite distinctly separate

---

[14] Already transposed from a four-part genealogical story by its inclusion in the chain of narration linking the Noah story with that of Abraham.

[15] One might also understand the relationship between Genesis-2 Kings and 1-2 Chronicles in this manner.

narratives and traditions of narratives. However, they relate what is commonly understood by both the ancient and the modern audience as recurrent events, and can even encourage belief—both ancient and modern—in recurrence as a pattern of historical event brought about by the influence of the god(s). Such varieties of tradition have unfortunately attracted the interest of historians of Israel as they offer immediate access to questions of historicity. The variations can be quite minor or may involve great complex traditions. We might understand the variety of conquest traditions in this light, especially the great contrast overemphasized by historians between Joshua 1–12 and Judges 1. This is also an appropriate classification for the variety of traditions relating to Moses's origin and his rise to prominence in emergent Israel. Certainly such a classification can be most helpful in analyzing the many interesting historiographical and historiographical like accounts such as the conquest of *Jerusalem,* of which we have at least three wholly separate traditions: the conquest by Joshua in Joshua 12:13; that by the patriarch Judah in Judges 1, and the magnificent tale of the conquest of *Jerusalem* by David, which itself has a multiple of variants. The editorial techniques involved in the inclusion of such multiple tales relate to redactional efforts to create a moderately coherent whole. This, of course, is perceived both in its later stages of development and in its final form as an historiographical tradition recounting distinct events.

E) *Motif and Episode Variants.* A fifth form of narration variant is indicated in those independent narratives in which one finds a common use of traditional motifs and episodes, as well as in tale types that reflect divergent or variant forms of narration. For example, a motif of the Exodus wandering narrative is that Israel is guided by a pillar of fire by night and a cloud by day. However, in the story of Israel's crossing of the *Red Sea,* the pillar of cloud is used no longer as a guide but as a protection. It moves behind Israel, and hides Israel from the Egyptians. A further variant of this motif is found when, once the ark and the tent of meeting are built, the pillar of cloud is used as a sign of Yahweh's presence in the camp. All of the variant functions and significations of this motif do not adhere to each of the tales in which the motif is found. Variants of traditional episodes have been frequently noted by various scholars, and reflect a story telling technique whereby commonly narrated episodes in a wide variety of stories are recited on the basis of a stock or traditional pattern. Among the best known of the traditional episodes in biblical narrative are the heroic birth pattern, the sending of a messenger and the call of the prophet or savior.[16]

F) *Variant Stories.* Different narrations sharing a common story structure, but not belonging to the same tale type, are much more difficult to identify, and such identifications are frequently open to serious debate. Perhaps the most striking variants of this sort are the variants of Genesis 19 and Judges 19 or the Judah-Tamar story and the Book of Ruth. This type of variation must not be confused with variations of narration of a single narrative, such as the two stories of the flood, in which variations are on the level of motif and theme. It is also to be distinguished from traditional episodes and motif variants of a thematic nature, such as the classical "success of the unpromising" variations. There is no evidence of awareness in the use of such variations. The doubling is on the level of story narration. Technique and the raw materials of narration are at issue rather than the level of intentionality, meaning and purpose of narration. There are some examples where variants of several kinds becomes conscious and explicit and the variation itself functions as an element of plot in the narration. Clear examples of this are the use of the famine motif as a cause of a hero wandering in Genesis 12 and 20 (An unreflective, merely technical variant of this same motif can be found in Ruth 1.). Here it is abundantly clear that the differences in the use of this motif lie on the level of awareness and intentionality. Another example of a conscious use of a variant motif is the motif of Israel's crossing of the sea in Exodus 14 and of the *Jordan* in Joshua 2.

G) *Repetitions.* Text repetitions have a wide spectrum and are a form of variant that has long been recognized as most important for an understanding of tradition development. There are at least six significant types of repetitions: a) word for word copying of one narration by another or of a common source by both; b) a summary repetition of an earlier tradition; c) expansions; d) quotations; e) summary references (Og in Joshua); and f) broad allusions to the real or literary world outside our specific narration.

a) Examples of rote repetition are Joshua 13:16's repetition of Joshua 13:9, or the endless repetitions in 1–2 Kings. Even when the repetition is exact, such duplications by rote are true variants, which might properly be classified as functional variants. In every example, the narrative

---

[16] D. Irvin, *Mytharion, AOAT* 32 (Neukirchen, 1978).

context is significantly altered. In Joshua 13, the grammatical context differs. In examples of such, at times seemingly mindless repetitions, one must exercise caution in interpretation. Each example must be understood in its own context and syntax. A direct relationship to its variant is perhaps unnecessary as both may draw from other sources. Such texts give us an important entrance into questions of spontaneity and originality of narration.

b) Paraphrase or summary repetitions share many of the characteristics of rote repetition. One may, however, ask more directly after the cause or motive of the summation. A good example of a summation variant is the narration of the conquest of *Transjordan* in Numbers and Deuteronomy. An ever recurrent difficulty in the interpretation of paraphrase or summary variants regards the uncertainty that the summation is based on the particular text we assume as referent. Most instructive in this regard is Exodus 15's paraphrase in song of the prose tradition of Exodus 14's crossing of the Red Sea. The summary referent to the Eden story of Ezekiel 28:13-19, on the other hand, indicates a rather significant tradition variant of the garden story as its referent rather than the story we find in Genesis.

c) While a paraphrase or summation variant retells a story in a reduced or altered form, there are often many indications that allow us to judge whether we are dealing with the same or substantially altered narrative. In Expansion variants, the narrative adds new detail, motifs, and themes. Genealogical expansions and minor motifs added to a tradition by attraction are certainly the most common examples of this form of variant. Particular examples of expansion variants are Genesis 4 (Tubal Cain) and Genesis 6:1-4. It is always a great temptation in biblical scholarship, which has so many unanswered and unanswerable historical questions, to interpret such structurally and editorially motivated variations within a chronological or ideological framework of interpretation, leading to judgments of redaction, which, however logical, may not be and are rarely warranted historically.

d) Quotations in narratives should be considered as a type of doubling variant, if for no other reason than that the new context in which a quotation is used can significantly alter its meaning. There are a wide variety of quotations, many of which are specifically cited, such as the quotes from a decree of Cyrus in 2 Chronicles 36:23, Ezra 1:2-4, or the letter to Darius in Ezra 5:7-15. Such cited quotations and analogous citations as we find, for example, to the Book of Jashar in

Joshua 10:13 or from the Book of the Wars of Yahweh in Numbers 21:14 need to be critically evaluated within the context of a spectrum of citations and quotation referents that would include the literary motif of pseudo-verification which is a hallmark of both ancient historiography and folktale, functioning at times as an intentional argument of historicity within the narration and at times as a fictional contextualization or even as a comic closure. Many quotations are self conscious attributions of the meaning of the quotation to the specific narrative in which it is used. Such is clearly the case of the citation of Genesis 2 ("This is the bone of my bone," etc.). The use of most poems and proverbs within the prose narrative traditions have a basis in such quotations; they are not compositions original to their present context, and provide us with a major avenue into the greater literary world of our texts.

e) A fifth form of repetitive use of traditions is by way of reference. Examples abound in which earlier traditions and earlier passages within the same tradition are referred to. References are made to both texts and to past events of significance. The pentateuch, Joshua and Judges frequently refer back to characters, events, and interpretations of the "past" tradition. However, references are also often made to narratives and traditions which are nowhere found in the received biblical narratives such as, "You carried me on eagles' wings," suggesting to a modern reader, a reference perhaps to Inanna, but nothing we know in Hebrew literature. Similarly, Deuteronomy 26:5's reference, "A wandering Aramaean was my father and he went down into *Egypt*" likely refers to a variant or lost tradition rather than the received traditions of Genesis, in contrast, for instance to Sirach 44:21's citation of the extant patriarchal traditions. Other references, though relating to a known and recognizable tradition, make reference not to the specific narration we have, but to a variant of the received tradition. So Joshua 14:9 refers to the story of Caleb's faithfulness recounted in Numbers, and, in doing so, quotes a promise given to him by Moses. Although substantially similar to the statement of Moses narrated in Numbers 14:24, the words of Joshua 14:9 clearly do not represent a paraphrase of that text but a direct quote of an unknown variant of Moses's promise to Caleb.

f) Finally, broad allusions to past tradition are closely related to the clearer and more direct quotations and references discussed above. Given the limited quantity of narrative that has survived in the received tradition and the large amount of written tradition alone that has obviously been lost, the scholarly identification of allusions is frequently partial and sometimes misleading. For example, allusions to "The God of our-your fathers" is not to be taken as necessarily a referent to the "god of Abraham" or even "the god of Abraham, Isaac, and Jacob," but may also and sometimes clearly refer to the god of other fathers than the three great patriarchs of the canonical tradition, as in Joshua 24:14. Similar critical evaluations need to be made regarding the multivariant references to a variety of promises and covenants referred to in both the prophetic and narrative traditions. Evidence is needed before we can identify the specific reference made. One also occasionally finds intentionally hidden or "secret" allusions as in Genesis 14:14's reference to 318 fighting men as a play on the enigmatic Genesis 15:2's Eliezer, and in the Isaac puns of Genesis 18 and 20.

This brief summary of the literary and narrative techniques involved in the formation and composition of Genesis—2 Kings relates directly to the conclusions of Chapter 3 above that questions oriented to the historicity of biblical tradition are fundamentally dysfunctional in the effort of modern scholarship to develop a positive reconstruction of Israel's historical origins. First of all, questions of historicity have a strong negative *Tendenz*; that is, answers to such questions of historicity are often most clearly and satisfactorily answered when that answer is negative. Moreover, even such negative answers are rarely decisive, but relate to the lack of or inadequate evidence for affirming historicity.[7] The development of independent analyses of biblical tradition within the context of ancient Near Eastern, and especially Persian and Hellenistic composite tradition and the reconstruction of a history of Israel within the context of the historical geography of greater *Palestine,* offers the hope of limiting both questions of historicity and efforts at synthesizing biblical and extrabiblical materials to what may be truly viable and historically warranted. On the basis of the present state of research, much of the secondary and redactive framework of biblical narrative tradition can be expected to fail any rigorous test of historicity. However, this cannot be said of many of the units of traditions that have been structured by the redactive process of tradition formation. Indeed, when some of them are clearly separated from the fictive contexts within which they are imbedded, and when issues of both ancient historiography and

---

[7] So Th.L. Thompson, *The Historicity of the Patriarchal Narratives, BZAW* 133 (Berlin, 1974).

the quality of historical referents are considered, their historicality and historicity can often be demonstrably shown as plausible and likely. Dynastic lists and some genealogical narratives particularly stand out, as do many texts which are strongly marked as tendentious and propagandistic, or may be recognized as transparent forgeries. Moreover, many laws, cultic and ritual regulations, prophetic poems, songs and wisdom sayings relate realistically to a potentially reconstructible past. The historical value of such materials, however, is extremely limited, unless we first have an independent understanding of the manner in which tradition has preserved the refractions of the past that it transmits, as well as of the historicality of the extremely diverse referents and historical contexts in which these traditions were formed and preserved as meaningful. The task proposed is difficult, but hardly impossible.

2. Biblical Chronology

The general acceptance and assumption of the existence in the bible of a coherent chronological system of the bible as a whole, that could be associated with the absolute chronologies of historians, has had a history since as early as the late Hellenistic and Greco-Roman periods and has been followed in its many variants that have their origins in the numerous text recensions of the Bible in late antiquity.[18] This historiographically based distortion has continued with a variety of attempts at critical revision into modern times, and continues to influence both our understanding of Israel's history and the external chronologies of Palestinian archaeology and of extrabiblical texts. However, in spite of the many chronologically amenable elements and motifs in the traditions, no system of chronology as such is intrinsic to the narrations, and the earliest efforts imposed on the tradition as a whole, such as that used in the massoretic traditions, are demonstrably late, and might reasonably be judged to be secondary.[19] The perception of a linearly based progression of narrated events rests on the sequential demands of narration, and the understanding that this is a chronological and potentially coherent progression has been created by the received tradition's harmonization of the succession of heroes and great leaders

---

[18] See the discussion in Th.L. Thompson, *ibid.*

[19] *Ibidem.*

with the succession of epochal events that had independently established a progressive order out of originally independent biblical traditions.

This perception of a comprehensive internal chronology of the traditions has also undergone serious modification, especially since the nineteenth-century. The development of a tradition of historical criticism with its interests in sources, forms, redaction and tradition history, has systematically undermined most attempts to date traditions to the time of their referents to a potential external history, but rather has sought to place them in originative contexts appropriate either to the times of their literary authorship (especially the history of J-E-D and 2 Isaiah) or to a period ideologically consonant with their times and perspectives (one must think here above all of the traditions and redactions associated with concepts of a deuteronomistic reform and of "post exilic" priestly interests). These results of historical criticism have been extremely fragile. Although scholarly traditions stemming from Albright and Alt have sought confirmation of the historiographical referents of various aspects of the biblical tradition through archaeology and extrabiblical texts (particularly in their efforts to establish the historicity of the periods of the patriarchs, the conquest and the judges), their failure in this has not led to an affirmation of the results of source and redaction criticism or any of the aspects of tradition history. It has rather clarified the extent to which the traditional methods of historical criticism have been dependent on internal circular argumentation, rooted in a view of Israelite history and society that was fundamentally dependent on biblical historiography's view of Israel's past.

The development of historical-critical scholarship on issues of chronology has proceeded from significantly false premises. For example, the assumption that traditions that are redactive or secondary must have an originating context that is substantially later than those which are redacted or expanded, is persuasive only on the basis of an assumption that the literary traditions we have were the essential and critical media of transmission in history. Such an assumption, however, is difficult to confirm. This historical-critical tradition of scholarship is furthermore based on the false assumption that we are dealing with a tradition that was in the process of an ever increasingly coherent transformation, and had at its base a centralizing, univocal perception; that is an ideology. Such assumptions are not obvious in the received tradition. The demonstrable collective or envelope nature of the literary structure of our biblical books such as the Toledoth structure of Genesis and the

farewell speeches of Deuteronomy's Moses, or even the linearly
developed moral lessons of 1–2 Kings and the genre dominated
collections of Leviticus, Judges, Wisdom, and the Psalms (let alone such
incoherent complexes of tradition that we find for example in Exodus
3–9, Qohelet and Job) betray a motivation that is not so much
ideological as it is antiquarian in nature. The rationalistic assumptions
inherent in redaction criticism are misleading in their belief that we can
recreate the historical motivations that led to the formation and
transformation of traditions without the benefit of any independent
history in the context of which they can be judged. Not only are we
increasingly aware of the immense discrepancies that exist in any
correspondence of biblical historiography with the little known history
of *Palestine*, but we can affirm only a skeleton of both a "pre-exilic" or
a "post exilic" period in any history of ancient Israel. Indeed, the very
existence of an "exilic" period and its relationship to either of the
aforementioned is open to very serious challenge. What we do know is
that our understanding of these so-called periods rests in concepts
indispensibly and intrinsically dependent upon the composite of received
tradition that holds the "exile" as a central creative concept. This central
theological concept is a cardinal perception that does much to explain
the current scholarly historiography that continues to inform the
continuities assumed of the narratives when they are perceived as a
whole. Yet, we have always known that the transmission of the traditions
as a whole is very late.

The methodologies of tradition history and redaction history are also
fatally flawed in their dependence on a wholly inadequate data base.[20]
To the extent that most of the received traditions have roots in the early
Persian, Neo-Babylonian, or Assyrian periods,[21] they are based on the
prior existence of written or folk traditions, however accurate we may
judge them historically and whatever precision we use to define them. To
the extent that these tradition were oral, our written traditions reflect
only what must be a totally inadequate representation of such traditions,
if our purpose is to reconstruct anything of their originative historical
contexts. Unfortunately, we do not have the ability to determine the
degree of transformation that such oral traditions underwent in their

---

[20] Th.L. Thompson, *op.cit.,* 1987, pp.49ff.

[21] E. Knauf, (*Ismael, ADPV,* Wiesbaden, 1989) has raised very serious arguments in favor
of seeing this as likely—at least for some of the traditions.

procession towards a written form.[22] If these sources had been originally written,[23] we must ever remain uncertain about the extent to which they have been transformed by their present context within the received works. That the tradition is capable of accepting such literary or oral elements without radical or ideologically motivated transformation is strongly suggested, not only by the inclusion of geographical lists, collections of legal texts and the survival of narrative segments that only have significance within an Assyrian period context, but also by the larger tradition's acceptance of so many ideologically conflicting narrations and traditions without significant ideological revision or harmonization. Some of the most striking of these we find in the so-called deuteronomistic revision of Genesis and in the final reconstructions of Job. Certainly one must reflect on the survival of Deuteronomy 32, Leviticus 16 or Qohelet 1–6, as well as that remarkable collection of narratives found in Genesis 1–11.

Some conclusions do follow from such observations. Howevermuch ideology may have played a role in the formation of individual traditions and texts, ideology does not seem to have been the sole or dominant, motivating factor in the formation of the tradition as a whole. While one might see a quantitative dominance of one or other perspective within successive traditions, the final texts of especially the larger of the biblical books represents a variety of significantly variant and adamantly conflicting ideologies and theologies. One does well to doubt any assumed ideological or theological superiority of the collective embrace represented by the final redactions or by the tradition "as a whole." The pluralism of our text is so obvious that one must entertain, at least as a question, the possibility that the collectors of the tradition were indeed aware of the multiple significations of the traditions they collected. This line of argument opens us to further observations. The first is axiomatic. Intrinsic to the publication in written form of any specific portion of the biblical tradition as a significant whole is the necessity that the components of that tradition unit existed contemporaneously (whether written or oral) and commanded significance. That is, the traditions

---

[22] Th.L. Thompson, *op.cit.*, 1987, pp.41–48.

[23] Here one must not only think of partially corroborated, dynastic lists, but also the various references to such written sources as the Book of the Wars of Yahweh, the Book of the Acts of Solomon, and the like which are analogous to the extant "Book of the Toledoth of Adam" of Genesis 5.

collected by the larger redactive frameworks, whether of the pentateuch, the so-called deuteronomistic history, the prophetic books or any of the works collected in "The Writings," had meaning for their collectors, even if such value and significance be limited to that of tradition past.

One is driven to raise the question seriously whether this kind of writing in the period of the formation of the greater tradition had in a key way a creative function, or whether the primary function of writing was that of transmission. This issue is basic to our understanding of the received tradition. Why—for what purpose or function—were such texts written? The answer to this question may not be singular or univocal for most of the traditions. This, however, compounds both the complexity and importance of our answer. The difficulty of the question is further exposed when we ask simply and directly whether the texts were written to be read. As soon as the question is asked, the obvious answer evaporates and we begin to reflect upon the specific written biblical traditions to which the question is addressed. An understanding of hundreds of the anomalies in the tradition that have created the point of departure for modern historical criticism is at stake. Who today would venture to assert without substantial qualification that Genesis 6–9, Exodus 3–9, Exodus 14–15 or 19–40, Leviticus, Ezekiel or the book of Wisdom were ever readable? This is significant; for if they were not (and we refer here only to a few of the more obvious among the myriad of anomalies—and few can be explained away by the nodding of a Homer) then we must ask anew: why not? Certainly the domaine assumption of a creative ideologically motivated authorship of these written traditions is woefully inadequate. Certainly the concept of a biblical view of history, within which individual biblical traditions render signification, is patently absurd. Moreover, any question which addresses the significance of these traditions for reconstructing a history of the Israelite people, must address the manifest redirections of that tradition, and cannot be satisfied with any reconstruction that does not take these transformations seriously, for not a single historiographical assertion of consequence within the tradition remains coherent or univocal in any of our extant texts.

If one accepts such anomalies as an essential key to a critical understanding of the formation of the biblical tradition, explanations such as Garbini's of a dominant monotheistic ideology of "the tradition as a whole," needs to be rejected from the outset. Whether occasional LXX readings and Hellenistic influences transform the tradition in terms of an exclusive universalistic monotheism, the greater tradition, in both its Greek and Hebrew recensions, seems unresponsive to such univocal readings. Howevermuch one might wish to read Jeremiah's caustic diatribes as interpretively normative, Zachariah, Deuteronomy, Genesis, Qohelet and Job cannot be read through the eyes of Jeremiah. Whatever the "tradition as a whole" may be, it must be recognized as the tradition we have—and this does not display the theologically motivated ideology commonly asserted of it. Pluralism is ever an exceedingly difficult perspective to affirm amidst the passionate, ideologically motivated certainty of some of our texts.

The tradition of modern scholarship has often asserted that those traditions that reflect an awareness of the exilic or post exilic periods, of the United Monarchy, divided monarchy or even—in reflection on the pentateuch—of the period of sedentarization in *Canaan* are to be dated accordingly. Appropriate association of texts with a corresponding period in Israel's history has typically been a significant means of disassociating an originative core of traditions from subsequent amplifications. This was not only the methodology pursued by Alt in his distinctions between Canaanite cult and that of an originative Israelite "God of the Fathers," and of Israelite apodictic from Canaanite casuistic laws, but also was the methodology that underlay such distinctions as that asserted between 1 and 2 Isaiah and pre-exilic and post exilic psalms. Fundamental to such arguments has been the assumption that early texts could be distinguished from later texts through the identification of allusions and referents within a "known" or perceived history of Israel. A prejudice of this, however, has been that those traditions that purported to be original were accepted as such as long as there was an absence of countervailing evidence. Such opinions have been particularly tenacious regarding the collections of prophetic poems whether they were attributed to Amos, Hosea, Isaiah, Jeremiah or Ezekiel. The simple assertion that they were the *ipsissima verba* of the main characters of these literary works has been deemed—absent contradicting data—adequate evidence for their authenticity. This resulted in the sorry situation in which, for example, prophecies of doom are accepted as authentic and early merely because they make no specific reference to what are seen as the classical exilic and Persian period markers of repentance or salvation. Few, however, have asked why prophecies of doom were recorded and preserved. The explanation that they were preserved to explain *Israel*'s and *Judah*'s destruction has a certain minimal appeal, but it does not convince.

Prophecies of condemnation—or such narrative traditions as that of 2 Kings—do not present themselves as ideologically meaningful apart from an implied awareness of a reversal of condemnation. Such concepts—already familiar to us from Isaiah, Amos, and Hosea—of Israel's total condemnation as the result of an unforgivable crime (Exodus 23) has meaning as preserved tradition primarily in terms of the mercy of Yahweh who forgives the unforgivable. That is, reference to the unforgivable crimes of Israel seem to imply a post exilic consciousness of forgiveness. Otherwise they do not bear signification for their tradents nor merit preservation. All elements of texts cast along an historical trajectory imply an historical context subsequent to the trajectory's targeted goal. Such traditions of wrath and condemnation are only understood in terms of the success of what is in its very root unpromising. Nor is the coherence of such a prophetic motif with comparable narrative motifs accidental. All reflect a context and an understanding of the divinity as forgiving. If the ideologies of Exodus-Numbers and 2 Kings, of Isaiah, Amos and Hosea are consonant with that of 2 Isaiah, Jeremiah, Ezekiel and Ezra-Nehemiah, what basis do we have for our chronological distinctions, on which both tradition and redaction criticism stand?

3. *Historiography*[24]

Since the middle of the nineteenth-century, under the influence of the historicism of Herder and Hegel and in reaction to the empiricism of French and English scholarship, the genre of historiography has been increasingly used to describe biblical narrative. Although throughout the history of its use in biblical scholarship, and in modern usage generally, the term historiography often loosely refers to any of the many genres of prose narrative including tale and story, whether imaginary or real, the ancient and particularly the classical Greek genre of historiography used the term in a much narrower, more restrictive sense. This more distinctive meaning has been maintained also in its present usage,

---

[24] The following is a revision of my article, "Historiography: Israelite" in the forthcoming *Anchor Bible Dictionary*.

namely, as a specific literary genre relating to critical descriptions and evaluations of past reality and events, in contrast to more fictional varieties of prose. For example an essential aspect of early Hittite historiographical texts is that the truth of statements about historical or mythical time is explicitly maintained or challenged.[25] The concepts of truth, facticity and historicity is a central, pivotal concept in the writing of the Annals of Hattusili I and especially of Mursili II.[26] Similarly, the Babylonian Chronicle Series (747–539 B.C.), in contrast for example to the religiously tendentious Assyrian annals, also seem to hold historicity as a central structural value.[27] It is certainly from such annals and Chronicles that ancient Near Eastern historiography has its earliest beginnings, separate and independent of the epical and literarily fictive narrative traditions.

Within Greek literary traditions, a similar concern for historicity developed among the *logographoi* ("prose writers") who considered their task one of *historia* ("research"), seeking to offer a true and correct version of both the traditional past and of mythology. The first to systematically evaluate and criticize traditional Greek folk narrative with logic and rationality was Hecateus of *Miletus* who had a wide personal experience of travel and a considerable knowledge of both geography and ethnography. While much of the work of his successors, including Herodotus, was ethnographic, archival, and antiquarian in nature, the critical task which Hecataeus had established with *historia* became the dominant factor in the "scientific" history of Thucydides's account of the Peloponnesian War. Early Greek historiographers, like their ancient Near Eastern counterparts, developed the genre of *historia* in terms of rational critical research and as an evaluative science, in contrast to the more imaginative literary and poetic traditions of epic and mythology. The criterion for this discipline of historiography was historicity: the truth of the events recounted.

In sharp contrast to this extensive historiographical tradition of *Greece* from the early fifth-century B.C. on, and to some extent, even to that of the Hittites of a much earlier age, biblical tradition does not present us with any critical historiographical production prior to the Hellenistic work of Jason of *Cyrene* which 2 Maccabees professes to

---

[25] H. Cancik, *op.cit.,* 1970, pp.7-8.

[26] *Ibid.,* pp.101-184.

[27] J. Van Seters, *op.cit.,* 1983, pp.79-80.

summarize (2 Maccabees 2:23). Certainly it is that from the time of the
Assyrian Empire, the minor political courts of *Syria-Palestine*, and those
of *Samaria* and *Jerusalem* among them, maintained the kinds of lists,
inscriptions, and annals, and even perhaps court chronicles of the sort
we find in Assyrian and Mesopotamian records. However, such early
historical forms we know only by way of later reference[28] and such
references may either have been invented, or perhaps like the Books of
Jashar (Joshua 10:13), of the Wars of Yahweh (Numbers 21:14), of the
Acts of Solomon (I Kings 11:41), of the Toledoth of Mankind (Genesis
5:1) of the Law of Moses (Joshua 8:31) had been non-historiographical
sources for the biblical tradition.

Although it is a commonplace today to refer to "the historical
books," to deuteronomistic and even Yahwistic "histories," to
"patriarchal biographies" and a "court history" of David, an equivalent
of the word "history" does not exist in Hebrew, and a developed genre
of historiography is particularly difficult to associate with the kind of
prose narratives collected in the Hebrew Bible. Historiography proper
seems unlikely to have been part of the Palestinian literary culture prior
to the Hellenistic period. Both 2 Maccabees and Josephus stand fully
within the tradition of Greek historiography in striking contrast to
Hebrew prose narrative. The role of historiography in biblical literature
is an issue of wide disagreement among biblical scholars. This debate has
taken quite distinct but closely interrelated directions: The definition of
historiography has been broadened to include a wider range of narrative
prose. Dominant examples of this tendency are both the common
perception of biblical narrative as an account of Israel's past, ordered
chronologically, and the adoption of J. Huizinga's more theoretical
definition of history writing as "the intellectual form in which a
civilization renders account to itself of its past."[29] Such broader views
of early Israelite historiography allow many modern scholars to
understand the documentary sources of the pentateuch, the final editions
of the "former prophets," and the compilations of 1–2 Chronicles, Ezra
and Nehemiah as historiographies, and to speak of their authors as
historians. In this they define a genre and a tradition that stands in

---

[28] E.g., of Tyre: Josephus *Antiquities* VII:144-146, IX:283-285; *Contra Apionem* I:155-157;
of Byblos: Philo of Byblos (H.W. Attridge and R.A. Oden, *op.cit.*); of Israel: 1 Kings 14:19,
etc.; of Judah: 1 Kings 14:29, etc.

[29] J. Van Seters, *op.cit.*, 1983, p.1.

direct contrast to the genre and traditions of Mesopotamian, Hittite and Greek historiography, which bear the hall mark of critical reflection in contrast to both ethnography and the collections of folk and heroic literature and traditions.[30]

Closely related to this broadening of the genre of historiography, is the understanding of biblical historiography as an intellectual tradition of morally and religiously critical commentary on Israel's past, reflected in the biblical texts. This intellectual tradition, most notably centering on themes of "promise," "covenant," and various forms of "divine providence," has been seen to inform a wide range of literature. In terms of "salvation history," it is seen to form the core of the pentateuch, especially of the so-called Yahwistic theology. It has also strongly influenced both the content and collection of the prophetic books and has been seen as the central and dominant motivating force behind the formation of the so-called deuteronomistic history. Similar theological *Tendenz* is recognizable in almost all of Hebrew narrative: in Ruth, Jonah, Chronicles, Ezra and Nehemiah. The recognition of an ever recurrent concern for and judgment about Israel's past is so marked in this scholarship that Israel's faith is commonly understood as preeminently an historical faith. This view of biblical "historiography" as a theory or philosophy of history makes of biblical historiography not so much a genre but a frame of mind, and in doing so both blurs the boundaries between genre which were of such importance to late antiquity and confounds current attempts to understand the variety of very distinctive functions that were active in the formation of ancient literature.

These tendencies to understand historiography as playing a decisive role in the form (genre) and content (themes) of biblical tradition have been strongly influenced by two related developments within critical scholarship: The "biblical theology" movement, which until the 1960's understood "salvation history" not as a literary subgenre within the tradition but as a viable historical view about Israel's past, centered focus of the Bible's theological content on assumptions about both the historicity and the historiographical intent of the tradition. Similarly, the long standing efforts of historical-critical scholarship since Wellhausen and Meyer has attempted to reconstruct a critical modern history of

---

[30] *Contra* J. Van Seters, *op.cit.,* 1983; W.W. Hallo, "Biblical History in its Near Eastern Setting: Contextual Approach," *Scripture in Context* (New Haven, 1980) pp.1-26.

Israel by using biblical narrative as its primary source. Prose narratives, whether historical or fictional, typically proceed through successive actions or events; that is they speak chronologically. Both fictional and historical narratives speak from the historical context of the narrator in terms of what has happened, whether real or imagined; that is, they speak of a past. What distinguishes them, and what distinguishes historiography from other narrative genres, is neither their content nor mode of speech, and certainly not such tangential issues as their plausibility and verisimilitude, but rather their referent as perceived by their author. The referent of historiography lies within a world of the past understood as true and real, and as probable in terms of evidence. The referent of fictional literature, on the other hand, lies within a conceptual realm, understood as valid and possible, in terms of the author's own making. The distinction between the two lies within the intentionality of the authors and in their assumptions regarding the reality of the past of which they write. There is little difficulty in distinguishing historical from fictional literature when the author's intention is clear and explicit. However, such is rarely the case with biblical literature. Moreover, when the received tradition presents itself in large complexes of interrelated units of tradition, extending themselves over enormous reaches of time, the interplay of the motives of multiple authors necessarily precludes any simple or indeed any comprehensive designation of genres based on authorial intention. The adoption of Huizinga's definition of historiography by biblical scholars[31] understands historiography in primarily fictive categories, placing the early forms of ancient Near Eastern historiography such as lists, inscriptions, annals and the like into the category not of historiography but of mere record keeping, and preserving the category of historiography for history interpreted. Such a definition also ignores the origins of Greek and Hittite historiography specifically as a critical discipline, and blurs the distinctions of a wide variety of literary and narrative genres from aetiology to propaganda. The adoption of this understanding of historiography for the biblical traditions is dependent on a perception of the larger blocks of prose narrative as substantially unitary, historiographically motivated, productions of literary authors, and denies both the fragmentary nature (and the potentially oral and

---

[31] W.W. Hallo, "Assyrian Historiography Revisited," *EI* 14 (1978), *1-*7; J. Van Seters, *op.cit.,* 1983, p.1.

folkloric roots) of the smaller units collected within the literary contexts of the larger frameworks. Moreover, while moral, ideological and theological tendentiousness is a common trait of these larger frameworks that collect Israel's traditions, to understand such literary perspectives in terms of Israel seeking self understanding not only confuses *pars pro toto*, but also attributes to a peripheral and occasional characteristic of only some historiography the essence of the genre itself. Such a definition centering on a nation's self understanding is far more appropriate to ethnography, to genealogies and constitutional narratives, to origin stories and to much mythology than it is to historiography.

To define the genre of historiography one must of necessity distinguish in prose narrative traditions a considerable number of discrete formal types. One must also distinguish simple from compound tales, and these from various forms of chains of narratives. Similarly, occasional historiographical tales (Genesis 14?) must be sharply distinguished from identifiable historiographic intentionality that has informed the collection and transmission process of the tradition (Exodus 1–15), and both of these must be distinguished from those greater literary works of tradition collection which may or may not have assumed that the tradition sources had reflected a real or only a usable past. When dealing with the biblical tradition on the level of the specific units of the tradition, the genre of historiography is rare. Only very few Hebrew narratives involve historiography at a primary level. This genre is rather most notably present in the larger redactions and the final forms of composition. However, even there, a comprehensive historiographically motivated critical perspective only very occasionally surfaces in our literature (Genesis 11:26–12:5?) and is nowhere dominant.

Of greater importance is the observation that the redactional techniques of the comprehensive tradition reflect the antiquarian efforts of curiosity and preservation. Such intentionality is specifically inimical to that of historiography. Historians ask the question of historicity and critically distinguish and evaluate their sources. They "understand" history, and therefore at times slip into tendentious ideologies and theologies. The antiquarian on the other hand shows the more ecumenically pluralistic motivations of the librarian: classifying, associating, and arranging a cultural heritage that is both greater than the compiler or any single historiographical explanation. So, for example, we notice that in the larger blocks of tradition, narrative development has only the appearance of chronological progression. The process is rather plot oriented, as in the Torah story of Exodus 16–23 or most clearly in the narration of Abraham's travels from story to story, allowing among other things Sarah to be an old woman in Genesis 18 and 21 but a young marriageable beauty in Genesis 20. The recounting of such passages as Genesis 6–9, Exodus 1–12, Exodus 14–15, and especially Exodus 19–21, which collect so many different seemingly disharmonious tale variations, clearly is inimical to historiographical narration, for these collections present not accounts (whether critical or uncritical) of what is understood as past events, but rather they narrate variations existing within a tradition, self consciously rendering accounts (not events) past, and in doing so, clearly reflecting the intentionality of our collector and redactor: to preserve what is old: an antiquarian intentionality which is both pluralistic and in its own way objective. A similarly non-historiographical motivation is also noticeable in some of the compositional links of the larger redactions. So, for example, the Toledoth structure of Genesis encloses this extensive composition through a patterning of episodes (death bed scenes, burials, genealogies, etc.), introductory and closing formulae, post introductory inclusions, as well as through the conjunction of motifs (Exodus 16–17), themes (Genesis 10 and 11:1–9), and parallel, not consecutive, narratives (five genealogies of Esau: Genesis 36:1–5. 9–43). Indeed, disjunction is such a common phenomenon in what is only apparently a chronological progression of tradition from Genesis to 2 Kings that one must view this appearance of historical development and change as (if not entirely accidental) at least late and secondary.

As argued above, this extended tradition is internally structured very loosely as a succession of heroic biographies. However, this structure, although apparent, clearly stands at a distance from the narratives themselves, and is for the greater part a very secondary ordering of stories that are individually wholly independent of this structure. Externally, Genesis–2 Kings is structured as a succession of great periods. It is extremely difficult to see in this any purpose beyond that of a general classifying or cataloguing function. The post compositional and peripheral significance of this progression of texts, of necessity, excludes this aspect of the tradition from any such self conscious literary genre as historiography. An understanding of the intellectual tradition of judgments or critical commentaries on Israelite tradition reflected in the biblical text has been closely associated with scholarly efforts to trace the history of the formation of the Bible and to identify the ideological and theological biases of the larger compositional sources contained within the various biblical books.[32] Central to this discussion has been the elucidation of what was understood to be a particularly biblical view of Israel's past commonly referred to as *Heilsgeschichte* or "Salvation History." This concept of "Salvation History" was one of the primary issues on the agenda of the Biblical Theology movement. However, considerable confusion was introduced by its use both to designate the biblical view of history (a form of theologically motivated *Tendenz* in Israel's view of its past) and as a concept of revelation (a view of the history of Israel itself as salvific). In this latter, modern, theological understanding, the concept today has been largely discredited, because, as a view of history and as an affirmation about the past, it is open in every way to historical-critical research and can neither be equated with revelation nor seen as an object of faith alone.[33] Moreover, by associating revelation with the events of Israel's history, this tendency of the "biblical theology movement" implicitly rejected the Bible as the foundation of "biblical theology" in understanding the Bible as "revelatory" only to the extent that it recounted the external historical events of the past in which revelation was understood to have occurred.[34]

As an understanding of a biblical view of history, however, the concept of "Salvation History" can be seen to epitomize a significant aspect of ancient Israel's intellectual perception of its tradition. In this perspective, scholarly discussion of "Salvation History" has concentrated above all on the identification and description of the theological *Tendenz* of the collectors and redactors of biblical narrative, most notably in the understanding of the Yahwist (of the pentateuch's documentary hypothesis) as a theologian, who developed his narrative about the origins of Israel and of all humanity in a theologically motivated historiographical framework of progression from sin to grace and from promise to fulfillment.[35] This interpretation grew out of the

---

[32] N. Whybray, *The Intellectual Tradition of the Old Testament, BZAW* 135 (Berlin, 1976).

[33] R. Gnuse, *Heilsgeschichte as a Model for Biblical Theology, CTSSR* 4 (New York, 1989) p.23; J. Barr, *Biblical Words for Time, SBTh* 33 (Naperville, 1962) pp.66–69.

[34] Th.L. Thompson, *op.cit.,* 1974, p.327.

[35] G. Von Rad, "Theologische Geschichtsschreibung im alten Testament," *ThZ* 4 (1948), pp.166–176.

understanding of the Yahwist as an historian. Nevertheless, both the understanding of the Yahwist as a theologian, and indeed as an independent source of the pentateuch at all, has undergone serious criticism over the past decade,[36] and continues to be an issue of serious debate today.[37]

Also closely associated with the biblical theology movement's use of the concept of "Salvation History" has been an effort to create a special value of Israel's historical understanding as unique in the ancient Near East, both in light of the biblical concepts of time, as well as in the understanding of an unparalleled relationship that Israel was seen to have with its God, particularly in terms of Yahweh guiding Israel's destiny as well as controlling and acting in history. The Israelite concept of time was thought to be dynamic and linear, a fundamentally historiographical perspective in which events occurred, definitively establishing causal chains of unrepeated results through time. In contrast, the ancient Near Eastern understanding of time was described as static and circular, not historiographical but mythical, creating an understanding of the past as ever recurring in the present. Such stereotypes of both ancient Near Eastern and biblical thought have been thoroughly discredited today, and it is now widely recognized that substantial portions of ancient Near Eastern thought understood both linear progression of time and established considerable causally oriented historiographies. Moreover, the concept of time as circular is no more characteristic of ancient Near Eastern literature than it is of biblical. Rather, the biblical tradition shared a literary and conceptual mode of typology and analogy. Its writers frequently described the past and its traditions in terms of patterns of recurrence, a technique by which one tradition or event might be seen as a commentary on another, rendering meaning to the whole. Similarly, the recurrent biblical motif of God guiding Israel, playing an active role in historical events, and controlling world history is a motif in no way unique to Israel, but is a typical description of divine action found throughout ancient Near Eastern historical records, and was a dominant motif in literature from the

---

[36] R. Rendtorff, op.cit., 1977; H.H. Schmid, *Der sogenannte Jahwist* (Zurich, 1976); E. Blum, *Die Komposition der Vätergeschichte, WMANT* 57 (Neukirchen, 1985); Th.L. Thompson, op.cit., 1987.

[37] J. Van Seters, *Der Jahwist als Historiker, ThS* 134 (Zurich, 1987).

Assyrian period onwards.[38] Finally, it is difficult to maintain an understanding of the motif of "Salvation History" in the pentateuch as an intellectual view of Israel's past. Unlike the deuteronomistic tradition and Chronicles, the pentateuch is integrally an origin tradition and holds as its primary referent not any Israel of the past so much as an Israel contemporary with its own self formation as a tradition of origins, defining Israel's essence and significance as an ethnic community of faith. The motifs of promise and fulfillment are not elements from past history so much as they are assertions meaningful in the tradition's contemporary world.[39] As such, the genre of the pentateuch is not historiographical but rather constitutional narrative, a complex subgenre of aetiology, which uses stories and traditions from the past in what is an illustrative and paradigmatic mode.

Central to what might be described as a biblical view of Israel's past is the critical commentary of the world and the past that we find in the prophetic collections and redactions. Illustrating the more than a millennium old West Semitic tradition of the prophet and seer as a moral and political critic of the government and the populace[40], the books of the classical prophets collect many early poems and oracles that condemn the governments of *Israel, Judah*, and neighboring states, as well as their populace, for a variety of major crimes such as war atrocities, injustices, moral indifference and cultic hypocracies. These collections understood the destructions of the states of *Israel* and *Judah* by the Assyrians and Babylonians as a divinely guided punishment and laid the implicit foundation of what was a future oriented religious understanding of divine mercy and forgiveness. This prophetic tradition cast a trajectory towards a new *Jerusalem* of peace and justice in which Israel would finally carry out its destiny that was accordingly understood to have been established by Yahweh in the forgotten, broken, and lost traditions of the past. Historiographically, the focus of the redactions of the prophetic traditions was not so clearly directed towards any real past except insofar as it served as a justification for the moral and cultic

---

[38] B. Albrektson, *History and the Gods* (Lund, 1967); H. Cancik, *op.cit.*, 1970, and *op.cit.*, 1976; H.W.F. Saggs, *Encounter with the Divine in Mesopotamia and Israel* London, 1978); J. Van Seters, *op.cit.*, 1983.

[39] Th.L. Thompson, *op.cit.*, 1974, p.329.

[40] F. Ellermeier, *Prophetie in Mari und Israel, Theologische und Orientalische Arbeiten aus Göttingen* 1 (Göttingen, 1977).

reorientation demanded by the composite tradition in terms of the Persian world. That the critical judgment involved in this literature related more to the genres of religious interpretation, ideology and propaganda,[41] than that of historiography is clearly indicated in the idealistic and utopian orientation of the historical trajectory cast by the redactors. The historical referent of such ideologically motivated. collections was of course not the past at all but the contemporary need. Comparable to the pentateuchal narrative's preference for an heroic past to illustrate the meaning of Israel in constitutional aetiologies, the Persian period redactions of early Palestinian prophecy created a revolutionary future by reference to the failed past as a paradigm of glory shattered.

The intellectual assumption at the core of the West Semitic prophetic traditions that biblical prophecy continued, is that gods interfere in human affairs and control the political and military events of history, as well as of the cult, of fertility and other aspects of reality, rewarding and punishing their subjects for good or ill. With the help of this common ancient Near Eastern perspective,[42] the collectors of prophetic poems were able to create a theological understanding and self identity in terms of a restoration of traditions past. The fittingness of the Assyrian and Babylonian conquests and their ancestors' subsequent humiliation, presented as Israel's punishment under the wrath and anger of Yahweh, and the appropriateness of the role of Cyrus as Messiah and savior of a chastised remnant, are not historical reflections analyzing what happened in Israel's past so much as they are explanations of piety, illustrative of future demands. This judgment about the past was not drawn from reflection about past events. Rather, a tradition of the past was collected and interpreted to stand both as warning and basis for an idealized ethnicity of the future. It was this future as the true Israel that determined the past remembered.

Comparably pious explanations of tradition are found occasionally in the pentateuch: fulfillment as confirming of promises cast yet in the future (Genesis 22:17–18 and 28:13b–15), the use of the wilderness murmuring motif as a pattern of Israel's recurrent history (Exodus 24:2–8), as well as the self conscious anachronism of the passover festival (in Exodus 12:3, 14, 17, 24 and 26–27) and even more frequently in the

---

[41] G. Garbini, *History and Ideology in Ancient Israel* (London, 1988).

[42] H.W.F. Saggs, *op.cit.*; B. Albrektson, *op.cit.*

collections of the traditions of Joshua–2 Kings, where the condemnation of Israel for immorality, injustice and loss of cultic integrity formed a recurrent leitmotif. In 2 Kings, this critical judgment is indistinguishable from the redactional framework itself. The motifs of the divine control of Israel's destiny by Yahweh, of Yahweh's jealous anger at Israel's unfaithfulness and the ever recurrent need for reform, were didactic and moralizing theological reflections on the traditions sometimes haphazardly gathered from the past. They echo many motifs from the Mesha stele and Assyrian texts,[43] but ideologically they belong to the Persian period circles which developed the collections of sayings and oracles in the prophetic works. Instead of prophetic oracles, the traditional tales and other early stories were used in the prose collections as narrative illustrations of ideology and theology.[44] Although central to this literature (both prophetic and narrative) was the national self understanding claimed by some today to be essential to the genre of historiography, this intellectual tradition in its entirety neither presents a history nor has an abiding interest in historical events. It deals, rather, with what one might better describe as ethnographic aetiology, an intellectual effort that was pivotal in creating the *ethnos* of Israel, reflecting a literary motivation that is characteristic of Persian period literary works throughout the ancient world.

4. Questions of Context and Reference[45]

The dictum of Wellhausen that a biblical document reflects the historical context of its own formation rather than the social milieu of its explicit referents to a more distant past,[46] is one that has hardly been overcome by any of the attempts to synthesize traditio-historical and archaeological research during the past century. In spite of substantial changes, the essential thrust of Wellhausen's axiom continues to haunt us, illustrating

---

[43] B. Albrektson, *ibid.*, pp.106f.

[44] J.W. Rogerson, *Myths in Old Testament Interpretation*, BZAW 134 (Berlin, 1974) pp.182f.

[45] This section is a revision of my earlier article, "Text, Context, and Referent in Israelite Historiography," in *The Fabric of History*, ed. by D. Edelman (Sheffield, 1991) pp.65-92.

[46] J. Wellhausen, *Prolegomena zur Geschichte Israels* (Berlin, 1905) p.316. This dictum played a central role in the development of his evolutionary history of Israelite religion.

a perspective necessary to an understanding of the biblical traditions through their historical context. As archaeologically oriented historical scholarship has finally adjusted its assumption that biblical and extrabiblical research are open to direct synthesis, mutual confirmation and conjectural harmonization, much progress in the secular history of *Palestine* for the Bronze and Iron Ages has become possible.[47] Moreover, as traditio-historical assumptions of an historical core to biblical traditions have been questioned and gradually abandoned, this direction of research has found value and legitimacy as an aspect of compositional theory.[48] It has also become a viable method for one significant aspect of Israel's history. The development of the tradition reflects the historically significant formative process by which "Israel" was created out of the fragments of Palestinian folk traditions and literature that survived the political and historical disasters of the Assyrian and Neo-Babylonian periods. The formation of biblical narrative—the ethno-creative theologically motivated originating process that rendered Israel—had its earliest roots in the period of *Assyria*'s domination of *Palestine*. At the latest, the Israel we know from the tradition came to be during the prehellenistic period.[49] In the aftermath of the destructions of the states of *Samaria* and *Jerusalem*, and in the renaissance born of the Persian restructuring of its conquered territories, the Israel of tradition first presented itself to history, like the phoenix, specifically in the form of an *Israel redivivus*, whose true essence and significance—and implicitly its future glory—was traced in the tales of the patriarchs, the stories of the wilderness and of the judges, and the great legends about the golden age of the united monarchy. Idealistic sentiments of futuristic incipient messianism ring throughout this revisionist tradition with the recurrent affirmation of one people and one God. It is this God, the only true king and emperor, who would some day, finally, really rule from his throne in the temple of the future *Jerusalem* and who would draw all nations to him through his chosen remnant. This is the Israel of tradition.

---

[47] H. Weippert, *Die Archäologie Palästina in vorhellenistischer Zeit* (Munich, 1988); G. Ahlström, *The Early History of Ancient Palestine* (Sheffield, 1992).

[48] Th. L. Thompson, *op.cit,* 1987.

[49] See also on this E.A. Knauf, *Midian: Untersuchungen zur Geschichte Palästinas und Nordarabiens am Ende des 2.Jahrtausends, ADPV* (Wiesbaden, 1988), and his paper at the *SBL* International Congress in Copenhagen in 1989.

To understand the orientation of this literature to any real world of history, renewed focus needs to be given to the context and referent of the text. The text cannot be divorced from its historical context without loss or grave distortion. Certainly, the near generational hemorrhaging of literary critics from any serious effort at historical criticism is a huge disaster, diminishing biblical studies through growing ignorance of the world from which our text comes. No text is understood apart from its context. All meaning bearing structures, to the extent that they are translatable, have an historical contingency or context that must be unlocked if we are to make them ours. Meaning does not signify apart from an historical context, real or assumed. However, the final form of most biblical texts rarely purports to be a unit whole in itself. Anthological, historiographic and archival motives and functions are so common that the signification of much of what the extant form brings together bears meaning primarily in marked independence from the context in which it is collected and only secondarily as an element of a larger context. This distinctive peculiarity of so many of the units of biblical tradition is the result of their having been collected as meaningful traditions. They are voices apart from the collector, historiographer or archivist. They spoke to them, as they do to us, from the past.

The specific manner in which we find this historical context and conceptual world refracted by the tradition requires yet further discussion. Unfortunately, pentateuchal scholarship, and traditio-historical literary criticism generally, are not yet at the point at which we can reconstruct history directly from tradition. The interpretive problem involving the historical changes that moved the people of ancient *Palestine* to forge a sense of ethnicity is one that can hardly be dealt with apart from an understanding of the initial formulation and development of the specific traditions and ideologies that first gave expression to this ethnicity. These traditions and ideologically motivated perspectives are not so much direct refractions of ancient Israel's past as they are themselves intrinsically and substantially causative forces in the development of what we today, in spite of our dependence on these perceptions, understand as Israel.[50] As Max Miller has clearly and

---

[50] This does not involve a judgment about the historicity of many aspects of the biblical tradition, especially of 2 Kings, but addresses only the process by which older narratives and historiographical sources are understood as traditions about an Israel, which, transcending

convincingly argued, any examination of the origins of Israel is forced to move in lock step with an examination of the development of Israelite tradition.[51] Apart from biblical tradition, this Israel never existed as an historical reality open to independent historical research and judgment. It was in the formation of the tradition as such that—to reiterate Malamat's phrase—what we recognize as biblical Israel, for the first time, became a dominant reality in the history of ancient *Palestine*.[52] From this perspective, one must agree with Miller's conviction that Israel's tradition is in a radical and fundamental way our starting point for the history of Israel.[53] Without it, we can not write a history of Israel, because, within the context of the Persian renaissance, the tradition itself created the population of *Palestine* as Israel out of the ashes of the Assyrian and Babylonian empires.

Biblical tradition is related to Israelite history when we use it teleologically and understand Israel as the end result of a literary trajectory. If, however, we use the tradition as historical evidence for a history prior to the historical context of the tradition, such a history can hardly avoid being anachronistic in its essence. Nevertheless, when understood teleologically, the tradition gives focus and direction to our research; for it is the Israel of tradition that we need to explain historically. The stories within this extended tradition generally bear the character of "traditional narratives" that stand somewhat apart from both history and historiography.[54] Chronicles, Ezra and Nehemiah also do not stand substantially closer to a recoverable "history," for they too took their shape long after the events of which they might be thought to speak. The purported referents of these later works are also distinct from their contexts. Nor is the intent underlying their collection so obviously an historiographic one, howevermuch they have been structured chronologically.[55] Any interpretative matrices, which we may

---

its pre-exilic status as the State of *Samaria*, takes on the contours of the Israel of tradition (also G. Garbini, *History and Ideology in Ancient Israel*, London, 1988).

[51] Orally at the annual convention of *SBL*, Chicago, 1988.

[52] A. Malamat, "Die Frühgeschichte Israels: eine Methodologische Studie," *Theologische Zeitschrift* 39 (1983), pp.1–16.

[53] J.M. Miller and J.H. Hayes, *A History of Ancient Israel and Judah* (Philadelphia, 1986).

[54] Following here D. Gunn, *The Stories of King David*, JSOTS 4 (Sheffield, 1976).

[55] P. Welten, *Geschichte und Geschichtsdarstellung in den Chronikbüchern*, WMANT 42 (Neukirchen, 1973); H.G.M. Williamson, *Israel in the Book of Chronicles* (Cambridge, 1977); R.L. Braun, "Chronicles, Ezra, and Nehemiah: Theology and Literary History,"

be tempted to draw from the biblical story itself, render for us only hypothetical historical contexts, events and situations whereby our texts only seem to take on meaning as literary responses. The matrix, however, remains imbedded in the literary vision and is not historical. This danger of eisegesis is particularly serious when assumptions akin to Eissfeldt's imaginary *Stammesgeschichte* are present,[56] where fictional stories are understood as refracted pantomimes of supposedly real political and social struggles. As with other forms of allegorical interpretation, these efforts bypass all critical evaluation.[57] Fairly mainstream historical-critical exegetical efforts are implicated in this criticism. For example, recent scholarly efforts have tried to associate such a central tradition complex as Numbers 16–18 with a presumed historical Levitical conflict in a "pre-exilic" period or in an equally imaginary "post exilic" Aaronide hegemony over the cult.[58] Both options are unverified fictions, created wholly from the traditions themselves. They share the common categorical error of assuming the very history they seek to reconstruct. Similarly, the increasingly common temptation to associate the Abraham wandering tales or the Exodus stories with an historical context in an "exile," interpreting these stories as implicit reflections of the "return" and of the "exiles'" self understanding as *gerim*, is equally suspect,[59] for no other reason than that the language of "exile" they use is not so much historical as it is traditional. Not even the pentateuch's golden calf story or Bezalel's construction of the ark and tent of meeting can, with any reasonable security, be related to any alleged historical matrices by making them retrojections of presumably reliable depictions of cultic

---

Studies in the Historical Books of the Old Testament, ed. J.A. Emerton (Leiden, 1979) pp.52–64.

[56] O. Eissfeldt, "Stammessage und Menscheitserzählung in der Genesis," *Sitzungsberichte der Sächsischen Akademie der Wissenschaft zu Leipzig*, Phil-hist Kl 110,4 (Leipzig, 1965) pp.5–21.

[57] See Th.L. Thompson, "Conflict Themes in the Jacob Narratives," *Semeia* 15 (1979), pp.5–26.

[58] J. Milgrom, "The Rebellion of Korah, Numbers 16–18: A Study in Tradition History," *SBL Seminar Papers* (Atlanta, 1988) pp.570–73 and E. Rivkin, "The Story of Korah's Rebellion: Key to the Formation of the Pentateuch," *SBL Seminar Papers* (Atlanta, 1988) pp.574–81.

[59] Here I am reacting to my own inclination to reinterpret these traditions as stories originating in an exilic or early post-exilic context. Th.L. Thompson, *op.cit.*, 1987, pp.194–198.

innovations undertaken by the Jeroboam and Solomon of 2 Kings. The accounts of 2 Kings are also stories not history, and as stories in the tradition they are fully equivalent to their variants set in yet more hoary antiquity. One does well to reflect on both the multivalent and distinctive nature of so many of the traditions found within biblical historiography. Apart from a consideration of the many lost traditions unavailable to us, the immense complexity involved in the history of the extant traditions alone must give pause to any scholar employing a method of historical research that prefers one element of the tradition as more viable historically than another. Without concrete external evidence, such selective preference is not critical. As long as we continue to work with historical contexts that are not based on independent evidence, plausibility and verisimilitude cannot be recognized as valid criteria for historicity. Plausibility and verisimilitude are characteristics that are to be attributed far more to good fiction. Reasonableness is a characteristic of the fictional not the historical genres of literature. History happens, and our knowledge of it is based on evidence not reason.

When we are dealing with univocal traditions without extant variants we have precious few[60] means which enable us to recognize and confirm positively a reference to a real past,[61] or to measure in any significant way the manner and extent to which the tradition reflects its own historical context. Valid negative conclusions are many, come immediately to hand, and certainly do not need emphasis.[62] However, the recognition and clarification of explicit and implicit referents and conceptual contexts do not define the limits of the positive contributions to be expected from a study of the historical world of our narratives. Of equal importance is the growing realization that the redactional techniques of the comprehensive traditions of the pentateuch, of the so-

---

[60] This lack is rapidly diminishing in recent years, not only through the dozens of monographs and hundreds of articles that have revolutionized the history of Palestine, but also through the recent comprehensive handbooks of H. Weippert, *op.cit.*, 1988 and G. Ahlström, *op.cit.*, forthcoming.

[61] For an earlier discussion of some of these issues, *op.cit.*, 1979.

[62] One might note the discussions in M. Weippert, *Die Landnahme der israelitischen Stämme in Palästina* (Göttingen, 1967); Th.L. Thompson, *op.cit.*, 1974; J.H. Hayes and J.M. Miller (eds.), *op.cit.*, 1977; J.A. Soggin, *The History of Israel* (Philadelphia, 1984); N.P. Lemche, *Early Israel* (Leiden, 1985); J.M. Miller and J.H. Hayes, *A History of Israel and Judah* (Philadelphia, 1986); G. Garbini, *op.cit.*, 1988.

called deuteronomistic tradition and of their variants in Chronicles-Ezra-Nehemiah reflect not merely the occasional historiographical intentions of the redactors, but also and much more importantly for modern efforts to reconstruct the world of *Palestine*'s past, the pedantic efforts of antiquarian-motivated curiosity and preservation.[63] These are not only distinct from historiography but at times inimical to it. Rather than the politically motivated ideology of historiography, we might rather look for the more pluralistic activity of ethnographers and librarians. The choice is important. Many passages in the narrative sections of the pentateuch, the so-called deuteronomistic tradition and Chronicles–Ezra–Nehemiah are unreadable in any sense of linear narrative continuity, plot development or either chronological or historiographic coherence (for example, the five lists of Edom in Genesis 36, the call and instructions to Moses of Exodus 3–6 and the aetiology on the clean and unclean of Leviticus 10). Many of these passages, especially Exodus 3–6, occur at the crossroads of tradition, where, if our redactions were historiographical, one would least expect some complex dissonance. If they are not historiographical one can then entertain the possibility that these passages may indicate that our extant texts may not have been written to be read—at least not in the way that we read historiographical narrative.

Historians ask the question of historicity and critically distinguish and evaluate their sources. They "understand" history, and therefore often slip into tendentious ideologies and theologies—so Thucydides.[64] The antiquarian, on the other hand, shares the more ecumenically pluralistic motivations of the librarian (not without significant discrimination and occasional critical control) classifying, associating, and arranging a

---

[63] Recent comparisons of biblical narrative with Greek authors, especially Herodotus (J. Van Seters, *op.cit.,* 1983, and R.N. Whybray, *op.cit.,* 1987) underscore the importance of this more detached scholarly aspect of our traditions. *Pace* Van Seters. Such detachment is to be contrasted to the more politically and ideologically motivated genre of historiography.

[64] The issue here is not one of historicity but of historiography, and pertains to the intention of the author, not his success. On this, see the interesting discussions of W.R. Connor, "Narrative Discourse in Thucydides," *The Greek Historians: Literature and History: Papers Presented to A.E. Raubitschek,* ed. by W.R. Connor (Saratoga, 1985) pp.1-17; P. Robinson, "Why Do We Believe Thucydides? A Comment on W.R. Connor's 'Narrative Discourse in Thucydides'," *Greek Historians,* pp.19-23; and S.W. Hirsch, "1001 Iranian Nights: History and Fiction in Xenophon's Cyropaedia," *Greek Historians,* pp.65-85.

cultural heritage that is greater than both the compiler and any single historiographical explanation—so perhaps Herodotus,[65] Philo of Byblos,[66] and certainly the pentateuch![67]

The recent discussions of G. Garbini, A. Knauf, and especially of D. Jamieson-Drake,[68] about the ancient scribal profession and a variety of

---

[65] For recent discussions of historiography in Herodotus, H.R. Immerwahr, *Form and Thought in Herodotus*, *Philological Monographs* 23 (Cleveland, 1966); H. Fahr, *Herodot und altes Testament*, *Europäische Hochschulschriften* 266 (Frankfurt, 1985); P.R. Helm, "Herodotus' Medikos Logos and Median History," *Iran* 19 (1981), pp.85-90; K.D. Bratt, "Herodotus' Oriental Monarchs and Their Counsellors" (Princeton University dissertation, 1985); J.M. Balcer, *Herodotus und Bisitun*, *Historia* 49 (Stuttgart, 1987); H. Sancisi-Weerdenburg, "Decadence in the Empire or Decadence in the Sources?" *Archaemenid History* I, ed. H. Sancisi-Weerdenburg (Leiden, 1987) pp.33-45; F. Hartog, *The Mirror of Herodotus* (London, 1988).

[66] H.W. Attridge and R.A. Oden, *op.cit.* Other ancient Near Eastern historiographic ethnographies and related genres might profitably be compared with Old Testament literature and themes. W.W. Hallo, *op.cit.*, 1978; *idem*, "Sumerian Historiography," *History, Historiography, and Interpretation*, ed. H. Tadmor and M. Weinfeld (Leiden, 1984) pp.9-20; *idem*, *op.cit.*, 1980; N.E. Andersen, "Genesis 14 in its Near Eastern Context," *Scripture in Context*, pp.78; P. Veyne, *Did the Greeks Believe in Their Myths?* (Chicago, 1988); F. Rochberg-Halton, "Fate and Divination in Mesopotamia," *Archiv fur Orientforschung* 19 (1982), pp.363-371; M. Liverani, "The Ideology of the Assyrian Empire," *Power and Propaganda, Mesopotamia* 7 (Copenhagen, 1979) pp.297-317; P. Michalowski, *The Lamentation over the Destruction of Sumer and Ur* (Winona Lake, 1989); M. Weinfeld, "Divine Intervention in War in Ancient Israel and in the Ancient Near East," *History, Historiography and Interpretation*, pp.121-47; H. Tadmor, "Autobiographical Apology in the Royal Assyrian Literature," *History, Historiography and Interpretation*, pp.36-57; H. Cancik, *op.cit.*, 1970; *idem*, *op.cit.*, 1976.

[67] J. Van Seters, *op.cit.*, 1983; N. Whybray, *op.cit.*, 1987; Th.L. Thompson, *op.cit.*, 1987. For a dissenting voice on the comparison between the pentateuch and Herodotus, R.E. Friedman, "The Prophet and the Historian: The Acquisition of Historical Information from Literary Sources," *The Past and the Historian*, HSS 26, ed. R.E. Friedman (Cambridge, 1983) pp.1-12. Some important recent studies of Israelite historiography are: H. Schulte, *Die Entstehung der Geschichtsschreibung im alten Israel*, BZAW 128 (Berlin, 1972); M. Weippert, "Fragen des israelitischen Geschichtsbewusstseins," *VT* 23 (1973), pp.415-41; G.W. Trompf, "Notions of Historical Recurrence in Classical Hebrew Historiography," *Studies in the Historical Books of the Old Testament*, SVT 30, ed. J.A. Emerton, (Leiden, 1979) pp.213-29; D.I. Block, "The Foundations of National Identity: A Study in Ancient Northwest Semitic Perceptions" (University of Liverpool dissertation, 1981); R. Schmitt, *Abschied der Heilsgeschichte?*, *Europäische Hochschulschriften* 195 (Frankfurt, 1982); J.A. Soggin, "Le Origini D'Israele Problema per lo Storiografo?" *Le Origini di Israele* (Rome, 1987) pp.5-14; B. Halpern, *The First Historians* (San Francisco, 1988); G. Garbini, *op.cit.*.

[68] G. Garbini, op.cit.; E.A. Knauf, *Midian*, ADPV, 1988; and D. Jamieson-Drake, *op.cit.* See the earlier related studies of J. Rogerson, *op.cit.*, 1974; A. Lemaire, *op.cit.*, 1981; and

issues involved in book formation and library collections, have all agreed
that we cannot seek an origin of literature in *Palestine* prior to the
eighth, or perhaps even better the seventh-century. Such an *a quo* dating
of course pertains not only to the conceptual world of the narrators of
biblical traditions, but equally as powerfully to the world that began to
collect those narrations.[69] A date earlier than the late Assyrian period
for such activity in *Palestine* cannot be seriously entertained today, and
even this date is very early indeed. In a world that knows libraries, not
only does the non-utilitarian function of writing find room to expand
and proliferate, but the genre of the collected literature itself undergoes
structural alteration. Tales are linked and become chains of narration,
which in turn, can extend in a theoretically infinite succession of chains.
In the broad conceptual context of a library, chronology, the linear
progression of a series of heroic persons, or the great periods and
epochs of the past, steps outside of the semantic and historiographic
nuances of past, present and future, and provides an order and structure
that is uniquely external to the literature itself. Such chronology,
specifically because it is fictive and rationalizing, becomes capable of
relating a multiplicity of literature within a comprehensive framework.
It is in the intellectual world of the Persian reconstruction that we first
find a context for the formation of a comprehensive great tradition
reflected in the prophetic books and the collection of prose narrative
from Genesis–2 Kings, further expanded in the late Persian or early
Hellenistic period with Chronicles, Ezra and Nehemiah, and perhaps
even later with the *Megilloth*.[70] Many of the extended traditions
contained in this library have survived successive dislocation because
they found echo and meaning in the lives of their tradents; the handful
of collectors and those limited few who used books for leisure. For
them, these traditions held relevance to both their political and social

---

B. Halpern, *op.cit.*

[69] That the Old Testament is a "collection" or even a library of literature, authored by
many different persons, is a commonplace of biblical studies. The perception, however, that
this description also accurately describes the function of the collection of traditions of
Genesis-Ezra-Nehemiah as library, substantially explaining the textual context of the works
included in this collection, was first granted me by the observations of S.E. Janke in a
seminar in Jerusalem in 1985. That there is not a normative role in such collections or
anything at all similar to a canon is obvious.

[70] One of course must be aware that the dating here is based more on the tradition of
scholarship than on unequivocal evidence; cf. above, note 10.

worlds, often lending these fragmented worlds of experience interpretive contexts of their own. One ought not assume, however, that such *Sitze im Leben* lie *im Leben des Volkes*. Rather, we are dealing only with scholarly bibliophiles.[71]

We cannot assume that the collected traditions as such reflect either indirectly or explicitly the real world of their tradents and collectors. They are only meaningful to that world in terms of contemporary resignification or of more distant future oriented intellectual projections. The issue of the sources for the final compositions and collections is of critical importance in understanding our text. It is in the context of the discrete traditions themselves being from the past that we come to deal for the first time with the originating signification of their historical context. Our understanding of collectors and redactors, such as the author of the *Toledoth* structure of Genesis or the collector of the wilderness variants found in the second half of Exodus and in Numbers, does not supply us with that primary context which can be understood as an historical matrix of tradition. Nor can the world of such compilers be understood as the referent of the tradition; i.e., the situations or events which the tradition is about. Rather, research into the historical context of such redactions, even of a "final" redaction, renders only a secondary usage and perspective, only a world in which our traditions have become meaningful or useful. From the perspective of the world of the collectors, we do not understand the historical referent of a story or poem collected. Nor can we expect to reconstruct specific historical and socio-political contexts that somehow (with Knauf) must be reflected in such traditions from the past whether or not they have been fragmented and transformed by these secondary contexts. Furthermore, the more the narrator or collector of such composite traditions is convinced that the "realities" of such traditions represent the distant past, or more recent events, or as significant to his worldview, the less we will be able to understand his sources in relation to their original context and signification. To the extent, on the other hand, that they have not been transformed by their inclusion in this "library" and by their association with the other discrete works that surround them—each with its own context, referent and intention—to that extent they become amenable to an historical-critical analysis of both their originating context and their

---

[71] For the scribal class as a social elite, B. Lang, *Monotheism and the Prophetic Minority*, *SWBAS* 1, Sheffield, 1983.

historicity, and open to being understood in their own terms, meanings and intentions, apart from what they have been made to mean in the accumulating, distinct contexts of their tradents.

The issues of whether or not the biblical traditions of Genesis–2 Kings and Chronicles-Ezra-Nehemiah are literarily unified, dealing with Israel's past *ex novo*, whether they are primarily tendentious, ideological and/or theological historiographic redactions of traditions, whether they are oral or literary, or whether they are the gatherings of a bibliophile or librarian are of immense interpretive importance. That they are from or about the past, however, is the primary *raison d'être* of their inclusion in the growing tradition. How past they are is a subject of examination for each recognizably distinct tradition collected. The nature of both the manner of composition and the tendentiousness of historiography renders it exceedingly difficult to recognize and distinguish the discrete sources of historiography. What we can know is largely restricted to the understanding of the world and of tradition at the time of its written forms. Even when a more ancient source is claimed by the putative historian, our judgment regarding the veracity of such claims must derive almost totally from the world we understand to be contemporary with its establishment as tradition. The pursuit of a specific *Traditionsgeschichte* must by necessity be limited to the analysis of changes that are specifically observable in the text. Even such observable transitions may reflect a variety of contemporary understandings rather than an evolutionary development that might theoretically carry us into a prehistory of the text. The unproven assumption that the pentateuch tradition is historiographical and the creation of a single literary hand—perhaps undergoing successive revisions and editions by subsequent authors[72]—can speak only to the successive secondary contexts within which the growing tradition found a home. In only a limited fashion can it speak to the tradition's originating matrices or significant referents. Such secondary structures, whether or not they may be historiographic in intent, must be seen as largely irrelevant to critical historical reconstruction. The historical contexts of the successive assumptions and perspectives of such revisions or redactions are basically closed to us. Also lacking is any criterion for establishing either a relative or an absolute chronology for strata within the tradition. To

---

[72] I am thinking here for instance of such as J. Van Seter's revisionist hypothesis in *Abraham in History and Tradition* (New Haven, 1975).

assume that J², for example, is to be dated to an "exilic" period because it is easier to interpret it within that context is wholly inconsequent as an historical-critical evaluation because such a period is not known to exist apart from the tradition. Howevermuch the process of this tradition formation might presumably reflect the worlds of the redactors or collectors, each with their distinctive political, social and religious realities, it can hardly be used directly for reconstructing these worlds of reference that are largely unknown to us.

The tradition, within its field of semantic references, lives within both a real and a literary world. Without a detailed and independent understanding of the historical contexts within which a tradition has relevance, our ability to distinguish or even identify the historical contexts of the tradition is fleeting and sporadic. Furthermore, both the historiographic and antiquarian concerns, that sought to preserve traditions after the collapse of the old order, do not pretend to present any coherent or univocal truth about the past.[73] However, the specific content of the narratives that have been suspended out of their own time and held as meaningful to these Persian period traditionists does not directly reflect either the late Persian or early Hellenistic world in which the traditions found their final form. The narratives do not even reflect the pre-destruction world they so desperately tried to revive and preserve. Like the traditions of *Yavneh*, the biblical traditions reflect but incoherent part fictive remnants of a past that the survivors of the destruction and their descendants were able to put together and give meaning to in the radically new worlds into which they were thrown. It is their significance as meaningful expressions of the old order, giving hope and direction to the new that affected these traditions' preservation, not their dependability in preserving past realities, so painful and ineffective as they were. Both the form and the content of the preserved past have been strongly affected—I hesitate to use the word determined—by the needs of the tradents. Understandably, the realities of the referents were often perceived as having less significance.

It is indisputable that many elements of the received tradition reflect the exigencies of the Assyrian period. Yet other elements refer to what has become a fictionalized or literary past. Clear examples of a past

---

[73] One might note an analogous indifference to a thoroughgoing ideology in the efforts made to collect the traditions of the schools of Hillel and Shammai by Hillelites after the fall of Jerusalem in 70 A.D. J. Neusner, *From Politics to Piety* (New York: 1979) p.100.

phrases in Exodus 15:26d and 23:21. The appeal to "Yahweh, your healer," in 15:26d is out of context in the tale episode of 15:22–26, wherein Yahweh neither plays nor is called upon to play the role of healer. Nor does this divine title derive from the larger context of Exodus 1–23, where Yahweh provides and protects, guides and saves, but never heals. On the other hand, the close variant tradition found in Numbers 21:4–9 presents a deity with whom the motif of healing might be associated. Another variant in Deuteronomy 7:12–15, not only presents Yahweh as healer, but also refers to a now lost account of an episode in Egypt in which Israel, too, suffered disease. It is noteworthy that Yahweh's healing is presented as a reward for obedience to his ordinances in both Exodus 15:22ff. and Deuteronomy 7:12–15. A process of literary allusion, not historical reference, is apparent here. Even more striking is Yahweh's speech to Moses in Exodus 23. In its context of the early constitutional tradition of Exodus 1–24:8, the speech by Yahweh who is sending his angel to lead Moses and his people against his enemies in "the place [he] has prepared," refers to a future transgression, which Yahweh will not forgive (v.21). The immediate and original context (23:1–24:8) makes it very clear that the unforgivable transgression to which this speech directs us is Israel's entering into covenants with the peoples and gods of *Eretz Israel*. The referent then is historiographical and external to the tradition. The threatened punishment for this unforgivable transgression refers to the destruction of either *Jerusalem* or *Samaria*, understood theologically and ideologically as having been caused by their own God as a result of what is here attested as Israel's fault. The suggested historical context of this original narration is obviously then the post destruction period, either of the seventh or the sixth-century. Within the context of the whole of the pentateuch our pericope of Exodus 23:20–24:8 radically alters its referent. No longer does Yahweh's speech reflect immediate preparations for the conquest of *Palestine*. It rather serves as an opening to the wilderness wandering. The book of the covenant that Moses wrote (Exodus 24:4. 7) is quickly displaced by Yahweh's tablets (Exodus 24:12), themselves displaced by Moses's copy (Exodus 34:4ff. 27ff) as he runs up and down the mountain for successive variations on the traditions of Exodus 19 and 20. Within this context, the referent is literary and internal. It is the transgression of continued murmuring and the sins of Miriam and Aaron, and of Aaron and Moses, in the growing conglomerate of narrative, explaining the entrance into the promised

conglomerate of narrative, explaining the entrance into the promised land of a new generation rather than the generation addressed by Yahweh in Exodus 23. The historical context of this literary referent is apparently a situation in the Persian period in which the tradition supports the hope of a new generation in *Palestine* who have identified themselves spiritually with a return from the "wilderness" of exile to the promised land. This hope is born, or promises to find its fulfillment, in their lives in the Persian Period.

Although many primary elements of the tradition reflect the historical contexts of periods earlier than the received tradition's formation, their narrative contexts, both primary and secondary, imply an historical context associated with the complex secondary level of the tradition. This suggests in turn that the compilation of the extant tradition is, in terms of intellectual history, clearly distinct from its sources. Such a distinction between an originating historical context (i.e. historical matrix) and a secondary historical context is particularly pertinent when dealing with traditions that appear to be largely irrelevant to their received contexts, yet assumed by this secondary context to derive from hoary antiquity. Here one might well think of Leviticus 16, but perhaps also those tales introduced into larger narratives by means of "post introductory inclusion"[74] such as Genesis 12:10–20, Genesis 26, and Genesis 38. It is equally necessary for the historical critic to sort out the potentially distinctive literary and historical referents and contexts of narratives that appear to exhibit historiographical or literary harmony (e.g. Genesis 11:26–12:4)[75] or an editorial dovetailing of successive variant narrations of what was perceived as an equivocal episode or tale (e.g., Genesis 6–9; Exodus 5–13; and Exodus 14).[76]

Given the complex manner in which the tradition has functioned as survival literature, our ability to relate the historical context of various redactive moments to late Assyrian times, to the early or to the later Persian periods, does not substantially help our arriving at either the specific historical and intellectual milieu of their received form or, ultimately, the specific socio-historical matrix of their origins, except in the grossest and most general terms. As survival literature, the traditions

---

[74] Th.L. Thompson, *op.cit.,* 1987, p.169.

[75] Th.L. Thompson, *op.cit.,* 1974, pp.308-11.

[76] Th.L. Thompson, op.cit., 1987, pp.74-77. 139-146.

render a composite ideological understanding of these periods. The traditions are not so much a direct reflection of or reference to their periods of origin and composition as they are an explanation that gives meaning to them. That is, the ideological and theological *Tendenz* of the received or extant traditions, to the degree that they are oriented to the world of the final stages of the tradition's formation, may well preclude their use for any historical reconstruction based on assumed events from a greater past. For such past worlds refracted from the redactions are constructs of a world contemporary to the redaction. Indeed, they stand outside of any historical field of reference other than intellectual history. The historical significance of the received tradition, holistically perceived, lies primarily in its dual function as meaningful literature and as library in post compositional times. One must indeed incline towards the late Persian period for the historical context in which our narratives have their significance as a tradition of Israel. At such a date considerable portions of the tradition's original contextual content have already lost much of their intrinsic relevance. While these traditions have been transvalued in the process of transmission and have acquired an even wider meaning than they bore as reflections of the often opaque world of their original historical context, they have also lost much cohesion with their specific origins in antiquity.

Unlike the problems surrounding the historical context of a literary unit, the problem dealing with their intentional referent involves one immediately with the many variant degrees of fictional and historiographical intent as well as with the externally oriented issues of accuracy and historicity. Internally, one necessarily distinguishes a number of discrete formal categories as relevant: a) aetiologies, b) traditional tales, c) *Standesgeschichte*, d) *Stammesgeschichte*, e) genealogical tales, f) romances, g) ethnographies, and h) historiographies.[77] Their intentional referent distinguishes them. For instance, aetiology is different from historiography in that the referent of an aetiology is typically some contemporary reality, while historiography refers to the perceived past. Historiographical narrative is distinct from the often literarily comparable traditional tale in that historiography involves a critical reflection on sources for an understanding of the past with the intention of presenting the reality of the past, while traditional narratives are preserved either for antiquarian motives (because they are from the

---

[77] Th.L. Thompson, op.cit., 1979, pp.5-26.

past) or because of their hermeneutical and heuristic value to the tradent. Propaganda, on the other hand, and other ideologically tendentious literature, are vitally anti-critical, intending to distort or to create a past for extraneous reasons. *Stammesgeschichte*, *Standesgeschichte*, and genealogical tales, with their signification born of attraction to the tradents, are all categorically subvarieties of historiography, propaganda, or romances. Romances are distinct from traditional tales in that they are fictional histories and literary expressions of the aura surrounding the heroes and events of the past. Certainly Genesis 14 fits this category, perhaps the song of Deborah in Judges 5, and with little doubt the song in Exodus 15. Only very few Israelite narratives involve historiography at a primary level of the tradition.[78] This genre is most notably present in the larger redactions and final forms of composition. Even there a comprehensive, historiographically motivated critical perspective rarely surfaces in our literature. The sweeping assertions common today that boldly refer to "historians" and the like, existing long before Thucydides[79] say much more than they properly can.

In suggesting that the essential interpretative context of the narrative tradition of Genesis–2 Kings is that period during which the tradition achieved its role as survival literature, a perspective is recommended which is quite different from that usually taken by tradition history. It is unlikely that we will be able to correlate adequately the earlier strata of the tradition with concrete historical events in the past history of ancient *Palestine*, or even with any of the episodes of the tradition, as if they were—somehow—memories of a real past. Determining the potential historical referents of the tradition and determining that tradition's relevance to the writing of a history of Israel is theoretically more

---

[78] On this particular issue, see the early chapters of either J.M. Miller and J.H. Hayes, *op.cit.*, 1986 or J.A. Soggin, *op.cit.*, 1984. The more recent and more radical presentations of N.P. Lemche, *Ancient Israel: A New History of Israelite Society* (Sheffield, 1988) and G. Garbini *op.cit.*, 1988, though less comprehensive, are closer to the writer's position.

[79] I am thinking here of such otherwise helpful studies as J. Van Seters, *op.cit.*, 1983. One might also refer to similar assumptions of B.O. Long ("Historical Narrative and the Fictionalizing Imagination," *VT* 35, 1985, pp.405-16) and C. Meyers ("The Israelite Empire: In Defense of King Solomon," *Backgrounds for the Bible*, ed. M.P. O'Connor and D.N. Freedman, Winona Lake, 1987, pp.181-97). See, on the other hand, the very interesting discussion of H.M. Barstad ("On the History and Archaeology of Judah during the Exilic Period: A Reminder," *Orientalia Louvaniensa Periodica* 19, 1988 pp.25-36).

possible the closer we are to the extant form of the tradition. However, this is true only to the extent that these latest formulations and revisions relate to or are identical with those issues and events informing these ultimate redactions. The hypothesis that the received traditions once existed in antiquity in substantial form at a time prior to these latest redactions needs reinvestigation. Certainly Wellhausean forms of "documents" dating from as early as the United Monarchy must now be abandoned—if only because of the tenuous hold on existence a period of a United Monarchy has. Furthermore, much recent scholarship has questioned the existence of such extensive and coherent portions of the received text at such an early period, and variously recommends an historical context in the late Assyrian, or the early Persian period.[80] An early date certainly seems impossible now. However, too specific late dates appear arbitrary and seem based on circular arguments. Our understanding of the Josianic reform and of the prophetic and covenantal ideologies that presumably supported it is crucially based on an historicistic and naive reading of 2 Kings, which is after all a product of the same spectra of traditions that use 2 Kings for their referential context. Similarly, in dating the prophets—Amos, Hosea, First Isaiah, Ezekiel—we too quickly identify the characters of stories as historical persons and assume that the prophetic traditions had original *nuclei* deriving from actual events and persons narrated by the traditions, which continued to have significance in a post destruction world. In fact, however, we know historically little of any such events or persons. External confirmatory evidence we have for these assumptions is both fragmentary and oblique. The very knowledge of "exilic" or "post exilic" periods rests on the presupposition that Jeremiah, Ezekiel, Chronicles, Ezra and Nehemiah can somehow be translated into reflections of historical reality. Yet we know that these traditions were also written and edited as substantial traditions of Israel's distant past. Any assumption that they render history is no longer self evident.

---

[80] H. Vorländer, *Die Entstehungszeit des Jehowistischen Geschichtswerkes, EHST* 109 (Frankfurt, 1978); J. Van Seters, *op.cit.,* 1975; *idem, op.cit.,* 1983; H.H. Schmid, *Der Sogenannte Jahwist: Beobachtungen und Fragen zur Pentateuchforschung* (Zurich, 1976); N.P. Lemche, *op.cit.,*1985; E. Blum, "Die Komplexität der Überlieferung: Zur synchronen und diachronen Analyse von Gen 32:23-33," *DBAT* 15 (1980), pp.2-55; *idem, Die Komposition der Vätergeschichte, WMANT* 57 (Neukirchen, 1984); M. Rose, *Deuteronomist und Jahwist, AThANT* 67 (Zurich, 1981); and F. Kohata, *Jawhist und Priesterschrift in Exodus 3-14, BZAW* 166 (Berlin, 1986).

CHAPTER NINE

CONCLUSIONS: AN INDEPENDENT HISTORY OF ISRAEL

1. *The Separate Origins of "Israel" and "Judah"*

The focus of this book has been on the implications of interdisciplinary historical research in *Palestine* in the hope of developing an understanding of the history of "Israel" within the context of a comprehensive regional and historical geography of *Palestine*. The history of "Israel" twenty years ago had been understood essentially as a part of biblical studies. However, both the history of "Israel" and of *Palestine* require a broad, interdisciplinary perspective that extends throughout the humanities to the natural and social sciences. Developing and maintaining such a perspective is very important, because the history of "Israel" and of *Palestine* is a significant component of our historical and cultural heritage. As current political developments suggest, understanding this heritage remains of vital importance not only to the academic community but also to the community at large.

The broad interdisciplinary scope of the history of "Israel" and *Palestine* has not always been understood. Until the mid-1970s, all modern histories of "Israel" and *Palestine* had been developed on the basis of an integration or synthesis of three very different types of sources: biblical traditions, ancient Near Eastern texts and material culture discovered through archaeological exploration. Critical historical interpretation centered on the determination of historicity, especially on the degree to which extra-biblical information was seen to confirm, amplify, contradict or modify the history of "Israel" as presented in biblical tradition. Historical description was developed through a chronologically progressive synthesis of the three source fields, following principles of coherence, plausibility and verisimilitude. The presentation of the history of *Palestine* proceeded through a succession of periods defined by material cultural remains derived from archaeology and interpretively marked by an association with major events drawn from written sources, whether from contemporary ancient Near Eastern texts or from much later biblical traditions. For example, the Early Bronze IV transition period was understood in terms of Egyptian and Mesopotamian texts that referred to conflicts with nomadic groups. The onset of Middle Bronze II was understood in the light of the rise of the Twelfth Dynasty. Middle Bronze IIb prosperity was viewed in terms of a Levantine based "Hyksos" conquest of *Egypt*. The Middle Bronze–Late Bronze transition was interpreted as the result of the expulsion of these "Hyksos" from *Egypt*. The Late Bronze–Iron I transition was fixed as the context for the Israelite conquest, settlement or revolt of Joshua and Judges. Finally, the Iron I–Iron II transition was explained either in terms of the rise of 2 Samuel's "United Monarchy" or as marking 1 King's devolution of this "United Monarchy" into the "divided" states of *Israel* and *Judah*.

Several unintended and unfortunate developments resulted from the essentially circular methodologies involved. Archaeological periodization became fixed by an absolute chronology of texts that both interpreted and were interpreted by archaeological remains. Moreover, because of the coherence of biblical tradition and the bias of "biblical archaeology," what was after all an essentially prehistoric *Palestine* came to be understood as a unified entity, and was uneasily separated from southern *Syria*, the *Transjordan* and the steppe and desert regions to the South and Southeast. A univocal and interlocking historical interpretation was assumed for all the subregions of *Palestine*. In fact, historical geography in Palestinian studies was almost universally understood merely in terms of the identification of toponyms (i.e., as a support for textual and especially biblical studies). Perhaps the most serious drawback of this direct synthesis of archaeological and written sources, with its focus on integrating the history of *Palestine* into the larger and textually much richer worlds of the Bible, classical historiography and ancient Near Eastern literature, lay in the neglect of internal Palestinian and archaeologically derived explanations of change of both material culture and forms of settlement. This neglect has led to the impoverishment of our abilities to write a history of *Palestine* beyond descriptive illustrations within the externally fixed causal framework that was provided by the uncorroborated historiographies of antiquity.

The extent of this problem is very pervasive. For example, in most recent serious introductory handbooks to biblical studies, whether liberal or conservative, the primary function of Palestinian archaeology is that of illustrating the text. The history of "Israel" is seen as derivative of a synthesis of biblical studies and archaeology, and, in biblical studies of a fundamentalist slant, largely identifiable with biblical historiography. Only very recently has the writing of the history of "Israel" begun to function in biblical research in the manner of history long established in other literary fields, by providing context and background to texts. However even today the history of "Israel" rarely provides an interpretive matrix for biblical studies.

One of the focal issues today concerning the question of the history of "Israel" or of "Israel's" origins is or ought to be that of method. So many of our central problems pivot on it, and every one of our major comprehensive reconstructions must out of both truth and modesty hesitate before using the adjective "sound" to describe its historical methods. While the purges brought about by the historicity debates, the increasingly popular late datings of biblical traditions and the growth and greater complexity of our archaeological and extra-biblical information, have helped build an appearance of an emerging consensus around such topics as the indigenous nature of early "Israel," its emergence contemporary with the establishment of a Saulide or Davidic state and the blurring of distinctions separating Canaanite from Israelite, none of these gains stand on entirely firm methodological grounds. If we reflect on how easy it is to challenge the historicity not only of a David or Solomon but of events in the reigns of Hezekiah or Josiah, or on how persuasive a dating to the Persian period or later of biblical traditions might appear today, the very substance of any historical project that attempts to write a history of the late second- or early first-millennium B.C. in *Palestine* on the basis of a direct integration of biblical and extrabiblical sources, bridging a gap not only of centuries but of a near total political, social and cultural dislocation, must appear not only dubious but wholly ludicrous.

Integrity and the search for historical competence, however, demands that we also recognize (if our ignorance is not willful) that much of what we have presented as a critical history of "Israel" or *Palestine*—even that resting on a basis independent of biblical historiography—is equally dubious, subject perhaps to less trenchant criticism only because it is less ambitious: a thin history is not as easy a target as a fat one. Not only is, with Lemche, the Canaanite-Israelite polarity a tendentious biblical tradition, but the protagonists are *eo ipso* literary, not historical realities, and the concept of an "indigenous Israel" in the twelfth–tenth centuries

B.C. is historically meaningless. Similarly, to begin the origins of biblical Israel with Merneptah or even with the Assyrian texts' *Bit Humri* on the grounds that we have extra-biblical rather than biblical attestation is willful. These texts are, *mirabile dictu*, even less relevant than the biblical traditions, if only because of the logical imperative that requires us to establish an association of them with the Israel of tradition. With the "Israel" stele we have only a name in an historical context in which the shifting signification and dislocation of regional and gentilic toponymy over centuries is a commonplace. And with *Bit Humri* we are faced with the additional embarrassment that the tradition itself rejects the association. If we are to look for the historical origins of the biblical Israel, we must methodologically begin with the Israel of tradition as logically prior, and we are forced to cast our trajectory backwards into the past, holding fast to the *rote Faden* of continuity.

The methodological crux of reconstructing the history of "Israel's" origins lies in the manner of our integration of whatever biblical and extrabiblical data we have: that difficult process of transubstantiation of "data" to "evidence." This crux is also very appropriately Janus-faced. The one face presents the chronological dilemma of all origin questions: by definition, the historical reality of biblical Israel is *post quem*, but the historical evidence for its origins is *ante quem*. The other face presents us with the dilemma of our evidence, which comes to us in radically different genres: the primary evidence of contemporary data, with a variety of distinctive type: textual, archaeological and geographical, and the secondary evidence encompassed by the *Mischgattungen* of biblical and extrabiblical traditional literature. The recognition of these serious difficulties is not a brief fostering despair; it is rather a procedural prolegomenon seeking the appropriate *hodoi*, along which we might progress historically rather than merely apologetically or polemically. In this effort, we must define history as disciplined research rather than as ideologically motivated assertions about the past.

Even when we argue for a history of "Israel" independent of the Bible, we rarely get further than a revisionist correction and reconstruction of biblical historiography; *i.e.*, a reorganized "Bible History". The psychologically more astute among us might see in the current malaise of historical research a pattern akin to post-partum depression. The child we have created in the 1980's is a *Mischwesen*: no longer a bible history, but even less is it a history of "Israel." We have given mere lip service to the principle of independent analysis of sources; we have rather created archaeologically structured sociological models based on deuteronomistic historiography.

In history, meaning is created, arbitrary and additional. The past, however, is a given to be discovered in its fragments and refractions, to be described as history. Hence, the requirement of evidence. The difficulty of relating our historical reconstructions to evidence is very serious. History as a descriptive science dependent on observation is not one we can subject to proof. Rather, historical reconstruction finds its criteria in accuracy and adequacy of portrayal independently confirmed. It did not have to be so; it was so.

In using sociology for historical research, we investigate the known patterns that human societies have taken: not what is intrinsic to society but what characterizes it! What is amazing about the "models" of Mendenhall and Gottwald (and one could easily add Coote and Whitelam here) is not that their theories were unsupported by evidence, but that these theories, lacking evidence, were ever proposed. Logic, discipline and method were never entertained. Their focus on anthropology, sociology and economics, however, is of immense importance, since most atextual approaches to historical change and development must proceed *á là longue durée; i.e.,*more in terms of societal and structural changes than in terms of events and personages.

A sound sociological approach must allow evidence to precede theory. Evidence, moreover, is always circumstantial. Historical judgment seeks not proof but accumulating conviction, corroboration and the absence of reasonable doubt. What we need to overcome this crisis in the historiography of early "Israel" is a structurally dependable, correctable and expandable history, which, independent of biblical historiography, might render the context of the tradition's formation and the background of its referents. Ultimately, we are attempting to integrate what we understand of geography, anthropology, sociology, archaeology, historical linguistics, Assyriology, Egyptology and biblical studies broadly conceived. But the methods of each of these fields—like their data—are extremely diverse, and none alone readily renders historical evidence of "Israel's" origins.

Since the early 1970s, attempts have been made to develop methods for integrating data from regional geography, anthropology and sociology with Syro-Palestinian archaeology, in the hope of describing major changes that affected the population of *Palestine* over time. Some of the major difficulties involved the accuracy and dependability—indeed the lack of standards—for surface surveys and their evaluation by historians, as well as very well founded doubts about the data and relevance of some of the then dominant sociological models used in the field.

In the 1980s, however, some real progress has been made. We have gained much in accuracy of reporting and in sophistication of the interpretation of settlement patterns. A great many scholars are responsible for this, but the surveys and studies of D. Esse, I. Finkelstein, and the recent Moab survey of J.M. Miller are exemplary. Problems remain—especially those of a seriously inadequate archaeological chronology and the still difficult task of corroboration. Settlement patterns are particularly useful in describing historical change if they can be integrated not only with traditional historical data but also with the palaeo branches of regional geography, anthropology and sociology. N.P. Lemche's *Early Israel* and H. Weippert's *Archäologie Palästina* are not only a great help in their use of anthropology in making sociological methods historically relevant, but Lemche also presents a good demonstration of what we have been referring to as a "spectrum studies" approach.

This method is based on efforts to interrelate a wide variety of taxonomies or spectra which organize ancient data that are potentially related to our historical questions and hence to our reconstructive interpretations. The integration of our analysis of multiple, overlapping spectra brings into our historical purview hundreds of data-sensitive variables relating to such important historical factors as economics, politics, social organization, linguistics, religion, ethnicity, art and material culture. When these spectra can be isolated in discrete chronological units, our analysis becomes open to the intrinsically historical issues of stability, development and change. We are now capable of establishing such spectra in great variety: settlement types, taxonomies of political structures, economic forms and types of food production. We can correlate these with geographic settings and climatic zones, as well as with regionally and chronologically related changes in rainfall and climate, vegetation, land use, roads and demographics. The pursuit of such an analysis creates a number of correlations that are relevant to the process of settlement during the Iron Age in the central hills of *Ephraim* and *Manasseh* and in the southern highlands of *Judaea.* The contrast of patterns that these regions reflect, when compared to each other and to other regions of *Palestine,* supports rather interesting lines of historical reconstruction.

A) *1600–1250 B.C.* During the Late Bronze dry spell, climatic stress correlates with the dislocation of small village and hamlet based agriculture throughout most of *Palestine* and also with the centering of the population in the larger towns of the lowlands and in the agriculturally most viable great highland valleys. Settlement in some regions are abandoned—most notably in those regions most affected by the radical shift in the border of aridity northwards.

B) *1250–1050 B.C.* The great Mycenaean drought correlates with East Mediterranean collapse and migrations into *Syria-Palestine* and the Egyptian Delta. Dislocations and deterioration of the lowland towns in the Mediterranean climatic zones of *Palestine* correlate with a substantial growth in the number of small villages within not only regions of established agriculture but also in many new regions and subregions that were for the first time opened to agricultural exploitation. Small and impoverished new village settlements are found in three distinct ecological zones of the central highlands of *Ephraim:* semi-steppe, fertile plateaus and valleys and the rugged western slopes. These three zones correspond respectively to high potentials for the economic regimes of grain agriculture and pastoralism, intensive forms of farming and horticulture-viniculture. The occupation involves full sedentarization in the central region of intensive agriculture, but also forms of transhumance pastoralism in the eastern sector and transhumance agriculture in the western sector. The requirements of symbiotic ties that are necessary for the economies of the eastern steppe and the western slopes to become viable, as well as clearly marked material cultural relationships with the Palestinian lowlands, suggests a very high probability that we have in the central hills during the Iron I period, a population that is economically rooted in an interrelated market or cash-crop economy of sheep and goats and their products, grains, intensive field crops, olives, wine and timber; *i.e.,* the product of a typical Mediterranean economy. A regime of subsistence farming on the other hand, must be excluded for many of the subregions that are newly settled at this time. The sources of the population of these new settlements were essentially of three types: a) people dislocated by the climatic and demographic stresses on lowland agriculture; b) some neighboring steppe dwellers under stress from the deterioration of the climate; and c) non-sedentary groups indigenous to the central highlands. Here one must think of the *'apiru* and *Shasu.* The continuities of the material culture suggest that the lowland immigrants were the more dominant.

C) *1050–850 B.C.* The Mycenaean drought comes to an end sometime before 1000 B.C. There are some indications of an agriculturally better than normal climate during the first two centuries of the first-millennium. This corresponds with the relative prosperity of *Palestine* during the Iron II period and an explosion of population during this poeriod in all regions of *Syria-Palestine*. The expansion of population correlates closely with the revival of international trade and, with it, an expected increase in the demand for oil, lumber, wine, meat and dairy products, and the largest development of new settlements in those areas where terraced-based horticulture was alone viable or normally dominant. In this context, *Samaria* was built—not as a city state (*i.e.*, the essentially agriculturally based market town with an indigenous *Hinterland* supporting it traditional to *Palestine*) but as a capital city with dominant public structures. *Samaria*, nevertheless, developed a true town with a base in agriculture and an immediate *Hinterland* supporting a considerable population as befits the capital of a state wholly dependent on agriculture and timber. That *Samaria* was the capital city of much of the region of the central highlands is corroborated by Assyrian texts that suggest a tripartite competitive struggle for the control of the *Jezreel* and the *Galilee* between *Damascus, Tyre* and *Samaria*. A Moabite text refers to a similar struggle over the *Gilead* between *Moab* and *Israel*, a competition which may also have included *Damascus* and *Ammon*. All of this corresponds well with Assyrian and biblical references to dynastic rule centered in *Samaria*.

One of the central changes distinguishing Iron I from Iron II in the central highlands, corresponding to the development of a capital center, was an economic shift from regionally and subregionally based markets to a dominance of interregional and international markets, giving increased importance to the trade routes and their access. This shift goes far to explain the concurrent shift towards centralization in these geographically decentralized central hills. An evolutionary explanation based in a city-state imperial form of expansion (as one might expect, for example, from *Shechem*, recreating its *Amarna* Period dominance) probably should be excluded because it runs counter to the proclivities of the regional state structure that the building of *Samaria* seems to require. At *Samaria*, the establishment of a political base of power is logically prior to the actual building of the city. What was established here was new to *Palestine*. Moreover, the lack of geographically unifying factors in the geological structure of the central hills, and the development of numerous subregional centers throughout the central highlands militated strongly against an expanding dominance of a single city over such a diverse population. This context was radically different from that of Labaya's *Shechem*. The motive force behind the development of Samaria was the end result of the rationalization of trade to accommodate the rising demands of markets external to the central hills, a development that small scale trade simply could not foster. This led to the formation of a region-wide agricultural cartel with an autonomous center free of any single subregion's dominance. Samaria was built to monopolize and funnel oil production, timber and other products to the trade routes of the *Jezreel*, linking *Samaria*'s fate inexorably to the *Jezreel* and to the greater world of politics, caravans and soldiers.

The origin of the population of the Judaean highlands reveals both analogies and contrasts to that of the state of *Israel*.

A) *1600–1000 B.C. Jerusalem*'s heartland from the Middle Bronze Age through the Iron I period comprises the rich and stable agricultural zones of the *Jerusalem* saddle and the *Ayyalon* Valley that are dominated by a number of small agricultural market towns of which *Jerusalem* was among the most prominent. In contrast, the Judaean uplands lay south of the border of aridity, that reached nearly as far north as *Jerusalem* itself throughout this very long period. The corresponding lack of any significant sedentary population in the Judaean highlands is to be expected. South of the highlands, the Northern *Negev* hosted only the short-lived dimorphic, pastoral-market town of *Tell el-Meshash* during the height of the Mycenaean drought, a factor most important in understanding its economic role in the heart of *Palestine*'s steppe. The rolling *Shephelah* hills to the West of the highlands maintained a fragile stability among an impoverished indigenous population that was settled geographically, ecologically and economically separate from the *Jerusalem* heartland.

B) *1000–700 B.C.* During the first part of Iron II, *Jerusalem* was a small provincial town at best, not significantly superior to such *Shephelah* towns as *Lachish* and *Gezer*. One *Arad* letter implies that *Arad* was politically independent from *Jerusalem,* and one text from *Kuntillet Ajrud* refers to a Yahweh of *Samaria* and a Yahweh of *Teman* but makes no mention of *Jerusalem*. Similarly, Shoshenk moves his army against the *Ayyalon* Valley but does not list *Jerusalem* among the towns it attacks. While these are negative references and perhaps insignificant, one may be excused for doubting that *Jerusalem* was a major power in the region at this early date. During the Iron II period, a number of forts were built in both the Northern *Negev* and the *Judaean Desert*. This period also witnessed the development of a large number of small villages in the Judaean highlands in areas where either pastoralism or terraced-based horticulture were ecologically supported and traditionally dominant. On the basis of these correlations, I would suggest that the sedentary population of the Judaean highlands resulted initially from either an expansion of the *Shephelah* or from the coastal plain's efforts to meet the growing demand for olive production made by interregional and international trade (supported by logging and terrace construction). To enhance security and to support the expansion of the oil industry, the town based agriculturalists forced the sedentarization of nomadic pastoralists in both the Judaean highlands and the Northern *Negev*.

Prior to the seventh-century, *Jerusalem* may have been competitive with *Hebron, with* the *Shephelah* and with the Northern *Negev* towns for the control of the cash crops of the highland's timber, pastoral and horticultural production. *Jerusalem*'s easy road-access to the highland villages along the watershed would have supported any ambitions *Jerusalem* may have had in this direction. The processing plants of such towns as *Ekron*, however, could easily bypass *Jerusalem*, and the funnelling process moving olives from production to the presses and ultimately to markets may well have gone through such towns as *Lachish* or *Hebron*. *Lachish*'s possible subordination to *Jerusalem* is both unknown and unexplained, and should not be assumed. Indeed, it should be suggested that not only the *Shephelah* towns, but *Hebron* and the towns of the Northern *Negev*, had been independent from and competitive with *Jerusalem* until at least the end of the eighth-century. It seems unlikely that the small town of *Jerusalem* could have extended its power base so far southward and have developed settlements in both the Judaean highlands and the Northern *Negev*. Although the biblical traditions encourage us to look in this direction, they hardly give us warrant to affirm this against the more likely claims of *Hebron* and the *Shephelah* towns.

C) *The seventh-century B.C.* In the seventh-century, *Jerusalem* became a city with a population and a prosperity many times that of earlier periods. It is first in this period that *Jerusalem* acquired the character of a regional state capital. One must doubt *Jerusalem*'s capacity for such political aggrandizement at any earlier period. It is unlikely that

Jerusalem's growth was driven simply by the opportunity, following *Lachish*'s destruction, to expand imperially southwards, since Sennacherib's campaign had decidedly trimmed *Jerusalem*'s influence in *Judaea*. It also seems difficult to assume that *Jerusalem* had expanded as the result of an influx of refugees from the destruction of *Samaria*. Not only would this have drawn *Jerusalem* in the direction of a hopeless confrontation with *Assyria*, but *Jerusalem* had been a long-standing enemy of *Samaria*, and whatever refugees from *Samaria* there might have been would have found more likely refuge among its more durable allies in *Phoenicia*. The economic support of *Jerusalem*—now a great city in the seventh-century—could not have been maintained solely by the *Jerusalem* saddle and the *Ayyalon* Valley. *Jerusalem*'s expansion might be seen as partially analogous to *Ekron*'s comparable expansion to a position of hegemony on the coastal plain, that is as the result of a cooperative effort with the Assyrian empire to establish the center of a vassal state in *Judaea*. After the destructions at the hands of the Assyrian army, the eighth-century *Shephelah* towns were not resettled. Rather, during the seventh-century, *Judaea*, and with it the *Shephelah*, was reorganized around a number of new fortified towns, apparently subject to *Jerusalem*, rather than on the patterns of the eighth-century and earlier periods. *Jerusalem*'s expansion of its *Hinterland* southwards seems clearly explained in terms of a concerted effort to establish control over the Judaean highlands, the *Shephelah* and perhaps the Northern *Negev*. However much *Jerusalem* had the blessing or the support of *Assyria* in this move, one must characterize it as an imperial-type expansion of a city-state over subject peoples. *Jerusalem*'s growing size alone gave it warrant to assert authority over *Hebron* and the towns of the Northern *Negev* and to fill the power gap left by the collapse of the *Shephelah* towns. It is unlikely, however, that the exercise of this warrant was carried out in opposition to the firmly established Assyrian authority in the region.

Our conclusion, then, is that *Jerusalem* became the capital of a regional state in the course of the seventh-century. However, unlike *Samaria*, its political structure was that of an imperial city-state. *Jerusalem*'s potential as a capital of a nation-state can only with great difficulty be asserted for any period of the Iron Age. Such a development came about only with the ideological and political changes of the Persian period, centered around the Persian supported construction of a temple dedicated to the transcendent *elohe shamayim*, identified with Yahweh, the long neglected traditional god of the former state of *Israel,* who, in his new capital at the center of the province of *Yehud,* might, like Ba'al Shamem of Aramaic texts, be best described as a Palestinian variant of the Neo-Babylonian divine *Śin* and of Persia's *Ahura Mazda.*

2. *"Israel" as a National Entity*

When this reconstruction is related to Assyrian texts, biblical traditions and linguistic data, the conclusion becomes difficult to avoid that just as the origin of the ninth and seventh-century states of *Israel* and *Judah* were wholly separate, they were also unlikely to have any more common an ethnic base than had any other two neighboring states of the Southern Levant. *Israel,* having developed out of the geographical dislocation of the lowland agricultural population in response to the great Mycenaean drought, and *Judah,* having originated in the expansion of the olive industry supported by international trade that brought about a forced sedentarization of pastoralists in the course of early Iron II, were, throughout the ninth to seventh centuries, at most small petty states largely confined to the hill country, and although *Israel* indeed played a role in power politics prior to *Assyria*'s entry into the region, neither were ever dominant in *Palestine.* The existence of the Bible's "United Monarchy" during the tenth-century is not only impossible because *Judah* had not yet a sedentary population, but also because there was no transregional political or economic base of power in *Palestine* prior to the expansion of Assyrian imperial influence into the southern Levant.

The population of the central highlands might be understood as reasonably coherent and stable for a period of more than four centuries. This coherence took on state form in the ninth-century under the Omride dynasty, and lasted until the fourth quarter of the eighth-century. This state of *Israel* had expansive ambitions, and, during the course of the period of Assyrian hegemony in the Levant, *Samaria* found itself in recurrent conflict over the control of the *Gilead,* the *Jezreel* and possibly the *Galilee.* We know that during this period *Israel* had asserted its control over part of the *Transjordan* highlands of *Gilead,* and it is likely that it was occasionally successful in its claims on the *Jezreel.* However, its control in the *Gilead* is likely to have remained at the level of economic and political influence, as, while there are clear similarities in the type of agriculture between *Israel* and the *Gilead,* the forms of political and military hegemony typical of the southern Levant was commonly that of political subordination and vassalage, with an economic exploitation in the forms of booty, tribute or taxes, but not in forms of colonization or population absorption. During the time that *Gilead* was subject to *Israel,* the essential core of its population could be expected to have remained distinct. Whatever *Samaria*'s influence over the *Jezreel* was, and whatever the shifting economic and military controls over the region were, the population of the *Jezreel,* with its roots going back to the Bronze Age, with its centers in large agricultural towns and with its openness to the cosmopolitan influences of the international trade networks, maintained its diverse distinctiveness from that of the more isolated central highlands. The *Jezreel,* though politically decentralized, with a huge agricultural population and a lucrative trade network with towns of considerable size, must have been difficult for any of the regionally based powers in Northern *Palestine* to hold permanently. The *Galilee* could not have been held by *Samaria* without it first having established control over the *Jezreel.* Control over the *Galilee* by *Samaria* seems unlikely, as the *Galilee* continued to reflect strong influences from the North and the Northwest, and was markedly Phoenician in character. We have no reason to associate its population with that of *Israel.*

The diversity of *Palestine*'s population during the first half of the first-millennium B.C. is underscored by our limited linguistic evidence. First it is necessary to separate the Hebrew of biblical tradition from the extensive linguistic diversity of epigraphic finds. Not only do the morphological distortions of the massoretic traditions require us to deal with these sources in methodologically different ways, but Ullendorf and Knauf have given us reason to view biblical Hebrew as an artificial literary construct, a *Bildungssprache,* with a history from the mid-first-millennium B.C. to the mid-first-millennium A.D. In analyzing the dialectical variances of the epigraphic finds from greater *Palestine* of the early first-millennium B.C., the various dialects of "Canaanite," with roots in Early West Semitic ("Amorite") display some interesting distinctions and associations. "West Canaanite" (Phoenician, two or more dialects of Israelite and Judaean) distinguishes itself from "East Canaanite" (Ammonite, Moabite and Edomite). Even more clearly, a "Core Canaanite" (Israelite and Phoenician) can be distinguished from "Fringe Canaanite" (Judaean, Ammonite, Moabite and Edomite).

Certainly, Halpern's argument that we need to be more attentive to the geographic and sociological displacement of epigraphic finds is well founded. The proto-ethnic developments of the central highlands under the centralized rule from *Samaria* (which is the *"Israel"* of the Assyrian and Moabite texts) do not resolve the questions of either ethnicity nor of the origins of the Israel of biblical tradition. There is continuity neither of population nor of ideology between the *Israel* of *Samaria* and the Israel of tradition. In biblical tradition, *Samaria* is the false Israel. The reasons for this transvaluation of the signification of the name Israel are both clear and enlightening.

If the population of *Palestine* during Iron I and early Iron II was mixed, that of the later Assyrian period was even less unified. This was an intentional and a direct outcome of Assyrian imperial policy. When in the fourth quarter of the eighth-century *Assyria* suppressed the state of *Israel* and subordinated Northern *Palestine* under a provincial authority, it also systematically destroyed the coherence of the population and the economic and political infrastructures that had been the foundation of *Israel*'s solidarity and the source of its strength. *Assyria* did this through highly sophisticated policies of mass deportation and population transference. Not only were the elite deported, but craftsmen, corvée laborers, women for the slave trade and men for the army, and indeed entire villages and towns were moved across great distances of the empire. The admittedly limited and incomplete number of Assyrian deportation texts we have, nevertheless number well over one hundred and fifty, and are more than adequate to show that the minimum number of people in the Middle East affected by these policies were in the hundreds of thousands, and the number is more likely to have been in the millions. These policies of population deportation and relocation were multifunctional: terror, punishment, extortion, reward, systems of hostage taking, royal building projects, the slave trade, the development of economic monopolies in crafts and trade, military induction, the security of borders, the destruction of indigenous bases of power, the destruction of the social fabric within conquered territories, forestalling revolution, the resettlement of previously decimated regions and towns and the creation of dependents and groups faithful to the Assyrian empire. When *Samaria* was destroyed, much of *Samaria*'s and *Israel*'s population was resettled in *Assyria, Media* and Northern *Syria*. They were partially replaced by groups from Northern *Syria, Babylon, Elam* and *Arabia*.

Similarly, Sennacherib claims to have deported parts of the population of forty-six villages of *Judah* (a considerable portion of this region in any period) and to have divided the Judaean *Hinterland* among *Assyria*'s allies: *Ashdod, Eqron* and *Gazza.* The story of 2 Kings 18:19 of Sennacherib's siege of *Jerusalem* is wonderfully reflective of *Assyria*'s policy—especially the Assyrian general's teeth-baring propagandistic speech to the people, pitting them against their rulers, offering reward rather than punishment": "Make peace with me, surrender to me, and every one of you will eat the fruit of his own vine and of his own fig tree, and drink the water of his own cistern, until I come to deport you to a country like your own, a land of corn and good wine, a land of bread and vineyards, a land of oil and honey, so that you might not die but live." *Jerusalem,* and with it, some part of its core periphery, survived Sennacherib, and in the course of the seventh-century, under Assyrian vassalage, even prospered. However, neither *Jerusalem* nor *Judah* survived the Babylonian armies of Nebuchadnezzar. *Judah* was pillaged, *Jerusalem* was destroyed and at least a three-fold deportation followed. Judging from the many new towns and villages that were created in this region beginning already with the mid-seventh-century Assyrian period settlements and continuing new settlement during the Iron III or Persian period, a substantial relocation of foreign peoples took root throughout *Judaea* and the *Shephelah*. By the end of the sixth-century, the *Jerusalem* and *Judah* of the Assyrian period had ceased to exist as thoroughly as had the *Samaria* and *Israel* of the eighth-century. If this region had ever developed a coherence or national ethnicity, that did not survive the dislocations and displacements of the sixth-century. The Iron Age population of the Palestinian highlands entered the Persian period radically transformed.

3. *The Intellectual Matrix of Biblical Tradition*

Deportation was not primarily a policy of punishment. The deportees were also protected by the Assyrians and the Babylonians, receiving not only land and property but also support against the indigenous populations among whom they became representatives of imperial control. Even in the central cities of the empire, the deportees formed pockets of imperial influence against unrest and rebellion. While our best evidence for such practices come from Assyrian texts, both the

Babylonians and the Persians continued these policies on a large scale. However, as successors to rather than as creators of empire, both the Babylonians and the Persians added significantly to the propagandistic component of their population policies, seeking through this practice of massive manipulation of peoples to create an imperial citizenry faithful to the government, educated by the government and supported by the government, without substantial regional power except insofar as they were subject to and dependent on the empire. In these aims they were largely successful.

As successors to an already established empire, the Babylonians and the Persians did not need to defend the right of conquest over indigenously independent networks of traditional power and wealth. They were dealing with already conquered peoples, and the needs of the new imperial administration turned rather to issues of legitimation and right of succession rather than conquest. Their propaganda consequently was oriented away from policies of terror and towards winning support for a change of administration. Efforts were made to demonstrate that *Babylon*—and Persia in its turn—were the legitimate successors to imperial power, and hence worthy of allegiance. The nature of imperial power was a given, already long established by *Assyria*. The new leadership was free to concentrate on winning support and loyalty. No longer did one deal with a dominant need for a politically suppressive force. Infrastructures could now be rebuilt as an enhancement and support to economic prosperity because they were no longer directly threatening to imperial control. In this new context, the propagandistic function of deportation texts take on a more persuasive character. Simply put, the Babylonian and Persian administrations had the luxury of presenting themselves as the liberators and benefactors of their subject peoples, and were able to cast their predecessors (the Assyrians, and the Babylonians in their turn) as barbaric oppressors of the people. This genre of propaganda is transparent.

Among the most extraordinary stelae of the ancient Near East are the double pair of Nabonidus and Nabonidus's mother in the temple of *Sin* at *Harran*. In these texts, it is very clear that a new world order was being created at *Harran,* but the establishment of the new order is put in the language of "restoration." Nabonidus, the servant of the god *Sin,* is in the act of restoring the long lost cult of the god to *Harran.* In doing this, he brings people from *Babylon, Syria* and *Egypt,* but *Harran*'s restoration is also theirs; for he establishes them as citizens of and heirs to the forgotten traditions of *Harran*, rebuilding the city in its former glory and bringing all the old gods back to their homes: *Sin, Nirsku, Sudarnunna* and *Ningal*. Here this new god of a new population in this newly reconstituted city is declared to be the true and original ancient god of *Harran*, their forgotten god of their lost tradition. This ideological transference is enabled by the identity of the traditional deity of the region—who is indeed *Sin*—with the God of heaven, the ultimate, spiritual representative of all that is divine in the Neobabylonian world. This theme of the emperor as the "restorer" of the gods and of the "indigenous" populace is found throughout the Babylonian deportation inscriptions. Conversely, in these texts,the destruction of the cults and temples of the subject peoples is blamed either on the Assyrians or on barbaric allies. The Babylonians take the high ground as champions of the oppressed population, acting under Marduk's instruction, restoring cities and their populations, rebuilding the temples and dedicating deportees as temple servants of the gods.

The ideological thrust of deportation policy was perfected by the Persians. The Cyrus cylinder, as we have seen, claims that the former Babylonian king had destroyed the integrity of religion. Instead of the real, heavenly, spiritual God of tradition, only replicas—mere clay statues—were worshipped throughout the land. Even the rituals, offerings and prayers were all wrong. The Babylonian king had enslaved the people; towns were in ruins, fields were abandoned and the gods were so upset at having been forced away from their homes into *Babylon* that they abandoned the city. Marduk, however, had had mercy and had called Cyrus to reestablish justice among all the people whom Marduk himself had (out of his goodness and righteousness) caused Cyrus to take *Babylon*. Cyrus, of course, didn't need weapons for this conquest. The people greeted Cyrus their new ruler with open arms, tears of joy and song. Rather than murder and pillage, Cyrus tirelessly restored both gods and peoples to their homes. This transportation of gods and populations under the title of "restoration" is indeed declared by the scribe as the primary function of empire, a literary policy which is continued under both Xerxes and Darius II.

However they may be related to a specific historical transportation of deportees from *Babylon* to *Palestine*, or to the actual onset of construction on the temple in *Jerusalem*, I see no reason to doubt the authenticity of references to a decree of Cyrus in 2 Chronicles 36, Ezra I and Isaiah 45. 2 Chron 36:22–23 and Ezra 1:1–11, after all, do nothing more than identify the heavenly, spiritual, divine *elohe shamayim* with the name of the long neglected indigenous deity of the former state of Israel: *Yahweh*. As Nabonidus at the command of the God of heaven restored the temple and the ancient cult of *Sin* at *Harran*, so Ezra sees Cyrus, acting under the command of the supreme God of heaven, as ordering the restoration of the temple and the ancient cult of *Yahweh* at *Jerusalem*. It is within this intellectual context that Isaiah 40–48 understands Cyrus as "restoring" the traditional people of the land—of course now misunderstood by the Persian administration and Isaiah as "Israel"—the people destroyed by the Assyrians some two centuries earlier—in *Jerusalem* and as "restoring" their ancestral faith in the one true God. It is, of course, clear that we are not dealing with the restoration of exiles to their homeland anymore than we are dealing with the restoration of an ancient forgotten cult or the rebuilding of a temple. The texts reflect the transportation and creation of a new people with a new cult, expressing an understanding of the divine that is central to the imperial administration and identified with a divine name common to the larger region's traditional past. This can be described as the creation of a new society centered on a new temple and administered by the Persian administrator, who himself identifies with these people (Nehemiah 1:1–11). Whatever people were being transported or returned to *Palestine*, they certainly were not Israelites. However, they were identified by the Persians and in the development of a written tradition came to understand themselves as the population of long lost Israel returning to *"Eretz Israel"* from bitter exile after having been delivered from *Babylon* by their savior and master: Cyrus. With the help of the Persians, they set as their goal the reestablishment of the ancient cult of *Yahweh*, now, of course, understood and identified with *elohe shamayim*, who was not merely the head of a divine pantheon, but was the very essence of the divine—throughout the empire—and who, in *Palestine*, went by the name *Yahweh*.

Under Darius, the Persians began to centralize the legal and economic structures of the empire. This was done by enforcing the "King's law" given by *Ahura Mazda* in terms of the "restoration" of "traditional" and local legal custom and practice. The propagandistic form that this reorganization took should not mislead us into seeing this as an inauguration of a regionally-based "home rule." Rather, it was centralized administration with a local, regional face. Ezra 4–6 reflects some of the administrative difficulties endemic to imperial policies that introduced new population elements, new central cults and new interpretations of tradition into a region and the self-understanding of its established population. These tensions and conflicts reflect the realities of the intrusive nature of Persian relocation and deportation policies. To the indigenous population, which had long been structured by the prior Assyrian and Babylonian polity, the formation of a centralized cult of Yahweh and the imposition of a legal and economic restructuring of society under the authority of a resurgent *Jerusalem,* would certainly appear as a substantial threat to the established order. This is exactly what the indigenous population protests in Ezra 4–6, and it is exactly the issue that the New Israel had to address. In the collection and restructuring of tradition that followed, there emerged for the first time in *Palestine* an Israel that is recognizable as the Israel of biblical tradition.

The central historical question that needs to be raised regarding these transitions from the Assyrian to the Persian periods rests in part on our evaluation of the nature and the effects of these policies of population transference as they relate to the people of *Palestine.* Certainly a recognition of the propagandistic quality of the language of return and restoration encourages us to question the modern chronological categories of pre-exilic, exilic and post-exilic in our judgment about the history of "Israel." Both the nature of deportation policies and the lack of an independent precise definition of the exilic community suggest that the perception and identification of the formers of the biblical tradition as post-exilic is indeed essentially prior both chronologically and in terms of self-understanding. That is to say: the understanding of themselves as "saved" in a return from exile cast the understanding of the formers of biblical tradition in the pattern of identification with the victims of Assyrian and Babylonian deportation practices. This, in turn, engendered an understanding of a pre-exilic period as the matrix of both divine wrath and a lost glory to be restored. The logic of the argumentation requires us to ask whether the scholarly language of "pre-exilic," "exilic," and "post exilic" periods reflects realities of history or is not rather an attribute of Persian-biblical ideology. Are the "returnees" from *Babylon,* with whom the biblical tradition finds identification, in fact exiles who effectively restore "Israel's" real past, or does the self-understanding of themselves as exiles serve as an ideological matrix for a new Israel, now centered in a temple in

Jerusalem dedicated to a reestablished Yahweh the God of Israel, and identified with *elohé shamayim*?

This question, relating to the literal validity of Persian propaganda, is not easily answered as we possess little more than the Persian texts themselves and their derivatives in the biblical tradition. At stake is both an historical understanding of the received view of Cyrus as *Messiah* of Yahweh, on the basis of which the reforms of Ezra and Nehemiah are understood as restorations rather than innovations, and the understanding of Yahweh as *elohé shamayim* as derivative of the Persian administration of the province of *Yehud* supporting a restoration of religious traditions that were indigenous to the region.

One effect of the Assyrian policies of deportation, which might properly be recognized as a goal of their imperial administration, was the systematic destruction of the infrastructure of conquered territories. Primary targets for transportation were the ruling elite, skilled craftsmen, scribes and educators, and the military and the cultic personnel: all those who structure a society as a functional whole. In some regions, societal destruction went even further as whole villages were transported, dislocating agriculture and the economic foundation of lands conquered. While vassal states maintained their indigenous infrastructure, territories included within the borders of *Assyria* were ruthlessly exploited both for their population and for their material wealth in lumber and minerals. In place of the productive core of their populations, subject territories received, when they received anything at all, dislocated elements who could only with the greatest difficulty be integrated into a disoriented and depressed economy. The lack of ethnic discrimination in Assyrian military and administrative policy seriously undermined regional coherence and destroyed the potential for regional solidarity. The effects in *Palestine* of these policies is born out in the archaeological records. Settlement in the *Galilee* collapses and is not revived until the hellenistic period. The prosperity of the *Jezreel* and the central hills is replaced by an economic depression contemporary with their incorporation into the Assyrian empire, and the population of *Judah* rapidly deteriorated from the end of the seventh-century until nearly the end of the Persian period. That such deterioration was intentional is perhaps too harsh a judgment. *Assyria*'s efforts to create a common language (Aramaic), and the development of schools throughout the empire that fostered the amalgamation of the diverse populations created by transportation, certainly indicates active policies to reverse the deleterious effects of deportation. Nevertheless, the dynamic cosmopolitan character of the Assyrian cities and the major trading centers of the Levant were created at the cost of massive dislocation and the weakening or destruction of the ethnic, religious and economic infrastructures of the provinces. By the end of the sixth-century, *Palestine* was without unity or any meaningful coherence. Ethnically, linguistically, religiously, economically and politically it lacked cohesion. Its elite had been transported to serve imperial aims, and the core of its populations was scattered and divided among incoherent groupings of indigenous and resettled peoples. It is instructive that the primary opposition to the efforts of the so-called returnees in their efforts to create a centralized cult and political center in *Jerusalem* came from *Samaria* that had a history of some two centuries in the region, rather than from *Judea*. The political opposition of *Samaria* was, however, never whole-hearted, and an ethno-religious consolidation among the concept of return became viable, resulting in the construction of a temple in *Jerusalem* and the subsequent development of an ethno-centric core around the worship of Yahweh, the traditional deity of both *Samaria* and *Judaea*, but now understood in universalist monotheistic terms.

A significant benefit of establishing the historical context of the origin of the Israel of tradition is that one creates thereby an entry into the intellectual matrix or *Zeitgeist* that had formed the central core of Israel's tradition as a whole, that complex composite of legal, cultic and folk tradition, whose preservation was central to both the formation and the survival of Israel's self understanding. The physical and editorial unities that hold Genesis-2 Kings together (and gives coherence to Israel) is a cumulative, collected tradition—a survival literature if you will—certainly a literature aimed at a self-understanding in terms of a surviving remnant. The tradition comes truly from the past: fragments of memory: written and oral, chains of narrative, complex literary works, administrative records, songs, prophetic sayings, the words of philosophers, lists and stories: all perceived as meaningful within a cohering and cumulative whole, discriminatingly assembled and organized: interpreted as a past shattered.

The "Babylonian Exile" plays a central role in the formation of tradition not as the historiographical point in time to which the tradition is directed in its closure in 2 Kings, nor even that period of the past from which new beginnings were launched. It rather plays the role of interpretive matrix of the tradition in its function as a self understanding of the people of Yahweh, a remnant saved. Radical trauma of exile is used as a literary paradigm in terms of which both the newly formed tradition and its collectors acquired identity as Israel. In the Persian period, one takes on the identity of Israel through association with this remnant, whether or not one's ancestors had originally come from *Babylon, Nineveh and Egypt* or had always been in *Palestine.* To identify with the true Israel was to assert one's roots in exile, and through it in the lost glory of the Davidic empire, in the conquest with Joshua, in the wilderness with Moses, in the exodus from *Egypt,* as a *ger* with Abraham and with *Yahweh* at the creation.

This central core of tradition, this *Torah* of instruction, is marked by both a universal and an inclusive monotheism, comparable to both the Neobabylonian concept of a spiritual, heavenly supreme deity, such as *Sin* at Harran, and of the universal God of heaven and creator of all known by the Persians as *Ahura Mazda.* This worldview seems to have been significantly prior to the exclusivistic tendencies of Persian religion under Xerxes and the nationalistic proclivities of later Yahwism. It seems possible that one might do well to mark the inclusive and exclusive forms of monotheism so evident in the biblical traditions as reflections of a mid- and a late-Persian period intellectual milieu in *Palestine.* The former seems to have been marked with the expansive euphoria of empire and world order with an ecumenism born of confidence, while the latter seems driven by fears of external threat and loss of tradition that was brought about in this western fringe of *Persia*'s empire by the encroachment of a new and competitive worldview of syncretistic polytheism born of incipient hellenism.

The linguistic and literary reality of the biblical tradition is folkloristic in its essence. The concept of a *benei Israel*: a people and an ethnicity, bound in union and by ties of family and common descent, possessing a common past and oriented towards a common futuristic religious goal, is a reflection of no sociopolitical entity of the historical state of Israel of the Assyrian period, nor is it an entirely realistic refraction of the post-state Persian period in which the biblical tradition took its shape as a cohering self understanding of *Palestine*'s population. It rather has its origin and finds its meaning within the development of the tradition and within the utopian religious perceptions that the tradition created, rather than within the real world of the past that the tradition restructured in terms of a coherent ethnicity and religion. In this, the religion of "Israel" is not identifiable with the religion of

Palestine of the past, however much it echoes and reasserts aspects of that past religion. It is in the Persian period, quite specifically to be identified with the theologized world of the biblical tradition, within which Israel itself is a theologumenon and a new creation out of tradition. Concepts of syncretism are not immediately relevant to the formation of the tradition. The limited religious centrism of Iron Age *Samaria* and *Jerusalem* do not survive the transformation of the populations that took place during Iron II. Yahwism was the central state cult in *Samaria*. That it survived into the Persian period and beyond is a characteristic more of its conceptual flexibility and its ability to be subsumed under the inclusive universalist understanding of *Elohim* than of the continuity of its adherents. The shift of the religious center from *Samaria* to its former competitor *Jerusalem*—with its new temple—is an aspect of Persian administrative rationalization supported by the for *Palestine* new worldview of inclusive Yahwism.

TOPONYMS

AUTHORS

GENERAL INDEX

BIBLIOGRAPHY

Aharoni, M. "The Pottery of Strata 12-11 of the Iron Age Citadel at Arad," *Eretz Israel* 15 (1981), pp.181-204.

Aharoni, Y. *The Settlement of the Israelite Tribes in Upper Galilee* (Hebrew University, dissertation 1957).

—— "Galilee, Upper," *EAEHL*, vol. I, pp.74f. 82-89.

—— "Forerunners of the Limes: Iron Age Fortresses in the Negev," *IEJ* 17 (1967), pp.1-17.

—— "New Aspects of the Israelite Occupation in the North," in J.A. Sanders (ed.) *Near Eastern Archaeology in the Twentieth Century: Essays in Honor of Nelson Glueck*, ed. by J.A. Sanders (Garden City, 1970) pp.254-265.

—— "Excavations at Tell Beersheba," *BA* 35 (1972), pp.111-127.

—— "The Settlement of the Tribes in the Negev: A New Picture," *Ariel* 41 (1976), pp.3-19.

—— "Nothing Early, Nothing Late: Rewriting Israel's Conquest," *BA* 39 (1976), pp.55-76.

—— "The Negev During the Israelite Period," *The Land of the Negev*, ed. by A. Schmueli and Y. Grados (Tel Aviv, 1979) pp.209-225.

Ahituv, S. "Economic Factors in the Egyptian Conquest of Palestine," *IEJ* 28 (1978), pp.93-105.

Ahlström, G.W. *Aspects of Syncretism in Israelite Religion* (Lund, 1963).

—— *Administration and National Religion in Ancient Palestine* (Leiden, 1982).

—— *An Archaeological Picture of Iron Age Religions in Ancient Palestine*, Studia Orientalia 55,3 (Helsinki, 1984).

—— "The Early Iron Age Settlers at Hirbet el-Msas (Tel Masos)," *ZDPV* 100 (1984), pp.35-52.

—— and Edelman, D. "Merneptah's Israel," *JNES* 44 (1985), pp.59-61.

—— *Who Were the Israelites?* (Winona Lake, 1986).

—— *The Early History of Ancient Palestine from the Palaeolithic Period to Alexander's Conquest* (Sheffield, 1992).

Albrektson B., *History and the Gods* (Lund, 1967).

Albright, W.F. "Historical and Mythical Elements in the Joseph Story," *JBL* 37 (1918), pp.111-143.

—— "The Archaeological Results of an Expedition to Moab and the Dead Sea," *BASOR* 14 (1924), pp.1-12.

—— "The Israelite Conquest of Palestine in the Light of Archaeology," *BASOR* 74 (1939), pp.1-23.

—— *From the Stone Age to Christianity* (Garden City, 1940, ³1957).

—— *The Excavations at Tell Beit Mirsim III: The Iron Age*, AASOR 21 and 22 (1943).

—— *The Archaeology of Palestine* (London, 1949).

—— *Archaeology and the Religion of Israel* (Baltimore), 1953).

—— "Albrecht Alt," *JBL* 75 (1956), pp.169-173.

—— "Abram the Hebrew, A New Archaeological Interpretation," *BASOR* 163 (1961), pp.36-54.

—— *The Biblical Period from Abraham to Ezra* (New York,1963).

—— *Yahweh and the Gods of Canaan* (London,1968).

Ålin, P. "Mycenaean Decline—Some Problems and Thoughts," *Greece and the Eastern Mediterranean, Ancient History and Prehistory*, ed. by K.H. Hinzl (Berlin, 1977) pp.31-39.

Alt, A. "Ein Reich von Lydda," *ZDPV* 47 (1924), pp.169-185.

—— *Die Landnahme der Israeliten in Palästina: Reformationsprogramm der Universität Leipzig* (Leipzig, 1925).

—— "Die asiatischen Gefahrzonen in den Ächtungstexten der 11ten Dynastie," *ZÄS* 63 (1928), pp.39-45.

—— *Die Staatenbildung der Israeliten in Palästina: Reformationsprogramm der Universität Leipzig* (Leipzig, 1930).

—— "Erwägungen über die Landnahme der Israeliten in Palästina," *PJ* 35 (1939), pp.8-63.

—— "Die älteste Schilderung Palästinas im Lichte neuer Funde," *PJ* 37 (1941), pp.19-49.

—— "Herren und Herrensitze Palästinas im Anfang des zweiten Jahrtausends v.Chr." *ZDPV* 64 (1941), pp.21-39.

—— *Kleine Schriften I-III* (Munich, 1953).

—— *Essays on Old Testament History and Religion* (Oxford, 1966).

Amiran, R. *Ancient Pottery of the Holy Land* (Jerusalem, 1969).

Andersen, N.E. "Genesis 14 in its Near Eastern Context," *Scripture in Context*, ed. by W.W. Hallo (New Haven, 1980) p.78ff.

Anderson, G.W. *«Israel: Amphictyony:'Am; Kahal; Edah,"* Translating and Understanding the Old Testament: Essays in Honor of Herbert Gordon May*, ed. by H.T. Frank and W.L. Reed (Nashville, 1970) pp.142f.

Applebaum, S. Porath, Y. and Dor, S. *The History and Archaeology of Emeq-Hefer* (Tel Aviv, 1985).

'Aref, 'Aref el and Häfeli L. *Die Beduinen von Beerseba* (Luzern, 1938).

Asaro, F. Perlman, I. and Dothan, M. "An Introductory Study of Mycenaean IIIC:1 Ware from Tel Ashdod," *Archaeometry* 13 (1971), pp.169-175.

Ashkenazi, T. *Tribus Semi-Nomades de la Palestine du Nord* (Paris, 1938).

Attridge, H.W. and Oden, R.A. *Philo of Byblos: The Phoenician History, CBQMS* 9 (Washington, 1981).

Aufrecht, W.E. "The Ammorite Language of the Iron Age," *BASOR* 266 (1987), pp.85-95.

Bächli, O. *Amphiktyonie im Alten Testament*, (Basel, 1977).

Balcer, J.M. *Herodotus und Bisitun, Historia* 49 (Stuttgart, 1987).

Balensi, J. "Tell Keisan, Lémoin original de l'apparition du 'Mycenien IIC 1a', au Proche Orient," *RB* 88 (1981), pp.399-401.

Banning, E.B. "Peasants, Pastoralists, and Pax Romana: Mutualism in the Highlands of Jordan," *BASOR* 261 (1986), pp.25-50.

Barnett, R.D. "The Sea Peoples," *Cambridge Ancient History* (Cambridge, 1975) pp.359-378.

Barr, J. *Biblical Words for Time, SBTh* 33 (Naperville, 1962).

Barstad, H.M. "On the History and Archaeology of Judah during the Exilic Period: A Reminder," *Orientalia Louvaniensa Periodica* 19 (1988), pp.25-36.

Baruch, U. "The Late Holocene Vegetational History of the Kinneret," *Paléorient* 12 (1986), pp.37-48.

Beck, B.L. *The International Role of the Philistines during the Biblical Period* (Southern Baptist Theological Seminary dissertation, 1980).

Beckerath, J. von. *Untersuchungen zur politischen Geschichte der zweiten Zwischenzeit in Ägypten, ÄgF* 23 (1964).

Behrens, P. "Wanderbewegungen und Sprache der frühen Saharanischen Viehzüchter," *Sprache und Geschichte in Afrika* 6 (1984-1985), pp.135-216.

Beit-Arieh, I. and Gophna, R. "The Early Bronze Age II Settlement at 'Ein el Qudeirat (1980-1981)," *Tel Aviv* 8 (1981), pp.128-135.

—— "Canaanites and Egyptians at Serabit el-Khadim," *Egypt, Israel, Sinai*, ed by A. Rainey (Tel Aviv, 1987) pp.57-67.

Bell, B. "The Dark Ages in Ancient History I: The First Dark Age in Egypt," *JNES* 75 (1971), pp.1-26.

—— "Climate and the History of Egypt: The Middle Kingdom," *American Journal of Archaeology* 79 (1975), pp.223-269.

Ben-Tor, A. "Tell Qiri: A Look at Village Life," *BA* 42 (1979), pp.105-113.

Bernhardt, H.-H. *Der alte Libanon* (Munich, 1976).

Bienkowski, P. *Jericho in the Late Bronze Age* (Westminster, 1986).

Bimson, J.J. *Redating the Exodus and Conquest, JSOTS* 5 (Sheffield, 1981).

Bintliff, J.L. "Climatic Change, Archaeology, and Quaternary Science in the Eastern Mediterranean Region," *Climatic Change in Later Prehistory*, ed. by A.F. Harding (Edinburgh, 1982) pp.143-161.

Biran, A. "Tel Dan," *BA* 37 (1974), pp.26-51.

—— "Notes and News: Tel Dan," *IEJ* 26 (1976), pp.54f.

—— "Tell Dan—Five Years Later," *BA* 43 (1980), pp.168-182.

—— "Die Wiederentdeckung der alten Stadt Dan," *Antike Welt* 15 (1984), pp.27-38.

—— "The Collared Rim Jars and the Settlement of the Tribe of Dan," *Recent Excavations in Israel: Studies in Iron Age Archaeology*, ed. by S. Gitin and W.G. Dever (Winona Lake, 1989) pp.71-97.

Block, D.I. *The Foundations of National Identity: A Study in Ancient Northwest Semitic Perceptions* (University of Liverpool dissertation, 1981).

Blum, E. "Die Komplexität der Überlieferung: Zur synchronen und diachronen Analyse von Gen 32:23-33," *DBAT* 15 (1980), pp.2-55.

—— *Die Komposition der Vätergeschichte, WMANT* 57 (Neukirchen, 1984).

—— *Studien zur Komposition des Pentateuch, BZAW* 189 (Berlin, 1990).

Boling, R.G. *The Early Biblical Community in Transjordan, SWBAS* 6 (Sheffield, 1988).

Bondi, S.F. "The Course of History," *The Phoenicians*, ed. by S. Moscati (Milan, 1988) pp.38-45.

—— "The Origins in the East," *The Phoenicians*, ed. by S. Moscati (Milan, 1988) pp.28-35.

Boraas, R.S. and Horn, S.H. "The First Campaign at Tell Hesban: 1968," *AUSS* 7 (1969), pp.97-239.

—— and Horn, S.H. "The Second Campaign at Tell Hesban: 1971," *AUSS* 11 (1973), pp.1-144.

—— and Horn, S.H. "The Third Campaign at Tell Hesban: 1973," *AUSS* 13 (1975), pp.101-247.

—— and Geraty, L.T. "The Fourth Campaign at Tell Hesban: 1974," *AUSS* 14 (1976), pp.1-216.

—— and Geraty, L.T. "The Fifth Campaign at Tell Hesban: 1976," *AUSS* 16 (1978), pp.1-303.

——"Iron IA Ceramic at Tell Balatah: A Preliminary Examination," *The Archaeology of Jordan and Other Studies* (Berrien Springs, 1986) pp.249-263.

Borowski, O. *Agriculture in Iron Age Israel* (Winona Lake, 1987).

Bottero, J. *Le Probleme des Habiru à la Rencontre d'assyrilogique internationale, Cahiers de la societè asiatique* 12 (Paris, 1954).

—— "Habiru," *RLA* 4 (1972) pp.14-27.

—— "Entre Nomades et Sèdentaires: les Habiru," *DHA* 6 (1980), pp.201-213.

—— "Les Habiru, les nomades et les sedentaires," *NSP* (1981), pp.89-107.

—— "Eastern Society Before the Middle of the 2nd Millennium, B.C.," *Oikumene* 3 (1982), pp.7-100.

Brandfon, F.R. *The Beginning of the Iron Age in Palestine* (University of Pennsylvania dissertation, 1983).

—— "Kinship, Culture and Longue Durée," *JSOT* 39 (1987), pp.30-58.

—— "Archaeology and the Biblical Text," *BAR* 14 (1988), pp.54-59.

Bratt, K.D. *Herodotus' Oriental Monarchs and Their Counsellors* (Princeton University dissertation, 1985).

Braun, R.L. "Chronicles, Ezra, and Nehemiah: Theology and Literary History," *Studies in the Historical Books of the Old Testament*, ed. J.A. Emerton (Leiden, 1979) pp.52-64.

Brentjes, B. "Zu den Ursachen der Herausbildung zu Domestikation in Vorderasien," *Paléorient* 1 (1973), pp.207-211.

Brett, M.G. "Literacy and Domination: G.A. Herion's Sociology of History Writing," *JSOT* 37 (1987), pp.15-40.

Briant, P. *Etats et pasteurs au Moyen-Orient ancien* (Cambridge, 1982).

Briend, J. and Humbert, J.-B. *Tell Keisan, 1971-1976: Une Cité phenicienne en Galilée* (Paris, 1980).

Bright, J. *Early Israel in Recent History Writing, SBTh* 19 (London, 1956).

—— *A History of Israel* (Philadelphia, ³1981).

Brinkman, J. "Settlement Surveys and Documentary: Regional Variations and Secular Trends," *JNES* 43 (1984), pp.175-179.

Broshi, M. "The Expansion of Jerusalem in the Reigns of Hezekiah and Manasseh," *IEJ* 24 (1974), pp.21-29.

—— and Gophna, R. "The Settlements and Population of Palestine During the Early Bronze Age II-III," *BASOR* 253 (1984), pp.41-53.

Buccellati, G. *Cities and Nations of Ancient Syria: An Essay on Political Institutions with Special Reference to the Israelite Kingdoms* (Rome, 1967).

Buhl, M.-L. and Holm-Nielsen, S. *Shiloh* (Copenhagen, 1969).

Bulbach, S.W. *Judah in the Reign of Manasseh as Evidenced in Texts During the Neo-Assyrian Period and in the Archaeology of the Iron Age* (New York University dissertation, 1981).

Burckhardt, J. *The Age of Constantine the Great* (New York, 1949).

Burney, C.B.M. "The Archaeological Context of the Hamitic Languages in N. Africa," *Hamito Semitica*, ed. by J. and T. Bynon (The Hague,1975) pp.495-506.

Butzer, K.W. "Environment and Human Ecology in Egypt during Predynastic and Early Dynastic Times," *Bulletin de la Société de Géographie d Égypte* 32 (1959), pp.65ff.

—— "Pleistocene History of the Nile Valley in Egypt and Lower Nubia," *The Sahara and the Nile*, ed. by M. Williams and H. Faure (Rotterdam, 1980) pp.253-280.

Callaway, J.A. "New Evidence on the Conquest of Ai," *JBL* 87(1968), pp.312-320.

—— "The Significance of the Iron Age Village at Ai (et-Tell)," *Proceedings of the Fifth World Congress of Jewish Studies* (Jerusalem, 1969) pp.56-61.

—— and Cooley, R.E. "A Salvage Excavation at Raddana in Bireh" *BASOR* 201 (1971), pp.9-19.

—— "Excavating 'Ai (et-Tell): 1964-1972" *BA* 39 (1976), pp.18-30.

—— *The Early Bronze Age Citadel and Lower City at Ai (Et-Tell)* (Cambridge, 1980).

—— "Village Subsistence at Ai and Raddana in Iron Age I," *The Answers Lie Below: Essays in Honor of Lawrence Edmund Toombs*, ed. by H.O. Thompson (Lanham, 1984) pp.51-66.

—— "A New Perspective on the Hill Country Settlement of Canaan in Iron Age I," *Palestine in the Bronze and Iron Ages: Papers in Honour of Olga Tufnell*, ed. by J.N. Tubb (London, 1985) pp.31-49.

Campbell, E.F. "The Amarna Letters and the Amarna Period," *BA* 23 (1960), pp.11-15.

—— "The Shechem Area Survey," *BASOR* 190 (1968), pp.19-41.

—— "Tribal League Shrines in Amman and Shechem," *BA* 32 (1969), pp.104-116.

—— and Miller, J.M. "W.F. Albright and Historical Reconstruction," *BA* 42 (1979), pp.37-47.

Cancik, H. *Mythische und Historische Wahrheit*, SBS 48 (Stuttgart, 1970).

—— *Grundzüge der Hethitischen und alttestamentlichen Geschichtsschreibung*, ADPV (Wiesbaden, 1976).

Cangh, J.M. Van. Thompson, Th.L. and Gonçalvez, F. *Toponomie Palestinienne* (Louvain, 1988).

Carpenter, R. *Discontinuity in Greek Civilization* (Cambridge, 1966).

Cerny, J. "Fluctuations in Grain Prices during the Twentieth Egyptian Dynasty," *Archiv Orientalni* 6 (1934), pp.173-178.

—— "Egypt: From the Death of Ramses III to the End of the Twenty-First Dynasty," *Cambridge Ancient History* (Cambridge, 1975) pp.606-657.

Chaney, M.L. "Ancient Palestinian Peasant Movements and the Formation of Premonarchic Israel," *Palestine in Transition* (Sheffield, 1983) pp.42-44.

Cogan, M. *Imperialism and Religion: Assyria, Judah and Israel in the 8th and 7th Centuries B.C.E.*, SBLMS 19 (Missoula, 1974).

Cohen, R. and Dever, W.G. "Preliminary Report of the Pilot Season of the 'Central Negev Highlands Project'," *BASOR* 232 (1978), pp.29-45.

—— and Dever, W.G. "Preliminary Report of the Second Season of the 'Central Negev Highlands Project'," *BASOR* 236 (1979), pp.41-60.

—— "The Iron Age Fortresses in the Central Negev," *BASOR* 236 (1980), pp.61-79.

—— "Excavations at Kadesh Barnea 1976-1978," *BA* 44 (1981), pp.93-107.

—— and Dever, W.G. "Preliminary Report of the Third and Final Season of the Central Negev Highlands Project," *BASOR* 243 (1981), pp.57-77.

—— *The Settlement of the Central Negev* (Hebrew University dissertation, 1986).

Connor, W.R. "Narrative Discourse in Thucydides," *The Greek Historians: Literature and History: Papers Presented to A.E. Raubitschek*, ed. by W.R. Connor (Saratoga, 1985) pp.1-17.

Cooley, R.E. and Callaway, J.A. "A Salvage Excavation at Raddana in Bireh" *BASOR* 201 (1971), pp.9-19.

Coote, R.B. and Whitelam, K.W. "The Emergence of Israel: Social Transformation and State Formation Following the Decline in Late Bronze Age Trade," *Social Scientific Criticism of the Hebrew Bible and its Social World: The Israelite Monarchy, Semeia* 37 (1986) pp.107-147.

—— and Whitelam, K.W. *The Emergence of Early Israel in Historical Perspective SWABAS* 5 (Sheffield, 1987).

—— "Settlement Change in Early Iron Age Palestine," *Early Israelite Agriculture: Reviews of David C. Hopkins' Book The Highlands of Canaan*, ed. by O.S. Labianca and D.C. Hopkins (Berrien Springs, 1988) pp.17-27.

Cross, F.M. "Yahweh and the God of the Patriarchs," *HThR* 55 (1962), pp.225-259.

—— *Canaanite Myth and Hebrew Epic* (Cambridge, 1973).

—— "Biblical Archaeology: The Biblical Aspect," *Biblical Archaeology Today*, ed. by A. Biran (Jerusalem, 1985) pp.9-15.

Crown, A.D. "Toward a Reconstruction of the Climate of Palestine 8000 B.C.-0 B.C.," *JNES* 31 (1972), pp.312-330.

Currid, J.D. "The Deforestation of the Foothills of Palestine," *PEQ* 116 (1984), pp.1-11.

Dalman, G. *Arbeit und Sitte in Palästina* (Gütersloh, 1928-1942; reprinted in seven volumes, Hildesheim: 1964-1987).

Davies, G.I. "Megiddo in the Period of the Judges," *Crises and Perspectives, Oudtestamentisches Studien* 24 (Leiden, 1986) pp.34-53.

Davies, P.R. and Gunn D.M. (eds.) "A History of Ancient Israel and Judah: A Discussion of Miller-Hayes (1986)," *JSOT* 39 (1987), pp.3-63.

Davis, J.B. *Hill Country Village Subsistence in the Period of the Judges* (Southern Baptist Theological Seminary dissertation, 1984).

Delitsch, F. *Neuer Commentar über die Genesis* (Leipzig, 1887).

Dever, W.G. *The Pottery of Palestine in the Early Bronze IV-Middle Bronze I Period, ca.2150-1950 B.C.* (Harvard University Dissertation, 1966).

—— "Gezer," *EAEHL II*, pp. 428-443.

—— *et alii, Gezer I* (Jerusalem, 1970).

—— "The People of Palestine in the Middle Bronze Period," *HThR* 64 (1971), pp.197-226.

—— "The EB IV-MB I Horizon in Transjordan and Southern Palestine," *BASOR* 210 (1973), pp.37-63.

—— *et alii, Gezer II* (Jerusalem, 1974).

—— "The Beginning of the Middle Bronze Age in Syria-Palestine," in *Magnalia Dei: The Mighty Acts of God*, ed. by F.M. Cross *et alii* (Garden City, 1976) pp.3-38.

—— "The Patriarchal Traditions," *Israelite and Judaean History*, ed. by J.H. Hayes and J.M. Miller (Philadelphia, 1977) pp.102-120.

—— and Cohen, R. "Preliminary Report of the Pilot Season of the 'Central Negev Highlands Project'," *BASOR* 232 (1978), pp.29-45.

—— and Cohen, R. "Preliminary Report of the Second Season of the 'Central Negev Highlands Project'," *BASOR* 236 (1979), pp.41-60.

—— "New Vistas on the EB IV ('MB I') Horizon in Syria-Palestine," *BASOR* 237 (1980), pp.35-64.

—— and Cohen, R. "Preliminary Report of the Third and Final Season of the 'Central Negev Highlands Project'," *BASOR* 243 (1981), pp.57-77.

—— "Be'er Resisim—A Late Third Millennium B.C.E. Settlement," *Qadmoniot* 16 (1983), pp.52-57.

—— "From the End of the Early Bronze Age to the Beginning of the Middle Bronze Age," *Biblical Archaeology Today*, ed. by J. Aviram (Jerusalem, 1985) pp.113-35.

—— "Village Planning at Be'er Resisim and Socio-Economic Structures in EB IV Palestine," *EI* 18 (1985), pp.18-28.

—— *Recent Archaeological Discoveries and Biblical Research* (Seattle, 1990).

Diakonoff, I.M. *Semito-Hamitic Languages* (Moscow, 1965).

—— "Earliest Semites in Asia," *Altorientalische Forschungen* 8 (1981), pp.23-74.

Diebner, B. "Forschungsgeschichtliche Einführung," *DBAT* 6 (1986), pp.217-241.

Donley, D.L. *Analysis of the Winter Climatic Pattern at the Time of the Mycenaean Decline* (University of Wisconsin dissertation, 1971).

Donner, H. *Geschichte des Volkes Israel und seiner Nachbarn in Grundzügen: Grundrisse zum Alten Testament: ATD* Ergänzungsreihe 4/1-2; 2 vols. (Göttingen, 1984, 1986).

Dor, S. Applebaum, S. and Porath, Y. *The History and Archaeology of Emeq-Hefer* (Tel Aviv, 1985).

Dornemann, R. "The Beginning of the Iron Age in Transjordan," *SHAJ* I (Amman, 1982) pp.135-140.

—— *The Archaeology of Transjordan in the Bronze and Iron Ages* (Milwaukee, 1983).

Dossin, G. "Benjaminites dans les Textes de Mari," *Mélanges Syriens offerts à monsieur René Dussaud: Secretaire perpetuel de l'Academie des inscriptions et belles lettres par ses amis et ses élèves; Bibliotheque archeologique et historique*, vol. 30 (Paris, 1939) pp.981-996.

Dothan, M. "The Fortress at Kadesh-Barnea," *IEJ* 15 (1965), pp.134-151.

—— and Freedman, D.N. *Ashdod I, Atiqot VII* (Jerusalem, 1967).

—— Perlman, I. and Asaro, F. "An Introductory Study of Mycenaean IIIC:1 Ware from Tel Ashdod," *Archaeometry* 13 (1971), pp.169-175.

—— *Ashdod II-III, Atiqot IX-X* (Jerusalem, 1971).

—— "Akko: Interim Excavation Report: First Season 1973/4," *BASOR* 224 (1976), pp.1-48.

—— "Archaeological Evidence for Movements of the Early 'Sea Peoples' in Canaan," *Recent Excavations in Israel: Studies in Iron Age Archaeology,* ed. by S. Gitin and W.G. Dever (Winona Lake, 1989) pp.59-70.

Dothan, T. "Philistine Material Culture and Its Mycenaean Affinities," *The Mycenaeans in the Eastern Mediterranean* (Nicosia, 1973) pp.187ff.

—— "Anthropoid Clay Coffins from a Late Bronze Age Cemetery near Deir el-Balah: Preliminary Report II," *IEJ* 23 (1973), pp.129-146.

—— *Excavations at the Cemetery of Deir el-Balah, Qedem* 10 (Jerusalem, 1979).

—— *The Philistines and their Material Culture* (New Haven, 1982).

—— and Gitin, S. "Notes and News: Tell Miqne (Ekron)," *IEJ* 32 (1982), pp.150-153.

—— and Gitin, S. "Notes and News: Tell Miqne (Ekron)," *IEJ* 33 (1983), pp.128f.

—— "The Philistines Reconsidered," *Biblical Archaeology Today* (Jerusalem, 1985) pp.165-176.

—— and Gitin, S. "Notes and News: Tell Miqne (Ekron)," *IEJ* 35 (1985), pp.67-71.

—— "Aspects of Egyptian and Philistine Presence in Canaan During the Late Bronze-Early Iron Ages," *The Land of Israel: Cross-Roads of Civilizations*, ed. by E. Lipinski (Leuven, 1985) pp.55-75.

—— and Gitin, S. "Notes and News: Tell Miqne (Ekron)," *IEJ* 36 (1986), pp.104-107.

—— and Gitin, S. "The Rise and Fall of Ekron of the Philistines: Recent Excavations at an Urban Border Site," *BA* 50 (1987), pp.197-222.

—— "The Arrival of the Sea Peoples: Cultural Diversity in Early Iron Age Canaan," *Recent Excavations in Israel: Studies in Iron Age Technology*, ed. by S. Gitin and W.G. Dever (Winona Lake, 1989) pp.1-15.

Dugan, J.A. *Martin Noth and the History of Israel* (Brandeis dissertation, 1978).

Dupont, F.R. *The Late History of Ugarit* (Hebrew Union College dissertation, 1987).

Dus, J. "Die Ältesten Israels," *CV* 3 (1960), pp.232-242.

—— "Das Sesshaftwerden der nachmaligen Israeliten im Land Kanaan," *CV* 6 (1963), pp.263-275.

—— "Die altisraelitische amphiktyonische Poesie," *ZAW* 75 (1963), pp.45-54.

—— "Die Sufeten Israels," *Archiv Orientalni* 31 (1963), pp.444-469.

—— "Die Stierbild von Bethel und Dan und das Problem der 'Moseschar'," *AION* 18 (1968), pp.105-137.

—— "Mose oder Josua? Zum Problem des Stifters der israelitischen Religion," *Archiv Orientalni* 39 (1971), pp.16-45.

—— *Israelitische Vorfahren: Vasallen palästinischer Stadtstaaten, Europäische Hochschulschriften* (Frankfurt, 1991).

Dussaud, R. "Nouveaux Renseignements sur la Palestine et la Syrie vers 2000 avant notre Ere," *Syria* 8 (1927), pp.216-231.

—— "Nouveaux Textes Égyptiens d'Éxecration contre les peuples Syriens," *Syria* 21 (1940), pp.170-182.

Edelman, D. and Ahlström, G. "Merneptah's Israel," *JNES* 44 (1985), pp.59-61.

—— *The Rise of the Israelite State under Saul* (University of Chicago dissertation, 1987).

—— "Doing History in Biblical Studies," *The Fabric of History, JSOTS* 127, ed. by D. Edelman (Sheffield, 1991) pp.13-25.

Edelstein, G. and Eisenberg, E. "Emeq Refaim," *Excavations and Surveys in Israel,* 3 (Jerusalem, 1984) pp.51f.

—— and Eisenberg, E. "Emeq Refaim," *Excavations and Surveys in Israel* 4 (Jerusalem, 1985) pp.54-56.

Edens, C. Review of *Biblical Archaeology Today, AJA* 93 (1989), pp.289-292.

Edzard, D.O. "Mari und Aramäer," *ZA* 22 (1964), pp.142-149.

Einsele, G. *et alii,* "Sea Level Fluctuation During the Past 6000 yr at the Coast of Mauritania," *Quartenary Research* 4 (1974), pp.282-289.

Eisenberg, E. and Edelstein, G. "Emeq Refaim," *Excavations and Surveys in Israel,* 3 (Jerusalem, 1984) pp.51f.

—— and Edelstein, G. "Emeq Refaim," *Excavations and Surveys in Israel* 4 (Jerusalem, 1985) pp.54-56.

Eissfeldt, O. "Stammessage und Novelle in den Geschichten von Jakob und von seinen Söhnen," *Eucharisterion, Festschrift H. Gunkel* (Leipzig, 1923) pp.56-77.

—— "Achronische, anachronische, und synchronische Elemente in der Genesis," *JEOL* 17 (1963), pp.148-164.

—— "Stammessage und Menscheitserzählung in der Genesis," *Sitzungsberichte der Sächsischen Akademie der Wissenschaft zu Leipzig,* Phil-hist Kl 110,4 (Leipzig, 1965) pp.5-21.

Ellermeier, F. *Prophetie in Mari und Israel, Theologische und Orientalische Arbeiten aus Göttingen* 1 (Göttingen, 1977).

Emerton, J.A. "New Light on the Israelite Religion: the Implications of the Inscriptions from Kuntillet Ajrud," *ZAW* 94 (1982), pp.2-20.

Emery, K.O. and Neev, D. *The Dead Sea Depositional Processes and Environments of Evaporites* (Jerusalem, 1967).

Ephál, I. *The Ancient Arabs* (Leiden, 1982).

Esse, D.L. *Beyond Subsistence: Beth Yerah and Northern Palestine in the Early Bronze Age* (University of Chicago Dissertation, 1982).

Evenari, M. *et alii, The Negev* (Cambridge, 1971).

Ewald, H. *Geschichte des Volkes Israel I,* (Berlin, 1876).

Fahr, H. *Herodot und altes Testament, Europäische Hochschulschriften* 266 (Frankfurt, 1985).

Fairbridge, R.W. "Effects of Holocene Climatic Change," *Quartenary Research* 6 (1976), pp.532-538.

—— "Shellfish Eating Preceramic Indians in Coastal Brazil," *Science* 191 (1976), pp.353-359.

—— "An 8000-yr Paleoclimatic Record of the 'Double-Hale' 45-yr Solar Cycle," *Nature* 268 (1977), pp.415ff.

—— and Hillaire-Marcel, C. "An 8000 Year Palaeoclimatic Record of the 'Double Hale' 45 Year Cycle," *Nature* 268 (1977), pp.415ff.

Fargo, V.M. and O'Connell, K.G. "Four Seasons of Excavation at Tell el Hesi," *BA* 41 (1978), pp.165-182.

Finkelstein, I. "Shiloh 1981," *IEJ* 32 (1982), pp.148-150.

—— "Shiloh 1982," *IEJ* 33 (1983), pp.123-126.

—— "Excavations at Shiloh 1981-1984" *Tel Aviv* 12 (1985), pp.123-180.

—— "Shiloh Yields Some, But Not All, of its Secrets," *BAR* 12 (1986), pp.22-41.

—— *'Izbet Sartah An Early Iron Age Site near Rosh Ha'ayin, Israel, BAR* 299 (Jerusalem, 1986).

—— *The Archaeology of the Israelite Settlement* (Jerusalem, 1988).

—— "Arabian Trade and Socio-Political Conditions in the Negev in the Twelfth-Eleventh Centuries, B.C.E.," *JNES* 47 (1988), pp.241-252.

—— "The Emergence of the Monarchy in Israel: The Environmental and Socio-Economic Aspects," *JSOT* 44 (1989), pp.43-74.

—— "Further Observations on the Socio-Demographic Structure of the Intermediate Bronze Age," *Levant* 21 (1989), pp.129-140.

—— "The Emergence of Israel in Canaan: Consensus, Mainstream and Dispute," *SJOT* 1,2 (1991), pp.47-59.

Flemming, N.C. "Mediterranean Sea-Level Changes," *Science* (1968), pp.51-55.

Foerster, G. "Dor" *EAEHL I*, pp.334f.

—— "Recent Archaeological Research in Israel," *International Journal of Nautical Archaeology* 10 (1981), pp.297-305.

—— "Recent Archaeological Research in Israel," *International Journal of Nautical Archaeology* 12 (1983), pp.229-238.

—— "The Ancient Harbors of Israel in Biblical Times," *Harbor Archaeology*, ed. by A. Raban (Oxford, 1985) pp.23-27.

Fohrer, G. *Überlieferung und Geschichte des Exodus. Eine Analyse von Ex 1-15, BZAW* 91 (Berlin, 1964).

—— "Altes Testament: 'Amphiktyonie' und 'Bund'?," *Studien zur alttestamentlichen Theologie und Geschichte (1949-1966), BZAW* 115 (Berlin, 1969) pp.84-119.

Fokkelman, J.P. *Narrative Art in Genesis* (Assen, 1975).

—— *Narrative Art and Poetry in the Book of Samuel* (Assen, 1981).

Forbes, R.J. *Studies in Ancient Technologies*, 9 vols. (Leiden, 1964ff.).

Foster, B.R. "Agriculture and accountability in Ancient Mesopotamia," *The Origins of Cities in Dry-Farming Syria and Mesopotamia in the Third Millennium, B.C.* ed. by H. Wiess (Guilford, 1986) pp.116ff.

Frankel, R. *The History of the Processing of Wine and Oil in Galilee in the Period of the Bible, the Mishnah, and the Talmud* (University of Tel Aviv dissertation, 1984).

—— "The Galilee in the Late Bronze and Iron Age," *The Land of the Galilee*, ed. by A. Schmueli (Haifa, 1984).

—— "Oil Presses in Western Galilee and the Judaea: A Comparison," *Olive Oil in Antiquity*, ed. by M. Heltzer and D. Eitam (Haifa, 1988) pp.63-73.

Franken, H.J. "Deir 'Alla," *EAEHL* I, pp.321-4.

—— *Excavations at Tell Deir 'Alla* I (Leiden, 1969).

Freedman, D.N. and Dothan, M. *Ashdod I, Atiqot VII* (Jerusalem, 1967).

—— "The Real Story of the Ebla Tablets: Ebla and the Cities of the Plain," *BA* 41 (1978), pp.143-164.

—— and Graf, D.F. *Palestine in Transition: The Emergence of Ancient Israel, SWBAS* 2 (Sheffield, 1983).

Frick, F. *The City in Ancient Israel, SBLDS* 36 (Missoula, 1977).

—— *The Formation of the State in Ancient Israel, SWBAS* 4 (Sheffield, 1985).

Friedman, R.E. "The Prophet and the Historian: The Acquisition of Historical Information from Literary Sources," *The Past and the Historian, HSS* 26, ed. R.E. Friedman (Cambridge, 1983) pp.1-12.

Friis, H. *Die Bedingungen für die Errichtung des davidischen Reiches in Israel und seiner Umwelt, DBAT* 6 (Heidelberg, 1986).

Fritz, V. "Erwägungen zur Siedlungsgeschichte des Negeb in der Eisen I Zeit (1200-1000 v. Chr.) im Lichte der Ausgrabungen auf der Hirbet el-Msas," *ZDPV* 93 (1975), pp.30-45.

—— "Bestimmung und Herkunft des Pfeilerhauses in Israel," *ZDPV* 93 (1977), pp.30-45.

—— "Die Kulturhistorische Bedeutung der früheisenzeitlichen Siedlung auf der Hirbet el-Msas und das Problem der Landnahme," *ZDPV* 96 (1980), pp.121-135.

—— "The Israelite Conquest in the Light of Recent Excavations at Khirbet el-Meshash," *BASOR* 241 (1981), pp.61-73.

—— "The Conquest in the Light of Archaeology," *Proceedings of the Eighth World Congress of Jewish Studies* (Jerusalem, 1982) pp.15-22.

—— and Kempinski, A. *Ergebnisse der Ausgrabungen auf der Hirbet el-Msas* (Tel Masos) I-III (Wiesbaden, 1983).

—— "Conquest or Settlement? The Early Iron Age in Palestine," *BA* 50 (1987), pp.84-100.

—— "Die Landnahme der israelitischen Stämme in Kanaan," *ZDPV* 106 (1990), pp.63-77.

Fronzaroli, P. "Le origini dei Semiti come Problema Storico," *Accademia Nazionale dei Lincei Rendiconti della Classe di scienze morali, Storiche e Filologiche* 15 (1960) pp.123-144.

—— "Studi sul Lessico Commune Semitico" I-VI, in *Academia Nazionale dei Lincei, Rendiconti della Classe di scienze morali, Storiche e Filologiche Series* 8, vols. 19-20. 23- 24 (1964-1969).

Gal, Z. *Ramat Issachar* (Tel Aviv, 1980).

—— "Tel Rechesh and Tel Qarnei Hittin," *Eretz Israel* 15 (1981) pp.213-221.

—— "The Settlement of Issachar: Some New Observations," *Tel Aviv* 9 (1982), pp.79-86.

—— *The Lower Galilee in the Iron Age* (University of Tel Aviv dissertation, 1982).

—— "Ramat Issachar" *Tel Aviv* 12 (1985), pp.123-180.

—— "The Late Bronze Age in Galilee: A Reassessment," *BASOR* 272 (1988), pp.79-84.

Galili, E. and Weinstein-Evron, M. "Pre-History and Palaeoenvironments of Submerged Sites along the Carmel Coast of Israel," *Paléorient* 11 (1985), pp.37-52.

—— and Raban, A. "Recent Maritime Archeological Research in Israel," *IJNA* 14 (1985), pp.332-349.

Galling, K. *Die Erwählungstraditionen Israels, BZAW* 48 (Berlin, 1928).
—— *Textbuch zur Geschichte Israels*, 2nd. ed. (Tübingen, 1968).
Garbini, G. *I Fenici: Storia e Religioni* (Naples, 1980).
—— "Philistine Seals," *Biblical Archaeology Today* (Jerusalem, 1985) pp.443-448.
—— *History and Ideology in Ancient Israel* (London, 1988).
Gardiner, A.H. Peet, T.E. and Cerny, J. *The Inscriptions of Sinai I-II* (London, 1952-55).
Garr, W.R. *Dialect Geography of Syria Palestine, 1000-586 B.C.E.* (Philadelphia, 1985).
Gelb, I.J. *Prisoners* (Chicago, 1966).
Geraty, L.T. and Boraas, R.S. "The Fourth Campaign at Tell Hesban: 1974," *AUSS* 14 (1976), pp.1-216.
—— and Boraas, R.S. "The Fifth Campaign at Tell Hesban: 1976," *AUSS* 16 (1978), pp.1-303.
—— and LaBianca, O.S. "The Local Environment and Human Food Producing Strategies in Jordan: The Case of Tell Hesban and its Surrounding Region," *SHAJ* II (Amman, 1985) pp.323-330.
—— and Willis, L.A. "Archaeological Research in Transjordan," *The Archaeology of Jordan and Other Studies*, ed. by L.T. Geraty and L.G. Herr (Berrien Springs, 1986) pp. 3-72.
—— *et alii*, "Madeba Plains Project: A Preliminary Report of the 1987 Season at Tell el-Umeiri and Vicinity," *BASOR* supplement 26 (1990) pp.33-58.
Gerstenblith, P. *The Levant at the Beginning of the Middle Bronze Age, ASORDS* 5 (Winona Lake, 1983).
Geus, C.H.J. de. "De Richteren van Isräel," *Nederlands teologisch Tijdschrift* 20 (1965), pp.81-100.
—— "The Amorites in the Archaeology of Palestine," *Ugarit-Forschung* 3 (1971), pp.41-60.
—— "The Importance of Archaeological Research into the Palestinian Agricultural Terraces, with an Excursus on the Hebrew Word *gbi*," *PEQ* 107 (1975), pp.65-74.
—— *The Tribes of Israel: An Investigation into Some of the Presuppositions of Martin Noth's Amphictyony Hypothesis, Studi Semitica Neerlandica* 18 (Assen, 1976).
—— "Agrarian Communities in Biblical Times: 12th to 10th Centuries B.C.E.," *Recueils de la Société Jean Bodin pour l'histoire Comparatives des Institutions* 41 (1983) pp.207-237.
—— *De Israelitische Stad* (Kampen, 1984).
Geva, S. "The Settlement Pattern of Hazor Stratum XII," *Eretz Israel* 17 (1984), pp.158-161.
Geyer, J.B. "The Joseph and Moses Narrative: Folk-Tale and History," *JSOT* 15 (1980), pp.51-56.
Gilbert, A.S. "Modern Nomads and Prehistoric Pastoralists: The Limits of Analogy," *JANES* 6 (1974), pp.53-71.
Gitin, S. and Dothan, T. "Notes and News: Tell Miqne (Ekron)," *IEJ* 32 (1982), pp.150-153.
—— and Dothan, T. "Notes and News: Tell Miqne (Ekron)," *IEJ* 33 (1983), pp.128f.
—— and Dothan, T. "Notes and News: Tell Miqne (Ekron)," *IEJ* 35 (1985), pp.67-71.
—— and Dothan, T. "Notes and News: Tell Miqne (Ekron)," *IEJ* 36 (1986), pp.104-107.
—— and Dothan, T. "The Rise and Fall of Ekron of the Philistines: Recent Excavations at an Urban Border Site," *BA* 50 (1987), pp.197-222.
Giveon, R. *Les Bedouins shosou des documents égyptiens. Documenta et Monumenta Orientis antiqui* 18 (Leiden, 1971).
—— "Le Temple d'Hathor à Serabit el-Khadem," *Archealogia* 44 (1972), pp.64-69.

—— "Investigations in the Egyptian Mining Centres in Sinai," *Tel Aviv* 1 (1974), pp.100-108.

—— *The Impact of Egypt on Canaan, OBO* 20 (Göttingen, 1978).

—— *The Stones of Sinai Speak* (Tokyo, 1978).

Glock, A.E. "Taanach," *EAEHL* III, pp.1138-1147.

—— "Texts and Archaeology at Tell Ta'annek," *Berytus* 31 (1983), pp.58-63.

Glueck, N. *Explorations in Eastern Palestine* I, *AASOR* XIV (Cambridge, 1934).

—— *The River Jordan* (1946).

—— *Explorations in Eastern Palestine* IV, *AASOR* 25-28 (New Haven, 1951).

—— "The Age of Abraham in the Negev," *BA* 18 (1955), pp.10-22.

—— *Rivers in the Desert* (New Haven, 1959).

—— *The Other Side of the Jordan* (New Haven, 1959).

Gnuse, R. *Heilsgeschichte as a Model for Biblical Theology, CTSSR* 4 (New York, 1989).

Goldwasser, O. "The Lachish Hieratic Bowl Once Again," *Tel Aviv* 9 (1982), pp.137f.

—— "Hieratic Inscriptions from Tel Sera' in Southern Canaan," *Tel Aviv* 11 (1984), pp.77-93.

Gonçalvez, F. Thompson, Th.L. and Cangh, J.M. Van. *Toponomie Palestinienne* (Louvain, 1988).

Gonen, R. "Urban Canaan in the Late Bronze Period," *BASOR* 253 (1984), pp.61-73.

Gophna, R. and Kochavi, M. "An Archaeological Survey of the Plain of Sharon," *IEJ* 16 (1966), pp.143-144.

—— and Beit-Arieh, I. "The Early Bronze Age II Settlement at 'Ein el Qudeirat (1980 - 1981)," *Tel Aviv* 8 (1981), pp.128-135.

—— and Broshi, M. "The Settlements and Population of Palestine During the Early Bronze Age II-III," *BASOR* 253 (1984), pp.41-53.

—— "Middle Bronze Age II Palestine: Its Settlement and Population," *BASOR* 261 (1986), pp.73-90.

—— and Portugali, J. "Settlement and Demographic Processes in Israel's Coastal Plain from the Chalcolithic to the Middle Bronze Age," *BASOR* 269 (1988), pp.11-28.

Gordon, C.H. "The Patriarchal Age," *JBR* 21 (1953), pp.238-243.

—— "The Patriarchal Narratives," *JNES* 13 (1954), pp.56-59.

—— "Abraham and the Merchants of Ura," *JNES* 17 (1958), pp.28-31.

—— *The World of the Old Testament* (New York, 1958).

—— *Before the Bible* (New York, 1962).

——"Abraham of Ur," *Hebrew and Semitic Studies: Essays in Honour of G.R.Driver*, ed. by D.W. Thomas and W.D. McHardy (Oxford,1963) pp.77-84.

—— "Hebrew Origins in the Light of Recent Discovery," *Biblical and Other Studies*, ed. by A. Altmann (Cambridge, 1963) pp.3-14.

Gottwald, N.K. "Domain Assumptions and Societal Models in the Study of Pre-Monarchic Israel," *VTS* 28 (1975) pp.89-100.

—— "Early Israel and the Asiatic Mode of Production in Canaan," *SBL Seminar Papers* (1976) pp.145-154.

—— *The Tribes of Yahweh: A Sociology of the Religion of Liberated Israel 1250-1050 B.C.E.* (Maryknoll, 1979).

—— "Early Israel and the Canaanite Socio-economic System," *Palestine in Transition* (1983) pp.26ff.

—— "Two Models for the Origins of Ancient Israel: Social Revolution or Frontier Development," *The Quest for the Kingdom of God: Studies in Honor of George E.*

Mendenhall, ed. by H.B. Huffmon, F.A. Spina and A.R.W. Green (Winona Lake, 1983) pp.5-24;

Graf, D.F. "The Saracens and the Defense of the Arabian Frontier," *BASOR* 229 (1978), pp.1-26.

—— and Freedman, D.N. *Palestine in Transition: The Emergence of Ancient Israel, SWBAS* 2 (Sheffield, 1983).

Graf, K. *Die geschichtlichen Bücher des alten Testaments. Zwei Historisch-kritische Untersuchungen* (Leipzig, 1866).

Grant, E. and Wright, G.E. *Ain Shems Excavation V* (Haverford, 1939).

Greenberg, R. "New Light on the Early Iron Age at Tell Beit Mirsim," *BASOR* 265 (1987), pp.55-80.

Gressmann, H. "Sage und Geschichte in den Patriarchenerzählungen," *ZAW* 30 (1910), pp.1-34.

—— "Ursprung und Entwicklung der Joseph-Sage," in *Eucharisterion*, Festschrift H. Gunkel (Leipzig, 1923) pp.1-55.

—— *Altorientalische Texte zum alten Testament*, 2nd. ed. (Berlin, 1926).

—— *Altorientalische Bilder zum alten Testament*, 2nd. ed. (Berlin, 1927).

Gross, W. *Verbform und Funktion: Wayyiqtol für die Gegenwart?, Alttestamentliche Studien* 1 (St. Otilien, 1976).

Gunkel, H. *Genesis, Handkommentar zum alten Testament* (Göttingen, 1901).

Gunn, D.M. *The Story of King David* (Sheffield, 1976).

—— *The Fate of King Saul*, JSOTS 14 (Sheffield, 1980).

—— and Davies, P.R. (eds.) "A History of Ancient Israel and Judah: A Discussion of Miller-Hayes (1986)," *JSOT* 39 (1987), pp.3-63.

Gunneweg, J. *et alii*, "On The Origin of Pottery from Tel Miqne-Ekron," *BASOR* 264 (1986), pp.3-16.

Hackett, J.A. *The Balaam Text from Deir 'Alla*, HSM 31 (Chico, 1984).

—— "The Dialect of the Plaster Text from Tell Deir 'Alla," *Orientalia* 53 (1984), pp.57-65.

Häfeli L. and 'Aref, 'Aref el. *Die Beduinen von Beerseba* (Luzern, 1938).

—— *Spruchweisheit und Volksleben in Palästina* (Luzern, 1939).

Haldar, A. *Who Were the Amorites?* (Leiden, 1971).

Halligan, J.M. "The Role of the Peasant in the Amarna Period," *Palestine in Transition: The Emergence of Ancient Israel* (Sheffield, 1983) pp.15-24.

Hallo, W.W. "Assyrian Historiography Revisited," *EI* 14 (1978), *1-*7.

—— "Biblical History in its Near Eastern Setting: Contextual Approach," *Scripture in Context*, ed. by W.W. Hallo (New Haven, 1980) pp.1-26.

—— "Sumerian Historiography," *History, Historiography, and Interpretation*, ed. H. Tadmor and M. Weinfeld (Leiden, 1984) pp.9-20.

Halpern, B. *The Emergence of Israel in Canaan*, SBLMS (Chico, 1983).

—— "Dialect Distribution in Canaan and the Deir Alla Inscriptions," *Working With No Data*, ed. by D.M. Golomb (Winona Lake, 1987) pp.119-139.

—— *The First Historians* (San Francisco, 1988).

Hammond, P. "Hebron: Chronique Archaeologique," *RB* 72 (1965), pp.267-270.

Hanbury-Tenison, J.W. "The Jerash Region Survey, 1984," *ADAJ* 31 (1987), pp.129-158.

Hankey, V. "Mycenaean Pottery in the Middle East," *BSA* 62 (1967), pp.127-128.

Harding, A.F. "Introduction: Climatic Change and Archaeology," *Climatic Change in Later Prehistory*, ed. by A.F. Harding (Edinburgh, 1982) pp.1-10.

—— (ed.) *Climatic Change in Later Pre-History* (Edinburgh, 1982).

Hartog, F. *The Mirror of Herodotus* (London, 1988).

Hauser, A.J. "Israel's Conquest of Palestine: A Peasants' Rebellion?," *JSOT* 7 (1978), pp.2-19.

—— "Response to Thompson and Mendenhall," *JSOT* 7 (1978), pp.35-36.

—— "The Revolutionary Origins of Ancient Israel: A Response to Gottwald (*JSOT* 7, 1978, 37-52)," *JSOT* 8 (1978), pp.46-49.

Hauser, C. "From Alt to Anthropology: The Rise of the Israelite State," *JSOT* 36 (1986), pp.7ff.

—— "Anthropology in Historiography," *JSOT* 39 (1987), pp.15-21.

Hayes, J.H. and Miller, J.M. *A History of Israel and Judah* (Philadelphia, 1986).

—— "On Reconstructing Israelite History," *JSOT* 39 (1987), pp.6ff.

Hayes, J.L. *Dialectical Variation in the Syntax of Coordination and Subordination in Western Accadian of the El-Amarna Period* (University of California, Los Angeles dissertation, 1984).

Helck, W. *Die Beziehungen Ägyptens zu vorderasien im 3. und 2. Jahrtausend* (Wiesbaden, 1962).

Helm, P.R. "Herodotus' Medikos Logos and Median History," *Iran* 19 (1981), pp.85-90.

Heltzer, M. "Problems of the Social History of Syria in the Late Bronze Age," *La Siria nel Tardo Bronze*, ed. by M. Liverani (Rome, 1969) pp.31-46.

—— "Soziale Aspekte des Heerwesens in Ugarit," *Beiträge zur sozialen Struktur des alten Vorderasien*, ed. by H. Klengel (Berlin, 1971) pp.125-131.

—— *The Rural Community in Ancient Ugarit* (Wiesbaden, 1976).

—— *The Internal Organization of the Kingdom of Ugarit* (Wiesbaden, 1982).

Henry, D.O. "The Pre-History and Paléoenvironments of Jordan; An Overview," *Paléorient* 12 (1986), pp.5-26.

Hensley, L.V. *The Official Persian Documents in the Book of Ezra* (University of Liverpool dissertation, 1977).

Herion, G.A. "The Role of Historical Narrative in Biblical Thought," *JSOT* 21 (1981), pp.25-57.

—— "The Impact of Modern and Social Science Assumptions on the Reconstruction of Israelite History," *JSOT* 34 (1986), pp.3-33.

Herr, L.G. *The Scripts of Ancient Northwest Semitic Seals* (Missoula, 1978).

—— "The Formal Scripts of Iron Age Transjordan," *BASOR* 238 (1980), pp.21-34.

Herrmann, S. *A History of Israel in Old Testament Times*, revd. ed. (London, 1981).

Herzog, Z. *Beer-Sheba II: The Early Iron Age Settlements* (Tel Aviv, 1984).

—— *et alii*, "The Israelite Fortress at Arad," *BASOR* 254 (1984), pp.1-34.

Hesse, B. and Wapnish, P. "The Contribution and Organization of Pastoral Systems," *Early Israelite Agriculture*, ed. by O.S. LaBianca (1989) pp.29-41.

Hillaire-Marcel, C. and Fairbridge, R.W. "An 8000 Year Palaeoclimatic Record of the 'Double Hale' 45 Year Cycle," *Nature* 268 (1977), pp.415ff.

Hirsch, S.W. "1001 Iranian Nights: History and Fiction in Xenophon's Cyropaedia," *The Greek Historians: Literature and History*, A.E. Raubitschek Festschrift ed. by W.R. Connor (Saratoga, 1985) pp.65-85.

Holm-Nielsen, S. and Buhl, M.-L. *Shiloh* (Copenhagen, 1969).

Holtyzer, J. *A search for Method: A Study in the Syntactic Use of the H-Locale in Classical Hebrew, Studies in Semitic Languages and Linguistics* 12 (Leiden, 1981).

Hopkins, D.C. *The Highlands of Canaan, SWBAS* 3 (Sheffield, 1985).

Horn, S.H. and Boraas, R.S. "The First Campaign at Tell Hesban: 1968," *AUSS* 7 (1969), pp.97-239.
—— and Boraas, R.S. "The Second Campaign at Tell Hesban: 1971," *AUSS* 11 (1973), pp.1-144.
—— and Boraas, R.S. "The Third Campaign at Tell Hesban: 1973," *AUSS* 13 (1975), pp.101-247.
Horowitz, A. "Preliminary Polynological Indications as to the Climate of Israel during the last 6000 Years," *Paléorient* 2 (1974), pp.407-414.
—— *The Quaternary of Israel* (New York, 1979).
Horwitz, L.K. "Sedentism in the Early Bronze IV: A Faunal Perspective," *BASOR* 275 (1989), pp.15-25.
Hübner, U. *Die Kultur und Religion eines transjordanischen Volkes im 1. Jahrtausend* (Heidelberg dissertation, 1991).
Humbert, J.-B. and Briend, J. *Tell Keisan, 1971-1976: Une Cité phenicienne en Galilée* (Paris, 1980).
Hunt, M.L. *The Iron Age Pottery of the Yoqneam Regional Project* (University of California, Berkeley dissertation, 1985).
Hütteroth, W.-D. *Palästina und Transjordanien im 16. Jahrhundert*, *BTAVO* 33 (Wiesbaden, 1978).
Ibach, R. "Archaeological Survey of the Hesban Region," *AUSS* 14 (1976), pp.119-126.
—— "Expanded Archaeological Survey of the Hesban Region," *AUSS* 16 (1978), pp.201-213.
Ibrahim, M. "The Collared-rim Jar of the Early Iron Age," *Archaeology in the Levant*, ed. by P. Parr and R. Mooney (London, 1978) pp.116-126.
Immerwahr, H.R. *Form and Thought in Herodotus, Philological Monographs* 23 (Cleveland, 1966).
Inbar, M. and Sivan, D. "Paleo-Urban Development of the Quaternary Environmental Changes in the Akko Area," *Paléorient* 9 (1983), pp.85-91.
Irvin, D. *Mytharion, AOAT* 32 (Neukirchen, 1978).
Irvine, S.A. *Isaiah, Ahaz, and the Syro-Ephraimitic Crisis, SBLDS* 123 (Atlanta, 1990).
Ishida, T. "The Leaders of the Tribal Leagues 'Israel' in the Pre-monarchic Period," *RB* 80 (1973), pp.514-530.
Isserlin, B.S.J. "Some Aspects of the Present State of Hamito-Semitic Studies," *Hamito-Semitica*, ed. by J. and T. Bynon (The Hague, 1975) pp.479-485.
—— "The Israelite Conquest of Canaan: A Comparative Review of the Arguments Applicable," *PEQ* 115 (1983), pp.85-94.
Jackson, K.P. *The Ammonite Language of the Iron Age, HSM* 27 (Chico, 1983).
Jagersma, H. *A History of Israel in the Old Testament Period* (Philadelphia, 1983).
Jamieson-Drake, E. *Scribes and Schools in Monarchic Judah: A Socio-Archaeological Approach* (Sheffield, 1991).
Janssen, J.J. *Commodity Prices from the Ramesside Period: An Economic Study of the Village of Necropolis Workmen at Thebes* (Leiden, 1975).
Jaussen, A. *Coutumes des Arabes au Pays de Moab* (Paris, 1903).
Jepsen, A. *Das Gilgamesch-Epos*, 2 vols. (Berlin, 1924-1926).
Jones, A.H. *Bronze Age Civilization: The Philistines and Danites* (Washington, 1975).
Kallai, Z. *The Tribes of Israel* (Jerusalem, 1967).
—— *Historical Geography of the Bible* (Jerusalem, 1986).

Kamp. K.A. and Yoffee, N. "Ethnicity in Ancient Western Asia during the Early Second Millennium B.C.: Archaeological Assessments and Ethnoarchaeological Perspectives," *BASOR* 237 (1980), pp.85-104.

Kaplan, J. "Jaffa (Joppa)," *EAEHL II*, pp.532-541.

Kaucky, F.L. and Smith, R.H. "Lake Beisan and the Prehistoric Settlement of the Northern Jordan Valley," *Paléorient* 12 (1986), pp.27-36.

Kaufman, S.A. "The Aramaic Texts from Deir 'Alla," *BASOR* 239 (1980), pp.71-74.

Kelso, J.L. *The Excavations of Bethel, AASOR* 39 (1968).

Kempinski, A. "Tel Masos," *Expedition* 20 (1978), pp.29-37.

—— *The Rise of an Urban Culture, Israel Ethnographic Society Studies* 4 (Jerusalem, 1978).

—— *et alii*, "Excavations at Tel Masos 1972, 1974, 1975," *Eretz Israel* 15 (1981), pp.154-180.

—— "Baal-Perazim and the Scholarly Controversy on the Israelite Settlement," *Qadmoniot* 14 (1981), pp.63f.

—— and Fritz, V. *Ergebnisse der Ausgrabungen auf der Hirbet el-Msas (Tel Masos) I-III* (Wiesbaden, 1983).

Kenyon, K. "Palestine in the Time of the Eighteenth Dynasty," *CAH* vol 2,1 (London, 1971) pp.526-566.

—— *Amorites and Canaanites* (Oxford, 1967).

Khazanov, A.M. *Nomads and the Outside World* (Cambridge, 1983).

Kitchen, K.A. *Ancient Orient and the Old Testament* (London, 1966).

Klein, G.L. and Mazar, A. "Three Seasons of Excavations at Tel Batash—Biblical Timnah," *BASOR* 248 (1982), pp.1-36.

Klein, M. and Sneh, Y. "Holocene Sea Level Changes at the Coast of Dor," *Science* 226 (1984), pp.831f.

Klengel, H. *Benjaminiten und Hanäer zur Zeit der Könige von Mari* (Berlin dissertation, 1958).

—— "Zu einigen Problemen des altvorderasiatischen Nomadentums," *Archiv Orientalní* 30 (1962), pp.585-596.

—— "Aziru von Amurru und seine Rolle in der Geschichte der Amarnazeit," *Mitteilungen des Institut für Orientforschung* 10 (1964), pp.57-83.

—— "Sesshafte und Nomaden in der alten Geschichte Mesopotamiens" *Saeculum* 17 (1966), pp.205-222.

—— *Geschichte Syriens im 2. Jahrtausend v.u.Z.* Teil II: *Mittel- und Südsyrien*, (Berlin, 1969).

—— *Zwischen Zelt und Palast: Die Begegnung von Nomaden und Sesshaften im alten Vorderasien* (Leipzig, 1972).

—— *The Rural Community in Ancient Ugarit* (Wiesbaden, 1976).

—— *Handel und Händler im alten Orient* (Vienna, 1979).

—— *The Internal Organization of the Kingdom of Ugarit* (Wiesbaden, 1982).

Kling, B. "Comments on the Mycenaean IIIC:1b Pottery from Kitian Areas I and II," *Kitian V* (Nicosia, 1985) pp.38-56.

Knauf, E.A. "Midianites and Ishmaelites" in J.F.A. Sawyer and D.J.A. Clines (eds.) *Midian, Moab, and Edom, JSOTS* 24 (Sheffield, 1983) pp.147-162.

—— "Supplementa Ismaelitica," *BN* 40(1987), p.20.

—— and Maani, S. "On the Phonemes of Fringe Canaanite," *Ugarit-Forschungen* 19 (1987), pp.91-94.

468   BIBLIOGRAPHY

—— *Midian: Untersuchungen zur Geschichte Palästinas und Nordarabiens am Ende des 2ten Jahrtausends, ADPV* (Wiesbaden, 1988).
—— *Ismael: Untersuchungen zur Geschichte Palästinas und Nordarabiens im 1sten Jahrtausend vChr, ADPV* (Wiesbaden, 2nd ed., 1989).
—— "The Migration of the Script and the Formation of the State in South Arabia," *PSAS* 19 (1989), pp.79-91.
—— Review of G. Ahlström, *Who Were the Israelites?, JNES* 49 (1990), pp.81-83.
—— "War 'Biblisch-Hebräisch' eine Sprache?," *Zeitschrift für Althebräistik* 3 (1990), pp.11-23.
—— "From History to Interpretation," *The Fabric of History: Text, Artifact and Israel's Past, JSOTS* 127, ed. by D. Edelman (Sheffield, 1991) pp.26-64.
—— "Bedouin and Bedouin States," *Anchor Bible Dictionary*, ed. by D.N. Freedman (forthcoming).
Knight D.A. (ed.), *Julius Wellhausen and His Prolegomena to the History of Israel, Semeia* 25 (1982; Chico, 1983).
Knudtzon, J.A. *Die El-Amarna Tafeln* (Leipzig, 1915).
Kochavi, M. and Gophna, R. "An Archaeological Survey of the Plain of Sharon," *IEJ* 16 (1966), pp.143-144.
—— *The Settlement of the Negev in the Middle Bronze (Canaanite) I Age* (Hebrew University dissertation, 1967).
—— *Judaea, Samaria, and the Golan: Archaeological Survey 1967-1968* (Jerusalem, 1972).
—— "Khirbet Rabud = Debir," *Tel Aviv* 1 (1974), pp.2-33.
—— "The Conquest and the Settlement," *Et-Mol* 7 (1982), pp.3-5.
—— "The Period of the Israelite Settlement," *The History of Eretz Israel, II: Israel and Judah in the biblical Period*, ed. by I. Ephal (Jerusalem, 1984) pp.19-84.
—— "The Land of Israel in the 13th.-12th. Centuries, B.C.E.: Historical Conclusions from Archaelogical Data," *Eleventh Archaeological Conference in Israel* (Jerusalem, 1985), pp.16ff.
Kohata, F. *Jawhist und Priesterschrift in Exodus 3-14, BZAW* 166 (Berlin, 1986).
Kuenen, A. *Historisch-kritische Einleitung in die Bücher des alten Testaments hinsichtlich ihrer Entstehung und Sammlung I. Die Entstehung des Hexateuch* (Leipzig, 1887).
Kupper, J.R. *Les Nomades en Mesopotamie au temps des rois de Mari, Bibliothèque de la Faculté de Philosophie et Lettres de l'Université de Liège*, 182 (Liège, 1957).
Kuschke, A. "Hiwwiter in Ha-'Ai?" *Wort und Wahrheit, AOAT* 18, ed. by H. Rösel (Neukirchen, 1973) pp.115-119.
—— Mittmann, S. and Müller, U. *Archäologischer Survey in der nördlichen Biqa', Herbst 1972: Report on a Prehistoric Survey in the Biqa'* (by I. Azoury), *BTAVO* 11 (Wiesbaden, 1976).
LaBianca, O.S. and Geraty, L.T. "The Local Environment and Human Food Producing Strategies in Jordan: The Case of Tell Hesban and its Surrounding Region," *SHAJ* II (Amman, 1985) pp.323-330.
—— *Sedentarization and Nomadization: Food System Cycles at Hesban and Vicinity in Transjordan* (Brandeis dissertation, 1987).
Laheyrie, J. "Sea Level Variations and the Birth of the Egyptian Civilization," *Radiocarbon Dating*, ed. by R. Berger and H. Suess (Berkeley, 1979) pp.32-35.
Lamb, H.H. "Reconstruction of the Course of Postglacial Climate over the World," *Climatic Change in Later Pre-History*, ed. by A.F. Harding (Edinburgh, 1982) pp.11-32.
Lang, B. *Monotheism and the Prophetic Minority, SWBAS* 1 (Sheffield, 1983).

—— "The Yahweh Alone Movement and the Making of Jewish Monotheism," *Monotheism and the Prophetic Minority* (Sheffield, 1983) pp.13-59.

Lemaire, A. "Excursus II: Le Clan D'Aprill et Israël, les Origines de la Confederation Israélite," *Inscriptions Hebraiques Tome I: Les Ostraca* (Paris, 1977) pp.283-286.

—— *Les Écoles et la Formation de la Bible dans l'Ancien Israël, Orbis Biblicus et Orientalis* 39 (Göttingen, 1981).

—— "Deux origines d'Israel: la montagne d'Ephraim et le territoire de Manassé," *La Protohistoire d'Israel*, ed. by E.-M. Laperrousaz (Paris, 1990) pp.183-292.

Lemche, N.P. "The Greek 'Amphictyony'—Could it be a Prototype for the Israelite Society in the Period of The Judges?" *JSOT* 4 (1977), pp.48-59.

—— "'Hebrew' as a National Name for Israel," *StTh* 33 (1979), pp.1-23.

—— "'Hebraeerne': Myths over habiru—hebraeerproblemet," *DTT* 43 (1980), pp.153-190.

—— "Det Revolutionaere Israel. En Praesention af en Moderne Forskningsretning," *Dansk Teologisk Tidsskrift* 45 (1982), pp.16-39.

—— "On Sociology and the History of Israel: A Reply to Eckhardt Otto—and Some Further Considerations," *BN* 21 (1983), pp.48-58.

—— "Israel in the Period of the Judges—The Tribal League in Recent Research," *Studia Theologica* 38 (1984), pp.1-28.

—— *Early Israel: Anthropological and Historical Studies on the Israelite Society Before the Monarchy, VTS* 37 (Leiden, 1985).

—— *Ancient Israel: A New History of Israelite Society* (Sheffield, 1988).

—— *The Canaanites and Their Land* (Sheffield, 1991).

Leonard, A. "The Jarash-Tell el-Husn Highway Survey," *ADAJ* 31 (1987), pp.343-390.

Liebowitz, H. "Excavations at Tel Yin'am: the 1976 and 1977 Seasons: Preliminary Report," *BASOR* 243 (1981), pp.79-94.

Lipschitz, N. "Overview of the Dendrochronological and Dendroarchaeological Research in Israel," *Dendrochronologia* 4 (1986), pp.37-58.

—— "Olives in Ancient Israel in View of Dendroarchaeological Investigations," *Olive Oil in Antiquity*, ed. by M. Heltzer and D. Eitam (Jerusalem, 1988) pp.139-145.

Liverani, M. "The Amorites," *Peoples of Old Testament Times*, ed. by D.J. Wiseman (Oxford, 1973) pp.100-133.

—— Review of R. De Vaux, *L'Histoire ancienne d'Israel I-II, OA* 15 (1976), pp.145-159.

—— " Un ipotesi sul nome di Abramo," *Henoch* 1 (1979), pp.9-18.

—— "Economia delle fattorie palatine ugaritiche," *Dialoghi di Archeologia* 1 (1979), pp.7off.

—— "The Ideology of the Assyrian Empire," *Power and Propaganda, Mesopotamia* 7 (Copenhagen, 1979) pp.297-317.

—— "Le 'Origini' d'Israele progetto irrealizzabile di ricerca etnogenetica," *Rivista Biblica Italiana* 28 (1980), pp.9-31.

Long, B.O. *The Problem of Etiological Narrative in the Old Testament, BZAW* 108 (Berlin, 1968).

—— "Historical Narrative and the Fictionalizing Imagination," *VT* 35 (1985), pp.405-16.

—— "On Finding the Hidden Premises," *JSOT* 39 (1987), pp.10-14.

Loretz, O. *Habiru-Hebräer: Eine sozio-linguistische Studie über die Herkunft des Gentiliziums 'ibri vom Appelativum Habiru, BZAW* 160 (Berlin, 1984).

Luke, J.T. *Pastoralism and Politics in the Mari Period* (University of Michigan dissertation, 1965).

—— "Abraham and the Iron Age: Reflections on the New Patriarchal Studies," *JSOT* 4 (1977), pp.39ff.

—— "'Your Father Was an Amorite' (Ezek 16:3. 45): An Essay on the Amorite Problem in Old Testament Traditions," *The Quest for the Kingdom of God: Studies in Honor of George E. Mendenhall*, ed. by H.B. Huffmon, F.A. Spina, and A.R.W. Green (Winona Lake, 1983) pp.226ff.

Maani, S. and Knauf, E.A. "On the Phonemes of Fringe Canaanite," *Ugarit-Forschungen* 19 (1987), pp.91-94.

Magny, M. "Atlantic and Sub-Boreal: Dampness and Dryness," *Climatic Change in Later Pre-History*, ed. by A.F. Harding (Edinburgh, 1982) pp.34-47.

Maisler, B. (Mazar), "The Excavations at Tell Qasile: Preliminary Report," *IEJ* 1 (1950/51), pp.61-76. 125-140. 194-218.

Malamat, A. "Die Frühgeschichte Israels: eine Methodologische Studie," *Theologische Zeitschrift* 39 (1983), pp.1-16.

—— "The Head of All These Kingdoms," *JBL* 79 (1960), pp.12-19.

Matthews, V.H. *Pastoral Nomadism in the Mari Kingdom (ca. 1830-1760 B.C.), ASORDS* 3 (Cambridge, 1978).

—— "The Mari Texts and Enclosed Nomadism," typescript of SBL paper (Anaheim, 1990).

Mayerson, P. *The Ancient Agricultural Regime of Nessana and the Central Negeb* (London, 1960).

Mayes, A.D.H. *Israel in the Period of the Judges, Studies in Biblical Theology* 29 (Naperville, 1974).

—— "The Period of the Judges and the Rise of the Monarchy," *Israelite and Judaean History*, ed. by J.H. Hayes and J.M. Miller (Philadelphia, 1977) pp.285-331.

Mazar, A. "Giloh: An Early Israelite Settlement Site Near Jerusalem," *IEJ* 31 (1981), pp.1-36.

—— and Klein, G.L. "Three Seasons of Excavations at Tel Batash-Biblical Timnah," *BASOR* 248 (1982), pp.1-36.

—— "The Emergence of the Philistine Material Culture," *IEJ* 35 (1985), pp.95-107.

—— "The Israelite Settlement in Canaan in the Light of Archaeological Excavations," *Biblical Archaeology Today* (Jerusalem, 1985) pp.61-71.

Mazar, B. "The Philistines and the Rise of Israel and Tyre," *Israel Academy of Sciences and Humanities Proceedings* 1 (Jerusalem, 1964) pp.1-22.

—— "The Middle Bronze Age in Canaan," *IEJ* 18 (1968), pp.65-97.

—— "The Book of Genesis," *JNES* 28 (1969), pp.73-83.

—— "A Philistine Temple at Tell Qasile" *BA* 36 (1973), pp.42-48.

—— *Canaan and Israel* (Jerusalem, 1974).

—— "Excavations at Tell Qasile," *BA* 40 (1977), pp.81-87.

—— "The Early Israelite Settlement in the Hill Country," *BASOR* 241 (1981), pp.75-85.

—— *The Early Biblical Period: Historical Studies* (Jerusalem, 1986).

McCarter, P.K. "The Balaam Texts from Deir 'Alla: The First Combination," *BASOR* 239 (1980), pp.49-60.

McClellan, T.L. "Chronology of the 'Philistine' Burials at Tell el-Far'ah (South)," *Journal of Field Archaeology* 6 (1979), pp.57-73.

McClure, H.A. *The Arabian Peninsula and Prehistoric Populations* (Miami, 1971).

McGovern, P.E. "Environmental Constraints for Human Settlement in the Baq'ah Valley," *SHAJ* II (Amman, 1985) pp.141-148.

—— *The Late Bronze and Early Iron Ages of Central Transjordan: The Baq'ah Valley Project, 1977-1981, University Museum Monograph* 65 (Philadelphia, 1986).

—— "Central Transjordan in the Late Bronze and Early Iron Ages: An Alternative Hypothesis of Socio-Economic Transformation and Collapse," *SHAJ* 3 (Amman, 1987) pp.267-274.

—— "Baq'ah Valley Project—Survey and Excavation," *Archaeology of Jordan* II, 1, ed. by D. Homes-Fredericq and J.B. Hennessy (Amman, 1989) pp.25-44.

Mendenhall, G.E. "Covenant Forms in Israelite Tradition," *BA* 17 (1954), pp.50-76.

—— "Law and Covenant in Israel and the Ancient Near East," *BA* 17 (1954), pp.26-46.

—— "The Hebrew Conquest of Palestine," *BA* 25 (1962), pp.66-87.

—— *The Tenth Generation: The Origins of Biblical Tradition* (Baltimore, 1973).

—— "The Monarchy," *Interpretation* 29 (1975), pp.155-170.

—— "Between Theology and Archaeology," *JSOT* 7 (1978), pp.28-34.

—— "Ancient Israel's Hyphenated History," *Palestine in Transition: The Emergence of Ancient Israel, SWBAS* 2, ed. by D.N. Freedman and D.F. Graf (Sheffield, 1983) pp.91-103.

Merner, S. *Das Nomadentum im nordwestlichen Afrika* (Berlin, 1937).

Meshel, Z. "Horvat Ritma: An Iron Age Fortress in the Negev Highlands," *Tel Aviv* 4 (1977), pp.110-135.

Meyer, E. *Geschichte des Altertums* I-V (Stuttgart, 1884-1902).

—— *Forschungen zur alten Geschichte* (Halle, 1892).

—— *Die Entstehung des Judenthums* (Halle, 1896).

—— *Julius Wellhausen und meine Schrift Die Entstehung des Judenthums: Eine Erwiderung* (Halle, 1897).

—— *Die Israeliten und ihre Nachbarstämme* (Halle, 1906).

Meyers, C. "Kadesh-Barnea: Judah's Last Outpost" *BA* 39 (1976), pp.148-151.

—— "Of Seasons and Soldiers: A Topographical Appraisal of the Pre-monarchical Tribes of Galilee," *BASOR* 252 (1983), pp.47-59.

—— "The Israelite Empire: In Defense of King Solomon," *Backgrounds for the Bible*, ed. M.P. O'Connor and D.N. Freedman (Winona Lake, 1987) pp.181-97.

Michalowski, P. *The Lamentation over the Destruction of Sumer and Ur* (Winona Lake, 1989).

Milgrom, J. "The Rebellion of Korah, Numbers 16-18: A Study in Tradition History," *SBL Seminar Papers* (Atlanta, 1988) pp.570-73.

Miller, J.M. "The Israelite Occupation of Canaan," *Israelite and Judean History*, ed. by J.H. Hayes and J.M. Miller (Philadelphia, 1977) pp.213-284.

—— "Archaeological Survey of Central Moab: 1978," *BASOR* 234 (1979), pp.43-52.

—— and Campbell, E.F. "W.F. Albright and Historical Reconstruction," *BA* 42 (1979), pp.37-47.

—— "Approaches to the Bible through History and Archaeology: Biblical History as a Discipline," *BA* 45 (1982), pp.211-216.

—— "Recent Archaeological Developments Relevant to Ancient Moab," *SHAJ* II (1982) pp.169-173.

—— and Hayes, J.H. *A History of Ancient Israel and Judah* (Philadelphia, 1986).

—— and Pinkerton, J.W. *Archaeological Survey of the Kerak Plateau* (Atlanta, 1991).

Miroschedji, R. de. *L'Époque pré-urbaine en Palestine, CRB* 13 (Paris, 1971).

Mittmann, S. *Beiträge zur Siedlungs- und Territorialgeschichte des nördlichen Ostjordanlandes, ADPV* (Wiesbaden, 1970).

—— *Deuteronomium 1, 1-6, 3: Literarkritisch und Traditionsgeschichtlich Untersucht, BZAW* 139 (Berlin, 1975).

—— *et alii*, "Palästina: Israel und Juda in der Königszeit und Siedlungen der Eisenzeit (ca.1200-550 v.Chr.)," *TAVO* Karte B IV 6 (forthcoming).

Moscati, S. *I Predecessori D'Israele, Studi orientali publicati a cura della scuola orientale IV* (Rome, 1956).

—— *The Semites in Ancient History* (Cardiff, 1959).

—— *et alii, An Introduction to the Comparative Grammar of the Semitic Languages* (Wiesbaden, 1969).

—— *I Fenici* (Milan, 1988).

—— "Who Were the Phoenicians?," *The Phoenicians*, ed. by S. Moscati (Milan, 1988) pp.24f.

—— "Territory and Settlements," *The Phoenicians*, ed. by S. Moscati (Milan, 1988) pp.26f.

Musil, A. *Arabia Petra*, vols. I: *Moab;* II: *Edom;* III: *Ethnologisches Reisebericht*, (Vienna, 1907f.).

Na'aman, N. *The Political Disposition and Historical Development of Eretz-Israel According to the Amarna Letters* (University of Tel Aviv dissertation, 1975).

—— "The Inheritance of the Sons of Simeon," *ZDPV* 96 (1980), pp.136-152.

—— "Economic Aspects of the Egyptian Occupation of Canaan," *IEJ* 31 (1981), pp.172-185.

—— "The Political History of Eretz Israel in the Time of the Nineteenth and Twentieth Dynasties," *The History of Eretz Israel*, vol. I, ed. by I. Eph'al (Jerusalem, 1982) pp.241-251.

—— "Pharaonic Lands in the Jezreel Valley in the Late Bronze Age," *Society and Economy in the Eastern Mediterranean, ca. 1500-1000 B.C.*, ed by M. Heltzer and E Lipinski (Leuven, 1988) pp.177-185.

Namiki, K. "Reconsideration of the Twelve-Tribe System of Israel," *AJBA* 2 (1976), pp.29-59.

Nashef, K. "Ausgrabungen, Forschungsreisen, Geländebegehungen: Jordanien (1980-82)," *AfO* 29/ 30 (1983/84), pp.241-292.

—— "Ausgrabungen, Forschungsreisen, Geländebegehungen: Jordanien II,"*AfO* 33 (1986), pp. 148-308.

Neev, D. and Emery, K.O. *The Dead Sea Depositional Processes and Environments of Evaporites* (Jerusalem, 1967).

Neuman, J. and Parpola, S. "Climatic Change and Eleventh-Tenth Century Eclipse of Assyria and Babylonia," *JNES* 46 (1987), pp.161-182.

Neusner, J. *From Politics to Piety* (New York, 1979).

Newberry, P.E. *Beni-Hasan I-IV* (London, 1893ff.).

Niehr, H. *Der Höchste Gott, BZAW* 190 (Berlin, 1990).

Niemann, H.M. *Die Daniten: Studien zur Geschichte eines altisraelititschen Stammes, FRLANT* 135 (Göttingen, 1985).

—— *Stadt, Land, und Herrschaft* (Habilitation, University of Rostock, 1990).

Nissen, H.J. *The Early History of the Ancient Near East* (Chicago, 1988).

Noth, M. *Die israelitischen Personennamen im Rahmen der gemeinsemitischen Namengebung, BWANT* 10 (Stuttgart, 1928).

—— "Zum Problem der Ostkanaanäer," *ZA* 39 (1930), pp.214-216.

—— *Das System der zwölf Stämme Israels, BWANT* IV/ I (Stuttgart, 1930).

— "Die syrisch-palästinische Bevölkerung des zweiten Jahrtausends v.Chr. im Lichte neuer Quellen," *ZDPV* 65 (1942), pp.34f.

— *Überlieferungsgeschichtliche Studien* I (Halle, 1943).

— *Überlieferungsgeschichte des Pentateuch* (Stuttgart, 1948).

— "Überlieferungsgeschichtliches zur zweiten Hälfte des Josuabuches," *Alttestamentliche Studien: Friedrich Nötscher zum sechzigsten Geburtstag, 19 Juli 1950, gewidmet von Kollegen, Freunden und Schülern, BBB* 1, ed. by H. Junker and J. Botterweck (Bonn, 1950) pp.152-167.

— "Das Amt des 'Richters Israels'," *Festschrift, Alfred Bertholet zum 80. Geburtstag gewidmet von Kollegen und Freunden,* ed. by W. Baumgartner *et alii* (Tübingen, 1950) pp.404-417.

— "Mari und Israel: Eine Personennamenstudie," *Geschichte und altes Testament; Beiträge zur historischen Theologie:* Festschrift A. Alt (Tübingen, 1953) pp.127-152.

— *Geschichte Israels* (Göttingen, 1959).

— *The History of Israel* (New York, 2nd. ed., 1960).

— "Der Beitrag der Archäologie Zur Geschichte Israels," *VTS* 7 (1960) pp.262-282.

— *Die Ursprünge des alten Israel im Lichte neuer Quellen, Arbeitsgemeinschaft für Forschung des Landes Nordrhein-Westfalen,* 94 (Cologne, 1961).

— *Die Welt des Alten Testaments, Theologische Hilfsbücher* 3 (Berlin, ⁴1962).

Nützel, W. "The Climatic Changes of Mesopotamia and Bordering Areas ca 14000-2000 B.C.," *Sumer* 32 (1976), pp.11-24.

O'Connell, K.G. and Fargo, V.M. "Four Seasons of Excavation at Tell el Hesi," *BA* 41 (1978), pp.165-182.

Oded, B. *Mass Deportation and Deportees in the Neo-Assyrian Empire* (Wiesbaden, 1979).

Oden, R.A. and Attridge, H.W. *Philo of Byblos: The Phoenician History, CBQMS* 9 (Washington, 1981).

Ohata, K. *Tel Zeror* I-III (Tokyo, 1966-75).

Olami A. "Daliya," *Survey of Israel,* (Jerusalem, 1981) Pal. grid sq. 15-22, maps 2 and 3.

Oppenheim, M. Frhr. von, Bräunlich E. and Caskel, W. *Die Beduinen I-III* (Berlin, 1939-1952).

Oren, E. "The Overland Route between Egypt and Canaan in the Early Bronze Age," *IEJ* 23 (1973), pp.198-205.

— "Governors' Residencies' in Canaan under the New Kingdom: A Case Study in Egyptian Administration," *Journal of the Society for the Study of Egyptian Antiquities* 14 (1985), pp.37-56.

— "The 'Ways of Horus' in North Sinai," *Egypt, Israel, Sinai: Archaeological and Historical Relationships in the Biblical Period,* ed. by A. Rainey (Tel Aviv, 1987) pp.69-119.

Orlinsky, H.M. "The Tribal System of Israel and Related Groups in the Period of the Judges," *OA* 1 (1962), pp.11-20.

Ottosson, M. *Gilead: Tradition and History* (Lund, 1969).

Overstreet W.C. *et alii, The Wadi al-Jubah Archaeological Project,* vol. IV (Washington, 1988).

Paltiel, E. "Ethnicity and the State in the Kingdom of Ugarit," *Abr-Nahrain* 19 (1980), pp.43-58.

Parker, S.T. "Peasants, Pastoralists, and Pax Romana: A Different View," *BASOR* 265 (1987), pp.35-51.

Parpola, S. and Neuman, J. "Climatic Change and Eleventh-Tenth Century Eclipse of Assyria and Babylonia," *JNES* 46 (1987), pp.161-182.

Pearse, C.K. "Grazing in the Middle East," *Journal of Range Management* 24,1 (1966), pp.13-16.

Pedersen, J. *Early Israel*, vols.I-IV; (Copenhagen, 1926/40).

Perlman, I. Asaro, F. and Dothan, M. "An Introductory Study of Mycenaean IIIC:1 Ware from Tel Ashdod," *Archaeometry* 13 (1971), pp.169-175.

Petrie, F. *Beth-Pelet* I (London, 1930).

—— *Ancient Gaza I-IV* (London, 1931-1934).

Picard, L. and Solomonica, P. "On the Geology of the Gaza-Beersheba District," *JPOS* 16 (1936), pp.180-223.

—— and Solomonica, P. *On the Geology of the Gaza-Beersheba District*, (Jerusalem, 1936).

Pinkerton, J.W. and Miller, J.M. *Archaeological Survey of the Kerak Plateau* (Atlanta, 1991).

Pitard, W.T. *Ancient Damascus, A Historical Study of the Syrian City-State from Earliest Times until Its Fall to the Assyrians in 732 B.C.E.* (Winona Lake, 1987).

Porath, Y. Dor, S. and Applebaum, S. *The History and Archaeology of Emeg-Hefer* (Tel Aviv, 1985).

Portugali, J. and Gophna, R. "Settlement and Demographic Processes in Israel's Coastal Plain from the Chalcolithic to the Middle Bronze Age," *BASOR* 269 (1981), pp.11-28.

Prag, K. "The Intermediate Early Bronze-Middle Bronze Age: an Interpretation of the Evidence from Transjordan, Syria, and Lebanon," *Levant* VI (1974), pp.69-116.

—— "Continuity and Migration in the South Levant in the Late Third Millennium: A Review of T.L. Thompson's and Some Other Views," *PEQ* 116 (1984), pp.58-68.

Prausnitz, M.W. "Acho, Plain of," *EAEHL* I (Jerusalem, 1975) pp.23-30.

Pritchard, J.B. *Ancient Near Eastern Texts Relating to the Old Testament* (Princeton, 1968).

—— *The Cemetery at Tell is Sa'ideyeh* (Philadelphia, 1980).

Provan, I.W. *Hezekiah and the Book of Kings, BZAW* 172 (Berlin, 1988) pp.114-130.

Raban, A. and Galili, E. "Recent Maritime Archeological Research in Israel," *IJNA* 14 (1985), pp.332-349.

—— "The Harbor of the Sea Peoples at Dor," *BA* 50 (1987), pp.118-126.

—— "The Constructive Maritime Role of the Sea Peoples in the Levant," *Society and Economy in the Eastern Mediterranean*, ed. by M. Heltzer and E. Lipinski (Leiden, 1988) pp.261-294.

Raban, I. "Nahalal," *Survey of Israel* (Jerusalem,1981) Pal. grid Sq.17-23, maps 2 and 3.

Rad, G. von. "Theologische Geschichtsschreibung im alten Testament," *ThZ* 4 (1948), pp.166-176.

—— *Das erste Buch Mose: Genesis übersetzt und erklärt* (Göttingen, 1949-1953).

—— *Theologie des Alten Testaments* (Munich, 1957).

—— "History and the Patriarchs," *Expository Times* 72 (1960/61), pp.213-216.

—— *The Problem of the Pentateuch and Other Essays* (Edinburgh, 1966).

Rafferty, J.E. "The Archaeological Record on Sedentariness: Recognition, Development and Implications," *Advances in Archaeological Method and Theory*, vol. 8, ed. by M.B. Schiffer (Orlando, 1985) pp.113-156.

Rainey, A. "The Identification of Philistine Gath," *Eretz Israel* 12 (1975), pp.63-76.

—— *El Amarna Tablets 359-379, AOAT* 8 (Neukirchen, 1978).

—— "Toponymic Problems," *Tel Aviv* 9 (1982), pp.130-136.

—— "The Biblical Shephelah of Judah," *BASOR* 251 (1983), pp.1-22.

—— Review of *Biblical Archaeology Today, BASOR* 273 (1989), pp.87-95.

Ramsey, G.W. *The Quest for the Historical Israel: Reconstructing Israel's Early History* (Atlanta, 1981).

Range, P. *Die Küstenebene Palästinas* (Frankfurt, 1922).

—— *Die Isthmuswüste und Palästina* (Hamburg, 1926).

—— "Wissenschaftliche Ergebnisse einer genealogischen Forschungsreise nach Palästina in Frühjahr 1928," *ZDPV* 55 (1932), pp.42-74.

Rast, W. *Taanach I* (New Haven, 1978).

Raveh, K. "A Concise Nautical History of Dor/ Tantura," *International Journal of Nautical Archaeology* 13 (1984), pp.223-241.

Reinhold, G. *Die Beziehungen Altisraels zu den aramäischen Staaten in der israelitisch judäischen Königszeit* (Frankfurt, 1989).

Rendtorff, R. *Das überlieferungsgeschichtliche Problem des Pentateuch, BZAW* 147 (Berlin, 1977).

Richard, S. "Toward a Consensus of Opinion on the End of the Early Bronze Age in Palestine-Transjordan," *BASOR* 237 (1984), pp.5-34.

—— "From the End of the Early Bronze Age to the Beginning of the Middle Bronze Age," *BAT* (Jerusalem, 1985) pp.113-135.

—— "The Early Bronze Age: The Rise and Collapse of Urbanism," *BA* 50 (1987), pp.22-43.

—— "The 1987 Expedition to Khirbet Iskander and its Vicinity: Fourth Preliminary Report," *BASOR* supplement 26 (1990) pp.33-58.

Richter, W. *Traditionsgeschichtliche Untersuchungen zum Richterbuch, BBB* (Bonn, 1968).

Ritter-Kaplan, H. "The impact of drought on Third Millennium BCE Cultures on the Basis of Excavations in the Tel Aviv Exhibition Grounds," *EI* 17 (1983), pp.333-338.

Rivkin, E. "The Story of Korah's Rebellion: Key to the Formation of the Pentateuch," *SBL Seminar Papers* (Atlanta, 1988) pp.574-81.

Robinson, P. "Why Do We Believe Thucydides? A Comment on W.R. Connor's 'Narrative Discourse in Thucydides'," *The Greek Historians: Literature and History, A.E. Raubitschek Festschrift, ed. by W.R Connor* (Saratoga, 1985) pp.19-23.

Rochberg-Halton, F. "Fate and Divination in Mesopotamia," *Archiv fur Orientforschung* 19 (1982), pp.363-371.

Rogerson, J.W. *Myths in Old Testament Interpretation, BZAW* 134 (Berlin, 1974).

—— *Anthropology and the Old Testament* (Sheffield, 1984).

—— *Atlas of the Bible* (Oxford, 1985).

Ronen, A. "Late Quaternary Sea Levels inferred from Coastal Stratigraphy and Archaeology in Israel," *Quaternary Coastlines and Marine Archaeology*, ed. by P.M. Masters and N.C. Flemming (London, 1983) pp.121-134.

Rose, M. *Deuteronomist und Jahwist: Untersuchungen zu den Berührungspunkten beider Literaturwerke: AThANT* 67 (Zurich, 1981).

Rössler, O. "Verbalbau und Verbalflexion in den semitohamitischen Sprachen," *ZDMG* 100 (1950), pp.461-514.

—— "Der semitische Charakter der lybischen Sprache," *ZA* 50 (1952), pp.121-150.

—— "Eine bisher unbekannte Tempusform im Althebräischen," *ZDMG* 111 (1961), pp.445-451.

—— "Ghain im Ugaritischem," *ZA* 54 (1961), pp.158-172.

—— "Das Ägyptische als semitische Sprache," *Christentum am Roten Meer*, ed. by F. Altheim and R. Stiehl (Berlin, 1971) pp.263-326.

Rothenberg, B. *Negeb* (Ramat-Gan, 1967).

—— *Timna* (London, 1972).

Rowton, M.B. "Enclosed Nomadism," *JESHO* 17 (1974), pp.1-30.

—— "The Topological Factor in the Hapiru Problem," *Assyriological Studies* 16 (1965), pp.375-387.

—— "Enclosed Nomadism," *JESHO* 17 (1974), pp.1-30.

—— "Economic and Political Factors in Ancient Nomadism," *Nomads and Sedentary Peoples*, ed. by J.S. Castillo (El Colegio de México, 1981) pp.25-36.

Saggs, H.W.F. *Encounter with the Divine in Mesopotamia and Israel* (London, 1978).

—— "Assyrian Prisoners of War and the Right to Live," *Archiv für Orientforschung* 19 (1982), pp.85-93.

Sancisi-Weerdenburg, H. "Decadence in the Empire or Decadence in the Sources?" *Achaemenid History* I, ed. H. Sancisi-Weerdenburg (Leiden, 1987) pp.33-45.

Sapin, J. "La géographie Humaine de la Syrie-Palestine au Deuxième millénaire avant J.C. comme Voie de Recherche Historique I," *JESHO* 24 (1981), pp.1-62.

—— "La géographie Humaine de la Syrie-Palestine au Deuxième millénaire avant J.C. comme Voie de Recherche Historique II," *JESHO* 25 (1982), pp.1-49.

—— "La géographie Humaine de la Syrie-Palestine au Deuxième millénaire avant J.C. comme Voie de Recherche Historique III," *JESHO* 25 (1982), pp.113-186.

Sauer, J.A. *Heshbon Pottery, 1971: A Preliminary Report on the Pottery from the 1971 Excavations at Tell Hesban, Andrews University Monographs* 7 (Berrien Springs, 1973).

—— "Prospects for Archaeology in Jordan and Syria," *BA* 45 (1982), pp.73-84.

—— "Ammon, Moab, and Edom," *Biblical Archaeology Today*, ed. by J. Amitai (Jerusalem, 1985) pp.206-214.

—— "Transjordan in the Bronze and Iron Ages: A Critique of Glueck's Synthesis," *BASOR* 263 (1986), pp.1-26.

Schachermeyer, F. *Die Agäische Frühzeit*, vol. 4: *Griechenland im Zeitalter der Wanderungen* (Vienna, 1982).

Schickele, R. *Die Weidewirtschaft in den Trockengebieten der Erde* (Jena, 1931).

Schley, D.G. *Shiloh: A Biblical City in Tradition and History, JSOTS* 63 (Sheffield, 1989).

Schmid, H.H. *Der sogenannte Jahwist: Beobachtungen und Fragen zur Pentateuchforschung* (Zurich, 1976).

—— "Auf der Suche nach neuen Perspektiven für die Pentateuch-Forschung," *VTS* 32 (Leiden, 1981) pp.375-394.

Schmitt, R. *Abschied der Heilsgeschichte?, Europäische Hochschulschriften* 195 (Frankfurt, 1982).

Schulte, H. *Die Entstehung der Geschichtsschreibung im Alten Israel, BZAW* 128 (Berlin, 1972).

Schumacher, G. *Tell el-Mutesellim*, vol. I, (Leipzig, 1908).

Seale, M.S. *The Desert Bible: Nomadic Tribal Culture and Old Testament Interpretation* (London, 1974).

Seger, J.D. *The Pottery of Palestine at the Close of the Middle Bronze Age* (Harvard University dissertation, 1965).

—— "Investigations at Tell Halif, Israel," *BASOR* 252 (1983), pp.1-23.

Sellers, O. *The 1957 Excavations at Beth Zur, AASOR* 38 (1968).

Seters, J. Van. *The Hyksos: A New Investigation* (New Haven, 1966).

—— *Abraham in History and Tradition* (New Haven, 1975).

—— *In Search of History: Historiography in the Ancient World and the Origins of Biblical History* (New Haven, 1983).

—— *Der Jahwist als Historiker, Theologische Studien* 134 (Zurich, 1987).

Shanks, H. "The Exodus and the Crossing of the Red Sea according to Hans Goedicke," *BAR* 7/5 (1981), pp.42-50.

Shannon, I. "Problems of Correlating Flandrian Sea Level Changes and Climate," *Climatic Change in Later Prehistory*, ed. by A.F. Harding (Edinburgh, 1982) pp.52-67.

Shea, W.H. "The Conquests of Sharuhen and Megiddo Reconsidered," *IEJ* 29 (1979), pp.1-5.

Shehadeh, N. "The Climate of Jordan in the Past and Present," *SHAJ* II (Amman, 1985) pp.25-37.

Shennan, I. "Problems of Correlating Flandrian Sea Level Changes and Climate," *Climatic Change in Later Pre-History*, ed. by A.F. Harding (Edinburgh, 1982) pp.52ff.

Shiloh, Y. *Excavations at the City of David I: 1978-1982, Qedem* 19 (Jerusalem, 1984).

—— "The Material Culture of Judah and Jerusalem in Iron Age II: Origins and influences," *The Land of Israel: Cross-Roads of Civilizations*, ed. by E. Lipinski (Leuven, 1985), pp.113-147.

—— "Judah and Jerusalem in Eighth-Sixth Centuries B.C.E.," *Recent Excavations in Israel: Studies in Iron Age Archaeology*, ed. by S. Gitin and W.G. Dever (Winona Lake, 1989) pp.97-105.

Simpson, K.C. *Settlement Patterns on the Margins of Mesopotamia: Stability and Change along the Middle Euphrates, Syria* (University of Arizona dissertation, 1983).

Singer, I. "Takuheinu and Haya: Two Governors in the Ugarit Letter from Tel Aphek," *Tel Aviv* 10 (1983), pp.3-25.

—— "The Beginning of Philistine Settlement in Canaan and the Northern Boundary of Philistia," *Tel Aviv* 12 (1985), pp.109-122.

—— "Dating the End of the Hittite Empire," *Hethitica* 8 (1987), pp.413-421.

—— "The Origin of the Sea Peoples and Their Settlement on the Coast of Canaan," *Society and Economy in the Eastern Mediterranean*, ed. by M. Heltzer and E. Lipinski (Leuven, 1988) pp.239-250.

—— "Merneptah's Campaign to Canaan and the Egyptian Occupation of the Southern Coastal Plain of Palestine in the Ramesside Period," *BASOR* 269 (1988), pp.1-10.

Sivan, D. and Inbar, M. "Paleo-Urban Development of the Quaternary Environmental Changes in the Akko Area," *Paléorient* 9 (1983), pp.85-91.

Smend, R. *Jahwekrieg und Stämmebund, Erwägungen zur ältesten Geschichte Israels, FRLANT* 84 (Göttingen, 1966).

—— "Zur Frage der altisraelitischen Amphiktyonie," *Evangelische Theologie* 31 (1971), pp.623-630.

Smith, R.H. and Kaucky, F.L. "Lake Beisan and the Prehistoric Settlement of the Northern Jordan Valley," *Paléorient* 12 (1986), pp.27-36.

Sneh, Y. and Klein, M. "Holocene Sea Level Changes at the Coast of Dor" *Science* 226 (1984), pp.831f.

Soggin, J.A. "The Davidic and Solomonic Kingdom," *Israelite and Judaean History*, ed. by J.H. Hayes and J.M. Miller (Philadelphia, 1977) pp.332-380.

—— "The History of Ancient Israel: A Study in Some Questions of Method," *Eretz Israel* 14 (1978), pp.44-51.

—— *A History of Israel: From the Beginnings to the Bar Kochba Revolt, AD 135* (London, 1984).

—— "Le Origini D'Israele Problema per lo Storiografo?" *Le Origini di Israele* (Rome, 1987) pp.5-14.

—— *Einführung in die Geschichte Israels und Judas* (Darmstadt, 1991).

Solomonica, P. and Picard, L. *On the Geology of the Gaza-Beersheba District,* (Jerusalem, 1936).

Spannuth, J. *Die Phönizier: Ein Nordmeervolk in Lebanon* (Osnabrück, 1985).

Speiser, E.A. *Genesis, Anchor Bible,* Vol.1 (Garden City, 1965).

Sperber, D. "Drought, Famine and Pestilence in Amoraic Palestine," *JESHO* 17 (1974), pp.272-298.

Stager, L.E. *Ancient Agriculture in the Judaean Desert* (Harvard University dissertation, 1975).

—— "Farming in the Judaean Desert during the Iron Age," *BASOR* 221 (1976), pp.145-158.

—— "The Archaeology of the Family in Ancient Israel," *BASOR* 260 (1985), pp.1-35.

—— "Merenptah, Israel, and Sea Peoples: New Light on an Old Relief," *Eretz Israel* 18 (1985), pp.56*-64*.

Staubli, T. *Das Image der Nomaden* (Göttingen, 1991).

Steele, C.S. *Early Bronze Age Socio-political Organization in Southwestern Jordan* (MA Thesis, State University of New York,1983).

Steuernagel, C. "Der 'Adschlun nach den Aufzeichnungen von G. Schumacher," *ZDPV* 47 (1924), pp.191-240.

—— "Der 'Adschlun nach den Aufzeichnungen von G. Schumacher," *ZDPV* 48 (1925), pp.1-144. 201-392.

—— "Der 'Adschlun nach den Aufzeichnungen von G. Schumacher," *ZDPV* 49 (1926), pp.1-167. 273-303.

Stiebing, W.H. "Another Look at the Origins of the Philistine Tombs at Tell el-Far'ah (S)," *AJA* 74 (1970), pp.139-143.

—— "The End of the Mycenaean Age," *BA* 43 (1980), pp.7-21.

—— *Out of the Desert? Archaeology and the Exodus/ Conquest Narratives* (Buffalo, 1989).

Tadmor, H. "The Southern Border of Aram," *IEJ* 12 (1962), pp.114-122.

—— "Autobiographical Apology in the Royal Assyrian Literature," *History, Historiography and Interpretation,* ed. H. Tadmor and M. Weinfeld (Leiden, 1984) pp.36-57.

Thomas, C.G. *The Earliest Civilizations* (Washington D.C., 1982).

Thompson, Th.L. Review of P.R. Miroschedji, *L'Epoque Pre-Urbaine en Palestine,* *ZDPV* 90 (1974), pp.60f.

——"The Settlement of Early Bronze IV-Middle Bronze I in Jordan," *Annual of the Department of Antiquities in Jordan* (1974), pp.57-71.

—— *The Historicity of the Patriarchal Narratives,* *BZAW* 133 (Berlin, 1974).

—— *The Settlement of Sinai and the Negev in the Bronze Age,* *BTAVO* 8 (Wiesbaden, 1975).

—— "Beth-Sean," *BRL,* ed. by K. Galling (Tübingen, 1977) pp.46f.

—— "Thaanach," *BRL,* ed. by K. Galling (Tübingen, 1977) pp.342-344.

—— "The Joseph and Moses Narratives," *Israelite and Judaean History,* ed. by J.H. Hayes and J.M. Miller (Philadelphia, 1977) pp.149-180. 210-212.

—— "A New Attempt to Date the Patriarchs," *JAOS* 98 (1978), pp.76-84.

—— "The Background of the Patriarchs: A Reply to William Dever and Malcolm Clark," *JSOT* 9 (1978), pp.2-43.

—— "Palästina in der Übergangszeit der Frühbronze/ Mittelbronzezeit," *Tübinger Atlas Des vorderen Orients,* map B II 11b (Wiesbaden, 1978).

—— "Palästina in der Frühbronzezeit," *TAVO,* B II 11a (Wiesbaden, 1978).

—— "Historical Notes on Israel's Conquest of Palestine: A Peasants' Rebellion?" *JSOT* 7, 1978, pp.20-27.

—— "Conflict Themes in the Jacob Narratives," *Semeia* 15 (1979), pp.5-26.

—— *The Settlement of Palestine in the Bronze Age, BTAVO* 34 (Wiesbaden, 1979).

—— "Palästina in der Spätbronzezeit," *TAVO*, B II 11d (Wiesbaden, 1980).

—— "Palästina in der Mittelbronzezeit," *TAVO*, B II 11c (Wiesbaden, 1980).

—— "History and Tradition: A Response to J.B. Geyer," *JSOT* 15 (1980), pp.57-61.

—— *The Origin Tradition of Ancient Israel I, JSOTS* 55 (Sheffield, 1987).

—— Gonçalvez, F.J. and Cangh, J.M. Van. *Toponomie Palestinienne: Plaine de St Jean D'Acre de Jérusalem, Publications de L'Institut Orientaliste de Louvain* (Louvain La Neuve, 1988).

—— "Text, Context, and Referent in Israelite Historiography," *The Fabric of History: Text, Artifact and Israel's Past*, ed. by D. Edelman (Sheffield, 1991) pp.65-92.

—— "Palestinian Pastoralism and Israel's Origins," *SJOT* 6 (1992), pp.1-13.

—— "W.F. Albright as Historian," *Proceedings of the Midwest Regional Meeting of SBL* (1992, forthcoming).

—— "Historiography: Israelite," *Anchor Bible Dictionary* (forthcoming).

Tigay, J. *You Shall Have No Other Gods: Israelite Religion in the Light of Hebrew Inscriptions, HSS* 31 (Atlanta, 1986).

Timm, S. *Die Dynastie Omri* (Göttingen, 1982).

—— *Moab zwischen den Mächten: Studien zu historischen Denkmälern und Texten, ÄAT* 17 (Wiesbaden, 1989).

Toombs, L.E. "Shechem: Problems of the Early Israelite Era," *Symposia*, ed. by F.M. Cross (Cambridge, 1979) pp.69-83.

Tournay, R. "Nuzi," *DBS*, vol. VI (Paris, 1967) col.644-674.

Trompf, G.W. "Notions of Historical Recurrence in Classical Hebrew Historiography," *Studies in the Historical Books of the Old Testament, VTS* 30, ed. J.A. Emerton, (Leiden, 1979) pp.213-29.

Tubb, J. "The MB IIA Period in Palestine: Its Relationship with Syria and its Origin," *Levant* 15 (1983), pp.49-62.

Tufnell, O. "Reviews and Notices: Hazor II," *PEQ* 93 (1961), pp.94-98.

Tyloch, W. "The Evidence of the Proto-Lexikon for the Cultural Background of the Semitic Peoples," *Hamito-Semitica*, ed by J. and T. Bynon (The Hague, 1975) pp.55ff.

Ullendorf, E. *Is Biblical Hebrew a Language?, Studies in Semitic Languages and Civilizations* (Wiesbaden, 1971).

Ussishkin, D. "Excavations at Tel Lachish 1978-1983: Second Preliminary Report," *Tel Aviv* 10 (1983), pp.97-175.

—— "Levels VII and VI at Tel Lachish and the End of the Late Bronze Age in Canaan," *Palestine in the Bronze Age*, ed. by J.N. Tubb (London, 1985) pp.213-230.

—— "Lachish: Key to the Israelite Conquest of Canaan?" *BAR* 13 (1987), pp.18-39.

Vaux, R. de. *Die hebräischen Patriarchen und die modernen Entdeckungen* (Stuttgart, 1959).

—— *Les Institutions de l'Ancien Testament*, 2 vols. (Paris, 1958), ET = *Ancient Israel* (New York, 1959).

—— *Die Patriarchenerzählungen und die Geschichte* (Stuttgart, 1965).

—— "Method in the Study of Early Hebrew History," *Biblical and Other Studies*, ed. by J.P. Hyatt (1966), pp.15-29.

—— "On Right and Wrong Uses of Archaeology," *Near Eastern Archaeology in the Twentieth Century: Essays in Honor of Nelson Glueck*, ed. by J.A. Sanders (New York, 1970) pp.64-80.

—— *L'Histoire ancienne d'Israel* I. *Des Origines à l'installation en Canaan* (Paris, 1971).

—— *The Early History of Israel* (Philadelphia, 1978).

Vergote, J. Joseph en Égypte: Genèse chap. 37-50 à la lumière des études égyptologiques récentes (Paris, 1959).

Veyne, P. *Did the Greeks Believe in Their Myths?* (Chicago, 1988).

Vorländer, H. *Die Entstehungszeit des jehowistischen Geschichtswerkes. Europäische Hochschulschriften*, Reihe 23, 109 (Frankfurt, 1978).

Vries, S. de. «*A Review of Recent Research in the Tradition History of the Pentateuch,*» *SBL Seminar Papers* 26 (1987), pp.459-502.

Wagner, M. "Beiträge zur Aramäismenfrage im alttestamentlichen Hebräisch," *VTS* 16 (Leiden, 1967) pp.355-371.

Waldbaum, J. "Philistine Tombs at Tell Fara and their Aegean Prototypes," *AJA* 70 (1966), pp.331-340.

Wapnish, P. "Camel Caravans and Camel Pastoralists at Tell Jemmeh," *JANES* 13 (1981), pp.101-121.

—— and Hesse, B. "The Contribution and Organization of Pastoral Systems," *Early Israelite Agriculture*, ed. by O.S. LaBianca (1989) pp.29-41.

Ward, W.A. "The Shasu 'Bedouin': Notes on a Recent Publication," *JESHO* 15 (1972), pp.35-60.

Weinfeld, M. "Divine Intervention in War in Ancient Israel and in the Ancient Near East," *History, Historiography and Interpretation*, ed. H. Tadmor and M. Weinfeld (Leiden, 1984) pp.121-47.

Weingreen, G. "The Theory of the Amphictyony in Pre-Monarchical Israel," *JANESCU* 5 (1973), pp.427-433.

Weinstein, J.M. "The Egyptian Empire in Palestine: A Reassessment," *BASOR* 241 (1981), pp.17-28.

—— "The Egyptian Empire in Palestine: A Reassessment," *BASOR* 241 (1981), pp.1-28.

Weinstein-Evron, M. and Galili, E. "Pre-History and Palaeoenvironments of Submerged Sites along the Carmel Coast of Israel," *Paléorient* 11 (1985), pp.37-52.

Weippert, H. *Palästina in vorhellenistischer Zeit, Handbuch der Archaeologie, Vorderasien* II/1 (Munich, 1988).

Weippert, M. *Die Landnahme der israelitischen Stämme in der neueren wissenschaftlichen Diskussion, FRLANT* 92 (Göttingen, 1967).

—— *The Settlement of the Israelite Tribes in Palestine SBT* 21 (London, 1971).

—— "Abraham der Hebräer? Bemerkungen zu W.F. Albright's Deutung der Väter Israels," *Bb* 52 (1971), pp.407-432.

—— *Edom: Studien und Materialien zur Geschichte der Edomiter auf Grund schriftlicher und archäologischer Quellen* (Tübingen dissertation, 1971).

—— "Das geographische System der Stämme Israel," *VT* 23 (1973), pp.76-89.

—— "Fragen des israelitischen Geschichtsbewusstseins," *VT* 23 (1973), pp.415-41.

—— "Semitische Nomaden des zweiten Jahrtausends. Über die *shasw* der ägyptischen Quellen" *Bb* 55 (1974), pp.265-280. 427-433.

—— "The Israelite 'Conquest' and the Evidence from Transjordan," *Symposia*, ed. by F.M. Cross (Cambridge, 1979) pp.15-34.

—— "Edom und Israel," *TRE* 9 (1982), pp.291-299.

Wellhausen, J. *Geschichte Israels* (Berlin, 1878: 2nd. ed.= *Prolegomena zur Geschichte Israels*, 1883).

— *Skizzen und Vorarbeiten*, Vols.1-6 (Berlin, 1884-1899).

— *Israelitische und jüdische Geschichte* (Berlin, 1894).

— *Die Composition des Hexateuchs und der historischen Bücher des alten Testaments* 3d. ed. (Berlin, 1899).

— *Grundrisse zum alten Testament*, ed. by R. Smend (Kaiser, Munich, 1965).

Welten, P. *Geschichte und Geschichtsdarstellung in den Chronikbüchern*, *WMANT* 42 (Neukirchen, 1973).

Whitelam, K.W. and Coote, R.B. "The Emergence of Israel: Social Transformation and State Formation Following the Decline in Late Bronze Age Trade," *Social Scientific Criticism of the Hebrew Bible and its Social World: The Israelite Monarchy, Semeia* 37 (1986) pp.107-147.

— and Coote, R.B. *The Emergence of Early Israel in Historical Perspective, SWBAS* 5 (Sheffield, 1987).

Whybray, N. *The Intellectual Tradition of the Old Testament, BZAW* 135 (Berlin, 1976).

— *The Making of the Pentateuch, JSOTS* 53 (Sheffield, 1987).

Widengren, G. Review of S. Moscati, *Le antiche Divinita Semitiche, JSS* 5 (1960), pp.397-410.

Williamson, H.G.M. *Israel in the Book of Chronicles* (Cambridge, 1977).

Willis, L.A. and Geraty, L.T. "Archaeological Research in Transjordan," *The Archaeology of Jordan and Other Studies*, ed. by L.T. Geraty and L.G. Herr (Berrien Springs, 1986) pp. 3-72.

Winkler, H. *Altorientalische Forschungen* I-III (Leipzig, 1893-1906).

— *Religionsgeschichtlicher und Geschichtlicher Orient* (Leipzig, 1906).

Wolf, E.R. *Peasants* (Englewood, 1966).

Wright, G.E. *The Pottery of the Early Bronze Age* (Cambridge, 1938).

— and Grant, E. *Ain Shems Excavation V* (Haverford, 1939).

— "The Literary and Historical Problem of Joshua 10 and Judges 1," *JNES* 5 (1946), pp.105-114.

— *The Old Testament Against its Environment* (London, 1955).

— *Biblical Archaeology* (Philadelphia, 1957).

— *God Who Acts* (Garden City, 1962).

— *Shechem, The Biography of a Biblical City* (New York, 1965).

— "Fresh Evidence for the Philistine Story," *BA* 29 (1966), pp.70-86.

— "Beth-Shemesh," *EAEHL I*, pp.248-253.

Wüst, M. *Untersuchungen zu den Siedlungsgeographischen Texten des Alten Testaments I: Ostjordanland, BTAVO* 9 (Wiesbaden, 1975).

Yadin, Y. *Hazor I, III-IV* (Jerusalem, 1958, 1961).

— "Hazor," *Archaeology and Old Testament Study*, ed. by D.W. Thomas (Edinburgh, 1967) 245-263.

— *Hazor: The Head of All Those Kingdoms, 1970 Schweich Lectures* (Oxford, 1972).

— *Hazor: The Rediscovery of a Great Citadel of the Bible* (London, 1975).

— "The Transition from a Semi-Nomadic to a Sedentary Society in the Twelfth Century B.C.E.," *Symposia*, ed. by F.M. Cross (Cambridge, 1979) pp.57-70.

— "Megiddo," *EAEHL*, pp.85of.

Yoffee, N. and Kamp. K.A. "Ethnicity in Ancient Western Asia during the Early Second Millennium B.C.: Archaeological Assessments and Ethnoarchaeological Perspectives," *BASOR* 237 (1980), pp.85-104.

Yurco, F. "Merenptah's Palestinian Campaign," *Society for the Study of Egyptian Antiquities Journal* 8 (1978), p.70.

Zeder, M.A. "Understanding Urban Process through the study of Specialized Subsistence Economy in the Near East," *Journal of Anthropological Archaeology* 7 (1988), pp.1-55.

Zeist, W. Van. "Past and Present Environment of the Jordan Valley," *SHAJ* II (1985) pp.199-204.

Zertal, A. *Arubbath, Hepher, and the Third Solomonic District* (University of Tel Aviv dissertation, 1986).

—— "The Water Factor During the Israelite Settlement in Canaan," *Society and Economy in the Eastern Mediterranean, Orientalia Lovaniensia Analecta* 23, ed. by M. Heltzer and E. Lipinski (Leuven, 1988) pp.341-352.

Zevit, Z. "Archaeological and Literary Stratigraphy in Joshua 7-8," *BASOR* 251 (1983), pp.23-35.

Zori, N. "An Archaeological Survey of the Beth-Shean Valley," *The Beth Shan Valley* (Jerusalem, 1962).

—— *The Land of Issachar Archaeological Survey* (Jerusalem, 1977).

Zyl, A.H. Van. *The Moabites* (Leiden, 1960).

SCHOLARS' LIST

*Through its Scholars' List Brill aims to make available
to a wider public a selection of its most successful
hardcover titles in a paperback edition.*

Titles now available are:

AMITAI-PREISS, R. & D.O. MORGAN, *The Mongol Empire and its Legacy*.
2000. ISBN 90 04 11946 9, price USD 29.90

COHEN. B., *Not the Classical Ideal*. Athens and the Construction of the Other
in Greek Art. 2000. ISBN 90 04 11712 1, price USD 39.90

GRIGGS, C.W., *Early Egyptian Christianity* from its Origins to 451 CE.
2000. ISBN 90 04 11926 4, price USD 29.90

HORSFALL, N., *A Companion to the Study of Virgil*. 2000.
ISBN 90 04 11870 5, price USD 27.90

JAYYUSI, S.K., *The Legacy of Muslim Spain*. 2000.
ISBN 90 04 11945 0, price USD 54.90

RUTGERS, L.V., *The Jews in Late Ancient Rome*. Evidence of Cultural
Interaction in the Roman Diaspora. 2000.
ISBN 90 04 11928 0, price USD 29.90

TER HAAR, B.J., *The Ritual and Mythology of the Chinese Triads*.
Creating an Identity. 2000. ISBN 90 04 11944 2, price USD 39.90

THOMPSON, T.L., *Early History of the Israelite People* from the Written &
Archaeological Sources. 2000. ISBN 90 04 11943 4, price USD 39.90

WOOD, S.E., *Imperial Women*. A Study in Public Images, 40 BC – AD 68
2000. ISBN 90 04 11950 7, price USD 34.90

YARBRO COLLINS, A., *Cosmology & Eschatology in Jewish & Christian
Apocalypticism*. 2000. ISBN 90 04 11927 2, price USD 29.90

———